Pentecost, Mission and Ecumenism
Essays on Intercultural Theology
Festschrift in Honour of Professor Walter J. Hollenweger

Band 75

PETER LANG
Frankfurt am Main · Berlin · Bern · New York · Paris · Wien

Jan A. B. Jongeneel, a. o.
(Eds.)

Pentecost, Mission and Ecumenism Essays on Intercultural Theology

Festschrift in Honour of Professor Walter J. Hollenweger

PETER LANG
Frankfurt am Main · Berlin · Bern · New York · Paris · Wien

Die Deutsche Bibliothek - CIP-Einheitsaufnahme

Pentecost, mission and ecumenism's essays on intercultural theology : Festschrift in honour of Professor Walter J. Hollenweger / Jan A. B. Jongeneel (ed.). - Frankfurt am Main ; Berlin ; Bern ; New York ; Paris ; Wien : Lang, 1992
(Studien zur interkulturellen Geschichte des Christentums ; Bd. 75)
ISBN 3-631-44010-3

NE: Jongeneel, Jan A. B. [Hrsg.]; Hollenweger, Walter J.: Festschrift; GT

ISSN 0170-9240
ISBN 3-631-44010-3

Printed in Germany 1 3 4 5 6 7

Contents

Part 2
Historical Case Studies and Statistics on Pentecostalism and the Charismatic Renewal in Missiological and Ecumenical Perspective

Preface

In 1989 a conference on 'Pentecostal and Charismatic Research in Europe' took place at Utrecht University. At this Conference, the idea was born to prepare a Prof. Walter J. Hollenweger - *Festschrift*. Many former students, friends and colleagues of Hollenweger who were present at that conference were consulted; they all responded positively to this idea and invited Prof. Jan Jongeneel, Dr. Cornelis van der Laan and Dr. Paul van der Laan to do the editorial work. These Dutchmen accepted this responsibility, but invited Dr. Martin Robinson and also Dr. Peter Staples to join the editorial board to be both more representative and more equipped to solve language problems.

Nine people present at the above mentioned Utrecht Conference have contributed to this *Festschrift*. With all the other authors a link was established by correspondence. Nearly all people approached by the editorial board have responded positively to our invitation. It would not be difficult at all to find 50 persons willing to write a *Festschrift*-article, but in consultation with Peter Lang as publisher, we decided to limit the number of contributions to ca. 25. In this collective work there is a great variety of contributors with quite different backgrounds and relationships to Hollenweger: both colleagues and former students, either belonging to the Roman Catholic Church or to the Ecumenical Movement, the Evangelical Movement and the Pentecostal Movement, black and white, male and female. We are very pleased to have found such a broad group of authors willing to contribute. They all finished their work, except Prof. Dr. J. Reiling, New Testament scholar at Utrecht University, who, because of a heart attack, was not able to finish his article on 'narrative exegesis'.

Although the editorial board invited the approached authors to write in English, some manuscripts were offered in other languages. The three manuscripts offered in German are published in that language; because it is the mother language of Hollenweger. Although Hollenweger is able to read Dutch as well, we invited drs. A. Pellegrom to translate the article of Professor Jan Veenhof into English; we thank him for accepting this task. Both Dr. Robinson and Dr. Staples checked the English, especially in the articles written by non-native-speaking-English writers; they did not, however, solve the outstanding question of the difference between American and British spelling, nor the difficult problem of capitalization.

All articles in this *Festschrift* are new, except one, the article of Richard Friedli, which was already published by Herder Verlag in Basel-Freiburg-Wien. We thank this Verlag very much for his spontaneous willingness to let this article *pro Deo* be reprinted in this *Festschrift*.

The Bibliography was compiled by Dr. Paul van der Laan; the List of Students of Professor Hollenweger by Dr. Cornelis van der Laan. Marten Visser, student-assistant in missiology at Utrecht University, took care of the List of Contributors and Index of Persons. Mrs. Joan Pearce, the former secretary of Prof. Hollenweger at Birmingham, prepared the *tabula gratulatoria*, which is included here as a loose-leaf inset. The Pentecostal Bible School at Lunteren undertook the job of preparing the camera-ready text. Dr. Cornelis van der Laan controlled the work done at Lunteren.

We trust that this publication will be appreciated by Prof. Hollenweger. We hope that it is a good reflection of his broad theological, missiological and ecumenical thinking in the light of Pentecost.

Utrecht - Birmingham
Spring 1992

Editorial Board
Jan A.B. Jongeneel
Cornelis van der Laan
Paul N. van der Laan
Martin Robinson
Peter Staples

Introduction

Jan A.B. Jongeneel

This *Festschrift* has three parts.

The first part deals with the biography of Professor Walter J. Hollenweger. After a general introductory chapter (Paul N. van der Laan), Hollenweger is described as theologian (Richard Friedli), as ecumenical (Werner Ustorf), as Professor of Mission (Emmanuel Y. Lartey - George M. Mulrain), and as poet and liturgist (Marianne Heuberger - Gloor). The article on The Centre for Black and White Christian Partnership at Birmingham (Roswith Gerloff) is an appendix to the article on Hollenweger as Professor of Mission at Birmingham.

The second part deals with historical case studies and statistics on Pentecostalism and the Charismatic Renewal in missiological and ecumenical perspective. It opens with two articles on the early history of Pentecostalism: the black roots of Pentecostalism (Iain MacRobert), and William H. Durham and the finished work of Calvary (D. William Faupel). Thereafter, it offers eight case studies at the local, national or continental level: the United States (Cecil M. Robeck), Mexico (Kenneth D. Gill), Norway (David Bundy), The Netherlands (Cornelis van der Laan), South-Africa (both Martin Robinson and J. Nico Horn), Korea (Boo-Woong Yoo), and Indonesia (I. James M. Haire). At the end of this second part, two articles deal with global developments in the Pentecostal Movement and the Charismatic Renewal, including statistics (David B. Barrett; Todd M. Johnson).

The third and last part has a systematic character: missiological and ecumenical reflections on inculturation and encounter, with special reference to Pentecostalism and the Charismatic Renewal. The first two articles deal with the basic topics of inculturation (Theo Sundermeier) and encounter (Charles H. Kraft). The following two articles investigate in a comparative way the impact of Pentecostalism and the Charismatic Renewal on mission (Jan A.B. Jongeneel) and liturgy (Jean-Jacques Suurmond). Thereafter the relation of Pentecostalism to ecumenical theology (Peter Staples) and the ecumenical movement (Martin Conway) are topics of reflection. The two final articles deal with the significance of the Charismatic Renewal from a protestant perspective (Jan Veenhof) and a Roman-Catholic perspective (Peter Hocken).

The bibliography includes a survey of all books and articles published by Walter J. Hollenweger (Paul N. van der Laan).

Part 1

Biography of Professor Walter J. Hollenweger

1

Walter J. Hollenweger: A Pluriform Life

Paul N. van der Laan

Outline of his life

1 June 1927	Birth in Antwerp, Belgium
1934-1943	Primary and Secondary school in Zürich, Switzerland
1943-1948	Apprentice and employee at the Bank Dr. Friedrich, Zürich, and at the Union Bank of Switzerland, La Chaux-de-Fonds
1948-1949	Student of the International Bible Training Institute at Leamington Spa, England
1949-1958	Youth leader and Pastor in the Swiss Pfingstmission in St. Gallen and Zürich, Switzerland
30 June 1951	Married to Erica Busslinger
1955-1961	Theological study at Zürich and Basel
1961-1964	Research Assistant for Church History and Social Ethics at the University of Zürich with Prof. F. Blanke and Prof. A. Rich
1964-1965	Study-director of the Evangelical Academy at Boldern, Switzerland
1965-1971	Executive Secretary of the Department on Studies in Evangelism and Secretary for Evangelism in the Division of World Mission and Evangelism of the World Council of Churches at Geneva, Switzerland
9 July 1966	Completed his inaugural dissertation and became Doctor in Theology at Zürich
1971-1989	Professor of Mission at the University of Birmingham and Selly Oak Colleges at Birmingham, England
1989-1992	Retired - Guest Professor at Bern and Zürich

Raised in Poverty

The Hollenweger's familytree is rooted for 800 years in Zürich, Switzerland.[1] However, Walter J. Hollenweger, our central figure, was born at Antwerp. His parents called their firstborn after his father: Walter Jacob. Later their family would be completed with two daughters (born in 1929 and 1942). At the time of his birth Hollenweger's father served as a steward on an English liner, which hired its crew in Belgium. His mother earned some extra money by working as a servant in a rich Belgian family.

In 1929 they went back to Switzerland. During the thirties his father had to perform all kind of odd jobs to keep the family going. Among other things he served as a waiter and sold chocolate at the railway-station. Later he became a book-seller and ended up as the director of the book-shop. Both of his parents had been involved with the Salvation Army; but, back in Zürich, his mother attended the Reformed Church. In the period of unemployment she was converted and started to teach her son out of a children's Bible. The family was so poor that young Walter had to go barefoot to his primary school, much to the mockery of both his fellow-students and his teachers.[2] For this reason he was determined to become rich. After his schooling he was accepted as an apprentice at the Bank Dr. Friedrich in Zürich. At the stock exchange he saw how one could get rich and poor overnight.

Occasionally his creative talents revealed themselves. Already as a youngster he played the horn and composed music, even some cantatas.

Pentecostal Period

The Sunday-School of the Reformed Church in Zürich-Aussersihl, which young Walter had to visit was so noisy that he protested to his mother: "If I am not allowed to play football on Sunday morning, let me go to some place where I can at least learn something".[3] For this reason his mother sent him to the Pentecostal church she occasionally visited. As he grew up he became involved in the youth-work of the local Pentecostal assembly. Here he first met Erica Busslinger, a secretary at a lawyer's office who later became his wife. His call to the ministry clashed with his initial ambition to become rich. For two years he fought an inner struggle, but in the end he gave his life to the Lord. As he was searching the baptism in the Holy Spirit he prayed:

> Dear Father in heaven! When you still want to use such a stubborn and proud man like me, who has opposed your call for two years, then take my life, I surrender it to You.

As an answer to his prayer he experienced God's power and simultaneously was healed of a skin disease.[4] To be better equipped for the ministry he travelled together with his future wife to England and attended from 1948-1949 the International Bible Training Institute at Leamington Spa. This Bible school was founded soon after World War II by the flamboyant evangelist Fred Squire to provide a basic training for Pentecostal youngsters worldwide. Although the school was simple and way below his capacities, it did implant a love for the Bible which would mark him for the rest of his life.[5] He was also taught how to communicate the Bible in non-abstract terms.

Back in Switzerland he was appointed as assistant pastor in Winterthur and later in Zürich. After his marriage on 30 June 1951 he became assistant pastor in St.

Gallen, a church with a total membership of 200. During this period he started to question whether Pentecostal hermeneutics did match its theology and experience. Once he wanted to find out why his Zürcherbibel commented at several scriptures (for instance the genealogies of Jesus) that the old manuscripts gave different versions of the text. He consulted a Reformed minister and to his utter amazement he was given the answer that some liberal theologians had smuggled these remarks into the Bible. Most Pentecostal pastors would have been more than satisfied with such an answer, but Hollenweger was determined to go to the bottom of this. If this was true, these liberal theologians had to be exposed. After forty days of praying and fasting, together with his wife, he decided to study theology. By private lessons and self-study he managed to complete his grammar school education (*Eidgenössich Maturität*) and in 1955 he entered the Faculty of Theology at the University of Zürich. Most of his church-members were suspicious about these intellectual endeavours and prayed he would fail. But to their disappointment Hollenweger proved to be too good a student.

In the meantime he had grown to a considerable stature in his own rank and file. During the Pentecostal World Conference in London (1952) he acted as an interpreter and led a Swiss choir and brass band. He proved to be a productive author[6] and was known nationwide as the translator of the famous American healing-evangelists William Branham and Tommy Hicks. Hicks even called Hollenweger the 'Martin Luther of the 20th Century'.[7] Already at that time Hollenweger learnt to relativize the exaggerated remarks of these American preachers. Nevertheless he was one of the most gifted and successful evangelists. Attendance in his local church grew from 300 to 1500. He even became the treasurer of the national movement. At some point, however, his critical attitude and open spirit had to clash with the rigid ethics and narrow-mindedness of his Pentecostal brethren. In the end the conflict centered around trivial matters such as whether women were allowed to cut their hair and wear ornaments.[8] When it was discussed whether or not he should be suspended because of his 'liberal convictions', Hollenweger resigned as a pastor of the Swiss Pfingstmission in February 1958. His natural curiosity could not stop him from asking questions. Finally his broad mind simply did not fit any more in the tight thought-pattern of his Pentecostal peers.

Growing to Academic Maturity

For a while he must have felt like a bird liberated from its cage. Freed from suspicion of and obligations towards his fellow-believers, Hollenweger continued his quest for truth. One important guide in this period was his *Doktorvater*, the church-historian Professor Fritz Blanke. Blanke was a specialist in the Free Churches and the Anabaptists. Unlike most of his colleagues, he did not judge the

Anabaptists by the writings of their critics, but by searching their own sources.[9] Blanke also had the gift of making complicated matters simple.

In 1961 Hollenweger finished his graduate studies in Theology. Among his teachers were Hans Conzelmann, Eduard Schweizer, Karl Barth and Emil Brunner.[10] Brunner showed him how to combine the method of critical historical exegesis with a genuine love for the Bible and a desire to communicate it.[11]

In 1961 Hollenweger became an ordained minister of the Swiss Reformed Church in the canton Zürich. Although he only had a parish for a period of six months, he preached almost every Sunday during his residence in Switzerland. Professor Blanke asked him to become his personal assistant at the University and challenged him to write an extensive dissertation on the worldwide Pentecostal Movement: including a historical, dogmatic and sociological analysis. For six years Hollenweger methodologically worked on this vast subject, which was still an academic *terra incognito*. In order to be able to read the sources in their original tongue, he himself learnt twenty foreign languages. In December 1966 he finished this *magnum opus* of ten volumes entitled *Handbuch der Pfingstbewegung*[12], which was awarded a *magna cum lauda*. In 1969 the core of this dissertation was published in the book *Enthusiastisches Christentum*.[13] In the dedication of the revised English translation, Hollenweger pithily summarizes his feelings concerning his past by stating:

> To my friends and teachers in the Pentecostal Movement who taught me to love the Bible and to my teachers and friends in the Presbyterian Church who taught me to understand it.[14]

Ecumenical Work

While he was working on his dissertation, his gifts as a creative communicator already came to the fore. From 1964 till 1965 he served as the study director for the Evangelical Academy (a socio-theological training centre) at Boldern near Zürich. In 1965 Hollenweger was asked by the World Council of Churches (WCC) to develop a number of bible courses in which he would combine the method of critical exegeses with evangelical statements. He accepted the position, moved to Geneva and was appointed as Executive Secretary of the Department on Studies in Evangelism and finally as Secretary for Evangelism in the Division of World Mission and Evangelism. In these positions he was confronted with the multi-cultural nature of Christianity. He recognized the need for a communication code which would be relevant in both Western Academic Christianity and other cultural settings, especially in the Third World.[15] It was the time of experimenting with different types of church varieties, which would be more relevant for contemporary Christians and non-Christians. He was deeply involved in the publication of the report entitled 'Church for Others'. This document was the result of the North American and European study groups, which had worked on an assignment given by the WCC Assembly at New Delhi (1961) to investigate various missiological structures of the Church.[16] Retrospectively, Hollenweger would refer to this document and the subsequent draft resolution for Section II of the WCC-Assembly at Uppsala (1968) as precursors of the later 'Narrative Theology'.[17] In spite of the opposition at Uppsala, especially by the German, Scandinavian and Anglo-Saxon delegates[18], Hollenweger seemed determined to develop this new approach to experimental activities and narrative communication. Many of his articles were devoted to this topic.[19] Gradually, he realized the necessity of an intercultural theology to advance the cross-fertilization of the global Church.

During his years at the WCC, Hollenweger built up an international reputation through his creative contributions at the German *Kirchentag*.[20]

In his own way he tried to raise interest for the ecumenical cause among his Pentecostal brethren. In October 1966 he organized a consultation between European Pentecostals and WCC-representatives at Gunten, Switzerland.[21] He made several journeys, especially to Latin America, in order to encourage the Pentecostals to enter into a dialogue with other denominations.[22] As a result of these visits a number of Pentecostals participated in the WCC-Assembly at Uppsala. Here, at Hollenweger's initiative, Christian H. Krust, a German Pentecostal, was enabled to address the meeting.[23] In 1969 the 'Evangelical Pentecostal Church Brazil for Christ' became the third Pentecostal denomination to join the WCC[24]

Much more of Hollenweger's ecumenical endeavours can be found in the contributions of Werner Ustorf and Martin Conway in this *Festschrift.*

A Foreign Professor

On March 20th 1970, the Council of the Selly Oak Colleges and the University of Birmingham (U.K.) signed an agreement to set up a Chair in the field of Mission Studies. Hollenweger was invited to become the first holder of this chair. Although he had different options, he accepted the position at Birmingham because he was given the opportunity to experiment with a new type of theological education[25], with room for narrative thinking and the integration of oral cultures.

From 1971 till 1989 he served as the only professor in this subject in an English-speaking university East of the Atlantic. In this capacity he had a threefold task[26]:

1. Education of undergraduate students in theology at the University of Birmingham. He not only gave courses in missiology, but also in wider subjects such as Modern Theological Thought, Political Theology and

Systematic Theology.

2. Personal supervision of postgraduate students. This may well have been Hollenweger's most prominent task. Nearly a hundred postgraduates of all ages, cultures, professions and denominational backgrounds worked under his guidance on a large variety of topics[27], ranging from the culture of economism in Great Britain to shamanism in Korea. All of those involved will never forget the Doctoral Seminars (usually three every term), which were held at his home. After the presentation of a subject by one of his postgraduates, there was always ample time for reflection and fellowship. The fact that Hollenweger was loved and admired by many of his students is shown extensively by the contribution of Emmanuel Lartey and George Mulrain in this *Festschrift*.
3. Education at the Selly Oak Colleges. Every term Hollenweger supervised a number of weekly lectures concentrating on one particular subject. The variety of topics presented at these seminars once again demonstrates Hollenweger's broad field of interest.[28] Of particular significance was his participation in the Centre for Black and White Partnership at Selly Oak on which the article of Roswith Gerloff in this *Festschrift* expands.

An important personal help during these years was his faithful secretary Joan Pearce, who not only proved to be a very competent and prompt administrator but also one of his most fervent supporters.

A Pluriform Life

It seems impossible to comprehend such a pluriform life in a few pages. By all means someone, preferably a Swiss, should write a doctoral dissertation on Hollenweger's life and work. This will prove to be an immense task. Just to scan through his writings, as the bibliography shows, will take considerable time.

Hollenweger proved to be a passionate innovator and creative communicator. Historically this may be explained by the fact that his life was a non-stop search to blend the emotional and the rational, the creative and the structural, the poor and the rich.

He had the courage to build bridges. As in the natural world, this is a dangerous task, especially when the gaps are wide and the surface is rough. Once the bridge is finished the crossing is easy and seems obvious. Who remembers the people who risked their lives to make it possible? As a real Christian, following his Master, Hollenweger built his bridges towards those who are living on the fringes of society. He supported the emancipation of women and the liberation of the blacks. He earned their self-esteem by challenging them to use their own particular qualities, rather than denying them. He set the example himself by promoting a new way of communication. His revaluation of stories and art as important metaphors of universal values was a step ahead into our era of mass-media, where images and experiences are more important then the written word. Since his retirement in 1989 he can devote even more energy in what he has come to love most: writing plays, musicals and drama's in order to communicate his conception of the gospel.[29] The article of Marianne Heuberger in this *Festschrift* deepens this subject. In my interview with Hollenweger, he said:

> My highest ambition is to be remembered as a theologically trained artist. The plays are a summary of my ministry, because they are accessible to all people.[30]

After his Pentecostal period he felt like a liberated bird. One may wonder, however, whether he ever found a place to settle down again. He seemed indefatigable looking for Utopia, where the best of his past and present would be blended. This stimulated him to do the seemingly impossible: to join both the Pentecostals and the Ecumenicals, both the Blacks and the Whites, both the Illiterates and the Academics. He shared this burden with his life-companion Erica, a beautiful wife, a wonderful host, a reflecting sounding board[31], but also a competent author in her own right.[32] Their marriage was not blessed with children, but certainly the prophecy once given to Israel[33] also applies to this invaluable couple:

'Sing o barren woman
you who never bore a child;
burst into song, shout for joy,
you who were never in labour;
because more are the children of the desolate woman,
than of her who has a husband,' says the Lord.
'Enlarge the place of your tent,
stretch your tent curtains wide,
do not hold back;
lengthen your cords,
strengthen your stakes.
For you will spread out to the right and to the left;
your descendants will dispossess nations
and settle in their desolate cities.'

Notes

1. Kurt Studhalter, *Walter J. Hollenweger: Christsein in einer multikulturellen Gesellschaft*, Protokoll des Abendgesprächs vom 27 März 1990 - Romero-Haus Protokolle 24 (Luzern: Romero-

Haus, 1990), 3.

2. W.J. Hollenweger, "Aus meinem Leben", *Jugendbote der Freien Christengemeinden in Österreich*, Heft 3 (Vienna: July 1953), 2.
3. W.J. Hollenweger, "Glanz und Elend der Theologie: Autobiographical sketch", Introduction to seminars and lectures, 1987, 1.
4. W.J. Hollenweger, "Aus meinem Leben", 3.
5. Jac. Roos, "Dr. Walter Hollenweger: van Pinksterbeweging naar Wereldraad", *Hervormd Nederland* 24/1 (6 January 1968), 2.
6. See bibliography at the end of this *Festschrift* under Articles over the period 1948-1955.
7. Personal interview with Walter J. Hollenweger, Birmingham 7th July 1988.
8. W.J. Hollenweger, "Kommentar über die Begegnung des Gebetskreises mit dem Brüderrat vom 16. Dezember", Manuscript, 16 December 1956.
9. Kurt Studhalter, 5.
10. For Hollenweger's publications on Barth and Brunner see:: "Es began mit Karl Barth", Manuscript, 1966; "Karl Barth in seinen Briefen", *Leben und Glauben* 50/12 (22 March 1975), 6 ff.; Foreword: "Karl Barth as a Narrative Theologian", in: David Ford, *Barth and God's Story*, Studies in the Intercultural History of Christianity (1981), 6-8; "Karl Barth Tells Such Good Stories", *Reform* (1 October 1981), 9; "Karl Barth erzählt biblische Geschichten", *Leben und Glauben*, 56/45 (4 November 1981), 6 ff.; "Aus dem weltweiten Echo auf Emil Brunners Theologie", *Reformatio* 12/8 (1 August 1963), 441-48; "Wurzeln der Theologie Emil Brunners. Aus Brunners Theologischer Entwicklung von ca. 1913 bis 1918", *Reformatio* 12/10 (1 October 1963), 579-87; "Emil Brunner, Ein Geschichte in Porträts", in: H.J. Schulz (ed.), *Tendenzen der Theologie im 20. Jahrhundert* (1966), 360-67; " Emil Brunner: Ein Theologe, den alle verstehen können", *Leben und Glauben* 57/27 (30 June 1982), 6 ff.
11. G. Puchinger, "Gesprekken met dr. J.W. Hollenweger over: Zending en Ontwikkeling", *Maandblad Reunisten Organisatie Societas Studiosorum Reformatorum* no. 7 (June 1971), 2.
12. Walter J. Hollenweger, *Handbuch der Pfingstbewegung*, 10 vols. - dupl. Geneva, (Dr. Theological Dissertation: University of Zürich, 1966). Available from ATLA, Board of Microtexts, Divinity School, Yale University.
13. Idem, *Enthusiastisches Christentum: Die Pfingstbewegung in Geschichte und Gegenwart* (Zürich/Wupperthal: Zwingli-Verlag und Theol. Verlag R. Brockhaus, 1969).
14. Idem, *The Pentecostals* (London: SCM Press Ltd., 1972), xvi.
15. Idem, "Glanz und Elend der Theologie, Autobiographical sketch", Introduction to seminars and lectures, 1987, 5.
16. W.J. Hollenweger (ed.), *The Church for Others and the Church for the World: A Quest for Structures for Missionary Congregations*, Final Report of the Western European Working Group and North American Working Group of the Department on Studies in Evangelism (Geneva: WCC, 1967); W.J. Hollenweger, "The Church for others in Belgium: Can the Church be pluralistic?", *Study Encounter* 4/1 (1 June 1968), 162-65; Idem, "The Church for others: Discussion in the DDR", *Study Encounter* 5/1 (1 June 1969), 26-36; Idem, "The Church for Others - Ten Years After", *Research Bulletin ISWRA* 1977 (1 June 1977), 82-96; Idem, "The Church for Others: On the ecumenical and intercultural understanding of mission from 1961 to 1976", Lectures, 1976. See also: Idem (ed.), *Kirche, Benzin und Bohnensuppe: Auf den Spuren dynamischer Gemeinden* (Zürich: TVZ, 1971).
17. Idem, *Umgang mit Mythen: Interkulturelle Theologie 2* (München: Chr. Kaiser Verlag, 1982), 35.
18. *Ibid.*, 33.
19. See for instance: Idem, "Analysis of a Parish", *Monthly Letter About Evangelism* (1 May 1968), 1 ff.; Idem, "Bible Study in the post-literary Age", *Monthly Letter about Evangelism* (1 January 1969), 1 ff.; Idem, "Flowers and Songs in Mexico. Bible Study in the Post-Literary Age: An

Example'', *Monthly letter about Evangelism* (1 December 1970).

20. Jac. Roos, ''Dr. Walter Hollenweger: van Pinksterbeweging naar Wereldraad'', *Hervormd Nederland* 24/1 (6 January 1968), 2.
21. At this consultation at the Parkhotel in Gunten, from 22-24 October 1966, there were 23 Pentecostals and 12 WCC-representatives. For a complete list of participants cf. Walter J. Hollenweger (ed.), *Die Pfingstkirchen - Selbstdarstellungen, Dokumente, Kommentare,* Die Kirchen der Welt Vol. VII (Stuttgart: Evangelisches Verlagwerk, 1971), 288. For more information on the conference at Gunten: Idem, ''Pfingstbewegung und Ökumene'', *Ökumenische Rundschau* 17/1 (January 1968), 57-59; Idem, ''Pentecostalia'', Department on Studies in Mission and Evangelism SE 67:14, Geneva: WCC, 1967.
22. WCC, *Von Neu-Delhi nach Uppsala 1961-1968: Bericht des Zentralausschusses an die Vierte Vollversammlung des Ökumenischen Rates der Kirchen* (Geneva: Ökumenischer Rat der Kirchen, 1968), 82. See also: G. Puchinger, ''Gesprekken met dr. J.W. Hollenweger over: Zending en Ontwikkeling'', *Maandblad Reunisten Organisatie Societas Studiosorum Reformatorum* no. 7 (June 1971), 4-5.
23. Christian Krust, ''Pentecostal Churches and the Ecumenical Movement'', Appendix VIII in: Norman Goodall ed., *The Uppsala Report 1968. Official Report of the Fourth Assembly of the WCC Uppsala 4-20 July 1968* (Geneva: WCC, 1968), 340-43.
24. Literally: Igreja Evangélica Pentecostal 'O Brasil para Cristo' - 1,100,000 members. Already in 1961 at New Delhi two Chilean Pentecostal denominations with a Methodist background were accepted as members of the WCC : The 'Pentecostal Church of Chile' (Iglesia Pentecostal de Chile - 90,000 members) and the 'Pentecostal Mission Church' (Mision Iglesia Pentecostal - 12,000 members).
25. W.J. Hollenweger, ''The Chair of Mission at the University of Birmingham'', *Selly Oak Journal*, no. 4 (1 January 1986), 12-13.
26. W.J. Hollenweger, ''Beschreibung des 'Professor of Mission' an der Universität Birmingham'', Manuscript, 1980, 1-2.
27. Walter J. Hollenweger, ''The Future of Mission and the Mission of the Future'', *Selly Oak Colleges: Occasional Paper 2* (Birmingham: Selly Oak Colleges, 1989), 3-4; 12-13.
28. To mention a few: Scripture in Dialogue; Light from the East; Spirit and Matter: A New Look at the Holy Spirit; Jesus of Nazareth seen through Jewish, Christian and Muslim eyes; The Quest for God; Narrative Theology - Problems and Promises.
29. For examples of narrative theology, plays, musicals and drama from W.J. Hollenweger see article of M. Heuberger-Gloor in this *Festschrift.*
30. Personal interview with W.J. Hollenweger, Birmingham, 7th July 1988.
31. In his preface to *The Pentecostals* Hollenweger thanks his wife for putting up with numerous conversations at home on the subject of the Pentecostal movement (W.J. Hollenweger, *The Pentecostals* (London: SCM Press, 1971), xx.
32. Erica Hollenweger, ''Aus meinem südafrikanischen Tagebuch'', *Leben und Glauben* 52/4 (22 January 1977), 10 f.; Idem, ''Aus meinem karibischen Tagebuch'', *Leben und Glauben* 53/12 (25 March 1978), 8 f.; Idem, ''Aus meinem karibischen Tagebuch'', *Leben und Glauben* 53/16 (22 April 1978), 10 f.; Idem, Wer hat dich so entstellt, du schöner Wald, *Leben und Glauben* 61/1 (3 January 1986), 15..

33, Isaiah 54:1-3, New International Version.

2

Als Christ zusammen mit Gleichgültigen und Ungläubigen das Evangelium entdecken: Hollenweger als Theologe

(Discovering the Gospel as Christians in Cooperation with the 'Indifferent' and Unbelievers: Hollenweger as Theologian)

Richard Friedli

> Ein Christ steht nicht links.
> Ein Christ steht nicht rechts.
> Ein Christ steht auch nicht in der Mitte.
> Ein Christ geht vorwärts.
> [W.J. Hollenweger]

Während den vergangenen Jahren hat der am. 1 Juni 1927 in Antwerpen geborene Zürcher Walter J. Hollenweger in ökomenischer und missionarischer Zusammenarbeit an der Universität Freiburg i. Ue. öfters Gastvorlesungen, Kolloquien und Seminare gehalten. Der Lehrerfolg, dessen er sich hier erfreut, beruht im Wesentlichen auf der Eröffnung einer Dimension von Erfahrungen, Fragen, Thesen und Folgerungen, mit denen den Hörern und Teilnehmern, unseren Studenten und Studentinnen aus Brasilien und Mexiko, aus Zaire und Rwanda, aus Korea und Japan, aus der Schweiz und Frankreich überraschenderweise das Ganze von Theologie ebenso ansichtig wurde wie ihre kulturelle Plurifomität. Mit einer rigorösen, oft aber bereits post-akademischen theologischen und humanwissenschaftlichen Kompetenz, die häufig vermengt ist mit ansteckendem Humor, dann wieder mit tiefer Betroffenheit vom Leiden der Menschen, läßt der begabte Schweizer-Universitätsprofessor von Birmingham (1971-1989) eine ganzheitliche Betrachtung und Beurteilung vom Leben in der Welt von heute erahnen. Die Lehrveranstaltungen werden so zu *Erfahrungen der Leibhaftigkeit* (1979). Erlebt, verpflichtend erörtert und präzise dokumentiert wird dabei, "daß die Kirche Jesu Cristi größer ist als mein kultureller Kontext, und daß darum die Theologie diese Universalität der Kirche Jesu Christi widerspiegeln muß, wenn sie denn wissenschaftliche Theologie sein muß (z.B. China, Brasilien, Westafrika, die Arbeiterkultur)".[1] Die theologische *Disziplin, die sehr wohl weiß, daß sie einer bestimmten kulturellen Ausprägung des Evangeliums verpflichtet ist*, und gerade deshalb *Brücken finden* muss, um *die Solidarität der Menschheit unserer Kirchen sichtbar werden zu lassen,* ist für den ehemaligen Bankangestellten (1943-48), Prediger der Schweizerischen Pfingtmission (1949-58) und weitgereisten Exekutivsekretär beim Ökumenischen Rat der Kirchen in Genf (1961-71) *interkulturelle Theologie.*

Leitsätze interkultureller Theologie

> Da ich nicht an eine objektive, wertfreie Wissenschaft glaube, muß ich den Gesichtspunkt angeben, von dem aus ich mein Thema angehe, nicht um ihn als den wichtigsten (oder gar als einzig möglichen) zu verteidigen, sondern um meine Argumentation verständlicher zu machen. Ein einzelner Mensch kann keine umfassende Interpretation des uns beschäftigenden Phänomens leisten. Er hat keine globale Perspektive und kann das zur Diskussion stehende Phänomen nicht von allen Gesichtspunkten aus gleichzeitig betrachten. Die Synthese aller Gesichtspunkte ist - theologisch gesagt - das Vorrecht Gottes. Zu beanspruchen, daß ich die Welt von seinem Gesichtspunkt aus, nämlich vom Gesichtspunkt Gottes aus betrachte, ist für einen Theologen unmöglich, denn Gott hat uns diese globale Vision der Welt nicht mitgeteilt.

Die vorausgehenden knappen biographischen Angaben lassen bereits ahnen, daß beim reformierten Pfarrer Hollenweger die interkulturelle Sensibilität existentiell verwurzelt ist. Seine internationalen Kontakte und Verantwortungen ließen ihn realisieren, wie sehr gilt: "Die Theologie der Frauen ist wichtig für die Theologie der Männer. Sie ist nicht einfach ein Seitenthema der Haupttheologie. Die Theologie der Schwarzen ist wichtig für die Weißen. Sie ist nicht einfach unterentwickelte Theologie".[2] Für eine in all diesen Bereichen nicht nur hermeneutisch, sondern auch heuristisch arbeitende Theologie sind dann "Grenzüberschreitungen zu anderen Kulturen, Religionen und Menschen, die uns fremd, unverständlich oder gar absurd vorkommen"[3], methodologisch notwendig. Nur mit dem Ausbruch aus dem *monokulturellen Gefängnis* wird es möglich, das, *was an Bleibendem in der europäischen Theologie geschaffen wurde, nicht zu verlieren, und den Anschluß an die neuen Weisen des Theologisierens in den neu entstandenen Kirchen nicht zu verpassen.*[4]

Kulturbedingtheit jeder Theologie

> Interkulturelle Theologie ist diejenige wissenschaftliche, theologische Disziplin, die im Rahmen einer gegebenen Kultur operiert, ohne diese zu verabsolutieren.

Es gibt somit nicht die reine Theologie oder den reinen Glauben. Vielmehr ist der religiöse und theologische *Pluralismus als Gabe und Aufgabe* zu verstehen. Bereits von der Arbeit in der Pfingstmission her und durch seine Dissertation bei Fritz Blanke, Kirchengeschichtler an der Universität Zürich zu den Pfingstbewegungen (1969), ist der Prediger und Liturge Hollenweger vor allem dafür sensibilisiert, daß Theologie nicht in ausschließlich rational argumentierenden Kategorien geleistet werden kann. Aber das kulturelle Eintauchen in die Welt der unabhängigen schwarzen Kirchen Afrikas und Mittelamerikas, von denen 120 in Birmingham vertreten sind, und die intensiven Auseinandersetzungen mit seinen Doktoranden und Doktorandinnen aus den verschiedensten Kulturen und Subkulturen, beruflichen Schichten und wissenschaftlichen Disziplinen Europas und der Dritten Welt ließen ihn noch globaler erfahren, wie sehr seelisches Heil und körperliche Heilung zusammengehören: "Der Ort, wo Heilung im weitesten Sinne des Wortes erwartet werden darf und wo nicht nur darüber geredet wird, ist die Gemeinde Jesu Christi. Gesundheit und Krankheit sind nicht Privatsache, sondern Sache der Liturgie".[5]

Der ghanesische Theologe Kofi Appiah-Kubi, sagt das programmatisch so: "der Mensch behandelt, Gott aber heilt" (Man cures, God heals), denn "ich bin krank in meinem Nachbarn".[6]

Was hier vom Umgang mit kranken Menschen gesagt ist, gilt auch für alle anderen - gesellschaftlichen,wirtschaftlichen, politischen - Wirklichkeiten, die theologisch situiert und geöffnet werden sollen, denn "die Welt gibt die Tagesordnung".[7] Hollenweger illustriert das an Zwinglis Reformation[8], wo der Kontext seiner Auslegung des Evangeliums die Republik Zürich ist. Dort stellte sich zu Beginn des 16. Jahrhundertes Zwingli z.B. die Fragen von Recht und Unrecht der Soldverträge mit dem Ausland, von der Ehelosigkeit der Priester oder von Recht und Unrecht des Kapitalzinses. "Zwingli wich diesen Fragen nicht in theologische Abstraktionen aus, die immer korrekt, aber nie konkret sind. Er beugt sich aber auch nicht der Meinung der damaligen Experten, sondern er versucht, im Gespräch mit ihnen die theologischen Dimensionen dieser Fragen ans Licht zu bringen und die Entscheidungen auf Grund der biblischen Offenbarung zu treffen".[9]

Revelanz theologischer Methoden

> Die Methoden zur Erreichung dieses Zieles, der universalen und sakramentalen Dimension des christlichen Glaubens gegenüber offen zu sein, sind auf Grund ihrer Tauglichkeit zu wählen. Die Mittelmeer-Tradition kann dabei nicht a priori als eine der Möglichkeiten ausgeschaltet werden, jedoch sollte man sie nicht als die einzige oder gar die wichtigste heranziehen, außer man habe Gründe, welche die großen Geschichten der Bibel, inclusive die Gleichnisse Jesu, als wissenschaftliche Theologie disqualifizieren.

Diese methodischen Ansätze sind pluriform. Die Westkirche Euramerikas hat -

entsprechend einer seiner Grundrhythmen - in der systematischen Theologie dem rational-argumentativen Potential des Menschen und in der Bibel-Exegese der historisch-kritischen *Methode* den Vorzug gegeben. Professor Unrat mußte zwischen Bangkok und Birmingham aber erfahren (1975), daß diese Bibel-Interpretationsweise von einzelnen Beobachtern "für bankrott erklärt wird, weil sie - anstatt uns zum Ursprung mit alten und neuen Mythen anzuleiten - diese einfach eliminiert oder glaubt zu eliminieren".[10] Viel mehr sollten situationsgemäß und komplementär andere relevante Methoden eingesetzt werden: z.B. die Ansätze der *Prozeß-Theologie* (1971) oder die vor allem in Basisgemeinden verwendete Weise der *Wurzeltheologie* (1977).

Grosse Chancen gibt Hollenweger, weil er diesen Weg auch meisterhaft begehen kann, der *narrativen Vorgehensweise* und ordnet so die Erzählungen der Deduktion vor, denn "Ich vermute, daß die erzählerische und biographische Darstellung komplizierter abstrakter Denkprozesse eine der Möglichkeiten interkultureller Theologie ist".[11]

Hierher gehört auch - theoretisch und praktisch glänzend dargestellt (1982) - das Spiel, das Lied, die Musik und der Tanz (1985, 1986 und 1987). Die Choreographie gehört dann zur Missiologie. Ob dadurch verhindert werden kann, daß "unsere Gottesdienste zu einer Mischung aus Predigt, kirchenmusikalischem Seminar und liturgiegeschichtlichem Exkurs"[12] werden? Dadurch wird aber wenigstens die Dimension des wahren Mythos in der interkulturellen Theologie wieder geweckt. Mit "Mythen können sich ja Menschen verschiedener Kulturen identifizieren, denn ohne Mythenrahmen ist die Kommunikation von Informationen, Überzeugungen und Urteilen undurchführbar".[13]

Es geht aber Hollenweger hier nicht darum, den Begriff 'Mythos' zu definieren, sondern vielmehr darum, *die Funktion von Mythos* zu illustrieren: "Ich suche eine Exegese, die dem denkenden Christen hilft, von den biblischen Mythenarbeitern den rechten Umgang mit den heutigen Mythen zu lernen".[14]

Der ganze zweite Band der "interkulturellen Theologie" widmet der Geschichtenerzähler und Theologe Walter Hollenweger alten und neuen Mythen: dem *schweizerischen Selbtsgefälligkeitsmythos von Wilhelm Tell*, dem *Elite-Mythos des Engländers*, den *Weinachtsmythen*, dem *Mythos der Gottesbegegnung* im Jakobskampf (Gen. 32) und *Versöhnungsriten*. In diesen beispielhaften Mythen wird illustriert, wie sehr *der Mythos ein Datum des Menschseins des Menschen* ist, ebenso wie der *Traum, das Frau- und Mannsein und die Sprache*.[15]

Um sich theologisch verantwortlich mit dem Mythos auseinanderzusetzen, schlägt Hollenweger folgende Kriterien für einen wahren Mythos vor:[16]

1. Bezug zu gegenwärtigen gesellschaftlichen, kulturellen und wirtschaftlichen Konflikten (Sozialisierung);
2. im wahren Mythos wird die Verankerung im Kreuz historisch (Relativierung)

und

3. er drückt einen "Mehrwert der Verheißung über die Geschichte" aus (Antizipation).

Wie narrative, choreographische und mythische Methoden - immer kombiniert mit seriöser historisch-kritischer Exegese - in einem wahren Mythos Wirklichkeit werden kann, illustriert die "Schule für schwarze Arbeiterpfarrer" in Birmingham (am Center for Black and White Christian Partnership an den Selly Oak Colleges). An dieser "Arbeiteruniversität" sind z.B. im Fach "christliche Glaubenslehre" Gottesdienste, Gebet, Lied und Zeugnis so wichtig wie Vorlesung und Examen.[17]

Alternative Formen des Theologisierens

> Da wir bis anhin der Mittelmeer-Tradition in unseren Forschungsmethoden den Vorzug gaben, schlage ich vor, daß wir nun nach den alternativen Formen des Theologisierens Ausschau halten.

Das eben erwähnte Beispiel einer nach der Paolo-Freire-Methode arbeitenden Volks-Universität, die aber dem akademischen Standard im Endeffekt keinen Abbruch tut[18], läßt erahnen, in welcher Richtung sich solche, für zünftige Universitätsprofessoren unerhörte Weisen des Theologisierens entwickeln können. Dann ist nämlich das "Medium der Kommunikation nicht die Definition, sondern die Deskription, nicht die These, sondern der Tanz, nicht die Lehre, sondern das Lied, nicht das gelehrte Buch, sondern Geschichte und Gleichnis, nicht das Formulieren von Konzepten, sondern das Feiern von Banketten".[19]

Für die theologische und evangelisierende Arbeit kann so das Chanson "Pardon" von Jacques Brel, das Märchen Rumpelstilzchen, ein marxistischer Text, die Leidenssituation des ausgebeuteten Volkes (*Minjung*) in Korea, die Erinnerung an den Propheten Simon Kimbangu aus dem heutigen Zaire oder ein Lied des Jodelchoires im Dorf Hilterfingen am Thuner See zum Ausgangspunkt genommen werden.[20] Dazu ist aber *eine andere Exegese* verlangt (wie der schwarze Nordamerikaner James Cone oder Juan Luis Segundo in Montevideo es bereits tun). "Die Exegese der Zukunft ist eine Exegese, zu der alle Charismen einen Beitrag leisten, alle Interessen, alle Kulturen, Männer und Frauen, alle Gaben im Leibe Christi".[21]

Selbstkritik des Theologen

> Interkulturelle Theologie ist nicht eine Form von Pop-Theologie. Sie dispensiert uns nicht von den Methoden der in unserer Kultur akzeptierten kritischen Wis-

senschaft, aber sie verlangt von uns, daß wir diese nicht nur auf den Inhalt unserer Disziplin, sondern auf den Gesamtprozeß der Kommunikation anwenden, auf das Feld zwischen Sender und Empfänger, kurz, auf den Prozeß des Theologisierens innerhalb des Leibes Christi.

W. Hollenweger weiß aus den unzähligen Debatten, Diskussionen und Streitgesprächen, die er weltweit hält und halten mußte, das zwar die Hermeneutik und die Exegese auch aus der oben skizzierten Perspektiven *nicht weniger wissenschaftlich als die übrige Exegese* sein darf, daß aber während dem interkulturellen Umsetzungsprozeß sich notwendigerweise Wertverschiebungen ereignen: "Die Ungenauigkeit ist der Preis, der zu bezahlen ist für die Kommunizierbarkeit kritischer Exegese in ein mehrbödiges soziales Leser-(oder Hörer-) Feld."[22] Neben den Reaktionen der Basis auf seine biblischen Interpretationen und homiletisch-liturgischen Interventionen sind für den einfühlsamen und fordernden Lehrer Hollenweger "die Fragen und Einwände meiner Studenten. Ich kann nicht an ihnen vorbei Theologie betreiben".[23] Immer wieder und voller Bewunderung - und wer, wie ich, die Chance hatte in der Wohnung von Erica und Walter Hollenweger an der Harborne Road in Birmingham einem solchen 'Doctoral Seiminar' teilzunehmen, weiß um ihre Fähigkeit zum kritischen und weiterführenden Hinhorchen und Nachfragen - kommt Hollenweger auf *diesen Einfluß der Dritt-Welt-Studenten* zu sprechen.[24] Hier wird in reziproker Verbundenheit und Verbindlichkeit, Ernsthaftigkeit und Freude, die interkulturelle Theologie gepflegt, getestet und radikalisiert. Das ist "Diakonie des Denkens".[25]

Leitbilder der Mission

Die intensive, glaubende und hoffende, im Konflikt zwischen 'Evangelikalen' und 'Ökumenikern', zwischen 'Vertikalen' und 'Horizontalen' erhärtete Betroffenheit und Solidarität zwischen den Exekutivsekretären für Evangelisation am Ökumenischen Rat der Kirchen in Genf - Johannes Chr. Hoekendijk (1949-53), Hans Jochen Margull (1961-1967) und Walter J.Hollenweger (1967-1971) - hat ihre Suche nach dem *Christus intra et extra muros ecclesiae* nie erlahmen lassen. Im Gegenteil: in ihrer Studie "Kirche für andere"[26] freuten sie sich darüber, daß "Christus schon vor der Kirche da war, weil er schon immer größer gewesen ist als die Kirche".[27] Mission ist dann "jener Prozeß, durch den Christen zusammen mit den Gleichgültigen und Ungläubigen das Evangelium entdecken".[28]

Kirche für andere

Der Entdeckungsprozeß, in welchem der Evangelist durch das Geschehen der Evangelisation etwas über das Evangelium erfährt, heißt nach Hollenweger 'Evangelisation'.[29] Evangelisation verläuft - eben weil Christus den Christen vorausgeht (Mk. 16:7) - nicht entlang einer missionierenden und proselytischen Einbahnstraße, sondern in der je für alle Menschen gemeinsamen Heilsgeschichte, in der auch die kirchliche Gemeinschaft mit Gläubigen und Ungläubigen aus allen Kulturen auf dem (Pilger-)Weg ist. Modellhaft ist diese Gegenseitigkeit in der Mission ablesbar in der Begegnung zwischen Petrus und dem römischen Hauptmann Cornelius in Caesarea (Apg. 10)[30] und zwischen dem Kongo-Missionar Placide Tempels in der Jamaa-Bewegung mit Christus, der schon da war.[31] In beiden Situationen *hat sich der Evangelist bekehrt.*

Wie kann sie dabei in kritischer Solidarität auf Jesus den Christus hinweisen und zugehen? "Wie bauen wir eine Kirche, die sich nicht selbst im Wege ist, deren organisatorische Struktur dem, was sie predigt nicht dauernd widerspricht, ... eine Gemeinde, der man glaubt, daß sie für andere ist, weil sie sich nicht selber sucht?".[32] Für viele Theologen sind solche "Anwälte einer Kirche für die anderen" *Säkularisierer.* Hinter solchen Anklagen ist oft viel Angst verborgen. Wie *ändert man Mentalitäten und Strukturen?* Hollenweger ist davon überzeugt, dass man "Angst nicht überwindet, indem man die Ängstlichen verspottet, beschimpft oder anpredigt, sondern indem man mit einigen beherzten Freunden zusammen durch das Feld marschiert, vom dem die andern wähnen, es sei voller Mienen".[33]

Umgang mit Konflikten

Dadurch kann die kirchliche Gemeinschaft modellhaft vorleben, wie unter dem Zeichen des biblischen *Schalom* mit den für jede Gemeinschaft von Menschen unausweichlichen Konflikten umgegangen werden könnte. Norm ist dabei, wie es W. Hollenweger in seiner meisterhaften exegetischen Analyse und narrativen Umsetzung des Konflikts in Korinth[34] gezeigt hat, nicht das zerstörerische Rechthaben (Orthodoxie), sondern das Aufbauen des Leibes Christi (Orthopraxis). Es geht in einer eucharistischen Gemeinde um die "Transsubstantiation der Leute und nicht der Elemente".[35] Und die Theologie, "insofern sie Leib-Christi-Theologie ist, deutet diese sozialen und kulturellen Konflikte als notwendige Wachtstumkrisen einer theologischen Reflexion".[36]

Strukturprinzip Dialog

Damit ist auch bei der Eucharistiefeier das interkulturelle Anliegen im Zentrum: "Jesus hat durch seinen Umgang mit Zöllnern, Dirnen und Sündern nicht nur damalige politische und soziale Tabus durchbrochen, sondern er hat - um den Willen Gottes zu tun - das verletzt, das man damals für den Willen Gottes hielt. Dadurch, daß er nicht kultfähige Personen zu seinen Mahlfeiern einlud, hat er neu bestimmt, was Gottesdienst ist".[37] *Aufgabe der Liturgie ist es also, den Dialog zu ermöglichen und im Zusammenhang mit der Tradition der Kirche die 'Stimme des Geistes' zu vernehmen.*[38] In seiner Pneumatologie (*Interkulturelle Theologie III*) thematisiert und exemplifiziert Hollenweger einige Dialogfelder in der heutigen

Zeit: Islam (z.B. Korankritik und Kreuzestheologie, islamische und christliche Christologien), *Religion civile* (z.B. Volkskirche und 'Leutereligion'; der neue Patriotismus) oder Friedenspraxis.

Unter den Vielfältigen Dialogorten - Straße und Büro, Konferenzsaal und theologische Akademie, Familie und Massen-Medien - erwähnt Hollenweger wissenschaftliche Instrumente, bei denen er in Birmingham Mitinitiant war: das wichtigste Dokumentationszentrum der Welt für 'New Religious Movements', dessen Direktor Harold W. Turner, ein Theologe der Presbyterianischen Kirche von New Zealand, ist[39] und das Institut für angewandte Religionswissenschaft 'Multi Faith Resource Unit', das seine ehemalige Doktorandin aus Irland, Mary Hall, gegründet hat und leitet.[40] Es sind diesse Dialogorte, *wo die Vertreter verschiedener Religionen ihre eigene Religion im Kontext einer modernen Großstadt artikulieren.* Wie und nach welchen Kriterien diese dialogische Modell vorgeht, zeigt Hollenwegers Suche nach dem theologischen Stellenwert der Reinkarnationslehre.[41]

Darnach geht es bei der 'Wiedergeburt' um einen *wachsamen Kampf, die persönliche und soziale Verantwortung wahrzunehmen* (vgl. Tit. 3:5; Joh. 3:3-8), und nicht um das "Wie einer Seele, die zwischen verschiedenen Körpern wandert".[42]

Nachwort: Das Gebet

Im vorausgehenden Versuch, die Anliegen, Methoden und Grenzen der Interkulturellen Theologie aus dem so umfang- und facettenreichen Werk von Walter J. Hollenweger herauszukristallisieren, ist sicher Vieles eingeebnet und vereinfacht worden. Beim erneuten Nachlesen seiner Schriften und beim erinnernden Nachdenken unserer Gespräche finden sich zwei Leitmotive seiner Theologie - oder noch umfassender seiner Spiritualität: die theologische und ethische Rück- und Vor-Verwurzelung im Leib Chisti als existentielle Richtschnur und der Platz des persönlichen und gemeinschaftlichen Gebetes im Alltag. In Solidarität mit Walter J. Hollenweger schließe ich daher diese Darstellung mit dem gleichen Gebet, das er zum Ausklang seiner dreibändigen interkulterellen Theologie formuliert hat:

Froschgebet

> Lieber Gott,
> manchmal komme ich mir vor wie eine Frosch.
> Wenn ich im Wasser bin, dann geht mir die Luft aus und ich muß wieder an die Luft.
> Und wenn ich auf einem Seerosenblatt sitze und die Sonne auf meine Haut scheint, dann wird es mir zu heiß und ich muß wieder ins Wasser zurück.

Warum muß ich ein solches Zwischengeschöpf sein, weder Fisch noch Vogel,
weder im Wasser noch auf dem Trockenen wirklich zu Hause?
Wenn ich bei den Christen bin, so sagen sie, ich sei kein Christ, weil ich viele
Fragen habe und mir manchmal die Luft ausgeht.
Und wenn ich bei den Nichtchristen bin, so sagen sie, ich sei ein Christ, weil ich
an Jesus Christus glaube.
Wenn ich bei den politisch Engagierten bin, so sagen sie, ich sei ein Frommer,
weil ich glaube, daß das Gebet wichtig ist für die Politik.
Und wenn ich bei den Frommen bin, so sagen sie, ich sei zu weinig fromm, weil
ich glaube, daß wir etwas tun müssen für unsere arme Welt.
Wenn ich bei den Offizieren bin, so sagen sie, ich sei kein rechter Schweizer, weil
ich glaube, daß wir die Kriegsdienstverweigerer nicht einsperren sollten.
Wenn ich bei den Kriegsdienstverweigerern bin, so sagen sie, ich sei ein Militär-
kopf, weil ich die Sweizer Armee nicht abschaffen will.
Warum muss ich immer dazwischen sein?
Warum muss ich ein Frosch sein?
Warum kann ich kein Flamingo, oder ein Löwe oder ein Adler sein.
Nur so ein gewöhnlicher Frosch, über den alle lachen.
Hilf mir, daß ich meine Existenz bejahe, daß ich sehe, daß es solche Evangelis-
ten, solche Zwischengeschöpfte braucht in deinem Reich.
Mach mich zu einem fröhlichen Frosch! Amen.

Anmerkungen

— Früher erschiehnen als "Walter J. Hollenweger (* 1927) als Christ zusammen mit Gleichgültigen und Ungläubigen das Evangelium entdecken" in: Stephan Leingruber und Max Schoch (Hrsg.), *Gegen die Gottvergessenheit; Schweitzer Theologen im 19. und 20. Jahrhundert* (Basel/Freiburg/Wien: Herder, 1990), 652-62.

1. Die in Kursivschrift wiedergegebenen Ausdrücke, Formulierungen oder Kurzsätze sind dem Werk von W.J. Hollenweger entnommen. Um die Lesbarkeit dieses Beitrags nicht zu zerhacken, sind aber nur für längere Zitate die genauen bibliographischen Rechtfertigungen angegeben.
2. W. Hollenweger, *Umgang mit Mythen; Interkulturelle Theologie II* (München: 1982), 97.
3. W. Hollenweger, *Geist und Materie; Interkulturelle Theologie III* (München: 1988), 195.
4. Die vier folgenden "Leitsätze zur interkulterellen Theologie"(I 50-51) sind die hermeneutisch-theologische Begründung, um die Stadt Korinth im 1. Korinterbrief als "ein Laboratorium interkultureller Theologie" (I 34-38) darzustellen (vgl. 1978). Diese missionsmethodologisch für die aktuelle Inkulturationsdiskussion entscheidenen Prinzipien sind von R. Friedli generalisiert und weitergeführt worden: Artikel "Interkulturelle Theologie", in: K. Müller und Th. Sundermeier (Hg.), *Lexikon missionstheologischer Grundbegriffe* (Berlin, 1987), 183-184; ferner R. Friedli, *Mission oder Demission; Konturen einer lebendigen, weil missionarischen Gemeinde* (Freiburg i. Ue., 1982), 75-84.
5. W. Hollenweger, *Geist und Materie*, 22 f.
6. *Ibid.*, 48-52.
7. Im Schlußbericht der westeuropäischen und nordamerikanischen Arbeitsgruppe des Referats für

Fragen der Verkündigung des Ökomenischen Rates der Kirchen *Die Kirche für andere und die Kirche für die Welt im Ringen um Strukturen missionarischer Gemeinden* (Genf 1967) ist diese Option "Die Welt setzt die Tagesordnung" (23-27) theoretisches und praktisches Referenz-Kriterium für die Evangelisation. Hollenweger bleibt damit in kritischer Solidarität zu seinem Vorgänger am ökumenischen Rat der Kirchen (siehe unten Abschnitt II), J. Chr. Hoekendijk. Zu den hoffnungsstarken Horizonten dieses holländisch-indonesischen Missionars und Missiologen vgl. J.Chr. Hoekendijk, Zur Frage einer missionarischen Existenz (Anhang von 1966 zu seiner 1948 veröffentlichten Dissertation *Kirche und Volk in der deutschen Missionswissenschaft* (in: Theologische Bücherei 35, München, 1967, 297-354). Vgl. ferner Hollenweger II 29-45 (*Die Kirche für andere*) und 45-62 (Hoekendijk).

8. W. Hollenweger, *Erfahrungen mit Leibhaftigkeit; Interkulturelle Theologie I* (München, 1979), 299-328.
9. *Ibid.*, 299.
10. W. Hollenweger, *Umgang mit Mythen*, 12.
11. W. Hollenweger, *Erfahrungen mit Leibhaftigkeit*, 349.
12. *Ibid.*, 246.
13. W. Hollenweger, *Umgang mit Mythen*, 63.
14. *Ibid.*, 14.
15. *Ibid.*, 231.
16. *Ibid.*, 161-63.
17. *Ibid.*, 182.
18. *Ibid.*, 178-88.
19. W. Hollenweger, *Erfahrungen mit Leibhaftigkeit*, 80 f.
20. Ausgehend vom immer gleichen Prinzip, daß sich das Volk selbst evangelisieren soll, ist auch das Festspiel 'Friedensmahl' zum 700jährigen Bestehen der Schweiz (1991), welches an mehr als 50 Orten unter Zusammenarbeit mit den ortsansässigen Gesangs-und Musikvereinen gestaltet werden soll, konzipiert. Dieses choreographisch, musikalisch und textlich von W.J. Hollenweger durchkomponierte Theater, welches die 'Arbeitsgemeinschaft Christlicher Kirchen der Schweiz' bei ihm in Auftrag gegeben hat, soll - in Anlehnung an das bekannte Bild 'Abendmahl' von Leonardo da Vinci - determinieren, welche Schweizerinnen und Schweizer (H. Zwingli, H. Dunant, Nikolaus und/oder Dorothea von Flüe, Abbé Bovet usw.) am Abendmahltisch Platz nehmen dürfen.
21. W. Hollenweger, *Umgang mit Mythen*, 136.
22. W. Hollenweger, *Erfahrungen mit Leibhaftigkeit*, 49 f.
23. *Ibid.*, 344.
24. W. Hollenweger, *Geist und Materie*, 63; 88-94.

Zur Bedeutung der Dritt-Welt-Studenten für das theologische Schaffen von Hollenweger vgl. seine Analyse, Synthese und Perspektiven der in Birmingham unter seiner Leitung ausgearbeiteten Dissertationen:" Towards an Intercultural History of Christianity", in: *International Review of Mission* 304 (Oct. 1987), 526-556. Zur zwischenmenschlichen Bedeutung der Dritt-Welt-Studenten im Leben von W.J. Hollenweger: vgl. folgenden Abschnitt aus seiner Abschiedsvorlesung in Birmingham (Sommer 89):

The only limits of my work were not the limits of institutions and organisations, but my own limits, the limits of my ignorance, of my inertia, of my lack of perception. And what discoveries did we make! 99 postgraduates came of all ages (the oldest of them over 70, the youngest in their early twenties), many pastors, teachers, church leaders, even a trade union leader, college and university teachers from such countries as Korea and Kenya, East Germany and Ghana, the Caribbean and West Africa, Mexico and Malaysia, Argentina and Australia, India and Indonesia, Romania, Ireland, Switzerland, Holland, Germany, Britain and the United States, men and women, catholic nuns, priests and lay people, Baptists, Methodists, Presbyterians, Lutherans and Anglicans, even

Eastern Orthodox, Seventh Day Adventists, Pentecostals, members of African independent churches and of black British cultures.

Their topics ranged from a study of the culture of economism (the state religion of Britain) to Vaudouism (the folk religion of Haiti), from research into the gospel of prosperity in Argentinian Pentecostalism to the ecumenical promises of Dutch pentecostalism, from intercultural pastoral care in Ghana to shamanism in Korea, from a theological reading of Dürrenmatt to a rigorous and hihgly technical debate on gene manipulation in the Soviet Union and the U.K. (with the help of our own Medical Faculty), from worship and theology in a communist country to business ethics (or the lack of it) in the USA, from non-Christian religions to the churches in China, from a critical reading of Fynn's *Mister God, Here is Anna* to Forster's *A Passage to India*, from biographies of missionaries, ecumenical leaders, pentecostal pioneers to an analysis of the fears and faiths of Birmingham workers, from an interpretation of the songs of Zambia to the stories of independent churches in India, Africa or Latin America, from a study of the liturgies in the Orthodox churches to an analysis of worship, preaching style and the role of women in British black churches... You can imagine that the research of my students opened my eyes to the problems and promises of the worldwide ecumene, the universal church. Coming from a small country like Switzerland, I received at the University of Birmingham an education in global theology, liturgy, economics and educational theories, from my student researchers.

25. W. Hollenweger, *Erfahrungen mit Leibhaftigkeit*, 15.
26. W. Hollenweger, *Umgang mit Mythen*, 29-38.
27. W. Hollenweger, *Erfahrungen mit Leibhaftigkeit*, 155.
28. *Ibid.*, 160.
29. *Ibid.*, 121.
30. Cf. *Ibid.*, 127-30.
31. W. Hollenweger, *Evangelisation gestern und heute* (Stuttgart, 1973), 14-19.
32. W. Hollenweger, *Erfahrungen mit Leibhaftigkeit*, 246.
33. *Ibid.*, 225.
34. W. Hollenweger, *Konflikt in Korinth* (München, 1978), 9-45; ders., *Erfahrungen mit Leibhaftigkeit*, 38-47.
35. W. Hollenweger, *Erfahrungen mit Leibhaftigkeit*, 218.
36. W. Hollenweger, *Geist und Materie*, 229.
37. W. Hollenweger, *Umgang mit Mythen*, 176.
38. *Ibid.*, 175; cf. 240 f.
39. W. Hollenweger, *Geist und Materie*, 134-37.
40. *Ibid.*, 171-73.
41. *Ibid.*, 263-66.
42. *Ibid.*, 265.

3

The Magpies Gotta Know: Hollenweger as an Ecumenical

Werner Ustorf

> Ja, was man so kennen heißt. Du hast dunkle Augen und lockiges Haar und einen feinen Teint und sagst immer zu mir: lieber Georg! Aber (er deutet ihr auf Stirn und Augen) da, da, was liegt hinter dem? Geh, wir haben grobe Sinne. Einander kennen? Wir müßten uns die Schädeldecken aufbrechen und die Gedanken einander aus den Hirnfasern zerren.
> Ich glaube, man muß... die Bildung eines neuen geistigen Lebens im Volke suchen und die abgelebte moderne Gesellschaft zum Teufel gehen lassen. Zu was soll ein Ding wie diese zwischen Himmel und Erde herumlaufen? Das ganze Leben derselben besteht nur in Versuchen, sich die entsetzlichste Langeweile zu vertreiben. Sie mag aussterben, das ist das einzige Neue, was sie noch erleben kann. [Georg Büchner][1]

Starting an attempt to portray W.J. Hollenweger as an ecumenical from these quotations by an artist and a revolutionary, a scientist, an emigrant, a lover of and a sufferer from life, and an atheist critic of the godlessness of modernity (G. Büchner, 1813-1837), implies a strong if onesided focus. However, the focus is neither to 'explain' Hollenweger through Büchner or vice versa, nor to compare the two. Büchner's words - relics of a torn and fragmented life - have here a catalytic function: They produce the sobering realisation of the limited nature of our attempts to escape from loneliness, not to impose our images on others, and, hence, the difficulty of understanding one another.

A portrayal might easily and unconsciously slip into betrayal, to use a phrase by Anton Wessels. That holds even more true if only one part of the full picture, a detail of Hollenweger's theological engagement, which may be called his 'ecumenical' contribution, is being treated. And who would be more appropriate to weigh this contribution than the *oikoumene* itself, Christians from all over the world, and particularly, I guess, those theologians who previously were his doctoral candidates? What I am doing here, therefore, is merely offering for further discussion some hypotheses of how to understand this essential, if all-embracing 'detail'. And in that regard there is something more to be gained from Büchner's words. Büchner was probably one of the first thinkers on the continent who really unreservedly encountered all the uncertainties and dead ends of modernity and the hopelessness of the human condition. And this is exactly what I think I 'discovered' as a fundamental ecumenical ethos in Hollenweger's thinking - the attempt to unreservedly encounter what is realized as 'reality', and to resolutely understand the gospel in relation to this reality, notwithstanding that this may go beyond the framework and constructional patterns of our worldview, our ecclesiological or denominational convictions and our theological fixations.

Therefore, I regard his ambition to include in his theological thinking what normally was left aside by academical theology - namely e.g. the Christian experience in the diversity of its oral and often non-western expression, the theological quality and structure of charismatic phenomena, the marxist critique, the usage of art, drama, narrative and music as 'theological' languages, and his abandonment of watertight theological systems - not as a return to a past naivety or to a pre-enlightened simplicity, but just the other way round as an attempt to leave the narrow confines that theological discourse has erected in order to get out of the troubled waters of the post-Christendom era. In my opinion, Hollenweger opts for a real theological encounter, the exposure of one's belief to the plurality of Christian experience, and to the explicitly non-religious, multireligious and multicultural modernity of our time. Perhaps, he wants to go beyond modernity, and he knows, as G. Büchner foretold, that this can only be done with 'the people'. This perspective is suggested and tentatively applied to the following brief *tour d'horizon* of Hollenweger's ecumenical contribution.

Being Rigorously Ecumenical

If the church universal really is one of the most important agents for peace and reconciliation, then, "it is doubly important that when they become indigenous the churches in the Third World do not follow the nationalistic and provincial theological methodology of their European/American mother churches, but become - perhaps for the first time in church history - truly ecumenical and catholic. And for this to happen they have to be exposed to an international and intercultural context", - here we have one of Hollenweger's basic insights at the height of his activity as a professor, and in fact, the one and only Professor of Mission in a British University.[2]

The preparation for this was very special, and indeed very much 'ecumenical': Having worked on one hand as a clerk in the Zürich stock exchange before becoming a Pentecostal minister for ten years on the Continent (Zürich 1949-1958), ordained a Minister of the Swiss Reformed Church in 1962, and as such in Britain a regular churchgoer for whom speaking in tongues was "a natural part" of his prayer life[3], he engaged on the other hand in a years-long detailed and very critical study of worldwide Pentecostalism, and from 1965 to 1971 in the ecumenical movement, first as Executive Secretary of the Department on Studies in Evangelism, then as a Secretary for Evangelism in the Division of World Mission and Evangelism of the WCC, editing e.g. two of the most pioneering ecumenical reports of the time.[4] A third field in which he was engaged at the same time was radio and television. In order to overcome the limitations of a theology which was discursive and divided people by its definitions, he made use of songs, music, even pop music, and enabled people to articulate theologically in their own way.

All his findings led him to the conclusion that what is usually called the western form of Christianity did not cover the wider Christian reality, not even in the West. In fact, the well established traditions of Rome, Wittenberg, Geneva or Canterbury are nowadays minority forms and other Christians are very different from that, because they belong to the majority culture of this world which is that of oral culture. Oral theology, as in the case of scriptures, operates through the medium of the story, not the statement. It uses descriptions, not definitions. But not only that. He realized that Marxist, Agnostic, Hindu and Muslim followers of Jesus write and think about the story of Jesus of Nazareth. Jesus, as a matter of empirical fact - not simply as a propositional claim - has become an universal figure, breaking through the Christians' attempts to regard him as their property only. Now, having in mind that being Christian in the diversity of cultures means different things, one inevitably starts to apply the question of Christian pluralism also to the history of Christianity.

This may lead to a confrontation with the 'dangerous memories' (J.B. Metz) of the past, when reconstructing a reality which was surprisingly pluriform: discovering e.g. the pre-god-like Jesus of the early Hebrew Christians, a Christology which was declared to be heretical by the victorious gentile Christians. "Shall we ever be able to correct this mistake?", asks Hollenweger. He regards it as a mistake to silence what is and was different, because the images of Christ Jesus as expressed by others and by those who call themselves non-Christians are necessary for a global understanding and essential for the search for a just, peaceful and ecological world order.

This would include the point of view of those who declare themselves as non-believers, because they are the ones who enable those who regard themselves as believers to discover and theologically express their 'unbelief'. The other way round: the critical method of academic Christian theology can become an asset when used dialogically by Muslim and Christian theologians in order to discover the "underlying pluralistic treasures, the promises of flexibility and intercultural theology in Islam". This listening to that which the other Christians and the non-Christians have to offer and to criticise, Hollenweger calls being "rigorously ecumenical".[5]

The Need for Constant Reinterpretation

In the summer term of 1963, when he was a Research Assistant for Church History in the University of Zürich (1962-1964) and offering a lecture course on the relationship between church and sect for the extra-mural department, Hollenweger gave a paper on 'piety' (Frömmigkeit). Surprisingly, he defined piety in relation to its 'value'. Not valuable seemed to him that type of piety "which leads us back to God," because this was "phenomenologically not ascertainable". Valuable was that type "which leads us back to the neighbour".[6] Here already, 'reality' in its empirical sense is regarded as a subject of theological dignity. Personal belief or theological tradition have to be tested by the criterion of its relatedness to this reality.

This basic assumption takes Hollenweger so far as to honestly declare his personal decision for Christ as (1) socially and culturally conditioned in the first instance. This background made his confidence in the reliability of Jesus of Nazareth possible. However, Hollenweger is aware of the fact that there he is dealing with a presupposition (2) which is seen as a valuable one unless (3) being taught otherwise. The criterion applied certainly is not 'truth' (meaning a collection of words, a judgmental proposition of the mind, claiming to state 'what is the case'). Hollenweger does not claim to know whether his understanding of revelation is true or not. The criterion is the usefulness of "Jesus' reliability" for the realities of life. The *theologia crucis* "so far served us well", and "so far", Hollenweger did not encounter any "more reliable" understanding other than the one offered through Jesus of Nazareth.[7]

The person-affirmed dimension in Hollenweger's approach makes the person and his/her experiences of reality[8] the *locus* of "Jesus' reliability" to such an extent that I ask myself where the 'What' of this reliability, i.e. that which stands up against us, really turns up. On the other hand, it is quite justifiable to assume that all our fundamental presuppositions are conditioned, preliminary, relative, partial, provisional. There is a reality which is not known and which lies 'beyond' all the realities which might be experienced. That is the justification for experimenting also with a non-personal or panentheist image of God.[9] How can the problem of the relationship between 'truth 1', which stands up against us, and 'truth 2', which is the one experienced in the unreserved encounter with the realities of life, be resolved?

Hollenweger's response to this question is that religions themselves, and that includes the Christian traditions, are as partial and provisional as our encounters with the realities of life are. Religions are given in an historical context, "they mirror truth in a contingent and historical situation and therefore have to undergo constant reinterpretations."[10]

Beyond Our Cautious Agreements

Hollenweger never understood the historical attempt of doing *oikoumene* as an enterprise which would finally lead to the creation of a single Christian church in the world. His concept of unity is not to be found in the fields of organisation or definition, but more in an attitude which allows for the experience of the brother- and sisterhood of humankind: enjoying the mutual differences in spirituality, theology and morality; trusting each other; being genuinely curious and not afraid of one's courage.[11] To overcome fear and worry, that is precisely what Hollenweger, following Bangkok 1973, regards as an expression of God's grace - or of "the charm of God".[12] This vision of an *oikoumene* which is moving and being moved seems to be modelled on the history of the Pentecostal movement with the diversity of its forms. Pentecostalism is in itself an ecumenical movement, unified particularly by its black roots, which Hollenweger describes as the orality of liturgy, the narrativity of theology, maximum participation at the levels of reflection, prayer and decision-making, and the inclusion of dreams, visions and the body/mind relationship into worship.

Could this be a viable, namely a catholic, ecumenical and universal form of unity, capable of integrating the partial Mediterranean theological approach - can D. Bonhoeffer so to speak be related to W.J. Seymour?[13] In other words, does the future lie with the pluriform and communicating church, a diversity of theological, spiritual, ethical and political traditions - engaged with each other in friendly and creative conflict? Perhaps. However, the church is like all our different forms of piety and spirituality, for others. If they do not lead us back to our neighbours, that is right into the realities of life, they are of no value.

At the end of the day, Hollenweger's contribution can also be seen as an attempt to bring mission to the official factories of theology, namely to the academic departments and faculties. Tell all this to the 'magpies'! Who are these magpies? They sometimes walk up and down, all majestic in black and white, and they peck those who neither feel quite at home within nor above the earth, neither are they sufficiently radical in the eyes of the revolutionaries, nor sufficiently pious in the eyes of those who claim to be the shareholders of heaven. Magpies are the 'haves', the knights of intellectual systems and religious truth, the great reducers of reality, and particularly numerous in academic settings. Hollenweger says:

> And so I am what I am, an earth-worm.
> 'Til that moment when you, God, whisper into my ear:
> Earth-worm, you are important! Without you there is no life, no plants, no vegetables, no animals, no people, no university, no government, no science and art and no magpies in all their academic glory.
> What can I say to this, dear God?

I know what I say: I say, thank you, dear God, thank you indeed.
I am important.
But, dear God, I wonder whether you couldn't tell that to the magpies too.[14]

Certainly, to regard oneself as a 'Hollenwegerite' is a contradiction in itself. Don't make him a magpie. I am grateful to the earth-worm which helped me to discover - and to struggle with it - that I am a theologian.

Notes

1. First quotation from Büchner's *Dantons Tod*; for second quote of Büchner see Erich Fried in: *Frankfurter Rundschau*, 21st October 1987, 14 f.
2. Undated [presumably from the early eighties] and unpublished assessment of the 'Chair in Mission', University of Birmingham, by W.J. Hollenweger, p. 5. The paper is called "The First Professor of Mission in U.K." and starts with the year 1970. Obviously, this formulation relates to the University of Birmingham's *News Release* of 17th March 1971 which had as its title "First British Professor of Mission appointed in the University of Birmingham". Not mentioned, however, in the two papers is the name of Godfrey E. Phillips, who in 1938 became Professor of Mission at the Selly Oak Colleges, at that time the only holder of a Mission Chair in Great Britain. Of course, the history of British chairs in mission goes even further back and started in 1867 with Alexander Duff at Edinburgh.
3. Cf. interview in *Church Times*, 18th January 1974.
4. In cooperation with G. Casalis and P. Keller (eds.): *Vers une église pour les autres, à la recherche de structures pour des communautés missionaires*, Geneva 1966 (following the German edition which was edited in 1965 by H.J. Margull); and: *The Church for Others, and The Church for the World*, Geneva, 1967.
5. These thoughts and quotation are taken from his "Farewell Lecture" at Birmingham University, see note 14.
6. "Kirchen, Freikirchen und Sekten". Volkshochschule Zürich, Manuscript.
7. Cf. *Intercultural Theology*, Vol. III (Munich: Chr. Kaiser Verlag, 1988), 331-34.
8. In Vol. III, p. 18, of his *Intercultural Theology* Hollenweger made the statement that his theological thoughts are adressed to those topics: "Where I was able to collect experience of life. It goes against my principles to write on subjects conceptualised only, not experienced". On p. 334 he writes: "In the first place, I want to face the world, the experiences of people within and without church... before I regard them as 'weed' or 'edible'" (my own translation).
9. Cf. again *Intercultural Theology*, III, 17 and 195.
10. *Farewell Lecture*, 7.
11. Hollenweger in an interview in *Church Times*, 18th January 1974.
12. Hollenweger in his (alias Mr. Chips' or Professor Unrat's) analysis of the WCC/DWME conference at Bangkok, cf. here *Evangelische Kommentare* (1973), 149.
13. See Hollenweger's article on these two in *Norsk Tiddsskrift for Mission* (1985), 192-201.
14. Quotation is taken from W.J. Hollenweger's "Farewell lecture", *Selly Oak Colleges, Occasional Paper No. 2* (Birmingham, 1989), 11 ff., however, my 'explanatory' remarks relate also to a prior version which is to be found in Vol. III, of his *Interkulturelle Theologie* (Munich: Chr. Kaiser Verlag, 1988), 339 ff. The 'frog poem' occured frequently in Hollenweger's contributions.

4

Hollenweger as Professor of Mission

Emmanuel Y. Lartey and George M. Mulrain

The Chair in Mission

In 1970 the University of Birmingham was preparing to do something new in the realm of theological education in Britain. Three decades before this, in 1940, it had established a Department of Theology. Now with the dawning of the seventies plans had been well underway for establishing a Chair of Mission. Although new to Birmingham and indeed to Britain, the idea of Mission as an academic discipline had long been accepted in universities across the continent of Europe and in the United States of America. The impetus for such a Chair came from the Federation of Selly Oak Colleges which had been involved in preparing men and women for Christian service overseas since the beginning of the century. The Colleges' Council offered financial help on the understanding that the professor would teach, conduct seminars and supervise postgraduate research at both institutions.

1970 therefore saw the University of Birmingham advertising for a Professor of Mission. It was the hope that someone with an interest in the very broad aspects of Mission would be found to fill this post. Seven related areas were identified in the university's paper, "Chair in the Field of Mission - Further Particulars": history, comparative religion, the philosophy of religion, the relation of religion and culture, the sociology of religion, indigenization, systematic theology. "The successful candidate would be expected to be interested in this broad field, but not a specialist in each and every item."[1]

The Makings of a Professor

Walter J. Hollenweger was the University of Birmingham's first Professor of Mission, a position which he occupied from 1 October 1971 until 30 September 1989. Academics are sometimes regarded as persons who have little or no experience in the practicalities of life. Hollenweger's life history suggests otherwise. Born on 1 June 1927, his first taste of working life was as a clerk in the Zürich Stock Exchange. He then pastored the Swiss Pentecostal Mission in Zürich (1949 -1958), pursued formal theological studies at the universities of Zürich and Basel, after which he was ordained as a minister of the Swiss Reformed Church. This was in

1962. In the same year he began a two-year stint as a Research Assistant for Church History at the University of Zürich. The university awarded him the degree of Th.D. for extensive research on the Pentecostal Movement. This was in 1966. A year earlier he had joined the staff of the World Council of Churches (WCC) in Geneva. When he accepted the appointment to the Chair of Mission, he had been serving the WCC as Secretary for Evangelism in the Division of World Mission and Evangelism for five years.

Walter Hollenweger brought to the professorship both practical and academic expertise. He served on several committees: the Selly Oak Colleges' Council, Library Committee, the University's Nominations Committee for Honorary Degrees, Resources Committee of the Faculty of Arts and the Faculty's Board of Postgraduate Studies. It must be said that as a foreigner to Britain, he often viewed issues from a distinct perspective and was able to inject creativity into the way he contributed to matters under discussion. He was a very effective communicator, having himself been involved in radio and television programme production. Both Geneva and Scottish televisions had benefitted from his scripts for religious programmes. This is how a 1971 release from the WCC, Geneva, described him:

> Basically Walter Hollenweger is an innovator. He wants to do things that have not been done before. When an experiment succeeds - whether it be in revolutionizing worship services or doing Bible study or communicating with the unchurched - he then moves on to another experiment, leaving others to continue the pattern he has pioneered.[2]

Throughout his tenure he maintained the marks of distinction which must undoubtedly have been evident to the selection committee that singled him out for the post.

It seems helpful in appreciating Hollenweger as Professor of Mission that we see him in the following light, namely as (1) a true scholar, (2) a prolific writer, (3) a creative and innovative theologian, (4) an inspiring supervisor, and (5) a caring counsellor.

A True Scholar

Hollenweger brought to the Chair of Mission a wealth of scholarship. It could honestly be said that he was fully committed to research. He was an avid reader, ever searching books, journals and other literature in German, French, English and other languages. "He impressed me with bibliography in Spanish, demonstrating enough control of this language. So, it was possible to work with him without losing violently my personal roots," writes one of his research students from Chile.[3]

His breadth and depth of scholarship meant that he was well-equipped as a Christian theologian to enter into dialogue with other faiths, with Science, with Marxism, in fact with several other disciplines which are usually regarded as being outside the scope of theology. Another student who was researching the area of Christian-Marxist dialogue in Czechoslovakia found Professor Hollenweger to be "ingenious in attempting to find cohesion in the disparate endeavours of his students."[4] This student's study hovered on the boundary between theology and the sociology of knowledge. Through the professor's ingenuity, he was helped to address the problems created by inter-disciplinary dissertations and therefore to navigate creatively through the rigours and pitfalls of such study.

Much ought to be attributed to Hollenweger's broadmindedness. In fact, having students from the Selly Oak Colleges hailing as they did from diverse nationalities, meant that the Professor of Mission could not be parochial in this outlook. "As a foreigner, he could empathize with foreign students. He suffered similar humiliation like us. He allowed us to be our 'authentic' selves," stated a South African postgraduate student.[5] He could handle perspectives different from his own without feeling in any way threatened by them. Flexibility was a characteristic of his. He was not afraid to expose himself to new ideas. On the contrary, he actively promoted experimentation with new ways of thinking, expression and learning.

As a true scholar, he inspired others to take scholarship seriously. "Tutorials could be nerve-wracking," admitted one student. "Shoddy thinking and expression were anathema to him."[6] It was no wonder that those persons who were supervised in their research by Walter Hollenweger felt duty-bound to aim at excellence, not mediocrity.

A Prolific Writer

There are some scholars who make their contribution to the academic world by writing articles for journals. Others put the bulk of their effort into producing a book. But there are still others who continue writing essays for specialist journals and producing books at the same time. Walter Hollenweger, as Professor of Mission, fitted into the third category. He was a prolific writer.

When he began his duties at the University of Birmingham, he had already published extensively in theological journals and had written *Enthusiastisches Christentum*, *Die Pfingstkirchen* and the *Handbuch der Pfingstbewegung*. As the years rolled on, he never ceased to write. He is renowned as a leading authority on Pentecostalism. As Professor of Mission, he managed to stimulate thinking on the subject through putting his ideas in print. He wrote on ecumenism, inter-faith dialogue, inter-cultural theology and a host of other topics. But he did not merely write. The truth is, he wrote 'with conviction'; because he was convinced that the insights which he, together with his researchers, had should be shared with others.

Walter Hollenweger was doubtless one of the major publishing professors at the University of Birmingham. His writings appear in English, Spanish, Dutch, Italian, French, German and Indonesian. His three volumes on *Intercultural Theology* are being translated into English and a second volume to *The Pentecostals* is in preparation. One must not forget the encouragement which Hollenweger has given to scholars to have their writings published. His editing of the series on the *Intercultural History of Christianity* bears testimony to this. The bibliography at the end of this book speaks for itself.

A Creative and Innovative Theologian

One of the most remarkable aspects of Walter Hollenweger as a theologian was his almost inimitable styles of presentation. He did not give dry, boring lectures. Rather, he has been widely appreciated for using story, music, art and drama when presenting his topics. It was as though he lived for what he believed in, and therefore did all in his power to truly 'enjoy' his work. According to one researcher: "Walter Hollenweger, as I knew him as my supervisor, was a 'professor' in the precise sense of someone who professes something, is stating a creed, is animated by a belief in what he is doing in the role of an academic."[7] Because he was so fully committed, he instinctively made *academia* interesting, so that whether he was giving a lecture or leading a seminar, memorable and exciting things took place. Writes one postgraduate researcher: "...it was the evening monthly seminars at his home which were really exciting. You never knew who would be there and what personal stories and insights they would bring to the meeting. My passion for liberation theology was begun at these meetings."[8] And another: "I found Professor Hollenweger's seminars in his home particularly helpful... I was also pleased to be able to invite my wife so that she felt a part of things."[9]

One of the highlights of life at the University of Birmingham was the Department Day for Theology. Hollenweger used such occasions to experiment with drama which he himself had produced, such as his *Conflict in Corinth* and *A Bonhoeffer Requiem*. In so doing, he effectively revolutionized theological discourse, presenting it as he did in a dramatic format.

The truth is that Walter Hollenweger did not want theology to be imprisoned by academic theologians. This is why he experimented and offered it as something for the housewife or the worker on the docks to be interested in. No wonder the self-styled 'non-academics' could find it 'interesting' and 'relevant'. As a theologian lecturing at a British university, he did not regurgitate other theologies. Instead he 'did' theology, interpreting current situations with a creative, theological mind.

His treatment of the subject of Mission needs special mention here. He challenged many of its accepted definitions and concepts. The way he treated Christianity in relation to other faiths was refreshing, yet at the same time disturbing. An African researcher commented on his experiences following a lecture by the professor:

> It seemed that Hollenweger had extolled all religions including African traditional religions which the students regarded as pagan, therefore of no profit. Hollenweger, it seemed, had given the impression that such 'pagan' and other religions had a common but essential identity, which is a peculiar understanding of God from which Christianity could learn some aspects of God in which it lacks insight.[10]

To those committed to an understanding of mission as Christians from the west 'giving' to the rest, this would indeed be disturbing. However, it is important that we appreciate that persons of other faiths and cultures have valuable messages from God which they can share with western Christianity.

Creative and innovative as he was in ideas and activities, Hollenweger saw fit to encourage at the University of Birmingham and in the Selly Oak Colleges a continuing dialogue between the established churches of the west and the independent black churches within Britain. Pastorin Roswith Gerloff, one of his students, researched the presence of independent black churches.[11] The establishment of a Centre for Black and White Christian Partnership came out of her research. The University now validates a certificate programme in theology designed to meet the needs of pastors and lay persons, many of whom would not otherwise have had an opportunity to pursue Biblical and theological studies at the tertiary level. Hollenweger was indeed a brave academic.

An Inspiring Supervisor

In dealing with his students Walter Hollenweger showed a profound respect for them. He took each and every individual seriously. One student, now a professor in Australia, pays the following tribute:

> Research students came before everyone else. Work was corrected and returned within days. Criticisms and suggestions were precise and for the aid of the researcher... Most of all, I remember those moments when tears came to his eyes, whether in interviews or in teaching... when the magnitude and indescribable depth of the Grace of God became apparent to him. Here was a person beyond denomination or cultural background for whom God's action was quite overwhelming.[12]

Hollenweger was an enabler, for he succeeded in motivating his researchers and encouraging them to pursue their task with seriousness of purpose. During his term of office, he saw about eighty students to the completion of postgraduate research projects. One slightly older than usual research student has ventured the following comment: "What impressed me most was the simple fact that he was willing to give everyone a chance, and especially the geriatrics... What he did was to give the kind of encouragement and stimulation that suited my situation."[13] Another tribute mentions the tremendous patience and sensitivity which the professor showed towards students who were researching under pressure.

> He was always most understanding and accommodating. He allowed me to set the pace and he always had words of encouragement to offer as well as helpful criticism when reading my work. There was something about his approach which enabled humble students to realize they were being treated, quite genuinely, as equals, and that their work was respected and valued. His enthusiasm - even excitement - over many issues demonstrated his passion for the work in which he was involved. This, I found contagious and stimulating.[14]

The other way whereby respect was shown for students was his insistence that they spoke out of their own cultural backgrounds. "I can't see nor hear the people of Latin America in your writing," was the constant challenging remark which he made to one Chilean researcher.[15] Hollenweger earned the respect and admiration of his students, especially those from countries outside Europe; because he allowed them to be their authentic selves and not carbon copies of others.

A Caring Counsellor

Hollenweger's sensitivity to the needs of students from so-called 'Third World' countries highlights his skills as a counsellor. With tremendous patience and understanding, he would talk their ideas through with students. Sometimes these ideas might have been blurred through their inability to articulate competently in English, or through the difficulty encountered in any form of cross-cultural communication. In so doing, each student was helped to develop greater self-confidence, and to feel that he or she was the expert in his or her chosen field of research. Students from overseas often remarked about how relaxed they felt in the professor's presence. "His home was open to the students: his office could be considered our working place."[16] Clearly, his human touch was appreciated by the vast majority.

Hollenweger often encouraged his students to look critically at their own religious beliefs and practices in the light of their culture. He hoped that their Christianity would not be considered a burden, with a series of negative attacks on culturally accepted behaviour-patterns. It is more important to have a faith which leads us into the realm of positive thinking about ourselves and our potential as children of God.

An interesting story has been told by a Latin American research student:

> The first time I met Professor Hollenweger was at a Mexico City restaurant. The waiter came and asked what we wanted to drink. Professor Hollenweger showed that he was well acquainted with all brands of Mexican beer and ordered one that, he assured me, was of excellent quality. Then he asked me what I wanted. As a good Mexican Pentecostal, of course, I do not drink beer, and my answer, what could perhaps be judged as a little ironic, was: 'I am a Christian, I do not drink beer.' Professor Hollenweger did not show any displeasure at my ungracious reply. His only words were: 'Don't say that when you go to Europe. They will think you are not as intelligent as you are.'[17]

Anyone writing a postgraduate thesis will be well-advised to have a plan for starting, continuing and completing one's research. One of Hollenweger's earliest students pays tribute to him for seeing that such good advice did not go unheeded: "He was relentless in demanding a plan, a timetable, and getting one to stick to it. This was invaluable for me when I was 'writing up', but demanded a lot..."[18] The same student paid tribute to his ability as a caring counsellor to women: "...what always struck me was his ability to empathize with women... He seemed to understand women's problems in a way equalled only by Leo Tolstoy... I think he had so many women students because they responded to his confidence in them."[19]

Without doubt, Walter Hollenweger enjoyed what he was doing. It is small wonder, then, that he made an impression - a positive one at that - upon all those with whom he came into contact. Of course one is not implying that he was a model of perfection. He has sometimes been criticised for not being kindly disposed towards those who did not share his insights. One of our correspondents lamented the fact that a national of Britain was not appointed as his successor in the Chair of Mission. But she did admit that it was not his responsibility to choose one to follow in his post.[20] The fact is, the majority of former students were full of praise for his work among them.

What then can we say to conclude? Without doubt the University of Birmingham and the Selly Oak Colleges owe a tremendous debt of gratitude to Walter Hollenweger. Mention should also be made of two persons who ably supported him in his role. His wife Erika and his competent secretary Joan Pearce, although they kept a low profile, were towers of strength. Around the world, Walter Hollenweger is well-known for his writings. But those of us who have had him as our professor are fortunate for having known him personally.

Notes

1. "Chair in the Field of Mission - Further Particulars", Department of Theology, University of Birmingham, 7th April, 1970.
2, Extracted from University of Birmingham *News Release*, March 1971.
3. Tomas A Stevens Noel, M.Litt. (1986), pastor of Primera Iglesia Metodista in Concepcion Chile in correspondence with the authors. In preparing this paper former students and researchers under Hollenweger's supervision were invited to contribute their reflections for inclusion.
4. J. Martin Haworth, Ph.D. (1982), Sheffield, U.K. - Correspondence.
5. Bongani A. Mazibuko, Ph.D. (1983), professor, Department of Missiology, Science of Religion and Pastoral Studies, University of Zululand, South Africa - Interview.
6. John Rutherford, Ph.D. (1983), Greystoke, Cumbria, U.K. - Correspondence.
7. Harold Tonks, Ph.D. (1981), Raintal 4, Germany. - Correspondence.
8. Charles Bradshaw, M.A. (1976), parish priest, Leicester, U.K.- Correspondence.
9. J. Martin Haworth, Ph.D. (1982), Sheffield, U.K. - Correspondence.
10. Sydney Nkosi, researching "Intercultural Theology in South Africa" - Correspondence.
11. Roswith Gerloff, researching "Black Churches in Great Britain", Frankfurt, Germany.
12. I. James M. Haire, Ph.D. (1981), professor of New Testament Studies, Trinity Theological College, Queensland, Australia. - Correspondence.
13. George Hood, Ph.D. (1985), Threlkeld, Cumbria, U.K. - Correspondence.
14. David Major, Mini M.A. (1982), senior lecturer in Religious Studies, Chester College, U.K. - Correspondence.
15. Thomas A Stevens Noel from Chile cites this as one of Professor Hollenweger's permanent questions while revising his research.
16. Quote of Thomas Stevens Noel. - Correspondence.
17. Manuel J. Gaxiola-Gaxiola, Ph.D. (1990) Mexico. - Correspondence.
18. Eleanor M. Jackson, M.A. (1972), Ph.D. (1976), translator and researcher, Birmingham U.K. - Correspondence.
19. *Ibid.*
20. *Ibid.*

5

Theological Education in Black and White: The Centre for Black and White Christian Partnership (1978 - 1985)

Roswith Gerloff

Introduction

The Centre for Black and White Christian Partnership and the experience as Tutor in Mission of the Certificate in Theology Course, run in conjunction with the University of Birmingham, confronted me - and others - to be in touch with a reality quite different from the traditional monocultural system. Even though we began our venture with a course designed to provide pastors from black independent churches with some form of 'recognized' theological education, we soon found ourselves dealing with much more basic facts and needs. The words of Walter J. Hollenweger, without whose insights the Centre would not have been conceived, still serve as a blueprint today:

> Solidarity with Black Theology implies such a challenge to our European monocultural way of doing theology that repercussions and even animosity are bound to arise from those who fear for their privileges. Of course, they will not formulate their animosity in terms of power. They will camouflage it in speaking of academic standards and the like. By this they mean those standards according to which they are experts and will easily forget the standards of oral theology according to which they are inferior.[1]

Those who came to the Centre, predominantly black and some white, were, with rare exceptions, ministers whose profession or occupation was anything but 'academic' or church-directed: such as train-drivers, nurses, clerks, midwives, teachers, labourers in car-factories, supervisors of inner-city transport systems, employed, underemployed or unemployed. Some were middle-aged, others young adults. Yet, all of them had been called into the Christian ministry within a particular local congregation for a specific task: pastors, deacons, administrators, evangelists, missionaries, exhorters, teachers, prophets, apostles, youth leaders, choir directors, exercising spiritual gifts such as described by Paul for the Corinthian Church. They arrived at the Centre already well trained in pastoral and leadership skills, in knowledge of the Bible and of the theological traditions of their churches, appointed on the grounds of their personal integrity and spiritual maturity, and tested as to their physical and intellectual capacity, by daily work. All of them had been inspired by 'spiritual parents', both mothers and fathers, Afro-Caribbean or West African, and most of them had received their vocation in a vision - not in the church, but somewhere on the shop-floor, in an office, or bedroom: a vision to care for certain people in a given neighbourhood. They could identify with the disadvantaged, immigrants and underdogs, had indeed been part of them, and had therefore developed a high sense of mission in taking on the burden of their communities. Their's was an immensely valuable contribution to post-war Britain as a whole, in places where the professional English clergyman or social worker could never reach, at nobody's expense except their own; indeed without any acknowledgement or remuneration. Quietly but persistently they led their people towards the path of cultural identity, moral integrity, and spiritual liberation in areas of social unrest and racial polarization. As one of the first students on the course, Rosalind Edwards of the Cherubim and Seraphim Church, wrote:

> Our churches have grown out of European missionary activities. But then, we have awakened to the reality that we don't have to be 'shadow Englishmen'. We don't have to reject our culture and entire way of life to be Christians. The Church of Black People today is practically the only means of reviving our native cultures, beliefs and forms, the basis of our social and spiritual lives. The Church has given us dignity... (and) it is one of the greatest means of liberation. It helps in the fight for the liberation from injustice, sin and oppression and is the bearer of liberation already won.[2]

The starting point of the Centre for Black and White Christian Partnership has been this contribution of black ministers of independent churches to the British church and academic circles. Perhaps not so extreme in Britain as in Germany, Western academic theology has generally lost for too long its roots in the common lives of people. It is now confronted on its own soil with Christian communities with experiences of human feeling in worship; of mutual instruction in church life; and with a concept of wholeness ('holiness') which embraces the 'whole bundle' of human existence. From 1972, when Hollenweger started me on what we then considered a small research project in West Indian Pentecostalism, and more so from 1978, when we formally established the educational experiment, it became increasingly apparent how indispensable for the welfare of society these ministers without professional training and university degrees had been. They were competent in looking after their own affairs, building stable congregations and headquarters, administering human and material resources, and functioning as good shepherds and counsellors of their flock. Some, of course, did better than others. Most of them, especially the older pastors, lacked basic education which would put them on equal footing with their white partners. But all of them exercised their talents not through the bureaucratic channels of white society, but by applying black patterns of movement organization such as charismatic leadership; face-to-face recruitment; an itinerant ministry; a consistent message; and opposition from the established order.[3] They succeeded - at least from the mid-1970s - to cover the country with a highly effective, if oral, network of human relations: cutting across the barriers of organization; denomination; class; and even race.

Nevertheless, the historical churches of Britain ignored these new Christian communities or suspected their ministers to be 'self-styled' leaders without proper standing. Black Christians who were utterly convinced to operate on a biblical understanding of one's calling by God in society were long denied this very sense of vocation by their white fellow-Christians. This feature has already changed, but still exists in subtle ways. Not so long ago, the Church of England offered as its main solution to the racial problem among British Christians the ordination of more black Anglican clergy: and thus pumps much more money into its own Black Theological Institute than into partnership programmes.[4] At least in Europe as a whole, pastors and bishops of flourishing movements, 'overseers' in the New Testament sense, still suffer from a widespread lack of respect from traditional theologians. They are treated as lay-people without 'theology proper' or 'valid orders'; as duly appointed ministers of the Gospel of Jesus Christ. Even the discussion of the Lima paper on *Baptism, Eucharist and Ministry* which defines the ministry as the calling of the *whole* people of God, did not lead much further, as it emphasized the ordained ministry as a set-apart ministry from the rest of the Christian community and made the traditional threefold office of bishop, presbyter and deacon the predominant pattern - which in no way corresponds to the quite different forms of ministerial formation in black independent movements.[5]

It is obvious, however, that the black churches have in some peaceful but unyielding protest established themselves in two directions. They have now entered into ecumenical dialogue with other Christians and play an increasingly active role in the social and ecumenical life of the nation, which is reflected in co-operation with the 'New Instrument' of the British Churches. This is due partly to their own efforts, partly to the effects of the joint educational programme we are going to describe. They have also - much earlier - set up their own educational projects. First, in the local congregations: worship which serves as a training ground for various skills and talents, Sabbath and Sunday schools for children and adults alike, and supplementary education. Second, in Bible Colleges such as the Central Bible Institute in Birmingham, Overstone College in Northampton, or regional Bible courses. Third, in theological education by extension such as the correspondence courses developed by the Shiloh United Church of Christ Apostolic (which also serves people in the Caribbean, Africa and parts of Asia). Some of these programmes run on very conservative lines, both theologically and methodologically, using Evangelical materials from the USA or the UK. Others are highly innovative, both in content and methodology, adapting to the real needs of the communities they serve. Certainly no black Pentecostal or Sabbatarian church in Britain today would be taken seriously by their own members if they did not embark upon various educational projects to help the deprived. Yet, in all of these, there is a secret battle between the white, mostly Fundamentalist overlays, and the actual questions of a dispossessed people. Whatever their form, they all contradict the notion that proper theological education and legitimate ministerial formation can only be channelled through the 'main-line' institutions. Indeed, all of them would rightly insist that most of our traditional ways of doing theology are out of touch with reality: the reality of the people; the reality of the Bible; and most important the reality of God. Therefore they would not wish to be indoctrinated by education which alienates people from daily life and destroys the sense of joy and dedication experienced in genuine worship. They would not want to lose a training pattern which makes everybody participate, instead of developping the elitist potential of only a few. They would not want to be co-opted into English institutions for fear of further exploitation and of losing power and relevance. As Malachi Ramsay, a prominent black Pentecostal Bishop in Britain, wrote to a white agnostic scholar:

> You must rearrange your theology... God cannot work for you from the outside. No man gets drunk by having strong drink poured out all over his body. He will only have the smell of liquor, but if he drinks the strong drink, then the difference is an experience to him and a testimony to those who saw him, because he will have no more control of the liquor; the liquor is on the inside and is now in control... You have stayed sober for too long. Start as a little child again and you will see the beauty and the power of God in your life. Your teaching will no more be just a theory, but a practical experience, too.[6]

Setting up an Intercultural Christian Project

Against this background, the educational work of the Centre for Black and White Christian Partnership must be seen, examined, evaluated, encouraged and also warned. In Hollenweger's own words:

> Here was a challenge to invent an educational programme which was acceptable on academic grounds and at the same time did not estrange these pastors from their own culture. I told my colleagues at the university that such a thing would be possible by combining the formal process of teaching with elements from the black religious culture. Worship, prayer, song, dance and personal witness would

> be as important in this school as lectures and examinations. When I presented this programme to my university colleagues, they smiled and reminded me that we were part of a secular university where such things were not customary. I argued for my approach... that for these Black pastors to talk *about* God without talking *to* God did not make sense: an analysis of biblical texts without dance, song and witness, a discussion of the difficult race relations in Britain without an intercultural feast of reconciliation, was not understandable.[7]

This is how we began. The Centre, then under the name of the 'Project in Partnership between Black and White', was officially set up in September 1978, and started its first university course in December the same year. Long-term preparation was necessary. One was my five-years research under the supervision of Hollenweger, which uncovered a far wider spectrum of black Christian traditions than any of us had anticipated. By 1976, it contained information on hundreds of Afro-Caribbean and African congregations in Britain in some eleven theological families, the foundation for a fascinating educational experiment between black and white traditions in the years to come. It led to several pioneering events such as the meeting at Handsworth Methodist Church when for the first time black pastors met white ministers and the Bishop of Birmingham. How obvious the intense search for mutual exchange, coming-together, sharing-together and learning-together shone through! There was the Dartmouth House Conference under the auspices of the British Council of Churches (BCC) which for the first time looked closely into black-white church relations and laid the foundation for future sharing in worship, buildings and education. There was the Luton Conference at the Calvary Church of God in Christ, attended by more than seventy black leaders, which gave birth to the Joint Working Party between black-led and white-led churches of the BCC. To facilitate the latter, a deliberate decision had to be taken: namely to open the research files for these practical purposes, despite the danger that such information might be misused by racist and fascist organizations. It could not have happened without black encouragement at all. Many today have forgotten about these two pillars of the experiment, responsible academic research not ending in the ivory tower of a university, and the black leaders' outspoken co-operation who hoped for increasing equality, at least in the Church, and the betterment of the conditions of their people by improved education, very much in the tradition of the great black American educationalist William E.B. Dubois. Olu Abiola of the Aladura International Church, now Co-president of the Council of Churches for Britain and Ireland, wrote in 1977:

> Education and re-education, theological and spiritual, is therefore needed on both sides of the fence... by the creation of a centre... Thus the black-led churches will by practical demonstration educate and guide the white-led churches towards spirituality, and the white-led churches will by theoretical knowledge educate and

> reshape the black-led churches... in systematic biblical education. Both groups will by mutual understanding once again lighten the world.[8]

I will never forget when we met in the president's office at Selly Oak Colleges in 1977. Black leaders, such as Martin Simmonds (First United Church of Jesus Christ Apostolic), Samuel Owusu-Akuffo (Divine Prayer Society), and Olu Abiola - with the support of others - approached the Department of Mission to provide them with systematic theological education. After the meeting, which as usual offered much goodwill but no concrete ideas, Hollenweger caught me on the stairs of Central House and said with great excitement: "This is far too serious than to leave the matter to some form of adult-education without a recognized award at the end. This is a challenge to the taken-for-granted privileges and powers of the church and academic world. This *must* be linked to the university." So he persuaded the Department of Theology to sponsor a pilot project in December 1977. Again in his own words:

> It is quite remarkable that the British mission societies, which are famous for their ecumenical and missiological pioneering work in the Third World, have almost totally missed the opportunity for a renewing intercultural dialogue in their own country. The Labour Party also, which cannot criticize South African apartheid enough, are unable in their own country to recognize the cultural, political and spiritual leadership potential of these churches. To discover this, two foreign 'missionaries' were needed, a German lady pastor and a Swiss university professor.[9]

This was the second necessary priming. The 'Small Beginning', as we had called the pilot project, turned out to be a great success. It was attended by forty-five leaders from fifteen different churches spread out over Britain, Pentecostal, Sabbatarian, Holiness, African Indigenous and other independent traditions, including Simmonds, Abiola, Owusu, Malachi Ramsay (Shiloh United Church of Christ Apostolic), S.A. Abidoye (Holy Order of Cherubim and Seraphim), J.M. Odonkor (Church of the Universal Prayer fellowship), Owen Lynch (Seventh Day Baptist Church), and S.E. Thomas (Full Gospel Revival). Their partners in the exercise were the white academic theological staff of Birmingham University - including the Dean of the Department of Theology, Gordon Davies, and the Staff Tutor of the Department of Extramural Studies, Michael Goulder - and Martin Conway of the Divisions of Ecumenical Affairs. Together we began to explore the training and experience of ministers in black churches; how to encourage intercultural dialogue cutting across the barriers of creed, race or class; how to teach mission in a multi-cultural society; and to help promote competent leadership for the building up of partnership between black and white Christians. As a result, lecturers of the university and the Selly Oak Colleges offered their support and competence for re-designing an already-existing Certificate in Theology course to meet the needs and aspirations of these working people. By introducing a significant black element into European studies, to our knowledge this was the first cross-cultural form of theological education in Europe, but not in the entire world, because similar projects such as the 'Black Church Leadership and Faculty Development Project' initiated by Gayraud Wilmore at Rochester Divinity School in the United States were already underway:

> This development has the potential of opening up a new area of academic excellence where the hope of 'workers' universities and the like - so much desired and argued for but never realised - might come attainable without asking students to sacrifice the competence of their own culture.[10]

The first regular course began in December 1978. It was preceded by a number of theological and methodological considerations. A support group, consisting mainly of black members of the Joint Working Party, was to help the young and vulnerable child to 'grow in wisdom, stature and favour with God and people', and not collapse with unforeseen expectations, obstacles and expansion in years to come. With their advice, a small group of academics drafted the curriculum for the first year. Michael Goulder and myself were asked to serve as Tutors in New Testament and Mission, followed in the second year by Frances Young and David Ford to teach in Old Testament and Christian Doctrine. Under the guidance of Hollenweger, and following the insights of my own research, I outlined the contents of a course, 'Towards an Intercultural Understanding of Mission', which never existed before and included strong elements of British black traditions. Also, I remember that even before the first weekend was in sight, and in close consultation with Hollenweger as the Consultant, I had drafted a paper on the educational strategies which were to apply in such a venture. They were based on the methods developed by Paolo Freire, the well-known Latin American educationalist, transferred into the reality of a multiracial society in Europe. I recall vividly the originally-appointed Tutor in New Testament, Dr. Birdsall, withdrawing from the experiment after we met; because he became so frightened by such an educational approach within university studies that he refused to co-operate. Perhaps it was the Holy Spirit's doing that Michael Goulder as Staff Tutor had to step in, as he marvelously matched with the black pastors and proved an excellent adult teacher. Both of us, so to speak, took one another's hand, he helping me to embark on university teaching, and me helping him to understand something of the communication structures of the black community. During this time, Hollenweger's advice, support and prayers were indispensable, especially when it came to the inherently racist structures of the institutions involved. From the inside he saw through them more clearly than others. In his own words:

> Some White Christians and educationalists might fear the consequences of such an experiment in black education, because it could lead black church leaders to question hitherto unchallenged assumptions in the empires of science and academia. They could well introduce new concepts and competence which so far have not only been absent in our academic world but which have been positively ridiculed or considered to be of decorative rather than scientific value. When expressed in a competent way, such a challenge would be of vital significance not only in black studies but for the rigour of academic research which aids us all. It might also realign the pecking order of the academic world, and that is always frightening.[11]

Goals and Struggles

The project, later to be called the Centre for Black and White Christian Partnership, was initiated to meet at least three objectives:

First, to offer ministers and workers of independent mostly black congregations a recognized educational programme and a Certificate in Theology which would acknowledge their competence, open the door to continuing studies (including research in hitherto unknown traditions) and remove some of the obstacles in communication between the black and the white communities. This, naturally, involves a major shift from indoctrinating teaching to building on the experience of participants and developing their own potential.

Second, to open to white educational institutions such as the University of Birmingham, the Selly Oak Colleges and other theological seminaries the opportunity to listen to the voices, perspectives and global insights of the oppressed, in this case, Christians from other than European shores; in short, to encourage an intercultural approach to mission and theology which pleads for a plurality of theologies 'on either side of the fence'. This, evidently, implies a major shift from considering the theological faculty, the Bible college and the mission school as the sole producers of 'theology proper', to understanding theology as owned by the whole people of God in streets, homes, jobs and acting within the framework of Christian worship. Ministerial formation then takes place where these people are considered the primary agents of the theological task of the church. Or with the words of Martin Luther King Jr, the theologian must from within the struggle of life relate the Christian faith to the conditions which affect both body and soul. There must be a 'praxiological focus'.[12]

Third, to help traditional educators, faculty and college staff, to become motivators and facilitators of the people they serve, rather than remain 'experts', and thus to promote informed leadership for diverse communities. This means re-education of the white tutors in terms of the 'wounds of the oppressed', constant exposure to one another, even if it hurts, and entering 'communion' with one another beyond the limits of the intellect. It involves a major shift from teachers regarding themselves as the proprietors of knowledge, to listening how others articulate their faith in concrete situations, and how they re-create the gospel of Jesus Christ spiritually and bodily in a given cultural and socio-political context. Theological work together then pays tribute to the diverse, in our context black and white, dimensions, and the challenge that derive from them, and it builds itself carefully around these various approaches. With Bongani Mazibuko, the Co-director of the Centre from 1981, in his thorough analysis of the experiment:

> Many educators have not fully grasped or appreciated the value of this new approach. Too many of them still employ the teacher-tell methods and the transmitter-receiver techniques which are normally employed when they teach young children. They are the poorer by doing so.[13]

It was here where the greatest difficulties occurred; because both academic tutors and traditional clergy have to work within a given system and are more or less trained in mono-cultural standards only. Thus they often fear to lose their 'expertise' and privileges, and stick to language and symbols they are acquainted with. Yet, as the black experience itself uses a 'passionate' and contextual language, education of this kind cannot afford to be an 'abstract, dispassionate discourse' on the nature of God and the essence of humanity unrelated to cultural, political and ethical implications.[14] In Hollenweger's interpretation:

> One, if not the most important feature of theological education is to help Christians to articulate their religion clearly and intelligibly. If Black Christians can express their aspirations and values clearly, then it follows that they will apply this very same skill to the articulation of their social, cultural and political insights.[15]

This excludes some of the purposes for which the Centre was *not* set up, albeit occasionally mistaken. It was *not* founded as a replacement scheme for the educational programmes ventured by the black Churches themselves in favour of a more academic or 'critical' approach; on the contrary, this would only have revealed a rather uncritical stance about its own inherent dangers in professionalising the ministry and suggesting theological bankruptcy for the laity of the white churches. It was *not* conceived as a 'black school' where whites could learn something about blacks, nor as a 'white school' which would teach only blacks; this would have implied another and even more subtle form of control and exploitation! It was *not* initiated as a substitute training scheme of some lower standing for voluntary clergy and for those who do not fit into the 'normal' theological system; this would have been an insult to the competence of the black churches!

The Centre was conceived rather as a *turntable* between the historic and the charismatic traditions; between the 'third' and the 'first' worlds on our doorstep; between the oral and the literary cultures; between poor and rich, labourers and academics, black and white.

The Centre was also envisaged as a *partnership scheme* on all levels, within the courses, within the committees, within staff, in order to loosen the bonds of tradition and to break through inherited discriminatory and exploitative structures.

The Centre thus developed into an *alternative model in ecumenism* which builds on relationships from the bottom up rather than from the top down, and which operates by commitment rather than by proportional representation.

In this way we hoped to equip ourselves - God's people from different cultural backgrounds, races and traditions - for a joint Christian mission in a segregated and disjointed society.

Yet, there always remained the problem of language, or what people understood by what we said. Hollenweger always spoke and wrote about the 'black school'. What he meant, however, was a challenge to the all-white educational system. He certainly never did encourage white teachers to imitate black speech, thought and behaviour patterns "in some desperate attempt to become honorary blacks". He supported the project as a searching and challenging 'test' of inter-cultural competence of the institutions, and as an 'enquiry' as to the usefulness 'or otherwise' of their methods in integrative education.[16] He certainly opposed the attempt to turn blacks into 'shadow Englishmen' in order to assimilate them into the existing social and educational order, "a system whose viability in its present form is in question even amongst the English, in particular as to its usefulness as a tool to ensure the survival of the humanity of humankind in our world".[17] He understood the programme as a 'joint struggle' to unveil alternative methods of social and political integration.[18] So he warned us more than once, that the Centre could run out of funds, or lack widespread recognition from established theological boards in education. As none of the blacks from independent bodies who had received the Certificate ever intended to come 'under the umbrella' of the traditional churches, but all returned - strengthened in spirit, intellect and action - to their own organizations; this fear was (and perhaps still is) justified. As one former student, Clive Browne (Bethel Christian Fellowship), wrote in an essay:

> No Christian witness can hope to communicate the gospel effectively, if we ignore the cultural life of those to whom we proclaim the gospel. Sometimes people resist the gospel, not because they think it is false but because they become aware that it is a threat to their culture, their national and tribal solidarity. To some extent this cannot be avoided. For Jesus Christ is a disturber as well as a peacemaker. He is Lord, and He demands our total loyalty... I personally believe that the unity of the church is a given fact and truth, whereby we, as Black and White Christians, have the responsibility to maintain this unity, to make it visible or

> known, and to grow up into the fullness of a new humanity in Christ. The people of God are by his grace a multi-cultural, multi-national and multi-lingual community.[19]

This is mentioned with some constructive criticism. Together we have travelled through the years from 1978 to 1985 when, even in the initial period, there has been the great danger of losing that constant flow of communication between black and white members of the Advisory Committee, which is the life-blood of such a joint venture. Together we have encountered the betrayal of interracial partnership by the taken-for-granted contacts and procedures within white institutions. Together we have experienced the attempt of historical bodies to co-opt the programme into the 'normal' bureaucratic or hierarchical structures and to take away its indispensable autonomy. This all happened, not from outspoken racists, but from what our black friends term 'white liberals' who, perhaps totally unintentionally, block the open and participatory styles of the black community, and thus become a handicap to the principle of power-sharing, and the spirit of communication (Pentecost!) which alone transcends natural human barriers. Thus the hidden trends of white-dominated society have often run counter to our progress. Established structures have been showing more rigidity than anticipated. The Theological Department has sometimes felt threatened about the 'clarity' of theology, or the Western analytical approach, and has accused us of "lowering academic standards". Historical denominations have tried to exercise undue influence, counter to the conceived 'balance' between theirs and the independent traditions, and to turn the project into a more traditional English venture. All these problems will accompany the Centre as long as it exists, particularly with an increase of students from the 'main-line' churches. However, the way they are tack-led will add to or detract from its credibility with the black, both Afro-Caribbean and African, community.

Ten years later I feel that all of us, including Hollenweger, underestimated the question of power and power-sharing. We, workers in the Centre, due to our Christian naivety, failed to some extent in theoretical reflection. He himself lost ground practically faced with repercussions from the powers-that-be. I can also say that the approach was too individualistic. Although we deliberately structured the Advisory Committee to keep a 'balance' between black and white members, procedures lapsed easily back into lack of transparency, and the might - or competition! - of the institutions overpowered the voices from the grass roots embodied in the courses. What would have been necessary was more solidarity among the whites and more strategies among the blacks. On the surface, there is now certainly more black representation and participation on Britain's academic and ecumenical platforms, and this as a direct result of the work in these years. However, as Alvin Blake, another graduate of the Centre, said, this has not changed the overall social climate. Racism, also in Church, is now more subtly handled and more skillfully applied than in earlier years.[20]

Yet, it is also true what we once expressed in summarizing our experience in a Biblical image:

> The friends of the lame man in the gospel broke through the roof because they were convinced that Jesus was in the house. We too have broken through the roof, we have protected underprivileged people, because we are convinced of their spiritual and intellectual potential and because we know that Christ has something to say to our academic and ecclesiastical institutions. It was not confidence in the goodness of these institutions which prompted us to act in this way. It was confidence in the Christ who calls these institutions to repentance. In this process something like conversions were possible, conversions of so-called uncritical students to clear thinking and conversions of so-called unspiritual scholars to an experience in faith.[21]

Organization and Content

There is no space to describe many of the Centre's activities even in the first six years. So much should be said that from the start the project's regular programmes have been centered around the Certificate in Theology Course, spread out over seven weekends (later including a residential week) annually, in two years. 'Sponsored' by the British Council of Churches (now the Council of Churches for Britain and Ireland), the Selly Oak Colleges, and the University of Birmingham, it was a joint effort with the Department of Extramural (now Continuing) Studies providing the model for adult education, the Department of Theology determining the academic standards and setting the examinations, and the 'Project in Partnership' organizing and directing the weekends and ensuring the links with the churches. The four subjects - Old Testament, New Testament, Christian Doctrine and Mission - appear at first glance rather traditional. One of the strategies of Hollenweger was to use already-existing channels as a means, so to speak, to 'revolutionary' purposes. I mention two examples. One is that we grouped the weekends around concerted topics in New Testament (NT) and Mission, or Old Testament (OT) and Christian Doctrines (e.g. The Holy Spirit, The People of God, Incorporation, Healing, or The Future). This warranted a close interaction between themes and lecturers, and implied a highly critical element. It linked the Bible with today's hopes and aberrations. For instance, the weekend which discussed the Church in the NT would also deal with the rise of indigenous churches in Africa, the Caribbean or North America. The weekend which raised the question of Living Before God would relate the OT understanding of law and wisdom to the issue of Christian maturity in a racist and sexist society. An even more illuminating example may be the way we tackled topics in the Mission course. Themes such as the history and effects of slavery, the experience of the Church as a place of resistance and survival, or Christian worship in a multi-faith society, became self-evident. I wrote into the syllabus 'Awareness Training'; but this was rejected by the university as 'psychology' rather than 'theology'. Hollenweger smiled: "Listen, why don't you say: 'Who is a missionary?' Nobody can be a missionary without knowing him- or herself, and our racial and cultural limitations!"

In the educational experiment, Hollenweger had three functions. He served as a Consultant to both the Director(s) and the Advisory Group, and formed the link to the Department of Theology. He set, in consultation with the Tutor, the exam papers for the Mission course. He taught two courses annually: one was 'Types of Mission' when he delighted the students by clearly stating a difference between the 'colonial' and the 'dialogical' forms of Mission and suggesting the latter as the original type in the NT; the other was 'Healing and Miracles' when he drew a line between the rational and superrational, or conscious and subconscious aspects of the human mind - and also between black pastors and the medical profession! - and suggested a connection of the 'maximum participation at the levels of reflection, prayer and decision-making' in black Pentecostal Churches, and the 'inclusion of dreams and visions into personal and public forms of worship', to an understanding of the body-mind relationship 'which is formed by experience' and therefore carries a healing and reconciliatory capacity.[22] When one sceptical Tutor was puzzled after an 'Exhorter' at Small Heath New Testament Church of God had publicly encouraged him to be prayed for at the altar-call - without knowing his name or his disability! - and he had found relief, he enquired from me afterwards whether this was 'pure manipulation'. Hollenweger, with whom I discussed the matter, commented cunningly: "You see, these things happen in the Kingdom of God, only we in our culture have lost this intuitive power".

Extremely important in the exercise was that both group interaction and communication were based on oral as well as literary, verbal as well as non-verbal modes and expressions. Prayer, singing, dancing, meals, visitors, worship, and an Annual Celebration which combined all these elements, were regarded as basic didactic components besides formal lectures. The Celebration of the year 1983 which took place in the Great Hall of the university became (after St. Paul's Cathedral the previous year) a national event, weaving diverse denominational, cultural and even political aspects into one great Feast of Love in Britain. The preacher, Jerisdan Jehu-Appiah (Musama Dico Christo Church), was a graduate of the Centre. One of the speakers, Paul Boateng, became shortly afterwards one of the four black members of the Westminster Parliament. Hence hospitality was not just a pragmatic but an immensely theological ingredient, inviting one another into the sharing of liturgies, customs, insights and feelings. This above all created a spirit of trust in which many risks could be taken without anybody ever walking out for good. It also created friendship between natural antagonists such as white professors and black shift-workers. Most significant, it promoted participation and leadership training; because from the start there was always a 'student' chairing the session when the lecturer was talking, so that now after a decade those former 'students' can become themselves 'associate lecturers' at the weekend courses. John Adegoke, Senior Apostle of the Cherubim and Seraphim Church, and long-term treasurer of the project, wrote in 1980:

> When I was a child in Nigeria, I experienced non-discrimination among the religious groups in my country... I am convinced that whatever happens in any country or society, the fault in racial prejudice is not in the religion but in the people. Did Jesus not teach us in his sermon on the mountain that if your friend asks you to go one mile, go two miles with him - beyond expectation? This is Christianity in practice. This is anti-prejudice... The Project in Partnership between Black and White has within a short time achieved more than it can realize in bringing minds closer... People have met in lecture rooms, over dinner and buffets and in worship. This small beginning could serve as a mustard seed. Throughout the length and breadth of British society there should be such projects actively working among the people to do the work of renovation and restructuring the fundamentals of British culture, its hospitality, its tolerance, its charity, its understanding of other's people problems, and - first and foremost - its Christian re-education.[23]

The teaching methods were - and hopefully still are - based on Paolo Freire's conscientization programme, doing away with "the conceptual language of the oppressor" and opting "instead for the oral language of the common people".[24] This, as Hollenweger affirms, was "both a cultural and a political decision".[25] The language had to be contextual, or relevant to members of the working-class and of a black 'subculture'. Contents, especially history and doctrine, had to be taught from the perspectives of the participants, or their own cultural and religious heritage. Teaching did not imply imposing knowledge on previously ignorant students but helping them to work through their own - perhaps unreflected - experiences. Learning and teaching became a process of constant exchange in which both students and teachers were partners, subjects rather than objects in the exercise. Lecturers had to be motivators and facilitators, and often found themselves at the receiving end. Truth was experienced as an encounter between those who respect one another's opinions. Forums on Saturday night with visitors from the churches, the city, and the university ensured non-homogeneous seminars. Interaction was never dominated by one group alone. Worship on Sunday morning, and the overall sense of humour and spirituality, became the means of finding distance to oneself and of sharing agreements and controversies in the presence of God.

In all this the Bible served as common ground, adding, however, to the analytical approach of European Biblical theology, the understanding of Scripture as a source for vision and inspiration. This African approach challenged all those for whom the historical-critical school alone would provide proper 'evidence'. On the other hand, supposedly fundamentalist and 'pious' black pastors (unlike some of their white colleagues) were not at all afraid of the critical analysis of a Bible text, and the contradictions involved in it. It linked the Bible with their own reality, both in terms of actual dilemmas and of the kerygmatic pattern of a story. It made them enjoy the dynamics of text and form criticism. It rendered both Testaments close to the features of black religion. It spread out the historical, social, material and cultural contexts of Scripture. Thus it paved the way to better communication of blacks with whites, and whites with blacks.[26]

Finally, the examinations or the Certificate in Theology not only gave accreditation to educationally disadvantaged people and opened the doors for further academic studies. They also introduced, for the first time, elements of black studies into a European university. Hollenweger formulated intriguing questions such as, "Compare the practice of healing in the black independent churches with that in the British National Health Service"; or, "Christians did not help the abolition of slavery: Discuss!" These functioned as eye-openers not just to our own course members but to other students who sat the exams in the Great Hall.

The Theological Challenge

In a discussion on British television, a Hindu woman professor of English said, "There has been a long, long history or itinerary of silencing throughout human history." It can be said that the Centre for Black and White Christian Partnership has been an attempt to undo at least part of that silencing. Or, as the black American scholar Eric Lincoln wrote:

> White theology has excluded Black people from its universe of discourse and from its meaningful concern. In so doing, white theology....has contributed significantly to the involuntary invisibility of Black people - to Black oblivion.[27]

Black oblivion has existed in British schools, town-halls, trade unions and political parties until very recently. Even now, institutions and organizations have only scratched the surface of what the new voices, insights and challenges among us entail. We live in a world in which Christianity is no more 'A white man's religion', in which the fastest growing Christian movements are precisely those which have arrived on our doorsteps, and in which the survival of basic human values depends on progress in intercultural learning. People are still silenced or condemned to oblivion, even as our neighbours. As Hollenweger himself analyzed it, the fundamental reasons for refusing black competence a place in the academic and political world "are not themselves academic, but of a power-political-nature".[28]

In this way, the human substance of the task at hand is linked up with pain without which the liberation of God's people will not be ours: pain of blacks; pain of women; pain of the powerless and dispossessed; pain of all those for whom the decision-machinery of the powerful is anything but transparent. This is even reflected in this *Festschrift* where many of the Third World scholars and women whom Hollenweger supported are not represented. The Centre certainly followed a different line. From its inception, it tried to care for those who cannot afford the luxury of full-time education, are not funded by mission-boards, and belong to the lower-income strata of society. Hence sufficient funding will remain a problem. Donors put their money where their interests are. However, this is precisely the fundamental task: to inspire people to share financially and spiritually with *all* God's children.

So we have to dig anew into the vision of the Kingdom of God where people will gather from South and North, East and West, and sit at table; and the first will be last, and the last will be first (Luke 13:29). What we need is a Church which builds itself carefully around the personal desires and spiritual gifts of human beings regardless of colour, origin and creed. What we need is an education for the incarnation and contextualization of the Gospel of Jesus Christ. In the words of William J. Seymour, the Black Apostle of Pentecostalism: "If God can get a people around in one accord, in one place, of one heart, mind and soul, believing for this great power, it will fall and Pentecostal results will follow".[29] It is no coincidence that all of us who have worked with black Pentecostals have also found categories for intercultural learning, especially with other religions!

Yet, there is still another aspect, the issue of staffing within the project. A Swiss professor, an English secretary and a German woman pastor, together with a mixed Executive, would not have been enough. After my return to Frankfurt, I found it strange to be put back into the monocultural atmosphere made up by all-white German Protestants: after the experience in Birmingham I cannot see this as a responsible way of doing theology! In other words, the intercultural nature of the project's staff was and is of tremendous theological significance. There was Martin Simmonds, now a bishop in Ipswich, who from 1981 served the Centre as Associate Director and brought his delightful Afro-Caribbean and Pentecostal gifts into the venture. He later did a Master's degree with Hollenweger. There was Bongani Mazibuko from 1982-1985 who, after the completion of his doctorate on the project's educational methods, became Co-director and, from his South African experience, added not only an educational but also a political element. His plea for 'decolonizing the mind' both of whites and blacks will not be forgotten.[30] Besides Brenda Rae, an English woman free from any racial prejudice, there were two black secretaries, Pamela McIntyre and Mavis Braham, who, brought up in England, introduced a healthy element of black British identity into the work, and became true link-persons between the British and Afro-Carribean cultures.

When my own contract ended with the Centre, Mazibuko was left as the only Director, as there was no money to replace the Co-director. When he too departed to take up work with the South African Council of Churches, he encouraged Patrick Kalilombe, White Father and Third World lecturer at Selly Oak Colleges, to look after the Certificate course at least voluntarily. For more than a year the Centre was left without paid academic staff and almost collapsed. When the post was re-advertised, Kalilombe, an African Roman Catholic bishop, applied for it, for he had never enjoyed work so much. This time not only the whites but also the blacks had made up their minds. Today the Centre, even with one Director and reduced means, has re-gained strength, still operating with modifications on the original pattern and running two Certificate courses simultaneously.[31]

In 1988, the Centre celebrated its ten years 'of spiritual (and political?) challenge' in St. Francis Hall. I was invited to preach the sermon on Philippians 3, or the athlete 'pressing on toward the goal'. In this service Hollenweger was given his Farewell. People presented him with an African gown to do away with his dull academic European 'talar'. Eric Pemberton, another graduate in Afro-Caribbean studies under him and also a poet, sang a song in his honour. Professor E.W. Ives, Dean of the Faculty of Arts, addressed the congregation. He said: "Walter, you have written many, many books. Your dissertation alone consists of twelve volumes. But I am sure that The Centre for Black and White Christian Partnership will still exist when you are reduced to a footnote." Martin Simmonds added: "If you have written perhaps 500,000 pages or more, there will be soon five kilometers written by all whom you inspired to do black studies."

In July 1991, Hollenweger processed into the Great Hall in his African gown when eventually my own dissertation in two volumes on 'A Plea for British Black Theologies' earned me a doctorate. It contains the story of the black Church movement in Britain in its transatlantic cultural and theological interaction and - indirectly - the journey of the Centre. Once inspired by Hollenweger who taught me to understand the dynamics of oral theology, it is the research behind the project or, as Kalilombe said, the 'foundation' on which it is built. I quote from Hollenweger's Foreword:

> For many years the World Council of Churches and the more enlightened members of the theological teaching profession have made themselves the advocates of the under-privileged, the oral and silenced people in our society. Now these very people begin to speak for themselves. And what happens? Do we adapt our theological education, our forms of teaching, our examination structure, our qualifications for studies to this new, important and life-enhancing clientele?... There is not even one specialist in any European or American university with a proper

> institute, library, facilities, etc., to study the beginnings of the future of a new church which is happening under our noses... What kind of scholarship is that! Should scholarship not also be interested in what really happens in the Church worldwide?[32]

It is my wish that his dream of these specialized institutes for intercultural education, research and reflection will come true some day. I am also sure that his name will be never reduced to just a footnote. However, I agree that the Centre for Black and White Christian Partnership for which he formed such important links will be one of the major contributions of his ministry.

Notes

1. Walter J. Hollenweger, "The Challenge of Black Theology", unpublished paper, Birmingham 1982, quoted in: *Christian Action Journal*, The Centre for Black and White Christian Partnership, edited by R. Gerloff and E. James (London: Autumn 1982), 11.
2. Rosalind Edwards in: Roswith Gerloff/Martin Simmonds, *Learning in Partnership*, Third report by the Joint Working Party between White-led and Black-led Churches (London: The British Council of Churches, 1980), 11.
3. See for this the doctoral dissertation by the author: *A Plea for British Black Theologies: The Black Church Movement in Britain in its cultural and theological interaction*, Studies in the Intercultural History of Christiantiy 77 (Frankfurt: Verlag Peter Lang, 1992), chapters 2 and 3.II.
4. "Children of an Imperial God", Open University programme, approx. 1983. Simon of Cyrene Theological Institute, London.
5. *Baptism, Eucharist and Ministry*, Faith and Order Paper No. 111 (Geneva: World Council of Churches, 1982).
6. Letter of Bishop Malachi Ramsay to Michael Goulder, 15 December 1981.
7. Walter J. Hollenweger, "A Revival in Black and a New Way of Learning" in *Reform* (April 1981). Cf. *Ten Years of Spiritual Challenge*, Dialogue between Rev. Roswith Gerloff and Rev. Bongani Mazibuko (Birmingham: The Centre for Black and White Partnership, 1988), 16-21.
8. Olu Abiola in: Roswith Gerloff, *Partnership in Black and White* (London: Methodist Home Mission, 1977), 27 f. ("Spiritual and Theological Re-education within the Christian Ministry").
9. Walter J. Hollenweger, "Interaction between Black and White in Theological Education" in: *Theology* 90 (September 1987), 342.
10. Walter J. Hollenweger, "Black Competence" in: *Christian Action Journal* (Autumn 1982), 17.
11. *Ibid.*
12. Noel L. Erskine, essay on Martin Luther King Jr, in: *Biographisch - Bibliographisches Kirchenlexikon* (Göttingen: Verlag T. Bautz, 1991).
13. Bongani A. Mazibuko, *Education in Mission/Mission in Education. A Critical Comparative Study of Selected Approaches*, Studies in the Intercultural History of Christianity 47 (Frankfurt: Verlag Peter Lang, 1987), 39.
14. *Ibid.*, 68.
15. Walter J. Hollenweger, *op. cit.*
16. *Ibid.*
17. *Ibid.*
18. *Ibid.*

19. Clive Brown, in: *Learning in Partnership*, 8, 14.
20. Alvin Blake, Pastor of the Calvary Church of God in Christ, Luton, in a meeting of the Forum for Ecumenical Intercultural Learning, 1989.
21. Roswith Gerloff quoted by Walter J. Hollenweger, in: "Interaction between Black and White in Theological Education", *op. cit.*, 344.
22. Cf. Walter J. Hollenweger, "Priorities in Pentecostal Research", in: Jan A.B. Jongeneel (ed.), *Experiences of the Spirit: Conference on Pentecostal and Charismatic Research in Europe at Utrecht University 1989*, Studies in the Intercultural History of Christianity 68 (Frankfurt: Verlag Peter Lang, 1991), 9 ff.
23. John Adegoke, in: *Learning in Partnership*, 12.
24. Walter J. Hollenweger, "Interaction between Black and White in Theological Education", 345, where he compares the introduction of black competence in Church and university with the *ochlos* in the Gospel of Mark, and with the *Minjung* theology of Korea.
25. *Ibid.*
26. Cf. Roswith Gerloff, *A Plea for British Black Theologies*, 12-15.
27. C. Eric Lincoln, *The Black Church since Frazier* (New York: Schocken Books, 2nd printing, 1975), 144 ff.
28. Walter J. Hollenweger, in: *Christian Action Journal* (Autumn 1982), 17.
29. William J. Seymour, quoted in: Douglas J. Nelson, "For such a Time as This" (Ph.D. dissertation, University of Birmingham, 1981), 202-05.
30. Bongani Mazibuko also did his doctorate under the supervision of Hollenweger, and is now Professor of Mission at the University of Zululand.
31. See current information and course materials of the Centre for Black and White Christian Partnership, edited by Patrick Kalilombe, present Director of the project, Selly Oak Colleges.
32. Walter J. Hollenweger, Foreword to R. Gerloff, *A Plea for British Black Theologies*, ix-x.

6

Die Bibel, verkündigt und ausgelegt in Wort, Musik, Tanz und Spiel: Hollenweger als Dichter und Liturgiker

(The Bible Proclaimed and Interpreted in Word, Music, Dance and Play: Hollenweger as Poet and Liturgist)

Marianne Heuberger-Gloor

Als Prof. Walter J. Hollenweger vom Deutschen Kirchentag die Einladung bekam, als Nachfolger des damaligen Münsterpfarrers Dr. Walter Lüthi dessen Bibelarbeit fortzusetzen, übernahm er diese Aufgabe. Inhaltlich setzte er sich dasselbe Ziel: eine theologisch verantwortete, klare Exegese, bezogen auf die Probleme der jeweiligen Stunde auf den Ebenen von Politik, Soziologie, Wirtschaft und Seelsorge. Seine künstlerische Begabung auf musikalischem und dramaturgischem Gebiet liessen ihn jedoch neue Formen suchen, und er fand sie in den 'Bibelspielen'. Mit dem deutschen Choreographen und Tänzer Hansjürgen Hufeisen und seinem 'Stuttgarter Theater der Bilder', und mit dem Schweizer Musiker und Komponisten David Plüss bekam er begabte und begeisterte Helfer, mit denen er über Jahre hinaus immer neue Bibeltexte durchsichtig machte und herausfordernd gestaltete.

Immer mehr deutsche Gemeinden erkannten die mannigfachen Möglichkeiten, die sich auftaten bei der Uebernahme solcher Bibelauslegung. Sie verbreiteten sich über die Landesgrenzen hinaus, und seit 1980 hat diese Form der Bibellektüre auch in der Schweiz immer mehr Freunde gefunden unter Theologen und Laien, die mit Hollenwegers Texten Gemeindegottesdienste feiern.

Theologische Hintergründe

Damit ist es bereits deutlich ausgesprochen: es handelt sich hier nicht um 'Laienspiele', wie sie schon lange seit den 50-er Jahren von einzelnen Theatergruppen, vor allem auch von Jugendverbänden und Konfirmandengruppen in die Gottesdienste eingebracht wurden.

Was hier geboten wird, ist Exegese, ist Universitäts-Theologie, die nun aber nicht im akademischen Raume gefangen bleibt, sondern den Weg findet zum 'Laien'. Es geschieht hier, was jede Predigt zu leisten hat: Vermittlung von Lehre, von neuer Erkenntnis, aber nun nicht im oft schwer verständlichen und oft langweiligen Gewand des Lehrvortrages, sondern als 'Spiel', dem alte und junge Gemeindeglieder bis hin zu den Kindern gut und gerne folgen können. Es ist 'Theologie zum Anlangen', Lehre, die leiblich, sinnlich geworden ist, ohne ihren Ernst, ihre Mitte zu verlieren. Lehre, bei der ich nicht Zuhörer bleibe, sondern Mitbeteiligter am Geschehen und dadurch auch am theologischen Prozess. Hollenweger selber formuliert sein Anliegen mit folgenden Worten:

> ...Darum herrscht heute weitherum ein biblischer Analphabetismus. Um dem abzuhelfen, schrieb ich zum Beispiel verschiedene Choreographien, dramatische und musikalische Auslegungen und Monodramen für das säkulare Theater. Diese Art von Theologie spart die kritische Arbeit am Text nicht aus. Aber sie macht sie augenfällig und erlebbar. So kann sie verstanden und aufgenommen werden, auch von Nichtakademikern. Die Leitfrage ist dabei nicht: 'Was sagt mir dieser Text heute? Was fühle und erfahre ich, wenn ich ihn höre?', sondern: 'Was wollte der Autor damals sagen?' Werktreue sind gemeinsame Qualitäten der Künstler und der Exegeten. Meine Erfahrung ist, daß, je näher ich dem biblischen Verfasser auf die Spur komme, desto näher bin ich auch beim heutigen Hörer und Zuschauer.[1]

Welche theologischen Anliegen, welche Motivation steht dahinter?

Mission und Evangelisation

Prof. Hollenweger hatte in Birmingham den Lehrstuhl für Missionswissenschaft inne. Dass heute auch die ganze westliche Welt zum Missionsgebiet erklärt worden ist, ist nachgerade kein Geheimnis mehr. Wie aber missioniert man im nach-christlichen Raum? Die Form der Großevangelisation im gemieteten Sport-Stadion oder im Zelt hat zwar ihre Funktion behalten als Treffpunkt der Gläubigen und zu ihrer Bestätigung und Ausrüstung. Ein Neuwerden der Gemeinden konnte aber dadurch nicht erreicht werden. In der einzelnen Ortsgemeinde selber müsste das Interesse an der Bibel neu geweckt, das Gespräch untereinander in Gang gebracht werden. Solches ist aber nur möglich, wenn man die Bibel so aufschließt, daß sie 'neu' gelesen werden kann. Daß das geschichtliche Umfeld, in das die Texte hineingehören, dem Leser gegenwärtig wird; daß es in Bezug gestellt wird zu seiner Welt; daß er sich in den Gestalten, die ihm begegnen, selber findet; daß er sich mit ihnen identifizieren kann. Und echtes Gespräch kann nur da entstehen, wo man sich gegenseitig ernst nimmt und achtet; wo man aufhört, auszusondern in 'Gläubige' und 'Ungläubige', in 'Bekehrte' und 'Unbekehrte'; wo man sich vielmehr anerkennt als Weggefährten auf der Suche nach Gott, nach der Wahrheit; wo man bereit ist, gegenseitig voneinander zu lernen; wo Evangelisation nicht mehr so verstanden wird, daß der 'Wissende' den 'Sünder' in sein Bild, in seine Glaubensform umgestaltet; wo der eine nicht alles hat, und der andere nichts, sondern wo man von vornherein akzeptiert, dass bei diesem Suchen nicht jeder dasselbe findet. Echte Evangelisation setzt den Freiraum der Toleranz voraus. Aus diesem Anliegen, aus dieser Sicht heraus sind die Bibelfestspiele entstanden.

Die narrative Theologie

Die Bibel ist vordergründig ein Buch der Geschichten. Wäre sie es nicht, wäre sie längst in Vergessenheit geraten. Die grossen theologischen Texte des Apostels Paulus zum Beispiel bleiben bis heute den meisten Bibellesern in ihrem Zusammenhang verschlüsselt. Die Trostworte, die helfen und begleiten, sind aus dem Zusammenhang herausgefallen. Geschichten hingegen werden von einer Generation zur andern weiter erzählt: Grossmütter erzählen sie den Enkeln, Eltern den Kindern; sie sind der Inhalt von Sonntagsschule und Unterricht; man kann sie zeichnen und malen in Büchern und auf den Fensterscheiben der Kirchen und Kathedralen: sie sind 'an-schaulich'. Was macht nun aber ihre Besonderheit aus im Vergleich zum theologischen Lehrtext?

Jesus selber hat seine Lehre in Geschichten weitergegeben. Seine Gleichnisse sind Antworten auf knifflige Theologenfragen.

Die Geschichte entlässt in die Freiheit; die Lehre legt mich fest. Ich muss ihr zustimmen oder ich muss sie widerlegen. Der Geschichte kann ich entnehmen, was mich im Moment betrifft, was ich verstehe: als Kind oder als Professor. Ich blamiere mich nicht durch mein Verständnis. Es ist nicht falsch oder richtig; es ist die mir jetzt angemessene Auslegung. Vor einer Geschichte muss ich mich deshalb nicht fürchten. Ich darf 'mit dabei sein'.

Eine Geschichte ist nach vorne offen. Sie erlaubt mir, sie weiter zu denken, weiter zu erzählen, zu ergänzen. Wohl ganz bewusst hat Jesus Fragen offen gelassen. Wir wissen nicht, ob der ältere Sohn sich vom Vater hat mitnehmen lassen zum Fest (Luk. 15:25-32). Es wäre eine interessante Sache, diesen Versuch des Weitererzählens einmal bewußt zu wagen.

Bibelfestspiele erzählen und geben so den Raum frei zum eigenen Nachdenken und zum Gestalten. Der Phantasie des Glaubens steht die Türe offen.

Die interkulturelle Theologie

Was Hollenweger im Gespräch mit seinen Doktoranden aus der dritten Welt gelernt hat, macht er hier fruchtbar für unsere eigenen Begegnungen. Unser Christsein ist ja viel stärker geprägt von unserem kulturellen Umfeld als wir uns dessen meist bewusst sind. Die landeskirchlichen Gottesdienste erreichen den bürgerlichen Mittelstand. Die Arbeiterschaft, geschweige denn Menschen die aus dem Rahmen der 'Normalität' herausgefallen sind, haben hier praktisch keinen Platz, auch wenn sie theoretisch in der Predigt oft und gerne vorkommen. Man spricht hier die Sprache des 'Gebildeten'. Wer sich dabei nicht wohlfühlt, bleibt weg oder wandert aus in eine Gemeinschaft, die seinem Lebensstil eher entspricht; wo das Alternative seine Sprache findet; wo man Gefühle zeigen und leben darf.

"Wie aus Grenzen Brücken werden" hat Hollenweger eines seiner Bücher betitelt. Diese Möglichkeit bietet sich im gemeinsamen Erarbeiten und Feiern der Bibeltexte. Ich werde später noch näher darauf eingehen. Es kann hier deutlich werden, daß das Evangelium nicht eine besondere Kultur voraussetzt, wie das lange angenommen wurde, sondern daß es fähig ist, jede Kultur zu erlösen, zu heiligen, das heißt sie zu dem zu machen, zu dem sie wirklich fähig ist, damit in ihr Menschen angstfrei ihr Leben finden. Und dies gilt, wie gesagt, nicht zur zwischen den großen Kulturunterschieden verschiedener Kontinente und ihrer Religionen, sondern auch für die aufgerichteten Abgrenzungen zwischen den Bewohnern eines einzigen Dorfes!

Aufbau und Stil der Bibelfestspiele

Von diesem theologischen Hintergrund aus gestaltet Hollenweger seine Dramaturgien.[2] Sie bestehen wesentlich aus folgenden 'Bausteinen':

1. Exegese durch *das Wort*. Es wird dabei nicht geredet 'über' den Text, sondern die 'Beteiligten' selber kommen zu Wort. Im *Ostertanz der Frauen* erzählen diese, was ihnen geschehen ist bei ihrer Begegnung mit Jesus. Dasselbe tun in der Pfingst-, in der Passions- und in der Weihnachtsliturgie die 'Akteure' des Geschehens. In einem zweiten Teil sprechen dann die 'Interpreten', Menschen von heute, in Analogie zu ihren biblischen Gesprächspartnern.
2. Die Exegese durch den *Tanz*. Die Bilder sind nicht einfach Wiederholung des im Wort Gesagten. Sie führen die Gedanken der Sprecher(innen) selbständig weiter, sind so selber Exegese, überlassen sich der Deutung des Zuschauers.
3. Die Exegese durch *die Musik*. Sie begleitet den Tanz und das Wort mit allen ihr zur Verfügung stehenden Möglichkeiten. Einmal ist es die meditative Sprache eines einzelnen Instrumentes, improvisierend, Flöte, Geige, Cello u.a.; ebenso oft beteiligt sich ein kleines Orchester: Kammermusik, Blasmusik oder Schlagzeuger; in der *Jüngermesse* spielen diese drei Gruppen gemeinsam! Einmal singt der Kirchenchor, ein ander Mal ein Gesangverein des Dorfes, oder ein Kinderchor (bei 'Jona' im *Das Fest der Verlorenen*). Wichtig ist, daß die Gemeinde selber immer wieder mit einbezogen wird ins Geschehen durch das Singen der ihr bekannten Kirchenlieder, die die einzelnen Teile miteinander verbinden. Sie ist ja nicht Zuschauerin; man feiert gemeinsam einen Gottesdienst.

4. Auch *die Farben* haben ihre wesentliche Aussage. Farben sind symbolträchtig. Sie wecken beim Betrachter bewusste oder unbewusste Assoziationen, die zum Verstehen helfen. Diese Farben werden überall sichtbar gemacht. Sie verbinden Sprecher und Tänzer, 'Beteiligte' und 'Interpreten' und machen so die Zusammenhänge deutlich.

Mit diesen Erzähl-Elementen wird der Mensch ganzheitlich angesprochen. All seine Sinne werden betroffen; auf allen Ebenen 'berührt' ihn der Text. Gleichzeitig können so möglichst viele Gemeindeglieder in den Prozess der Auslegung integriert werden. Voraussetzung zum Mitmachen ist nicht der rechte Glaube, der fleissige Kirchenbesuch, sondern die Gaben, die man einbringt, die Freude, sich auf das Fest einzulassen. Nicht nur der, der gut lesen kann, ist gefragt. Es braucht ja auch Leute, die sozusagen 'im Hintergrund' mithelfen: beim Schmuck des Raumes, mit Malen und Bauen der Requisiten, beim Nähen der Kleider und vielem mehr.

Statt daß einer den Text auslegt, höchstens noch assistiert vom Organisten, sind an der Gestaltung eines solchen Gottesdienstes bald einmal 50-150 Leute beteiligt. Dabei ist es die Stärke dieser Dramaturgien, daß sie den Gestaltenden den Raum frei lassen zur Eigenbestimmung. Tanz und Musik richten sich nach den vorhandenen Möglichkeiten: sind Solisten da oder ein Chor? Sind es 'Profis' oder 'Laien'? Wie gross ist der Raum, der zur Verfügung steht; wie ist er gestaltet? 'Bausteine' nennt Hollenweger das, was er der Gemeinde in die Hand gibt. Daraus kann etwas sehr Grosses und Aufwendiges entstehen, aber auch etwas Bescheidenes, Schlichtes. Hauptsache ist: es soll Freude machen; Menschen sollen ihre Gaben und Möglichkeiten entdecken; es soll Gemeinschaft entstehen. Und dies ist umso leichter möglich, weil man es diesen Texten anspürt, daß sie zwar am Schreibtisch geschrieben wurden mit einem klaren Konzept, daß aber der Ansporn dazu jedesmal neu gegeben wurde durch ein Gespräch; durch eine Begegnung, die auf diese Weise Gestalt annahm; durch ein engagiertes Teilnehmen am lebendigen Prozess von Gemeindeleben und -wachstum.

Praktische Erfahrungen

Natürlich gibt es Pfarrer und Gemeinden, die sich auf das Wagnis solcher Exegese nicht einlassen wollen. Sie fürchten sich vor einem grossen Aufwand; davor, wie Ungewohntes, zum Beispiel der Tanz in der Kirche, aufgenommen würde. Auch theologische Gründe werden ins Feld geführt. Und Hollenweger hat es tatsächlich auch unserer Gemeinde nicht immer einfach gemacht. Seine Texte wurden zur Herausforderung. Altvertraute Worte und Geschichten rückten in ein neues, fremd anmutendes Licht; sie wurden hinterfragt. Man konnte ihnen nicht mehr ausweichen. Die Sprache war dort angesiedelt, wo Luther sie suchte: nicht in den Buchstaben des gewohnten kirchlichen Stils, sondern in der Ausdrucksweise "der Mutter im Hause, der Kinder auf der Gasse, des gemeinen Mannes auf dem Markte". Seine 'Tiergebete' machten betroffen; sie wurden nicht immer verstanden, gerieten einigen 'in den falschen Hals'.

Wer immer es aber unternommen hat, diese Texte im Gottesdienst zum Leben zu erwecken, hat wohl dieselben Erfahrungen gemacht, die ich selber mit einer Gemeinde über Jahre hinweg erleben durfte. Ich zähle hier nur zwei der wichtigsten auf. Sie wären beliebig zu vermehren.

1. Die Vorbereitung ist mindestens so wichtig wie das Fest selber. Es beginnt vom ersten Moment an ein Prozess: die Helfer müssen gesucht werden mit ihren Gaben; in gemeinsamen Proben nehmen allmählich Bilder und Gedanken ihre Formen an, wobei jedes die Möglichkeit hat, seine eigene Ideen und Vorstellungen einzubringen. Dass man dabei auch miteinander streiten lernt, ist vielleicht nicht nur eine negative Erfahrung!
   Es ist auch empfehlenswert, den entsprechenden Bibeltext und seine theologische Aussage mit der Gemeinde über längere Zeit vorzubereiten auf verschiedenen Ebenen: in der Predigt, in Bibelkreisen, in Unterricht und Sonntagsschule. Dann wird das Fest für alle Abschluss und Zusammenfassung eines gemeinsamen Wegabschnittes. Die Texte sind nicht mehr fremd, sondern bereits ein Stück 'Eigentum' geworden.
2. Das 'interkulturelle' Moment ist voll zum Tragen gekommen. Die Altersgrenzen wurden überschritten. Vom 4-jährigen Engel, der mittanzte in *Hiobs* 'Tanz der Engel' und dann, von Müdigkeit übermannt, auf der Bühne einfach einschlief, bis zur über 70-jährigen Frau, die mitwirkte im Sprechchor der *Gomer*, waren alle Alter vertreten. Die Konfirmanden machten mit als Kühe im 'Tanz der Tiere' bei *Hiob*; und bei *Mirjam*, dem Monodrama des Marienlebens, gestalteten sie die begleitenden Bilder. Im Sprechchor der *Gomer*, in Gesangsgruppen, trafen sich die Mitglieder der Landeskirche mit den Angehörigen verschiedenster Freikirchen: der Methodisten, der Pfingstgemeinde u.a.

Am Stärksten wurde dieses Anliegen sichtbar bei der *Jüngermesse*, weil hier die Texte nicht einfach übernommen und auswendiggelernt wurden, sondern weil echte Vertreter der jeweiligen gegensätzlichen Ansichten untereinander ins Gespräch kamen und ihre Verschiedenartigkeit dann auch offen bekannt gaben. Als im selben Gottesdienst Vertreter des Kammerorchesters, der Dorfmusik und junge Schlagzeuger miteinander spielen sollten, musste das Ungewohnte tatsächlich zuerst gelernt werden, nicht nur im musikalischen Bereich! Nach Ueberwindung der Widerstände wurde das gemeinsam gefeierte Abendmahl zu einem Schlüsselerlebnis, das sich in den Alltag hinein auswirkte.

Es hat sich auch erwiesen, dass die Texte tatsächlich nicht als Schauspiele, sondern als Gottesdienste zu verstehen sind. Wir haben sie bewusst jedesmal hineingenommen in den gottesdienstlichen Rahmen unserer gewohnten Sonntagsliturgie. Hier haben dann auch Taufe und Abendmahl ihren jeweiligen besondern Ort gefunden.

Folgen und Ergebnisse

Werden die, von diesen Gottesdiensten anvisierten Ziele erreicht? Ich möchte diese Frage mit einem überzeugten 'Ja' beantworten.

1. Die Bibel hat sich neu erschlossen. Sie wurde in einer andern als der gewohnten Sicht gelesen. Die Gestalten begannen zu leben. Ihre Aussagen wurden zu den eigenen. Konfirmanden, kirchenferne Leute fingen an, selbständig die Bibel zu lesen. Das hatte man vorher so nicht gewusst.
2. Man lernte neu zu hören. Wer die Texte selber vor der Gemeinde las, sie auslegte, wollte und musste dies verantworten können. Aussagen, die man bis dahin ohne Ueberlegung von der Kanzel her kritiklos angenommen hatte, wurden kritisch hinterfragt, abgelehnt, neu formuliert.
3. Es erwachte die Freude, selber in dieser Art Texte liturgisch zu gestalten in gemeinsamer Arbeit. Es entstanden so neue Gottesdienste.
4. Es öffnete sich in unerwarteten Ausmasse die Möglichkeit ökumenischer Zusammenarbeit. Die katholische Kirche entdeckte hier die Wiederaufnahme ihrer Tradition der Mysterienspiele. Hier ist die Voraussetzung geschaffen für eine gemeinsame Verkündigung des Evangeliums durch die Traditionen des Wortes und der Liturgie.
5. Es ist wohl kein Zufall, dass aus diesen Gottesdiensten heraus die Segnungsgottesdienste mit der Salbung gewachsen sind. Wo das Wort 'leiblich', 'zum Anlangen' wird, da wagt man auch die liturgische Berührung zu Segen, Heil und Heilung. Und wo das Wort gelebte Gegenwart wird, wagt man es auch, daran zu glauben, daß uns die biblischen Geschichten nicht dazu überliefert sind, daß unsere Pfarrer gute und schöne Predigten darüber halten, sondern damit unter uns dasselbe geschieht. Man nimmt es ernst, daß das Wort 'Dynamit' ist, Kraft des Schöpfergeistes; daß es nicht leer zurückkommt (Jes. 55:11); daß es tut, was es verspricht; daß der Heilige Geist auch der Schöpfergeist ist.

Bei der Vorbereitung zur *Gomer*, im Nachdenken darüber, was der Segen Gottes sei und bedeute, wurde der Wunsch laut nach eigener Segenserfahrung im Gottesdienst.

Antworten auf die Bibelfestspiele

Lassen wir zum Schluss noch zwei Teilnehmerinnen solcher Gottesdienste zu Worte kommen.

Eine junge Frau, die als Mutter eines Täuflings an der *Jüngermesse* teilgenommen hatte, schreibt:

> Liebe Frau Pfarrer,
> Ich möchte Ihnen danken für den unvergeßlichen Taufgottesdienst vom letzten Sonntag. Es war ein tiefes Erlebnis, an dieser Abendmahlsfeier teilzunehmen und zu wissen, daß ich selber auch angenommen bin. Ich fühlte mich vorher nie berechtigt oder erwartet. Durch die Zweiergruppen Menschen, die sich in ihrer Verschiedenheit vorgestellt haben, 'ging auch mir ein Licht auf'. Seit meiner Konfirmation war es das erste Abendmahl, zu dem ich gegangen bin. Gleich den Kerzenlichtern kam mir die Erleuchtung, daß ich trotz zweifelndem, ungefestigtem und in Frage gestelltem Glauben zum Tisch gehen konnte. Es war schön, dieser Gottesdienst, ich werde noch lange daran und darüber nachdenken.
> Mit freundlichen Grüssen, R.S.

Zur Passionsliturgie schreibt eine junge Theologin:

> ...am Sonntag Abend konnte ich zwar nicht mehr dabei sein. Aber die beiden ersten Gottesdienste waren in jeder Hinsicht ausgezeichnet, so weit ich es beurteilen kann. Ausgezeichnet durch ihre inneren und äusseren Aussagen, durch die Verbindung von ausgesprochenen und kreativen Elementen, von Vergangenem und dem gespannten Bogen zu unserer Situation. Ich kam natürlich kritisch, skeptisch daher wie immer, aber ich bin sehr glücklich über all den Reichtum, der sich auftut. Die beeindruckendste Szene war für mich beide Male die der Maria, sie hätte nicht besser gesprochen und getanzt werden können. Der Kampf darum, etwas Liebgewordenes wieder hergeben zu müssen, ohne souveränes Verstehen oder 'gut damit fertig werden können', das gehört sicher menschlich gesehen zum Schmerzvollsten und ist doch nie verlorener Kampf. Das sind so einige Gedanken.
> Mit liebem Gruss, R.G.

Anmerkungen

1. W.J. Hollenweger, Das Evangelium sinnlich verkündigen. In: *Evang. Information* 30/91, Gastkommentar.
2. Eine Liste der wichtigsten Dramaturgien:

— *Glaube, Geist und Geister; Professor Unrat zwischen Bangkok und Birmingham* (Frankfurt: O. Lembeck, 1975). Auszug im Englischen in verschiedenen Zeitschriften.

— *Konflikt in Korinth: Memoiren eines alten Mannes* (München: Kaiser, 1978). English: *Conflict in*

Corinth; Memoirs of an Old Man (New York: Paulist, 1982). Auch im Französischen, Italienischen und Indonesischen.
— *Erfahrungen in Ephesus: Darstellung eines Davongekommenen* (München: Kaiser, 1979). Auch im Italienischen.
— *Besuch bei Lukas* (München: Kaiser, 1981).
— *Jüngermesse/Gomer: Das Gesicht des Unsichtbaren* (München: Kaiser, 1983). Auch im Französischen.
— *Zwingli zwischen Krieg und Frieden, erzählt von seiner Frau* (München: Kaiser, 1983). Auch im Französischen.
— *Das Fest der Verlorenen; Die Bibel erzählt, getanzt und gesungen* (München: Kaiser, 1982).
— *Der Handelsreisende Gottes/Totentanz zum neuen Leben (Passionsliturgie): Im Rössli zu Emmaus (Osterliturgie)* (München: Kaiser, 1985).
— *Im Schatten Seines Friedens* (Renningen: P. Marquardt, 1986). Christmas Oratorio.
— (mit Hans-Jürgen Hufeisen,) *Das Wagnis des Glaubens: Ein Spiel über die Mission für Sprecher, Instrumentalisten, Bewegungstheater und Gemeinde* (München: Kaiser, 1986).
— *Mirjam, Mutter/Michal; die Frauen meines Mannes* (Freiburg, Switserland: Exodus, 1987).
— *Ostertanz der Frauen* (Kindhausen: Metanoia, 1991).
— (mit Heyno Kattenstedt,) *Ecce homo: Jürg Ratgeb, Maler und Bauernkanzler erlebt die Passion Jesu Christi: Eine musikalische Dokumentation* (Kindhausen: Metanoia: 1992).
— *Veni Creator Spiritus; Pfingstliturgie* (Kindhausen: Metanoia, 1991).
— *Hiob oder die Wette Gottes* (Kindhausen: Metanoia, 1991).
— *Requiem für Bonhoeffer* (Kindhausen: Metanoia, 1991).
— *Kommet her zu mir alle, die ihr mühselig und beladen seid* (Salbungsliturgien) (Kindhausen: Metanoia, 1991).
— *Die Basler Mission und der Trumph-Buur* (1990). Manuskript.
— *Fontana; die Frau am Brunnen und der siebte Mann* (Kindhausen: Metanoia, 1991).
— *Der Knabe und die Mondin* (München: Strube, 1991).
— *Das Friedensmahl* (1991). Manuskript; ein Schauspiel zur 700 jährigen Gedächnisfeier der Schweiz. Ein Auftrag van den Römisch Katholischen, den Reformierten und den Freien Kirchen. Gespielt durch berufmäßige Schauspieler, Chor und 'brassband' in ungefähr 50 Orte der Schweiz.

Part 2

Historical Case Studies and Statistics on Pentecostalism and the Charismatic Renewal in Missiological and Ecumenical Perspective

7

The Black Roots of Pentecostalism

Iain MacRobert

In 1965, at a time when most white American Pentecostal authors had either written William Joseph Seymour and his black prayer group out of their Movement's history or trivialised his central role, Walter Hollenweger recognised that:

> The Pentecostal experience of Los Angeles was neither the leading astray of the Church by demons... nor the eschatological pouring out of the Holy Spirit (as the Pentecostal movement itself claims) but an outburst of enthusiastic religion of a kind well-known and frequent in the history of Negro churches in America which derived its specifically Pentecostal features from Parham's theory that speaking with tongues is a necessary concomitant of the baptism of the Spirit.[1]

The historical origins of Pentecostalism in the United States lie primarily in the Wesleyan-Holiness, Keswick and Higher Life Movements, and in the black American church.[2] While the white influences on the early Pentecostal Movement have been recognised by Pentecostal historians, they have often disparaged and sometimes completely ignored the crucial influences of Afro-American Christianity. White pioneers and early leaders like Charles Fox Parham or Ambrose Jessup Tomlinson have been recognised - even eulogised - whereas Seymour, one of the most influential of the pioneers, has generally been marginalized and his important role even denied by the myth of no human leadership, and this in spite of the recognition accorded him by such diverse people as Frank Bartleman in the United States, Alexander A. Boddy in Britain and G.R. Polman in the Netherlands.[3] Parham may have been accused of homosexuality and Tomlinson of financial mismanagement and megalomania, but Seymour was less acceptable to most North American Pentecostal historians than either of them. They were white, he was black.

A more scholarly and rigorous historian, James R. Goff, continues to maintain that "Parham, more than Seymour, must be regarded the founder of the Pentecostal movement", because "it was Parham who first formulated the theological definition of Pentecostalism by linking tongues with the Holy Spirit baptism."[4] For Goff, glossolalia as the initial evidence of Spirit baptism is "the *sine qua non* of the experience" and "the central theological corpus which has always defined the movement."[5] To characterise Pentecostalism in terms of the evidence doctrine is, however, to accept a narrow, inadequate, white, North American definition which is belied, not only by Pentecostals in the two-thirds world, but also by some white classical Pentecostals in Britain and by many black-majority Pentecostal churches both in Britain and in the United States itself.[6]

Because Pentecostalism is primarily founded not on a theological proposition, but on a shared perception of human encounter with the divine, it has roots in many Christian traditions and in a diversity of cultures; but it is first and foremost an experiential rather than a cognitive movement. Goff maintains that, "the primacy of theological formulation" labels Parham as chronologically the founder of Pentecostalism.[7] While doctrine was important to some early Pentecostals (though generally less so to black worshippers), all theological formulations were both secondary to their pneumatic experience and, to a greater or lesser extent, inadequate in their attempts to understand or explain the Pentecostal phenomena. The Pentecostal movement did not spread to fifty nations within two years of the Azusa Revival or grow to its current size of some 360 million adherents world-wide as a result of Pentecostal 'theology' or Parham's evidence doctrine, although his understanding of tongues as *xenoglossa* did encourage early Pentecostal foreign missions.[8]

The particular attraction of Pentecostalism to people around the world and the ease with which it has been indigenized in non-Western societies lies in its black experiential roots which provide a substratum of enduring values and themes for the bulk of the Movement outside of white North America and Europe.

One historian who has taken Seymour's role seriously is the Methodist clergyman, Douglas J. Nelson. In 1981, Nelson completed his thesis - under Hollenweger's supervision - on "The Story of Bishop William J. Seymour and the Azusa Street Revival".[9] His historical and biographical research made Seymour's crucial role clear. Seymour, however, was not simply an American with a black skin. Nor was his socialization solely determined by his negative encounters with the aftermath of American slavery and enduring discrimination and racism. Seymour and the other black worshippers who brought to birth the Azusa Street revival and the world-wide Pentecostal Movement which flowed from it shared an understanding and practice of Christianity which had developed in the African diaspora out of a syncretism of West African primal religion and culture with Western Christianity in the crucible of New World slavery.

African Roots and the Black Leitmotif

Africans, brought as slaves to the Americas, did not arrive *tabula rasa* nor did forced acculturation totally eradicate their primal religious beliefs. On the contrary, both in Africa and in the Americas these pre-literate beliefs were transmitted from generation to generation by oral tradition and symbolism. In narratives - myths, legends and folk tales -, songs, parables and other aphorisms, ritual, drama, dance and the rhythms and tones of 'talking' drums African religious ideas were preserved to be syncretized with the Christianity of white America and thus produce a distinctively black form of Christianity. Albert J. Raboteau has well summarised this process:

> Shaped and modified by a new environment, elements of African folklore, music, language, and religion were transplanted to the New World by the African diaspora... One of the most durable and adaptable constituents of the slave's culture, linking African past with American present, was his religion. It is important to realise, however, that in the Americas the religions of Africa have not been merely preserved as static 'Africanisms' or as archaic 'retentions'... African styles of worship, forms of ritual, systems of belief, and fundamental perspectives have remained vital on this side of the Atlantic, not because they were preserved in a 'pure' orthodoxy but because they were transformed. Adaptability, based upon respect for spiritual power wherever it originated, accounted for the openness of African religions to syncretism with other religious traditions and for the continuity of a distinctively African religious consciousness.[10]

The primal religious beliefs brought from Africa with the diaspora included a powerful sense of the importance of community in establishing and maintaining both the personhood of individuals and an experiential relationship with the spirit world of ancestors and divinities. They inhabited a world in which the sacred and profane were integrated and the ability to tap into the *force vitale* by means of divination and spirit possession was considered essential to the welfare of the community, the wholeness of the individual and the success of any major undertaking in the material world.[11]

To attune themselves to the power of the spirits, both in Africa and in the New World, they used rhythm and music. Polyrhythmic drumming, singing, dancing and other motor behaviour opened up the devotee to spirit possession. In Africa, these were understood as the spirits of the ancestors and divinities. In the Americas new understandings grew out of the pragmatic syncretism of their primal religion with Western Christianity. The possessing spirits of Africa became identified with the apostles, prophets, saints, angels and Holy Spirit of the white missionaries but phenomenologically there was considerable continuity.[12]

In spite of missionary attempts to demythologise the perceptions of slaves, literacy brought them into contact with the world of the Bible which, like their own, was concerned with the relationship between the spiritual and the natural. The biblical accounts of miracles, healings, exorcisms, spiritual power and the presence of the Holy Spirit in peoples' lives did not seem so different from their own experiential ancestral religion. Furthermore, their identification with the story of Israel's bondage in Egypt and their subsequent Exodus to the promised land meant that freedom was understood as more than liberation from the power and consequences of personal sin. An African concept of sin as antisocial activities was reflected in an understanding of the work of the devil as predominantly in the concrete realities of enslavement. The Lord of Hosts who delivered his people from Pharaoh's oppression was the God of liberation from political and social evil.[13]

The adventism of evangelical revivalism was also particularly attractive to black Christians for it proclaimed an apocalyptic revolution to be inaugurated by the Second Coming of Christ. The high, the mighty and the oppressor were to be put down, while the humble, the powerless and the oppressed - the Saints - were to be exalted. This eschatological status-reversal was believed to be immanent. Thus the black church in the Americas embraced an inaugurated eschatology which was congruent with an African sense of the future which is so close that it has almost arrived. And if at any moment they were to put on their golden slippers "to walk the golden streets" it was because - in spite of their bondage and sub-human status - they were the children of God now! Others were inspired by the scriptures and their Christian faith to plan insurrections during Sunday services and other ostensibly religious gatherings.[14]

The revivalism of the late 18th and early 19th centuries attracted black people because it stressed an experiential conversion of the heart rather than an intellectual or catechetical religion. "The powerful emotionalism, ecstatic behaviour, and congregational responses of the revival," writes Robateau, "were amendable to the African religious heritage of the slaves, and forms of African dance and song remained in the shout and the spirituals of Afro-American converts to evangelical Protestantism". "In addition," continues Robateau, "the slaves' rich heritage of folk belief and folk expression was not destroyed but was augmented by conversion."[15]

Thus much of the primal religion of West Africa was syncretized with Western Christianity and, in particular, with those themes which were of primary importance to the survival and ultimately the liberation of an oppressed people. Certain leitmotifs which echo both their African origins and their sojourn in the 'Egypt' of chattel slavery surface again and again in the black church of the Americas. An integrated holistic world view, the immanence of the divine, belief in spirit possession, spirit healing and spirit power, the importance of dreams and trances, the extensive use of rhythm, certain types of motor behaviour, antiphonal participation in worship, baptism (immersion) in water and the centrality of community all had African antecedents and reemerged during the revivalist camp meetings of the 18th and 19th centuries where they also influenced whites.[16]

Other leitmotifs of white evangelical or biblical origin became particularly important in the black Christian community: the imminent Parousia, an inaugurated eschatology and an 'Exodus' theology which perceives freedom in socio-political as well as spiritual terms. These leitmotifs were expressed, not in systematic propositions but in the oral, narrative, sung and danced liturgy and theology of the black Christian community.[17]

By the beginning of the 20th century, many of the black churches in the United States - particularly in the North - had largely conformed to white, middle-class conservative evangelicalism. Both the black and white Holiness people - who were mainly proletarian - were dissatisfied with the 'deadness' and 'worldliness' in many churches and looked for a world-wide revival as the harbinger of the imminent Second Advent of Christ. One such Holiness preacher was William J. Seymour.[18]

William Joseph Seymour and the Azusa Street Revival

Born in the South in 1870, the son of emancipated slaves, Seymour grew up in the midst of violent racism. Nelson writes that during his first twenty-four years of life:

> Seymour receives little or no formal schooling but works hard, educates himself... drinks in the invisible institution of black folk Christianity, learns to love the great Negro spirituals, has visions of God, and becomes an earnest student of unfulfilled scriptural prophecy.[19]

That invisible institution of black folk Christianity with its black leitmotif formed the cultural and religious basis for Seymour's subsequent role as the leader of the Azusa Street revival.

Seymour was "seeking for interracial reconciliation" but was aware that this could only be brought about with the aid of divine power.[20] Leaving the interracial Methodist Episcopal Church, he joined another less bourgeois interracial group, the Evening Light Saints, who taught - in addition to holiness, divine healing, racial equality and a kind of ecumenism - that a final great outpouring of the Spirit was about to take place before the end of world history. Their holiness doctrine, like that of the rest of the Holiness Movement, was based on a simplistic understanding of Wesley's teaching and stressed that a second crisis experience of entire sanctification should follow conversion. Some, following the teaching of Charles G. Finney, also stressed the social aspects of Wesley's teaching and defined sanctification as a willingness to become involved in social action as an outworking of personal faith and consecration.

After recovering from smallpox, which left him blind in one eye, Seymour was ordained by the Evening Light Saints and, during the summer of 1905, was serving as the pastor of a black Holiness church in Jackson, Mississippi. In October he received reports that glossolalia as an evidence of the power of the Holy Spirit was being experienced at the Bible School of Charles F. Parham in Houston, Texas. While outbursts of glossolalia have recurred again and again throughout the history of the Church from the day of Pentecost to the present, in 1901 Parham was responsible for the teaching that it is both the initial evidence of Spirit baptism and the ability "to preach in any language of the world."[21] While the former tenet has become widely, but by no means universally, accepted by Pentecostals, the latter, like his Anglo-Saxon Israel, anti-medicine and conditional immortality teaching, has been largely rejected.[22]

Seymour enrolled at Parham's Bible School. At nine o'clock each morning, he attended classes "segregated outside the classroom beside the door carefully left ajar by Parham" who "practices strict segregation".[23] Leaving Houston, Seymour travelled to the cosmopolitan city of Los Angeles to become pastor of a small black (Church of the Nazarene) Holiness mission on Santa Fe Street. At nightly meetings he preached on conversion, sanctification, divine healing and the imminent Second Advent; and on Sunday morning he spoke on glossolalia as a sign accompanying Spirit baptism, and this in spite of the fact he had not yet spoken in tongues himself. Returning to the mission for the evening service he found the doors locked against him. He lived and worshipped in the home of Edward S. Lee and his wife and later with Richard and Ruth Asbury. Both couples were black. On Friday the 6th April, Seymour and a small group began a ten-day fast. Three days later Lee asked Seymour to pray for his recovery from illness. After anointing and prayer Lee felt better and requested that Seymour pray for him to receive the Holy Spirit with the evidence of tongues. He was not disappointed.[24]

Later that night in the Asbury home, a group of black "sanctified wash women" were singing, praying and testifying. As Seymour rose to preach on Acts chapter 2, verse 4, he recounted the events that had taken place earlier that evening but could preach no longer because as soon as he had completed his account of Lee's experience, Lee burst forth in tongues. Nelson describes what followed:

> The entire company was immediately swept to its knees as by some tremendous power. At least seven - and perhaps more - lifted their voices in an awesome harmony of strange new tongues. Jennie Evans Moore, falling to her knees from the piano seat, became the first woman thus to speak. Some rushed out to the front porch, yard, and street, shouting and speaking in tongues for all the neighbourhood to hear... Teenager Bud Traynor stood on the front porch prophesying and preaching. Jennie Evans Moore returned to the piano and began singing in her beautiful voice what was thought to be a series of six languages with interpretations.[25]

Within three days the original all-black group was receiving visits from whites as well as blacks to witness and experience glossolalia, trance and healing. On the 12th April Seymour spoke in tongues himself.[26]

The revival rapidly outgrew the Asbury home and a rundown former African Methodist Episcopal chapel was leased at 312 Azusa Street. Cleared of construction materials which had been stored there, sawdust was spread on the dirt floor and pews fabricated from odd chairs, nail kegs and boxes with planks laid across them. The three services which were conducted each day often overlapped. Some meetings only attracted about a dozen people but within a month Sunday attendance had risen to 750 or 800 with a further four or five hundred, for whom there was no room, crowding outside.[27] Nelson declares that, "multitudes converged on Azusa including virtually every race, nationality, and social class on earth, for Los Angeles contained the world in miniature... Never in history had any such group surged into the church of a black person."[28] Multi-racial congregations were unusual. Black leadership of such congregations, while not unheard of, was extremely rare.

Spirit baptism was, for Seymour, more than a glossolalic episode. It was the power to draw all peoples into one Church without racial distinctions or barriers. Seymour's newspaper *The Apostolic Faith* of September 1906, declared that "multitudes have come. God makes no difference in nationality. Ethiopians, Chinese, Indians, Mexicans, and other nationalities worship together."[29] Black witnesses to those events recalled that, "everybody went to the altar together. White and colored, no discrimination seemed to be among them."[30] "Everybody was just the same, it did not matter if you were black, white, green or grizzly. There was a wonderful spirit. Germans and Jews, black and whites, ate together in the little cottage at the rear. Nobody ever thought of color."[31] White witnesses echoed the same theme: "The color line was washed away in the blood."[32] Visiting from England, the Church of England clergyman, Alexander A. Boddy, recorded that:

> It was something very extraordinary, that white pastors from the South were eagerly prepared to go to Los Angeles to the Negroes, to have fellowship with them and to receive through their prayers and intercessions the blessings of the Spirit. And it was still more wonderful that these white pastors went back to the South and reported to the members of their congregations that they had been together with Negroes, that they had prayed in one Spirit and received the same blessings as they.[33]

Within five months of the birth of this Movement, thirty-eight missionaries had gone out from Azusa. In only two years it had spread to over fifty nations worldwide, but the radical challenge to racism was by this time being subverted and rejected by some arrogant and pusillanimous whites. Parham, who propagated the

Anglo-Saxon Israel teaching of white supremacy and wrote for the notoriously racist Ku Klux Klan, was horrified at the de-segregation and the adoption of black liturgy by whites which had taken place and castigated Azusa for having "blacks and whites mingling" and "laying across one another like hogs".[34] In 1912 he wrote that:

> Men and women, whites and blacks, knelt together or fell across one another; frequently, a white woman, perhaps of wealth and culture, could be seen thrown back in the arms of a big 'buck nigger', and held tightly thus as she shivered and shook in freak imitation of Pentecost. Horrible, awful shame![35]

Dissociation and Replication

In 1914 the white-dominated Assemblies of God was formed, thus ending, in the words of Vinson Synan, "a notable experiment in interracial church development."[36] Two years later, the 'new issue' controversy over the baptismal formula and the nature of the Godhead resulted in the withdrawal of the 'Jesus Name' Oneness Pentecostals and the further purging of black people and elements of the black leitmotif from the Assemblies of God. Thus, writes Robert Mapes Anderson, "the Assemblies became an all but 'lily white' denomination... Since 1916, except for a few black faces here and there in urban congregations in the Northeast, the Assemblies has remained a white man's church."[37] The moralistic Oneness Pentecostals fared little better. The same desire for white 'respectability', racial segregation and the rejection of the black leitmotif tore them apart so that by 1924 there were separate white and black organizations. When the Pentecostal Fellowship of North America was set up in 1948 with the ostensible purpose of demonstrating to the world the fulfillment of Christ's prayer for Christian - in this case Pentecostal Christian - unity, only white organizations were invited to join. In 1965, having added a further nine organizations to the original eight, it was still exclusively white.[38]

What began in April 1906 as a black revival under Seymour's leadership incorporated the leitmotif of black Christianity in the Americas and Parham's distinctive doctrine of glossolalia as an evidence of Spirit baptism and the instrument of world evangelization. Almost immediately it became interracial and spread at a phenomenal rate, both in the United States and throughout the world. White Pentecostals in the United States, however, exploited doctrinal disagreements to dissociate themselves from their black brethren, distance themselves from the black origins of the Movement and to purge it of its more obviously black and radical elements which, however, re-emerge again and again wherever Pentecostals of the African diaspora meet for worship.

In Britain, for example, the black Pentecostal congregations which have been established by settlers from the Caribbean from the early 1950's, fall into three broad categories. Those which are part of the white-dominated, three-stage, Trinitarian organizations in the United States, like the Church of God (Cleveland) [known in Britain as the New Testament Church of God] and the Church of God of Prophecy, or the white-dominated, moralistic United Pentecostal Church, tend to be culturally ambivalent and there is often considerable tension between white-defined fundamentalist 'orthodoxy' and 'orthopraxis' and the black leitmotif which can never be totally stifled. Other three-stage, Trinitarian, 'Church of God' type congregations have broken free from white headquarters in the United States and are significantly more 'black' in their beliefs, liturgy and practice. But the congregations which demonstrate the most overt commitment to the black leitmotif tend to be the Oneness groups with black headquarters in the United States or the Caribbean which pre-date the West Indian migrations of the late 1940's and early 50's.

These groups continue to pulsate most clearly with the liturgical characteristics of the Azusa Revival[39]: orality, narrativity, dance and liturgical motor behaviour with the extensive use of music and rhythm; an integrated and holistic world view incorporating Spirit possession[40] and trances; the importance of dreams, healing and the need for spiritual power to change the material (and social) world; the importance of community and human relationships - including the abolition of the colour line - if life and religion are to be worthwhile; freedom as a socio-political as well as a spiritual issue; the imminence of a revolutionary world order inaugurated by the Second Advent of Christ, which is already to some extent present in an inaugurated eschatology. These themes were all in evidence at Azusa as they had been in the church of the African diaspora in the United States and they are replicated among black Pentecostals in Britain and in the two-thirds world where the overlay of white, North American 'orthodoxy' is often quite superficial and in many situations - when the North Americans have gone home - totally absent. Parham's evidence doctrine, while of real importance to most white North American Pentecostals, some European Pentecostals and a few mission churches, is largely irrelevant to most Pentecostals in the underdeveloped and developing nations and serves only as a redundant symbol of Pentecostal 'orthodoxy' for most black Pentecostals in Britain.

Does It Matter?

"Directly or indirectly," writes Synan, "practically all of the Pentecostal groups in existence can trace their lineage to the Azusa Mission".[41] If this is true, then Seymour rather than Parham or Tomlinson is the most significant historical figure in the early Pentecostal Movement. But does it actually matter who the person primarily responsible was: Parham, who taught that glossolalia is the evidence of Spirit baptism and who advocated and practiced racial segregation; Tomlinson who forbade political involvement and led a racially divided church[42], or Seymour who, as part of the African diaspora, believed in and lived out a Pentecostal experience with socially revolutionary implications? It matters to many black Pentecostals in the United States, Britain and South Africa who have to confront the social, economic and political sins of racism, discrimination and apartheid.[43] It matters - though they may not realise it - for many white Pentecostals who in the denial of their Movement's roots perpetuate the racial arrogance and support for an oppressive socio-political and economic *status quo* which makes them the enemies of the Gospel to the poor. And it matters so that Pentecostalism does not become - or indeed remain - an individualistic ideology used by the powerful to control the powerless, or an alien ideology internalised by the powerless to control themselves, but returns to its original emphasis on God's pneumatic empowering of the powerless to be agents of transformation in both the Church and the wider society.

Notes

1. Walter J. Hollenweger, *The Pentecostals* (London: SCM Press, 1972), 23-24; originally in his ten volume *Handbuch der Pfingstbewegung* (Geneva, 1965-67).
2. See Vinson Synan, *The Holiness-Pentecostal Movement in the United States* (Grand Rapids, Michigan: William B. Eerdmans, 1961), and Vinson Synan (Ed.), *Aspects of Pentecostal-Charismatic Origins* (Plainfield, NJ: Logos International, 1975).
3. Frank Bartleman, *Azusa Street* (Plainfield NJ: Logos International, 1980 [originally 1925]), especially 46; A.A. Boddy in *Confidence* (September, 1912); G.R. Polman, letter to G.A. Wumkes, 27th February 1915.
4. James R. Goff, *Fields White Unto Harvest: Charles F. Parham and The Missionary Origins of Pentecostalism* (Fayetteville: University of Arkansas Press, 1988), 11.
5. *Ibid.*
6. The Elim Pentecostal Church in Britain, following the teaching of George Jeffreys, maintains that any of the gifts of the Spirit are evidence of Spirit baptism. While most of the black Pentecostal organizations have articles of faith - largely inherited from their white co-religionists - which state their belief in glossolalia as the initial evidence, in practice it is largely ignored and displaced by an implicitly inclusive charismatology.
7. Goff, 15.
8. Barrett's estimate of 360 million Pentecostals may be a little too high for the narrower definitions of Pentecostalism because it includes traditions which pre-date both Parham (1901) and Seymour (1906). David B. Barrett, "The Twentieth Century Pentecostal/Charismatic Renewal in the Holy Spirit, with it's Goal of World Evangelization" in *International Bulletin of Missionary Research*, Vol. 12, No 3, (July 1988).
9. Douglas J. Nelson, "For Such Time As This: The Story of Bishop William J Seymour and the Azusa Street Revival" (unpublished Ph.D. dissertation, University of Birmingham, 1981).

10. Albert J. Raboteau, *Slave Religion: the Invisible Institution in the Antebellum South* (Oxford: Oxford University Press, 1978), 4-5.
11. Iain MacRobert, *The Black Roots and White Racism of Early Pentecostalism in the USA* (Basingstoke: Macmillan Press, 1988), 9-14.
12. *Ibid.*, 14-15.
13. *Ibid.*, 15-18.
14. *Ibid.*, 20-23, 33-36.
15. Raboteau, 149.
16. Melville J. Herskovits, *The Myth of the Negro Past* (Boston: Beacon Press, 1958), 227-31.
17. MacRobert, *Black Roots*, 31-34.
18 *Ibid.*, 38-42.
19. Nelson, 31,153-8.
20. *Ibid.*, 161.
21. Sarah E. Parham (Comp.), *The Life of Charles F Parham: Founder of the Apostolic Faith Movement* (Joplin, Missouri: Tri-State Printing Co, 1930), 51-52.
22. On Parham's theories of racial supremacy see: Charles Fox Parham, *A Voice Crying in the Wilderness* (Joplin, Missouri: Joplin Printing Co, 1944 [originally 1902]), 81-84, 92-100, 105-118; and Charles Fox Parham, *The Everlasting Gospel* (Baxter Springs, Kansas, 1942), 1-4.
23. Nelson, 35.
24. *Ibid.*, 187-90; MacRobert, *Black Roots*, 51-52.
25. Nelson, 191.
26. *Ibid.*, 191-92.
27. *Ibid.*, 192-94, 196; *The Apostolic Faith* Vol. 1, No 1 (September 1906), 1, col. 1; Bartleman, 47-48.
28. Nelson, 196.
29. *The Apostolic Faith*, *op. cit.*, 3, col. 2.
30. Quoted in Synan, *Aspects*, 133.
31. Quoted in Nelson, 234, n. 91.
32. Bartleman, p 54.
33. *Confidence* (September 1912).
34. Parham, *Everlasting Gospel*, 1-3.
35. Charles Fox Parham, *Apostolic Faith*, Baxter Springs, Kansas (December 1912).
36. Synan, *Holiness-Pentecostal*, 153.
37. Robert Mapes Anderson, "A Social History of the Early Twentieth Century Pentecostal Movement" (Ph.D. Thesis, Columbia University, 1969), 319-20; published in a revised form as *Vision of the Disinherited: The Making of American Pentecostalism* (New York: Oxford University Press, 1979).
38. Synan, *Holiness-Pentecostal*, 179-80.
39. Iain MacRobert, "Black Pentecostalism: Its Origins, Functions and Theology with special reference to a Midland Borough" (unpublished Ph.D. dissertation, University of Birmingham 1989), 39.
40. Even Bartleman, a white Pentecostal pioneer, constantly refers to the baptism with, in or of the Holy Spirit as 'possession'. Bartleman, 72 ff.; see also Seymour in *The Apostolic Faith* Vol. 1, No 4 (December 1906), 1, col. 4.
41. Synan, *Holiness-Pentecostal*, 114.
42. A.J. Tomlinson, *Answering the Call of God*, 9-10, quoted in Lillie Dugger, *A.J. Tomlinson* (Cleveland, Tennessee: White Wing Publishing House, 1964), 21; A.J. Tomlinson, quoted in C.T. Davidson, *Upon This Rock* (Cleveland, Tennessee: White Wing Publishing House and Press, 1973), 437-38, 448, 518, 552-53, 594; "Minutes of 45th Assembly (1950)", quoted in *Church of God of*

Prophecy Business Guide (Cleveland, Tennessee: White Wing Publishing House and Press, 1987), 45.

43. See, for example, Nico Horn "The Experience of the Spirit in Apartheid South Africa" in *Azusa Theological Journal*, Vol. 1, no 1, Durban, South Africa: Relevant Pentecostal Witness Publications (March 1990), 19-42.

8

William H. Durham and the Finished Work of Calvary

D. William Faupel

Introduction

During the first four years of the Pentecostal revival, 1906-1910, all persons coming into the Pentecostal Movement on the North American scene embraced a Five-fold or Full Gospel. This gospel included justification by faith, entire sanctification as a second definite work of grace, Spirit-baptism evidenced by speaking in tongues, divine healing as part of the atoning work of Christ, and the premillennial return of Christ. These five cardinal doctrines were seen as 'first principle' truths of the Apostolic Faith by which the Church had initially been established. These truths, early adherents proclaimed, had been lost during the dark ages. Since the time of the Reformation, however, God had been restoring them to the Church.

It never occurred to the early Pentecostal leaders that any of these tenets would be challenged from within the Movement's ranks. However, in 1910, a Pentecostal pastor from Chicago, William H. Durham, did just that. He declared that the second tenet, the doctrine of entire sanctification, was not of Apostolic origin. Rather, he asserted, this doctrine was unscriptural. The biblical understanding of sanctification, he argued, was part of Christ's 'Finished Work of Calvary.'

Within five years, Durham's message rent the Pentecostal Movement from top to bottom. By the time the controversy had subsided, sixty per cent of the Movement had adopted Durham's 'Finished Work' message. Only in the Southeastern United States did a significant number (seventy-five per cent) retain the original doctrine of entire sanctification. In the rest of North America a full eighty per cent had embraced Durham's teaching.[1]

Little is known about Durham. What has been written to date suggests that he was motivated by a desire to gain personal control of the Movement, or at best to impose a Keswick understanding of entire sanctification upon what had been an essentially Wesleyan tradition. The purpose of this article is to take a fresh look at the man, set forth his theological position, assess the motives that have been attributed to him and present an alternative reading of his actions.

Durham's Ministry

William Durham became a Christian in 1898 at the age of 25 in a Baptist church. Three years later he received the Wesleyan experience of entire sanctification. In 1903 he accepted the call to pastor the Gospel Mission Church, a holiness mission, in Chicago.[2]

Durham heard about the Azusa Street Revival in the spring of 1906. Like many holiness adherents at that time, he expected that the gifts of the Spirit would be restored to the church in the last days. In February 1907 he decided to go to Los Angeles to judge for himself whether that time had come. He arrived at Azusa in February, 1907. Like others who made their *hajji* to Los Angeles in the early days of the revival, he experienced the meetings as being completely controlled by the Holy Spirit. After seeking for five days the gift of languages began to flow. William Seymour, pastor at Azusa, seeing Durham 'slain in the spirit' raised his hands over him and prophesied that wherever this man would preach "the Holy Spirit would fall upon the people."[3]

It was not long before Seymour's prophecy began to be fulfilled. Durham returned to Chicago transformed. He began holding revival meetings at his mission every night. Soon people were coming in such numbers that the building could not hold them.[4] News of the revival spread quickly. Hundreds and then thousands came to Chicago to hear Durham preach and left with the conviction that he was a new pulpit prodigy. Chicago began to rival Los Angeles as the Movement's centre, and North Avenue Mission became the new 'Mecca' for the Pentecostal faithful.[5]

Durham's Message

In May 1910, Durham addressed the annual Pentecostal Convention at the Stone Church in Chicago which was attended by many of the Pentecostal leaders of the Mid-west. His sermon was entitled "The Finished Work of Calvary."[6] The message was quite simple: "Identification with Jesus Christ saves and sanctifies, no second work of grace [is] taught [by Scripture] or necessary."[7] According to him, perfection was something that must be maintained by accepting the historical reality of the cross. As long as this was done, inbred sin was crucified with Christ and imputed righteousness would bear fruit in the believer's life. If, however, sin appeared, it was a sign that the relationship with Christ had been severed and the carnal nature was raising its ugly head. Perfection could be restored to the individual by placing faith once again in the power of the cross.[8]

Durham set his view over against the prevailing second definite work theory. He concurred with the holiness theory to the extent that he acknowledged entire sanctification meant a crucifixion of the sinful nature. "We believed then, as now, that when God saves a man,... He cleanses him from all sin."[9] However, he denied that this was a separate experience apart from justification or that crucifixion meant the eradication of the sinful nature as the Holiness Movement understood it.[10]

Thus Durham collapsed the three-work theory: justification, sanctification, and spirit-baptism into two. These corresponded to Christ's objective work in history: His finished work at Calvary, and his sending the Holy Spirit on the Day of Pentecost.[11]

The content of Durham's message was a bombshell that one observer described as "A Shot Heard Round the World."[12] Leaders, from other parts of the country who had attended the meeting, invited him to take the message to their area. Everywhere he went he caused a fire storm. A few rejected his message but most who heard him ultimately embraced it.[13] In February, 1911, Durham resigned as pastor of the North Avenue mission to establish headquarters in Los Angeles.[14] After capturing the West coast to his point of view, he laid plans to return to Chicago in 1912 from which he expected to take his message to the Holiness stronghold, the Southeast.[15] However, in late June, his health failed. He returned to Los Angles where he died of pulmonary tuberculosis on July 7, 1912.[16]

Durham's Motives

Several reasons have been set forth in previous research seeking to discover both the undergirding motives that caused Durham to break the early Pentecostal unity and the compelling factors which enabled others to follow him.

Douglas Nelson has argued that "above all other concerns," Durham desired "to become the undisputed, dominant leader" of the Pentecostal Movement.[17] In short, Nelson contends that the 'Finished Work' doctrine was primarily a ruse by which Durham could divide and conquer until such time as he controlled the Movement.

Undoubtedly, there is much truth in this perspective. Durham's impact on his followers must have been incredible. Frank Bartleman observed that by 1912, "His word was coming to be almost law in the Pentecostal missions, even as far as the Atlantic Coast."[18] His close friend and co-worker, Frank Ewart, felt that he was "unconscious of the tremendous influence and power he wielded in the new religious world."[19] The impact Durham had upon the young Movement during the last two years of his life can also be seen in his writing. During that time 382,000 copies of his magazine *The Pentecostal Testimony* and 250,000 of his tracts were distributed across the continent and around the world.[20]

Durham's popularity, coupled with the strain of constant attack by his critics, also had negative effects. Bartleman parted company with him because he believed that Durham's message had degenerated into "carnal controversy."[21] Supporters of his teaching acknowledged that Durham 'ridiculed' those holding the second definite work position.[22] An outside observer noted that he must "rule or ruin."[23] Even friends observed: "Too much power is unsafe for any one man."[24] However, Durham's bid for undisputed leadership does not fully account for his motives. Long after his death, Pentecostals continued to convert to his point of view.

Robert Anderson has correctly observed that when the 'Finished Work' controversy finally subsided, those holding the position were predominantly whites from the North or West and were from Reformed and Baptist religious backgrounds. This imbalance, he suggests, indicates that those who adopted Durham's view were seeking to accommodate Pentecostalism to the racial, regional, and religious biases that adherents brought with them.[25] Once again, there is much truth in this perspective.

Nelson has demonstrated that William Seymour understood racial integration as a theological issue. He believed that the miracle of Pentecost was not speaking in tongues *per se* but, rather, that at Pentecost God brought a divided world back together and gave it a language by which people could understand one another once more. The Cross itself, he contended, was designed by God to draw all mankind together at their point of commonalty - their sinfulness. Pentecost was a gift of enablement that came upon the newborn children of God. However, Seymour insisted, if the Pentecostal Movement failed to heal "the deepest breaches of humanity" (racism), it would deny the gospel itself.[26]

In the first burst of enthusiasm that came at the outset of the revival, it appeared that Seymour's vision might be realized. An eyewitness reported:

> Different nationalities are now hearing the gospel in their own 'tongue wherein they were born'... The rich and educated were the same as the poor and ignorant and found a much harder death to die. We only recognized God. All were equal... No instrument that God can use is rejected on account of color or dress or lack of education.[27]

In a context where there was such a sense of solidarity, it was easy to believe that Bartleman might be right when he declared, "the 'color line' was washed away with the blood."[28] But as the revival abated, so did the sense of solidarity. Few white adherents understood, or at least acknowledged, integration as a theological issue.

When the time came to organize, the same attitude prevailed. The initial council of the Assemblies of God, for example, was clearly an attempt to unify the Movement on a national, if not international, basis. Despite Durham's efforts to make the 'Finished Work' doctrine a test of fellowship, most of his followers did not share that view. Every effort was made to include the second work people.

Both A.J. Tomlinson and J.H. King, leaders of regional second work groups, were issued personal invitations to join in the deliberations. When the Statement of Fundamental Truths was written two years later, the doctrine on 'entire sanctification' was worded in such a way that both 'Finished Work' and 'Second Work' adherents could embrace it.[29] Yet, all the evidence suggests that this inclusive national church was intended to be for whites only. No personal invitations were sent to blacks. Those who came were politely ignored.[30]

Anderson is also correct in suggesting that regionalism played a factor in determining those who accepted Durham's doctrine. The Civil War was still fresh in the memories of many adherents. Younger Southerners were still smarting from the policies and attitudes that came with Reconstruction. Synan, for example, acknowledges that "most southern white pentecostal churches expressed the Dixie viewpoint through the early part of the century."[31]

However, too much should not be made of the data Anderson cites. One can only speculate how different the landscape might have been had Durham lived long enough to focus his appeal on the South. He had experienced intense opposition in other parts of the country, yet prevailed in winning the majority of Pentecostal adherents. There appears to have been no concerted effort by Durham's followers to win the Southern churches to his position. Rather, they sought conciliation. The attacks that finally came from the Southern churches two to five years after Durham's death are essentially caricatures and show a fundamental misunderstanding of his message. Likewise, given Durham's appeal to Blacks and ethnics in Chicago, the racial equation between 'Finished Work' and 'Second Work' adherents might have been quite different had Durham lived to invade the South.

Anderson's analysis of the religious background of adherents to show who was predisposed to accept the 'Finished Work' message has enjoyed strong support among Pentecostal historians. At first glance, it does appear that those from Reformed and Baptist backgrounds tended to accept the 'Finished Work' doctrine, while those that came from a Wesleyan background did not. Upon closer examination, however, this analysis breaks down. Several who retained entire sanctification as a second definite work had been highly influenced by the Keswick tradition. Charles Parham, for example, in his spiritual pilgrimage rejected most of his Wesleyan heritage and was strongly influenced by Alexander Dowie, A.B. Simpson, D.L. Moody, R.A. Torrey, and Frank Sandford who all fell into the Reformed camp.[32] A.J. Tomlinson was a Quaker when he came upon the Church of God that had primarily Baptist roots.[33] Charles Mason and most of his early converts in the Church of God in Christ came from a Baptist background.[34] N.L. Holmes, who became a major leader in the Pentecostal Holiness Church, led a group of Presbyterian churches into that denomination in 1915.[35] Likewise, The Free-

Will Baptists who accepted the Pentecostal Message remained in the 'Second Work' camp.[36]

On the other hand, men like Howard Goss, M.M. Pinson, F.F. Bosworth, Robert Brown, and H.G. Rogers, and women like Elizabeth Sexton, Aimee Semple McPherson, Elizabeth Sisson and Hattie Barth had their roots in the Wesleyan tradition, but adopted the 'Finished Work' position.

J. Roswell Flower from a Christian and Missionary Alliance background became the General Secretary of the Assemblies of God. Despite being in a denomination that officially held the 'Finished Work' position, however, he retained belief in the 'Second Work' theory until the day he died.[37] It is, therefore, this investigator's conclusion that prior religious tradition, though important, clearly was not a determining factor. A complex set of conditions in each case, determined the direction an individual or a group would take. The ego factor was certainly present. Racial prejudice and regional bias were clearly in evidence. Religious predisposition is apparent. In the final analysis, however, no examination of the 'Finished Work' doctrine is adequate without coming to terms with the theological significance of Durham's message.

Durham's Significance

Walter Hollenweger has described William Durham as "the one original theologian of the Pentecostal Movement."[38] This perception is correct. Yet little exploration has been made. To date, Allen Clayton's highly provocative essay entitled "The Significance of William H. Durham for Pentecostal Historiography," is the only serious attempt to demonstrate this claim.[39]

Clayton seeks to refute the commonly held view that Durham was proclaiming a Keswickian or Reformed view of sanctification. First, he attempts to show that the 'Finished Work' doctrine is primarily Lutheran. As such, he suggests, it can hardly be classified as a view of sanctification at all. Indeed he points to several examples where the 'Finished Work' functioned as a slogan devoid of specific content in the subsequent history of the moment.

Secondly, he contends that conflicting views of sanctification was not the issue which caused the Pentecostal Movement to split. Rather, he suggests, a more fundamental underlying substructure divided the movement. Pneumatology functioned as the unifying centre for the 'Second Work' Pentecostals, he believes, while an emerging Christology came to the fore as the substructure for the 'Finished Work' adherents. By articulating the 'Finished Work' theology, Clayton maintains, Durham gave visibility to this Christological theme.

In terms of these specific assertions, Clayton is wrong. However, his instincts are fundamentally correct. First of all, in contrast to Clayton's contention, Durham was deeply concerned about the matter of sanctification. For example, Frank Bartleman acknowledged that some abused the doctrine by "declaring that because the work of redemption was fully accomplished on the cross it was of necessity finished in us also, the moment we believed," thereby denying "the principle of holiness itself." But, Bartleman implored, this was a fundamental misunderstanding of Durham's message.[40]

Clayton is also wrong in thinking that Durham's doctrine had Lutheran roots. There is absolutely no evidence that Durham had any exposure to the Lutheran tradition. Furthermore, his doctrine of "the gradual abandonment to the will of God" is remarkably similar to the Keswick position that was being articulated within the Reformed tradition. Finally, Clayton is wrong when he suggests that the fundamental division which caused the split was the underlying substructure. Donald Dayton has clearly demonstrated that this fundamental tension came into the holiness movement in the mid-nineteenth century when sanctification shifted from christological to pneumatological categories. Dayton's development of the 'Five-fold Gospel' theme has shown that all Pentecostals had a strong christological impulse at the centre of their theology. It was not the exclusive domain of the 'Finished Work' camp.[41]

Despite these short-comings, Clayton's analysis is suggestive to the person seeking to understand the significance of Durham's theology. First of all, Clayton can be forgiven for failing to recognize a Keswick understanding underlying Durham's articulation. Durham stated his theology within Pentecostal rather than Keswickian categories. Furthermore, his opponents charged him with 'Zinzendorfianism,' a form of Lutheran theology.

Secondly, though there was not a fundamental split in the substructure as Clayton suggests, he is none-the-less correct in pointing to the christological underpinnings inherent in Pentecostalism for the person attempting to understand Durham's theology.

Shortly after Durham proclaimed his 'Finished Work' theology at the Stone Church in Chicago in 1910, he wrote a lengthy account of his experience of Spirit-baptism. For several days he remained in a state of waiting, feeling empty of self, trusting God to "finish the work" in him. "Finally", he reports, on March 2, 1907:

> He, for Whom my soul had longed, did not leave me this time, but remained, and for a long time I could not help speaking in tongues. O, how glorious it seemed to have the blessed Holy Ghost abiding within me, so that I was as conscious of His presence as I was of my own life, and O, how real the precious Blood of Christ and all that pertains to His work of redemption on the Cross of Calvary was made to me.[42]

Durham's experience was not unique. In 1908, A.A. Boddy printed the testimony of similar accounts of Spirit-baptism.[43] The content of such experiences must be understood in the context of the Pentecostal world-view which preconditioned early adherents to focus on the work of Christ. Unlike others, however, Spirit-baptism had a jarring effect upon Durham. He reports:

> From that day to this, I could never preach another sermon on the second work of grace theory. I had held it for years, and continued to do so for some time, but could not preach on the subject again. I could preach Christ and... holiness, as never before, but not as a second work of grace.[44]

Something had happened. Instinctively, Durham sensed that the Acts account as well as his own experience at Azusa had not fully jibed at the theology he had previously proclaimed. The Acts account suggested that there were, at most, two major points of crisis experience in a person's life, conversion and spirit baptism, whereas he had been proclaiming three.

Durham's shift of position, however, did not come about simply as a result of an effort to square his doctrinal position with Scripture. Nor did it come simply because he had another significant religious experience at Azusa. Rather, Durham's theological transformation came directly as a result of the kind of experience he had at Azusa. Spirit-baptism brought him to a point of crisis which he had not anticipated. His internalized theological system had brought him to the point where Christ became alive for Him in a totally new way. As he noted in his testimony, "The works that I had formerly rejoiced in, and the experiences that I had gloried in could not help me now." His previous religious experiences, and his previous theological understanding of those experiences, had to be recast in light of his new insight. Unexpectedly, this experience had transcended the very theological categories which had brought him to it. He had to find new language to express what he now believed. It was a traumatic situation.

> It was so contrary to all that I had taught and had been taught, that I dared not admit, even to myself, that I could find nothing in the Word of God to establish the doctrine that sanctification was a definite second work of grace... This led me to pray and search the Word of God as never before, and the more I searched, the plainer it was to me that many Pentecostal preachers, myself included, were preaching a doctrine that God's Word did not teach.[45]

In the light of his new vision of the Cross, he came to see his past life, experiences, and theological understanding as a form of works-righteousness.[46] His friend, A.S. Copley, who was present for the famous Stone Church address in May, 1910, elaborated on this theme the following month in an article entitled "Sanctification - 'Jewish' and 'Christian'."

> There are two methods of sanctification taught. They may be distinguished as 'Jewish' and Christian. The first is taught by the holiness people generally. Of course they both aim at the same results, viz., deliverance from sin and victory in life. But the process for reaching these ends differ widely... 'Jewish' sanctification is... partly by works, i.e., being once freed from sin, the soul must itself, by God's help, live a holy life. Its aim now is human perfection, or a restoration to the innocent Adamic state.[47]

Thus, by his own testimony it is clear that Durham had not rejected the 'Second Work' doctrine because of his prior Baptist roots. Nor had he initially embraced the doctrine with an uneasy conscience when he came into the Pentecostal Movement to maintain unity as many Pentecostal historians have suggested. The 'Second Work' theory had been an intricate part of his experience and theological understanding until the point of his Spirit-baptism.

Durham's articulation struck a deep chord in other Pentecostal adherents, for it squared with their own experience as well. Some, like Frank Ewart, could accept it readily because of his prior religious background.[48] Generally, however, the reaction was similar to Durham's experience. They were stunned. They felt initial resistance, but the message struck deep. After searching the Scriptures through the lens that Durham offered, they often embraced his teaching.

A few, of course, did reject his message for some combination of the factors noted above. Durham died before he was able to direct his attention to the South. His successors attempted to heal the breach by being conciliatory in the interest of preserving unity. Thus, the Movement as a whole did not embrace his teaching.

In retrospect it is clear that Durham's theological significance went far deeper than a mere rejection of the second definite work doctrine of entire sanctification. Rather, his message provided the foundation for a truly distinctive 'Pentecostal theology.' Rooting his experience in conformity with the Acts of the Apostles, he took a stance that made this book the paradigm for Pentecostal faith and practice. This in turn sparked off further theological development such as the 'Jesus Name' issue.[49] At the same time, Durham's rejection of a Wesleyan theme enabled a far broader cross section of evangelicalism to be attracted to Pentecostalism and eventually allowed the Movement to be fully accepted as a legitimate part of the Evangelical tradition.[50]

Notes

1. Robert Mapes Anderson, *Vision of the Disinherited: The Making of American Pentecostalism* (New York, NY: Oxford University Press, 1979), 169.
2. *Pentecostal Testimony* 2 (July, 1912), 2-3; and W.H. Durham, ''A Chicago Evangelist's Pentecost'', *The Apostolic Faith* 1 (February-March, 1907), 4.

3. *Pentecostal Testimony*, 1 (July, 1912), 3-4.
4. Carl Brumback, *Suddenly... From Heaven: A History of the Assemblies of God* (Springfield, MO: Gospel Publishing House, 1961), 69.
5. Frank Ewart, *Phenomenon of Pentecost* (Houston, TX: Herald Publishing House, 1947), 73; and J. Roswell Flower, "History of the Assemblies of God", (Unpublished manuscript, Springfield, MO, 1949), 17.
6. Allen Clayton, "The Significance of William H. Durham for Pentecostal Historiography", *Pneuma: The Journal of the Society for Pentecostal Studies* 1 (Fall, 1979), 2;
7. William H. Durham, "The Finished Work of Calvary", *Pentecostal Testimony* 2 (January, 1912), 1.
8. *Ibid.*
9. William H. Durham, "Some Other Phases of Sanctification", *Pentecostal Testimony* 2 (July, 1912), 10.
10. Durham, "The Finished Work of Calvary", 3.
11. William H. Durham, "The Gospel of Christ", *Pentecostal Testimony* 2 (January, 1912), 8.
12. A.J. Tomlinson, "History of Pentecost", *The Faithful Standard* 1 (November, 1922), 8.
13. For a complete assessment of the Pentecostal response to Durham's message see my "Response to Durham's Message" in "The Everlasting Gospel: The Significance of Eschatology in the Development of Pentecostal Thought" (Ph.D. dissertation, University of Birmingham, 1989), 285-311.
14. *Ibid.*
15. William H. Durham, "The Great Chicago Revival", The *Pentecostal Testimony* 2 (July, 1912), pp. 14-5.
16. "In Memoriam", *Pentecostal Testimony* 2 (July, 1912), 2; and William H. Durham, California State Board of Health, Bureau of Vital Statistics, *Standard Certificate of Death* (Los Angeles, CA: Local Registration Number 3145, July 7, 1912).
17. Douglas Nelson, "For Such a Time as This: The Story of William J. Seymour and the Azusa Street Revival" (Ph.D. Dissertation, University of Birmingham, 1981), 251.
18. Frank Bartleman, *How Pentecost Came to Los Angeles* (Los Angeles, CA: The Author, 1925), 150.
19. Frank Ewart, *The Phenomenon of Pentecost*, 75.
20. *Pentecostal Testimony* 2 (January, 1912), 15; and *Pentecostal Testimony* 2 (July, 1912), 16.
21. Bartleman, *How Pentecost Came to Los Angeles*, 150.
22. Richard Crayne, *Pentecostal Handbook* (Morristown, TN: The Author, 1986), citing J. Roswell Flower, letter to Richard Crayne, 202.
23. Charles Shumway, "A Study of 'The Gift of Tongues'" (B.A. thesis, University of Southern California, 1914), 179.
24. Bartleman, *How Pentecost Came to Los Angeles*, 150.
25. Anderson, *Vision of the Disinherited*, 169-73.
26. Nelson, "For Such a Time as This", 201-05.
27. "Bible Pentecost", *The Apostolic Faith*, (Los Angeles) 1 (November, 1906), 1.
28. Bartleman, *How Pentecost Came to Los Angeles*, 54.
29. *Ibid.*, 170; *Word and Witness* (December 20, 1913), 1; and Carl Brumback, *Suddenly*, 356-60.
30. Vinson Synan, *The Holiness-Pentecostal Movement in the United States* (Grand Rapids, MI: Eerdmans, 1971), 170.
31. *Ibid.*, 181.
32. James Goff, *Fields White Unto Harvest: Charles F. Parham and the Missionary Origins of Pentecostalism* (Fayetteville, AR: University of Arkansas Press, 1988), 49-61.
33. Charles Conn, *Like a Mighty Army Moves the Church of God* (Cleveland, TN: Church of God Pu-

blishing House, 1955), 15-16, 50.

34. C.F. Range, "The Story of Our Church, the 'Church of God in Christ",' *Official Manual with the Doctrines and Discipline of the Church of God in Christ* (Memphis, TN: Church of God in Christ Publishing House, 1973), xxiii-xxvi.
35. Vinson Synan, *The Old Time Power* (Franklin Springs, GA: Advocate Press, 1973), 135-37.
36. Vinson Synan, *The Holiness-Pentecostal Movement*, 130-31; and *Discipline of the Pentecostal Free-Will Baptist Church, Inc.* (Dunn, NC: The Pentecostal Free-Will Baptist Church, n.d.), 5.
37. William Menzies, Interview with D. William Faupel, July 10, 1976.
38. Walter Hollenweger, *The Pentecostals: The Charismatic Movements in the Churches* (Minneapolis, MN: Augsburg Publishing House, 1972), 25.
39. Allen Clayton, "The Significance of William H. Durham for Pentecostal Historiography", *Pneuma*, 27-42.
40. Bartleman, *How Pentecost Came to Los Angeles*, 146.
41. Donald W. Dayton, *The Theological Roots of Pentecostalism* (Grand Rapids, MI: Francis Asbury Press, 1987), 19-23.
42. *Ibid.*
43. *Confidence* 1 (November 15, 1908), 6.
44. William H. Durham, "An Open Letter to My Brother Ministers", *Pentecostal Testimony* 2 (July, 1912), 14.
45. Durham, "An Open Letter", 14.
46. William H. Durham, "Some Other Phases of Sanctification", *Pentecostal Testimony* 2 (July, 1912), 10.
47. A.S. Copley, "Sanctification - 'Jewish' and 'Christian'", A Call to Faith (June, 1910), reprinted in *Confidence* 3 (July, 1910), 168-69.
48. Frank Ewart, *The Phenomenon of Pentecost*, 74-75.
49. Clayton, *Significance of William H Durham*, 34-42.
50. Anderson, *Vision of the Disinherited*, 173.

9

The Social Concern of Early American Pentecostalism

Cecil M. Robeck, Jr.

Interest and Participation in Matters of Social Concern

> The most beautiful thing about the Pentecostals was their ability to pour themselves into the power of the Holy Spirit. They could blend like nobody's business into the words of the Holy Scriptures and do their best to uphold their conception of Christianity. It was a miracle how they could shut out the hot and cold running cockroaches and king-size rats and all the added horrors of decaying rotten tenement houses and garbage-littered streets, with drugs running through the veins of our ghetto kids. It was a miracle that they could endure the indignities poured upon our Barrios. I knew that every one of them didn't get weaker. They got stronger. Their prayers didn't get shorter. They got longer. Those who looked for God to come closer were blessed with *El Bautismo del Espirito Santo*, and they spoke a language that I could not understand. Tia had said it was the tongue of the angels, and only a few could interpret it.[1]

Pentecostals are frequently criticized for a lack of interest and participation in matters of social concern and justice.[2] On the surface, this criticism possesses some merit. Pentecostals seem to be especially concerned with matters of the soul rather than matters related to the body.[3] But as Miroslav Volf has recently pointed out, appearances may be deceiving; for, in fact, Pentecostals have traditionally taken a positive position toward the 'materiality of salvation'.[4] The body has been important even if the soul has been given priority.

To be sure, Pentecostals have frequently chosen not to participate in matters of social justice as they are often defined today. They have placed considerable energy into the so-called 'compassionate ministries',[5] but, on the whole, few Pentecostals in the U.S. have become involved in the struggles which seek to identify and overcome evil in social structures and institutions. This is a generalization, to be sure, for many African-American Pentecostals have participated actively in the Civil Rights movement for decades.[6] But Civil Rights aside, this generalization can be made.

There is at least one very significant factor that may cast light on why this is the case. That factor is related to social location. While this factor does not provide adequate justification for the continued rejection of involvement in matters of social justice, it has clearly been a major factor in the past.

In the early days of the Twentieth Century when Pentecostals were beginning to develop an identity of their own, they were commonly representative of the lower class and the dispossessed.[7] They often found themselves to be effectively blocked from places of power cultural, educational, political, ecclesiastical, and financial. They were often oppressed people, former slaves or the children of former slaves, poor whites, or linguistically limited Hispanic Americans.

Early Pentecostals were ridiculed or harassed, in public; the brunt of private jokes.[8] The oppression they experienced on numerous fronts helped to direct them toward the needs of others who were marginalized like themselves the poor: the alcoholic, the prostitute, and the drug addict. They turned their attention to evangelistic preaching and compassion for the poor and disenfranchised, often ignoring the structures and institutions which they felt powerless to transform. They functioned like extended families or therapeutic encounter groups in their brush arbors and store fronts. They emphasized personal salvation, transformed lifestyles, developing relationships and hope for the future.[9]

Frank Bartleman's Criticism of War and Capitalism

> *Wow,* I thought to myself. *If ever there were an escape this has got to be it. Is God gonna make it up to us in heaven?*
> *Caramba, I smiled, maybe it ain't an escape, maybe like a sombre Pentecostal guy had once told me. Maybe, like he had said, they aren't interested in material wealth. God's Kingdom will provide enough for all in the sweet bye and bye. God's work and God's will be done. But ... 'How about starting here on earth, brother, with the nitty-gritty reality?' I had asked this Pentecostal guy. He had looked at me funny and had said, 'God's Kingdom is not of this earth'. 'But we are,' I had insisted. He just shook his head and walked away.*[10]

At the popular level, the idea that God's Kingdom was not part of the present world reality was widespread. Frank Bartleman, an early participant-observer of the Pentecostal Movement, was one of those who drew a clear distinction between the Kingdom of God and the kingdoms of this world. Jesus had noted that his kingdom was not of this world (John 18:36), Bartleman observed, and "as He [was], so are we in the world".[11] He argued as late as 1934 that "Our government is in heaven, not of this world.[12]

Unlike Frank Sandford, John Alexander Dowie, to some extent Dr. Finis Yoakum, and even Charles Fox Parham, Bartleman held no utopian dream of a church-run or church-based society.[13] Bartleman was too pessimistic for that. He constantly appealed to history, concluding that whenever the Church became enmeshed in the concerns of the State, the life and message of the Church were compromised.[14] For this reason he believed firmly in two facets of a doctrine of the separation of Church and State. First, the State has no right meddling in the affairs of the Church. The Church must be free from State domination. Second, the Church has no right to participate in the affairs of State.[15] Bartleman did believe, however, that Christians had not only a right, but an obligation to criticize the affairs of State on moral and ethical grounds. Indeed, his own continuous criticism, even harassment of public policies throughout the world suggest that he may be the most outspoken social critic the Pentecostal Movement has produced to date.

Most of Bartleman's social commentary is limited to the articles he authored. Few of these nearly 600 articles are extant today, but a survey of what does exist indicates that the outbreak of hostilities in Europe in 1914 changed him. By 1915, his writings were full of social analysis and criticism. One of his earliest such articles was published in March, 1915 under the title "The Situation in Europe."[16] Bartleman argued that the war was merely an act of God's judgment. He warned his readers to be objective and maintain neutrality lest they find themselves in rebellion against God's sovereign purpose. God had dealt patiently with the nations for years. Now, observed Bartleman, "The Lord has simply changed the tone of His voice. He is now speaking from the cannon's mouth". The targets of God's judgment were clear. "Russian despotism, German militarism and English imperialism together spell 'devilism'," he charged.[17]

Throughout the war, Bartleman kept readers of *The Bridegroom's Messenger* (Atlanta, GA), the Assemblies of God's *Weekly Evangel* (Springfield, MO), and *Word and Work* (Framingham, MA) regularly appraised of the moral and ethical issues which he judged as lying behind the war. Foremost among them were illegitimate quests for power, greed, and the ever present danger of hypocrisy.

Bartleman was particularly piqued by the lack of discernment among Pentecostals regarding the real reasons which lay behind the war. An ardent pacifist himself, he tolerated participation in the war by German Pentecostals on the grounds that because they had no exception clause in their conscription law, the churches in Germany did not have the same light on the subject as the British and Americans, and they believed they had to engage in the war effort to evangelize among their own troops. Still, Bartleman hoped they would choose not to serve and die as martyrs [traitors] for the sake of their faith.[18]

Bartleman was far less tolerant toward American Pentecostals. He resented their calls to enter the war following the sinking of the Lusitania. "We send shiploads of ammunition to Europe, and cover the cargo with American citizens, and then want to go to war if they got blowed up," he complained.[19] To respond in this fashion was, at best, hypocritical, but Bartleman dug more deeply than that. The reason that ammunition was sent to Europe was not the justness of the cause so much as it was capitalistic profit. "A handful of rulers, capitalists, and ammunition makers are exploiting the whole human race for gain," he contended.[20]

Concern with greed and profit as underlying motivations for American involvement in the war led Bartleman to criticize what went under the guise of patriotism. "The fact is," he declared, "American patriotism, except for the 'almighty dollar', is just about as cracked on the whole as our revered liberty bell. We sell to the highest bidder, even if he be an enemy. This sin is going to undo us."[21] So taken was he by this fact that he even suggested that Americans should "pluck out the stars from our flag and instate dollar marks in their place."[22]

As a result of his concern that the war was kept alive by American investors, Bartleman criticized capitalism and American economic policy more broadly. The war was, after all, a "commercial struggle... for final supremacy..."[23] By 1930 Bartleman was more adamant than ever about what he perceived to be the evils of capitalism. "The Capitalistic system is all unscriptural" he charged.[24]

Capitalistic practices were a favorite target of Bartleman's analysis. He believed in the idea that all things should be held in common in much the same way they had been in Acts 2 and 4. Capitalists were responsible for producing inequitable salary structures[25], artificially inflated markets affecting food prices[26], immoral policies which destroyed surplus food, and inequitable land distribution policies which, in the case of the United States, had been stolen from its rightful stewards in the first place, the Indians.[27] Ultimately this led Bartleman to conclude that while Soviet communism was wrong to be wedded to atheism, the spirit of communism was right, for it was consistent with New Testament practice.[28]

It may be that Bartleman's frustration with his own social location contributed to such ideas, for he clearly supported the poor over against the rich. "The Soviets have given the land to the people in Russia, for the common good" he wrote. "They have equalized rights and possessions. The system of selfish land ownership is broken. What a blessing if we all could have some land to till here in America. But, 'none but the wealthy'."[29] One cannot help but detect a tinge of wishfulness in this lionized description of Soviet reality.

Such class distinctions, he argued, were not limited to the United States, but were prevalent in England as well. "God is done with [the] class system in England," he maintained. People were starving to death while the wealthy kept vast hunting preserves which, if planted with potatoes, could feed the starving poor.[30]

Much more could be said of Bartleman's social criticism, but one item of injustice he seems to have left unaddressed was the issue of racism within the American context.

William J. Seymour's Criticism of Racism

The issue of racism was uniquely addressed by William J. Seymour, the soft-spoken African-American pastor of the Apostolic Faith Mission on Azusa Street.

Seymour was not nearly as vocal on social issues as Bartleman was. Bartleman was widely read, widely travelled, and made ready use of the press. Seymour was a pastor who instructed those who attended his church, but who, more than anything, modeled with his life the lessons he hoped to convey to those who heard him.

Elder Seymour arrived in Los Angeles, California on February 22, 1906. He came at the invitation of a group of what he called 'the colored people of the city...'[31] who had asked him to serve as their pastor. Almost from the start, he was locked out of the church to which he had been called. Undaunted, he met for several weeks in a home Bible study on Bonnie Brae Street. While the group to whom he ministered were largely Black, several Caucasians moved with ease and regularity in and out of the group.[32]

When in April 1906 people who attended this Bible study group began to speak in tongues, word spread rapidly and a mission was organized. The Azusa Street Mission quickly became known in the local press as 'the old negro church'.[33] Even the mission's leadership admitted to this description.[34] As the days went by, however, an increasing number of other nationalities joined the African-Americans at Azusa Street leading Bartleman to note that at Azusa, "the 'color line' was washed away in the blood."[35]

The Azusa Street Mission was established during a period of intense racial prejudice throughout the United States.[36] Because Los Angeles lay outside the South, Jim Crow laws, which enforced strict segregation elsewhere, were not in force there. To say this does not mean that racial prejudice did not exist in Los Angeles. It did. There were areas of the city in which African-Americans were not welcome.[37] Some restaurant owners attempted to discriminate on the basis of color, only to be rebuffed by city leaders.[38] There were churches which were organized along racial lines[39], but there were also churches which had held racially integrated services for years. Among them were churches associated with the Holiness Church of Southern California and Arizona.[40]

Seymour invited participation of both whites and blacks in the Azusa Street Mission from the outset. Not only were whites present from the earliest services, but in 1907 when the mission was incorporated, whites were listed among the trustees, as church secretary, business manager, and later, as camp-meeting organizer.[41] What caught the attention of the press, however, was Seymour's unorthodox willingness for blacks and whites to mingle so freely at the altar, including a good deal of physical contact. Many newspaper reports made mention of this phenomenon. Indeed, it appears to have been the fact found to be most offensive by outsiders.[42]

The freedom with which the races mingled under Seymour's leadership was apparently difficult even for some of those who were open to other aspects of his message. George B. Cashwell, an evangelist from North Carolina, noted that when he arrived at the mission "a new crucifixion began in my life and I had to die to many things..."[43] Carl Brumback and Vinson Synan both note that this 'crucifixion' had to do with Cashwell's willingness to be prayed over and touched by a black brother.[44] Still, the mission celebrated the fact that "No instrument that God can use is rejected on account of color or dress or lack of education."[45]

In spite of Seymour's commitment to the total integration of the races in all facets of life at the mission, there were those who disagreed with his policies. Charles Parham's attacks upon Seymour were relentless. He labelled Azusa Street "a cross between the Negro and Holy Roller form of worship," and made repeated racial sneers on the Mission.[46] Bartleman hints at more widespread racial dissatisfaction which was manifest when "most of the white saints" left Azusa Street when Elmer K. Fisher established the Upper Room Mission nearby.[47]

In 1915, Seymour reflected on the situation at some length. He expressed his sorrow at the divisions and problems which had sprung up along racial lines. He continued to maintain and affirm a deep love for white Pentecostals, articulating his teaching that Christ is all and for all. "He is neither black nor white man, nor Chinaman, nor Hindoo, nor Japanese, but God," Seymour argued.[48] Nevertheless, he declared the interracial character of the Azusa Street experiment to be at an end for the sake of peace among the churches.[49] It may be that the fully integrated character of the Azusa Street Mission in an otherwise segregationist society was a prophetic distinctive of the movement which was lost due to overriding jealousy and bigotry on the part of many.

Other Early Prophetic Figures: Ambrose J. Tomlinson, Finis E. Yoakum, a.o.

> Deeply entrenched moral biases, value preferences, and social prejudices, sometimes expressed systemically in structured forms of sexism, classicism, or racism, are ushered into eschatological judgment in the Spirit's charismatic restructuring of the church. All the dividing walls of the old social order are forever undermined in the *koinonia* that the Spirit creates. In replicating the kingdom ministry of Jesus through the *charismata*, the Holy Spirit creates *koinonia* that witnesses to the inclusive scope and the egalitarian nature of God's reign.[50]

Bartleman and Seymour are but two early Pentecostal pioneers who were moved by specific issues of social justice: war, economic oppression, and racism to name but three. Robert Mapes Anderson has astutely observed that "Pentecostalism was a movement born of radical social discontent, which, however, expanded its revolutionary impulses in veiled, ineffectual, displaced attacks that amounted to withdrawal from the social struggle and passive acquiesence to a world they hated and wished to escape".[51] It is clear that Bartleman and Seymour represented some of early Pentecostalism's social discontent. Each in his own way, Bartleman through well crafted words, and Seymour through the model of his life, hoped to effect some level of social change. They were not alone.

Considerable work needs to be undertaken by historians and theologians of the Movement to recover and restore to contemporary Pentecostalism some of its early prophetic edge. Ambrose J. Tomlinson, for instance, was greatly concerned with Appalachian poverty, with the lack of food and clothing for children and the unavailability of basic educational opportunities for young and old alike. For several years he raised money, bought land, taught school, and fed scores of poverty stricken children in the rural mountains of North Carolina, Georgia, and Tennessee.[52]

Finis E. Yoakum, M.D., established a medical practice in Southern California after a dramatic healing in his own life in 1895. As time passed he invested his entire personal savings and donations which he solicited to meet the needs of the chronically ill (especially those with tuberculosis and cancer), the poor and destitute, the alcoholic, prostitute, and other social outcasts. Often controversial, his Pisgah Home Movement grew to encompass a ministry in 1911 which provided 9,000 clean beds and fed 18,000 meals each month to the needy. He established a 'free' Pisgah store as a distribution center for donated clothing, canned goods, and fresh fruits and vegetables, Pisgah Ark, a halfway house for women with addictive behavior, Pisgah Gardens which fed the needy and acted as a rehabilitation center for the chronically ill, a small orphanage, and Pisgah Grande, a 3225 acre utopian-like community.[53] Some of the work continues to the present.

The names of others such as Aimee Semple McPherson, George and Carrie (Judd) Montgomery, and Lillian Trasher could be added to the list of early Pentecostals with ministries of social justice. Unfortunately, as these prophetic figures passed from the scene, their social ministries often went with them, or were continued on a much smaller scale.

The social location of Pentecostals in the United States has increased dramatically, especially since World War II. The relationship of the Kingdom of God to the present reality has become less partitioned in the thinking of many. It is time, once again, to question the construct of the contemporary social order in light of newer Pentecostal understandings of the Kingdom of God. The social concern expressed by several early American Pentecostals may yet help to inform and direct future Pentecostal thinking in constructive and powerful ways.

Notes

1. Piri Thomas, *Savior, Savior, Hold My Hand* (Garden City, NY: Doubleday & Company, Inc., 1972), 19-20.

2. J. Deotis Roberts, *Black Theology in Dialogue* (Philadelphia, PA: The Westminster Press, 1987), 59, says "It is notoriously short on social conscience and social justice. Corporate sins are seldom recognized, and there is little concern for social transformation". Similarly Richard J. Mouw, *The God Who Commands* (Notre Dame, IN: University of Notre Dame Press, 1990), 189, notes that "Unfortunately little has been done within either the older Pentecostal or newer charismatic movements by way of exploring the implications of a strong emphasis on the Holy Spirit for ethical theory...".
3. This idea is clearly expressed in "Sidetracked", *Mountain Movers* 31/3 (March, 1989), 3; Norm Correll, "Out to Change the World?", *Mountain Movers* 31/4 (April, 1989), 10-11; and "Dead Faith", *Mountain Movers* 31/6 (June, 1989), 3. For a more balanced approach see J. Philip Hogan, "Because Jesus Did", *Mountain Movers* 31/6 (June, 1989), 10-11.
4. Miroslav Volf, "Materiality of Salvation: An Investigation in the Soteriologies of Liberation and Pentecostal Theologies", *Journal of Ecumenical Studies* 26/3 (Summer, 1989), 447-467.
5. One celebrated example which extends from the earliest days of the movement is the work of Lillian Trasher among Egypt's orphans. See Beth Prim Howell, *Lady On a Donkey* (New York: E.P. Dutton & Company, Inc., 1960), and *Letters from Lillian* (Springfield, Mo.: Assemblies of God Division of Foreign Missions, 1983).
6. One example is that of Bishop Ithiel Clemmons of the Church of God in Christ who played a significant role in helping map the strategy of Dr. Martin Luther King, Jr. in New York during the early 1960s. See C. M. Robeck, Jr. "Ithiel Conrad Clemmons", in Stanley M. Burgess and Gary B. McGee, eds., *Dictionary of Pentecostal and Charismatic Movements* (Grand Rapids, MI: Zondervan Publishing House, Regency Reference Library, 1988), 222.
7. See, for instance Robert Mapes Anderson, *Vision of the Disinherited: The Making of American Pentecostalism* (Oxford: Oxford University Press, 1979).
8. Headlines were particularly cruel. Cf. "Religious Fanaticism Creates Wild Scenes" [subtitled: "Holy Kickers Carry on Mad Orgies"], *Los Angeles Record* (July 14, 1906), 1; "Howling Ground Is Offered to the Household", *Pasadena Evening Star* (July 18, 1906), 12; "Jumpers to Kill Children" [subtitled: "Holy Rollers Plan a Slaughter of Innocents"], *Los Angeles Herald* (July 20, 1906), 1-2; "Big Crowd Routs the Holy Rollers", *Whittier Daily News* (November 2, 1906), 1.
9. See especially Anderson, *op. cit.*, 195-222.
10. Thomas, *op. cit.*, 20.
11. Frank Bartleman, "Not of This World", *Word and Work*, 296.
12. F. Bartleman, "The Great Divide", *Maran-atha* 9/3 (February, 1934), 6.
13. Bartleman clearly sought to dissociate himself from Dowie and Sandford whom he classed among 'spiritual charlatans' in "All Things in Common", *Confidence* 6/4 (April, 1913), 79. On Frank Sandford see Shirley Nelson, *Fair Clear and Terrible: The Story of Shiloh Maine* (Latham, NY: British American Publishing, 1989); on Dowie see Gordon Lindsay, *John Alexander Dowie: A Life Story of Trials, Tragedies, and Triumphs* (Dallas, TX: Christ for the Nations, reprint 1986), and Grant Wacker, "Marching to Zion: Religion in a Modern Utopian Community", *Church History* 54/4 (December, 1985), 496-511; on Yoakum see Jennifer A. Stock, "Finis E. Yoakum, M.D.: Servant of the Disinherited of Los Angeles: 1895-1920" (unpublished paper presented at the Society for Pentecostal Studies in Dallas, Texas, November, 1990), and Robert H. Vine, *California's Utopias* (San Marino, CA: The Huntington Library, 1953), 153-154; and on Parham see James R. Goff, Jr. *Fields White Unto Harvest: Charles F. Parham and the Missionary Origins of Pentecostalism* (Fayettville, AR: The University of Arkansas Press, 1988).
14. F. Bartleman, "Last Day Conditions", *The Bridegroom's Messenger* No. 180 (March 1, 1916), 4; F. Bartleman, "The Great Divide", *Maran-atha* 9/7 (June, 1934), 7.
15. F. Bartleman, "The Great Divide", *Maran-atha* 9/3 (February, 1934), 6; F. Bartleman, "The Great Divide", *Maran-atha* 9/7 (June, 1934), 7.

16. F. Bartleman, "The Situation in Europe", *The Bridegroom's Messenger* Vol. 8 No. 168 (March 1, 1915), 1.
17. *Ibid.*
18. F. Bartleman, "Through the War Zone", *The Bridegroom's Messenger* Vol. 8 No. 171 (January 1, 1915), 3.
19. F. Bartleman, "The War Separation", *The Bridegroom's Messenger* Vol. 8 No. 166 (January 1, 1916), 4. Cf. F. Bartleman, "The Present Day Conditions", *Weekly Evangel* (June 5, 1915), 3.
20. Bartleman, "The War Separation", 4.
21. *Ibid.*
22. F. Bartleman, "The European War", *Weekly Evangel* (July 10, 1915), 3.
23. F. Bartleman, "In the Last Days", *Word and Work* (September 23, 1916), 393.
24. F. Bartleman, "Last Days Facts", *Maran-atha* 6 (March-April, 1930), 8.
25. F. Bartleman, "Christian Preparedness", *Word and Work* (circa 1916), 114.
26. F. Bartleman, "The World War", *Word and Work* (August 12, 1916), 296; "In the Last Days", 394.
27. F. Bartleman, "Last Day Facts", 9. Bartleman argued that judgment was coming to America because God was no respecter of persons. Besides, "We stole the U.S. from the Indians anyway."
28. *Ibid.*
29. *Ibid.*
30. F. Bartleman, "The European War", 3; "What Will the Harvest Be?" *Weekly Evangel* (August 7, 1915), 1.
31. W. J. Seymour, *The Doctrines and Discipline of the Azusa Street Apostolic Faith Mission of Los Angeles, Cal.* (Los Angeles: W. J. Seymour, 1915), 12.
32. F. Bartleman, *How Pentecost Came to Los Angeles* (Los Angeles: F. Bartleman, 1925), 43, 44. This work is reprinted in *Witness to Pentecost: The Life of Frank Bartleman* (New York: Garland Publishing, Inc., 1985).
33. "Religious Fanaticism Creates Wild Scenes", *Los Angeles Record* (July 14, 1906), 1.
34. "Bible Pentecost", *The Apostolic Faith* 1/3 (November, 1906), 1. Early descriptions place attendance as high as 700 with mostly black participants. Cf. "Weird Babel of Tongues", *Los Angeles Daily Times* (April 18, 1906), 2:1; "Rolling and Diving Fanatics 'Confess'", *Los Angeles Daily Times* (June 23, 1906), 1:7.
35. F. Bartleman, *How Pentecost Came to Los Angeles*, 54.
36. The fact has been amply demonstrated by Douglas J. Nelson, "For Such a Time as This" (Unpublished Ph.D. dissertation, University of Birmingham, England, 1981) and Iain MacRobert, *Black Roots and White Racism of Early Pentecostalism in the U.S.A* (New York: St. Martin's Press, 1988).
37. "Edendale Indignant Over Negro Neighbors", *Los Angeles Express* (October 2, 1907), 2:11; "Police Aid Negroes to Occupy House", *Los Angeles Herald* (October 8, 1907), 6.
38. Negroes Turned Down", *Pasadena Evening Star* (August 21, 1906), 1; "Puts Ban on Anti-Negro Signs", *Los Angeles Herald* (May 7, 1907), 12; "Negroes Thank Mayor Harper", *Los Angeles Herald* (May 12, 1907), 2:5.
39. G. R. Bryant, "Religious Life of Los Angeles Negroes", *Los Angeles Daily Times* (February 12, 1909), 3:7.
40. On this see Josephene M. Washburn, *History and Reminiscences of the Holiness Church Work in Southern California and Arizona* (South Pasadena, CA: Record Press, 1912; reprint New York: Garland Publishing, Inc., 1985).
41. Cecil M. Robeck, Jr. "Azusa Street Mission", in Stanley M. Burgess and Gary B. McGee, eds. *Dictionary of Pentecostal and Charismatic Movements* (Grand Rapids: Zondervan Publishing House, Regency Reference Library, 1988), 34.

42. "Religious Fanaticism Creates Wild Scenes", 1; "Women with Men Embrace", *Los Angeles Daily Times* (September 3, 1906), 11; "How Holy Roller Gets Religion",*Los Angeles Herald* (September 10, 1906), 7; etc.
43. G. B. Cashwell, "Came 3000 Miles for His Pentecost," *The Apostolic Faith* 1/4 (December, 1906), 3.
44. Carl Brumback, *Suddenly ... From Heaven: A History of the Assemblies of God* (Springfield, MO: Gospel Publishing House, 1961), 84; Vinson Synan, *The Holiness-Pentecostal Movement in the United States* (Grand Rapids, MI: William B. Eerdmans Publishing Company, 1971), 123.
45. "Bible Pentecost", *The Apostolic Faith* 1/3 (November, 1906), 1.
46. Untitled comments, *New Year's Greeting* (Baxter Springs, KS) (January 1912), 6. This parallels the comments of a Los Angeles pastor in "New Religions Come, Then Go", *Los Angeles Herald* (September 24, 1906), 7.
47. Bartleman, *How Pentecost Came to Los Angeles*, 84.
48. Seymour, *Doctrine and Disciplines*, 13.
49. Seymour, *op. cit.*, 12.
50. Murray W. Dempster, "Evangelism, Social Concern, and the Kingdom of God", in Murray W. Demptster, Byron D. Klaus, and Douglas Peterson, eds. *Called and Empowered: Global Mission in Pentecostal Perspective* (Peabody, MA: Hendrickson Publishers, 1991), 29.
51. Anderson, *op. cit.*, 222.
52. A. J. Tomlinson, "A Brief History of Mission Work in the Mountains of North Carolina, Georgia and Tennessee", *Samson's Foxes* (Culberson, NC: A. J. Tomlinson, no date) unpaginated.
53. See above, note 12.

10

The Oneness Doctrine as a Contextualized Doctrine of the Trinity for Mexico

Kenneth D. Gill

Shortly after the turn of the century, some members of the Pentecostal movement in the United States developed the Oneness Doctrine of the Trinity as a distinctive theological position. It began as a call to proper baptism or rebaptism in the name of Jesus as opposed to the traditional formula "in the name of the Father, and of the Son, and of the Holy Spirit."[1] From the rationale for baptism in the name of Jesus evolved the Oneness Doctrine of the Trinity. The doctrine focused on the unity of God. The terminology 'three persons' and 'Trinity' were rejected as referring to three beings or three gods. While explanations vary, the Oneness Doctrine of the Trinity is stated in functional terms or as three manifestations of God.[2]

One member of this new movement was a young Mexican lady named Romana Valenzuela. She was converted to the Pentecostal faith in Los Angeles, California. Valenzuela returned to Mexico in 1914 to convert her family and baptize them in the name of Jesus. A small congregation was established in Valenzuela's home town of Villa Aldama near Chihuahua, Coah.

Valenzuela became an evangelist and traveled throughout Northern Mexico. Through her efforts and that of many who followed, La Iglesia Apostólica de la Fe en Cristo Jesús was established as an indigenous Mexican denomination.

Iglesia Apostólica: Formal Statement of Beliefs

A formal statement of the beliefs of the Iglesia Apostólica is found in its "Principios Doctrinales," which is published with the constitution.[3] It contains eighteen main points, each supported by scripture references. The beliefs which are most significant for the purposes of this study are summarized below:

1. There is one universal Church composed of all who accept Jesus as their Saviour and have been baptized into the Church by the Holy Spirit.
2. There is only one God who has manifested himself to the world in different forms throughout the ages. Especially he has revealed himself as Father in the creation of the universe, as Son in the redemption of humanity, and as Holy

Spirit in the hearts of believers. God is eternal, possessing an absolute and indivisible divinity. He is known completely only to himself and is beyond human description.

3. Jesus Christ was born of a virgin and united the human and divine in one being. While manifested in human form, he was still the one true God and eternal Father. Because of the incarnation, he is also called Son of God and Son of Man.
4. Believers are baptized in the Holy Spirit, and this baptism is demonstrated by speaking in tongues. The Holy Spirit gives believers power to testify of Christ and develop Christian character. Every member of the Iglesia Apostólica should seek the Holy Spirit.
5. Believers should be baptized in water by immersion in the name of Jesus: by immersion because it represents the death of man to sin and in the name of Jesus because this is the form in which the Apostles administered baptism in the Early Church. Baptism should be administered by an ordained minister.[4]

Following the tradition of the Oneness Movement, the Iglesia Apostólica considers itself to be anti-trinitarian. The Doctrine of the Trinity is understood to be referring to three gods. "El Unico Dios Manifestado en Carne," an article by Manuel R. Ramírez, is an attack on trinitarians. He claims that there are people who believe in two, three, or many gods. Ramírez reiterates the Apostolic position that there is one God who has manifested himself in flesh. God manifests himself to the world in special ways, as Father in creation, as Son in redemption, and as Holy Spirit in the hearts of believers.[5]

Manuel J. Gaxiola makes the point that Apostolics do not believe that they have to accept or confess a trinitarian formula, but they do confess that Jesus is Lord. He feels that Apostolics have been misunderstood and accused of being heretics by those who have understood neither the Apostolic position nor the doctrines they themselves profess. Apostolics stress the deity of Jesus Christ.[6] This position has been stated very strongly throughout the history of the denomination.

In an effort to discount their position, many people have called the Apostolics heretics. Inaccurate correlations have been made with heresies of the past. Manuel J. Gaxiola asserts that Oneness Pentecostals are neither unitarian nor Arian. As good Pentecostals, they do not consider themselves bound by the decisions of the ecumenical church councils. However, they would agree with most of the decisions reached at Chalcedon.[7]

An article written in 1972 defends the church against the various Protestant groups that reject the Iglesia Apostólica as heretical. It suggests that the position of the trinitarian Protestants is inconsistent. If they accept the Doctrine of the Trinity, why do they reject other doctrines agreed upon at the various councils? The article specifically mentions the infallibility of the Pope, veneration of images, celibacy of priests, and oral confession.[8]

Apostolics speak about the manifestations of God as Father, Son and Holy Spirit. Here is found Sabellian terminology, but a different meaning. Unlike Sabellianism, the Apostolics consider God to be manifesting himself as Father, Son and Holy Spirit at the same time. Thus they use all of these three designations in reference to God. In practice, several terms are used to speak about and to God, just as may be found in most Christian churches. *Jesús, Jesucristo, Cristo, Dios, Señor,* and *Padre* are frequently heard in worship, teaching, and casual conversation.[9]

The *Espíritu Santo* is referred to as well. The Holy Spirit is spoken of as in any other Pentecostal church.[10] He is the *Poder de Dios*. God pours out his Spirit upon believers and gives them power to live holy lives and be his witnesses. However, the Holy Spirit is never referred to as a 'person' of the Trinity, but rather as a *modo* in relationship to God.[11]

A Bible study published in 1955 describes the work of the Holy Spirit. The discussion follows the same pattern as one would encounter in most Pentecostal churches. Fourteen points are listed concerning the work of the Holy Spirit. Among other things, the Holy Spirit is said to convince people of sin, reveal the things of Christ, cause people to speak in tongues, make believers one in the Lord, give liberty, and seal believers for God. In his manifestation as Holy Spirit, these are the things God accomplishes.[12]

Recent efforts reflect a more philosophical attempt to understand the problem than has been used previously.[13] This places the basis of theology on a very different plane. Such a departure from biblical language and thought-forms will result in a very different explanation and is likely to cause similar conflicts to those experienced in the Early Church. A basic premise for the Iglesia Apostólica is that God is beyond human understanding. Thus, He can never be fully known nor described. However, He has made himself known to man by revealing himself in Jesus Christ.[14]

Although few of the Apostolic ministers have read any of his work, their understanding of the Trinity approaches that of Karl Barth. Their use of the term *modo* mentioned above reflects this tendency. Each 'mode' is understood to be God himself in all of his fullness. Yet there remains one consciousness, one will, one personality, etc., manifesting himself to humanity through these three modes.

Manuel J. Gaxiola is familiar with the work of Karl Barth. While not committing himself to the position completely, he finds Barth's 'modes of being' intriguing. He views this as a more acceptable version of trinitarian doctrine than the use of the concept of 'person.'[15]

For the Mexican Apostolics the Oneness Doctrine of the Trinity brings Jesus Christ to the centre of the Christian faith in Mexico. Historically, that position was taken by the Virgin de Guadalupe, the most prominent Mexican manifestation of the Virgin Mary.[16] In 1531 Juan Diego, an Indian wood-cutter, reported that he had seen an apparition of the Virgin who appeared in the form of an Indian maiden. Very quickly the influence of the Virgin de Guadalupe spread throughout Mexico. In time she became the symbol of the country.

Part of the popularity of the Virgin was the location that was chosen for her shrine. It stands at Tepeyac, the former site of the Aztec shrine dedicated to Tonantzin, goddess of the Earth and mother of the Aztec gods. The result was the identification of the Virgin with the Aztec goddess. This union of Christian and Indian religious beliefs was a common missionary practice of the Roman Catholic Church. However, in Mexico it went further than anticipated. For, while the Virgin de Guadalupe remains central to the spirituality of the Mexican Catholic Church, she has become an object of veneration and worship in her own right apart from her son or the Catholic Church.[17]

The statement has been made by René Padilla, a well-known Latin American Evangelical theologian, that "the church in Latin America is a church without a theology."[18] What is meant is that there is no distinctively Latin American theology, and for much of the church that is true. Even many of the Pentecostal churches have imported their theology from abroad. Padilla refers to the abundance of foreign theological and religious books translated into Spanish and imported hymnology to substantiate this point.[19]

The assertion by Padilla is certainly true of Mexico. Pedro R. Rivera, a Mexican Catholic theologian, claims that the strongest part of Protestantism in Mexico is the large number of foreign mission agencies. He suggests that this demonstrates that Protestantism in Mexico is not as Mexican as one might suppose. The Mexican Protestants attempt to convince their fellow countrymen and the world that it is really Mexican. They want to eradicate the foreign image implied by the name 'Mexican Protestant.' Rivera is adamant that whatever Protestantism in Mexico may be, it certainly is not Mexican.[20]

Minutes of the early general conventions of the Iglesia Apostólica reflect the context in which the pastors worked out their belief and practice. Using only the Bible at first, they dealt with the concrete issues which faced them in their pastorates. Slowly, sometimes through trial and error, they developed a viable system of belief and practice. Even concerning their treaty with the Apostolic Assembly, a Mexican American sister denomination, they were determined to do things the Mexican way. The pastors reflected the social status and educational level of those to whom they ministered. Therefore, the decisions they reached were phrased in language all could understand.

The theology developed by the Iglesia Apostólica was a practical theology. Jesus was their God and obedience to him was foremost in their minds. Their often very literal understanding of the Bible was focused on doing the will of God. Only later, as more of the membership became highly educated, did the need for abstract discussion begin. Even now, the need for this philosophical discussion is questioned.

It must also be remembered that most of the doctrines espoused by the Iglesia Apostólica are consistent with Evangelical tradition. Manuel J. Gaxiola has called to the attention of his fellow ministers the fact that sixteen of the eighteen points of their doctrinal statement are upheld by the majority in the Pentecostal Evangelical community. It is only on the points of water baptismal formula and the Doctrine of the Trinity that they differ.[21]

Water Baptism Formula and the Doctrine of the Trinity

The practice of baptizing in Jesus' name is problematic only if those so baptized are the only ones considered to be Christians. Some may not agree with the practice or may consider the formula to be used in baptism unimportant. Yet, it is difficult to argue that baptism in the name of Jesus is un-christian in light of Luke's narrative in the book of Acts.

The Oneness Doctrine is another matter. Many Evangelicals are convinced that to deny the three 'persons' of the Trinity is to remove oneself from their ranks. It is so radical an idea as to be beyond their comprehension.

There are five criteria which appear to be crucial for the Evangelical community in determining a viable doctrinal formulation of the Trinity. First, the most important function of the Doctrine of the Trinity is to establish the divinity of Jesus Christ. He was not just a man, a good teacher, or the most wholesome example of humanity. Rather, he was God himself incarnated in human form. Second, God must be shown as having internal consistency, i.e., one centre of consciousness, one will, one personality, etc. Third, all three modes must function simultaneously. The passages in the Bible which reflect such simultaneous activity demand this interpretation to maintain the Evangelical Doctrine of scripture. Fourth, each mode must be God himself rather than an appearance of God or some type of artificial representation. In each is encountered the fullness of God. Fifth, God must be presented as existing eternally as Father, Son, and Holy Spirit. The three modes are not simply temporary or sequential manifestations of God, but part of his very being. All five criteria are necessary to a viable Evangelical Doctrine of the Trinity.

The first criterion, that of the divinity of Jesus, is the strongest facet of the Apostolic doctrine. To the Apostolics, Jesus is actually the name of God and in Jesus the totality of God is found.

The internal consistency of God is another major facet of the Apostolic position. Their firm assertion that God is one and adamant rejection of the idea of God as having three persons is based on a human analogy. Every human person has a mind, will, personality, etc., and it is precisely because of this reality that the

Apostolics reject the use of the term 'person' in relationship to God. They conclude that such a scenario could only result in three Gods who may act as one, but are in fact three separate deities.

The Apostolics believe that God manifests himself simultaneously as Father, Son, and Holy Spirit. They understand that each mode has identifiable activities which can be carried out at the same time. Their concern is that these modes do not constitute different persons.

The idea that the modes are only in appearance and not really God himself would be completely unacceptable to the Apostolics. Their literal understanding of scripture demands that it is God himself that they encounter as Father, Son, and Holy Spirit. They use the concept of the 'fullness' of God dwelling in Jesus to exemplify this point in relationship to the Son.

The fifth criterion has not yet been fully addressed by the Apostolics. Their insistence that Jesus is the name of God allows them to interpret biblical passages about him as referring to God as a unity rather than to the Son. The official statements they have made so far indicate that the eternal nature of the three modes is consistent with their understanding of the Trinity. However, the eternal sonship has been denied by some in other Oneness denominations.[22] It is this point which could potentially cause some conflict for the Iglesia Apostólica with the broader Evangelical Movement.

Diversity within Evangelicalism

Most Evangelical Christians have been taught that there is only one way of doing theology and interpreting the scriptures. Despite the great diversity within Evangelicalism, in most cases this instruction includes the understanding that all other ways are wrong or, at best, inferior. It is difficult, therefore, to entertain the possibility that other ways may, after all, be viable.

Paul G. Hiebert suggests that missionaries have a "theological shock" when they confront the pluralism of Christian theology in the Third World. There they find deeply committed believers interpreting the scriptures in many different ways. The initial reaction is to reject these differences as false without really examining them closely. Hiebert suggests that a differentiation must be made between the biblical data and one's theology. He goes on to reiterate the Evangelical concern that the Bible must control theologizing and not the reverse.[23]

Within the Evangelical community there is a wide variety of belief and practice. It should, therefore, be acceptable to the Evangelical community for a particular church to frame its theology as it wishes, as long as it falls within the general parameters of Evangelicalism outlined above.

In general, it can be affirmed that the Apostolic Doctrine of the Trinity conforms to the guidelines established by the Evangelical community. In addition, it emerged from a Mexican context and is meaningful within that context. It must be acknowledged that there are some inconsistencies among the Apostolics as to how certain aspects of their doctrine are understood. There are also some inconsistencies in the doctrine itself which may or may not be worked out in the future.

It should be taken into consideration that the Iglesia Apostólica and the Oneness Movement as a whole are very young. These Apostolics are attempting to formulate their theology to the best of their ability and desire to be consistent with biblical revelation. Even if one remains unconvinced as to the validity of the Apostolic position, he must at least be ready to grant the request of Manuel J. Gaxiola; that is, to allow the Iglesia Apostólica 'theological space.' What he means by this is that the church is in the process of formulating its doctrinal system and is in a fluid state. Like the Primitive Church, its theological statements should not be compared to those which have been refined over hundreds of years. Manuel J. Gaxiola simply asks that the Iglesia Apostólica should not be rejected as heretical or unitarian, but be accepted as a sincere group of believers who are attempting to be faithful to the Christian scriptures.[24]

Notes

1. Robert Mapes Anderson, *Vision of the Disinherited: The Making of American Pentecostalism* (New York: Oxford University Press, 1979), 176; and David Arthur Reed, "Origins and Development of the Theology of Oneness Pentecostalism in the United States," (Ph.D. dissertation, Boston University, 1978), 100-01.
2. I have discussed the development of the doctrine at length in "Toward a Contextualized Theology for the Third World: The Emergence and Development of Jesus' Name Pentecostalism in Mexico" (Ph.D. thesis, University of Birmingham, 1989), 31-41.
3. Iglesia Apostólica de la Fe en Cristo Jesús, *Constitución y Principios Doctrinales de la Iglesia Apostólica de la Fe en Cristo Jesús* (Mexico, D.F.: By the Organization, 1985).
4. My translation.
5. Manuel Ramírez R., "El Unico Dios Manifestado en Carne," *El Exégeta* (January 1951), 6.
6. Manuel J. Gaxiola-Gaxiola, "The Serpent and the Dove: A History of the Apostolic Church of the Faith in Christ Jesus in Mexico, 1914-1974," (M.A. thesis, Fuller Theological Seminary, School of World Missions, 1977), 186-187; and "The Unsettled Issue," paper presented at the Apostolic Faith Seminar, Hazelwood, MO, 5-8 December 1977.
7. Manuel J. Gaxiola-Gaxiola, "Serpent," 187.
8. "La Doctrina de los Apóstoles," *El Exégeta* (March 1972), 14-15.
9. Charles Bennett observed a service at an apostolic congregation in Tabasco in which both the Father and the Son were invoked in oral prayers. *Tinder in Tabasco: A Study of Church Growth in Tropical Mexico* (Grand Rapids, Mich.: William B. Eerdmans, 1968), 180-181. "El que me ha visto, ha visto al Padre" is the theme of an article written by Rafael Cepeda. He discusses what is known about God and uses references to the Father freely. Rafael Cepeda, "Como es Dios," *El Exégeta* (August 1951), 12.
10. Juan B. Casrejon, "El Espíritu y los Espíritus," *El Exégeta* (September 1973), 23-25; and Ysidro

Pérez Ramírez, "El Espíritu Santo en los Hechos de los Apóstoles," *El Exégeta* (December 1973), 6-7.

11. Casrejon, "Espíritu," 23; and Pérez, "Espíritu Santo," 6.
12. "Estudios Biblicos," *El Exégeta* (March 1955), 14-15.
13. Maclovio Gaxiola Lopez, *Teología Moral: Doctrina y Disciplina Cristiana* (Mexico, D.F.: Librería Latinoamericana, 1962), 15.
14. Manuel J. Gaxiola-Gaxiola, "The Unsettled Issue," (Paper presented at the Apostolic Faith Seminar, Hazelwood, Mo., December 5-8, 1977).
15. "Jesucristo," *El Exégeta* (November 1983), 23-24.
16. Numerous distinct manifestations of the Virgin Mary are found throughout Latin America. William B. Taylor, "The Virgin of Guadalupe in New Spain," *American Ethnologist* 14 (February 1987), 9.
17. Folk Catholicism in Mexico has also identified some of the other Indian gods with Catholic saints. This syncretistic practice is discussed in relationship to the Virgin de Guadalupe in John M. Ingham, *Mary, Michael, and Lucifer: Folk Catholicism in Central Mexico* (Austin, Texas: University of Texas Press, 1986), 180-193.
18. René Padilla, "The Contextualization of the Gospel," in: Charles H. Kraft and Tom N. Wisley (eds.) *Readings in Dynamic Indigeneity* (Pasadena, CA.: William Carey Library, 1979), 297.
19. Padilla, "Contextualization," 296-300.
20. Pedro R. Rivera, *Instituciones Protestantes en México* (Mexico, D.F.: Editorial Jus, 1962), 1. Manuel J. Gaxiola-Gaxiola discusses the characteristics of indigenous Mexican Protestantism found especially within the Pentecostal community. This is a sphere with which Rivera appears to be unfamiliar. Manuel J. Gaxiola-Gaxiola, "Mexican Protestantism: The Quest for Meaning and Relevance in a Pluralistic Society" (Ph.D. thesis, University of Birmingham, 1990).
21. Manuel J. Gaxiola-Gaxiola, "The Spanish-Speaking Oneness Churches in Latin America: Search for Identity and Possibilities of Doctrinal Renewal" (Paper presented at the First Occasional Symposium on Aspects of the Oneness Pentecostal Movement, Cambridge, Mass.: Harvard Divinity School, July 5-7, 1984), 21-23.
22. Reed, "Origins," 299-318.
23. Paul G. Hiebert, *Anthropological Insights for Missionaries* (Grand Rapids, Mich.: Baker Book House, 1985), 196-198.
24. Manuel J. Gaxiola-Gaxiola, *La Sana Doctrina* (Guadalajara, Jal.: By the Author, 1989), 104-105.

11

Thomas B. Barratt and *Byposten*: An Early European Pentecostal Leader and His Periodical

David Bundy

The story of the early North American Pentecostal periodical, *The Apostolic Faith* (Sept. 1906 - May 1908), is well known and has been recently reprinted and supplied with an extensive index.[1] Among the early European Pentecostal periodicals, only the English paper *Confidence* edited by A.A. Boddy, the Anglican rector at Sunderland, is generally familiar to scholars of Pentecostalism.[2]

However, a number of European papers had a similarly early beginning and many of them are still being published albeit under different names. The earliest was T.B. Barratt's *Byposten* (1904 - 1909).[3] This was quickly joined by *Confidence* (1908 - 1924) edited by A.A. Boddy, *De Spade Regen* (1908 - 1931) edited by G.R. Polman, *Verheissung des Vaters* (1909) edited by C.E.D. de Labiliere, and *Pfingstgrüße* (1904)[4] edited by Jonathan Paul. The early editors were all practicing clergymen from Methodist, Anglican, Lutheran or Holiness backgrounds. They were in constant contact with each other as well as with events in the rest of the world. However, the editor with the widest global vision was the peripatetic Methodist Holiness convert to Pentecostalism, Thomas Ball Barratt.

Barratt's Early Life and Ministry

Much is known about the life and ministry of T.B. Barratt. There are two autobiographical efforts, one edited posthumously, as well as volumes written by his wife and daughter.[5] He has attracted the attention of historians of Pentecostalism and a diverse secondary literature exists.[6] These sources record the evolution of an expatriate Norwegian miner's son who, under the tutelage of his mother, became an ecumenically-minded, innovative hard-working Methodist pastor, who after just a few months of service was called to work at a prestigious church in Christiania (Oslo). In that capacity, he was involved in the establishment of the Epworth League (a youth organization), a temperance mission, a deaconess ministry centre, and eventually a daring ministry program which used drama and classical music productions as well as charity programs to minister to the unchurched in the city.

Barratt was a frequent contributor to Methodist periodicals from the late 1880's onward. His writing was lucid and careful and dealt with issues he felt crucial to the development of the Church. In 1904, he established his own periodical *Byposten* (City Post). Barratt's editorial work is frequently mentioned by scholars but little attention is given to the periodical *Byposten* which, from late 1906 served as the basis for Pentecostalism in Norway and throughout Europe.

Byposten: From City Mission to Azusa Street Mission Reports

The periodical *Byposten* actually began as an effort to raise funds and provide a communication link to the diverse Oslo constituency of the Oslo City Mission (Bymission) in 1904.[7] Barratt had, despite considerable opposition among his Methodist Episcopal ministerial colleagues, begun an alternative evangelistic program which sought to reach the poor and secularized who would have no contact with a non-state church for social or economic reasons. With the Methodist periodical *Kristelig Tidende* closed to news and appeals for the City Mission an alternative was needed. *Byposten* chronicles the events which led to Barratt's trip to North America to raise funds for the Mission program, the frustrations experienced when American Methodist Bishops could not persuade the Mission Board to support his efforts as they had promised, and the efforts to diffuse the failure to raise funds in the face of direct opposition by the Mission Board. And, it supplies the basic narrative of the weeks spent penniless in the Mission Home of A.B. Simpson's ministry in New York. There he read a copy of *The Apostolic Faith* and described the phenomenon of the Los Angeles Azusa Street revival in glowing terms for his readers.[8] After correspondence with Azusa mission participants and extended prayer, he experienced the Pentecostal 'baptism in the Holy Spirit'.[9]

This was followed by an article which tied together John Wesley, Charles Cullis, Charles Parham, and Agnes Ozman borrowed from *The Apostolic Faith*, and which spoke perfectly to the needs of the Norwegian Methodist Holiness people who were beginning to feel cornered by the imperialism and manipulatory behaviour of the Methodist Mission Board.[10] His own reflections continued in the regular column from America.[11] It is this column which reported Barratt's own Pentecostal religious experience in December 1906.[12] The next issue continued to revise material published in *The Apostolic Faith* which described the worship and suggested in barest outline the theological maneuvers required by the doctrine of the 'latter rain'.[13] Perhaps most importantly, the periodical gave readers in Norway (about 3000 copies circulated) an intimate view of the struggle, searching and process of renewal which Barratt experienced. It was effective because it was totally spontaneous, unrehearsed and presented week by week without a clear direct agenda. As Barratt searched and found, so did his readers.

Byposten: Reporting the Revival in Norway and Around the World

Barratt's followers in Oslo quickly accepted the Pentecostal message as interpreted by Barratt in *Byposten* and personally after his return. The first issue in January reported that the Pentecostal Movement had begun in Christiania (Oslo).[14] From this point considerable space in the periodical is devoted to reports of the Pentecostal revival in Oslo. The worship, theological developments, personal histories and opposition are described in detail. The periodical circulated also throughout Scandinavia and among Scandinavian immigrants in the United States. Therefore there are already in late January 1907 letters published from new adherents in Sweden, Finland and Denmark as well as various points in Norway. An article is taken from a Danish periodical *Kirkeklokken* reporting on similar revivalistic activity at Pandita Ramabai's Mukti centre in India.[15] In that same issue, a testimony of the experience by a "state church member", identified otherwise only by the initials J.A.H., is published. Thereafter the letters flooded in from North America, India, China and throughout Europe. Most of the Europeans were responding to materials published in *Byposten* or 'private' correspondence with Barratt. The strength of the contacts was quite naturally to burgeoning numbers of villages and cities in Scandinavia with Pentecostal groups: Stockholm, Orebro, Surte, Skofde, Holmsbo, Skien, Arendal, Asker, Trondhjem, Spydeberg, Sandsvaer, Sarpsborg, Frederikshald, Larvik, Aalesund and beyond. In Norway the contacts are for the most part Methodist, but throughout Scandinavia materials were received from a variety of state and non-state church persons. The most detailed reporting was, as would be expected, of Pentecostal revivalist activities and results in Christiania (Oslo).

Beginning in April 1907, one finds the initial stages of theological reflection about the new tradition. There is a detailed book review of a volume entitled *Fyldt af Aanden* by C. Skovgaard-Petersen which serves as the lead article of the fascicle.[16] Barratt[17] then contributed articles on the new Pentecost and on glossolalia citing a variety of Methodist and Holiness writers, periodical articles and English language biblical commentaries.[18] Thereafter theological articles become standard fare. Some attention is given to clarifying relationships with the Methodist and Holiness revivals. This was necessary not only for Norwegian Holiness Methodists who were attracted to Pentecostalism, but for Barratt who was quickly being ostracized by the Methodist Episcopal Church. At the Methodist Annual Conference in July 1909, Barratt was forced to resign from the Methodist Episcopal Church and from the Bymission (City Mission) which he had founded. True to form, Barratt described the conference proceedings and printed his final communication to the Conference.[19] The only physical portion of that ministry which he took to his new headquarters in an Independent Holiness Church was *Byposten*.

Byposten: A European and Global Perspective on Pentecostalism

During the summer months of 1907, there is a distinct change in the orientation of *Byposten*. The initial tendency was to look to the model of the Los Angeles revival. Now, the model very clearly becomes Christiania (Oslo) as nuanced by the experiences in Germany, Sweden, Denmark, England, and especially India and China. And, except for occasional references to Pentecostal revival in Chicago among Scandinavians, references to North American Pentecostalism become increasingly fewer as the months progress. The events in Germany, Switzerland and especially England are given much more attention.[20] There are subsequently numerous reports from Sunderland and from another revivalist-editor, Jonathan Paul whose first article is published in September 1908.[21] The evolving network of European Pentecostal leaders is seen clearly in the reports from various countries sent to *Byposten*.

On 9 March 1909, after extensive travels in Norway to visit Pentecostal sites, Barratt headed for India to study and participate in the revival going on there. Typically he described in detail his impressions and experiences.[22] The narratives are most appreciative of India, Indian life and of the spirituality of the Indian Pentecostals. He was especially impressed by the Mukti Centre of Pandita Ramabai. His own intercultural experience in Norway had made him more open than many of his contemporaries to the activity of the Spirit of God outside European confines.

Based on his experiences on the trip to India, he decided that an alliance was needed to expedite Pentecostal revival around the world, beginning in Europe. He published in October 1908 an appeal for a 'Spirit Alliance' which would function like the Pietist mission societies. Each centre would be independent but responsible in fellowship to the larger corporate group. This he argued would facilitate the union of people who came to the Pentecostal experiences and tradition from ''state church, Methodist, Baptist, Free Mission and other'' backgrounds. Such a union would allow them to work together and present a common front to the rest of the world.[23]

It would appear to be this conviction that stimulated the series of Pentecostal 'Leader's Meetings' beginning in 1908. However the dream of an alliance would have to wait, vetoed as it were by the British participants. Not until 1911, would essentially the same vision even be published in *Confidence*.[24] And then, Boddy felt compelled to nuance Barratt's essay and insist on ''Unity, not Uniformity''.[25]

Beginning in December 1908, a detailed account of the international ecumenical conference in Hamburg is provided.[26] The June 1909 number of *Byposten* reports on the London conference of Pentecostal leaders held at Sion College, 23-27 May [27] and which seems to have continued as a combination preaching/evangelism and leaders conference at Sunderland with the involvement of George and Carrie Judd Montgomery.[28] The results of these conferences were also thus provided to the readers of *Byposten.* Through these reports and the narratives of the Pentecostal revivals throughout the world, the Pentecostal believers in Norway and throughout Scandinavia were exposed to a global and European perspective, framed by a European Pentecostal theological analysis, of what it meant to be part of the new communion: Pentecostalism.

Conclusion

Barratt used *Byposten* as an instrument to create a new Pentecostal reality which was European and global in character. It presented a paradigm based on respect for God's people and God's activity throughout the world. It was fiercely independent of American influence and did not attempt to impose its will on others either in Europe or beyond although it sought to provide a model of Pentecostal life based on Christiania (Oslo) experiences. It was ecumenical as well as internationalist. Earlier than any other Pentecostal leader, Barratt understood that the old structures were not being swept completely away by the flow of the new revival. He understood that ecumenical theological discussion and cooperation were imperative for the accomplishment of mission. All of this he presented through the pages of *Byposten* and in his personal appearances around the world.

Notes

1. *Like as a Fire,* A reprint of the Old Azusa Street Papers (Wilmington, MA, 1981); *Author-Subject Index, Like as a Fire,* A reprint of the Apostolic Faith (1906 - 1908) (Springfield, n.d.).
2. Photocopied versions have circulated widely among scholars and it is frequently cited. Cf. William K. Kay, *Inside Story, A History of the British Assemblies of God* (Mattersey, 1990), passim.
3. This has continued publication as *Korsets Seier* (1909-...).
4. Continued as *Heilszeugnisse.*
5. Thomas Ball Barratt, *When the Fire Fell and An Outline of My Life* (Oslo, 1927) reprinted in: *The Works of T.B. Barratt,* The Higher Christian Life 4, ed. by D.W. Dayton (New York, 1985); Idem, *Erindringer* (ed. by Solveig Barratt Lange, Oslo, 1941); Laura Jacobson Barratt, *Minner* (Oslo, 1946); Solveig Barratt Lange, *Et Herrens sendebud* (Oslo, 1979).
6. D. Gee, *The Pentecostal Movement; A Short History and Interpretation of the Pentecostal Movement* (London, 1941); L. Steiner, *Mit folgenden Zeichen: eine Darstellung der Pfingstbewegung* (Basel, 1954); S. Frodsham, *With Signs Following: The Story of the Pentecostal Revival in the Twentieth Century* (Springfield, 1928); H.R. Tomaszewski, *Grupy Chreseijanskio Typu Ewangeliezno-Baptystyeznegona Terenie Polski od 1885-1939* (Diss. Doctorate, Adademii Teologieznej w Warszawie, 1978); J. Kuosmanen, *Heratyksen historia* (Tikkurilla, Finland, 1979); M. Ski, *T.B. Barratt - dopt i And og Ild* (Oslo: Filadelfiaforlaget, 1979); A. Sunstedt, *Pingstväckelsen - des uppkomst och forsta utvecklingsskede,* Pingstväckelsen 1 (Stockholm: Normans Forlag, 1969); E. Briem, *Den moderna Pingströrelsen* (Stockholm: Svenska Krykans Diakonistryelses Bokforlag, 1924); N. Bloch-Hoell, *Pinsebevegelsen: En ondersokolso av pinsobevegelsen tilblivelse, utvik-*

ling og saerpreg med saerlig henblikk på bevegelsens utformning i Norge (Oslo: Universitetsforlaget, 1956), partially translated as: Idem, *The Pentecostal movement: Its Origin, Development and Distinctive Character* (Oslo, 1964); W. Hollenweger, *Handbuch der Pfingstbewegung* (Diss. Genf. 1965-1967). Par. 05.02; Idem, *Enthusiastisches Christentum; Die Pfingstbewegung in Geschichte und Gegenwart* (Zurich/Wuppertal, 1969); revised translation into English as: Idem, *The Pentecostals, The Charismatic Movement in the Churches* (Minneapolis, 1972); Idem, *El Pentecostalismo historia y doctrina* (Buenos Aires, 1976). For additional bibliography, see D. Bundy, "T.B. Barratt: The Methodist Years, Pentecostalism in the Context of the Holiness Revival", Society for Pentecostal Studies, 18th Annual Meeting, November 10-12, 1988 (Wilmore, 1988), 62-75; and Idem, "Barratt, Thomas Ball," *Dictionary of Pentecostal and Charismatic Movements* (Grand Rapids, 1988), 50.

7. On these developments, see D. Bundy, "T.B. Barratt's Christiania (Oslo) City Mission: A Study in the Intercultural Adaptation of American and British Voluntary Association Structures", presented at the Conference on Pentecostal and Charismatic Research in Europe 'Crossing Borders' (Kappel, 1991), 1-15.
8. T.B. Barratt, "Pintsefest paany: Los Angeles er nu besogt af er vackkelse, der minder om den beskrevet i Hel. Ap. Gj.2", *Byposten* 3/20 (6 october 1906), 86-87.
9. T.B. Barratt, "Glimt fra vesten, Da jeg fik min pintsedab," *Byposten* 3,22 (3 november 1906), 93-95. This article reprinted a letter from I. May Throp describing the events in Los Angeles and encouraging people to write for copies of *The Apostolic Faith.*
10. "Pintsedaaben fornyet, Den bebudede sildige regn udgydes over Guds ydmyge folk," *Byposten* 3/23 (17 November 1906), 97 from "The Pentecostalism Baptism restored, The Promised Latter Rain Now Being Poured Out on God's Humble People", *The Apostolic Faith* 1/2 (October 1906), 1.
11. T.B. Barratt, "Glimt fra vesten", *Byposten* 3/23 (17 November 1906, 97-98.
12. T.B. Barratt, "Glimt fra vesten", *Byposten* 3/24 (1 December 1906), 101-104; cf. Idem, *Byposten* 4/1 (12 January 1907), 4. Another version was published in a periodical edited by A.B. Simpson: T.B. Barratt, "The Seal of My Pentecost", *Living Truths* 6/12 (December 1906), 735-38.
13. T.B. Barratt, "Vaekkelsen i Los Angeles, Tegn og undergjerninger", *Byposten* 3/25 (22 December 1906), 106-107.
14. T.B. Barratt, "Vaekkelsen udbrudt i Kristiania", *Byposten* 4/1 (12 January 1907), 1-3.
15. "Daaben med den Hellig-aand og ild", *Byposten* 4/2 (26 January 1907), 7-8.
16. Review by T.B. Barratt[?] *Byposten* 4/9 (April 1907), 45-46. I have been unable to locate this volume.
17. Barratt appears to be the author of these articles although they are unsigned.
18. "Det nye pintse", *Byposten* 4/10 (May 1907), 49; "Tungetalen", *Byposten* 4/10 (May 1907), 49-50.
19. T.B. Barratt, "Min stilling tol methodistkirkens aarskonference", *Byposten* 4/16 (27 July 1907), 67-68. Methodist sources are remarkably silent. The *Forhandlings-Protokol for den biskoppelige Methodistkirkes norske Aarskonferences 32 te Modo afholdt i Larvik 10-16 juli 1907* (Kristiania, 1907), 27, merely reports his "location" (that is no longer assigned to ministry). Thereafter, he disappears from official Methodist records. Bishop Burt, "My Notes of European Conferences 1907", Manuscript, United Methodist Board of Global Ministries Archives, Drew University [OMC F 1152], notes: "Barratt left his appointment and went off to Sweden and Denmark on evangelistic work of a peculiar type. He professed to have the gift of tongues. His conduct this year caused considerable trouble. He will probably locate" (p. 67). Later he states: "T.B. Barratt was located at his own request. I insisted that he was not to be let into our churches to break up our regular order of work" (p. 72). In his "Notes on European Conferences 1908-1909", he expresses relief that "the Barratt movement appears not to have caused too much disturbance except at Saps-

borg'' (p. 63).

20. T.B. Barratt, ''Ilden er faldt i Sunderland, England'', *Byposten* 4/20 (September 1907), 83, is not the first report from England but is the first to mention Sunderland and A.A. Boddy. Cf. Idem, ''Besoget til England'', *Byposten* 4/20 (September 1907), 85-86; idem, ''Besoget til England'', *Byposten* 4/22 (September 1907), 87-88; Laura Barratt, ''Konferensen i Sunderland'', *Byposten* 5/13 (27 June 1908), 50-51.
21. Jonathan Paul, ''Et kjernesporgsmaal'', *Byposten* 5/18 (September 1908), 69.
22. T.B. Barratt, ''Turen til Indien'', *Byposten* 5/6 (21 March 1908), 22-23; *Byposten* 5/7 (4 April 1908), 26-27; *Byposten* 5/8 (18 April 1908), 30-31; *Byposten* 5/9 (2 May 1908), 41-43; *Byposten* 5/12 (13 June 1908), 46-47; *Byposten* 5/13 (27 June 1908), 49-50; *Byposten* 5/15 (11 July 1908), 54-55; *Byposten* 5/15 (11 July 1908), 58-60; Minnie F. Abrams, ''Fru Mukdi i Indien'', *Byposten* 5/16 (15 August 1908), 61; T.B. Barratt, ''I Indien'', *Byposten* 5/16 (15 August 1908), 61-62; *Byposten* 5/17 (29 August 1908), 66-68; *Byposten* 5/18 (12 September 1908), 70-72; *Byposten* 5/19 (26 September 1908), 73-75; Idem, ''I Palestina'', *Byposten* 5/20 (10 October 1908), 77-80.
23. 'Alliance-Aandd'', *Byposten* 5/21 (24 October 1908), 81.
24. T.B. Barratt, ''An urgent Call for Charity and Unity'', *Confidence* 2/4 (February 1911), 29-31; 2/5 (March 1911), 63-65.
25. A.A. Boddy, ''Unity, not uniformity'', *Confidence* 2/5 (March 1911), 60.
26. T.B. Barratt, ''Konferensen i Hamburg'', *Byposten* 5/24 (December 1908), 94-95; 6/1 (1 January 1909), 2-3; 6/2 (15 January 1909), 7-8; 6/4 (15 February 1909), 13-14. See analysis of this and other conferences by Cornelis van der Laan, ''The Proceedings of the Leaders' Meetings (1908-1911) and the International Pentecostal Council (1912-1914)'', *EPTA Bulletin* 6/3 (1987), 76-96.
27. Edvard Gerrard, ''Konferensen in London'', *Byposten* 6/12 (15 June 1909), 45-48.
28. T.B. Barratt, ''Konferensen i Sunderland'', *Byposten* 6/12 (15 June 1909), 48-52; *Byposten* 6/13 (1 July 1909), 54-56; *Byposten* 6/14 (15 July 1909), 58-60.

12

Discerning the Body: Analysis of Pentecostalism in the Netherlands

Cornelis van der Laan

In this historical analysis the main developments of Pentecostalism in the Netherlands are briefly traced with an emphasis on the formation of national bodies of Pentecostal assemblies.[1] Within the scope of this article it has not been possible to include the rise of the Charismatic Renewal.

Pentecostalism in the Netherlands started as an ecumenical revival movement. There was no intention to build a new church, but rather to be a blessing for the existing churches. Gradually the movement developed into separate denominations, consisting of loosely organized local assemblies with a more or less congregational structure. The beginning lies with an independent circle of believers in Amsterdam, searching for more power in their spiritual life. This group was largely made up of ex-Salvationists and was led by the couple Gerrit and Wilhelmine Polman.

Birth and establishment 1907-1930

Birth

Gerrit Roelof Polman (1868-1932) and his wife Wilhelmine J.M. Blekkink (1878-1961) were the undisputed leaders during the birth and formative years of Pentecostalism in the Netherlands (1907-1930). To a large extent they were responsible for the shape the movement assumed.

Gerrit Polman was born in a hamlet near Zwolle, son of a farmer. On Sundays his mother used to take him to the Netherlands Reformed Church in Zwolle. He experienced a religious conversion when he turned twenty. Shortly thereafter (1890) he joined the Salvation Army, which had just entered Holland. Through Arthur S. Booth Clibborn, commissioner of the Salvation Army in the Netherlands, Polman got acquainted with the healing evangelist John Alexander Dowie and his Christian Catholic Church in Zion, Michigan. In 1902 Booth Clibborn resigned from the Salvation Army and joined the Zion church of Dowie. Polman and other officers from the Salvation Army followed Booth Clibborn in this step.

In 1903 Gerrit Polman married Wilhelmine Blekkink, who had been raised in the Dutch Indies. The same year the couple moved to Zion to study theology and languages. In January 1906 they returned to Holland as messengers of the Zion church. The same month a prayer group was started in Amsterdam. Shortly after arrival Dowie was deposed causing the ties with the Zion church to be loosened.

Remembering the revival in Wales (1904) the members of the prayer circle in Amsterdam started to long for a new work of the Holy Spirit in their midst. By means of the *Apostolic Faith* paper they received news of the revival in Los Angeles (1906), where believers were baptized in the Holy Spirit and were speaking in tongues. In the course of 1907 these manifestations penetrated Europe as well: Norway, Germany, England and Switzerland. In October 1907 Mrs. Polman was the first of the prayer circle to receive the baptism with the Holy Spirit in this way. Many others were soon to follow. The relation with Zion was definitely broken.

Spreading the Message

In April 1908 Polman started the publication of the *Spade Regen* (Latter Rain) paper, that would continue till 1931. Next to *Spade Regen* the illustrated monthly *Klanken des Vredes* (Sounds of Peace - from 1915 till 1929) appeared for the purpose of evangelization. From Amsterdam the Pentecostal message gradually spread over the country. In 1912 the beautiful Emmanuel Hall was erected, one of the first buildings in Europe especially designed for Pentecostal gatherings. The larger part was allocated to lodgings. No wonder it became known as the Pilgrim's Home. Many believers from surrounding countries would travel to Amsterdam to receive the Spirit baptism in this centre. The Emmanuel Hall also housed a training school for missionaries. The mission program was connected with the British Pentecostal Missionary Union, until Polman in 1920 founded the Nederlands Pinksterzendingsgenootschap (Netherlands Pentecostal Missionary Society).

Under the dynamic and charismatic leadership of the Polmans the Dutch movement kept close contact with Pentecostals from neighboring countries. The couple were much appreciated speakers at international conferences and contributed to Pentecostalism in Great Britain, Germany, Switzerland, Belgium and France. Polman was part of the International Pentecostal Advisory Council, that during 1912-1914 held meetings in Sunderland and Amsterdam. During and after World War I Polman played a significant mediating role between the German and British Pentecostals culminating in the international conference in Amsterdam 1921, where the German and British brethren met again for the first time after the war. These international contacts, together with a considerable foreign mission program, gave the Dutch Pentecostals the self-respect needed in the face of blunt disapproval at home. It strengthened their unity and confirmed their desire to be loyal to the great commission of Christ.

During 1920-1930 the national figure of Pentecostals (including their children), estimated by this survey, reached about 2.000.[2] In Amsterdam (where the percentage of the unchurched was more than twice the national figure) probably one quarter of the Pentecostal members came from among the unchurched.[3] A survey among members of the Amsterdam Pentecostal assembly indicated that nearly two-thirds of the members were added through conversion. Pentecostalism had more success in urban, than in provincial areas. The members mostly came from the working class; supplemented with some from the middle-class (shopkeepers and tradespeople), and a few from the upper-class.

Pentecostal liturgy, with its appeal to human emotion and emphasis on equality in fellowship (all are brothers and sisters), was more inviting to members of the working-class than the traditional church services, and was better suited to meet the need of those who felt alienated from church and society. Urbanization, social dissatisfaction and the loss of function of the traditional churches most likely have been contributing factors in the decision of people to become Pentecostal. Through conversion and Spirit baptism they became members of a new community. The warm fellowship and encouragement (irrespective of education or social status) to fully participate in worship, compensated their adverse social circumstances.

From Frustration to Organization

The purpose of the Pentecostal movement in the eyes of Polman was not to build a church of its own, but the building up of the existing churches. With reference to Dowie's hostile attitude towards the churches, this represents a remarkable change. Dowie saw as the goal of the Christian Catholic Church of Zion "to smash every other church in existence".[4] After his Spirit baptism Polman wrote: "This blessing of God has filled my heart with overflowing love for my fellow-Christians and I cannot but love them all."[5]

Nevertheless the Dutch Pentecostal movement in its infancy years became marked by clergy of various churches as false or even demonic. The Berlin Declaration of 1909, in which 56 leaders of the German *Gemeinschafstbewegung* condemned Pentecostalism as demonic, had prejudiced many in the Netherlands.

Polman's longing "to loose ourselves as the Pentecostal movement into the larger body of Christianity" was frustrated.[6] Much to his regret he eventually organized the movement into Pentecostal assemblies and introduced membership cards. The wish to revive the churches slowly faded away. In the end Polman failed morally, which led to his withdrawal in 1930. This sad development caused many to turn away from the Pentecostal movement.

Reconstruction 1930-1950

The national unity that had characterized the first period disappeared with the removal of Polman. Three new leaders came to the fore: Peter van der Woude (1895-1978), Piet Klaver (1890-1970) and Nico Vetter (1890-1945). Klaver and Vetter were trained by Polman. Both returned from the mission field: Klaver from China and the Dutch Indies and Vetter from Venezuela. Van der Woude never met Polman. After a long stay in England, where he was converted and had become assistant pastor of the Pentecostal assembly of Summer Road Chapel at Peckam, London, he returned to Holland in 1932.

Van der Woude started a new work in Rotterdam under the name Assembly of God (Gemeente Gods). Through many evangelistic crusades, often with British evangelists, a number outposts were rapidly founded. From 1933 he published a periodical and gave it the familiar title *Spade Regen*. After World War II it was continued as the *Volle Evangelie Koerier* (Full Gospel Courier).

Klaver became pastor of the old Pentecostal assembly at Amsterdam in 1933. From there he tried to restore the national work of Polman, in part by the publication of *Kracht van Omhoog* (Power from on High - from 1937).

Vetter became pastor of the existing Pentecostal assembly at Haarlem. Vetter too started a national network and published a paper *Het Middernachtelijk Geroep* (The Midnight Cry - from 1937). Under the name Emmanuel six Pentecostal assemblies closely co-operated with Vetter.

Rivalry between the three leaders hindered a broad national co-operation. The war years brought the Pentecostals closer together. The United Pentecostal Assemblies in the Netherlands (Vereenigde Pinkstergemeenten in Nederland), founded in 1941, changed into the Pentecostal Assemblies in the Netherlands (Pinkstergemeenten in Nederland) in 1944, which as from 1947 was known as Full Gospel Assemblies (Volle Evangelie Gemeenten). A mission fund for the training of evangelists, pastors and missionaries was founded. Selected candidates were sent to the International Bible Training Institute (IBTI) that had just started at Leamington Spa, England. Among the first students of IBTI was also the young Walter J. Hollenweger and his fellow-countryman Ernst A. Graf. In 1952 a new start was made with the foundation of the Brotherhood of Full Gospel Assemblies in the Netherlands (Broederschap van Volle Evangelie Gemeenten in Nederland). The *Volle Evangelie Koerier* became its official paper.

Growth and Fragmentation since 1950

The growth of the present Pentecostal movement dates from the fifties. The visits of foreign healing evangelists, the repatriates from the Dutch Indies and the rise of

Streams of Power (Stromen van Kracht) were very influencial. After the Osborn crusade (1958) the developments began to move faster. The ministry of Johan Maasbach took large proportions. Under the inspiring leadership of businessman Peter van den Dries, the Full Gospel Business Men (Volle Evangelie Zakenlieden) organized mass meetings called Joy Days (Vreugdedagen). The Beukenstein conferences (1960-1968) and the developments around the periodical *Kracht van Omhoog* led to the 'Power from on High' persuasion, an important branch of Dutch Pentecostalism. Part of the Pentecostal assemblies, organized as the Brotherhood of Pentecostal Assemblies (Broederschap van Pinkstergemeenten), established a bible school. Other assemblies organized themselves as Full Gospel Fellowship (Volle Evangelie Gemeenschap). The 'One Way Day' youth rallies and the annual camp meetings around Whitsuntide (since 1974 held at Vierhouten) of Ben Hoekendijk and Foundation Revival (Stichting Opwekking) drew thousands of people. With the growth, fragmentation increased too. Hereafter the main developments, which led to the formation of national groups or streams are briefly outlined.

Healing Evangelists

The fifties were the hey-day of the healing evangelists, also in the Netherlands. The visit of the Indian evangelist Lam Jeeveratnam in January 1950 was small in scale, but had dramatic results. During meetings in Amsterdam and Rotterdam demons were expelled. Some people fell on the floor shouting. This was so unusual in Holland that the evangelist was arrested by the police and deported back to England. Jeeveratnam later sighed that he never met so many "pious demons" as in the Netherlands.[7]

Visits of Elaine Richards (1951-1952), a lay Anglican and member of the Order of St. Luke, and Hermann Zaiss (1952, 1953 and 1956), a German businessman, received considerable attention from the churches and made deep impressions. Their presence stirred much interest in the message of divine healing within the mainline churches. The arrival of Zaiss resulted also in the formation of a number of circles under the name Ecclesia, all of which have now ceased.

For the Pentecostal movement the visit of Tommy Lee Osborn in 1958 was the climax. The open-air meetings in The Hague and Groningen were prepared by an interdenominational committee. The public attendance was unprecedented. Some of the meetings in The Hague drew more than 100,000 people. Many touched by the crusade joined the Pentecostal movement.

For months debates were held in the ecclesiastical press between advocates and opponents of this healing *en masse*. Pentecostal leaders were active in making use of the new opportunities. Osborn's books were translated and sold by the thousands. The film *Holland Wonder*, a production of Osborn, was a success for many years. Young evangelists like Johan Maasbach and Ben Hoekendijk started their own healing crusades. In the advertisements Maasbach was announced as the interpreter of Osborn.

Johan Maasbach World Mission

Johan Maasbach was born in 1918 at Rotterdam. At the age of nine he was converted during a Salvation Army meeting. For many years he worked as a cook on an ocean liner. During World War II he lived for several years in New York. After the war he received his Spirit baptism in a small Pentecostal assembly at Rotterdam. From 1950 he crossed the country with his own evangelistic tent. In February 1952 he married Willy Klumper. Under the name Volle Evangelie Zending the couple pioneered a new assembly at Gouda. A deep valley, the death of their third child in June 1958, was followed by a peak: the Osborn crusade. In spite of protests from the organizing committee, Osborn chose the unknown Maasbach as his interpreter.

Hereafter the doors became wide open. Nearly every large city received a visit from the Dutch 'Osborn'. With his American style Maasbach managed to build up an impressive work. Next to the many meetings, literature was distributed on a large scale. From 1957 the paper *Genezing* (Healing) was issued sporadically and eventually replaced by the monthly *Nieuw Leven* (New Life) in 1962. In 1961 the weekly broadcast programmes through Radio Luxembourg commenced. When in 1968 the headquarters moved from Gouda to The Hague, the present name Johan Maasbach World Mission (Johan Maasbach Wereldzending) was chosen. Around this time Maasbach started his many evangelistic journeys abroad. Through buying several monumental church buildings and because of his striking appearance on television, Maasbach became a national figure.

By 1990 his work includes mission offices and children's homes at Semarang, Indonesia, and at Madras, India; an office in New York; a printing plant; publishing house; radio and video studio; travel agency; senior citizens' home; and ten church buildings. Weekly meetings are held in twelve places. In every place officers are appointed under the supervision of the headquarters in The Hague. The total attendance is 3,600 (1990).

Streams of Power

In 1952 the Canadian B.G. Leonard, an independent evangelist and leader of the Christian Training Centre at Calgary, gave courses on the spiritual gifts at the home of A. Njiokiktjien at Zeist. Among the students were the Pentecostal pastor Peter Quist and the Swiss missionary Ernst A. Graf, as well as Elisabeth Hoekendijk and Elma van Riemsdijk. Leonard taught that, by means of prayer and the laying on of hands for the baptism with the Holy Spirit, every believer would receive all nine gifts mentioned in 1 Corinthians 12:8-10.

The use of these gifts had, according to Leonard, nothing to do with mysticism and ecstasy but was a matter of down-to-earth faith. Where the old Pentecostal assemblies instructed believers to 'wait upon the Spirit' and to 'sanctify' themselves, Leonard stated that every believer simply had to pick up the gifts. Leonard saw speaking in tongues not as an act of the Holy Spirit, but as an act of the believer. The believer, not the Holy Spirit, speaks in tongues. Thereby Leonard emphasized the human element. Out of fear for 'foreign fire', most of the Dutch Pentecostal leaders repudiated the teachings of Leonard. Nevertheless through Streams of Power the same approach would greatly influence the Pentecostal and Charismatic movements.

Upon departure, Leonard laid hands on his students thus ordaining them as prophet, teacher or apostle (Quist) to spread the message in Holland. Elma van Riemsdijk, appointed as teacher, started to give courses on the spiritual gifts in Leusden and Amersfoort. Among her students were Wim Verhoef (who was to become the leader of the Charismatic Renewal), Albert H. van den Heuvel (who later served as the General Secretary of the Netherlands Reformed Church) and Karel Hoekendijk.

Karel Hoekendijk (1904-1987) was a son of the Netherlands Reformed missionary C.J. Hoekendijk. Karel's brother, Johannes C. Hoekendijk, was professor of Mission at the University of Utrecht. Karel spent his youth in the Dutch Indies, in West-Java. At the age of eleven he was sent to a boarding school in the Netherlands where he was trained as an architectural draughtsman. Returning to Java, he was converted on the boatdeck, age nineteen. All his applications to various bible schools were turned down, so he decided to become an artist. At the Academy of Fine Arts in Rotterdam he met Elisabeth la Rivière. They married in 1930.

Thereafter his artistic career commenced. He became completely absorbed by his work. Meanwhile, Elisabeth experienced a spiritual renewal. She was baptized by immersion in a Pentecostal assembly and followed the course from Leonard. A dangerous heart disease immobilized Karel. After prayer and the laying on of hands by a Pentecostal lady, he was instantly healed. It was Spring 1953, Karel was 48 years and grandfather. From then onwards he would be an itinerant healing evangelist.

Without any theological training, except for the course from Elma van Riemsdijk, he started to lead meetings in Bilthoven and from then on in other places. As from December 1953 the monthly *Levend Water* (Living Water) appeared. In April 1954 the name was changed to *Stromen van Kracht* (Streams of Power).

The new movement did not want to become a church. Therefore meetings were held during the week in the evenings. In 1957 meetings were held in 21 places and four full-timers carried on the work. Also the two sons of Karel, Ben and Frans, and the two daughters, Els and Liebje, were fully engaged in the ministry. Elisabeth led the songs, prophesied and taught. Following the pattern of Leonard, she gave fourteen-day courses on the spiritual gifts. The teachings of Leonard were translated and, against Leonard's will, published by Streams of Power.

The movement was looked upon with suspicion by both the Pentecostal assemblies and the mainline churches. When Hoekendijk in 1957 started to administer the Lord's Supper and baptism by immersion, he was completely denounced by the churches. The Netherlads Reformed minister Wim Verhoef, who had been a member of the editorial board of *Stromen van Kracht*, pulled out and with others commenced the periodical *Vuur* (Fire), which was the start of the charismatic renewal in Holland.

In his paper Hoekendijk now pleaded for the formation of autonomous local assemblies, free from every yoke of slavery and led by the Holy Spirit. Streams of Power, however, remained a movement and did not become an organization. At the end of the fifties the ministry of Karel and Elisabeth Hoekendijk extended to Switzerland, Germany and Belgium. From 1960 until the death of Karel in 1987, their ministry was largely abroad, leading large crusades in South-Africa, Surinam, West-Indies, Indonesia, Sri Lanka, India, Japan and Australia.

In some countries, missionaries of Streams of Power were left behind to follow up the work. In 1969 Kees and Fieke Goedhart returned from the mission field because of serious internal problems in Streams of Power in the Netherlands. Streams of Power fell apart as a national movement. Goedhart considered it his duty to build a solid homebase for the missionaries abroad. In the same year he therefore founded the mission society Mission and Assembly (Zending en Gemeente). From now on mission was carried out with the support of local assemblies. A number of Streams of Power circles in the Netherlands developed into independent local assemblies. In 1972 they united in the Federation of Full Gospel Assemblies (Federatie van Volle Evangelie Gemeenten). This federation amalgamated in 1978 with the Full Gospel Fellowship (Volle Evangelie Gemeenschap). The periodical *Stromen van Kracht* gradually changed into a newsletter of the missionary couple Hoekendijk and as from 1968 was simple called *Nieuwsbrief* (Newsletter).

Through the ministry of Streams of Power many thousands in the Netherlands received the Spirit baptism. Dozens of them became pastors and missionaries. Ben Hoekendijk followed in the footsteps of his father by becoming an independent evangelist. His organization Foundation Revival (Stichting Opwekking) is very active in evangelization. His periodical, baring the same name *Opwekking*, is read widely. In 1990 Ben suddenly left Foundation Revival, leaving the work to be continued by his sister Els and her husband Peter Vlug. Brother Frans Hoekendijk is director of the conference centre The Fountain Spring (De Bron) - originally set up by Streams of Power -, where the Charismatic Renewal holds its biannual National Conventions.

Conference Centre Beukenstein

During the period 1960-1968 the so-called Beukenstein conferences were held, named after the conference centre Beukenstein in Driebergen. The invitation for the first "Sanctification Meeting" in December 1960 read as follows: "These meetings are only for children of God searching for more holiness and power. There will be no praying for the sick and for those bound".[8] Practice, however, differed from precept. From the start exorcism had an important part. Jo van den Brink, editor of *Kracht van Omhoog*, reported: "Of course we did pray with the sick and bound during this weekend. After listening to the message of bondage and battle against the powers in the air, nearly all visitors came forward to be set free".[9] By means of prophecies, revelations and visions, the members of the team received insight in this new ministry.

The initiative for the conference came from Izaak Roose (born 1919). He and his wife, together with Mr. and Mrs. Hijink and Mr. and Mrs. De Groot, had spent many nights in prayer for revival during the preceding year. These three couples, together with Jo van den Brink, Jan van Gijs and Riemer de Graaf, formed the leading team of the Beukenstein conferences that were held on a regular basis for a period of eight years. Many weekends and 'edification weeks' followed. Christians from all churches and circles came and experienced the 'full gospel'. Every year hundreds were baptized by immersion in a swimming pool at Amersfoort.

In 1965 special days for pastors and elders with their spouses were held. These days served to unite the vision. From the young people's weekends the work Operation Pentecostal Fire (Operatie Pinkstervuur) developed. Young people received some training at Beukenstein for short term evangelization in Holland and abroad. From 1965 conferences, especially for foreign visitors, were organized.[10] In 1966 one edification week was held in Southern France, near Grenoble. Izaak Roose regularly preached in Brussels, Geneva, Kaiserslautern and Sheffield.

In 1964 Van den Brink wrote that the ministry at Beukenstein perhaps would have a temporal character, with the purpose of stimulating the assemblies to do the same. At the end of 1968, after the early death of Jan van Gijs, the conferences ended when the new owner of the Beukenstein centre had the building demolished. In the meantime the message brought here during eight years had carried fruit. Across the country new assemblies had deliberately chosen the name Full Gospel Assembly (Volle Evangelie Gemeente) of which many practiced the message of Beukenstein. For the time being *Kracht van Omhoog* remained to serve as the contact paper for all involved.

Power from on High

Kracht van Omhoog was founded in 1937 by Piet Klaver as a modest four-page periodical with a small circulation. In 1941 the brothers Henk and Jo van den Brink joined the editorial board. From 1945-1958 Henk van den Brink was editor-in-chief. Henk was much involved in the introduction of Youth for Christ in the Netherlands in 1946 and for several years served as chairman of their board. In the years after World War II, *Kracht van Omhoog* became the most influential periodical in Pentecostal circles.

Henk van den Brink (1904-1986) and Johannes Emmanuel van den Brink (1909-1989) grew up in an orthodox Reformed family at Haarlem. Both became teachers. Through their sister Maria they came into contact with the Pentecostal assembly at Amsterdam. In 1936 Jo received the baptism with the Holy Spirit. Although he received official recognition as a pastor of the United Pentecostal Assemblies in 1942, he kept his membership with the Gereformeerde Kerken (Reformed Churches) until 1944. When Henk withdrew from *Kracht van Omhoog* in 1958, Jo became the new editor-in-chief. In the same year Jo started a new assembly in Gorinchem and became its pastor. In 1960 he was one of the founders of the Full Gospel Business Men in the Netherlands.

The expelling of demons from Christians as occurred at Beukenstein met a lot of resistance from fellow-Christians. Van den Brink used his periodical to answer the objections. In trying to find a biblical legitimation for this practice, he developed several controversial teachings. He repudiated the traditional doctrine of original sin. Instead he claimed that human beings are not sinful in themselves, and that every sin is caused by contact with a demon. With this teaching he clashed with the Brotherhood of Pentecostal Assemblies, of which he was a member. In 1966 he withdrew. The controversies would only become stronger in the coming years. In 1966 his first article on spiritual Israel appeared. Van den Brink repudiated the expectation commonly held among Pentecostals that there would come a restoration of the natural Israel. In a series on eschatology, he blamed the Pentecostals for having uncritically accepted the dispensational eschatology of the Maranatha movement. Van den Brink also opposed the doctrine of the pre-tribulation rapture of the church.

At the end of the Beukenstein period, C. de Groot had a prophetic vision of a 'higher way'. Henceforth the new look at the battle against the demons in heavenly places would become known as the 'higher way' or the 'teaching of the kingdom of heavens'. According to Van den Brink it involved an absolute breach with the historic churches and the 'teachings of the fathers': "Although we admire the zeal and effort to serve the Lord many of the forefathers had, we can only think of them with pity, because they were unaware of the full salvation. Their zeal was a zeal without discernment".[11] But it also meant a separation among Pentecostals. Those who did not share the vision of the 'Higher Way' were called 'useless Pentecostal slaves', who together with the Maranatha Christians would be cast into outer darkness, where there is weeping and knashing of teeth (cf. Matt. 25:30).[12]

Van den Brink considered himself a "pioneer in the *terra incognita* of the heavenly regions" and believed that Jesus Himself had handed him the keys.[13] The use of three keys: (1) God is good, (2) the devil is evil, and (3) Christ is Lord, led to the understanding that God is only good: "If you do not accept this axiom, you are going astray in the heavenly places. God is the Father of Lights and you may never attribute something that is dark to Him".[14] This was also the starting-point for Osborn. Van den Brink, however, went further by applying it to Scripture itself. For instance by arguing that the commission to Abraham to sacrifice his son (Gen. 22) did not come from God, but from the devil, since a good God would not request a human sacrifice.

The contacts abroad established during the Beukenstein period led to the publication of foreign editions of *Kracht van Omhoog* in English, French, Italian and Portuguese: *Power from on High*, *Puissance d'en Haut*, *Pensieri dall'Alto*, *Podor do Alto*.[15] Some of Van den Brink's books have been published in four languages. An international cassette service mails the taped message in seven languages. Missionary work in Brazil and Italy is supported by the Dutch assemblies.

Through his articles in *Kracht van Omhoog*, his many books and lectures, Van den Brink had a strong influence in a large number of full gospel assemblies. Power from on High never became a denomination, but did become the designation for assemblies in agreement with the message of the periodical. These assemblies gradually became isolated from the other Pentecostal assemblies. National and regional gatherings for pastors and elders provided for mutual contact and a sense of unity.

Some pastors, not in agreement with the isolated position, started meetings at Utrecht in 1973. The group never received an official name, but became known as the Utrecht group. The assemblies involved chose for a milder position and for more contact with other Pentecostal assemblies. In 1987 the group amalgamated with the Full Gospel Assemblies in the Netherlands.

Van den Brink started to slow down in 1981. His son-in-law Peter Bronsveld took over as editor-in-chief of *Kracht van Omhoog* and as pastor of the assembly at Gorinchem. Van den Brink's prediction: "Peter will certainly work towards overcoming our isolated position", has proven to be right. Gradually the periodical assumed a more balanced position, without forsaking the specific teachings. In 1990 there were 37 assemblies with in total 6,000 members, involved in Power from on High. Some of these assemblies are unhappy with the new openness and as it seems now will move on independently in the 'Higher Way' of the Van den Brink era.

Brotherhood of Pentecostal Assemblies in the Netherlands

The search for national fellowship has already been mentioned. Out of the United Pentecostal Assemblies and the Full Gospel Assemblies came the foundation of the Brotherhood of Full Gospel Assemblies in the Netherlands in 1952. Only pastors and other ministers were member. As from January 1954 the *Volle Evangelie*

Koerier (Full Gospel Courier) became the official organ. Support came from the Swedish missionaries J. Hildring Brohede, Wendel J.D. Malmström, Stig R. Sagström and Göte Eugen Johansson. Weekly broadcast programmes through IBRA (International Broadcasting Radio Association), an initiative of the Swedish Pentecostals, resulted in many new contacts, especially in the southern (Roman-Catholic) provinces of Brabant and Limburg. Assemblies in Breda, Eindhoven and Treebeek were founded.

The Osborn campaign, co-organized by the Brotherhood, gave a tremendous impulse. Visits of David J. du Plessis were also of fundamental importance. This Pentecostal 'ambassador' made a strong contribution to the subsequent dialogue with the Netherlands Reformed Church. He stimulated the Brotherhood to open a bible school in Groningen and through him the contacts with the North American Assemblies of God were established.

The foundation of the bible school required a corporate body. This led to the foundation of the Brotherhood of Pentecostal Assemblies in the Netherlands (Broederschap van Pinkstergemeenten in Nederland) as a denomination in 1960. Although local assemblies could become members, in practice it remained a fellowship of pastors. The amalgamation of the periodicals *Volle Evangelie Koerier* and *Pinksterklanken* (Pentecostal Sounds) led to publication of *De Pinksterboodschap* (Pentecostal Message) in May 1960. In October 1960 the Netherlands Pentecostal Bible School was opened in Groningen with Ernst A. Graf as Director. A two-year programme was offered.

With fifty pastors in 1961 membership had doubled in two years. Annual conferences during Whitsuntide drew crowds of 1,000 people. The pastoral letter from the Netherlands Reformed Church *De Kerk en de Pinkstergroepen* (The Church and the Pentecostal groups) in 1960, was answered by the Brotherhood the following year with *De Pinkstergemeente en de Kerk* (The Pentecostal Assembly and the Church). The promising dialogue soon came to grief, partly because of internal tensions among Pentecostals. The Beukenstein conferences and the movement Streams of Power were opposed in Brotherhood circles. The mass meetings, 'Joy Days', organized by Full Gospel Business Men during 1963-1967 for a while managed to bring the whole range of Pentecostals under one roof, but ended in discord.

In 1966 the Brotherhood was reorganized. Again the bible school was the immediate cause. The bible school in Groningen failed and was closed in 1964. Support was secured from the Assemblies of God (U.S.A.) for a new start. In 1965 missionary R.L. Leach was sent to the Netherlands to lay a solid base for a new bible school. The co-operation with the Assemblies of God implied that the Brotherhood had to adapt the constitution, in particular the statement of faith, to the North-American model. Plans for this renewal were accepted in February 1966. It meant a choice for a firm union of local assemblies with a clear identity. A number of members preferred a less formal fellowship and stepped out. In 1967 the reorganization was finalized with the installation of the new executive council. The same year the Central Pentecostal Bible School was opened in The Hague with R.L. Leach as Director. The 22 students at the start of the new three-year program surpassed all expectations in terms of numbers.

After the presidency of Dirk Voordewind (1967-1969) and Johan J. Frinsel (1969-1975), Herman N. van Amerom has occupied this position since 1975. The membership of local assemblies has been increasingly emphasized. The 53 member-assemblies have in total 8,600 members (1991). Personal membership of the Brotherhood (130 in 1991) is open to pastors, evangelists, teachers, missionaries and pastoral workers with no restriction for women. In 1991 the first woman was elected to the executive council. The Brotherhood is a co-operation of autonomous local assemblies designed to execute tasks that usually cannot be done by a single local assembly. The Brotherhood has its own ministerial training institute; a training school for discipleship; a women's department; a youth department (with 4,000 members); a social outreach (Teen Challenge); a deparment for Sunday school materials (Ezra); a home mission's department; and periodicals: *Parakleet* (Paraclete), *Oogsttijd Magazine* (Harvest Magazine), *Christina* and *Out-Fit*.

As well as its affiliation with the Assemblies of God, the Brotherhood is a member of the Pentecostal European Fellowship. In the Netherlands the Brotherhood is one of the sixteen denominations participating in the official consultation between the churches and the government.

Full Gospel Assemblies in the Netherlands and Belgium

After World War II many Pentecostal assemblies showed a preference for the name Full Gospel Assembly. The predecessor of the present Brotherhood of Pentecostal Assemblies until 1959 was called Brotherhood of Full Gospel Assemblies. The names Pentecostal and Full Gospel were more or less synonymous. Assemblies derived from Streams of Power or from Beukenstein deliberately chose the name Full Gospel. They considered themselves 'new' Pentecostals in contrast to the 'old' Pentecostals, among whom the Pentecostal assemblies from before Osborn were categorized.

When the Brotherhood of Pentecostal Assemblies reorganized itself in 1966, in reaction a few months later the Federation van Full Gospel Assemblies was established by J.E. van den Brink, W.J. Lentink, P. Vlug and H. Blankespoor. The Federation wanted to break with every petrifaction and "Pentecostal papism" The initiative was not a success and did not survive the second meeting.

In May 1969 the Full Gospel Fellowship (Volle Evangelie Gemeenschap) was founded. Membership was open to assemblies represented by pastors and elders. The organizational part was minimal. The fellowship was basically formed by regular meetings for pastors and elders at Hilversum.

In 1972 eleven assemblies rooted in Streams of Power formed the Federation of Full Gospel Assemblies. After a few years the close relationship with the Full Gospel Fellowship in goal and structure became apparent. This resulted in an amalgamation in 1978. The Federation entered with four local assemblies (the other seven moved on independently) and the Fellowship with nine. The name changed into Full Gospel Assemblies in the Netherlands (Volle Evangelie Gemeenten in Nederland). Later on Belgium would be added to the name. The character of the meetings in Hilversum remained the same. In 1980 the Fellowship was officially registered as a denomination. Only assemblies have voting rights. Missionaries and evangelists may have personal membership without voting rights. Until now there have been no denominational activities in the areas of mission, evangelization, youth, education, publication and social outreach.

In 1987 an amalgamation with the Utrecht group was realized without changing the name. There are 42 member assemblies with a total of 8,400 members (1991). For several years the national boards of the Full Gospel Assemblies and the Brotherhood meet regularly for prayer and fellowship. Since 1989 these meetings have included representatives of Power from on High, the Full Gospel Bethel Church and since 1991 also Raphael Netherlands.

Churches from the Dutch East Indies

After the transfer of sovereignty of the former Dutch Indies to Indonesia in December 1949 ten-thousands of Indonesians emigrated to the Netherlands during the fifties. Among them were hundreds of Pentecostal believers. After the return of New Guinea to Indonesia in 1962, a second group followed. Rather than joining the existing Pentecostal assemblies, these believers often preferred to form their own assemblies. Five national groups developed: Christian Fellowship The Pentecostal Movmenent (Christelijke Gemeenschap De Pinksterbeweging), Bethel Pentecostal Temple Fellowship Netherlands, Bethel Fellowship Netherlands, Bethel Pentecostal Church Netherlands (Bethel Pinkster Kerk Nederland), Full Gospel Bethel Church (Volle Evangelie Bethel Kerk). Before discussing these groups one by one, a brief sketch of their background in Indonesia is given.

From 1909 Polman mailed *Spade Regen* to the Dutch Indies. In 1920 he announced a request from believers there to send a missionary to Java. Johan Thiessen (1869-1953) became one of the pioneers of the Pentecostal movement in the Dutch Indies. From 1901-1912 he had worked there as a missionary of the Dutch Mennonite church. During his furlough in Europe he became Pentecostal. In 1921 he returned to the Dutch Indies, this time as a Pentecostal missionary. At Bandung, in Java, he founded The Pentecostal Movement (Geraja Gerakan Pentekosta) and started publication of *Dit is het* (This is that - abbreviation of Acts 2:16)).

A new impulse came from the Bethel Temple Pentecostal Assembly in Seattle, U.S.A., founded by W.H. Offiler (1875-1950) in 1914. In 1921 this church sent the missionary couples C. Groesbeek and D. van Klaveren (both of Dutch descent) to the Dutch Indies. Initially they worked on Bali, but in 1922 moved on to Java. In 1924 Groesbeek, Van Klaveren together with W. Bernard (married to a sister of Mrs. Polman and a missionary of the Dutch Pentecostals), F.G. van Gessel and others founded at Bandung The Pentecostal Assembly in the Dutch Indies (De Pinkstergemeente in Nederlandsch Indië). The work grew rapidly and under the name The Pentecostal Church in Indonesia (Gereja Pentekosta di Indonesia) would become a national movement. In 1951 F.G. van Gessel and H.L. Senduk separated and founded the Full Gospel Bethel Church (Gereja Bethel Injil Sepenuh), since 1970 known as Bethel Church Indonesia (Gereja Bethel Indonesia). The Bethel Church Indonesia established an official relationship with the Church of God, Cleveland.

Shortly after the founding of the Bethel Church, Van Gessel separated and founded in New Guinea the Bethel Pentecostal Church. Van Gessel increasingly emphasized his 'Tabernacle Doctrine', which he had been teaching since 1935. After his death in 1957, he was succeeded up by his son-in-law C. Totaijs.

The following groups have in the meantime been formed in the Netherlands.

Christian Fellowship The Pentecostal Movement

Henk Thiessen, the son of Johan Thiessen, moved to the Netherlands in 1958 and founded the Christian Fellowship The Pentecostal Movement (Christelijke Gemeenschap De Pinksterbeweging). The mother-church in Indonesia (Gereja Gerakan Pentekosta) has since then been led by Indonesian believers. The Fellowship has four assemblies next to two groups that meet during weekdays, with in total 325 members (1990). President E. Cornfield is also pastor of the assembly in The Hague. The *Mannakorrels* (Manna Grains) paper appears from time to time. The small Fellowship has maintained contact with the old Pentecostal church at Mülheim, Germany.

Bethel Pentecostal Temple Fellowship Netherlands

C.J.H. Theijs, who had worked with Van Gessel in Indonesia, started home meetings in The Hague in 1952. Since 1956 he published the monthly *Het Volle Evangelie* (The Full Gospel), in which he propagated the tabernacle teachings. Around 1960 the Bethel Pentecostal Temple Netherlands was founded, later called Bethel Pentecostal Temple Fellowship Netherlands, or simply Bethel Temple. In 1963 Theijs moved to Seattle. When after a few months his deputy W.A. Hornung died, there was a vacuum in leadership. In this period C. Totaijs, coming from New Guinea, founded the Bethel Pentecostal Church Netherlands. Theijs returned after three years and regained leadership of the much reduced Bethel Temple. In 1980 Theijs moved to Spain, without arranging for a proper succession. New problems around leadership divided the group into two: Bethel

Pentecostal Temple Fellowship Netherlands and Bethel Fellowship Netherlands.

Bethel Pentecostal Temple Fellowship has six member-churches with a total of 300 members (1990). The periodical *Bethel Nieuws* (Bethel News) has been published since 1980. After the death of Theijs in 1981, official contacts with the Bethel Pentecostal Temple in Seattle were made, resulting in an affiliation. At the same time contacts are maintained with the Gereja Pentekosta di Indonesia, the large Pentecostal church in Indonesia.

Bethel Fellowship Netherlands

E. van der Worm (born 1915), also a pupil of Van Gessel, succeeded Theijs as editor of *Het Volle Evangelie* in 1962. Under the name the Netherlands for Jesus or the Full Gospel, he published a series of books and brochures by W.H. Offiler, F.G. van Gessel, C.J.H. Theijs and E. van der Worm. From manuscripts of Van Gessel he edited the book *Tabernakelonderzoek* (Study in the Tabernacle). After the departure of Theijs in 1980, Van der Worm and others tried to revive the lagging fellowship under the name Bethel Fellowship Netherlands. This resulted in a split from the original group. In 1987 Van der Worm ended the publication of *Het Volle Evangelie* and withdrew as pastor of the assemblies at Rotterdam and Utrecht. The presidency of the Bethel Fellowship Netherlands was taken over by H. Siliakus in 1988. Siliakus edits the bi-monthly *De Tempelbode* (The Temple Messenger), that became the official organ of the fellowship. The Fellowship has six member-churches with in a total of 350 members (1990). There is an increasing contact with the original group Bethel Pentecostal Temple Fellowship Netherlands.

Bethel Pentecostal Church Netherlands

C. Totaijs moved from New Guinea to the Netherlands in 1961. In Amsterdam he became pastor of an already-existing Pentecostal assembly. In 1963 he founded the Bethel Pentecostal Church Netherlands Bethel Pinksterkerk Nederland), which under his leadership developed into a firm, but closed and exclusive fellowship. Totaijs refined the tabernacle doctrine of his father in law Van Gessel and called it 'Bridal Doctrine'. There are twenty member-assemblies with in a total of 3,500 members (1990). The national board is formed by all assigned pastors and elders. A chairman is chosen for each meeting. Since 1977 the periodical *Bruidstijding* (Bride Tidings) has appeared. In order to propagate the bridal message abroad, Totaijs founded the Bride Tidings International, with the result that the bridal message has also reached Ghana, Nigeria, Zambia and the Philippines.

Full Gospel Bethel Church in the Netherlands

After a visit by H.L. Senduk to the Netherlands, some independent Indonesian assemblies united in 1975 as the Full Gospel Bethel Church in the Netherlands

(Volle Evangelie Bethel Kerk Nederland). Following the example of the mother-church in Indonesia (Gereja Bethel Indonesia), the Full Gospel Bethel Church affiliated with the Church of God in 1982. The fellowship has 16 member-churches with a total of 2,600 members (1990). There are departments for Sunday school, youth, women and education. Contrary to the other Bethel groups in the Netherlands, the Full Gospel Bethel Church does not teach the tabernacle doctrine and is more open to contacts with other Pentecostal groups.

The Door

The Door (De Deur) is a new phenomenon in Dutch Pentecostalism. Its spiritual father is the American Wayman Mitchell, pastor of the Potter's House Christian Centre, Preston, Arizona. In 1970 Mitchell, a former burglar and since 1960 minister of the International Church of the Foursquare Gospel, became pastor of a small church in Preston. Fascinated by the rise of the Jesus People, he started to attune all his church activities to evangelization and youth. Out of this rose a church with a special character. According to Mitchell, Christianity had become too 'female'. He taught his assembly to sing and praise in a 'masculine' fashion. As from 1973 the church began to grow and to extend to other cities, states and countries. Mitchell's antipathy to female leadership, bible schools and denominations led to a withdrawal from the Foursquare denomination in 1984. In 1989 there were 900 assemblies associated with the Preston church, of which 40 were in Europe (the Netherlands, Germany, England, Spain, Sweden, Norway, Belgium, Northern Ireland).

Mitchell's first visit to the Netherlands was in 1978. He addressed a small meeting at Haarlem. Supported by Mitchell a small assembly was launched at Steenwijk by Hugo Hisgen. After some initial problems Rudy van Diermen (born 1960) took over the leadership in 1980 and moved the assembly to Zwolle in 1981. Initially the work was financially carried by the Preston church. After some difficult years the Gospel Church The Door grew to 250 members in 1990. In 1991 there were 19 The Door assemblies with in a total of 700 members.

The meetings are noisy and enthusiastic and largely attended by young people. Following Mitchell, people reject female leadership, bible schools and denominations. Young people are trained in the local assembly. Characteristics are: aggressive evangelization, much (and noisy) prayer, and compulsory tithing. Every meeting is preceded by one hour of prayer. Rudy van Diermen frequently visits the U.S.A. At Zwolle he organizes annual international conferences attended by the sister-assemblies in Europe and representatives from the U.S.A.

Raphael Netherlands

Another recent addition to the Pentecostal family is Raphael Netherlands (Rafaël Nederland), founded by Henk Rothuizen in 1989. Henk Rothuizen, son of a Pentecostal pastor, started an assembly at Hoogblokland in 1980. As a conference speaker and author of *Vader wie ben ik?* (Father, who am I?), he developed a national ministry. In 1987 he established contact with the International Church of the Foursquare Gospel. In co-operation with the Foursquare church, Raphael Netherlands was founded. In 1991 there were 20 assemblies with a total of 1,400 members. The national body has a strong vote in the local assemblies, which is remarkable in Dutch Pentecostalism. The spiritual and organizational policy of local assemblies, including the calling and removing of a pastor, needs the approval of the national leadership.

Evaluation

Initially, Pentecostalism was regarded by outsiders as sectarian and of a temporary nature. Today the Pentecostals are increasingly recognized. Their growth has attracted the interest of academic researchers. Recent sociological research has shown that Pentecostals are above avarage in income and education in the Netherlands. Pentecostal faith is no longer limited to one class of the population, but is present in all layers of society.

The number of Pentecostal believers in the Netherlands in 1991 amounts to 77,000, spread over 560 assemblies. In this article only the groupings of assemblies have been described. The majority of the Dutch Pentecostal assemblies, however, are independent and do not fall under any of the mentioned fellowships. The axiom of the autonomy of the local church, behind which I detect a 'do-it-yourself' mentality, makes many averse to any kind of national organization. Such fragmentation entails a great variety in doctrine, spirituality, structure and liturgy.

A large number of the local assemblies originated by division. Sometimes this is done in harmony in order to found a new assembly. But more often this happens because of disagreements. For this reason, but also when there are differences in doctrine, it is often difficult for Pentecostal assemblies in one city to co-operate.

At the same time there is a general longing for national contacts on a free basis. The annual Agape meals, held since 1976, are a good example. Pastors and elders from all Pentecostal varieties meet round a relevant theme and a meal. Leadership conferences initiated by Youth With A Mission (ended in 1989) have received large attendances.

Next to the large number of independent assemblies, the do-it-yourself mentality of the Dutch Pentecostals is also apparent in an even larger number of foundations of every kind (evangelization, music, children's work, education, social outreach, prevention, mission etc.). Leaders with a different ministry than pastor, are used to instituting their own foundation and machinery to raise money. The do-it-yourself mentality does stimulate initiative and creativity, but at the same time much is done at cross purposes.

The Dutch Pentecostals give a lot of money towards foreign mission, but there is hardly any co-ordination, let alone a strategy. The Dutch Pentecostal missionaries are often pioneers who develop their own ministry on the field, usually independent of the already-existing work and institute their own foundations for raising money.

Pentecostal pastors get annoyed with the money-begging para-church organizations. All fish in the same pool. But the Pentecostal assemblies often have the same do-it-yourself mentality responsible for this development. Assemblies want to do everything themselves, for they are convinced that the assembly is autonomous and God's exclusive means in this end-time. If missionaries are sent out, they ideally must be completely taken care of by a local assembly, without the mediation of any external organization. In practice this ideal is often not attainable and therefore one has to settle for less. Because of the same attitude many assemblies are against bible schools for future ministers. The training, in their eyes, must be done in the local assembly.

The independent spirit might well have to do with Dutch character. But this national character has extra opportunities to develop because of the Pentecostal individualistic spirituality. There is a strong emphasis on the personal element. Rebirth must be a personal experience, the same is true of Spirit baptism and the calling for ministries. Through the baptism with the Holy Spirit Pentecostals claim to be led directly by the Spirit. Dreams, visions and prophecies are sometimes used to validate dictatorial leadership. Emphasis on the personal element is, of course, very important; but when we believe or act as if we do not need the other, we have gone too far. Then we are not discerning the body (1 Cor. 11:29).

Polman's longing for the Pentecostal movement was for it to lose itself in the larger body of Christianity. I see it as a challenge for Pentecostals today to learn from their ecumenical pioneers, among whom I wish to include Walter J. Hollenweger, to understand again what it means to be part of the larger body of Christianity. In Roman Catholic - Pentecostal dialogue, Roman Catholics have in the context of *koinonia* rightly challenged Pentecostals to think of the whole community as a temple of God in which the Spirit dwells (1 Cor. 3:16). May the Spirit of God help us to discern the body.

Notes

1. Source references for this article have been kept short. For extended documentation I refer to: C. van der Laan and P.N. van der Laan, *Pinksteren in beweging* (Kampen, J.H. Kok, 1981); C. van der Laan, *Sectarian Against His Will: Gerrit Roelof Polman and the Birth of Pentecostalism in the Netherlands* (Metuchen, N.J.: Scarecrow Press, 1991); P.N. van der Laan, "The Question of Spiritual Unity: The Dutch Pentecostal Movement in Ecumenical Perspective" (Unpublished Ph.D.

Dissertation, University of Birmingham, 1988).

2. Statistics in this article include children.
3. Stichting Noordholland Provinciaal Opbouworgaan, *Sociale atlas Noord-Holland* (Haarlem: Stichting Noordholland Provinciaal Opbouworgaan, 1963), table "Percentages kerkelijke gezindten per gemeente".
4. Rolvix Harlan, *John Alexander Dowie and the Christian Catholic Apostolic Church in Zion* (Evansville, WI: Press of R.M. Antes, 1906), 91.
5. G.R. Polman to J.H. Gunning J.Hz., Amsterdam, 12 March 1910.
6. *Spade Regen* 18/1 (April 1925), 16.
7. J.E. van den Brink, "De Christelijke Sadhu van India van ons heengegaan," *Kracht van Omhoog* 24/9 (28 October 1960), 7.
8. "Heiligingssamenkomst", *Kracht van Omhoog* 24/11 (25 November 1960), 13.
9. J.E. van den Brink, "Vijf jaar Beukenstein", *Kracht van Omhoog* 29/14 (22 January 1966), 10.
10. Four out of the eleven edification weeks in 1966 were with foreign participants from France, Switzerland, Germany and Belgium. The Dutch sermons were translated into French and English.
11. J.E. van den Brink, *Op hoger grond 3* (Baarn: VEZA, n.d.), 43.
12. J.E. van den Brink, *De tweede bergrede* (Gorinchem: Kracht van Omhoog, n.d.), 143-45.
13. Idem, "De sleutels van het Koninkrijk der Hemelen", *Kracht van Omhoog* 44/8 (6 June 1980), 13.
14. *Kracht van Omhoog* 45/5 (3 April 1981), 3.
15. These are financially independent publications, that translate articles from *Kracht van Omhoog*. Only the English edition is published from Gorinchem.

13

David du Plessis - A Promise Fulfilled

Martin Robinson

Introduction

Knowing of my interest in the Charismatic Movement, my advisor in the Department of Theology suggested that I talk to Professor Walter J. Hollenweger about the possibility of undertaking some post graduate work in the field of Pentecostalism. "What exactly did I have in mind?", the Professor wanted to know. I was a little unsure. My knowledge of Pentecostalism was new and largely experiential. Within a few minutes the Professor had suggested that I make a comparison between two Anglican priests. The one, Michael Harper, was then in the ecclesiastical limelight as the leader of the Charismatic Movement, especially, although not exclusively, amongst Anglicans. The other, Alexander Boddy, had been the Anglican priest in whose church the Pentecostal Movement in Britain had its origins.[1]

This sounded like a promising suggestion, at least it was a proposal and I didn't have another one to offer! I shifted a little uneasily in my seat. I knew who Michael Harper was, but who was Alexander Boddy? It was no good, if I was going to research him, I would have to admit it, I had never heard of him! The confession of my ignorance brought forth a triumphant "Aha" from the Professor and in an instant he was consulting what looked like several metres of bound heavyweights that was in fact his own Doctoral thesis, *Handbuch der Pfingstbewegung*. Sure enough, contained in one of the ten volumes and four hundred individual biographies, was a helpful section on the life of Alexander Boddy.

The *Handbuch* was to be consulted many more times during my Masters research and again during my later Doctoral research on the life and ministry of David du Plessis.[2] As my research progressed, I began to realise that the significance of the *Handbuch* did not just lie in its provision of vast quantities of data on the Pentecostal Movement, valuable as this was. The *Handbuch* represented the first serious attempt, not just to document the Pentecostal Movement, but to understand the very nature of the Pentecostal Movement itself. Hollenweger, in his book *The Pentecostals*, writing of the Pentecostal Movement put it this way:

> Thus when in Chile, Brazil and other countries it has more adherents than all other Protestants, when in France and Russia, Nigeria and South Africa it is far

> and away the most rapidly growing religious group, and when even the intellectuals of Europe and America rediscover with its aid long buried levels of human existence it is not surprising that Roman Catholic theologians and sociologists and even atheistic anthropologists and experts in African studies are beginning to take an interest in the phenomenon.[3]

As Hollenweger began this vital task, David du Plessis acted as an important catalyst. At its most simple level Du Plessis gave Hollenweger much practical assistance. During the 1950's David du Plessis had collected a great deal of information on the worldwide Pentecostal Movement. He was at that time arguably the best informed Pentecostal with regard to the scope, statistics and leadership of the global Pentecostal Movement. He almost certainly knew more leaders around the world on a personal basis than any other Pentecostal. When Hollenweger began work on his *Handbuch*, he began with Du Plessis' existing information. As Hollenweger puts it:

> The two volumes (ms) of Du Plessis were indeed extremely helpful to me at the beginning of my research. It gave me the first contact addresses where I could get more and more precise material.[4]

However, the importance that Hollenweger attached to the contribution of David du Plessis went far beyond the provision of research material. It was as if he recognised in the person of Du Plessis something of what he was trying to articulate in describing the Pentecostal Movement as a whole. It is in the inspirational contribution of Du Plessis to the work of Hollenweger that we come to see something of the importance of Du Plessis to the wider Christian church.

Unlikely Origins

By the time of his death in 1987, David du Plessis had become a recognised figure amongst ecumenical statesmen. He had been listed by a group of North American editors as one of eleven "shapers and shakers of twentieth century religious thought".[5] He had had an audience with the Pope, knew many eminent church leaders around the world on a first name basis and had received numerous honours of an academic and ecclesiastical nature.[6]

It would have been very difficult to have predicted any of these developments on the basis of his life before the age of forty. He was born in 1905, the eldest son of an Afrikaaner family. His father was a rather nominal Christian who had become very disillusioned with Christianity, partly as a result of his experiences fighting the British in the Boer war. His father's later conversion and entry into the newly emerging Pentecostal denomination, the Apostolic Faith Mission of South Africa, meant that the formative religious experiences of the young David du Plessis were of a religious group that exhibited both the experiential vigour and the aggressive sectarianism of the Pentecostal Movement in its infancy.

Du Plessis became a pastor in the Apostolic Faith Mission and then experienced a meteoric rise through the ranks of the denomination's hierarchy. He held a large number of posts, including that of editor of the movement's magazine, principal of their Bible college and general secretary from 1933 to 1947. By 1947 he had seen the dramatic growth of his denomination from approximately 25,000 members to some 50,000 members in a single decade. He had gained a great deal of experience and yet in the course of his rather activist secretaryship had made a number of enemies at the very heart of the movement that he served. At the age of 42 Du Plessis resigned as general secretary to begin a new ministry in Switzerland. In so doing, he left behind all that he had been familiar with: his post as general secretary; the church in which he had grown up; and his native country; all of this for a future that was none too certain.

That uncertain future was worked out first of all in relation to the emerging World Pentecostal Conferences. Following the 1947 World Pentecostal Conference in Zürich, Du Plessis became the new Secretary to the World Conference, a post which he held until 1953. Following the 1953 London Conference, he again launched out, this time into an even more uncertain future as an unpaid, unappointed, unaccountable and unrecognized Pentecostal ambassador to the very churches which had always regarded the Pentecostal Movement with the greatest of suspicion and which had been regarded by Pentecostals as at best sub-Christian but more likely not Christian at all!

It was this unusual, pioneering and ecumenical ministry that won for Du Plessis a special place in the Pentecostal Movement, one which Hollenweger both understand and applauded. However, the nature and scope of Du Plessis' new role was not immediately clear either to Du Plessis or to those who were none too happy with his emerging ministry.

Interpreting the Movement to Others

At the time of the London Conference in 1953, the larger white-led Pentecostal denominations had won for themselves an almost grudging acceptance in the National Association of Evangelicals in the United States. In many other lands, Pentecostals were actively opposed by the established churches. This was especially so in many European and South American countries which had maintained a strong Roman Catholic tradition. Even in countries such as Britain, Pentecostals were described in the pages of some evangelical publications as a cult along with

Mormonism and the Jehovah's Witnesses.[7]

The leaders of many other denominations knew little of Pentecostalism and had probably never met any Pentecostal leaders. So it came as some surprise to Du Plessis to begin to receive invitations to various ecumenical gatherings at which he was asked to give a description of the Pentecostal Movement.[8]

At first, Du Plessis' presentation of the Pentecostal Movement was restricted to a very basic interpretation which really did not go much beyond establishing some kind of personal contact. In his book, *A Man Called Mr. Pentecost*, he describes one of the earliest of his encounters with the leaders of other churches. The one he described took place at the Manhattan office of the World Council of Churches:

> I introduced myself to Dr. Rosswell Barnes, fumbling around for a good reason as to why I should be breaking in on them. But I needn't have worried. I was a Pentecostal, a curiosity. They were glad to see one in the flesh. And they were anything but ogres. They didn't have tails, and I didn't swing from the chandeliers. I spent a full day with them.[9]

The very act of beginning to interpret the Pentecostal Movement to others forced Du Plessis to reflect on the nature of the Pentecostal Movement himself. His research took him in two directions. On the one hand he began to look at the origins of the movement at Azusa Street, and on the other at the diversity of the movement around the world. Frankly, Du Plessis' attempts to understand the origins of the movement were somewhat basic. His efforts to understand the contemporary scene yielded a great deal more fruit. He began to become well-acquainted with the leaders of the predominantly black led Pentecostal churches in North America and with indigenous Pentecostal movements around the world, particularly in Africa and South America. Such intimacy was not likely to endear him to the leaders of the white-led Pentecostal churches with whom he also had to work. Du Plessis carried credentials as a minister from the Assemblies of God in the United States of America. The Assemblies were members of the Pentecostal Fellowship of North America, which although formed in 1948, still had no black-led Pentecostal churches in membership even by the mid 1960's.

Du Plessis' earlier involvement with the World Pentecostal Conference told him that there were considerable differences of view amongst Pentecostals as to who were in the family and who were not. These differences were not just a matter of race although that was clearly one factor. Sometimes there were local difficulties such as in Britain where there was a significant rift between the founder of the Elim Pentecostal Church and the leaders of that same church which resulted in the establishing of the Bible Pattern Church. On other occasions, the issues were more global in nature, such as the worldwide rift between the older Pentecostal groups and the newer Latter Rain element in the Pentecostal Movement. On other occasions, indigenous movements had broken away from the parent missionary body which would often be reluctant to see the breakaway group recognised as part of the Pentecostal family.

Du Plessis had a very inclusive attitude. In part this was related to his very open personality and to some extent he was anxious to demonstrate the numerical significance of the Pentecostal movement around the world as part of his apologetic. To this end, the larger the total number of members and adherents that he could legitimately demonstrate, the better. He began to collect statistical tables of the various movements around the world. Often, he was only able to gain access to this kind of material because of his personal relationships with so many Pentecostal leaders.

The process of collecting data and then interpreting the movement to others clearly led to a radical re-appraisal of the nature of the Pentecostal Movement on the part of Du Plessis himself. His starting-point was quite simple. Pentecostalism consisted of the sum total of Pentecostal churches wherever they may be found in the world. These Pentecostal churches were distinct from any other church by their adherence to and their advocacy of the 'baptism in the Holy Spirit'. Gradually, he began to realise that what connected these very diverse groups was not doctrine or ecclesiology since both of these elements were extremely diverse. He began to see that there was a common spiritual experience that cut across this range of denominational expressions which could be legitimately described and recognised as authentically Pentecostal. It was this distinct spirituality rather than any doctrinal statement that represented the heart of the Pentecostal Movement. This gradual realization not only changed the way in which he presented the Pentecostal Movement to others, but more particularly to those who were then becoming part of the movement.

Pentecost Outside of Pentecost

Such a conclusion regarding the nature of Pentecostalism would hardly be thought of as insightful today, but at that time it led to what was then a revolutionary concept for Pentecostals. Du Plessis called it 'Pentecost outside of Pentecost'[10], a term which was adopted by Hollenweger in his book, *The Pentecostals*[11], to describe the work of Du Plessis.

The process by which Du Plessis arrived at such a conclusion was a gradual one and there is not space in a chapter such as this to describe the development of his thinking in detail.[12] However, we can say that the issue arose because during the 1950's Du Plessis became aware of small numbers of individuals, including ministers, from the historic churches who were coming into an experience of 'baptism in the Holy Spirit'.[13] In many cases, this process came about not through the activities of Pentecostal denominations so much as through the various healing evangelists and organizations such as the Full Gospel Business Men's Fellowship International.[14] Du Plessis describes the heart of this process in a magazine article in the following way:

> ... I must admit that I often prayed and usually hoped that ministers and people from the churches would 'come out' and join our Pentecostal Movement. However, the process was a very slow one, and I began to realise that this could not be the way in which God would revive Christianity. A world shaking revival will have to be one where the Holy Spirit begins to move in the churches, and not only outside the churches. When He is poured upon all flesh he must fall upon the church members too.[15]

In the past, those coming into such an experience would normally have been urged to join a local Pentecostal church where they would receive the fellowship and encouragement that they would need following such an experience. Du Plessis was the first known Pentecostal leader to urge such people not to leave their churches but to stay and work for the renewal of the structures of which they were a part.[16] He said of such people: "They are PENTECOSTAL because of their experience and not because of membership in a full Gospel Church".[17]

Such advice was only possible because Du Plessis had a new vision of the nature of the Pentecostal Movement. Nor did his advice stop here. Because he had developed warm relationships with denominational leaders as he had sought to interpret the Pentecostal Movement to them, he undertook to intercede on behalf of any leaders who had pressure put upon them to leave their particular church.[18] In this way, the delicate nature of an emerging Pentecostal Movement in the historic churches was both protected and nurtured by Du Plessis. To use a term in current vogue, he developed 'networks' within the denominations of which these individuals were a part, putting them in touch with others in their own denomination who had received or were seeking a Pentecostal experience.

Such activity helped to foster the later development of the more structured Charismatic networks that emerged in the 1960's.[19] However, Du Plessis' vision did not end with the development of a Pentecostal Movement within the historic churches. The value of such a development for Du Plessis lay in exploiting the ecumenical possibilities that such a common experience could produce.

A New Pentecost

As long as the consequence of those in the historic churches receiving the 'baptism in the Holy Spirit' conformed to the sectarian scenario of such individuals joining Pentecostal churches, the leaders of Du Plessis' own denomination were more than happy. However, the recognition by Du Plessis of the validity of such individuals remaining in their own denomination caused some alarm. In past days, urging individuals to leave their denominations had not been necessary, they were simply expelled and such expulsions formed the popular rationale amongst Pentecostals for the existence of their own denominations.[20]

The fact that tolerance towards the Pentecostal experience was being practiced by those very denominations which were regarded by Pentecostal churches as being too worldly and as less than committed to an evangelical view of the Bible, aroused great hostility to the work of Du Plessis. Considerable pressure was placed on Pentecostal leaders by the leaders of those evangelical denominations in the National Association of Evangelicals who were hostile to the historic churches in general and to the ecumenical movement, as represented by the World Council of Churches, in particular.[21]

The leaders of the Assemblies of God were embarrassed by Du Plessis' work amongst ecumenical leaders and, in 1962, presented an ultimatum to Du Plessis. He must either cease his ecumenical ministry or lose his ministry-credentials with the Assemblies of God.[22] Naturally, given his new understanding of the nature of the Pentecostal Movement, it was impossible for him to agree to the demand of the Assemblies leadership and he was expelled as a minister. For Du Plessis this expulsion meant more than just the loss of his ministry-credentials. From now on it would be almost impossible for him to work with the official Pentecostal structures. Ironically, it was as if the Pentecostal leaders were wishing to place themselves outside of the new Pentecost that Du Plessis was discovering. Du Plessis did not miss the irony that it was the evangelical churches which had previously proved the most resistance to the 'baptism of the Holy Spirit' who were now successfully urging the Pentecostal churches to reject the development of this same experience in the more ecumenical of the historic churches.[23]

Immediately following his expulsion, Du Plessis developed a set of relationships far more controversial than any of those in which he had so far been engaged. Du Plessis had developed some personal relationships with a few Roman Catholic clergy as early as 1960.[24] These early contacts led in time to an invitation to attend two sessions of the Second Vatican Council during 1963.[25] His attendance at this event drew his attention to the remarkable prayer of Pope John XXIII at the Council: "Renew your wonders in this our day; give us a new Pentecost".[26]

Du Plessis' ecumenical quest did not just seek to document the existence of Pentecost outside of Pentecost, unexpected as this was in itself. Rather, he wanted to explore the promise of this Pentecost outside of Pentecost. His exploration included the fostering of a series of dialogues between the Vatican and the emerging Charismatic Movement, between the Vatican and Classical Pentecostals and between the World Council of Churches and the Charismatic Movement.[27]

His experience of the ecumenical potential of Pentecostal spirituality brought him to see that what he was witnessing was not just a kind of spiritual balm that would allow Christians of all denominations to feel that they had a unitive spiritual experience. After all, the Classical Pentecostals had received the same experience but had not chosen to see any ecumenical promise in such an experience. Rather, for Du Plessis, the experience of 'baptism in the Spirit' brought something much more fundamental into the life of the church. He described this process as he reflected on the address of Pope Paul VI to the 1975 Congress on the Charismatic Renewal in the Catholic Church:

> Had Pentecostalism finally penetrated the Catholic Church? Instantly I knew the answer. No, it was Pentecost, not an 'ism,' that was moving in the churches. They had not accepted Pentecostalism nor should they have. They had accepted Pentecost - the Holy Spirit, the baptism in the Holy Spirit, the work of Jesus.[28]

This indeed was a new Pentecost, an experience of God that would allow the church to address its mission in a new way. Du Plessis quotes Pope Paul VI as declaring on this same occasion:

> Nothing is more necessary to this more and more secularized world than the witness of this spiritual renewal that we see the Holy Spirit evoking in the most diverse regions and milieux... Today either one lives one's faith with devotion, depth, energy, and joy, or that faith will die out.[29]

A New Community of Pentecost

When Du Plessis first moved from his home in South Africa to the devastation of post war Europe in 1947, he was struck by the contrast between the progress of the church in Europe and the church as he had known it in Africa and North America. The historic churches in Europe seemed to be powerless and far removed from the lives of ordinary people. In those early days, he had seen the planting of Pentecostal churches as the obvious solution to the problem of re-evangelizing Europe.[30] His later discovery of Pentecost outside of Pentecost led him to see the potential for the mobilization of resources for mission outside of a purely Pentecostal framework. However, he later began to see that it was not just a matter of more resources for mission so much as the creation of the kind of missionary church which would be able to live out its mission because of the new Pentecost which would be exhibited in its midst.

Thus, Du Plessis' commitment to the prayer of Jesus in John 17, "That they all might be one, that the world might believe"[31], always contained both aspects of that prayer. The ecumenical content of the new Pentecost had as its intent the creation of a new community that would be empowered by its unity to so live out the gospel that evangelism would be the inevitable concomitant of such an experience. The constant danger for such a vision of a new Pentecost was that the creative tension between these two ingredients would be lost.

Du Plessis came from a Pentecostal tradition that had compromised the nature of Pentecost. They had interpretated unity as that unity which was experienced amongst Pentecostals. Such unity could only be achieved by coming out of the historic denominations and joining a Pentecostal church. The resultant movement would then use its uncompromised Pentecostal power to evangelise the world. However, this sectarian view of Pentecost not only compromised Pentecost itself, it was also a demonstrable failure in that the Pentecostals could not even agree on who was part of their own united family!

The emerging Pentecost outside of Pentecost was by contrast very inclusive. Although there were some debates concerning the entry of Catholics into the charismatic fold[32], it was a largely ecumenical view of Pentecost that emerged amongst the new leaders of the Charismatic Movement. However, their concern for ecumenism was primary, often to the exclusion of any discernible interest in evangelism beyond the rather naive hope that people would somehow be attracted to their more lively worship services. Such a hope has proved to be largely illusionary with the consequence that the mainstream Charismatic Movement has itself been challenged by the more radical 'house churches' who have exhibited a far greater concern for the evangelistic thrust of Pentecost but who in the process have reconstructed the same largely sectarian approach of the Classical Pentecostals.[33]

Such developments have been in danger of falling far short of the promise of a new community of Pentecost dreamed of by Du Plessis.[34] However, in more recent years there are some reasons for hoping that the Charismatics and indeed the Pentecostals themselves may recover a more authentic understanding of the new community that Pentecost seeks to bring.

As the pages of this chapter are being prepared, an International Charismatic Leaders Conference, Brighton '91, has been arranged as the response of the Charismatic Movement to the call for a major evangelistic thrust during the decade of the 1990's.[35] Three features of this event are worthy of notice.

First, the rekindling of a desire to emphasise evangelism returns the Charismatic Movement, not to a concern that it once had, for one suspects that evangelism has never really been a strong theme amongst charismatics, but to an emphasis upon Pentecost itself. Without such a concern, the Charismatic Movement can never be truly participants in Pentecost.

Second, the participation of the three streams of Catholics, historic Protestants, and Classical Pentecostals together with the newer independent Charismatic churches, restores the ecumenical dimension of Pentecost without which Pentecost is also denuded.

Third, an increasing sense of replacing a spirit of competition, not just with a non-aggression pact, but with a growing desire to actually assist each other in the task of mission, points to the kind of new community of Pentecost which will be necessary if the church is ever to fulfill its mission in relation to the Kingdom. The empires of competing denominations need to give way to the community of the King.

Pentecost on All Flesh - The New Language of Pentecost

However, the ultimate significance of Pentecost is not what it does for the Christian community but what it does in the world to which that new community seeks to relate. At Pentecost, God broke through to speak in the language of each nation group present so that each might understand. A similar community of nations was also present at the Azusa Street revival to which Pentecostalism traces its origins. Although there was no equivalent phenomenon of *xenolalia* at Azusa Street, nevertheless, there was an understanding that God was speaking and creating a new community from a disparate humanity.

The language of Pentecost points not just to the phenomenon of speaking in unknown tongues, important as that may be for giving voice to the dispossessed[36], but also to a world where God speaks through prophecy, through visions and dreams. Pentecost continually seeks to break into a world where God appears to be absent to demonstrate a sense of his immediate and vital presence.

It was very much as a Pentecostal that Du Plessis conducted his mission. His intuitive search for the heart of Pentecost was influenced more by prophecy and dreams, by the vital interpretation of God's leading, than by informed academic reflection.[37] He was fond of telling the story of his encounter with a German disciple of Bultmann. The disciple in question asked Du Plessis, "What is your programme?" Du Plessis replied, "To demythologise the scriptures." Curious at such a reply his questioner asked, "How do you do this?", to which Du Plessis responded, "It's very simple, we Pentecostals take the things in the Bible that you say are myths and we make them happen today so that they are demythologised!"[38]

Such stories were very much a part of Du Plessis' narrative approach which sought to open up people to new possibilities, ones perhaps ruled out by the very secular world-view to which they, as Western Christians, probably subscribed. This new and unexpected language about God was aimed at helping people to a God encounter which Du Plessis invariably called 'baptism in the Holy Spirit'.[39] The point of the experience was not that an individual should speak in tongues or exhibit any other particular phenomenon. Rather, the intention was that they should encounter God as one who breaks through into this world with the power of his coming Kingdom.

In his book, *Everyday Men*[40], Roger Edrington outlines his research undertaken amongst working-class men in the city of Birmingham. Each of the men who were interviewed claimed to be unbelievers. Dr Edrington demonstrated through his research that most of these men had in fact had significant religious experiences. Most of them had prayed at some time in their life and many could point to actual answers to prayer. However, the reality of their life was such that for them, the secular world-view which was thrust upon them from every side, eliminated the possibility of expressing or exploring faith in God in any serious way. Dr Edrington presents a picture of men who are truly lost, men whose souls are torn every day in the conflict between their existential experience of life and the actual rational options open to them to interpret their lives.

A few years ago, the exiled Roman Catholic Archbishop of Lusaka, Emmanuel Milingo, under suspicion by the Vatican for engaging in healing practices, was granted permission to conduct services in the empty churches of Rome. Here, in the very shadow of the Vatican, the poor amongst the forgotten masses filled the churches where he preached. The Archbishop ministered to the lost and torn souls of Europe's masses, bringing healing, casting out the demons of hopelessness and rejection. In Europe, in Rome, an African missionary spoke the new language of Pentecost, a language that seeks to create a new community of faith, one which gives dignity, purpose and meaning to those who hear and experience the new words of God's presence.

It is above all this new community of Pentecost that David du Plessis sought to speak of, recognise and encourage in his life and witness. It was this kind of intuitive concern that bound Du Plessis and Hollenweger together as kindred souls. Small wonder then that Du Plessis was glad to accept the designation given to him by his ecumenical friends, 'Mr. Pentecost'.[41]

Notes

1. For a detailed account of the life of Alexander Boddy see: M. Robinson, "Two Winds Blowing" (M.Litt. Thesis, Birmingham University, 1976).
2. M. Robinson, "To the Ends of the Earth" (Ph.D. Thesis, Birmingham University, 1987).
3. W.J. Hollenweger, *The Pentecostals* (London: SCM Press, 1972), xvii.
4. Letter from W. Hollenweger to M. Robinson, January 1991.
5. This took place in 1974 and is particularly referred to in the citation that accompanied the *Pax Christi* award made to David du Plessis by St. John's University, May 1976. See M. Robinson, "To the Ends of the Earth", 299.
6. The *Pax Christi* award mentioned above is one example of the recognition extended to Du Plessis, in this case by a Roman Catholic University.
7. See particularly H. Davies, *Christian Deviations* (London: SCM Press, 1954).

8. Du Plessis describes this process in Chapter 20 of his book, *A Man Called Mr. Pentecost* (Plainfield, NJ: Logos International, 1977).
9. David du Plessis, *A Man Called Mr. Pentecost*, 173.
10. The phrase "Pentecost outside of Pentecost", was used as the title for a 30 page pamphlet published privately by Du Plessis in 1960.
11. Hollenweger, *The Pentecostals*, 1.
12. The process by which Du Plessis arrived at the phrase "Pentecost outside of Pentecost" is described in: Robinson, "To the Ends of the Earth", 156 f.
13. Du Plessis describes this process in an article entitled, "He... established my goings", 2, a privately circulated paper, 1961.
14. For the story of the work of the Full Gospel Business Men's International see: D. Shakarian, *The Happiest People on Earth* (Plainfield, NJ: Logos International, 1975).
15. David du Plessis, "Upon all Flesh", *Comforter* (April 1957), 7.
16. David du Plessis describes his urging of ministers to stay in their denominations in the above cited private publication, "He... established my goings".
17. David du Plessis, "Pentecostal Revival and Revolution, 1947- 1957", *Pentecost* No. 41 (Sept. 1957), 17.
18. David du Plessis, "He... established my goings".
19. The model for many of the structured networks was that of the Fountain Trust, developed in England by Michael Harper.
20. David du Plessis reflects on this history and attitude within Pentecostalism in an article, "World Wide Pentecostal Revivals 1906 - 56", *Comforter* No. 36 (June 1956), 18.
21. This pressure is described in: M. Robinson, "To the Ends of the Earth", 176 f.
22. An account of this conflict is given in: M. Robinson, "To the Ends of the Earth", 173 ff.
23. David du Plessis, "Circular Letter", 29 June 1962. The contents of this letter are quoted in: M. Robinson, "To the Ends of the Earth", 176.
24. David du Plessis, *A Man Called Mr. Pentecost*, 201. His first contact was the Roman Catholic priest, Bernard Leeming.
25. *Ibid.*, 215.
26. Quotation taken from, L.J. Suenens, *A New Pentecost?* (London: Darton, Longman and Todd, 1974), x.
27. For a detailed account of these dialogues see: M. Robinson, "To the Ends of the Earth", 224 ff.
28. David du Plessis, *A Man Called Mr. Pentecost*, 242 f.
29. *Ibid.*, 241 f.
30. See M. Robinson, "To the Ends of the Earth", 115 ff.
31. John 17:20-21.
32. For detail on this debate see: M. Robinson, "To the Ends of the Earth", 224 ff.
33. For discussion of this tendency see M. Robinson, "To the Ends of the Earth", 251 ff.
34. *Ibid.*
35. Most of those who are heading this initiative are leaders who were helped in the early days of their ministry by David du Plessis.
36. Walter Hollenweger in his already cited work, *The Pentecostals*, 459, writes, "...the function of the Pentecostal movement is to restore the power of expression to people without identity and powers of speech, and to heal them from the terror of the loss of speech".
37. The central role of the Smith Wigglesworth prophecy in the ministry of Du Plessis is discussed in: M. Robinson, "To the Ends of the Earth", 5 ff.
38. This story was a favorite of Du Plessis and this author has heard him tell it on many occasions, albeit with a number of creative variations!
39. The phrase 'baptism in the Spirit' was one that was insisted on by David du Plessis. He strongly

resisted alternative phrases favoured by some leaders in the renewal such as 'filled by the Spirit'.

40. Roger Edrington, *Everyday Men: Living in a Climate of Unbelief* (Frankfurt: Lang, 1987).
41. David du Plessis' pleasure at such a designation is reflected in his selection of the term in the title of his autobiography, cited above, *A Man Called Mr. Pentecost*, 'ghosted' by Bob Slosser.

14

South African Pentecostals and Apartheid: A Short Case Study of the Apostolic Faith Mission

J. Nico Horn

The Pentecostal outpouring of the spirit in South Africa was no different from the outpouring in the United States. Racism in the Pentecostal movement in South Africa is not restricted to the apartheid era (i.e. after 1948 when the National Party gained power and introduced political apartheid). Only six months after the initial outpouring of the Holy Spirit in 1908, the executive counsel of the Apostolic Faith Mission (AFM) decided, "that the baptism of natives shall in future take place after the baptism of white people".[1] A few months later it was decided to separate the baptism of white and black people completely.[2] From then onwards, the AFM, the biggest and oldest Pentecostal movement in South Africa, moved towards separate congregations for white and black.

Before considering the way in which the AFM reacted to the policy of apartheid, it is necessary to establish if the church played any role in the formation of apartheid.

John Lake

John Lake's position on racial issues is somewhat dubious. He is both praised as the proclaimer of a non-racial historical Pentecostal gospel[3], and the father of segregation policy in South Africa.[4]

There seems to be a degree of truth in both views. Gordon Lindsay wrote a book on the life of John Lake, based on interviews with the latter. According to one of these oral traditions, Lake was the brain behind the segregation laws of the Union of South Africa. Lake gained influence with the Prime Minister, General Louis Botha, after he had assisted him during a national crisis. General Botha later invited Lake to address the parliament on the racial issue:

> I outlined a native policy and submitted it to the Government. In receipt of this I was invited to come to Cape Town and address the Parliament on this issue. I did so - something remarkable for an American in a foreign country. I framed the policy in harmony with our American policy involving the Indian tribes, having as

> an example the United States and other nations in regard to their handling of the native nations. This policy, as outlined by me was practically adopted by the Boer party in toto.[5]

De Wet concludes from this that Lake was a proponent of racial segregation.[6] However, a more balanced view would be that Lake supported racial segregation, but not necessarily church segregation. There is ample evidence that Lake did not conduct segregated meetings. He started his ministry in Johannesburg in a black Zionist church in Doornfontein. At Lake's second meeting, the first whites already attended.[7] When Elias Letwaba, the well-known black Pentecostal leader, attended the Bree Street Tabernacle, a predominantly white church, for the first time, Lake defended him against white attenders, even kissing Letwaba in front of the whole congregation. Lake immediately invited Letwaba to join him on a mission to Bloemfontein, a conservative white city in South Africa.[8]

Lake was paternalistic, and possibly even a proponent of political segregation, but he was not a racist. In one of his early letters to the Upper Room Mission in Los Angeles, Lake complained that the Afrikaner has, like the Southener, a strong prejudice against blacks, but added that God is changing the hearts of many white workers and caused them 'to love the natives'.[9]

It is very important to make a clear distinction between racial segregation and apartheid. Without trying to justify segregation as a policy, there is no evidence that the early governments of the Union of South Africa saw segregation as an all-embracing ideology of separation. Although many discriminatory laws were implemented during the segregation years in South Africa, amongst them the hated Natives Land Act of 1913 which restricted black farmers to certain secluded areas, the segregation politics never intended to separate blacks and whites in the way that the later ideology of apartheid did.

One has to agree with De Wet that "never in his wildest dreams would Lake have foreseen that the practical arrangement he advocated would change into the rigid apartheid ideology".[10] But unfortunately this typical Western paternalism, very popular even amongst early Pentecostal missionaries[11], laid the foundation for the AFM to plug into many apartheid laws when it was implemented in the post 1948 period.

Church Policy of the AFM

The decision to separate the children of God at the waters of baptism was like a light sea breeze that soon became a hurricane. Long before the National Party gained power and implemented its policy of apartheid or separate development, the AFM, like the Dutch Reformed Church, had separate congregations and later separate churches for the different races (although the AFM never called them ethnic churches, but ethnic sections of one and the same church).

At first sight it might be possible to presume that the AFM,like the Dutch Reformed Church, played a prominent role in the formation of apartheid. However, the facts point in another direction.

The AFM before 1948

De Wet makes the following comment on the racial attitudes of the Pentecostal pioneers in South Africa: "Driven by their feelings of white supremacy, the early white leaders followed closely a policy of paternalism".[12]

He goes on to show that there were no blacks amongst the first appointed elders (blacks were later appointed as elders in the Native work). Only a white could be appointed as superintendent of the so-called 'native work'. The Native Council that governed the native work from 1910 consisted of three white leaders and three black leaders. The white church was called the 'mother church', despite the fact that the Pentecostal revival actually started in a black church! De Wet points out in the mitigation of the racial attitudes of the pioneers, that many of these paternalistic actions were taken to meet the expectations of the government. Black churches were only recognized by the state if they were under white control.[13]

The AFM laid the foundation for racism in the church when they decided to separate the baptism of blacks and whites. I. Burger, historian of the AFM and presently President of the 'single section' (formally known as the white section), sees a socio-political reason for this decision:

> ...during the first few month White and non-White (*sic*) were even baptised together... at the end of 1908 some Afrikaans speaking brothers came on the executive council. The fact that they understood the history and the nature of the racial feelings in South Africa better, possibly contributed to the gradual separation of the races.[14]

Whenever an ideological decision is made in the church, it is very difficult to control its progress. Neither the pioneers nor Burger tried to give a theological reason for the separation or even question its validity. It is possibly correct to conclude that the pioneers deviated from non-racialism because of white racist pressure rather than theological conviction.

The decisions of 1908 to separate the baptism of blacks and whites took its course and at an executive council meeting of 1917 it was recognized that "White, Coloured and Native people have their separate place of worship... Further that in the case of certain worthy coloured families attending at the Central Tabernacle the matter be left in the hands of the Spiritual Committee''.[15] The term 'worthy coloured families' is not defined! At the same meeting it was also decided that ''we do not teach or encourage social equality between Whites and Natives''.[16]

Examples of this paternalistic and sometimes blatant racism of the AFM pioneers can be multiplied. Even a man of the stature of David du Plessis strengthened the growing alienation between blacks and whites by making the different 'sections' autonomous and gaving them their own separate constitutions in the thirties.[17]

There is, however, also ample evidence that the AFM was initially against ideological apartheid and even took an open stand against political racism and overemphasis on Afrikaner-nationalism, cornerstones of ideological apartheid. David du Plessis states that when he implemented segregation in the church, he never expected that segregation would grow into hard apartheid.[18]

Although politics was not high on the agenda between 1920 and 1948, the political sentiments in the church favoured the more liberal ruling United Party to the right wing National Party. When C.R. Wessels, who later became Vice-President and a Nationalist senator, was elected to the executive council in 1937, he was the only pro-Nationalist on the council.[19] Burger points out that the tension between the AFM and the three Afrikaans Reformed churches was not without political overtones.[20] The Dutch Reformed Church and the other two smaller Reformed churches were very closely linked to the ideals and aspirations of the Afrikaner and therefore also to the National Party. This approach was unacceptable to the AFM with its strong English constituency, its American history and its apolitical stance. It resulted in tension between the 'politically right wing churches' and the 'apolitical', but more politically liberal AFM.

P.L. le Roux, who succeeded Lake as President in November 1913 and remained in that capacity until April 1943, fought a long battle against Afrikaner nationalism, nazism and other right wing movements, in the columns of *The Comforter* (*Die Trooster*), the official publication of the church.

Shortly after the centenary festivals of the Afrikaner occupation of the northern parts of southern Africa, the so-called Ox Wagon Trek Centenary, Le Roux wrote an article in which he compared the rising Afrikaner-nationalism and white racism with fascism and nazism, which he called 'the spirit of the time'[21], being possibly a reference to the spirit of the Anti-Christ. Le Roux rejected the hero worship of the festivals and pointed out that God received no honour. On the contrary, the remembrance of white military victories and occupation of the land caused racism and anti-semitism, which is not of God, but of the spirit of the time and of the Anti-Christ.[22] He even hinted that the former Dutch Reformed minister and prominent leader in the National Party, who became the Prime Minister in 1948, Dr. D.F. Malan, was the false prophet of Revelation 13!

> The enemy knows that in our country he has to deal with a religious nation and he proves his cunning by using former ministers, who are still using their religious titles, but advancing (anti-semitism and nationalism). Is it not remarkable that the Anti-Christ uses people with a religious background? However, he will only use it (religion) to achieve his satanic end. We read that the first beast (dictator) will destroy the second beast (head of a worldly church) after the latter has made a statue for him and when the people will worship him.[23]

The influence of Le Roux and like-minded pioneers prevented the AFM in its early years from accepting ideological white racism, anti-semitism and the theology of the Afrikaner as an elect nation. However, their paternalism and reluctance to take an explicit stand against racism laid the foundation for later ideological influence upon the AFM.

The AFM after 1948

The change in the political attitude of the AFM coincided and was strongly influenced by the rise of a group of young pastors commonly known as the New Order. Their main objective was to rid the AFM of its sectarian image and to make the church more acceptable to the Afrikaner community. Although the AFM still had a strong English speaking contingent, the New Order concentrated mainly on the Afrikaners. The New Order wanted to change the church on two fronts: they wanted to bring the liturgy and worship of the church more in line with Reformed liturgy, and they wanted to link the church closely to Afrikaner culture.[24]

One of the first victories of the New Order was on the cultural front when the workers' council decided in 1946 to celebrate the Day of the Covenant with Christmas and Good Friday as a day of thanks and a sabbath.[25] The Day of the Covenant was an important symbol of the rising Afrikaner-nationalism. It celebrates a victory of a small band of Afrikaner settlers in Natal over a mighty Zulu army, as an act of God. Because of its nationalistic and political undertones, the AFM had never celebrated it before 1946.

Two years later the workers' council decided to encourage members to participate in the election of school committees.[26] Later, assembly boards were encouraged to affiliate with Afrikaner cultural bodies.[27]

During the fifties, the AFM, like many other international Pentecostal bodies, also forsook pacifism in practice, although it was never scrapped or removed from the old minutes.[28] In many of the assemblies where New Order pastors ministered, the liturgy also underwent radical changes.[29]

The election of G.R. Wessels as a Nationalist senator in 1955, gave the good intentions of the New Order a fatal blow. His election was both politically and spiritually controversial. The National Party gained power in 1948 with the election promise to implement 'apartheid'. One of its first aims was to remove the so-called coloureds[30] from the common voters roll. This removal could only be achieved by changing the constitution of the Union of South Africa. To change the specific article, a two thirds majority was needed at a joint sitting of both Houses of Parliament. After several unsuccessful attempts to change the constitution, the National Party decided to extend the Senate to give them the necessary majority. Wessels was one of the new appointed senators.[31] By allowing their Vice-President to become a senator in this controversial senate, the AFM became an active partner in the process of taking away the political rights of the coloured community, many of them members of the AFM and other Pentecostal churches.

From a spiritual perspective it was also an extraordinary decision by the AFM to allow a pastor to become a politician while keeping his credentials and staying on as Vice-President. This led to tension in the AFM and eventually to the breakaway of a substantial part of the church, which formed the Pentecostal Protestant Church.[32]

Heartbreaking stories of the influence of apartheid on the people come from the assemblies. In the early fifties the General Secretary sent a circular to all assemblies, both white and so-called coloured, asking them to see to it that white members worshipping in so-called coloured assemblies should be encouraged to join white assemblies, since joint worship was not the policy of the government (it was the time of the implementation of the Group Areas Act and the hated Separate Amenities Act), nor was it socially acceptable.[33]

The letter met with considerable resistance from some of the white workers in so-called coloured assemblies. A white sister leading a so-called coloured church with her husband raised the issue at a district council meeting in the Western Cape and said she would never resign from her church.[34]

After a while most of the whites left (a few-full time workers being the exceptions). The spirit of the letter soon produced its own momentum and coloured people worshipping in white congregations became the target. Goodwood, today one of the biggest assemblies in the so-called single or white section, is a good example of how apartheid was enforced in the assemblies.

At a special church board meeting on Friday July 20, 1956, the colour issue was recorded for the first time in the minutes.[35] A so-called coloured sister wrote a letter requesting an audience with the church board. She felt she was pushed aside by the assembly because of her colour.

> ...it was decided that we notify sister Willemse officially that she is no longer a member of this assembly, and as far as the colour issue is concerned, it was she who raised the idea, which was never mentioned by the pastor or the church board.[36]

It must be mentioned that pastor J.A. Wort, presently a senior executive member of the AFM single section, who was present as an elder at the meeting, told me that he remembers the case and that the sister's colour did not play a role in their decision. At that time, he points out, there were several other so-called coloured families in the assembly.[37] I have no reason to reject Wort's version of the meeting. It was nevertheless the first recorded action against a so-called coloured and the decision undoubtedly set the pace for further action.

On September 7, 1956, it was decided to seek the face of the Lord for guidance on the colour issue.[38] The minutes do not tell us what the result of their seeking God's face was, but at the board meeting of February 10, 1958, a brother was instructed to "find out if brother W. van Blerk was white or not" and two other brothers were appointed "to tell him that his children are no longer welcome in the Sunday School".[39] Brother Van Blerk was at one time vice-chairman of the church board.[40]

The pastor during these dramatic changes was a former policeman, P.N. Visser. He built the small assembly into a big, vibrant Pentecostal work, but he also advertised his meetings in the papers 'for whites only'. Some of those who were members at that time believe that it was his apartheid policies that filled the church[41], while others believe that the growth was the result of Visser's evangelistic ability.[42] This pattern was followed in several other assemblies. To my knowledge, Potchefstroom[43] and Oudshoorn[44] were among the assemblies which soon followed the example of Goodwood.

Du Plessis and probably most of the members of the New Order were undoubtedly sincere in their idealism to make the AFM more acceptable to society. However, they were not mere opportunists. It is clear that at least some of them fiercely believed in apartheid ideology. Wessels published a magazine during the fifties in which he attempted to influence Christians to participate in politics. This magazine propagated apartheid in its crudest form.[45]

The efforts of the New Order were not without success. The AFM was invited to conduct short devotions on the radio, the church gained a good image in white society and it built good relations with the government. But the price was very high. Du Plessis laments the close relations that developed between the church and the National Party, which he feels is paralyzing the church today. He has confessed his own participation in this process on several occasions.[47] Although Wessels resigned as Vice-President in 1969 and since then pastors were not allowed to participate in party politics, the bond between the AFM and the National Party remained strong, though more informal.

Since 1974 the executive council of the single or white section has tried to unify the former ethnic sections, but the attempts have always failed in the white workers' councils, were many layman and several pastors cannot rid themselves of the un-Pentecostal ideology proclaimed to them in the fifties.[48] One of my church board members told me that as a boy in the fifties his pastor told him apartheid was in the Bible, later he was told it was not in the Bible, but God is completely satisfied with it. He was unable to cross the border I expected from him - to see apartheid as a sin.[49]

In black South Africa the AFM has lost tremendous credibility over the years. It was only when the black churches stood up against church and political apartheid in the late seventies that it regained credibility. The fact that the three ethnic sections for Africans, so-called coloured and Indians unified in 1990 to form a non-racial church, known as the composite section, gave the church a great deal of momentum.

Throughout the years of Verwoerdian apartheid, the AFM never raised its voice against the crude oppression of the vast majority of the people. The forced removals of 3,5 million people, the banning of hundreds, if not thousands, without a chance to defend themselves, the detention of thousands without trial and the vulgar implementation of the dehumanizing Mixed Marriages Act and article 16 of the Immorality Act, never caused an eyebrow to be raised amongst white Pentecostals. On the contrary, there are, as we have seen, indications that the white section of the AFM actively supported the system.

The clearest sign of the church's insensitive political approach of those years is to be found in the new construction of 1961 which stated that members are white baptized members, while the church also has "non-white (*sic*), that is Indian, coloured and Bantu followers".[50] It was only when the era of reform started in South Africa that the AFM took a second look at itself.

With the help of the political reform of President F.W. de Klerk, the AFM will possibly rid itself of the church structures closely related to the political ideology of apartheid. But I predict that it will take many years to change the hearts of its members. This is true both of the whites and their superiority complex, still poisoned by the ideology of apartheid; and of the blacks, whose pain of many years has often turned into hatred[51] and other ideological alliances at worst, or to a desire to gain power in the church after all their years of powerlessness.[52]

'Blood on Our Hands, Hope for the Future'

The almost tragic history of the single section of the AFM serves as a warning to any Pentecostal church where people are flirting with ideology, no matter how good their intentions may be. This includes churches where support for liberation movements (many times not without good reasons), are once again paralyzing the prophetic witness of the church.[53] The saying 'he who rides a tiger can't get off' is applicable here. Anyone toying with ideological forces stands in danger of selling out the church and its values. This is equally true of white Afrikaners trying to improve their image, or black oppressed Pentecostals with a burning desire to liberate the oppressed and deliver the poor, plugging into a theology using Marxist analysis.[54]

However, this is not a good time for white South Africans to point to the growing ideological actions of our black brothers and sisters. We can only earn the right to play a positive and critical role in the future of a non-racial southern Africa if we are willing to walk the path of repentance, the acceptance of our corporate guilt in creating this monster, not hiding behind our good intentions. The road will be painful (we are already experiencing it in Namibia). Only when white Pentecostals will be prepared to cross the barriers to their black brothers and sisters, no matter how big the risks may be shall we be able to find our future in God and forgiveness in Jesus Christ.

Conclusion

The story of the South African Pentecostal churches and apartheid is by no means the story of the victorious church, not even for the black Pentecostals. In many ways the AFM is a microcosm of the international Pentecostal movement. Racism, right wing political attitudes and political power plays are not the prerogative of the AFM. It is not too surprising that the international Pentecostal community kept such a low profile when it came to apartheid. We all stand guilty before God: the liberals and conservatives, Africans and Europeans, whites and even blacks. May the Holy Spirit guide the Pentecostal movement through repentance and confession to cross racial barriers once again! May the spirit of Azusa Street be revived amongst us! And may the colour line (and also the cultural and ideological lines) be washed away in the blood!

P.S. Thank God for those who cared enough not to mind their own business, but to make apartheid their business, especially Walter Hollenweger, member of the Reformed Church, but from our ranks and at heart a Pentecostal. His writings play a major role in the thinking of progressive Pentecostals in Southern Africa, as is evident from *The Relevant Pentecostal Witness.*

Notes

1. I. Burger, *Geloofsgeskiedenis van die Apostoliese Geloofsending van Suid-Afrika 1908-1958* (Johannesburg: Gospel Publishers, 1987), 175.
2. *Ibid.*
3. W. Burton, *When God Makes a Pastor* (London: Victory Press, 1934), 30 ff.
4. I. Burger, *op. cit.*, 151.

5. G. Lindsay, *John Lake - Apostle to Africa* (Dallas: Christ for the Nations, 1981), 35-36. Lake's speech could not be traced in the minutes of parliament. It is possible that Lake addressed a select committee. See B. Sundkler, *Zulu Zion* (London: Oxford University Press, 1976), 54.
6. C. De Wet, "The Apostolic Faith Mission in Africa: 1908-1980. A Case Study in Church Growth in a Segregated Society" (Unpublished Ph.D. dissertation, University of Cape Town, Cape Town, 1989), 158 ff.
7. I. Burger, *op. cit.*, 167.
8. W. Burton, *op. cit.*, 52 ff.
9. Quoted in I. Burger, *op. cit.*, 422 ff.
10. C. De Wet, *op. cit.*, 160.
11. See W. Burton, *op. cit.* 1 ff.
12. C. De Wet, *op. cit.*, 161.
13. *Ibid.*, 162-63.
14. I. Burger, *op. cit.*, 176. Translation by the author.
15. "Minutes of the Executive Council of S.A., July 7, 1917", (AFM Archives, Lyndhurst), 33-35.
16. *Ibid.*
17. D. du Plessis and B. Slosser, *A Man Called Mr. Pentecost*, (Plainfield, New Jersey: Logos Int., 1977), 112.
18. *Ibid.*
19. Personal interview between Burger and Wessels, quoted in I. Burger, *op. cit.*, 325.
20. *Ibid.*
21. P. le Roux, "Die Gees van die Tyd en die Gees van God", in *Trooster* (Bethlehem, South Africa, February, 1939), 6-7.
22. *Ibid.*, 7.
23 *Ibid.* Translation by the author.
24. See my article "Quo vadis AGS?", in N. Horn and J. Louw, *Een Kudde! Een Herder*, (Kuilsriver: Ekklesia Publishers, 1987), 75-85, for more details on the ideals of the New Order. See also an article based on a conversation with J.T. du Plessis, younger brother of David du Plessis and a leading figure in the New Order: J. Theron, "Die Invloed van die Nederduitse Gereformeerde Kerk op Liturgiese Verwikkelinge binne die Apostoliese Geloofsending van Suid-Afrika: Die rol van Past. J.T. du Plessis", in *Ned. Geref. Teologiese Tydskrif*, Vol. XXX, no. 3 (July 3, 1989), 301-11.
25. M. van der Spuy, "Die Spanning tussen Vryheid en Formalisering ten Opsigte van die Liturgiese Verskuiwinge binne die Apostoliese Geloofsending van Suid-Afrika" (Unpublished M.A. thesis, University of South Africa, 1985), 155.
26. *Ibid.*
27. *Ibid.*, 156.
28. *Ibid.*, 156. See also I. Burger, *op. cit.*, 310.
31. I took over the assembly Krugersdorp Central from Eneas du Plessis, the youngest brother of David and J.T. du Plessis. Before me, J.T. du Plessis and his brother served in the assembly for more than thirty years. Members of the assembly often told me that no one clapped hands there for more than twenty years.
30. Under the race classification laws distinction was made between blacks and so-called coloureds. People who were neither black nor white nor Asian were classified 'coloureds'. It included amongst others Malaysian descendants and descendants from relationships and marriages between black and white.
31. I have dealt with this issue in more detail in an article, "Quo vadis AGS?", in *op. cit.*, 75-85.
32. See I. Burger, *op. cit.*, 324 ff.
33. A. Schoeman, "Circular from the General Secretary", (AFM Archives, Kuilsriver, date unreadable, probably between 1954 and 1955).

34. "Minutes of the Western Peninsula Coloured District Council", (AFM Archives Kuilsriver, date and page number unreadable, possibly in 1954-55).
35. "Minutes of the AFM of S.A., Goodwood, July 20, 1956" (AFM Archives, Lyndhurst), 75.
36. *Ibid.*
37. J.A. Wort, Personal Telephone Conversation, Windhoek/Kempton Park, May 31, 1991.
38. *Op. cit.*
39. *Ibid.*, 144.
40. J.A. Wort, *op. cit.*
41. K. du Toit, Personal Conversation, Windhoek, September, 1989.
42. J.A. Wort, *op. cit.* Wort points out that the growth started while there were still several coloured families in the assembly. He is convinced that the growth would have occurred even if the so-called coloured did not leave the assembly.
43. U. Bezuidenhout, Personal Conversation, Krugersdorp, 1987.
44. V. Isaacs, Personal Conversation, Uitenhage, 1984.
45. G. Wessels, "Die Bybel en Apartheid", in *Die Ou Paaie* (Jan.-March 1957). In this article he proclaimed separate races as an ordinance of God and defended the Mixed Marriages Acts as a Christian defence of civilization.
46. J. Theron, *op. cit.*, 308.
47. See my article "Quo vadis AGS?", *op. cit.*, 75-85 for examples.
48. I have elaborated on the dogmatic deviations from Pentecostal theology the AFM indulged in during the apartheid era, in my unpublished paper, "A Refutation of the Theology of Apartheid", delivered at the International Missionary Conference of the AFM, Lyndhorst, October 1985. The paper was distributed amongst the participants by the missionary department, together with my other paper, "The Pain of Apartheid", under the title "A Time for Repentance", but it was never officially printed.
49. L. Basson, Personal Conversation, Windhoek, November 6, 1989.
50. *Private Law* No. 24 of 1961, articles 1 and 2 of the statutes.
51. See the book by C. Lodewyk, *Love in a Hate Situation*, (Tulsa, Oklahoma: Christian Publishing Services, 1987) for a description of such an experience.
52. This was my experience in Namibia where the first workers council (January 1991) of the united AFM of Namibia was marked by a strong rejection of white leadership. Although one has no problem to understand this reaction from a sociological perspective, it does not contribute to reconciliation or the normalization of the church.
53. F. Joseph, Personal Conversation, Windhoek, September 1990. Pastor Joseph, presently President of the AFM of Namibia, had a very close relationship with Swapo during the years when the party was not allowed in Namibia. He saw it as his Christian duty to take up the just cause of Swapo and to speak on their behalf while they were forbidden to speak for themselves. However, when the atrocities of the Swapo detention came to the light, he refused to criticize it. Unlike the Council of Churches of Namibia, he defended the appointment of Simon Hawala, who was in charge of the Swapo camps, as head of the Namibian army.
54. It is common knowledge that Pentecostals played a prominent role in the writing of the *Kairos Document.* F. Chikane, Personal Letter, (Johannesburg, May, 1990). See the ICT on behalf of the Kairos theologians, *The Kairos Document. The Challenge to the Church. A Theological Comment on the Political Crisis in South Africa*, revised edition (Johannesburg: Skotaville Publishers, 1986), 17 ff.

15

Pentecostalism in Korea

Boo-Woong Yoo

Introduction

Though the Protestant Church in Korea is only one hundred years old, the growth of the Korean Church is generally recognized as the most remarkable in Asia, and, indeed, in the world. Because of that it has become the object of study for missionaries and evangelists.

Korea remained true to its name the 'Hermit Kingdom' until Christian missionaries arrived in 1884.[1] By 1890 Koreans *en masse* were openly asking for instruction.[2] In 1900 alone, Church membership increased by over thirty percent. Bible classes and the earnest simple witness of Korean Christians were primarily responsible. A third factor was this revival movement of 1907 that spread from Korea into Manchuria and China.[3]

The memory of this early spiritual climate and piety has remained with Koreans for many years. Throughout the Japanese occupation of 1910-1945, the Communist invasion from North Korea in 1950, and, in spite of Japanese Shinto persecutions and schisms from within during the 1950s, the Protestant community has continued to double in size every ten years.[4] Korean Protestant church-growth has been miraculous during the last three decades. Statistical tables are as follows:

1960	1,250,000
1970	2,200,000
1980	7,000,000
1983	8,500,000
1988	10,000,000

According to the latest statistics, there are over seventy active Protestant denominations.[5] These denominations can be divided into three types:[6]

1. Evangelical fundamentalism, emphasizing evangelism (the authoritative and supernatural character of the Bible as the Word of God), Sabbath observance and Church discipline;
2. Social groups, emphasizing the struggle for the liberation of suffering people, the struggle for human rights and social justice, from *Minjung* and *Han*

theological background;

3. Pentecostalism, emphasizing church-growth (concentrating on women and the masses), the baptism in the Holy Spirit and speaking in tongues, and *Gidowon* (prayer mountain) movement (fasting, prayer, and the ministry of healing).

Environmental Factors in the Early Stage

It would be useful to summarize here the contributory factors that have stimulated the Pentecostal Movement which have generally been agreed by Korean scholars.

A factor believed by many people to be most significant is the Korean people's innate religiosity, a trait thought to be basic to the Korean character or personality. Perhaps this is correct to some extent. However, the religious 'environment' in which the Korean Church has had the opportunity to cradle the Pentecostal Movement is also a highly important factor.[7]

Second, prior to the introduction of the Christian gospel, three major religions, Confucianism, Buddhism and Taoism, existed in a state of harmony for several centuries. These three major religions also came to Korea from other countries and took root in what was then a 'shamanistic' religious environment. These religions, in the course of time, became 'syncretized' in such a way as to create a new environment, which was sufficiently fertile to support Christian evangelism at a later stage. Certain scholars have expressed the view that this so-called religious syncretization is a major factor contributing to the Pentecostal Movement.

Linked to this idea is the fear that the present period (in which Christianity is partly influenced by a shamanistic 'prosperity theology') is now giving way to yet another new religious climate, which is influenced by what may well be a continuous process of religious syncretization that now includes the Christian Church.[8]

Third, despite the presence of major religions in Korea's earlier history, there existed something of a religious 'vacuum'; and I feel that this still exists in the hearts and minds of many Korean people. This vacuum could be described as a hunger, as a basic human need, and as a desire for a more meaningful life; and a more personal identification with God. I believe that the movement served to fill this vacuum and nourish people's hungry souls.[9]

Fourth, a further influential factor is what we recognize as 'social crisis'. Especially at the turn of the last century, Korea experienced tremendous turmoil and social upheaval. With the tragic circumstances surrounding the end of the Yi dynasty, the Japanese colonial invasion and enforced annexation, Korean social structure was beginning to change: with a new consciousness towards a more egalitarian society. Up to that period, Korean peasants and slaves were deprived of their basic human rights in a highly-stratified system consisting of *Yang-ban* (nobility), *Sang-min* (commoners) and *Chon-min* (slaves). In particular, the *Donghak* peasant revolt of 1894 shattered the stratified system of Korean society. In addition, the impact of the Japanese victory over China in the Sino-Japanese War of 1894-95 shocked the Confucian rulers of the Yi dynasty which had relied on the power of China for centuries. They saw Japan's victory, with its westernized military system and weaponry, and began to question the Confucian value system that had been the fundamental basis for the consciousness of the Korean people for centuries. For many Koreans, their faith was born out of misery, despair and tragedy. We cannot underestimate the influence of the 'new hope' being born out of these conditions and the very real human expectation that hopes could be achieved through the power of the Pentecostal Movement.[10]

Finally, the positive mission policies and strategies adopted by the early missionaries in their efforts to evangelize Korea were based upon the Nevius Plan, which encouraged self-propagation, self-government and self-support. The overall mission policy from the beginning was that evangelism in Korea must be initiated, administered and financed by the Korean people themselves. The Nevius Plan originated in China, having been developed by the early missionaries, but it failed there. In Korea, however, these approaches were implemented more successfully; and the experiences here have since served as examples of Christian evangelism and, to some extent, have inspired mission in other parts of the world.[11]

I have described five separate and possibly important factors that may have contributed significantly to the movement. There are obviously many more. It is clear that there is no single element that could account for the phenomenon. Perhaps all of these elements and others yet to be identified have combined to create this fertile environment which led to the Pentecostal Movement?[12]

Response to Korean Shamanism by the Pentecostal Church

The early missionaries focused on working class people and particularly women as the main targets for conversion. As a result, the basic character of the Protestant Church was formed by those people who were also the most familiar with Shamanism.[13]

Historically, the earliest religion in Korea was spirit worship or Shamanism. To this day Shamanism retains a powerful hold on the credulous folk, although other powerful religious forces and modes of thought entered Korean life in the process of its historical development.

Because Shamanism stems from pre-literate societies, and lacks a systematically expressed doctrine, it is difficult not only to comprehend, but also to distinguish from other religions. Moreover, because of its very nature, it has easily borrowed from others and has tended to vary in its expression in different times and places.

Because of its ready adaptability and accommodation it has penetrated and become part of other religions without experiencing any great resistance. Shamanism postulates a universe in which not only human beings but also lower animals and inanimate things have souls or spirits.[14]

Above all spirits stands *Hananim*. *Hananim* seems to dominate the lives of Korean people; for his name is continually on their lips. Curiously, however, they never really seem to worship him. Koreans believe that *Hananim*, the creator, is remote from the events of the world and rules the world through power delegated to lesser gods.

Shamanism believes in a three-level cosmos. In the upper level, the bright world above heaven, *Hananim* and benevolent spirits reside. The present world, where man and all animate and inanimate things live, constitutes the middle level. In the lower level, hell, live all evil spirits. It is said that man, after his present life, will either ascend to the upper level or descend to the lower one. Thus, Koreans seem to take immortality of some sort for granted, and the later form of Buddhism has also helped to give more content and meaning to this belief. Most Koreans also accept naturally the belief that everyone goes ultimately to *Jeuh-Seung* (the future world after this world) and to King Yumna (the king of judgement). Both of these have now become Buddhist terms, but these and many other ideas in Korean Buddhism represent much older tradition, and probably predate Buddhism.[15]

The above description illustrates the origin in Shamanism of some primal notions of sin and judgement and of some concern with morality.

Nevertheless, in the actual practice of Shamanism, people are primarily concerned with freeing themselves from the ever present, harassing spirits and the discomfort that they bring; and have little interest in the weightier matters implied in shamanistic belief. The characteristics that Koreans have developed in the practice of Shamanism are fatalism, moral indifference, self-centered interest, escapism, and also fanaticism with respect to its ceremonial rites.

Two factors should be noted, however. First, the beliefs of Shamanism have enabled Koreans to comprehend more easily the references in Christianity to the idea of God, to evil in the world, to heaven and hell, and to benevolent and evil spirits. Second, the above characteristics, developed through belief in Shamanism, greatly affected the Korean appropriation and expression of Christianity, through revival and Pentecostal enthusiasm and an other-worldly orientation.

All of the Protestant Churches adopted a critical attitude towards Shamanism; but most of them are influenced by it to a greater or lesser extent. In my understanding, the Pentecostal Church has a structure and world view very similar to that of Shamanism.[16]

To give an example, the Rev. Yonggi Cho's Full Gospel Central Church is a typical Pentecostal church in Korea. According to the January 1983 issue of *The Christian Life*, the Full Gospel Central Church in Seoul is the largest single congregation in the world in terms of numbers.

This congregation was started May 1958 by the Rev. Yonggi Cho with five members. The church building was a large military tent, easily available after the Korean War. The growth statistics for this congregation are as follows[17]:

1961	300
1973	18,000
1979	100,000
1983	250,000
1988	400,000

Within thirty years it has grown into the largest congregation in the world with 400,000 members. Its church building is equipped with the latest audio-visual equipment and can hold 40,000 people at one time. How was such growth possible?

Although this church has an excellent organization, as exemplified by a large well-equipped church building, a mammoth prayer centre on the Osanli mountain and, above all, 25,000 well-trained home-cell prayer unit leaders, all of which have contributed to this remarkable growth, I would nevertheless like to concentrate specifically on the preaching and ministry of the founder of this church, the Rev. Yonggi Cho.

First, his preaching philosophy is "Find need, and meet need."[18] What do the majority of Korean people need and how can the Korean church meet those needs? Why do the Korean working class and particularly the women go to the shaman? Because they need health, wealth, fertility and success in their life ventures. The Rev. Yonggi Cho's preaching meets those needs exactly. "Anything is possible if you have faith." This is his favorite subject on which to preach. He often says that the Christian faith is positive thinking and Jesus Christ is a positive thinker.

Second, Cho's preaching formula, "the threefold blessings of God"[19], is based on 3 John 2: "Beloved, I pray that all may go well with you and that you may be in health; I know that it is well with your soul." The threefold blessings of God are popularly interpreted by the Rev. Yonggi Cho as follows:

a. 'that all may go well with you' means business or material prosperity;
b. 'that you may be in health' means good health or longevity;
c. 'that it is well with your soul' means protection from evil spirits.

Shamanistic belief is concerned with these three blessings and the Rev. Yonggi Cho's preaching satisfies the needs of the majority of the Korean people.

Third, his healing ministry is based on the baptism of the Holy Spirit, speaking in tongues and driving away demons (evil spirits) from sick persons using the name of Jesus. His role in Sunday morning worship looks exactly like that of a *shaman* or *mudang*. The only difference is that a *shaman* performs his wonders in the name of the spirits, while the Rev. Yonggi Cho exorcises evil spirits and heals the sick in the name of Jesus.

A Recent Development: The Emergence of Pentecostal Minjung[20]

The *minjung* Theology arose in Korea in the middle of the mid-1970s. It arose against the background of political oppression of the dictatorial Park regime and the economic deprivation of city workers and rural peasants. The first thing that a non-Korean needs to understand about *minjung* theology is the meaning of *minjung*.[21] *Minjung* is a Korean word, but it is a combination of two Chinese characters *min* and *jung*. *Min* may be translated as 'people', and *jung* as 'the mass'. Thus *minjung* means 'the mass of the people' or 'the masses', or just 'the people'. But when we try to translate it into English, 'mass' is not adequate for our theological purpose; and 'the people' is politically dangerous in anti-Communist Korea, because it has become a Communist word. Although 'the People of God' may seem to be the safest and perhaps the most neutral expression both in Korean and English, theologically and politically *minjung* cannot be translated as 'the People of God'.

There is no agreement among Korean theologians regarding the precise definition of the *minjung*. The term is dynamic.

Ahn Byung-mu's "Jesus and the *Minjung* in the Gospel of Mark"[22] makes a sharper presentation of the notion of *minjung* in terms of Mark's use of the word *ochlos* as opposed to the word *laos*. For him the *minjung* is definitely *ochlos* rather than *laos*. His conclusion is that Mark does not define *ochlos* in a deterministic way, but rather describes the *ochlos* and uses the term in referring to a social historical context (2:4, 13; 3:9, 20, 32; 4:1; 5:21, 24, 31; 8:1; 10:1). On the other hand, the term *laos* refers to a national and religious group. He says that "Mark called Jesus' *minjung* the *ochlos* (*ochlos* = *minjung*)"[23] By quoting the characteristic saying of Mark 2:17b, "I came not to call the righteous, but sinners," Ahn draws attention to the partiality that Jesus showed in expressing his love. Ahn states, "He loved people with partiality. Whatever the situation he always stood on the side of the oppressed, the aggrieved, and the weak."[24]

The *minjung* is present where there is socio-cultural alienation, economic exploitation, and political suppression. Therefore, a woman is a *minjung* when she is dominated by man, by the family, or by socio-cultural structures and factors. An ethnic group is a *minjung* group when it is politically and economically discriminated against by another ethnic group or groups. A race is *minjung* when it is dominated by another powerful ruling race as is the case in a colonial situation. When intellectuals are suppressed for using their creative and critical abilities against rulers on behalf of the oppressed, they too belong to the *minjung*. Workers and farmers are *minjung* when they are exploited; their needs and demands are ignored; and they are trodden down by ruling powers.

Suh Kwang-sun, one of the representative *minjung* theologians, points out in his research how the majority of the Korean *minjung-ochlos* is charmed by the Pentecostal-Charismatic Movement. He says: "I have found the other side of *minjung* in the churches which have fast-growing non-denominational congregations".[25] If the majority of the Korean *minjung-ochlos* draws its consolation, encouragement, aspiration and strength of hope from the Charismatic fellowship of the Rev. Cho Yonggi's Full Gospel Central Church in Seoul and, as it usually happens, escapes from sickness, poverty and climbs up the social ladder with the help of Pentecostal-Charismatic ministry, how can *minjung* Theology help the Pentecostal-*minjung* with proper guidance; and how can they dialogue with each other?

Professor W.J. Hollenweger mentions the new direction of Pentecostalism in the third world, "Pentecost means more than speaking in tongues. It means to love in the face of hate, to overcome the hatred of a whole nation by demonstrating that Pentecost is something very different from the success-oriented American way of life".[26] According to him, the reason for fast growth of third world Pentecostalism does not lie in a particular Pentecostal doctrine. There are trinitarian and non-trinitarian, infant and adult baptizing Pentecostals and many other kinds... The reason for its growth lies in the black slave (*minjung*) spirituality of North America, which can be summarized as follows:[27]

- 'orality' of liturgy;
- 'narrativity' of theology and witness;
- maximum participation at the levels of reflection, prayer and decision-making and therefore a form of community that is reconciliatory;
- inclusion of dreams and visions into personal and public forms of worship;
- an understanding of the body-mind relationship, the most striking application of this insight is the ministry of healing by prayer.

We have discussed the two *minjung-ochlos* movements in Korea. One is the socio-political and the other is the Pentecostal-*minjung*. The discovery of the *minjung* in Korea led not only to the realization that it is *minjung-ochlos* which is the subject of history, but also that *minjung* is a subject in the making of reconciliation in Korea. The task of Pentecostal-*minjung* is to bear burdens; to heal a society which has had considerable class differences since the 1960s; to help create a new history of Korea; and, particularly, to reunify North and South Korea in the future.

Notes

1. Everett N. Hunt, *Protestant Pioneers in Korea* (New York: Orbis Books, 1980), 17-29.
2. David B. Barrett (ed.), *World Christian Encyclopedia; A Comparative Survey of Churches and Religions in the Modern World A.D. 1900-2000* (Nairobi: Oxford University Press, 1982), 442.
3. *Ibid.*
4. *Ibid.*
5. *A Study on the Pentecostal Movement in Korea* (Seoul: Korea Christian Academy, 1982), 300-01.
6. Boo-Woong Yoo, "Response to Korean Shamanism by the Pentecostal Church", *International Review of Mission*, Vol. LXXV, No. 297 (January 1986), 70-71.
7. Park Keun-Won, "Evangelism and Mission in Korea: A Reflection from an Ecumenical Perspective", *International Review of Mission*, Vol. LXXIV, No. 293 (Jan. 1985), 53.
8. *Ibid.*
9. *Ibid.*
10, *Ibid.*, 50.
11. Suh Kwang-Sun, "American Missionaries and a Hundred Years of Korean Protestantism", *International Review of Mission*, Vol. LXXIV, No. 293 (1985), 9; Min Kyung-Bae, *The Church History of Korea* (Seoul: Korea Christian Literature Society, 1972), 152.
12. A full account of "the 1907 Pentecostal Movement of Korea" by an American eye-witness is in William's Blair's Book, *The Korean Pentecost* (Edinburgh: The Banner of Truth Trust, 1977).
13. Boo-Woong Yoo, *op. cit.*, 71.
14. D.B. Barrett (ed.), *op. cit.*, 441. For a detailed study of this religion, the following materials are available: C.A. Clark, *Religion of Old Korea* (Seoul: Korea Christian Literature Society, 1961); *Korea; its Land, People and Cultures of All Ages* (Seoul: Hakwonsa, 1960); *Hankuk Moonwhasa Taekae: An Historical Outline of Korean Culture*, Vol. 6 (Seoul: Koryu University, Minjok Moonwhasa Yunkuso, 1970); Yun Sung-bum, *Christianity and Korean Thought* (Seoul: Korea Christian Literature Society, 1964); Ryu Dong-shik, *The Christian Faith Encounters the Religions of Korea* (Seoul: Korea Christian Literature Society, 1965).
15. C.A. Clark, *op. cit.*, 218.
16. Boo-Woong Yoo, *op. cit.*, 73.
17. *Korean Church Growth Explosion; Centennial of the Protestant Church 1884-1984* (Seoul: Word of Life Press and Asia Theological Association, 1984), 272.
18. Yong-Gi Cho, *Church Growth*, Vol. 3 (Seoul: Youngsan Press, 1983), 30.
19. *Ibid.*, 33-34.
20. Boo-Woong Yoo, *Korean Pentecostalism: Its History and Theology* (Frankfurt: Verlag Peter Lang, 1987), 205-10.
21. *Ibid.*, 191-92. Cf. *Minjung Theology; People as the subjects of history* (New York: Orbis Books, 1981).
22. Ahn Byung-Mu, "Jesus and the Minjung in the Gospel of Mark", *Minjung Theology*, 138-52; Idem, "The Transmitters of the Jesus-Event", *Bulletin of the Commission on Theological Concerns*, Christian Conference of Asia (CTC-CCA), Vol. 5, No. 3 - Vol. 6, No. 1 (1985), 26-40.
23. *Ibid.*, 140.
24. *Ibid.*, 141.
25. Suh Kwang-Sun, "The Korean Pentecostal Movement and Its Theological Understanding" in *A Study on the Pentecostal Movement in Korea*, 23-100; Idem: "Minjung and Holy Spirit", *Minjung and Korean Theology* (Seoul: Korea Theological Study Institute, 1985), 303.
26. Walter J. Hollenweger, "After Twenty Years Research on Pentecostalism", *International Review of Mission*, Vol. LXXV, No. 297 (1986), 5.
27. *Ibid.*, 6.

16

Animism in Indonesia and Christian Pneumatology

I. James M. Haire

Introduction

I have looked at that all-embracing facet of human and in particular religious life for which we use the code-words 'animism', 'primal religions' or 'pre-literary religions'. No term that I know of is totally appropriate in this field, and that is the opinion of many researchers in the area of interaction between the Gospel and cultures.

The term 'pre-literary' is used here to stress the fact that these religions have a long-developed tradition, the origins of which would appear to pre-date the appearance of literary forms in the various religions. The term, therefore, seems more neutral and purely descriptive in its use than many other terms (e.g., 'animistic', 'primal', 'primitive'). Other terms (e.g. 'tribal', 'customary', 'traditional') seem possible, but also appear to be applicable to other religions as well; when compared with the present use of 'pre-literary' they are not precise.

Throughout this paper, 'culture' and 'cultural' denote the total pattern of social life including religion, rather than the artistic as distinct from other activities; such as those of politics, trade or religion. The term is thus used as social anthropologists would use it, as compared with its use by historians of the arts.

Throughout this paper, 'the Gospel' is used in the Bultmannian sense of 'the Christ Event' or 'the Christ Event for us' or 'the Christ Event for them', etc. 'The Christian message' or 'gospels' are used for the written and oral traditions.

I wish on this occasion to use the term 'pre-literary' in relation to life-systems and world-views, including the religions, in the sense that these outlooks pre-date the manifestations of literary forms: although of course continuing after the arrival of such literary forms. I use the term, thus, in a purely descriptive way; no value-judgement is attached to it. It has its disadvantages. Other terms have, however, as great, if not greater, difficulties.

In the sense outlined above, pre-literary life-systems and world-views underlie all religious expressions in almost every part of the world. I have been involved in original research on this for some time, most recently in January, 1989. Moreover, I wish to look at the interaction of these pre-literary forms and certain aspects of other religions, in particular Islam and Christianity.

In doing so I wish to bear in mind such questions as: What is the God whom we as Christians know "in the face of Jesus Christ" (2 Cor. 4:6) saying to us (if anything) in these pre-literary forms and in their interactions?

The area in which I have been involved in research is the group of North Moluccan Islands in Eastern Indonesia. From an anthropological viewpoint it is an extremely useful area in which to carry out research. This is so for a number of reasons. First, a comparison of historical accounts by travellers over the past four centuries[1] indicates only the slightest changes to indigenous pre-literary forms over that period. This is very different from the situations, for example, in some South Pacific Islands [2] or among the various Australian Aboriginal groupings [3], where Asian or European influences have so influenced pre-literary forms that today we cannot really know what they were even two centuries ago. In such situations it is very difficult to comprehend how the whole system works, or even which are the genuine vestiges of any original system.[4] Second, population change through immigration has been very limited. Third, the heartlands of the pre-literary systems have been very isolated. An almost 'laboratory-type' situation has occurred.

When looking at these events, and when comparing them with others, we shall mainly be concerned to look at the beliefs, and the interaction of beliefs, from the standpoint of the believers: that is, of those involved in the life-systems. We shall not, therefore, be primarily concerned to discuss the various beliefs in terms of structural-functionalism or any other socio-anthropological theories.[5] In other words, we are vicariously involved in 'being there' in all senses, as far, of course, as that is possible. The words of S.G. Williamson concerning the Akan of Ghana could be applied to the North Moluccas, that "the integration of his religious views and practices lies not in the fashioning of theological and philosophical structures, but in his socially inculcated personal attitude to the living universe of which he is a part".[6]

It is impossible to dissociate in any way so-called 'religious beliefs' from a total understanding of life and the world. For theological reasons, however, we have chosen those particular parts or aspects of the totality of life which are the particular focus of the meeting of the Christian message with other beliefs as our departure-point in this investigation. When doing so, however, we must be aware that we are using one particular 'vantage-point' to view the whole.

Movements of the Holy Spirit in Animistic Terms

In the North Moluccas the term *gìkiri* is still used as a generic word for one of the many local or personal divinities. It is in this sense that in recent years the term has most usually been understood. However, it is clear that the word originally had a much wider meaning. A. Hueting in 1908 sees the basis of its meaning as 'living being, spirit, human being, somebody' ('levend wezen, geest, mensch, iemand').[7]

In other words, he sees in it the elements of *mana*[8], permeating nature in general and humanity in particular. What seems clear is that among the North Moluccans the *gìkiri* was originally a *mana*-type concept more connected with a Supreme Being.[9]

It is doubtless from the breadth of the applications of the *gìkiri* - concept that the term *Gìkiri Moi* was related to the concept of a High God. We can see that, from *gìkiri*, which we translate as 'spirit' or 'god', and *moi*, the general North Moluccan word for 'one', *Gìkiri Moi* implies 'the One God' or 'the One Spirit'. P.H. Thomas sums up the present understanding of *Gìkiri Moi* as "the One God (or 'Lord'), who is the head of all powers which are animistic, dynamistic or *mana*" (Indonesian: "Tuhan yang satu, yang mengepalai segala kekuatan-kekuatan yang animistis, dinamistis maupun mana").[10] However, it would seem to be inaccurate to think of *Gìkiri Moi* in terms of a *deus otiosus.*[11]

Below *Gìkiri Moi* are the great company of the *gòmànga*, the spirits of the dead; or, more accurately for the North Moluccans, the living dead.[12]

It would seem that the pre-literary understanding of evil was two-fold. First, there was always a tendency for the living-dead, especially of course those who had been insulted, to be jealous of the living[13], and so to cause evil. Second, there were simply those forces in nature and in the inter-relationships of the community[14] which militate against harmony and encourage what is considered evil. Below the *gòmànga*, then, is the world of these village-spirits, termed in the North Moluccas in general *roh-roh* (from the Indonesian).

From what we have seen, it can be observed that in the pre-literary religious understanding of the North Moluccans the security-creating harmony most closely related to the Christian concept of salvation concerns protection from the village-spirits; the correct relationship with other creatures and nature; the right ties with the *gòmànga*; and the desired respect to guarantee one's own future *gòmànga*-status. It seems that, for the North Moluccans in general, it is accurate to follow F.L. Cooley's observations in the Central Moluccas: that "the indigenous religion and *adat* should be seen as two halves of a whole".[15]

How the Dutch Mission came to the North Moluccas

The coming of Christianity to the North Mollucas involved significant movements of the Christian Spirit. It is the *modes* of this activity which we need to note.

The Utrecht Missionary Union (U.Z.V.) had begun work in New Guinea. It was formed in 1859, and in 1861 chose the northern coastline of western New Guinea as its first mission field.

At first, however, the work proved to be very disappointing. Both the Gossner-missionaries and the U.Z.V. missionaries were constantly beset by illness. It seemed very difficult to make contact with the local population; as a result, as Th. Müller-Krüger puts it, "Nach 25 Jahren mühevollster und entbehrungsreichster

Arbeit zählte man nicht mehr als 20 Getaufte''.[16]

Then, second, according to J. Rauws, on the night of 22nd-23rd May, 1864, an earthquake, "changed all plans and dealt the progress of the work a heavy blow''.[17] This event seems to have had a very considerable effect on the Mission Board, as on 15th March, 1865 it was decided to withdraw from New Guinea.[18]

Third, there was the influence of a tribesman named Moli upon the missionaries who were working at that time in New Guinea. This Moli had for a period worked for C.W. Ottow, one of the first Gossner-missionaries in New Guinea. Ottow arrived there in 1855 and died in 1862; presumably Moli had then returned to Galela. In 1865 Moli arrived from Galela in Ternate, with the aim of persuading G. Jaesrich of the Gossner-Mission and Th.F. Klaassen of the U.Z.V., who were both there at that time, to turn their attention to the North Moluccas. What is significant here is that Klaassen was impressed by Moli, and indeed "saw Moli as the Macedonian man was for Paul at Troas''.[19]

It is important for us to note the factors which the Moluccans themselves considered decisive in prompting the Mission to start work amongst them. Two factors stand out: first, the earthquake in New Guinea is regarded as decisive in turning the Mission's attention away from that area; second, the coming of Moli to Ternate is considered as vital in calling the Mission to the North of Moluccas.

Beginning of Mission Work in the North Moluccas

Hendrik van Dijken had received permission to set up his base on the fertile land surrounding the Lake of Galela and the other two nearby lakes in the interior. However, the actual point near the main lake which was suggested and granted to him by the Galelarese chiefs was a place greatly feared by the Galelarese population. The particular area had two Galelarese names: one, *Tomadoa* or *Tumadoa*, meant that it was the abode of the primeval giant who was the ancestor of the Galelarese and Lord of the Land[20]; the other name was *Morodoku*: "The meaning of the place where *Duma*[21] is in fact is the place of the Moros; so, its name is *Morodoku*, that is the place on the promontory; *morodoku* means 'the village belonging to the Moros'...''[22]

Like *Tomadoa* (or *Tumodoa*) *Morodoku* is Galelarese; *Tomadoa* is both the name of the giant primeval ancestor and the place of his continuing presence; *Morodoku* is the combination of two Galelarese words: *Moro* and *doku* meaning 'village', thus combining to mean: the village belonging to the *Moro* or *Moros*. According to Moluccan beliefs, the Moros were a group of Moluccans who formerly built a kingdom, mainly based on Galela and Morotai. Then they and their kingdom disappeared.[23] Therefore, for Moluccans, particularly in the north of the islands, the term 'the Moro man' means "the man who disappears but returns occasionally''. He is either a member of the original company of Moros who came to visit the area of their former kingdom or someone who joined them later. A.L.

Fransz cites an example in recent years of a Tobelorese tribeswoman disappearing after declaring that she was a Moro.[24] The Moros also show their powers; when the abandoned husband in Fransz's example re-married, signs of the former wife's presence, in particular earth thrown on the table at the wedding-feast from an unknown source, were noted[25]. More generally the Moros are associated with malevolent magical powers. It can be seen here that there are elements both of belief in the 'living-dead' ancestral spirits in general and of belief in various primeval ancestral giants in particular. In any case, *Morodoku* indicates a centre of power of one or more of these Moros.

Therefore, in directing Van Dijken to this particular point, the Moluccans were clearly arranging a direct confrontation between him and their ancestral heroes who were lords of the land and whose abode was at Tomodoa and Morodoku. Their motivation for this was probably two-fold: first, doubtless Muslims at the coastal trading-post, who disliked Van Dijken's insistence to the Sultan that he move inland, encouraged the Galelarese interior chiefs, who were almost entirely pre-literary religionists, to neutralise Van Dijken's influence in the area by bringing him face-to-face with their 'Lords of the Land' so that he would depart in fear from the area, if in fact he survived. Second, as A. Rooseboom points out, "they (i.e. the interior Galelarese) were afraid of his (i.e. Van Dijken's) 'god' or 'spirit'..." (Indonesian: *orang takoet gikinja*).[26] That is to say, they were afraid of his presence among them and its consequences if he had not previously met with their lords of the land. Therefore, it must doubtless have seemed most appropriate to the Galelarese that the issue of the viability of a Christian presence among them should be determined at Tomodoa/Morodoku. The Galelarese, of course, did not expect Van Dijken to survive.

Nevertheless, Van Dijken continued to build up his agricultural work. He was assisted by Moli and a number of Ternatenese. The Moluccans, however, would have no contact with him. As a Gossner-type missionary, he aimed through agriculture to provide something at least towards his own costs. From the Moluccan point-of-view, the life-and-death issue of the survival of Christianity was being determined at Tomodoa/Morodoku. The fact that Van Dijken survived was to be the first part of the Moluccan equivalent of the Exodus experience for the Israelites. Although no North Moluccan had yet been baptised, and no-one apart from Moli could be considered a serious adherent, Christianity in the Moluccan eyes was being established on Moluccan soil from the Tomodoa/Morodoku experience of 1886 onwards. For this reason, the beginnings of Christianity in the North Moluccas after the Portuguese period are dated not from the first baptisms on North Moluccan soil nor from Moli's baptism but from 19th April 1886, when Van Dijken started his work in Galela. It dates from that point, because of van Dijken's determination to enter the interior. For the North Moluccans, the Holy Spirit was meeting with the Lords of the Land: and yet still living.

The second part of the North Moluccan 'Exodus experience'[27] came in 1871. Before that, Van Dijken had renamed *Tomodoa/Morodoku, Duma*. He seems to have related it to *Duma* (or *Dumah*) of Isaiah 21:11, connecting that name with the isolation and tranquility of the place. However, the Moluccans were convinced that the name was related to the Galelarese phrase *Duma wi doohawa*, meaning "But he (i.e. Van Dijken) was not harmed", which at that time was the reaction in the area of van Dijken's survival. The Moluccans also noted that a price had been paid for Van Dijken's struggle. His fiancée died of cholera at Surabaya during this period, and in 1868 his house was destroyed by a hurricane. At that time too he married a Minahassan girl named Maria Soentpiet. The effect of these hopeful developments was to confirm to the Galelarese that there was a place for Christianity among them. Then, in December 1871, the issue of the future relationship between the Galelarese and Christianity (and indeed between the North Moluccans as a whole and Christianity) came to a head in the second part of the North Moluccan 'Exodus experience'. On the 14th, 15th and 16th December, there was continuous very heavy rain. As a result, a number of the villages around the lake were swamped as the waters in the lake rose.[28] Then, according to Rooseboom: "hundreds of people came to him (i.e. Van Dijken) and then Mr. Van Dijken told them that they must humble themselves (or 'bow themselves down') before God and together pray for the Lord to have pity on them".[29]

At that point, twenty-six people wished to become Christian, and many wanted their children to enter Van Dijken's school. In response to this Van Dijken held a prayer hour in the open air, and he on behalf of the Galelarese chiefs around the lake asked for the rains to stop and the flood-waters, now covering a number of villages, to recede; and according to Hueting, "the next day, Saturday, the rain stopped, we really can say, as a result of the prayer of Van Dijken".[30]

The effect of this experience on the Galelarese was to be crucial for the future of the Mission. For Church historians its importance was of a very great significance. Its importance was not simply related to the fact that a dangerous flood had subsided. Of far greater significance for the Moluccans was the meaning of the coming and departing of that flood. Clearly then the coming and departing of the flood was related to the meeting of the various divinities (*gìkiri*) of the Galelarese and those of Van Dijken and Klaassen, his colleague, in which those of the latter appeared now to be in control of the situation. However, another element was involved too. This was the theme of a new beginning related to a flood. This theme is found in the North Moluccas with the idea of a part of the population being destroyed and a new beginning made. However, it is not so developed as the tradition of a great flood and the re-peopling of the earth found in Ceram in the Central Moluccas.[31] From this we can see that, for the Moluccans, the experience of December 1871 clearly ensured not only that Christianity had a place in their society and demanded a certain allegiance among them, but also that this was to be the beginning of a re-orientation of their lives. For the Moluccans, although no-one (apart from Moli) had yet been baptised, this was the primary formative point in the history of modern Christianity in their islands. A real meeting had taken place between Christianity and the pre-literary religious system of Galela. A new beginning was required: Christianity demanded Moluccan allegiance. However, it is also important to note that, although Christianity rightfully required of the Moluccans a re-orientation of their loyalty in their eyes, it did not, in their view, necessitate a total break with the past. Their pre-literary religious system was being superseded by a new and more efficacious system. It was not being entirely annihilated by the new system; although it was now of course subservient to it. Such consequences of the 'Exodus experience' at Galela are significant.

Interaction with Christian Pneumatology

I now wish to look at the interaction between these beliefs and two world religions, Islam and Christianity, which came into the area. I wish to look mainly at some facets of the mutual interactions of this pre-literary outlook and Christianity; although I will also look briefly at the interactions with Islam. I wish to pick up certain salient features, rather than give an overview, as I have done elsewhere.[32] Of course there were mutual interactions between Islam and Christianity; but that is outside the scope of this paper.

Islam

First, Muslim concepts influenced pre-literary beliefs in a number of ways. There was clearly a strong Muslim influence on the development of the concept of *Gìkiri Moi* as the One High God. Second, pre-literary concepts influenced Islam as it developed in the region. J.F. Cady notes that: "A Sufi-type mysticism, a syncretistic faith overlaid with Koranic teachings, was transmitted to the Indies during the fourteenth and fifteenth centuries".[33]

For example, the pre-literary outlook of the North Moluccans influenced Islam as it entered the area by encouraging the Sufi mystical movement within Islam. It would seem that the pre-literary animistic, dynamistic and *mana* concepts encouraged the mystical and pantheistic tendencies of Sufism in the tradition of the ways of thinking originally associated with Ibn-al'Arabi of Murcia.[34] There was not a tendency towards asceticism; but there was an emphasis upon mysticism and the paths (*tarikas*) to achieving mystical and ecstatic union with Allah.

Christianity

We now go on to look at the interaction of Christianity and certain facets of the pre-literary system.

First, Christianity influenced this system in a number of ways, particularly in relation to the Christian doctrines of the sovereignty and grace of God. The North Moluccans felt that they were coming up against a God whose relationship with them could not be controlled as their relationship with *Gìkiri Moi* could be. The inference from the first part of their Exodus Experience was that unpredictably Van Dijken had not died at Tomadoa/Morodoku. The inference from its second part was that quite suddenly the flood had subsided. Therefore, the *gìkiri* associated with Van Dijken (and the local and particular appearance of his *Gìkiri Moi*) was not only more powerful than the Galelarese *gìkiri* (and *Gìkiri Moi*); he was also powerful in a new sense to the Moluccans: his actions and presence were totally unrelated to any concepts of control or predictability which they had. Thus the sovereign lordship of the Christians' God had first come to the Moluccans. The Christian sense of the sovereignty and self-giving grace of God had far-reaching consequences for the pre-literary outlook. It was this fact which seemed to be confirmed in the various appropriation events of the Exodus Experience in the tribal areas around the North Moluccas; although many did not immediately enter the Church - and indeed there was sometimes a movement back from Christianity into pre-literary belief again -, the pre-literary confidence in its system of being able to relate to *Gìkiri Moi* on its own terms and through its own clearly defined system had been broken.

Second, pre-literary influence on Christianity was and is considerable. A good example was the pre-literary influence on the relationship between the triune God and the varied *gìkiri* and village-spirits. Specifically, pre-literary beliefs influenced Christianity as follows:

First, a tendency towards Sabellianism could be expected in that *Gìkiri Moi* had been integrated into the greater Christian God. He was the unifying basis of all the *gìkiri*; and this in fact seems to have happened. In this tendency to Sabellianism 'à la North Moluccas', Christians regarded the varied *gìkiri* as the microcosmic presence in each place of one of the three facets of the triune God. Unlike the situation in Ceram in the Central Moluccas[35], in the North Moluccas the Christian God tended to be regarded more in terms of power-through-presence. Thus in Moluccan Christian thinking there seemed to be one of two possibilities in any situation. Either there was a continued dichotomy, where belief in God went in parallel with belief in the varied *gìkiri* within their own responsibilities, or there was the more integrated 'Moluccan Sabellian' concept of a macrocosm represented in a microcosm. Of these two possibilities the latter seems to have been the more prevalent.

Second, there was a strong but negative pre-literary influence on the doctrine of the Holy Spirit. As we have seen, the whole system had been related to that of Powerfulness-through-Presence. Thus, although the facet of the Holy Spirit was received, it was very greatly minimised. This came about not in opposition to the fact but because of the fact that the *gìkiri/Gìkiri Moi* system had been related to 'spirits'. So once it had been integrated into Fatherhood and Sonship ideas, there was no or little *Anknüpfungspunkt* for relationship with concepts of the Holy Spirit. This was further vitiated by the terms used in the island for the Holy Spirit. The North Halmaheran languages, which dominated the whole Church's thinking, used a number of variations on the same semantic theme for the translation of the term. *Womaha* and *Ngomasa* and their variants suggest a fine ethereal wind, while *Debi-debini* and its variants suggest that which is very pure. So, a very pure, ethereal wind was the vehicle given to carry the Holy Spirit concepts. In the first 1874 North Moluccan translation of the Apostles' Creed, the translators simply imported the Malay *Roh Elkoedoes* in their translation. But while in western Indonesia this Malay term had a connection with pre-literary and Muslim understanding, and through Arabic could be the vehicle to carry the meaning of the Old Testament *rûah* and the New Testament *pneuma*, which owed much of its understanding to *rûah*, in eastern Indonesia this was not possible. Thus, where the Malay/Indonesian *Roh Kudus* had both a connection with indigenous belief and a connection with Semitic thought, it would seem reasonable to expect that something within the Biblical range of meaning could be transferred to where the term was currently in use. In the Moluccas, this term was not well known. So the pure-ethereal-wind concept as a vehicle which was not associated with the *gìkiri*-complex was used. As, however, the *gìkiri*-complex had been incorporated into the Powerfulness-through-Presence ideas, the result was that the doctrine of the Holy Spirit became largely an incomprehensible *addendum*. Powerfulness-through-Presence was the vehicle for the Doctrine of the Holy Spirit.

At times there occurred an intensity of experience, belief and worship within the general North Moluccan pre-literary religious outlook. Related to this was a Messianic tendency in religious thinking until recent years. At various times the movement to raise up a "Just or Benevolent Prince" began in this area. It does not seem, however, that such a belief was indigenous. It was rather an imported concept; nevertheless it played an important part in the thinking in the area during the late-Nineteenth and Twentieth centuries. In this there was clearly a combination of religious and political motifs. This belief in the Coming-Just-Prince had considerable significance in their situation.

Christian Pneumatology 'in loco'

Transition, translation, transposing, transplanting, transferring, transforming, transfiguring are various expressions of the intercultural activity to which Christians are called and in which theologians bear a special responsibility. If we return to the question raised at the beginning, we can see how the Christ Event must live in, and yet transfigure, the culture in which it is placed: always at the same time struggling with the fact that it is the Divine which nevertheless has entered this world. The authentic Gospel or Christ-Event-for-us is not pre-packaged by cultural particularity but is living.

These stories of the Spirit's movements in Indonesia speak of 'Coming-without-conversion-yet' and 'Powerfulness-through-Presence'. The early dogmatic discussion within Christianity involved the interweaving of the Christ Event into, and transfiguration by the Christ Event of, Hellenism and its successors. But, if the Christ Event is interwoven into, and transfigures, another culture with a much more ancient and much richer background (as in the case of certain pre-literary cultures), then could not the impact of that Christ Event become clearer?[36]

So was it really that the Christ Event initially became interwoven with, and transfigured, Hellenistic culture and its successors? Much of Western Europe and North America inherited that Christ Event in Jewish, Greek, Latin, Celtic, Anglo-Saxon, German and French traditions, within succeeding nature-cultures. Do those interweavings of, and transfigurations by, the Christ Event, bring it out in total clarity? Or do other places do so more strongly?

The dichotomy between the Latin dogmatic understandings of the Holy Spirit and the experiential expression of Pentecostalism in the West reflects as much as anything the weakness of the paradigms of Hellenism and its successors. In the Latin tradition, theologians have been far too ready to make this an intellectual matter: i.e. a search for 'orthodoxy'. One of the greatest tragedies of the History of Dogma is that we have often so concentrated on our orthodoxy that we have forgotten the transforming power of the Holy Spirit. Without the power of the Spirit we cannot know the truth. The message of Pentecost is that Reality Itself, Truth Itself, sends his Spirit to lead us into all truth.

Notes

1. E.g.: J.M. Baretta, "Halmahera en Morotai", in *Mededeelingen van het Bureau voor de Bestuurszaken der Buitenbezittingen*, Vol. XIII (1917), 116 ff; C.F.H. Campen, "De Godsdienstbegrippen der Halmaherasche Alfoeren", *Tijdschrift voor Indische Taal-, Land- en Volkenkunde* Vol. XXVII (1882), 438-39; C.F.H. Campen, "De Alfoeren van Halmahera", *Tijdschrift voor Nederlandsch-Indië*, 4e Serie, Vol. XII, no. 1 (April 1883), 293.
2. J.R. Garrett, *To Live Among the Stars: Christian Origins in Oceania* (Suva/Geneva: University of the South Pacific/World Council of Churches, 1982), *passim*.
3. D.H. Turner, *Tradition and Transformation: A Study of the Groote Eylandt area Aborigines of Northern Australia*, Australian Aboriginal Sudies, No. 53 (Canberra: Australia Institute of Aboriginal Studies, 1974), 189; 192-193.
4. D.H. Turner, "Terra Incognita: Australian Aborigines and Aboriginal Studies in the 80's", typed manuscript, 1986, 18.
5. I.e. we are not dealing with the issue primarily from such a standpoint. On this, see J. Rex, *Key Problems of Sociological Theory* (London: Routledge and Kegan Paul, 1961), 175-90.

6. S.G. Williamson, *Akan Religion and the Christian faith: A Comparative Study of the Impact of Two Religions*, edited by K.A. Dickson (Accra: Ghana Universities Press, 1965), 86.
7. A. Hueting, *Tobèloreesch - Hollandsch Woordenboek, met Hollandsch - Tobèloreesch Inhoudsopgave* ('s-Gravenhage: Het Koninklijk Instituut voor de Taal-, Land- en Volkenkunde van Nederlandsch-Indië/Martinus Nijhoff, 1908), 100.
8. On this, see H. Hadiwijono, *Religi Suku Murba di Indonesia* (Primal Tribal Religion in Indonesia) (Jakarta: BPK Gunung Mulia, 1977), 11 and 17.
9. Hueting, *Tobèloreesch-Hollandsch Woordenboek*, 100.
10. P.H. Thomas, "Penjebaran Agama Kristen dan Pengaruhnja bagi Pendidikan Penduduk Halmahera" (The Spread of Christianity and its Influence on the Education of the Population of Halmahera) (Unpublished thesis; Ambon (Indonesia): Pattimura University, 1968), 20. *Tuhan* is the usual Indonesian word for (the Christian) 'Lord'; it is also frequently used for (the Christian) 'God', in order to avoid using the standard Indonesian for 'God' (including 'the Christian God'), *Allah*.
11. On this, see P.L. Tobing, *The Structure of the Toba Batak Belief in the High God* (Amsterdam: Jacob van Kampen, 1956), 21-23.
12. Hueting, *Tobèloreesch-Hollandsch*, 109. However, of course, not all *gìkiri* are *gòmànga*. North Moluccans say that the *gòmanga* are more refined than *gìkiri* (Indonesian: "lebih halus dari *gìkiri*"); by this it would seem that the *gòmanga* are deemed higher than the other types of *gìkiri* associated with birds, etc.
13. A. Hueting, "Geschiedenis der Zending op het eiland Halmahera (Utrechtsche Zendings-Vereeniging)", *Mededeelingen: Tijdschrift voor Zendingswetenschap*, Vol. LXXII (1928), 13.
14. In North Moluccan thought there is no great divide between what occurs in nature and what occurs in inter-personal relationshis. Cf. J.J. Fox, "Sister's Child as Plant: Metaphors in an Idiom of Consanguinity", in R. Needham, ed., *Rethinking Kinship and Marriage* (London: Tavistock Publications, 1971), 219-52 *passim*.
15. F.L. Cooley, "Altar and Throne in Central Moluccan Societies: A study of the relationship between the institutions of religion and the institutions of local government in a traditional society undergoing rapid social change" (Unpublished Ph.D. thesis; New Haven (Connecticut): Yale University, 1962), 482.
16. Th. Müller-Krüger, *Der Protestantismus in Indonesia: Geschichte und Gestalt*, Die Kirchen der Welt, Reihe B, Band V (Stuttgart: Evangelisches Verlagswerk, 1968), 155.
17. J. Rauws, "De Utrechtsche Zendingsvereeniging", Chapter XII of H.D.J. Boissevain, ed., *De Zending in Oost en West: Verleden en heden*, Vol. II (Hoenderloo (The Netherlands: Zendingsstudie-Raad, 1943), 26.
18. Hueting, "Geschiedenis der Zending", *Mededeelingen: Tijdschrift voor Zendingswetenschap*, Vol. LXXII (1928), 98.
19. J.A. Rooseboom, "Hikajat Zending" (The Story of the Mission) (Tobelo, 1938), 9. Notes given as a Course at the Training College for Teacher-Preachers in Tobelo and copied down by H. Simange, a pupil of Rooseboom.
20. Hueting, "Geschiedenis der Zending", *Mededeelingen: Tijdschrift voor Zendingswetenschap*, Vol. LXXII (1928), 109.
21. J. Haire, *The Character and Theological Struggle of the Church in Halmahera, Indonesia, 1941-1979*, Studien zur interkulturellen Geschichte des Christentums, Band 26 (Frankfurt-am-Main und Bern: Peter D. Lang, 1981), 138.
22. *Ibid.*, 165.
23. *Ibid.*, 166.
24. A.L. Franz, *Benih Yang Tumbuh IX: Suatu Survey Mengenai: Gereja Masehi Injili Halmahera* (The Growing Seed IX: A Survey on: The Evangelical Christian Church of Halmahers) (Jakarta: Lembaga Penelitian dan Studi Dewan Gereja-Gereja di Indonesia, 1976), 72.

25. A. Hueting, "De Tobeloreezen in hun Denken en Doen", *Bijdragen tot de Taal-, Land- en Volkenkunde van Nederlandsch-Indië* Vol. LXXVII (1921), 266-69; see too Fransz, *op. cit.*, 72.
26. Rooseboom, *op. cit.*, 9. See too R. Kennedy, "A Survey of Indonesian Civilization", in G.P. Murdock, ed., *Studies in the Science of Society* (New Haven (Connecticut): Yale University Press, 1937), 294.
27. By 'Exodus experience' is implied the founding experience which is constantly looked back to by the Church as the point in its history when the validity of Christianity was first made apparent to it; no further similarity with the Exodus is necessarily implied.
28. Hueting, "Geschiedenis der Zending", *Mededeelingen: Tijdschrift voor Zendingswetenschap*, Vol. LXXII (1928), 117.
29. Rooseboom, *op. cit.*, 10.
30. Hueting, "Geschiedenis der Zending", 117-18; and P. van der Crab, *De Moluksche Eilanden: Reis van Z.E. den Gouverneur-Generaal Ch. F. Pahud door den Molukschen Archipel* (Batavia (Java): Lange en Co., 1862), 212-13.
31. Haire, *op. cit.*, 237-73.
32. J.F. Cady, *Southeast Asia: Its Historical Development* (New York-San Francisco-Toronto-London: McGraw-Hill Book Company, 1964), 153.
33. Cady, *op. cit.*, 153.
34. C.E. Farah, *Islam: Beliefs and Observances*, 2nd ed. (Woodbury (New York): Barron's Educational Series, Inc., 1970), 215-17; H.A.R. Gibb, *Mohammedanism: A Historial Survey*, 2nd rev. ed. (London: Oxford University Press, 1969), 101; A. Guillaume, *Islam*, 2nd ed. (Harmondsworth: Pelican Books Ltd., 1961), 149.
35. Cooley, *op. cit.*, 490.
36. See R.H.S. Boyd, *Khristadvaita: A Theology for India* (Madras: The Christian Literature Society, 1977), *passim.*

17

Signs, Wonders, and Statistics in the World of Today

David B. Barrett

Some 203 times in the original Greek Bible (125 times in the Greek Old Testament, 78 times in the Greek New Testament) we come across the word *semeion* ('sign', plural *semeia*). Similarly the Greek word *teras* ('wonder', plural *terata*) occurs 46 times in the Old Testament, 16 times in the New. These lead into the fuller New Testament phrase *semeia kai terata* ('signs and wonders', 14 times), together with their range of synonyms in the English Bible ('miracle', 'mark', 'portent', 'work', 'power').

This complex, best represented in the English phrase 'signs and wonders', is clearly one of the hallmarks of God's dealings with His people, and especially of New Testament Christians, New Testament churches, the New Testament way of life, and the whole New Testament ethos. It is a hallmark of the way the New Testament envisages the kingdom of God spreading across the world.

Pentecostals and Charismatics (or, to use a single generic term, pentecostals/charismatics) like to feel that they are alert to God's signs and wonders of whatever kind, wherever they have already occurred, are occurring now, and will occur in the future. Usually the term conjures up physical healings inexplicable to medical science, extraordinary physical phenomena inexplicable to the earth sciences, strange coincidences that are statistically otherwise improbable, or sudden material provisions that confound the laws of logistics.

But even more important are signs and wonders relating directly to the spiritual life: sudden conversions, conversions of key individuals, unexpected people movements into the church, mass revivals, snowballing zeal for missions. From this standpoint, the 20th-century pentecostal/charismatic renewal itself can be regarded as the main and the major sign and wonder of our time. So also are the component elements of this renewal, including the means that communicate signs and wonders and give precision to them.

One of the major signs evident to us in the 1990s concerns the statistical way of investigating and describing the renewal. We can begin with the oft-quoted aphorism of Roger Schutz, founder of the Taizé Community in France: "Les chiffres sont les signes de Dieu--Statistics are signs from God." Statistics are the shortest and most concise form under which significant information can be represented. Thus the statistic "25 percent of all full-time Christian workers are pentecostals/charismatics" alerts us to one way in which God is at work. Again, the statistic

"There are 520 million people living in urban slums today" alerts us to the predicament of 10% of God's world of human beings.

One can see that even such statistics themselves have become for us both signs and also wonders. They have become for us 'signs' by pointing the way to what has happened, what is happening, and what will probably shortly happen (trends). They have become for us 'wonders' by startling us and shattering our inadequate stereotypes with otherwise incredible new information.

At the same time we need to realize that signs and wonders do not have the same value or meaning for everybody, everywhere, all the time. Take road signs, for instance. The neighbourhood you live in, or the town, or the city, probably has street signs at every corner. Most days you never look at them, because you are thoroughly familiar with the area. But if you visit a city new to you, or if you get lost somewhere you will need those signposts at every turn.

Similarly with 'wonders'. An eclipse of the sun is a strange, inexplicable, bewildering, frightening, terrifying event to millions unfamiliar with our Solar System and Newton's laws of gravity. Once we know the explanation, however - once we can fit an eclipse into our understanding of God's world - it is no longer anything to be frightened about.

'Signs' and 'wonders' in our usage therefore are primarily for those who are lost, or for those who are unfamiliar with God's ways and God's purposes.

This short essay will now briefly describe 11 contemporary characteristics of the renewal as a whole. Many of us are already familiar with these 'signs.' We need to remember that for thousands of other less-informed Christian leaders these characteristics will at first sound incredible, as 'wonders' indeed once they can overcome their initial incredulity. We have an urgent need to develop means of communicating information about these signs and wonders in ways that will convince the otherwise incredulous.

Growth

The first startling characteristic of the renewal, to the previously uninformed, is its meteoric growth over the last few years. Its church members have risen from some 3 million in 1900 to 71 million by 1970, 158 million by 1980, and 372 million by 1990. Today the annual increase is 19 million: 54,000 new persons every day become pentecostals/charismatics. It is important here for us not to exaggerate. This is where statistics come in useful: they help us to nail down precisely what it is that we are observing, and to do it according to the scientific method which permits others including skeptics to check all the steps and figures themselves independently.

Size

By mid-1991 the renewal had expanded to 392 million church members. Even the best-informed observers are regularly surprised by the magnitude of this new detail or that. The many components of the renewal may be studied in detail in my survey "The 20th Century Pentecostal/Charismatic Renewal in the Holy Spirit, with its goal of world evangelization" (*International Bulletin of Missionary Research*, July 1988), which breaks the world totals down by continents and then into 48 different types of pentecostals/charismatics. The 'startling' or 'wonders' aspects of this type of information depend entirely, of course, upon how well informed the reader already is.

There are literally hundreds of facts or pieces of information of this type now available. Here's one example. The renewal within the 25-million member Church of England began in 1907. Today it has some 800,000 charismatics in England itself. It is one of the major leaders in organized renewal activities. But readers unaware that 66% of all pentecostals/charismatics are found not in the West but in the Third World may be startled to hear that among the ancient civilization of the Tamils of South India there are already over one million pentecostal/charismatic church members - surpassing those in the Church of England. How do you, the reader, interpret this 'sign'?

Omnipresence

Geographically, the renewal is spread throughout the world. So also are the great pentecostal denominations. Most now have sizable diasporas on other continents. Thus a visitor to Oklahoma City, USA will be startled to find there 9 self-supporting Malayalam-speaking congregations of the immense Indian Pentecostal Church based in Kerala, South India. Again, if he visits the oil city of Dhahran, Saudi Arabia he may be surprised on encountering Urdu-speaking Pakistani pentecostals. And so on, and so on.

Uniqueness

The renewal is characterized by a number of unique features. Entirely new expressions of Christianity abound. One is the vast rash of huge congregations worshiping each in a single church building. The world's 5 largest of such congregations are all pentecostal/charismatic. Their membership is as follows: Yoido Full Gospel Church, Seoul (Korea), 800,000; Jotabeche Methodist Pentecostal Church, Santiago (Chile), 350,000; Visión del Futuro, Buenos Aires (Argentina), 145,000;

Brasil Para Cristo, Sao Paulo (Brazil), 85,000; Deeper Life Church, Lagos (Nigeria), 65,000.

Diversity

The ethnic and linguistic diversity in the renewal are startling indeed. Worldwide, members are found in 8,000 different ethnolinguistic cultures, speaking 7,000 languages covering 95% of the world's total population. We need to create a neologism here to help enumerate this phenomenon: a pentecostal/charismatic megapeople. This term defines an ethnolinguistic people with over one million pentecostals/charismatics. There are over 30 of these megapeoples in the world today. The best known are the Koreans with 13 million members renewed in the Spirit.

Complexity

The 1988 survey mentioned above employs a total of 20 new statistical categories in order to describe the phenomenon of the renewal. These include: prepentecostals, quasipentecostals, indigenous pentecostals, isolated radio pentecostals, postpentecostals, postcharismatics, crypto-charismatics, radio/TV charismatics, independent charismatics. Such complexity is only what we should expect. It is another modern parallel to the First Day of Pentecost itself when people were startled by the ethnic and linguistic diversity of those filled at that time with the Holy Spirit (Acts 2:6-12).

Transconfessionalism

From the earliest days of the renewal in the year 1900, protagonists were prophesying that it would spread to all parts of the Body of Christ. This has now been fulfilled. Today there are known to be pentecostals/charismatics in all of the 160 major confessions, traditions, and ecclesiastical families of which Christianity worldwide is made up. In a growing number, they are already in the majority.

Poverty

Not all of God's 'signs' to us are heartening. Some contain terrible indictments of the innate selfishness of Christians, of organized Christianity, and of the renewal itself. Some 60% of the renewal are urbanites living in cities. But around 50% of all pentecostals/charismatics today are forced to live as slumdwellers living wretched lives in absolute poverty. Another way of saying this is: 38% of the world's 520 million slumdwellers are pentecostals/charismatics. A tenth of these have to scavenge for food and live off huge urban garbage heaps every day. This is a shocking indictment of Western pentecostal/charismatic affluence and indifference to the reality of the Body of Christ.

Western missions

One of the 'signs' in the New Testament is the missionary one - the way in which the Twelve Apostles went out across the world in all directions, each eventually suffering the additional sign of martyrdom for Christ. Likewise today foreign mission is a notable mark of the renewal.

Unfortunately, anyone analyzing pentecostal/charismatic foreign missions will soon discover that their organized missions are deployed more among Christian populations than among non-Christians. If we examine the 14th edition of the *Mission Handbook of North American Protestant Ministries Overseas* (1989) we find that, of today's 820 North American foreign mission agencies (90 of which are pentecostal/charismatic) with a total of 72,000 foreign missionaries (a quarter of whom are pentecostals/charismatics), not a single agency or missionary is working with or targeting the world's least evangelized non-Christian countries, namely Albania, Brunei, Iran, Iraq, Libya, North Korea, Saudi Arabia, South Yemen.

So here are populations totalling 123,119,000 human beings which are being ignored by foreign missions because they consider them too difficult or too dangerous to work among.

These countries' names are not even in the list of countries of the world in that publication (*ibid.*, pages 297-410). Consider Iraq. In 1990 Iraq had the world's fourth largest military machine, and was thus a very significant country in world affairs. Yet it has been sent no pentecostal/charismatic foreign missionaries to confront it in the name of Christ.

This is in marked contrast to the world's response to Iraq's threat to Saudi Arabian oil. When Iraq seized Kuwait in August 1990, within days the USA immediately sent some 400,000 military personnel to confront the aggressor country. It is, again, startling (another 'wonder') to realize that of these troops, 88% were Christians, 34% were Evangelicals, and 25% were pentecostals/charismatics. It is sad that no agency attempted to send them to Arabia as emissaries of the gospel but only as emissaries of war.

Many of the renewal's 90 North American pentecostal/charismatic foreign mission agencies recognize this situation but have been powerless to do anything about it. In the face of hostility, they remain baffled, frustrated, and defeated. Most pretend in public that the problem does not exist. Instead, they concentrate on comforting accounts of harvests being reaped among choicer targets in the Christian world.

Shortage of money is often alleged to be the underlying cause of this situation. But wait a moment - call in the statistics. These show us that the 90 North American agencies control aggregate annual income of around one billion US dollars. And globally, pentecostal/charismatic mission agencies wield income of $1.5 billion a year. No shortage there.

Organized Western foreign mission is a 'sign', therefore, but in this case a sign of failure. In spite of its vast foreign mission activity, the renewal is still in the main attempting to renew unrenewed Christians in safe areas rather than taking the Good News to non-Christians.

Third-World missions

Another striking 'sign' since 1970 has been the emergence of some 800 new pentecostal/charismatic agencies for foreign mission begun and operated by Third-World Christians. Altogether these agencies field some 30,000 full-time foreign missionaries who are citizens of Third-World countries. Much of this follows New Testament patterns of origin and development. First, Christians migrate in search of trade or employment. Second, to serve them their home churches then send pastors and lay workers.

However, the same defect noted above with Western foreign mission agencies is also true here: 97% of these Third-World missionaries are targeting and living among Christian populations in heavily-christianized countries in the Western world - Britain, Spain, France, Italy, USA, Canada, *et alia*. Very few are actually in contact with non-Christians in non-Christian religions in non-Christian countries.

Unorganized mission

Now comes the final, really startling 'sign'. Although organized pentecostal/charismatic missions have been frustrated in reaching unevangelized countries, it is the case that, as stated above, unorganized witness has arisen 'spontaneously' on a massive scale. Among the 25 million Third-World citizens who now live as migrant workers in Europe and North America there are over a million pentecostals/charismatics. Thus Koreans are skilled in the construction industry, hence are found in building projects across the world and especially in the Middle East. Large numbers of their workers are pentecostals/charismatics, who then witness to Christ through and in their labour.

Even Iraq by mid-1990 had among its 1.5 million foreign workers around 80,000 pentecostals/charismatics from a wide range of Third-World countries. After Iraq invaded Kuwait, most of these Christians - brethren of ours in the Body of Christ - were then robbed of all their possessions, thrown out or otherwise forced to flee, with several hundreds killed or dying en route. Although these 80,000 lost everything, I am not aware of any financial assistance being offered to them (apart from token help to some individuals) by members of the organized Pentecostal/Charismatic Renewal, although the personal incomes of all pentecostals/charismatics have now (in 1991) reached a total of US$1,059 billion per year.

In other words, where human missionary organization and even elementary compassion had failed, God in His providence had already called His people to be present as His witnesses. And what is true for Iraq is true for all other countries in the unevangelized world. This situation has produced the whole gamut of signs and wonders, from personal miracles, personal healings, and personal theophanies (widespread across the Middle East), to mass witness, mass conversions, mass tribulation, mass sufferings of whole churches, mass martyrdoms, and so on.

Signs and wonders have thus become as numerous, all-pervasive, and universal today as they were in New Testament times. Our task is to assist in vigorously communicating them by all the media - person-to-person, print, electronic - to all persons unfamiliar with God's ways today. Especially to non-Christians in non-Christian religions in non-Christian countries.

Note

The subject of describing the phenomena, organizations, and statistics of the Pentecostal/Charismatic Renewal is so complex, that the author has developed a methodology for when to use capital letters and when to use lowercase. More information of this methodology and of the documentation and sources for material in this essay can be found in the author's survey "The 20th-Century Pentecostal/Charismatic Renewal in the Holy Spirit, With its Goal of World Evangelization" (1988), and in Barrett & Johnson's book *Our Globe and How to Reach It* (1990); see attached Bibliography.

Bibliography

Arndt, W.F. and Gingrich, F.W. *A Greek-English Lexicon of the New Testament and Other Early Christian Literature.* 2nd edition. Chicago, IL: University of Chicago, 1958.

Barrett, D.B., ed. *World Christian Encyclopedia: A Comparative Survey of Churches and Religions in the Modern World, AD 1900-2000.* Nairobi: Oxford University Press, 1982.

Barrett, D.B. *Cosmos, Chaos, and Gospel: A Chronology of World Evangelization from Creation to*

New Creation. Birmingham, AL: New Hope, 1987. (Documents 'signs and wonders' in the context of 40 centuries of biblical history).

Barrett, D.B. "The 20th-century Pentecostal/Charismatic Renewal in the Holy Spirit, With its Goal of World Evangelization", in *International Bulletin of Missionary Research* (July 1988).

Barrett, D.B. and Johnson, T.M. *Our Globe and How to Reach it: Seeing the World Evangelized by AD 2000 and Beyond.* Birmingham, AL: New Hope, 1990. (Places statistics of the Renewal in context of global Christianity).

Barrett, D.B. and Reapsome, J.W. *Seven Hundred Plans to Evangelize the World: The Rise of a Global Evangelization Movement.* Birmingham, AL: New Hope, 1988. (Places plans of the Renewal in context of global Christianity).

Bria, I., ed. *Martyria/Mission: The Witness of the Orthodox Churches Today.* Geneva: CWME, 1980. (On the 'sign' of witness in contemporary Orthodoxy).

Brown, L.R. et alii. *State of the World 1990: A Worldwatch Institute Report on Progress toward a Sustainable Society.* New York: W.W. Norton, 1990. Annual since 1984. (A classic series. Begins with a chapter "The illusion of progress". Documents secular 'signs' today).

Burgess, S.M. and McGee, G.B., eds. *Dictionary of Pentecostal and Charismatic movements.* Grand Rapids, MI: Zondervan, 1988. (Documents many personal and collective 'signs and wonders').

Carey, William. *An Enquiry into the Obligations of Christians to Use Means for the Conversion of the Heathens.* Leicester, UK: Anne Ireland, 1792. (First major statement of world mission using statistics as God's signs).

Darton, M., ed. *Modern Concordance to the New Testament.* Garden City, NY: Doubleday, 1976. (Word counts of Greek words in the New Testament).

Goodrich, E.W. and Kohlenberger III, J.R. *The NIV (New International Version) Complete Concordance.* Grand Rapids, MI: Zondervan, 1981. (See under 'signs', 'miracles', 'wonders').

Grubb, K.G. et al. *World Christian handbook.* London: World Dominion/Lutterworth, 1949, 1952, 1957, 1962, 1968 editions.

Guida delle Missioni Cattoliche 1989. Roma: Congregazione per l'Evangelizzazione dei Popoli, 1989. (Regularly-updated handbook of all Catholic missionary jurisdictions, with history, statistics as 'signs').

Kittel, G. and Friedrich G., eds. *Theologisches Wörterbuch zum Neuen Testament.* 10 vols. Stuttgart: W. Kohlhammer Verlag, 1932-1978.

Kittel, G. and Friedrich G., eds. *Theological Dictionary of the New Testament.* 9 vols. Translation from Kittel's German work by G.W. Bromiley. Grand Rapids, MI: Eerdmans, 1964-1974. One-volume edition, 1985. (Very detailed articles on *semeion*, 'sign', *et alia*).

Mott, John R. *The Evangelization of the World in this Generation.* New York: SVMFM, 1990. (A brilliant classic, establishing the case for world evangelization. Relates the task to such 'signs' as extensive secular statistical data on railways, navigation, *et alia*).

Robinson, D., ed. *Concordance to the Good News Bible.* London: The Bible Societies, 1983. (See under 'signs', 'wonders', 'miracles').

Wigram, G.V. *The Englishman's Greek Concordance of the New Testament.* Nashville, TN: Broadman, 1979 (first edition 1839). (Word counts and all references in context to *semeion*, et alia).

18

Global Plans in the Pentecostal/Charismatic Tradition and the Challenge of the Unevangelized World, World A

Todd M. Johnson

The information age and world evangelization

Alvin Toffler, writing of a global shift in the very nature of power and wealth as we head into the 21st century, states:

> Today, in the fast-changing, affluent nations, despite all inequities of income and wealth, the coming struggle for power will increasingly turn into a struggle over the distribution of and access to knowledge. This is why, unless we understand how and to whom knowledge flows, we can neither protect ourselves against the abuse of power nor create the better, more democratic society that tomorrow's technologies promise. The control of knowledge is the crux of tomorrow's world-wide struggle for power in every human institution.[1]

If Toffler is right, Christians in the developed world at the end of the 20th century will be bombarded with yet more information and will be forced to manage it properly. At the same time, Christians in the developing world will face the same challenges of survival under oppressive circumstances more akin to the industrial age. Pentecostals and Charismatics, who are spread evenly over the Americas, sub-Saharan Africa, and Europe (with growing numbers in Asia), will face both challenges.

The gospel will become increasing available to all peoples as global communications improve; but just how it is presented will depend largely on the success of plans the church currently has for world evangelization. In *Seven hundred plans to evangelize the world*, a historical survey of 788 global plans to implement world evangelization, authors David Barrett and James Reapsome point out both the potential and the perils of these plans.[2] Though the potential to evangelize the world is evident, these plans are each almost entirely stand alone in their mentality. Various Christian traditions and agencies simply carve up the world in different, sometimes divergent, fashions and then each proceed to get on with the job with little or no reference to each other. In the midst of this historical list of 788 global plans appear a good number of Pentecostal and Charismatic global plans. (These adjectives are capitalized here when used separately, but the blanket cover term 'pentecostal/charismatic' is not).

A survey of pentecostal/charismatic global plans

The list of pentecostal/charismatic plans (see Table 1) since 1901 shows a recent proliferation of plans as global communications improve and as more money and personnel are available. Some plans originate from mission agencies, such as the Assemblies of God with its Decade of Harvest. Others come from the vision of a single broadcasting evangelist, like Pat Robertson's vision to reach everyone through television.

It is important to note that 18 of the 78 megaplans (the largest currently expanding organized global plans) are pentecostal/charismatic in origin; and many others have significant pentecostal/charismatic influence (see Table 2). Of the 33 global gigaplans (each a current plan spending over a billion U.S. dollars in a decade) 12 are pentecostal/charismatic in origin. Thus 23% of all megaplans and 36% of all gigaplans are pentecostal/charismatic in origin; though only 23% of all Christians are in this tradition. Thus, the world of Spirit-filled renewed Christians has much to offer to the cacophony of active plans already in place by other traditions.

From 1900 to 2000

It is important to note the interesting fact that Pentecostal global plans, and Pentecostalism itself, emerged at the end of 30 years of determined efforts to see the world evangelized by the year 1900, efforts which clearly failed to reach their goal.

Before the first modern Pentecostal plan for world evangelization, a generation of evangelical Christians had focused their attention on evangelizing the world by the year 1900. Important figures such as D.L. Moody, A.B. Simpson, H. Grattan Guiness, and, especially, Arthur Tappan Pierson, all believed that every human being could hear the Good News if the church would take its mandate seriously. The year 1900 came and went with a good portion of the world's population still beyond the reach of the gospel. The end of the matter from Pierson's point of view was "A lack of consecration in the church—evidenced by a lack of giving, faith, personal holiness, and, perhaps most of all, prevailing prayer".[3] More than one leader of this movement bemoaned the lack of power from the Holy Spirit in the lives of Christians. But, as Hillel Schwartz has skillfully documented, when one century ends in panic another begins with hope.

> British and American Protestants, in particular those filling the pews and camp meetings of the Holiness Movement, had been anticipating a new Pentecost since at least the 1880s. When the Evangelical Alliance of the United States met in Washington D.C., in 1887, the assembly began by singing the hymn, 'Come Gracious Spirit, Heavenly Dove,' then reading Acts 2 ('And they were filled with the Holy Ghost, and began to speak with other tongues, as the Spirit gave them utterance'). At a major conference on the Holy Spirit convened in Baltimore in 1890, one speaker favorably comparing the pentecostal 'cloven tongues, like as of fire' to electricity and the ever impressive energy of the dynamo. In 1899 the millenarian evangelist Cyrus I. Scofield would claim with characteristic *fin de siècle* panache, 'Indeed, within the last twenty years more has been written and said upon the doctrine of the Holy Spirit than in the preceding eighteen hundred years.' Shortly before his death in December 1899, the transatlantic revivalist Dwight L. Moody professed, 'I think it is getting very dark but don't think for a moment I am a pessimist... Pentecost isn't over yet'.[4]

In this context, Pentecostalism was born.

Parham and xenoglossia

Charles F. Parham had just established a Bible training school and was holding an all-night prayer service at the dawn of the 20th century. He was concerned to write "The statistics show that there are 1,500,000,000 people in the world. Another fact is, as the statistics also show, that more [than] 1,000,000,000 of the world's population are yet without the Bible, and without the church, and without any missionary ministry".[5] With this foundation and Agnes Osman's experience of *xenoglossia* (speaking in known languages by the power of the Holy Spirit) that very night (January 1, 1901), Parham envisioned a world evangelized by a new wave of Pentecostal missionaries utilizing this gift and eventually formulated a plan (1906).

In many ways, Parham's plan was much more than just one of the first of many Pentecostal plans. In his eyes it signaled the advent of a new dispensation—one which he initially felt would no longer require the arduous task of language learning for new missionaries.

Though Parham's vision was a global one, it never really had the opportunity to be tested. *Xenoglossia* would never catch on as a major missionary strategy. Instead, Pentecostal missionaries had to learn languages just like other missionaries—the hard way. Then, it took non-global plans, like the founding of the Pentecostal

Missionary Union in January 1909, to focus on the least evangelized. Cecil Polhill, the founder, was closely connected with the China Inland Mission and sought to emulate its principles from a pentecostal doctrine. Though some missionaries went to India, most went to China, with a focus on Tibet. The PMU was run by Polhill until 1926 when it was absorbed by the Assemblies of God of Great Britain and Ireland.

Models for Pentecostal missions

Before 1920, three agencies, the Church of God (Cleveland), the International Church of the Foursquare Gospel, and the Assemblies of God, had clearly taken bold initiatives in foreign missions that would provide some kind of a model for Pentecostal mission in the future. After initially accepting missionaries from other agencies who had received the baptism of the Holy Spirit, each of these traditions began training institutes to prepare its own prospective missionaries. These persons were then deployed into the existing frontier mission fields of China, India, and Africa. Over time, however, a heavy proportion of missionaries were sent to peoples with strong non-Pentecostal Christian populations. As McGee observes, by 1945 "The highest number of missionaries could now be found in Africa and Latin America, a significant shift from earlier years when the number of missionaries to China and India had dwarfed the number serving in Latin America".[6]

Today's plans

By 1991 global plans have reached a level of sophistication previously unknown. Pentecostal evangelist Morris Cerrullo envisions one billion people coming to Christ under his ministry. Participants at a recent conference discussed in detail the territorial spirits over particular countries and peoples.[7] In 1979 the International Church of the Foursquare Gospel targeted 100 unreached peoples to be penetrated by the year 1990. By 1986 they raised their goal to 200. In 1987 the Assemblies of God announced the 1990s as a Decade of Harvest. The Roman Catholic Church is calling the 1990s 'The Universal Decade of Evangelization'. One Catholic plan, Evangelization 2000, is heavily supported by the Catholic Charismatic movement. But, as in the past, there is very little coordination between these plans creating a vast amount of overlap, duplication, and still untargeted areas. It is now abundantly clear that none of the global plans are likely to succeed without coordination with other Christian traditions.

The missing link

Another problem with most global plans (pentecostal/charismatic or otherwise) is the nature of their targeting. Though the emphasis in their promotion is on evangelizing the whole world, actual outreach is limited to a particular portion of humanity--the Christian world and the already evangelized non-Christian world. In other words, those non-Christian peoples who have little opportunity to hear the gospel have been completely ignored by global plans, Pentecostal or any other type. In the pentecostal/charismatic sphere one does not see missions targeting Muslims, Buddhists, Hindus, non-Han Chinese, or even tribal groups. Yet these effectively make up the bulk of the remaining task. About 4,000 distinct peoples in the world are thought to be less than 50% evangelized. These peoples have been termed World A (World B is those peoples 50-95% evangelized--approximately 2,700 peoples; World C is those peoples 95% evangelized or greater--approximately 4,800 peoples. For more details see *Our globe and how to reach it: seeing the world evangelized by the year 2000 and beyond*, by Barrett and Johnson, *1990 and AD 2000 global monitor*, No. 2, December 1990). A global plan that overlooks 4,000 of the world's 11, 500 ethnolinguistic peoples is certainly a contradiction in terms--wrongly conceived and unrealistic in its targeting.

Hope for focusing energy on the least evangelized

With all the enthusiasm over pentecostal/charismatic plans that has been generated in the past few years, there would seem to be hope that these plans could make a significant impact. Twenty-six missiologists and researchers from around the world have seen what this contribution could be and have called for an action step that would "explain to the leaders of all 410 existing, current, global plans that each of their plans forms an essential part of the mosaic of the big-picture global plan".[8] Thus, coordination between plans is the one as yet absent factor and condition essential for effective penetration of World A.

One new strategy that looks promising for pentecostal/charismatic missions is nonresidential missions. "A nonresidential missionary is a full-time, professional career foreign missionary who is matched up with a single unevangelized population segment for purposes of concentrating priorities of initial evangelization and eliminating gaps and inadvertent duplications with other agencies".[9] Though its roots are in the Evangelical world, very early on Pentecostal missions have shown interest and support. Within a short time, pentecostal/charismatic training schools for nonresidential missionaries should be up and running in Singapore, Malta, Berlin, and other locations around the world.

Conclusion: a view of the 1990s from 1895

In finally assessing where we stand in our day, perhaps the long look of a Methodist missionary bishop in India in 1895 speaking of the 1990s best describes our opportunity: "In such an age, with a world so revolutionized, and with all the terms of the problems so changed, the final conversion of all nations will no longer seem a far-off vision of a few enthusiasts, and the mention of a million converts will no longer startle timid or doubting Christians. We talk in hesitating tones of the possibility of seeing a million converts now; but those who will fill our places a century hence will look out upon a scene where not a million converts, but a million workers, appear".[10] He wrote these words in faith, without the knowledge that it was only moments before the genesis of the pentecostal/charismatic movement. Today, in a recent evangelistic campaign in Argentina, one million converts were claimed; and in 1991 pentecostal/charismatic full-time workers alone number just over one million for the first time ever. Will Parham and his legacy now take the lead in the preaching of the gospel among the remaining tongues, tribes, languages, and peoples with no gospel witness?

Notes

— The author followes Barrett's methodology for when to use capital letters and when to use lowercase. For more information see the note at the end of the article by David B. Barrett in this *Festschrift.*

1. Alvin Toffler, *Powershift: Knowledge, Wealth, and Violence at the Edge of the 21st Century* (New York: Bantam Books, 1990), 20.
2. David B. Barrett and James W. Reapsome, *Seven Hundred Plans to Evangelize the World: The Rise of a Global Evangelization Movement* (Birmingham, AL: New Hope, 1988).
3. Todd M. Johnson, *Countdowm to 1900: World Evangelization at the End of the Nineteenth Century* (Birmingham, AL: New Hope, 1988), 1.
4. Hillel Schwartz, *Century's End: A Cultural History of the Fin de Siècle from the 990s through the 1990s* (New York: Doubleday, 1990), 170.
5. *Apostolic Faith* (June 21, 1899), quoted in James R. Goff Jr., *Fields White unto Harvest: Charles F. Parham and the Missionary Origins of Pentecostalism* (Fayetteville, AR: University of Arkansas, 1988), 72.
6. Gary B. McGee, *'This Gospel... Shall Be Preached': A History and Theology of the Assemblies of God Foreign Missions to 1959*, Vol. 1 (Springfield, MO: Gospel Publishing House, 1986), 239.
7. C. Peter Wagner and F. Douglas Pennoyer (eds.), *Wrestling with Dark Angels: Toward a Deeper Understanding of the Supernatural Forces in Spiritual Warfare* (Ventura, CA: Regal Books, 1990), 84.
8. David B. Barrett and Todd M. Johnson, *Our Globe and How to Reach it: Seeing the World Evangelized by the Year 2000 and Beyond* (Birmingham, Alabama: New Hope, 1990), 95.
9. V. David Garrison, *The Nonresidential Missionary: A New Strategy and the People it Serves* (Monrovia, CA: MARC, 1990), 13.
10. J.M. Thoburn, *The Christless Nations* (New York: Hunt & Eaton, 1895), 72-73..

Table 1.

99 Global plans for world evangelization in the pentecostal/charismatic tradition since 1900*

Note. Column 1 is the year the plan originated, Column 2 is a brief name for the plan, Column 3 is the author of the plan, Column 4 is the country the plan originated in, and Column 5 is the ecclesiastical tradition the plan originated in.

Year 1	*Brief name for plan* 2	*Author* 3	*Country* 4	*Tradition* 5
1900	Pentecostalism (First Wave, Renewal in the Holy Spirit)	C.F. Parham	USA	Pentecostal
1901	Latter Rain restoration	D.W. Myland	USA	Pentecostal
1903	All Nations Flag Church/Church of God of Prophecy	A.J. Tomlinson	USA	Pentecostal
1904	Welsh revival	Evan Roberts	Wales	Methodist
1906	Glossolalia to accomplish world evangelization	C.F. Parham	USA	Pentecostal
1910	Church of God (Cleveland) World Missions	R.M. Evans	USA	Pentecostal
1915	Elim Foursquare Gospel Alliance	G. Jeffreys	Britain	Pentecostal
1917	True Jesus Church	Paul Wei	China	Pentecostal
1918	Worldwide Evangelism	Aimee S. McPherson	USA	Pentecostal
1921	Ecumenical Union of Pentecostal Believers	F.A. Hale	USA	Pentecostal
1921	Electric or electronic church	Aimee S. McPherson	USA	Pentecostal
1924	Global White leadership in world evangelization	R.E. McAlister	USA	Pentecostal
1924	United Pentecostal Church International	J.G. Scheppe	USA	Pentecostal
1926	Lighthouse of International Foursquare Evangelism	Aimee S. McPherson	USA	Pentecostal
1930	Association of Camps Farthest Out	Glenn Clark	USA	Charismatic
1933	Laodicean Church Age with Millennium in 1977	W.M. Branham	USA	Pentecostal
1934	Biblical Research Society	D.L. Cooper	USA	Messianic Jewish
1935	World Revival Crusade	G. Jeffreys	Britain	Pentecostal
1939	World-Wide Signs Following Evangelism	L.R.M. Kopp	USA	Messianic Jewish
1947	Oral Roberts Evangelistic Association	Oral Roberts	USA	Pentecostal
1948	New Order of the Latter Rain: Global Missions Broadcast	George Hawtin	Canada	Pentecostal
1949	Association for Native Evangelism	T.L. Osborn	USA	Pentecostal
1950	Evangelistic broadcasting/Cathedral of Tomorrow	Rex Humbard	USA	Pentecostal
1950	Full Gospel Businessmen's Fellowship International	D. Shakarian	USA	Pentecostal
1956	Charismatic Movement (Second Wave, Ren. in the Holy Spirit)	R. Winkler	USA	Charismatic
1957	Global Conquest	J.P. Hogan	USA	Pentecostal
1957	Nights of Prayer for World-wide Revival	George S. Ingram	India	Anglican
1960	World MAP (World Missionary Assistance Plan)	R. Mahoney	USA	Pentecostal
1960	Youth With A Mission	Loren Cunningham	USA	Pentecostal
1961	World Evangelism	Morris Cerullo	USA	Pentecostal
1961	Christian Broadcasting Network/CBN World Outreach	M.G. (Pat) Robertson	USA	Charismatic
1967	International Correspondence Institute	G. Flattery	Belgium	Pentecostal
1967	Crusade for World Revival	P. Yonggi Cho	Korea	Pentecostal
1968	African Independent Churches Service	D.B. Barrett	Kenya	Ecumenical
1969	Jimmy Swaggart Ministries	Jimmy L. Swaggart	USA	Pentecostal
1972	International Catholic Charismatic Renewal	Ralph Martin	USA	Roman Catholic
1972	'World evangelisation'/World Pentecost	Donald Gee	Britain	Pentecostal
1973	Summer Institute of World Mission	P. Yonggi Cho	Korea	Presbyterian
1973	Globe Missionary Evangelism	K. Sumrall	USA	Charismatic
1973	Trinity Broadcasting Network	Paul F. Crouch	USA	Pentecostal
1973	Ephesian Method: Breaking the stained-glass barrier	David A. Womack	USA	Pentecostal
1975	Full Gospel World Mission Association	P. Yonggi Cho	Korea	Pentecostal
1975	World Conference on the Holy Spirit	M. Benhayim	Israel	Pentecostal
1975	Total World Evangelization Vision	L. Southwick	USA	Charismatic
1976	Gabriel Olasoji World Evangelism	Gabriel K. Olasoji	Nigeria	Pentecostal
1976	Church Growth International Seminars	P. Yonggi Cho	Korea	Pentecostal
1977	Charismatic Renewal in the Christian Churches	K. Ranaghan	USA	Pentecostal/Charismatic

1978	International Conference on the Catholic Charismatic Renewal	L.-J. Suenens	Ireland	Roman Catholic
1979	Sharing of Ministries Abroad (SOMA)	Michael C. Harper	Britain	Anglican
1979	Foursquare Missions International	L. Edwards	USA	Pentecostal
1979	International Charismatic Pilgrimage to Lourdes	L.-J. Suenens	France	Roman Catholic
1979	12th Pentecostal World Conference	E. Dando	Canada	Pentecostal
1979	PTL Ministries	J. Bakker	USA	Pentecostal
1980	Operation World Begin From Here	Peter P.O. Alliu	Nigeria	Charismatic
1980	World Evangelization Crusade	P. Yonggi Cho	Korea	Evangelical/Charismatic
1980	Third-Wave Renewal in the Holy Spirit: Power Evangelism	C.P. Wagner	USA	Evangelical/Charismatic
1981	Charismatic TV evangelists	Oral Roberts	USA	Pentecostal/Charismatic
1981	Dominion Network/Video Satellite	R.W. Johnson	USA	Charismatic
1982	Project 223	Floyd McClung	USA	Charismatic
1982	Harvest Vision:1990	L. Edwards	USA	Pentecostal
1982	World Satellite Evangelism	P.I. McClendon	USA	Charismatic
1983	Lumen 2000	Bobby Cavnar	USA	Roman Catholic
1983	Committee on the Holy Spirit and Frontier Missions	G. Adkins	USA	Charismatic
1984	Worldwide Priests Retreat	Tom Forrest	Vatican	Roman Catholic
1985	Korean Churches' Plan for Entering Every Country	Han Ki Man	Korea	Interdenominational
1985	God the Evangelist	David F. Wells	Norway	Evangelical/Charismatic
1985	World Ambassadors	Mark A. Kyle	USA	Charismatic
1985	Amsterdam Prayer Conference for World Evangelization	David Bryant	Hollland	Evangelical/Charismatic
1985	EXPLO-85 Global Christian Training Teleconference	Bailey Marks	USA	Evangelical/Charismatic
1985	Association of International Mission Services	Howard Foltz	USA	Charismatic
1985	Power evangelism; Power healing; and Power encounters	John Wimber	USA	Charismatic
1986	Reaching the World's Cities by AD 2000	J.P. Hogan	USA	Pentecostal
1986	International Prophetic Ministry Convention	B. Maoz	Israel	Pentecostal/Charismatic
1986	International Conference for Equipping Evangelists	Terry Edwards	USA	Charismatic
1986	Leaders' Congress on the Holy Spirit & World Evangelization	H. Vinson Synan	USA	Pentecostal/Charismatic
1986	Intercontinental Broadcasting Network	J. Martin	Norway	Charismatic
1986	Televised Evangelism for All	N. Van Hamm	USA	Charismatic
1987	Evangelization 2000/New Evangelization 2000	Tom Forrest	Vatican	Roman Catholic
1987	Consultation on World Evangelization	Larry Christenson	Singapore	Pentecostal/Charismatic
1987	World Evangelization Strategy Committee	Gary Clark	Britain	Pentecostal/Charismatic
1987	AD 2000 Together	H. Vinson Synan	USA	Pentecostal/Charismatic
1987	Community Satellite Corporation	R.W. Johnson	USA	Charismatic
1987	Global Broadcasting System (Top Hat platform network)	Paul F. Crouch	USA	Evangelical/Charismatic
1987	Worldwide Prayer Crusade	Shelia Beatty	Vatican	Roman Catholic
1987	Decade of Harvest	J.P. Hogan	USA	Pentecostal
1987	COMIBAM '87/Ibero-American Missions Congress	Luis Bush	Brazil	Evangelical/Charismatic
1987	Decade of Destiny for Church of God World Missions	C. Moree	USA	Pentecostal
1987	Advance Ministries: Reaching the Unreached	Steve Shank	USA	Charismatic
1987	'The Missing Key to World Evangelization'	D. Shibley	USA	Charismatic
1988	Evangelistic mass campaigns: Christ For All Nations	Reinhard Bonnke	Germany	Interdenominational
1988	Charismatics United for World Evangelization	Larry Christenson	Singapore	Pentecostal/Charismatic
1988	Video churches and missions	K. Chareonwongsak	Thailand	Charismatic
1988	'88 World Evangelization Crusade	P. Yonggi Cho	Korea	Charismatic
1989	15th Pentecostal World Conference	Jakob Zopfi	Singapore	Pentecostal
1989	Jerusalem Charismatic Leaders Meeting	Michael C. Harper	Israel	Charismatic
1990	Decade of Universal Evangelization	John Paul II	Vatican	Roman Catholic
1990	World Congress on the Holy Spirit & World Evangelization	H. Vinson Synan	USA	Pentecostal/Charismatic
1991	Internat. Charismatic Consultation on World Evangelization	Michael C. Harper	Britain	Pentecostal/Charismatic
1991	Charismatic youth churches	Benson Idahosa	Nigeria	Charismatic

*derived from *Seven hundred plans to evangelize the world* by David B. Barrett and James W. Reapsome (New Hope,1988).

Table 2.

The top 78 current ongoing global megaplans, with the top 33 current gigaplans, 1988

All plans below are megaplans, those in bold are gigaplans,
those in italics are pentecostal/charismatic in origin

Origin	*Brief name of megaplan*	*Deadline*
1991	***International Charismatic Consultation on World Evangelization***	2000
1990	EXPLO-90 Worldwide Satellite Strategy	2000
1990	*Decade of Universal Evangelization*	2000
1989	International Bishops Retreat 2000	2000
1988	Third World Mission Advance	2000
1988	*Charismatic United for World Evangelization*	2000
1987	World Evangelism World Plan 1987-1991	1991
1987	COMIBAM '87/Ibero-American Missions Congress	2000
1987	***Decade of Harvest***	2000
1987	**New Life 2000: A Revolutionary Plan (Here's Life World)**	2000
1987	*AD 2000 Together*	2000
1987	***Evangelization 2000/New Evangelization 2000***	2000
1986	'Renew the Church—Reach the World'	2000
1986	*Reaching the World's Cities by AD 2000*	2000
1985	The World by 2000	2000
1985	**Global Strategy Committee, Seventh-day Adventists**	2000
1985	**Integrity Keepers Conventions**	1995
1985	Korean Churches Plan for Entering Every Country	2000
1983	Third-World Mission Societies	2000
1982	***Project 223***	2011
1979	**The Jesus Project ('Jesus' Film)**	2000
1976	**Bold Mission Thrust**	**2000**
1975	World Evangelical Fellowship Missions Commission	—
1974	**Synod of Bishops: 'Evangelization of the Modern World'**	—
1974	Lausanne Committee for World Evangelization	—
1973	***Trinity Broadcasting Network***	—
1972	***International Catholic Charismatic Renewal***	—
1969	***Jimmy Swaggart Ministries***	—
1967	**Sacred Congregation for the Evangelization of Peoples**	—
1961	***Christian Broadcasting Network***	—
1961	Commission on World Mission and Evangelism	—
1960	***Youth With A Mission***	—
1957	Operation Mobilization	—
1950	Missionaries of Charity	—
1950	*Full Gospel Business Men's Fellowship International*	—
1950	**World Vision International**	—
1950	Billy Graham Evangelistic Association	—
1948	World Council of Churches, 7th Function	—
1947	***Oral Roberts Evangelistic Association***	—
1946	**United Bible Societies**	—
1945	**Evangelical Foreign Missions Association**	—
1943	Conservative Baptist Foreign Mission Society	—
1942	New Tribes Mission	—
1934	Two Thousand Tongues to Go	—
1934	Youth For Christ International	—
1931	'Praised be Jesus Christ!'—Radio Vatican	—
1930	Bringing Christ to the Nations (The Lutheran Hour)	—
1930	Voice of Prophecy	—

(continued on next page)

Origin	*Brief name of megaplan*	*Deadline*
1924	*United Pentecostal Church International*	2000
1918	*Worldwide Evangelism (International Ch of Foursquare Gospel)*	—
1917	**Interdenominational Foreign Mission Association**	—
1913	Christ's Etceteras (Worldwide Evangelization Crusade)	—
1910	*Church of God (Cleveland) World Missions*	—
1899	Gideons International	—
1895	Association of Pentecostal Churches in America (Nazarenes)	—
1893	Africa Industrial Mission/SIM International	—
1890	Scandinavian/Evangelical Alliance Mission	—
1887	Christian & Missionary Alliance	—
1875	Verbites: 'Evangelizzazione dei popoli'	—
1872	Salesian Sisters: evangelization by works of charity	—
1870	**Watch Tower Bible & Tract Society**	1874
1865	Christian Revival Association (Salvation Army)	—
1863	**New Apostolic Church**	1880
1862	Scheutists: 'Evangelizzazione dei popoli'	—
1859	Salesians: Christian education across the world	—
1845	**Southern Baptist Convention**	—
1844	**Seventh-day Adventists**	1844
1830	**Church of Jesus Christ of Latter-day Saints**	—
1819	**Missionary Society of the Methodist Episcopal Church**	—
1804	Foreign-language Bible Societies: BFBS, ABS, et alia	—
1703	Spiritans: 'Evangelizzazione degli infedeli'	—
1680	Christian Brothers: evangelization by schools	—
1622	**Propaganda Fide: Spreading the Faith**	—
1588	**Consistorial Congregation (Sacred Congregation for Bishops)**	—
1580	Discalced Carmelite Sisters: evangelization by prayer	—
1523	**Conversion of Islam and the Whole World to Christ (Jesuits)**	—
1215	**Order of Preachers: 'Propagation of the Faith by Preaching'**	—
1209	**Order of Friars: mendicant orders of travelling preachers**	—

Part 3

Missiological and Ecumenical Reflections on Inculturation and Encounter, with Special Reference to Pentecostalism and the Charismatic Renewal

19

Inkulturation als Entäußerung

(Inculturation as Self-emptying)

Theo Sundermeier

Kultur war kein Thema der Missionare des 19. und frühen 20. Jahrhunderts. Kunst noch viel weniger. Das hat soziologische aber auch theologische Gründe. Die Kultur war Sache der Oberschicht, Kunst die der 'feinen Leute'. Zu diesen Kreisen gehörten die Missionare nicht. Sie kamen aus dem kleinen Bürgertum, dem Handwerkerstand, waren Kleinbauern. Wie sie selbst auf der sozialen Leiter aufsteigen wollten - Fernziel war das Pfarramt -, so fühlten sie sich eher als Vertreter der abendländischen Zivilisation, denn als Kulturträger im engeren Sinn des Wortes. Der Begriff der Kultur hatte nur eine komparatistische Funktion. Er definierte das Missionsgebiet. Man war entweder zu Natur- oder zu Kulturvölkern gesandt. Auch wenn die Grenzen als fließend empfunden wurden - Gustav Warneck (Halle) betont das in seiner *Missionslehre* ausdrücklich[1] -, so hatte diese Differenzierung dennoch Konsequenzen. Sie wurde zum Selektionsmaßstab für die Auswahl der Missionare. Die 'gebildeteren' unter ihnen wurden zu den Kulturvölkern gesandt, die anderen - von herausragenden Ausnahmen abgesehen - zu den Naturvölkern. Die Ostasien-Mission (1884 in Weimar als Allgemeiner Evangelisch-Protestantischer Missionsverein gegründet) verstand sich bewußt als Kulturträgerin mit klaren Selektionskriterien: Sie wußte sich zu den Kulturvölkern des Ostens gesandt. Kein Wunder, daß die Vertreter der liberalen Theologie - Ernst Tröltsch (Heidelberg, Berlin) u.a. - sich dieser Mission verbunden fühlten und gelegentlich auf ihren Missionsfesten als Redner auftraten. Sie wollten den Kulturaustausch. Die Durchdringung der Kulturen mit dem christlichen Glauben war für sie eine dem Christentum inhärente Aufgabe und entsprach seinem universellen Anspruch.

Der Pietismus, zumal seine durch die Erweckungsbewegung geprägte Gestalt des 19. Jahrhunderts, hatte auch aus theologischen Gründen zu Kunst und Kultur kein Verhältnis. Die dem Calvinismus inhärente Bilderfeindlichkeit hat die Erweckungsfrömmigkeit geprägt. Kunst und Kultur sind diesseitig, die Mission aber dient dem kommenden Reich. Die Mauern Jerusalems will man bauen, doch keine (Kultur) Schätze hier auf Erden sammeln. Der Unsichtbarkeit des Glaubens entspricht ein eher unansehnlicher Gottesdienst. Schönheit verführt, des Glaubens Charakteristikum aber ist im Sinne des Paulus Nüchternheit!

Diese Haltung ist bis heute in fundamentalistischen Missionskreisen zu finden.

Die Texte der Lausanner Konferenz (1974) sprechen eine eindeutige Sprache, und die Bemühungen des Ehepaares Kathleen und Bruce Nicholls, hier einen neuen Weg einzuschlagen stößt auf kein enthusiastisches Echo, trotz ihres großen Engagements und ihrer erfolgreich durchgeführten Workshops für Künstler in Afrika, Asien und Lateinamerika. Kultur kommt nur insofern in den Blick, als sie instrumentalisiert werden kann zur effektiveren Ausführung der Evangelisationsaufgabe. Doch wer Kunst instrumentalisiert, zerstört sie. Das gleiche gilt für eine einseitige Funktionalisierung der Kultur.

Akkommodation, Einheimischmachung

Das hier verhandelte Problem ist in der Missionstheologie der Konfessionskirchen auf katholischer Seite unter den Stichworten Akkomodation, Adaption und Assimilation vielfach verhandelt worden. Auf evangelischer Seite herrschen die Begriffe Einheimischwerdung, Indigenisierung vor, meinen aber ähnliches. Ziel ist jeweils - so besonders im II. Vaticanum und bei Warneck - die einheimische Ortskirche. Sie muß so konstituiert werden, daß sie selbständig geleitet wird und in der sie umgebenden Kultur verwurzelt ist. Die Ortskirche ist Spiegel der universalen Kirche im lokalen Gewand. Der Dreierschritt Akkomodation, Assimilation, Transformation, von Thomas Ohm O.S.B. (Münster) präludiert, hat im katholischen Bereich fast klassische Bedeutung gewonnen, wobei man unter Akkomodation eine bewußte Anpassung in Sprache und Stil an die missionarische Situation meint, die Assimilation auf die Übernahme dessen zielt, was in den vorgegebenen Kulturen 'wahr', 'gut' und 'wertvoll' ist, so daß dies zum Reichtum und zur Fülle der Weltkirche beitragen kann. Transformation schließlich meint die Reinigung, Läuterung und 'Erhebung' der Kulturen über sich hinaus, ihre Durchsäuerung mit dem christlichen Sauerteig, der sie von allem Schädlichen und Verdorbenen befreit zur Reinheit der ursprünglichen, gottgewollten Intention.[2]

Die Situation war im protestantischen Missionsdenken ähnlich. Die Fragwürdigkeit des Konzeptes der Einheimischwerdung wurde im deutschsprachigen Bereich jedoch durch die Koppelung an den Volksbegriff schneller deutlich. Darauf hat Johannes C. Hoekendijk (Utrecht) sehr früh in seiner Dissertation[3] aufmerksam gemacht. Nationalisierung, Provinzialisierung, Antimodernismus stehen mit diesem Konzept der Kirche ins Haus. Alternativen hat Hoekendijk dazu nicht aufgezeigt, jedoch eine Entschränkung der Kirche aus den lokalen Bindungen schlechthin gefordert. Der eigentliche Kontext der Mission ist nach ihm die ganze Welt, zumal in ihren sozialen und politischen Dimensionen.

Kontextualität

Ein neues missionstheologisches Konzept zur Sache hat erst der Theological Education Fund in den 70er Jahren vorgetragen. Sprecher war der chinesische Theologe Shoki Coe, doch darf die Rolle nicht übersehen werden, die der damalige Afrika-Referent beim TEF, Hans-Werner Gensichen (Heidelberg) bei der Entwicklung dieses Entwurfes gespielt hat. Seine Handschrift ist an verschiedenen Stellen erkennbar. Auch wenn Kontextualisierung den Kulturbegriff ursprünglich nicht ausschließen, sondern modernisieren und auf seine sozio-politische Relevanz hin erweitern und kritisieren wollte, er führte dazu, hier Gegensätze aufzubauen. Die befreiungstheologischen Entwürfe Südafrikas und Lateinamerikas haben die kulturtheologischen Aspekte entsprechend weitgehend übersehen, die asiatischen Theologen ihn in ihren kontextuellen Theologien um so deutlicher herausgestellt. Inzwischen ist eine Annäherung beider Standpunkte erkennbar. Hier kulturelle Wirklichkeit - dort die politische, hier Retrospektive - dort Zukunftsorientierung, hier der Nachbereich - dort der weltweite soziale Horizont, diese Alternativen sind schon längst nicht mehr gültig. Dennoch bleibt das sprachliche Dilemma, daß der Begriff der 'Kontextualität' inzwischen inhaltlich so festgelegt ist, daß er nur schwer die kulturelle Dimension der Wirklichkeit mitschwingen läßt.

Inkulturation

Mehr und mehr setzt sich deshalb der aus der katholischen Tradition stammende Begriff der 'Inkulturation' durch, auch im protestantischen Bereich. Trägt er, was man sich von ihm verspricht? Der Begriff selbst ist ein Neologismus und eine theologische Adaption des in der Kulturanthropologie beheimateten Begriffes 'Enkulturation', der jene Vorgänge umschreibt, wo vorgegebenes kulturelles Traditionsgut durch Erziehung und Sozialisation internalisiert wird. Die kleine sprachliche Veränderung orientiert sich bewußt an dem Begriff der Inkarnation. Beide Modelle, die Fleischwerdung des Logos und der im Umfeld der Pädagogik beheimatete Vorgang der Übernahme kultureller Werte, führten zu der sprachlichen Neubildung, die in gelungener Weise theologische und anthropologische Komponenten zusammenfügt.

Ermöglicht wurde solche Verbindung jedoch erst dadurch, daß der Kulturbegriff schon durch das II. Vaticanum seiner 'elitären' und 'aristokratischen' Konnotationen entkleidet und sozialwissenschaftlich tiefer angesiedelt wurde und umfassend die gestaltete Lebenswelt des Menschen beschreibt, die die Welt der Arbeit, der Familie, der bürgerlichen Gesellschaft u.a. einschließt (*Gaudium et spes* 53). Die Mission nimmt die Bewegung der Zuwendung Gottes zur Menschheit auf. "Wie der Logos eine konkret menschliche Natur annahm und als dieser konkrete Mensch eine Offenbarung Gottes wurde, soll sich auch die Botschaft Jesu in einer jeweils neuen Kultur 'inkarnieren', d.h. eine neue Gestalt annehmen, die dem jeweiligen Volk angemessen ist, auf eine neue Weise Offenbarung der allerbarmenden Liebe Gottes sein", interpretiert Karl Müller S.V.D. (St. Augustin) den Vorgang der Inkulturation.[4] Dem könnte man zustimmen, wenn so eindeutig das Subjekt der Inkulturation bestimmt wäre, wie es bei Müller zu sein scheint. Päpstliche Äusserungen hierzu sind jedoch eher unklar. Die Crux des Begriffes der Inkulturation liegt nämlich darin, daß sehr präzise bestimmt werden muß, wer das Subjekt dieses Vorganges ist. Darauf hat mit aller Schärfe Klauspeter Blaser (Lausanne) aufmerksam gemacht: "Wer inkulturiert was?".[5] An dieser Frage entscheidet sich erst, ob der Begriff der Inkulturation wirklich über den der Anpassung hinausführt, deren Subjekt naturgemäß immer nur die Kirche ist und sein kann. Die Kirche entscheidet darüber - und hat im Laufe der Kirchengeschichte immer wieder getan, man denke an den unseligen Ritenstreit in China - wieweit die Anpassung gehen darf. Sie legt Methode und Ziel fest. Sie tritt als Wächterin auf, sie ist Herrin dieses Vorganges. In der neuesten Missionsenzyklika *Redemptoris missio* (1991) findet gerade diese Umbiegung des Inkulturationsbegriffes in Richtung Anpassung erneut statt. Die Kirche 'macht' durch die Inkulturation "das Evangelium in verschiedenen Kulturen lebendig".[6] Die Kirche "wird in den Prozeß der Inkulturation eingebunden".[7] Hier wird die offene Weite des Inkulturationsbegriffes deutlich eingegrenzt. Inkulturation wird als 'heikler Bereich' beschrieben[8], bei dem 'zwei Prinzipien' leitend sein müssen: "Vereinbarkeit mit dem Evangelium und der Gemeinschaft mit der Gesamtkirche".[9] Ängstlichkeit herrscht vor. Die Hierarchie, so gewinnt man den Eindruck, hat wieder einmal die Sorge, daß die Dynamik der missionarischen Bewegung und ihrer Begegnung mit den Kulturen und Religionen der Welt ihr entgleitet. Die Offenheit des Glaubens für die Dynamik des Wortes selbst muß jedoch gewagt werden, wenn der Begriff der Inkulturation die ihm angemessene Bedeutung missionstheologisch und universal haben soll.

Entäußerung

Wenn Inkulturation sich *per definitionem* am Inkarnationsgeschehen orientiert, dann kann sein Subjekt nur das Evangelium von dem fleischgewordenen Wort sein. Den Weg des Evangeliums kann niemand bestimmen, noch festlegen; keine Methode ist ihm vorzuschreiben, und erst recht kann und darf nicht vorher festgelegt werden, welches Ergebnis der Weg zu zeitigen hat. Die Freiheit des Wortes Gottes in seiner Bewegung zu den Menschen in ihren Kulturen muß im Begriff der Inkulturation gewahrt bleiben. Deshalb muß er durch den Begriff der *Kenosis* qualifiziert werden. Inkulturation ist ein kenotischer Vorgang. Wie Christus selbst "es nicht wie einen Raub festhielt, Gott gleich zu sein, sondern sich entäußerte und Knechtsgestalt annahm" (Phil. 2:16), so geht das Wort in die Kulturen ein. Es nimmt die Kirchen auf diesem Weg mit, die deshalb ihre bisherige Gestalt nicht wie einen Raub festhalten dürfen, wenn sie "wie Christus gesinnt" sein wollen (Phil. 2:5). Auf diesem Weg lernen die Kirchen das immer neue Wirken des Geistes kennen, sie werden auf neue theologische Pfade geführt und entdecken neue Gestalten des Glaubens, neue Formen der Spiritualität und neue Gestaltungen des Zusammenlebens. Dabei geht es nicht darum, die Fülle der Kirche mit den Kulturen der anderen Völker anzureichern, sondern darum, "die Breite, die Länge und die Tiefe und die Höhe" des Geheimnisses von Christus selbst und seiner Liebe zu erkennen (Eph. 3:18 f.). Gewiß ist das ein Prozeß, "der das gesamte missionarische Leben begleitet"[10], er darf aber nicht durch die Furcht um den Verlust der Identität der Kirche verdunkelt werden. Dieser Prozeß ist ein Wagnis, das dem des Glaubens entspricht. Einen gesicherten Glauben gibt es nicht. Einen Weg der Inkulturation, auf dem wir dem Wort die Initiative nehmen und Vorschriften machen, hieße Gott vorschreiben, wie seine Kondeszendenz in die jeweilige Situation des Menschen und seiner Kultur auszusehen hat. Auf dem Wege der kenotischen Inkulturation bleibt niemand so, wie er zuvor war. Er erkennt die kulturelle Begrenzung seines bisherigen Wissens von Gott und läßt sich verändern. Verändern wird sich aber nicht nur der Missionar, sondern auch die sendende Kirche. Verändert wird durch das Evangelium auch die Kultur, in die hinein es inkarniert. Es verändert sich schließlich die Botschaft selbst! Der Prozeß der Inkulturation öffnet uns die Augen für die Veränderungen, die das Evangelium im Gang durch die Völkerwelt von seinem Ursprung an in Palästina erfahren hat. Er macht uns bescheiden, indem er uns die Begrenztheit der eigenen Erkenntnis unserer theologischen Aussagen und Überzeugungen zeigt. Das zu erkennen, ist jedoch kein Verlust, führt nicht in die Unsicherheit, sondern ist Erkenntnisgewinn. Die Studie der Evangelischen Kirchen in Deutschland *Religionen, Religiosität und christlicher Glaube* (1991), die den Begriff 'Inkulturation' nicht verwendet, sondern auf den früheren der 'Indigenisierung' zurückgreift, zeigt anhand der Dogmengeschichte diesen Vorgang auf, indem sie deutlich macht, wie schon im Übergang des Evangeliums von Palästina in die hellenistische Welt diese Veränderung der Botschaft stattfindet, ja, stattfinden mußte. Nur so kann die Botschaft das Herz der Völker und Kulturen treffen. Jenes Geschehen der Inkulturation und der Veränderungsprozeß der frühen Kirche als Veränderungsprozeß der Botschaft, die "ihre Identität in der Angemessenheit der jeweiligen Interpretation des Neuen Testamentes erweisen muß"[11], muß sich in Asien, Afrika und Lateinamerika fortsetzen. "In dem Bedenken dieses Geschehens steht die immer neue Selbstpreisgabe... Gottes als Heiliger Geist vor uns. Gott sucht die Menschen in ihren tief verschiedenen Denk- und Empfindungswelten auf und geht in sie hinein.

'Die' christliche Wahrheit, d.h. die Vergebung der Sünden, der Zugang zu dem nahen Gott, den wir in seinem Sich-Findenlassen suchen, geschieht aufgrund dieser Indigenisation in allen Kulturen. Aber keine Kirche kann in dem Bewußtsein leben, die reine Wahrheit zu besitzen oder zu 'verwalten'''.[12]

Tun sich mit dieser Interpretation erneut Gegensätze zwischen evangelischer und katholischer Missionstheologie auf? Das Zitat von Müller zeigt, daß das nicht der Fall ist. Wohl aber machen die Akzentverschiebungen deutlich, daß der ökumenische Austausch notwendig ist und fruchtbar sein kann.

Wie anregend solch ein ökumenischer Austausch ist, der immer zugleich ein interkultureller sein muß, da er weltweit zu führen ist, dafür legt Walter J. Hollenweger, dem diese Zeilen zum 65. Geburtstag gewidmet sind, in seiner missionarischen Existenz und seinen Entwürfen zu einer interkulturellen Theologie ein eindrückliches Zeugnis ab.

Anmerkungen

1. Gustav Warneck, *Missionslehre* III/1 (Gotha: Friedrich Andreas Perthes, 1899), 57 ff.
2. Vlg. hierzu besonders H. Rzepkowski, *Der Welt verpflichtet; Text und Kommentar des Apostolischen Schreibens Evangelii nuntiandi* (St. Augustin, 1976), 117 ff.
3. Johannes C. Hoekendijk, *Kerk en volk in de Duitse zendingswetenschap* (Amsterdam, 1948). Deutsche Übersetzung: *Kirche und Volk in der deutchen Missionswissenschaft* (München, 1967).
4. *Lexikon Missionstheologischer Grundbegriffe*, hrsg. von Karl Müller und Theo Sundermeier (Berlin: Dietrich Reimer Verlag, 1987) 178.
5. K. Blaser, "Kultur und Christentum", in: *Evangelisches Kirchenlexlicon*, Bd. II, 2. Auflage (Göttingen, 1989), 1518.
6. *Redemptoris missio* 52.
7. *Ibid.*
8. *Redemptoris missio* 53.
9. *Redemptoris missio* 54.
10. *Redemptoris missio* 52.
11. *Religionen, Religiosität und christlicher Glaube; eine Studie* (Gütersloh, 1991), 115.
12. *Ibid.*, 116.

20

Allegiance, Truth and Power Encounters in Christian Witness

Charles H. Kraft

Introduction

The subject of power encounter is one we hear increasingly discussed in missiological circles by charismatics and non-charismatics alike.[1] Many non-charismatic evangelicals have followed a path similar to my own in which we first were confronted with questions concerning spiritual power for which we had no answers, then began to learn more about the Kingdom of God theme in Jesus' teaching and finally have opened ourselves to the insights of Pentecostals and charismatics in this area. In my own case, the question of whether or not I took evil spirits seriously was put to me early in my missionary career in northern Nigeria. Unfortunately, I did not have a convincing answer.

After joining the Fuller faculty in 1969, however, I learned from colleagues such as A.F. Glasser and G.E. Ladd to take a 'Kingdom perspective' on the work of God in the world. Within this perspective, then, the insights of my colleague A.R. Tippett concerning power encounters (see below) began to make sense, first theoretically, then practically as I began to experience personally the joy of being used by God to free people from demons.

I must confess to a degree of uneasiness in this area, however, stemming from my evangelical concern for scriptural balance. For examples abound of the extremes to which many with a 'power focus' have gone, both in Euro-America and in the two-thirds world. Such people have often seemed to lose their way and to get into very questionable emphases and practices. In pondering this danger, then, I began to see the need raised by another of my colleagues, P.G. Hiebert, for paying at least as much attention to truth as to power in cross-cultural ministry, lest we mislead those whose primary concern is already for power into simply incorporating 'Christian power' into their experience in a syncretistic way.

These concerns have led to the following attempt to discuss what I believe to be a way to move and minister in spiritual power without losing biblical balance.

The Concept of Power Encounter

The term and initial discussion of power encounter come from A.R. Tippett (1971). Tippett observed that in the early days of Christian work in the South Pacific, the turning point for the acceptance of the Gospel usually occurred when there was an 'encounter' between the spiritual power of the Christian God and that of the traditional deity or spirit in which it was demonstrated that the power of God is greater than that of the other deity. Ideally such a demonstration would be accompanied by a visible desecration (an 'ocular demonstration') of the symbol(s) of the traditional deity by its priest or other official of that deity. In performing such an act, the priest who was previously devoted to that deity declares that he/she rejects that power and pledges allegiance to the Christian God on whom alone he/she will henceforth depend for spiritual power, including protection from any reprisals from the traditional deity.

Typical of such confrontations would be a converted priest of a given totem animal (e.g. a sacred turtle) openly eating and thus desecrating the totem to demonstrate that the power behind that totem has been defeated by the power of Jesus Christ.[2] A contemporary example (of many that could be cited) comes from Papua New Guinea where it was reported to me that a pastor, soon after moving to a new area (within his language group) to plant a church, chose to bathe in a sacred pool to demonstrate to the skeptical people of that area that the power of Christ is greater than the power of the spirits living in that pool. Seeing that the pastor suffered no ill effects from such bathing, the people accepted his successful confrontation as proving his point and opened themselves to the Gospel.

It was such confrontations and the classic power encounters of Scripture (e.g. Moses versus Pharaoh — Ex. 7-12; Elijah versus the Prophets of Baal — 1 Kings 18) that formed Tippett's view of power encounter. With a slight expansion of Tippett's concept, we will here use the term to label healings, deliverances or any other "visible, practical demonstration that Jesus Christ is more powerful than the spirits, powers or false gods worshiped or feared by the members of a given people group".[3]

The concept of 'taking territory' from the enemy for God's Kingdom is seen as basic for such encounters. Thus, Jesus' entire ministry is seen as a massive power confrontation between the power of God exercised through Him and the power of the enemy. The continuing ministry of the apostles and their disciples (including us) is then seen in these terms as the continuance of the exercise of the 'authority and power over all the demons and all diseases' given by Jesus to his followers (Luke 9:1).

What Tippett saw clearly was that large portions of the world's populations are more concerned with questions of spiritual power than with any of the other issues raised in the process of Christian witness. He observes: "In a power-oriented society, change of faith had to be power-demonstrated".[4] Christian messages and even demonstrations concerning faith, love, forgiveness and most of the other truths of Christianity are not, therefore, likely to have nearly the impact on such peoples as messages concerning and demonstrations of spiritual power. My own experience supports Tippett's insight and leads me to assert both from theoretical and practical perspectives that is extremely important for those engaging in cross-cultural witness to learn as much as possible about the place of power encounter in Jesus' ministry and in ours.

Theologically, though Jesus was the primary actor in the power encounters in which he participated, we also see the involvement of the Father and the Holy Spirit. It was from the Father that Jesus derived his authority (Matt. 28:18) and by the Father's power that he was resurrected (Acts 2:24; Col. 2:12) in victory over the enemy in the greatest power encounter of history. Jesus' basic empowerment for his tasks on earth came, however, from the Holy Spirit, starting when the Holy Spirit first came upon Jesus at his baptism (Luke 3:22) and continuing throughout Jesus' ministry (e.g. Luke 5:17; Acts 10:38). When Jesus left the earth, then, it was this Holy Spirit empowerment that he passed on to us his followers (Acts 1:4-5, 8) so that we can continue to engage the enemy in all the same ways Jesus did (John 14:12).

But, as important as power encounters are both theologically and in Jesus' ministry, and as relevant as they are today in winning and discipling people in 'power-oriented' societies, it is clear from Scripture that Jesus' battle with Satan is on a broader front. It is the purpose of a power encounter to bring freedom from the enemy. Whether the issue is illness or deliverance from demons or spiritual blindness (2 Cor. 4:4), people need a measure of freedom from the enemy's interference to experience the 'rest' (Matt. 11:28) Jesus offers them.

Beyond that rest, though, and enhanced by it are the needs for a relationship with God and some understanding of God and his activities. So Jesus' and our confrontations with the enemy and his kingdom also involve encounters over matters of allegiance (to establish and strengthen divine-human relationships) and truth (to build the necessary understandings). And these need to receive equal attention as encounters if we are to be biblically balanced. We may label these encounters 'allegiance encounter' and 'truth encounter'.

Allegiance and Truth Encounter(s)

What we mean by labeling the allegiance and truth aspects of Christian experience 'encounters' is that whatever choices we make with respect to Christianity, there are always alternatives. That is, there is always a contest over which allegiance or relationship and which 'truth' or understanding will be followed. Such encounters take place when a person considers which way to go, which choice to make in any given decision over the type and intensity of the allegiance (or commitment) one pursues and the source and nature of the truth one accepts. All three types of encounter take place throughout Christian experience, maturing, strengthening and defining initial commitments and understandings as well as continuing to free the Christian in areas of life where Satan still exerts influence.

Allegiance Encounters

The appeal for a relationship between humans and God based on allegiance/commitment and faithfulness is foundational to Scripture. Such allegiance/commitment is basic to the Old Testament covenants. It also forms the basis for the movement from darkness to light (Acts 26:18) promised in the New Testament to all who put their faith in Jesus (John 3:16). Without the relationship flowing from such commitment (John 1:12), there is no salvation.

With such a relationship, however, and the growth in faithfulness that issues from it comes increasing conformity to the image of Christ. With this develops the whole love dimension of Christianity, including the fruits of the Spirit (Gal. 5:22-23). And again, the whole Trinity is involved: the Father as the covenant maker, the Son as the model of faithfulness and the Spirit as the producer of fruit in the faithful ones.

Since this encounter is basic, any approach to Christian mission that ignores or obscures its primacy is deficient. However, such deficiency is sometimes the unintended result of either a power encounter oriented approach or one that exalts truth (especially philosophical truth) above all else. I have found both charismatics and those evangelicals who have newly come into the power dimensions of Christianity to be in danger of expecting power demonstrations in and of themselves to automatically lead people to allegiance. Such did not happen in Jesus' day. Nor is it likely in ours (see below).

Truth Encounters

Truth encounters are in their way just as basic as allegiance encounters. For the object of allegiance must be the true God, not a false one. And the power behind the power demonstrations must be the true Power, not an imposter. For knowing the truth from a scriptural point of view has a relational rather than an intellectual basis. We are to relate faithfully to the One who is both Truth and true to his commitments. At this point, then, the concern for truth and the pledge of allegiance come together, strongly reinforcing each other.

As with each of the other encounters, truth encounters involve each Person of the Trinity. The Father is the Source of truth; the Son the Exemplar of it (John 14:6); and the Spirit the One who leads his people into all truth (John 16:13).

In our concern for demonstrating and participating in the power of Christ, then, we dare not fall into the habit of ignoring or speaking with a lack of clarity concerning the crucial necessity of relating power encounters to these other two encounters. A diagram of what I am suggesting might help us to picture the perspective here in view:

JESUS CHRIST AND HIS FOLLOWERS CONFRONT SATAN:

Concerning POWER resulting in POWER ENCOUNTERS to release people from satanic captivity and to bring them into FREEDOM IN CHRIST

Concerning ALLEGIANCE resulting in ALLEGIANCE ENCOUNTERS to rescue people from wrong allegiances and to bring them into RELATIONSHIP TO JESUS CHRIST

Concerning TRUTH resulting in TRUTH ENCOUNTERS to counter error and to bring people to CORRECT UNDERSTANDINGS

Power Encounters Are not Adequate by Themselves

The need for Christian witnesses to deal effectively with spiritual power is obvious from the fact that in most parts of the two-thirds world large numbers even of those who have committed themselves to Christ continue to seek spiritual power from non-Christian diviners, curers, priests, fortune tellers and the like. Though they may have pledged allegiance to Jesus Christ as Lord and Saviour and may have embraced a large amount of Christian truth, they have not given up their pre-Christian allegiance and practice in the area of spiritual power. That area of their lives has not been properly confronted (encountered) and the pre-Christian power sources defeated in their lives by the power of Jesus. So they continue with a 'bifurcated' Christianity characterized by dual allegiance and a syncretistic understanding of truth.

The fact of such dual allegiance has led some to react by advocating healing and deliverance campaigns as the most effective way of presenting Christianity to the peoples of the two-thirds world. The assumption behind such a strategy seems to be that if such peoples are simply confronted with the superior power of Christ, they will turn to Him in droves. I have heard, however, of several such campaigns that have resulted in few or no lasting conversions to Christ. The problem arises when those who seek to win people through such power confrontations naively believe that people who experience God's healing power will *automatically* pledge allegiance to the Source of that power. They, therefore, do not do an adequate job of leading people from an experience of the power of Christ to a commitment (allegiance) to Him. The people, for their part, coming as they do from a background that accepts power from any source, see no greater compulsion to pledge allegiance to Christ than they have to any of the other sources of power they regularly consult.

In the dramatic, all-encompassing power encounters Tippett described, the risk of someone accepting help from God and then returning to his/her previous allegiance was not so great (although neither the Egyptians of Moses' day nor the Israelites of Elijah's seemed to turn to God as they should have in response to the dramatic power demonstrations God provided for them). For it was the official representative of the pre-Christian power source who deliberately desecrated the god, spirit or totem. And by so doing that person cut him/herself off from that power and threw him/herself on the mercy of the new Power, that of Jesus Christ. It was clear to such people and to their followers that they had pledged themselves to that new Power by going out on a limb and risking revenge from their previous power source. Acquaintance with this kind of power may mislead us into assuming that less dramatic power encounters experienced by ordinary people will be more effective in bringing people to allegiance and truth than they in fact usually are.

I would contend that Jesus expected power demonstrations that encounter and defeat the enemy to be as crucial to our ministries as they were to his (Luke 9:1-2). But I would also contend that any approach to Christian witness that advocates power encounter without giving adequate attention to the other two encounters is not as biblically comprehensive and balanced as it should be. The fact that many who saw and/or experienced power events during Jesus' ministry apparently did not turn to him in faith, should have alerted us to the potential inadequacy of power demonstrations as a total strategy.

On the other hand, much missionary endeavour has demonstrated that approaches which advocate allegiance and/or truth to the exclusion of power leave themselves vulnerable to the kind of dual allegiance spoken of above. Yet this recognition and the addition of a power encounter dimension to our ministries must not entice us into forgetting that a truly biblical approach to Christian witness needs to involve all three of these encounters.

A Balance of Encounters in Jesus' Ministry

In attempting to learn about the place and use of these encounters, it is instructive to note how and when Jesus employed them.

A quick survey of the Gospels leaves me with the impression that the authors gave more attention to Jesus' power demonstrations early in his ministry and more to his teaching of truth as time went on. Whether or not this means that Jesus focused more on one than the other at different points in his ministry we cannot say since the Gospel authors may have arranged their material more topically than chronologically. It may, however, suggest that in a discipleship training program, the focus should move from more to less emphasis on power with correspondingly more emphasis on truth.

Another impression is that Jesus regularly used power demonstrations when interacting with those outside his inner circle, but focused more on the teaching of truth with those committed to him. This observation suggests that once a person has successfully negotiated the allegiance encounter, the process of growth thereafter is primarily a matter of learning and practicing more truth.

From the early chapters of the Gospels we get the impression that a typical ministry situation for Jesus found him starting with teaching, followed by one or more healing events and then a return to teaching, at least for the sake of the disciples (e.g. Luke 4:31ff.; 5:1ff., 17ff.; 6:6ff., 17ff., etc.). In an event that seemed to precede the establishment of this pattern, however, Jesus did not perform a power demonstration during a visit to the synagogue in Nazareth (Luke 4:16-30).

Though we cannot know for sure, we may be justified in wondering if his teaching might have been more acceptable on that occasion had it been accompanied by a power demonstration. Might it be that Jesus learned in that event to accompany his teaching of truth and appeal for allegiance with a power encounter? We note, though, that, according to Luke, Jesus' appeal for the allegiance of His first five disciples (Peter, Andrew, James, John — Luke 5:1-11; and later Levi — Luke 5:27-28) occurred after significant power demonstrations. Jesus' ministry, then, provides grounds for suggesting that a power encounter can play a major part in stimulating allegiance, though it should not be divorced from the teaching of truth.

The Israelites of the first century were, like many/most of the peoples of our day, primarily concerned with spiritual power. In 1 Cor. 1:22 Paul speaks of the Jews as people who seek signs or miracles. Jesus' usual practice of healing and/or delivering from demons soon after entering a new area (e.g. Luke 4:33-35, 39; 5:12-13; 6:6-10, 18-19, etc.) may be seen as his way of approaching them at the point of their concern. When he sent out his followers into the surrounding towns to prepare the way for him, he commanded them to use the same approach he used (Luke 9:1-6; 10:1-9).

Jesus' reluctance to do miraculous works merely to satisfy those who wanted him to prove himself (Matt. 12:38-42; 16:1-4) would seem to indicate that his power demonstrations were intended to point to something beyond the mere demonstration of God's power. I would suggest that he had at least two goals he considered more important.

First, he sought to demonstrate God's nature by showing his love. As he said to Philip: "If you have seen me, you have seen the Father" (John 14:9). He freely gave his blessing to those who came to him and did not retract what he gave even if they did not return to thank him (Luke 17:11-19).

Secondly, he sought to lead people into the most important of the encounters, the allegiance encounter. This concern becomes evident in statements such as that to the Pharisees when they demanded a miracle. One such statement was that the people of Nineveh who repented in response to Jonah's message will accuse the people of Jesus' day who do not do likewise (Matt. 12:41).

The Nature and Aims of the Encounters

The encounters are not of the same nature. Each differs from the other two and serves a different purpose. But each is intended to initiate a process crucial to Christian experience and aimed at a specific goal. *The concern of the truth encounter is understanding and the vehicle of that encounter is teaching. The allegiance encounter is focused on relationship and is mediated through witness. Freedom, then, is the aim of the power encounter and spiritual warfare its vehicle.* Though the correspondence is not exact, it may be noted that truth and understanding have a lot to do with the mind, allegiance and relationship rest primarily in the will, and freedom is largely experienced emotionally.

The truth encounter, the encounter that seems to provide the overall context within which the others take place, seems to be aimed at solving the problem of understanding. Jesus constantly taught with the aim of bringing his hearers to ever-greater understandings of the person and plan of God. To do this, he led them in their involvement with him from an initial awareness into increasing understandings of truth through his communication of knowledge. Knowledge of truth, then, is the vehicle by means of which understanding is brought about. Note, however, that knowledge from a Scriptural point of view is relational and experiential, not simply philosophical. Thus, the truth encounter, like the other two, is primarily a personal encounter, not merely a matter of words and head knowledge.

A major function of the focus on knowledge and truth is to enable people to have enough information to be able to accurately interpret events such as those required by the other two encounters. A power demonstration, for example, has very little significance unless related to at least a modicum of accurate understanding of the Truth who is the Source of that power. Knowledge of the source of the power and the reason why the power was displayed are important ingredients in the interpretation of a power event. Erroneous knowledge leads to an erroneous interpretation: knowledge of the truth leads to a true interpretation.

To properly context the power and allegiance encounters, then, there needs to be enough knowledge presented to provide proper guidance for those who will interpret such events. Thus, Jesus usually started with a piece of teaching before a power encounter and continued teaching after it to bring people to the aims of the allegiance encounter.

Before turning to a discussion of those aims, I suggest the following diagram to summarize what I have been saying concerning the nature and aim of truth encounter(s).

START	PROCESS	AIM
Awareness —>	Leading to Knowledge —>	Understanding of Truth

The allegiance encounter is, as mentioned above, the most important one. For without allegiance to Jesus, there is no spiritual life. Initial allegiance, however, is designed to lead a person into a relationship with God involving a process of growth towards maturity lasting throughout life. This allegiance is linked tightly to truth, both by virtue of the fact that the allegiance encounter is contexted within the truth encounter and because Jesus is truth incarnate (John 14:6) and a relationship with God the true reason for human existence. We may diagram the process I am labeling allegiance encounters(s) as follows.

START	PROCESS	AIM
Commitment to Jesus —>	Growth in relationship —>	Maturity

Implied in the process labeled allegiance encounter(s) is the cultivation of the fruits of the Spirit, especially love, both toward God and toward the human community that God loves. We are to turn from love of (= allegiance to) the world that is under the control of the evil one (1 John 5:19) to the One who so loved the world that he both gave himself for it and set us an example that we should do likewise. Growing in our relationship with him, then, involves becoming like him both in person and in ministry, each of which contributes to movement toward Christian maturity. The latter may be defined alternatively as likeness to Christ to whom we relate and to whose image we are to conform (Rom 8:29).

The nature and aim of power encounter(s), then, contribute quite a different dimension to Christian experience. For the issue here, though involving truth and relationship, is focused on neither of these. Instead, the focus is on freedom, leading to victory over Satan. Satan is the blinder (2 Cor. 4:4), restricter, hinderer, crippler — the enemy who attempts to keep people from allegiance and truth. People need freedom from him if they are to cultivate those other dimensions.

We may diagram this encounter from two perspectives — that of the one who experiences power encounter(s) as release from captivity and that of the observer. Though our primary focus is on the former, we will note the latter as well. We may diagram the process as experienced by the person who is freed as follows.

START	PROCESS	AIM
Healing —>	Increasing freedom —>	Victory over Satan

As for the observer, the power encounter, if properly interpreted, leads him/her to believe at least certain basic truths concerning the power and love of God. The vehicle by means of which this process is carried out is demonstration. That is, the healer, if he/she is doing ministry in Jesus' way, provides for the observer a demonstration of God's power wrapped in God's love. This is designed to attract the observer's attention, demonstrate God and lead to belief that God is worthy of trust because He is able and willing to free people from the destructive hold of Satan. This process may be diagramed as follows.

START	PROCESS	AIM
Attract attention —>	Demonstration —>	Belief

With reference to this attention attracting function of power encounter(s), it should be noted that, though we are not referring to them as encounters, such things as demonstrations of love, acceptance and forgiveness, peacefulness in time of trouble and a large number of another characteristics of the Christian life can play the same role of attracting attention and leading to belief. These all witness to the presence of a loving God who is willing to give abundant live and to bring release from the enemy. If we were to refer to these as encounters, perhaps we could bundle them together and introduce a category labeled 'life encounter(s)'.

The Encounters Reinforce Each Other

Any total approach to Christian ministry needs to involve an integration of all three of these dimensions. People need salvation. But, according to 2 Cor. 4:4, a major hindrance to belief is the blindness caused by the enemy. Spiritual warfare may, therefore, be necessary in many (all?) situations before people are free enough from the enemy to understand God's message and commit themselves to him. Thus an appeal for commitment without the power encounter that frees people to confront and respond to the truth is likely to be ineffective.

Likewise, as noted above, a power encounter, if it is to serve its proper function, requires that those participating or observing it have enough understanding to rightly interpret the event. Power encounters free people from some aspect of satanic harassment. They also attract the attention of any who may be observing. But, if they are to be useful in teaching those attracted by them, they need interpretation. Otherwise, what they are intended to get across may be missed. They demonstrate the goodness, mercy and love of God only to those who correctly interpret him. One who has been healed by God and interprets his/her experience correctly usually has a firmer relationship with him than one who has not such an experience. But only if he/she interprets the experience properly.

The fact that power demonstrations only teach what they are intended to teach when those receiving or observing them know how to interpret them properly helps to explain why Jesus usually did his power demonstrations within a teaching context rather than simply performing them without reference to his teaching. Their meaning is not self-evident, especially to people (like the Jews and most contemporary two-thirds world peoples) who are quite used to power demonstrations brought about by the counterfeiter called by Jesus the 'ruler of this world' (John 14:30).

The need for allegiance to the Healer and Teacher, then, also has to be taught. And teaching is a matter of imparting knowledge and truth -- the truth encounter. The receivers are to be taught and thus encounter truth both in relationship to the other two encounters and as a continuing experience through which they will move toward greater maturity in Christ.

As the Christian grows, all three kinds of encounters are significant, for each contributes to growth and assurance. Any relationship involves a continuing series of challenges to one's will, culminating, hopefully for the Christian, in ever-renewed pledges of allegiance to Jesus Christ leading to an ever deepening relationship with him.

Nor is the function of power demonstrations limited to the start of Gospel witness. The truths of Jesus' victory over the enemy and of his continuing presence in human affairs are easily forgotten, however, if the kind of intellectualizing of truth common in our training institutions is allowed to take over. As we grow in Christ, our Lord seeks to keep before us the experiential and relational components of his truth by frequently healing, protecting and blessing us through power demonstrations that confront and defeat the enemy's use of his power to hinder, afflict and destroy us. Though many western Christians are not conscious of such activity, those who allow themselves to move into heightened awareness of God's presence and power discover that what we have referred to as miracles and considered infrequent are intended to be *normal* occurrences in Christian experience.

As implied above, the encounters with knowledge and truth provide the context in which the other two experiences occur and find their meaning. Such encounters are continual: involving a never ending succession of confrontations with new and deeper understandings of God and the meaning of our relationship with him. It is truth, particularly the experiential truth centered in our relationship with Christ, that enables us to understand and interpret both the other two encounters and all subsequent knowledge and experience. This relationship, then, involves a constant experience of the power dimension, bringing greater and greater freedom in all aspects of life and ministry.

We may diagram the total approach here recommended as a circle made up of three parts:

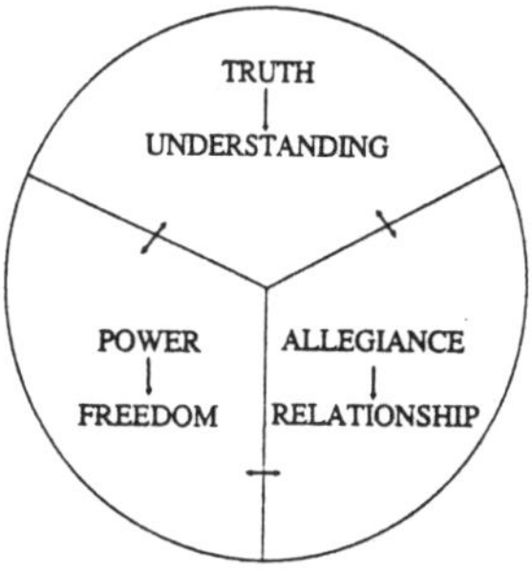

Read such diagram as follows: People need freedom from the enemy achieved through power encounters both to unblind their minds (2 Cor. 4:4) so they can receive and understand truth and to release their wills so they can commit themselves to a relationship with God. Christian truth is not, however, properly understood and applied, nor can power be properly exercised, without a continuing commitment to God. Nor will either truth or allegiance be maintained without freedom from the enemy won through continual power encounters.

A more detailed way of diagraming the interworkings of these three aspects of Christian life and witness is as follows:

	START	NEED	PROCESS	RESULT
	Satanic captivity	Freedom to understand	Power Encounter	
STAGE 1	Ignorance/ Error	Enough Under-Standing	Truth Encounter	Commitment to Jesus Christ
	Non-Christian Allegiance	Challenge to Commitment to Jesus Christ	Allegiance Encounter	
		Spiritual Warfare to Provide Proctection, Healing, Blessing, Deliverance	Power Encounter	
STAGE 2	Commitment to Jesus Christ	Teaching	Truth Encounter	Growing Relation-ship to God and His People
		Challenges to Greater Commitment and Obedience	Allegiance Encounter	

		Authoritative Prayer	Power Encounter	
STAGE 3	Growing Relationship to God and His People	Teaching	Truth Encounter	Witness to Those at the Beginning of Stage 1
		Challenge to Commitment	Allegiance Encounter	

Note that this diagram portrays three stages in the overall encounter process, the third of which results in witness to those at the start of the first. Read the diagram as follows: At the start, people are under satanic captivity in ignorance and/or error and committed to some non-Christian allegiance. They need freedom from that captivity through power encounter(s) from the blindness and will weakening of the enemy to open them up to the message. Then, through truth and allegiance encounters, they need to receive enough understanding to act on, plus enough challenge to induce them to commit themselves to Jesus Christ.

In the second stage a person or group, having made their commitment to Jesus, need the benefits of ongoing spiritual warfare to attain greater freedom from the enemy's continued efforts to harass and cripple. They also need ongoing teaching and challenges to greater commitment and obedience attained through continued encounters in all three areas to enable them to grow in their relationship to God and his people.

In stage three, then, this growing relationship issues in power encounters through authoritative praying to break the power of the captor to delude, harass, cause illness and demonization and the like. These encounters are accompanied by truth encounters involved in teaching and the continuance of allegiance encounters that challenge the believer to greater commitment and obedience, especially in the area of witness to those in stage one.

All three encounters are intended by God to be integral to every stage of his interactions with humans. Most committed Christians soon discover their need for understanding and the cultivation of their relationship with God. The need for a greater and greater freedom from the enemy's incursions into our lives is also evident. God intends, I believe, that a continuing series of each type of encounter should be a normal part of every Christian's experience.

Witness

Beyond experiencing these three dimensions of Christianity in our own growth, then, lies witness. At the end of his ministry, Jesus taught a good bit of truth both concerning his relationship to his followers and theirs with each other (e.g. John 14-16), and concerning the authority and power his followers were to receive (e.g.

Acts 1:8). These are, however, carefully related to witness (e.g. Matt. 28:19-20; Mark 16:15-18; Acts 1:8).

Witness is especially related to the power dimension. The disciples are instructed at Jesus' ascension to wait for spiritual power before they embarked on witness (Luke 24:49; Acts 1:4). They were to wait for the gift he had promised, the gift of the Holy Spirit who, when he came upon them, would empower them for witness (Acts 1:8). They were not to go forth to witness without that empowerment. In this they were to imitate Jesus' own experience. He appears to have done neither mighty works nor witnessing before he himself was empowered at his baptism (Luke 3:21-22): if we can judge by the startled reaction of the people from his hometown at the start of his ministry (Matt. 13:54-56).

Satan is a master of deceit and counterfeiting. So he counterfeits all three of these elements of Christianity and deceives people into committing themselves to him and his 'truth' and power. That is why we have to speak of *encountering* or *confronting* rather than simply ignoring. When we speak this way, though, we are speaking of encountering and confronting the enemy of God who specializes in blinding the minds and hearts of the peoples of the world (2 Cor. 4:4). The point is, we are fighting an enemy: not merely philosophizing about how to go about living for and serving our King.

We are taught that he who is in us is greater than he who is in the world (1 John 4:4) and that Jesus has 'stripped the spiritual rulers and authorities of their power' (Col. 2:15). But we are still at war and commanded to put on armour and fight against the 'wicked spiritual forces in the heavenly world' (Eph. 6:11-12) with 'God's powerful weapons' (2 Cor. 10:4). Furthermore, we are expected to know the enemy's devices (2 Cor. 2:11). We know how the war will come out, but there seem to be many battles yet to fight.

My appeal here is for completeness and balance: especially in view of two factors in contemporary missionary experience.

First, most of the world is primarily concerned about spiritual power. God has given us an abundance of this power. But only some of the representatives of Christ in the contemporary world have learned to use it.

Charismatic (including Pentecostal) Christianity offers the world spiritual power. And large numbers are attracted to such churches so that nearly all of the 25 or so largest congregations in the world fall into this group. It is often not clear, however, that they have avoided a syncretism that focuses more on the power demonstrations than on the Person behind the power. For many charismatic churches operate in the power dimension in such a way that the importance of the allegiance and/or truth dimensions of Christianity is obscured.

Non-charismatic evangelicalism, though, having provided the world with the majority of its missionaries, has been the source of large numbers of churches, some of them quite large. With all of its strong points, this brand of Christianity has drunk deeply at the fountains of rationalism and the other benefits provided for western societies by the 'Enlightenment'.[5] Evangelicals are really good at the knowledge and truth end of our faith. This is basically a knowledge-oriented tupe of Christianity. It has sided with the Greeks mentioned in 1 Cor. 1:22 in seeking wisdom or knowledge rather than with the Jews who seek power demonstrations. And a knowledge orientation is important.

But in a world in which most of its children have imbibed a focus on spiritual power with their mothers' milk, solid, lasting conversions to Christ are rarely achieved simply by presenting people with knowledge and truth. To those churches working either cross-culturally or in their homelands that are not working with the Holy Spirit in power, the call is to move into his dimension. For most of the world has sided with the Jews in seeking power.

Those observing or participating in non-charismatic churches usually conclude that the God of Christianity has no power. As they listen to the Christian Scriptures they learn that he once had a lot. But he seems to have lost it somewhere along the way. Those observing charismatic churches, then, often conclude that Jesus is just another curer to try when the efforts of the others don't work.

Second, either way, the second of our missiological problems emerges — the fact that large numbers of Christians both in the two-thirds world and in the West are practicing 'bifurcated' or 'dual allegiance' Christianity — a Christianity where people, including pastors, continue to go to shamans, priests, healers, fortune tellers and others working under satanic power. Those who have experienced a powerless Christ turn to traditional brokers of spiritual power rather than to the church when they need power. Those who see no difference between Christ and their traditional brokers of spiritual power also continue their allegiance to other powers, but for different reasons.

Satan has provided people with counterfeits of all three of the elements discussed above. He counterfeits truth, instills allegiance and provides power. He has, therefore, three arrows in his quiver. Non-charismatic evangelicals have had only two — allegiance and truth. They have encountered allegiance to other gods and spirits with the need for allegiance to Jesus Christ. And many have been attracted to this message. But when people seek healing, when they seek fertility, when there isn't enough rain, or there are floods, such churches can only offer partly effective secular answers — secular medicine, agriculture and schooling. So, if the converts stick with their commitment to Christ, their need for power to solve the problems of life leads them to follow the West and secularize.

Charismatic Christianity, on the other hand, has specialized in providing the other 'arrow' — the power one. Charismatics have not been unconcerned with allegiance and knowledge but, as Westerners, have often also fallen into the enemy's trap and led people into secularization through institutions more dependent on human knowledge and power than on the Holy Spirit.

Both groups have confronted Satan's counterfeit 'truths' with the exciting truths of Christianity. But we have often done it in such an abstract way that our hearers have seen very little verification of that truth in experience. And we may never have shared with them that we ourselves often suffer from the same lack of verification. Ofte they and we are both much more impressed with scientific truth than with biblical truth.

Effective Christian witness requires all three 'arrows'. We all need to experience together a genuine New Testament relationship with God issuing in the daily experience of his freeing power and growth in understanding what life with God is all about. When we move in all three of these dimensions of Christianity, both our own lives and the kind of witness we were called to give make sense — we can witness with power to a redeeming relationship with the true God and to the truths of life he has taught us.

And we can encounter the counterfeit allegiance, power, and 'truths' of Satan with something that is effective — saving allegiance, genuine truth and the power of God. We have failed to defeat Satan's power with our truth and knowledge. Some have attempted to fight power with truth. As important as truth is, it is not the proper weapon to pit against power. Satan's power needs to be countered with God's power. Satan's 'truth' is what God's truth is designed to combat. And the allegiance 'arrow' is the one that is confronted by presenting the option of allegiance to Christ.

In either case, the call is for the kind of completeness and balance in witness that occurs only when we give proper attention to each of the three dimensions in focus here. Let's engage biblically in all three encounters with all the weapons God has given us.

Notes

1. A previous and shorter version of this chapter appeared in *Evangelical Missions Quarterly* 27 (1991), 258-65.
2. Alan R. Tippett, *People Movements in Southern Polynesia* (Chicago: Moody, 1971), 206.
3. Peter C. Wagner, *How to Have a Healing Ministry* (Ventura, CA: Regal, 1988), 150; see also John Wimber, *Power Evangelism* (New York: Harper and Row, 1985), 29-32; Charles H. Kraft, *Christianity With Power* (Ann Arbor: Servant, 1989). Cf. Peter C. Wagner and F. Douglas Pennoyer, *Dark Angels* (Ventura, CA: Regal, 1990).
4. Tippett, *op. cit.*, 81.
5. See my *Christianiy With Power*.

21

Ecumenical, Evangelical and Pentecostal/Charismatic Views on Mission as a Movement of the Holy Spirit

Jan A.B. Jongeneel

> The coming of the Holy Spirit at Pentecost was the coming of a missionary Spirit [Roland Allen].

> The Holy Spirit is precisely the presence that accompanies the mission. He is the power of the mission. He is the leader of the mission. He is the light of the mission. He is the inspirer of the mission. Without the Holy Spirit the mission cannot be carried out. With him around, the mission *is* mission [Emerito P. Nacpil].

Introduction

In this article I call attention to the dynamic relation between the Holy Spirit (pneumatology) and Christian missions (missiology). I like to realize this programme by analyzing comparatively the views of some prominent theologians in the Ecumenical Movement, the Evangelical Movement and the Pentecostal Movement annex Charismatic Renewal who came to the fore and can be regarded as more or less representative.

In the first half of the twentieth century the Anglican missionary Roland Allen (1868-1947) has laid the foundations of a thorough reflection on the relation of the Holy Spirit - Christian missions. To my mind the *missionary pneumatology* of Allen is very significant for the above-mentioned movements; for that reason I take his writings[1] as the starting-point of my comparative analysis.

After 1945 several authors have given serious thought to the topic which my article covers. Here I call attention to the recent writings of ecumenical authors such as Harry R. Boer[2], Hendrik Berkhof[3] and Emerito P. Nacpil[4]; evangelical authors such as Alan R. Tippett[5], Graham Cheesman[6] and James I. Packer[7]; and Pentecostal and Charismatic authors such as John V. Taylor[8], Paul A. Pomerville[9] and Jack W. Hayford[10]. It is not difficult to enlarge this list of names[11]. However, I confine my research to the above-mentioned nine theologians. There are a few people among them who in so many words have referred to the publications of Allen: Boer, Tippett (cf. Cheesman who offers an introductory quotation of Allen) and Pomerville who come from the Ecumenical Movement, the Evangelical Movement and the Pentecostal Movement respectively.

People have often divided pneumatology - on the analogy of christology - into two parts: *the person and the work of the Holy Spirit.*[12] It is quite possible to divide my article accordingly: (a) the Holy Spirit as (sent and sending) person, and (b) mission as a (transforming) work of the Holy Spirit. However, the birth and progress of the Pentecostal Movement and Charismatic Renewal - studied very carefully by Walter J. Hollenweger - urge me to add one main point to this programme: *the fruit of the Spirit* (Gal. 5:22) *and the charismata* (1 Cor. 12:4-11), manifest in the life of the congregations and their members. These pneumatic realities can properly be regarded as the connecting link between the Holy Spirit as a missionary person, on the one hand, and his missionary work, on the other. Each of these topics has both a trinitarian-pneumatological and an anthropological-ecclesiological aspect; therefore, my article contains - apart from both the introduction and the conclusion - three sections and six subsections altogether.

In line with Berkhof, who has a keener eye for mission as *movement of the Spirit*[13] than all those other authors, I offer the next titles to the three sections of this article: the *origin*, the *equipment*, and the *activities* of mission as *movement of the Holy Spirit.*

The Origin of Mission As Movement of the Holy Spirit

In the Ecumenical Movement, the Evangelical Movement, the Pentecostal Movement and the Charismatic Renewal *trinitarian* thinking is current. This has consequences for pneumatology. Firstly, authors in these movements usually regard the Holy Spirit both as the Spirit of God who from the very beginning is active in creation - in the beginning already 'the Spirit of God moved upon the face of the waters' (Gen. 1:2) -, and as the Spirit of Jesus Christ who from the first day of Pentecost (Acts 2) transforms the world everywhere. Secondly, these authors put the Christian missionary movement as a rule not only in the perspective of the creation by God 'in the beginning' and of the redemption by Christ 'in the fullness of time', but also - and ultimately - in the perspective of being fulfilled with the Spirit 'in the last days': at Pentecost the Spirit of the Father and of the Son is poured out 'upon all flesh' (Acts 2:17). The missionary movement, rooted in the will of God (*missio Dei*) and inaugurated by Jesus Christ, turned out to be, *from Pentecost onwards*, a worldwide movement 'in demonstration of the Spirit and of power' (1 Cor. 2:4).

The Holy Spirit as Sending Missionary

Since the acceptance of the Athanasian Creed by Western Christianity it is customary to speak about the Holy Spirit as a *person.* This orthodox language is also adopted by a small number of missiologists.

In *Pentecost and the World; the Revelation of the Holy Spirit in the 'Acts of the Apostles'* (1917) Allen writes indeed on the Holy Spirit as a 'He' - not as an 'It'[14] -, and confers indeed upon him several epithets - for instance 'dictator and inspirer of missionary work'[15] -, but never speaks about him as a 'person'; in *Mission Activities Considered in Relation to the Manifestation of the Spirit* (1930), however, he calls attention to 'a personal, active, Spirit who works not only in us, as missionaries, but upon all with whom we deal and in all who will receive Him'[16]. Nearly all of the above-mentioned authors follow Allen wittingly or unwittingly: they write about the Spirit as a 'He', they confer epithets upon him, and they do not refer to him as a 'person'.[17] Berkhof, for instance, evades consciously the use of the term 'person'. Neither do we meet this term in the writings of Nacpil, Cheesman and Hayford. Therefore, Packer can write about 'the displaced person of the Godhead'; he stands up for a rehabilitation of the Spirit: "...the wind is God's picture of the activity of the person whom Charles Williams rightly and reverently called 'our Lord the Holy Spirit'...".[18] Tippett concurs directly with Michael Green: "Eschatology and mission unite in the person of the Spirit".[19] Last but not least I can quote Pomerville: "The crucial point is that the manner of God's working in contemporary times is by means of the ministry of the third person of the Godhead - the Holy Spirit. Significant mission issues are decided on this pivotal theological point".[20]

The understanding of the Holy Spirit as both *sent* and *sending* person is more important than the use of the term 'person'. In the course of the last five centuries, dozens of books and articles have dealt with the Spirit, but most of them have failed to connect him substantially with missions and have not typified him as 'missionary Spirit' (Allen; Berkhof)[21], as 'Missionary' (Allen)[22], as 'Spirit of witness/witnessing Spirit' (Boer)[23], as 'God the evangelist' (Packer)[24], as 'chief actor in the historic mission of the Christian church' (Taylor)[25], or as 'supreme strategist of world mission' and 'Lord of the harvest' (Pomerville)[26], etc. All of these in essence *a*-missionary pneumatologies[27], written in the context and for the benefit of the 'Christian Western world' (*corpus christianum*), make a very static impression upon missiologists.[28] The most important truth which can and must be attributed to the Spirit is precisely his being sent by the Father and the Son, by which he received the power at Pentecost to send out - in the name of the Father and the Son - both congregations and their members. Therefore, he has both a divine and a messianic mission, which becomes manifest in the dynamic mission of the congregations and their members. In other words: only in a dynamic and personalistic way can people speak adequately about the Holy Spirit as the one who both is sent - by the Father and the Son - and is sending - the congregations and their members.

The Roman Catholic author Adolphe A. Tanqueray affirms that the Holy Spirit is sent, but denies that he in addition sends.[29] I, however, believe that he is also a *sender*. Therefore, I am speaking about him as 'the sent one who is the sending one', or more clearly as 'the sending missionary'. In this matter I identify myself with both Allen who used the expression 'the Holy Spirit sent him'[30], and Berkhof who called the Spirit 'the divine subject of the mission' and who in addition wrote about 'the creative missionary work of the Spirit'.[31] The majority of the researched publications, however, speak more clearly about the Spirit as 'the one who is sent' than about him as 'the one who is sending'. Taylor and Pomerville, however, also value this last point highly: Taylor defines the sending Spirit as 'the director of the whole enterprise'[32], and Pomerville as 'the initiator, motivator, and superintendent of mission'.[33]

The Church as the Movement Sent by the Spirit into the World

The dynamic sending of the Holy Spirit by the Father and the Son enables the dynamic mission of the congregations and their members in the world. At the cradle of the missionary church there stands as messenger of God, moved with compassion, not only Jesus *with* us - Immanuel -, but also the Spirit upon/in - or *between*[34] - us.

Nacpil refers to the outpouring of the Spirit 'upon all flesh' (Acts 2:17) at the day of Pentecost - after the resurrection of Jesus from the dead at Easter - as 'the second founding act of mission'[35], whereas Boer correctly considers this event - after the creation of the world by God and the redemption by Christ - as the 'third great work of God'.[36]

Primarily, the Acts of the Apostles is the book of *the acts of the Holy Spirit*; it is, however, also the book of *the acts of the apostles*. In this book the origin of the church as a missionary movement is sketched. Allen has analyzed this book in a masterly fashion. He has rightly described it as 'a volume of Christian biography'.[37] He has typified the Spirit in this book as:

> ...a Spirit impelling those to whom He comes to carry to others that which they have received. He is revealed as a Spirit of redeeming love active in those to whom He comes rather towards others for their salvation than in themselves for their own personal perfection. The revelation of Him as a Spirit of personal holiness is brought out more clearly in St. Paul's epistles. The first sign of the Spirit's presence in the Acts is activity for the salvation of others; conviction of His personal work is the second and later sign.[38]

A biographical and personalistic understanding of the origin of Christianity as missionary movement occurs clearly in the writings of Allen, but is lacking in the majority of the publications consulted.

Since Pentecost (Acts 2) the Holy Spirit lives and works in the congregations and their members *personally* (not: *individualistically*!). He inspires the congregations and their members dynamically. By his indwelling, Christians learn primarily to call God and Christ *Thou* (*Du* in the German language); thereupon they learn to use this intimate word in their interaction with fellow-Christians; and finally they learn to use it missionarily in their contact with non-Christians. This reality, which is related to the origin of Christianity as a Spirit-movement, is either not discussed at all or explained in a very superficial way in this literature: Allen writes in passing, that we shall not speak 'impersonally' about the activity and zeal of the apostles[39]; thereafter Cheesman typifies briefly the missionary who is called, gifted and motivated by the Spirit as 'a person full of the Holy Spirit'[40]; and finally Hayford gives a casual reference to the Spirit as the one who "ensures the uniqueness of each personality. He does not violate the Father's handiwork by forcing any of us into a robot-like mold".[41] On this point Taylor is the only one who has penetrating thoughts: the *Abba* (= Father)-relationship of Jesus with God is a gift of the Spirit; it is the root of the *I-Thou*-relationships in human lives possessed by the Spirit; and it causes dynamics in the life of the churches and their 'personnel': "a constant pressure towards greater personhood, the creation of new occasions for choice, and the principle of self-surrender in responsibility for others. These must be the marks of any evangelism which is truly Christ's evangelism".[42]

In line with Taylor I would like to defend the following argument: since Pentecost (Acts 2) the church is a missionary movement inspired by the Holy Spirit which sends out people who *have become persons* in the Christian sense of the word, to approach other people with the message that they also *can become persons* in the Christian sense of the word, by faith in Jesus Christ and the outpouring of the Spirit. The messianic and pneumatic reality of the church as a movement sent into the world by God to be a paradigm of Christ-like Spirit-uality is, however, challenged from the very beginning. We know that already in the apostolic church (Acts 5: Ananias and Sapphira) the original ideal of every believer being 'a dynamic missionary person' was lost and that thereafter the missionary congregations and their members have not automatically been understood any more in the dynamic perspective of the missionary 'personhood' of the one God - Father, Son and Holy Spirit.[43]

Equipment for Mission As Movement of the Holy Spirit

In making our analysis of the equipment of the church doing its missionary work I concentrate my attention on 'the fruit of the Spirit' (Gal. 5:22) and the *charismata* (1 Cor. 12:4-11), which according to Berkhof are given by the Holy Spirit to equip the church "for the great work of transmission"[44], and according to Tippett are granted to enable him "to operate as the body of Christ in the world".[45]

Fruit and Charismata of the Missionary Spirit

In *Pentecost and the World* Allen explains in detail 'the gift of the Spirit (the sole test of communion)' (singular), but does not speak about 'the fruit of the Spirit' (singular), which in the mind of Paul (Gal. 5:19) is the opposite of 'the works of the flesh' (plural); nor does he write here in so many words about the *charismata* noticed by the same apostle in another context (1 Cor. 12:4-11). In his later work *Mission Considered in Relation to the Manifestation of the Spirit* we meet with the same gap.

The studies under review either leave *the fruit of the Spirit* undiscussed (Cheesman; Hayford), or note it only casually: Packer writes only about the Spirit who makes the encounter with God 'fruitful' in Christlike living, and Pomerville considers only the fruit of the Spirit as "the inward work of the Spirit in Christian initiation".[46] Boer and Tippett, however, pay real attention to this issue: the former underlines that Gal. 5:22 does not speak about nine separate fruits of the Spirit, but about one fruit only[47], and the latter agrees with Archibald M. Hunter who considers power, joy and faith as 'the concomitants of the Spirit's presence', which frequently occur together and are features of the church in times of spontaneous expansion.[48] In my opinion the presence of the fruit of the Spirit in the life of the congregations and their members is the primary condition of being successful in the missionary enterprise; a community of Christians which is still characterized by 'the lust of the flesh' (Gal. 5:16), has no real expressiveness and recruiting power.

As a matter of evidence Taylor, Pomerville and Hayford call a great deal of attention to the *charismata*, which I consider as the second essential condition for having success in missionary work. Hayford takes these gifts of the Spirit as 'supernatural operations and manifestations of the Holy Spirit'; he underlines that they are accompanied by signs and miracles.[49] Pomerville distinguishes two dimensions in the presence and work of God through the Holy Spirit: "God is present and actively working by means of the Holy Spirit, both inwardly as the source of spiritual life and outwardly in charismatic power"[50]. 'Inwardly' reminds Pomerville not only of 'the fruit of the Spirit', but also of regeneration and holiness, and 'outwardly' reminds him especially of the baptism in the Spirit, glossolalia and other gifts of the Spirit.[51] Pomerville associates *charismata* likewise with supernatural phenomena. In this matter Taylor clearly differs from Pomerville and Hayford: "The writings of most of the Pentecostals and other revivalists that I have read seem to me to look upon the Holy Spirit too much as a supply of superhuman power and wisdom and so to miss the fact that he works primarily by generating awareness and communion, and that whatever power and wisdom he gives derive from that".[52] Moreover Taylor is not at all willing to accept the genesis of an elite in the missionary church: people who possess *charismata* as opposed to people who do not possess these gifts.[53]

Boer deals with the question of the supernatural character of Pentecost and the *charismata* in a historic framework: "The past century of discussion about Pentecost has been largely controlled by the interest to remove or retain the supernatural character of the event and of the phenomena associated with it".[54] In our century nothing has changed in fact. That is apparent if we investigate how people think about *glossolalia* today. Boer speaks at some length about 'speaking with other tongues' (Acts 2:4) in the Early Church and thereafter[55]; however, he is not - like Pomerville and Hayford[56] - an advocate of glossolalia. To Berkhof, prophecy (cf. 1 Cor. 14:1-3) is more important than glossolalia.[57] Nacpil goes in the same direction: the confusion of tongues at Babel (Gen. 11) is totally undone by 'the miracle of tongues' at Pentecost which creates the Christian community.[58] And Taylor points out, that neither Von Zinzendorf nor Wesley has talked about this 'strange' gift, which in the New Testament is only mentioned by the authors of three books (the Gospel according to St. Mark, the Acts of the Apostles and the First Epistle to the Corinthians).[59] Neither Boer, nor Berkhof, nor Nacpil, nor Taylor looks at glossolalia as a supernatural phenomenon.

People clearly have different opinions about the equipment of the missionary church by the Spirit. In the researched literature I did not encounter any difference of opinion about 'the fruit of the Spirit' (Gal. 5:22), but I did concerning the supernatural character of the various gifts (linguistic talent versus glossolalia, etc.) and about their order. Hardly any of those theologians deals with the important question of the interrelation between 'the fruit of the Spirit' (of primary importance) and the *charismata* (of secondary importance). Only Pomerville devotes serious attention to it. I am, however, dissatisfied with his distinction between 'the fruit of the Spirit' as an inward working, and the *charismata* as an outward working of the Holy Spirit, because I consider 'the fruit of the Spirit' in no smaller measure than the *charismata* as an outward 'demonstration of the Spirit and of power'.

The Experience of the Fruit of the Spirit and the Charismata in the Missionary Church as Movement of the Spirit

Anyone who studies the History of Missions can examine *objectively* which fruit of the Spirit and which *charismata* are manifested and are becoming manifest in it. It is, however, also possible to speak about it *subjectively*. Hayford is the only one of those authors who strikingly tells about his *personal* experience with the Holy Spirit's miraculous power: after the experience of two healings in his own life (the last one through the laying on of hands and anointing with oil by the church elders) he became a dynamic evangelist.[60]

Ecumenical theologians such as Berkhof and Nacpil do not write about *the experience of the Holy Spirit*. Tippett touches upon this question.[61] Cheesman considers "openness, closeness to the Lord, experience" as needed in missionary work.[62] Packer is not willing to disconnect the knowledge of Christ and the experience of the Spirit, because he is afraid of ending up with the New Age movement.[63] Hayford is much less scared than Packer of aberrations in this field.[64] Taylor and Pomerville, however, deal with this subject extensively. In fact the whole book of Taylor is an irenic explication of "the mysterious experiences of encounter which the Spirit of God creates".[65] The explanation of the "dynamic, charismatic experience of the Spirit in the Christian life" given by Pomerville is determined not only very dogmatically, but also very polemically.[66]

Taylor, Pomerville and Hayford are the only authors who speak in so many words about *baptism in/of/with the Holy Spirit* as personal equipment for mission. Hayford deals with it in passing[67]; Taylor and Pomerville, however, at some length. Pomerville clarifies that not everybody in the Pentecostal movement has the same opinion about the baptism of the Holy Spirit: on the one side we encounter the Keswickian-Reformed view which considers the baptism of the Holy Spirit as 'enduement of power' for service, and on the other side the Wesleyan-Holiness view which interprets this event as 'cleansing from sin'.[68] Furthermore, Pomerville makes it clear that, in the Pentecostal movement, the gift of tongues is not uniformly held to be the initial evidence of the baptism of the Holy Spirit; other *charismata* as well are believed to be its initial evidence.[69] Taylor agrees partly with the Pentecostal view on the baptism of the Spirit, and partly disagrees with it:

> ...the Pentecostalist is right when he calls the bestowal of this gift 'Baptism in the Holy Spirit'. But I think he is distorting the evidence when he teaches that this is something subsequent to, and distinct from, becoming a Christian. In the last analysis it is the transforming gift of the Spirit that makes a man a Christian.[70]

A missionary pneumatology must steer clear of the Scylla of a purely objective equipment of the missionary church which entirely lacks experience, and the Charibdis of a purely subjective equipment, which only rests on the charismatic experience of the Spirit. On the one hand Pomerville rightly makes a stand against 'reductionism' in the Ecumenical Movement, which neglects the personal charismatic experience of the Spirit[71], on the other hand Taylor rightly puts up a vigorous fight against those Pentecostals who focus on glossolalia as the decisive evidence of the baptism of the Holy Spirit. Moreover, in the missionary church as a movement of the Spirit it is not only the experience of the *charismata* which is at stake, but also - and primarily - the experience of 'the fruit of the Spirit' which takes shape, at least ought to take shape, in the life of every church member.

The Activities of Mission As Movement of the Holy Spirit

The Holy Spirit is a dynamic missionary Spirit. Most of these writings treat at length 'the power (= *dynamis*) of the Holy Spirit'. Jim D. Douglas, for instance, does not recapitulate the lectures of Packer and Hayford at the International Congress on World Evangelization Lausanne II in Manila in 1989 under the heading 'the person and work of the Holy Spirit', but under the heading 'the power and work of the Holy Spirit'[72] And Tippett uses expressions such as 'the power and activity of the Spirit', 'the availability and the activity of the Holy Spirit as the source of power', 'the blessing and power of the Spirit', 'the presence and power of the Spirit'.[73]

Here I deal firstly with some aspects of what Hayford calls 'the Holy Spirit's mighty works'[74]; thereafter I discuss how these *magnalia Dei* act upon the missionary work of the congregations and their members: *ora et labora*; pray and work! There is above all much diversity of opinion as to 'the mighty works' of the moving missionary Spirit.

The 'Mighty Works' of the Missionary Spirit

It is very important to distinguish as Boer does between the operations of the Holy Spirit in *creation* and *redemption*. He is right in pointing out that in Luther *Spiritus animans* stands against *Spiritum sanctum sanctificantem*, and that Calvin has also distinguished both functions very clearly. Hence Boer can arrive at the following conclusion:

> The substratum of the life of man and of nature, the vital power informing and sustaining all cosmic processes, is the Spirit of the living God. This life-giving and life-sustaining function of the Spirit forms the basis for and finds its parallel expression in the redemptive renewal of the life of man and of nature. The operations of the Spirit in creation and redemption are therefore not disparate activities.[75]

In this literature, we encounter the tendency to overlook entirely the mighty missionary works of God's Spirit in *creation*. Here Taylor is, apart from Boer, the exception: in his opinion the Holy Spirit is "*universally* present through the whole fabric of the world, and yet *uniquely* present in Christ and, by extension, in the fellowship of his disciples"[76]; as eternal Spirit he has been at work "in all ages and all cultures making men aware and evoking their response, and always the one to whom he was pointing and bearing witness was the *Logos*, the Lamb slain before the foundation of the world".[77]

Most of these writers have merely an eye for the missionary work of the Holy Spirit in *redemption*. Boer considers the movement of the Spirit in redemptive history as a movement from universalism to universalism through a process of contraction and expansion, in five stages: 1. universal concern with mankind; 2. limitation to Israel; 3. concentration in the Messiah - the *Pneumatophoros*[78] - ; 4.

diffusion through the apostles; and 5. indwelling in the Church universal.[79] And Cheesman divides the transforming work of the Spirit (cf. Boer's stage 4 and 5) in the following points: 1. 'moving a man's heart to Christ'; 2. 'Church growth by manifestation of spiritual power'.[80]

Packer belongs to the authors who call attention to the work of the Holy Spirit in what Cheesman calls "moving a man's heart to Christ": *personal conviction and conversion.* He considers the Spirit as the author of conversion. The Spirit is "the direct agent. He illuminates, convinces, quickens, induces new birth, imparts repentance, and prompts the converted soul's confession 'Jesus is Lord'...".[81] Moreover he states that the Spirit cares for convergence: the lot of converts from different races, cultures, classes, sexes, etc. end up in the same place.[82]

Tippett, however, is interested in the work of the Holy Spirit in what Cheesman describes as "church growth by manifestation of spiritual power": *church planting and the conversion of social groups.* In explaining the missionary work of the Spirit he particularly thinks of "his relationship with responsive populations, with the winning of human communities to Christ'.[83]

Berkhof is confident that the Holy Spirit is not only the awakener of individual spiritual life in justification and sanctification (as he is conceived in protestant theology; cf. Packer), and at the same time that he is not only the soul and sustainer of the church (as he is thought of in Roman Catholic theology; cf. Tippett and the Church Growth Movement). He considers him primarily as the great mover and driving power on the way from the One to the many, from Christ to the world. Missionary work is the first work of the Spirit; logically it is prior to the mighty works of the Spirit in the conversion of individuals and in the edification of congregations.[84] The strong resistance of Berkhof to both the individualization and the institutionalization of the work of the Spirit does not lead at all in his case to the recognition of non-Christian religions as 'ways of salvation'[85], but it leads to the acceptance of *a missionary purpose which goes beyond the church and the individual believer*, namely that "the earth shall be full of the knowledge of the Lord, as the waters cover the sea" (Is. 11:9).

I hold the view that in fact anyone who limits the missionary work of the Holy Spirit either to the conversion of the individual or to the planting of churches and upbuilding of congregations is engaged in building missiological castles in the air. Boer has rightly observed that the work of the Spirit in creation is a premise of his work in redemption. The 'unique' missionary work of the Spirit 'in the last days' remains entirely disconnected if it is not strongly related to his preceding 'universal' work (from the very beginning up to Pentecost, and also thereafter, in the whole universe).

The Missionary Church as a Praying and Working Movement of the Spirit

The *magnalia* of the Holy Spirit intervene profoundly in the life and work of the missionary congregations and their members. According to Cheesman they demonstrate clearly that the power of the Spirit is supreme over satanic forces.[86]

Berkhof treats the human being as an instrument of the Spirit.[87] In accordance with his view I would like to define the missionary church as that instrument of the Spirit which, by *praying and working* (*ora et labora*), is dynamically present in world history and which exerts continuously - more or less - influence on it.

In these studies I did not encounter the following word of John Mott pronounced in 1902: "Before 'give' and 'go' comes 'pray'; this is the divine order". Beside Taylor, nobody has mentioned the outstanding *missionary prayer: Veni Creator Spiritus*. Neither the works of Berkhof and Nacpil, nor the works of Pomerville and Hayford, pay real attention to the role of prayer in missionary work. Tippett, Cheesman and Packer go into this matter very briefly: Tippett writes about "pray[er] for the gift of the Holy Spirit"[88], Cheesman about "prayer for His power"[89], and Packer about the view of some evangelical theologians on prayer as a means of evangelism.[90] Taylor, however, is the only one who has gone deeply into this topic. He considers prayer *in*, and not prayer *to* the Holy Spirit as the pattern of the New Testament.[91] In the last chapter of his book *The Go-Between God*, entitled "Prayer in the Spirit and the Silence of Mission", he remarks:

> Prayer is our response to both the privilege and the responsibility whereby we cry *Abba*, Father! To engage in the mission of God, therefore, is to live this life of prayer; praying without ceasing, as St Paul puts it, that is to say, sustaining a style of life that is focused upon God.[92]

The disconnection of prayer and work can have very harmful consequences for the missionary work of the congregations and their members. For it can lead to the situation that we, being short of missionary spirituality, take our - imperfect - 'good' works for the - perfect - work of the Holy Spirit. Allen has clearly discerned this danger; more perspicuously than anybody else of these authors, he has written about *the obscuration of the Spirit* in and also by missionary work. In his opinion, *the sole work* which the missionary church has to do in our world is "the ministration of the Spirit".[93] It must always be possible to reduce the multitude of missionary works by the congregations and their members into this sole essential work.

The missionary church as a praying and working community exists by the grace of the mighty works of the missionary Spirit. We are not able to give here an all-round explanation of the fruitful 'charismatic work of the Holy Spirit' (Pomerville)[93] nor of the transformations caused by it in the missionary church and through this body in the world, among other reasons because this topic is not discussed thoroughly in this literature. However, here I frankly admit that all spheres of life are involved in this work of the Spirit and in this process of transformation. Nacpil is the author who mostly has an eye for it. For he writes profusely about the changes which take place in the missionary church by the outpouring of the Spirit: changes in the understanding of the universality of the Lordship of Christ; in the language of the church; in the leadership of the church; in the cultural milieu of the church; in the church's understanding of the truth of its message, etc. All these changes impinge upon the encounter of the missionary church as movement of the Spirit with the world. According to Nacpil, the dynamic way in which the church encounters the world today may never take the shape of 'military raiding missions'.[94]

Conclusion

I present my conclusion in six points, in conformity with the six previous subsections of my article:

1. Most of the authors reviewed here put more emphasis upon the power and work of the Holy Spirit than upon his *personhood*. Despite this, everybody speaks about him as a 'He', and nearly everybody does confer upon him epithets (Packer for instance: God the evangelist). Pomerville is the author who most expressly refers to the Spirit as a person ('the third person of the Godhead'). The Spirit as a person is both *the sent one* (by the Father and the Son) and *the sending one* (the sender of the congregations and their members).

2. This literature, having paid little attention to the Holy Spirit as a person, also devotes little attention both to the members of the missionary congregations as peoples who *became persons* in the evangelical sense of the word, and to non-Christians who *can become persons* in this sense by the outpouring of the Spirit. In this case the views of Taylor are the most satisfying ones, among other reasons because they do justice to the *I-Thou* relationship, in which the Spirit personally places the members of the congregations to God, to one another in the communion of saints, and missionarily to the world.

3. This literature has reflected much less upon the *fruit of the Spirit* than upon the *charismata* which are emphasized by the Pentecostal Movement and the Charismatic Renewal. This literature has also hardly thought about the mutual relationship between the *charismata* and 'the fruit of the Spirit', which in my opinion (cf. Tippett) is of crucial importance in equipping the church to do her missionary work in the world. The way in which Pomerville construes this relationship - 'outwardly' against 'inwardly' - is not satisfying; logically priority must be given to 'the fruit of the Spirit', which also is an outward 'demonstration of Spirit and power'.

4. The *experience of the Holy Spirit* in general and *the experience of the baptism with the Spirit* in particular can neither theoretically, nor practically, be left out of

missionary reflection. In this case I follow Hayford readily, and therefore I differ from several ecumenical (and evangelical) theologians. At the same time I still believe that in church life the charismatic experience of the Spirit by some persons cannot be prescribed in compulsory way to others as some Pentecostal theologians are doing (especially in the case of glossolalia). We may expect 'the fruit of the Spirit' to be present in the life of every member of the congregation, but glossolalia is not bestowed upon every individual Christian.

5. The Holy Spirit works missionarily in two ways: in *creation* 'universally' as *Spiritus animans*, and in *redemption* 'uniquely' as *Spiritus sanctificans* (so rightly Boer - in accordance with Luther and Calvin - and Taylor). In my opinion, a limitation of the missionary work of the Spirit to redemption, i.e. to the conversion of 'heathens' and church growth (cf. Cheesman), leads to an illicit reduction of missionary pneumatology. Berkhof is right in giving a broader purpose to missions than only the conversion of the individual and the planting and edification of the church as community.

6. I trust that an explanation of missionary prayer is prior to an exposition of the activities of the missionary church. The peculiar works of the missionary congregations and their members can never be put on a par with the mighty works of the missionary Spirit, because the first ones are imperfect, the last ones perfect. All activities of the missionary congregations and their members are ultimately, at least should ultimately be, *ministration of the Spirit* (Allen). Of all the writers Nacpil is the one who mostly has an eye for the transforming significance of the fruitful charismatic work of the Spirit in the church and through this body missionarily in the world.

In connection with Jerry L. Sandidge, Pomerville declares that the Pentecostal Movement is a renewal of the charismatic ministry *in salvation history.*[95] I would gladly like to widen and deepen this view: the missionary movement of Christ's church 'in the last days' is a renewal of 'the mighty works' of the Spirit of God and the Spirit of Christ *in* world history, which started 'in the beginning' - in the creation of heaven and earth -, and which have been continued 'in the fullness of time' - through the cross and resurrection of Christ as the missionary *Pneumatophoros.*

Notes

1. David M. Paton (ed.), *The Ministry of the Spirit; Selected Writings of Roland Allen; With a Memoir by Alexander McLeish* (London: World Dominion Press, 1960).
2. Harry R. Boer, *Pentecost and the Missionary Witness of the Church* (Franeker: T. Wever, 1955). Dissertation Free University Amsterdam. Revised ed.; *Pentecost and Missions* (Grand Rapids: Wm.B. Eerdmans Publshing House, 1961).
3. Hendrik Berkhof, *De Leer van de Heilige Geest* (Nijkerk: G.F. Callenbach, 1964), 33-44: "De Geest en de zending". English ed.: *The Doctrine of the Holy Spirit* (Richmond, Virginia: John

Knox Press, 1964).

4. Emerito P. Nacpil, *Mission and Change* (Manila: The East Asia Conference, 1968), 80-98: "Pentecost and Mission".
5. Alan R. Tippett, *Introduction to Missiology* (Pasadena, CA: William Carey Library, 1987), 46-61: "The Holy Spirit and Responsive Populations".
6. Graham Cheesman, *Mission today; An Introduction to Mission Studies* (Belfast: Qua Iboe Fellowship, 1989), 28-31: "The director - The Holy Spirit".
7. James I. Packer, "The Power and Work of the Holy Spirit I: The Work of the Holy Spirit in Conviction and Conversion", in: Jim D. Douglas (ed.), *Proclaim Christ until He Comes; Calling the Whole Church to Take the Whole Gospel to the Whole World (Lausanne II in Manila, International Congress on World Evangelization, 1989)* (Minneapolis, Minnesota: World Wide Publications, 1990), 100-04.
8. John V. Taylor, *The Go-between God; the Holy Spirit and the Christian Mission* (London: SCM Press, 1973). In this work Taylor has not declared himself in so many words to be a 'charismatic theologian'; however, here I have used him as a representative of this movement because he has put emphasis upon the experiences of the Holy Spirit. I do not know any charismatic theologian who has developed his own 'charismatic missiology'.
9. Paul A. Pomerville, *The Third Force in Missions; a Pentecostal Contribution to Contemporary Mission Theology* (Peabody, MA: Hendrickson Publishers, 1985).
10. Jack W. Hayford, "The Power and Work of the Holy Spirit II: a Passion for Fullness", in: Jim D. Douglas (ed.), *op. cit.*, 108-15.
11. See also: Frederick W. Dillistone, "The Holy Spirit and the Christian Mission", in: Gerald H. Anderson (ed.), *The Theology of the Christian Mission* (New York/Toronto/London: McGraw-Hill Book Company, 1961), 269-80; Jan A.B. Jongeneel, *Missiologie; II: Missionaire Theologie* ('s-Gravenhage: Boekencentrum, 1991), 98-100 (offers a survey of literature).
12. Oepke Noordmans, *Herschepping; beknopte dogmatische Handleiding voor godsdienstige Toespraken en Besprekingen* (Amsterdam: Holland, 1956), 165-204: "Ik geloof in de Heilige Geest".
13. Berkhof, *op. cit.*, 33-44 passim; cf. Hayford, *op. cit.*, 113: "We need to be open to the moving of the Holy Spirit".
14. Paton (ed.), *op. cit.*, 90: "...it makes no small difference whether we speak of a 'spiritual force' or of 'the Holy Ghost'. In the one case we think and speak, and in the event act, as if we had to do with an impersonal force; in the other we think and speak, and in the event act, as if we had to do with a personal force".
15. Paton (ed.), *op. cit.*, 20.
16. *Ibid.*, 110-11.
17. Boer, *op. cit.*, 120-22 speaks by the way about "the person (and deity) of the Spirit"; and Taylor, *op. cit.*, 68 writes about an "overwhelming yet intensely personal meeting between the spirit of a man and the Spirit of God" in the book Ezekiel.
18. Packer, *op. cit.*, 100.
19. Tippett, *op. cit.*, 59.
20. Pomerville, *op. cit.*, 61. Pomerville speaks preferably about 'God the Holy Spirit': 8-9, 50, 51, 60, 61, 96, 98-99, 125, 141-143, 158, 159.
21. Paton (ed.), *op. cit.*, 21, 59, 60; Berkhof, *op. cit.*, 38 (English ed.: 35), quoted by Emerito E. Nacpil, *op. cit.*, 83.
22. Paton (ed.), *op. cit.*, 21.
23. Boer, *op. cit.*, 92-104, 113, 123.
24. Packer, *op. cit.*, 103.
25. Taylor, *op. cit.*, 3. \
26. Pomerville, *op. cit.*, 109, 121, 162, 163.

27. Cf. Paton (ed.), *op. cit.*, 21: "Missionary work as an expression of the Holy Spirit has received such slight and casual attention that it might almost escape the notice of a hasty reader. A few strong expressions here and there incidentally introduced do not satisfy the case".
28. Berkhof, *op. cit.*, 36 speaks about 'een introverte en statische pneumatologie'.
29. Adolphe A. Tanqueray (ed.), *Synopsis theologiae dogmaticae ad usum seminariorum, ad mentem S. Thomae Aquinatis, hodiernis moribus accommodata* II (Paris-Tournai-Roma, 1933), 407-414: "De divinis missionibus".
30. Paton, *op. cit.*, 48.
31. Berkhof, *op. cit.*, 33, 39.
32. Taylor, *op. cit.*, 3.
33. Pomerville, *op. cit.*, 190.
34. Taylor, *op. cit.*, 8: "Spirit is that which lies between..."; 19: "The Holy Spirit is the invisible third party who stands between me and the other, making us mutually aware".
35. Emerito E. Nacpil, *op. cit.*, 80.
36. Boer, *op. cit.*, 66.
37. Paton (ed.), *op. cit.*, 13.
38. *Ibid.*, 27.
39. *Ibid.*, 36.
40. Cheesman, *op. cit.*, 31.
41. Hayford, *op. cit.*, 114.
42. Taylor, *op. cit.*, 93, 94, 101, 136, 176; cf. 33: "...luring them towards ever higher degrees of consciousness and personhood..."; and 39: "...the missionary of the Holy Spirit learns how to recognize these issues and knows how to fight for the truly personal values in himself and in others".
43. In this context Allen speaks about an obscuration of the role of the Holy Spirit: "...we have put the means, our 'activities', into His place. When the activities usurp the place of the Holy Spirit, the Spirit is obscured and hidden, because He is in fact deposed from His rightful place" (Paton, *op. cit.*, 97).
44. Berkhof, *op. cit.*, 39.
45. Tippett, *op. cit.*, 59.
46. Packer, *op. cit.*, 103; Pomerville, *op. cit.*, 81.
47. Boer, *op. cit.*, 66, 78, 102, 123.
48. Tippett, *op. cit.*, 58-59.
49. Hayford, *op. cit.*, 108, 110, 112, 113.
50. Pomerville, *op. cit.*, 62.
51. Pomerville, *op. cit.*, 81-82.
52. Taylor, *op. cit.*, 200.
53. Taylor, *op. cit.*, 207: "The communal character of the gifts of the Spirit is... of equal importance... as a safeguard against the cult of a spiritual elite".
54. Boer, *op. cit.*, 46, 93.
55. Boer, *op. cit.*, 42-46: "Temporary linguistic endowment for evangelistic purposes".
56. Hayford, *op. cit.*, 114; Pomerville, *op. cit.*, 10, 101-02.
57. Berkhof, *op. cit.*, 39.
58. Nacpil, *op. cit.*, 86-87. The following authors write also about the confusion of tongues at Babel and Pentecost: Boer, *op. cit.*, 131-132; and Pomerville, *op. cit.*, 163.
59. Taylor, *op. cit.*, 218-19.
60. Hayford, *op. cit.*. 109.
61. Tippett, *op. cit.*, 58.
62. Cheesman, *op. cit.*, 30.
63. Packer, *op. cit.*, 101.

64. Hayford, *op. cit.*, 109, 112-13.
65. Taylor, *op. cit.*, 81; cf. 6, 49, 50, 59, 61, 85, 199, 209 en 225.
66. Pomerville, *op. cit.*, 11, 14, 63; cf. 79-104: "An experience with the Spirit".
67. Hayford, *op. cit.*, 111.
68. Pomerville, *op. cit.*, 12.
69. *Ibid.*, 101-02.
70. Taylor, *op. cit.*, 200; cf. 44, 104, 109, 111, 119, 200 en 218.
71. However, this reductionism is absent in *Baptism, Eucharist and Ministry (BEM)*, 1982. Cf. the article of P. Staples in this *Festschrift.*
72. Jim D. Douglas (ed.), *op. cit.*, 100, 108.
73. Tippett, *op. cit.*, 52, 53, 57, 58.
74. Hayford, *op. cit.*, 111, 113.
75. Boer, *op. cit.*, 58; cf. Taylor, *op. cit.*, 75: "...the Holy Spirit as both creator and restorer...".
76. Taylor, *op. cit.*, 180-81.
77. Taylor, *op. cit.*, 191; cf. 27: "The Spirit of Life is ever at work in nature, in history and in human living...".
78. Boer, *op. cit.*, 137.
79. *Ibid.*, 59-66.
80. Cheesman, *op. cit.*, 30-31.
81. Packer, *op. cit.*, 102.
82. *Ibid.*, 102.
83. Tippett, *op. cit.*, 52.
84. Berkhof, *op. cit.*, 33, 34, 36.
85. Cf. Paul F. Knitter, *No Other Name? A Critical Survey of Christian Attitudes toward the World Religions* (London: SCM Press, 1985). The so-called 'left wing' of the Ecumenical Movement, which reflects more upon dialogue than upon missions, and which by consequence speaks more about the relation Spirit-dialogue than about the relation Spirit-missions, is left out of consideration in this article.
86. Cheesman, *op. cit.*, 31.
87. Berkhof, *op. cit.*, 39.
88. Tippett, *op. cit.*, 61.
89. Cheesman, *op. cit.*, 31.
90. Packer, *op. cit.*, 103.
91. Taylor, *op. cit.*, 43-44.
92. *Ibid.*, 227.
93. Paton, *op. cit.*, 113.
94. Pomerville, *op. cit.*, 10.
95. Nacpil, *op. cit.*, 95.
96. Pomerville, *op. cit.*, 46, 56.

22

The Church at Play: The Pentecostal/Charismatic Renewal of the Liturgy as Renewal of the World

Jean-Jacques Suurmond

Professor Walter J. Hollenweger in his own person happily combines serious scholarship with a certain playfulness. In his academic writings, one often discerns a, for western Christendom, rather disturbing chuckle. On the other hand, his narratives, dramas and musicals evidence a background of research in the best Teutonic tradition. To my mind, he thus bears the true mark of an evangelist, a ministry he once told me he longed to pick up again after his retirement. That is to say, Dr. Hollenweger is a witness to that New World which will not be characterized by a repressive order, nor by a chaotic disorder, but by the playing order in which bride and bridegroom delight. It is this element of play which I will try to expound here as possibly the most important contribution of the Pentecostal Movement and Charismatic Renewal to the Church and, indirectly, to the world. This article, therefore, seems a fitting tribute to a missiologist who knows that the Spirit of Pentecost can bring alive the ancient symbol of Christ the clown.[1]

In the following, I will attempt to show that God has designed the world to be a play. It is obvious that the present world falls far short of that ideal. Next, therefore, the liturgy's potential to recreate the world into a play is described. Finally, the promise of Pentecostalism is found in its ability to enhance and actualize this potential of the liturgy. This is illustrated by way of the themes of the Conciliar Process (an ecumenical and missiological venture without precedent), i.e. peace, justice and the integrity of creation. Even when the Conciliar Process will have been officially concluded, these themes will undoubtedly continue to need our attention.

The World is Designed to Be a Play

God is not useful. He serves no earthly purpose. No matter how laudable our aim, when we try to use God for our own purposes we reduce him to an instrument and God will no longer be God. Growth in faith, therefore, always implies that we increasingly view God as having his aim in himself. This is the message of the mystics of all times. A technological age like ours, which is obsessed by efficiency and utility, is therefore bound either to turn God into a useful (and dreadfully boring) idol, or to experience Martin Buber's eclipse of God. This is in fact what we often witness today. The uselessness of God implies the uselessness of his creation. This is apt to relativize the grim ambition with which we often pull ourselves through life. Yet, there was and is for God no necessity to create. The world is superfluous, a luxury. So, why did God create it? For the same reason that Jesus at a wedding-party turned water into wine and not into a useful dairy-product. Out of pure joy and delight, God created the world as a play. To dust off a traditional term: we live by grace (*chen* in Hebrew, from which comes the Yiddish word *chein*, i.e. pleasure). God's Creator-Spirit is his Teamspirit inspiring 'all creatures great and small'[2] to play. The category of play therefore seems to be the key to understanding the nature and purpose of the universe. In play, creation comes to be re-creation.

Scriptural Data

The creation accounts in Scripture testify to the fact that the world is intended to be a play. In Genesis 1, God progressively creates ever higher forms of life. For a long time it was thought that human beings represent the crown of creation. Especially the influence of humanism contributed to this interpretation, with disastrous ecological effects. However, as Moltmann points out, not (wo)man created on the sixth day, but the sabbath which was created on the seventh and last day is the crown of creation.[3] Human beings are crowned with the glory and honour of the sabbath and, as such, they are the priests of creation (cf. Ps. 8:5-9) and image of the God who is aim-in-himself. The entire creative process is directed towards the sabbath, to the rest from necessity, to relaxation and play. The weekly sabbath points to the eternal sabbath-rest, to the new Jerusalem where the music never stops, vintage wines flow and the game of lover and beloved is played.

This is even more clearly brought out by the concept of wisdom. In Scripture, wisdom represents the principle of creation. God creates in, through and with (often personified) wisdom. In Proverbs 8, Lady Wisdom says:

> Yahweh created me at the beginning of his work... when he laid the foundations of the earth - then I was beside him as his favorite, and I was daily his delight, playing in front of him all the time, playing in his inhabited world and delighting in the sons of men.[4]

God's principle of creation is Wisdom at play. Those who play are wise because they are attuned to God's purpose for the world. According to Proverbs 1, in Wisdom is both a spirit (*rûach*) she pours out and a word by which she calls aloud in the street. God's Word and Spirit are joined in the concept of Wisdom.[5] Here we encounter precisely that combination of structure (Word) and dynamic (Spirit), of necessity and possibility, which is the mark of all genuine play.

In the New Testament, Lady Wisdom becomes the Lord Jesus. Now it is said of Jesus that God has created all things in, through and with him (e.g. Col 1). Jesus represents both the incarnate Word and the one who receives the Spirit without measure. Christ, therefore, is the wisdom of God (1 Cor 1:24). Jesus says that he came as one playing the flute and eating and drinking, yet nobody danced. But Wisdom, so he says about himself, is proved right by all her children (Luke 7:31-35). For a child, life is play. Without a playful, childlike receptivity one cannot enter the Kingdom of God (Mark 10:15). For the Kingdom of God is a Kingdom of play, the fulfillment and destiny of the process of creation. This explains why Jesus talked about the Kingdom in parables. Like a play, a parable is situated in this world, yet it is not of this world and therefore able to transform it. A parable represents our world with a shocking 'Kingdom difference'. We know what a landowner is, but here is one who pays his labourers a full day's wages for only one hour of work. We understand the joy of a parent when a lost child comes home, but are puzzled when the father between the dining table and the dancing floor not once seems to feel compelled to say: 'I told you so!' Like a play, a parable mirrors our world in the light of its sabbath fulfillment. As such, it has therapeutic power for it enables us to distance ourselves from the present situation, perceive possibilities hitherto undreamt of and thus understand ourselves and our world anew.[6] In this way we come to recreation (salvation). Through Spirit and Word, Jesus not only preached in parables but in his own person represented the Kingdom as a living parable. For he was a human being just like us, yet with that crucial 'Kingdom difference'. Like a superb play, his life was out of this world and therefore able to change it. Unexpected possibilities were opened up: publicans became Robin Hoods, giving away their money to the poor; frog-like lepers received royal health and dignity; ordinary Cinderella's became queens of the resurrection preaching. For those who let themselves be drawn into the gracious play of Jesus' life, fairy tales came true.[7] As such, Jesus embodied during his whole life the creative generosity of the cross, which is the wisdom of God but foolishness to the world. This mission he continues through the Church, which therefore is called the body of Christ (cf. 1 Cor 1:18-2:16; 12:27).

The Scientific View

The notion that God has designed the world to be a play is corroborated by modern science. Dutch historian Johan Huizinga has shown that the distinguishing mark of a human being is not the ability to think (*homo sapiens*), nor the capability to make things (*homo faber*), but the possibility of play (*homo ludens*).[8] Play is fundamental to being human. Huizinga points out that culture essentially is a play. In this he stood on the shoulders of Plato, the Greek philosopher who already thought out almost everything that is worth thinking about. In his last dialogue, Plato says that "while God is the real goal of all beneficent serious endeavour... all of us, men and women alike, must fall in with our role and spend life in making our play as perfect as possible". He immediately notes that this is a 'complete inversion' of the current state of affairs, which is dominated by serious attention to trifles and war.[9]

This central importance of play to being human, of the necessity of non-necessity,[10] is confirmed by modern psychology. No one is more obsessed by order and worried about the consequences of his or her behaviour than the neurotic or psychotic. Healthy is the one who can laugh about him- or herself and the world and playfully live by the day, open-handedly receiving life as a gift.[11]

Finally, I want to mention the recent discoveries of the natural sciences. These show that the world is not merely a stage on which the drama of life is acted out. The material world itself is built up according to the structure of play. Instead of the ordered, mechanistic world-view of Newton, modern physics and biology stress the idea of randomness. This should not be understood in the sense of blind chance, for there are fundamental constraints such as the species, space and time. These are the 'rules' of the cosmic play in which randomness represents the creative possibility of novelty and surprise. Word (necessity) and Spirit (chance) can thus be called, in the words of Irenaeus, the two creating hands of God. They are, so to speak, the '*yin* and *yang* of evolution', elaborating life like a great fugue of Bach.[12]

After this seven-league booted journey through Scripture and science, it is now time to summarize our findings by way of Huizinga's definition of play:

> Play is a voluntary activity or occupation executed within certain fixed limits of time and place, according to rules freely accepted but absolutely binding, having its aim in itself and accompanied by a feeling of tension, joy and the consciousness that it is 'different' from 'ordinary life'.[13]

Play is a voluntary activity, thus not necessary. The feeling of tension and joy is the only reason why we play. Furthermore, play is executed within certain limits of time and place. That is, it is in the world but not of the world; it possesses a 'Kingdom difference' distinguishing it from ordinary life. This parabolic character of play parallels the eschatological tension between the 'already' of the Kingdom and the 'not yet' of the present world; our consciousness of it is both revolutionary and healing. Next, play is marked by rules freely accepted but absolutely binding. This is the element of necessity, of the Word, which together with the Spirit (feeling of tension, joy) creates its own enchanting order in which all things are possible (for the outcome is open). Finally, play has its aim in itself; it is not subordinated to our own ends. Play is purposeless for meaningful in itself and exactly for this reason possesses recreative power. A good play attunes us to the eternal sabbath, to the end of creation, i.e. to God. We celebrate that we are ends in ourselves and this is balm for our harassed souls. In modern technocratic society, the children, the elderly, the handicapped and disabled therefore have become prophetic: signs reminding us that not our useful work but only useless grace can save us.

The Present World Is a Battle

It is obvious that the world resembles a battle more than a play. Already Plato observed that war is more in evidence than the 'play of peace'. Huizinga shows that war represents play in corrupted form. When play is no longer respected as having its aim in itself, but is subordinated to the players' ends, it degenerates into a battle. Not a few soccer matches end in a massacre. The play of the so-called free market is in essence a bitter struggle for survival. Instead of a partner in life's play, our neighbour has become a rival, a threat, and nature has become an object to exploit. Even the intimate play of lovers is often marred by the urge to score. However, when we thus allow play to degenerate into battle, we lower ourselves to the level of the animal kingdom. We are not so far removed from the higher animals as we would like to think. After all, we were created on the same day. Animal play generally has its end not in itself but serves the struggle for survival. When human play is corrupted into battle, culture, like nature, becomes red in tooth and claw. Thus we are faced with the vexing question: how can we fulfill our high mission to be stewards of creation and attune it to the play of the eternal sabbath? Are we not ourselves the greatest spoilsports? Heavy hangs the head that wears the crown of creation. The answer, I think, is provided by the liturgy of the Church.

The World-Recreating Potential of the Liturgy

The Liturgy As Eschatological Play

The word *leitourgia* denotes a work of service (*ergon*) for the people (*leitos, laos*). In Greek antiquity, it referred to the service of a wealthy citizen who sponsored the ceremonies at the games. In the ancient Christian church the word was often used figuratively, referring to a service rendered by a king to his people, particularly in times of disaster.[14] We may gather from this that the Church's liturgy implies God's service to his people in order that they may be able to play and save the world from destruction. Already in 1918, Romano Guardini described the liturgy as a play. According to him, in the liturgy we waste time for God. We recreate without reason or aim. The liturgy has no purpose, which would make it a means to something else. It has a meaning, and therefore has its aim in itself. Just as a child pours itself out in play, in the liturgy we merely express our true selves, giving ourselves to God and to each other.[15] Of course, this sounds like a curse to our efficient culture which continually battles for a goal it will never reach, because it can only be found in the celebration of life now. Hollenweger therefore rightly says that the pastor should be a 'priestly producer' enabling the people of God to play their own roles in the church and in the world convincingly.[16] In the liturgy, God gives himself to us in Christ in whom Word and Spirit are joined, thus liberating us for the eschatological play. Its intensity and joy involve an *ascesis* from the world and an openness for the Holy. We are free to worship God for who he is; to welcome our neighbour as equal partner in the play; and to draw creation into our playing through the use of bread, wine, water, incense, icons and so on. As eschatological play, the liturgy is both eternal life itself (the Eastern-Orthodox view) and the means of salvation (the Roman-Catholic view), but only because it has meaning in itself. We thus are again and again attuned to the eternal sabbath so that the liturgy has a world-recreating potential. In the liturgy, nothing less than the world is at stake. It is therefore not surprising that people living outside Christendom, including atheists, have always felt an intuitive need for their own secular liturgies.[17]

Plato already noted that play and ritual are identical.[18] Ritual behaviour has a parabolic character in that it implies controlled situations of dysfunction which stop our automatic way of living according to the pattern of this world and wake us up to the possibilities of the New World.[19] Von Zinzendorf tried to change the whole life of his Bohemian Brethren into one great liturgical play. As a result, this church was more liberated and equipped for service to the world than any other church since the Reformation.[20] A translation of this insight into theological terms is found in Karl Barth's *Church Dogmatics*, where he opens his section on ethics with a treatment of the Feast day. The play of the liturgy has integrating power for it brings together our spirituality and concern for the world; faith and facts; the future and the present; and the divine and the human (cf. the christological two-nature doctrine).[21] Our experience of God, who is useless because He is aim-in-himself, sets us free from our goal-oriented, play-corrupting attitude so that we can become a gift to the world, answering our call to be a partner and 'priestly producer' of the grand play of creation.

The Failure of the Liturgy

Just as it is obvious that the present world resembles a battle more than a play, it is clear that most liturgies do not realize their world-recreating potential. Many churches today experience a crisis of identity and wonder whether they have something to say to the world. To my mind, the chief cause is that the liturgy has lost much of its playfulness and therefore has no transforming power. In the attempt to be relevant, churches have adopted the instrumental thinking of the world and thus have become irrelevant. The priest or minister does not tell parables, but moralizes. The mass or service has been subjected to all kinds of political or social goals. The liturgy is no longer foolish enough, so that it no longer proclaims the wisdom of God. The balance has dipped into the direction of the Word, of structure, order, form, of useful didactics and ethics, to the detriment of the Spirit who inspires, surprises and renews. Feelings of joy and pain have been levelled to an almost stoic attitude which is powerless to change people, much less the world. This is the reason why the cult, like the modern money-oriented and bureaucratized sports world, has become culturally sterile.

All this explains why Pentecostals shudder at the word 'liturgy' and retain an a-liturgical stance. Yet, Pentecostal services certainly follow a planned order.[22] The refusal to admit this involves the inability to reflect on and improve their liturgical order, which may explain the spiritlessness of not a few Pentecostal churches. If the traditional churches often overemphasize the rules, the Pentecostal rules frequently are not adequate to the play. In both cases the play is spoiled, as any child can tell us. Too much weight on the rules breeds formalism; without good rules, the creative tension (the 'spirit') leaks away.[23] We observed that in wisdom, as well as in Jesus as also in the liturgy, Word and Spirit combine to work creatively. Neither order, nor disorder but a playing order is called for. Although the Liturgical Movement has recovered many treasures, with its catholicizing tendencies it is order-oriented and therefore unable to solve the present problem. The liturgy must again become a 'feast of fools' (H. Cox): a playful protest which disturbs and upsets the *status quo* in order to heal and redeem it. This is the *missio Dei* of the church and here, I think, lies the major promise of Pentecostalism.

The Promise of Pentecostalism: Renewal of the Liturgy As Renewal of the World

In his book *The Go-Between God*, Bishop John V. Taylor rightly describes Pentecostalism under the heading of 'Playing'.[24] The most striking thing about a well-conducted Pentecostal or Charismatic meeting is the 'jazz-factor', the creative integration of order and spontaneity. This is why such worship possesses the fascinating attraction of a good play. Witness the fervent devotion of millions to soccer or football matches! Nothing equals the missionary power of a good Pentecostal/Charismatic liturgy. It is moreover significant that Pentecostalism especially appeals to the poor of the Two-Thirds World. They are not as wedded to the present order as the well-to-do and are therefore more open to the foolish, generous play of God's Kingdom in which the last become the first.

I will now conclude by briefly sketching the contributions of the Pentecostal Movement and the Charismatic Renewal to the Church's liturgy and, indirectly, to the themes of the Conciliar Process.

Lack of Peace

Modern people suffer from a lack of inner peace, which prevents them from mak-ing peace in the world. We have an insatiable desire to justify our own existence, to prove that the human project is worthwhile after all. Since the Enlightenment, this striving for self-justification took the form of a striving for the perfect society. Now that the yoke of the Church had been shaken off and science and technology were soaring, (wo)man had become grown up and the ideal society had come within reach. Or so we thought. However, this grand goal was allowed to justify the means and recently both the capitalist and socialist paradises have proved to be morally bankrupt. With our dream of a perfect society we aimed too high, we wanted to become like God and fell miserably. There is a parallel here with the relationship between perfectionism and feelings of inferiority in psychology. Feelings of inferiority are the result of a mild megalomania, of an unrealistic ideal self-image. Naturally we cannot live up to this ideal, which time and again causes us to feel frustrated about ourselves. In the same way, our unrealistic belief in human progress had to lead to disillusionment.[25] Modern human beings are disappointed in themselves, which makes it very hard to live in peace with others. Moreover, because we still tend to rate our self-worth in terms of our ability to reach goals, we experience each failure to reach such a goal as a personal fiasco. Therefore, many have lowered their aims. In our 'post-modern' era, people have become wary of great dreams, lofty ideals and grand visions and largely settle for the *status quo*, however unsatisfactory this may be in terms of peace, justice and the integrity of creation.

Spirit-Baptism

The Pentecostal/Charismatic emphasis on the experience of God in the liturgy can heal our lack of inner peace. Our goal-oriented mentality by which we try to justify ourselves, turns life's play into a battle - not least of all with ourselves. But why do we continually have to justify ourselves? The answer is simple: because we are not so sure that we have permission to be. In the end, our fear of death is at the root of our goal-oriented behaviour. Death is the great spoilsport for it says: 'You are not allowed to be'. Death puts us under the necessity of having to be useful in order to prove that we have the right to exist. I think that, in Spirit-baptism, we experience time and again in many 'fillings' with the Spirit the resurrection life of Christ which liberates us from the fear of death.[26] This frees us from too much necessity which corrupts life's play into a struggle for survival.[27] At the same time, we experience that God himself is our goal and future. Thus we are able to flourish, to live childlike by the day and strive for peace, justice and the integrity of creation without letting ourselves be intimidated by the question as to the usefulness of our efforts. For these themes of the Conciliar Process are in themselves worthy to be busy about, even if the results are meager. Through Spirit-baptism, we can live playfully: taking the world seriously yet at the same time relaxing our hold of it. We are very much involved in our 'time is money' age, yet simultaneously we are wasting time for God by speaking in tongues.[28] Like Thomas Merton, we become useless fools in Christ, living parables which turn the world upside down and renew it.[29] For then something very remarkable happens. The less we worry about the results, the more our work will gain in quality. When we are no longer fixated upon our goal, we will reach it.[30] Only what we are able to lose, will we win. In the Spirit, the seventh-day recreation of the sabbath leavens the battle culture of our sixth day. The deposit of the 'Spirit of futurity' (Bultmann) sets us free to playfully walk the yellow brick road and grow day by day, instead of being obsessed by the goal of reaching the Emerald City and becoming weary of life. Thus the Spirit enables us to join the 'play of peace' and become truly human.

Injustice

The inner lack of peace modern (wo)man wrestles with has unleashed a huge wave of ideologies and a concomitant increase of unrighteousness. For if we are not content with ourselves, we are easily seduced into exchanging our unworthy self for the new identity ideological systems have on offer. Procrustes-like, an ideology cuts reality down to manageable size. This makes our goals in life attainable so that we can live with ourselves. Unlike e.g. the much more ambitious and therefore unrealizable aims of the Enlightenment, our highest purpose now is to convert somebody, or to veil women, or to send foreigners out of the country. But the price is high. For a reduced reality is, of course, a false reality which leads to a reduced, false self. The price is even higher for those who do not measure up to the ideological expectations. Requiring absolute allegiance, ideologies are served like gods. For a false self stands or falls with the ideology that justifies its existence, so that any deviation or criticism is experienced as a deadly threat. The Jewish author Richard Rubinstein says in so many words that, in this way, the Enlightenment dream to construct the new Jerusalem could turn into the nightmare of the concentration camp.[31] In a sense, the ovens of Auschwitz were stoked with the wreckage of our belief in human progress which had made us vulnerable to the Nazi-ideology that promised a solution for our problem: the *Endlösung*. The Third *Reich* became the reduced reality squeezing non-Arians. Ideologies lead to exclusion, repression and even elimination. This is injustice.

Charisms

The functioning of the gifts of the Spirit involves everybody in the Pentecostal/Charismatic liturgy, which can promote justice. While Calvin gave the psalms back in the mouth of the congregation, giving it active participation in the liturgy, Pentecostalism has expanded this. For here the Church as the body of Christ functions as an interplay of many different gifts. Freed by the Spirit to celebrate our own uselessness, we no longer take ourselves too seriously so that we dare to give ourselves away. Childlike, we pour ourselves out in the liturgical play, becoming a gift to others. Thus the dream of the political radicals of a participatory democracy is nurtured by an oral liturgy in which each can take part by means of a prophetic word, a prayer for the sick, a chorus and so forth.[32] For ages, the poor of Latin-America had been treated as dumb and unimportant instruments serving the goals of the rich, and this is also how they viewed themselves. Today, in the liturgy of the Charismatic base communities, the Spirit has begun to give them a voice. To their own surprise, they speak a prophetic word, or share an insight, or give a testimony. Thus they become self-conscious and grow in dignity and soon speak out against the repressive ideological structures of their society. In Latin-America today, the dumb begin to speak.[33] God's Teamspirit involves everybody in the Church's liturgical play. This is his answer to excluding ideologies. Let us not forget that, in the gospels, the charisms are especially promised to those who, in the courts, have to confront the high and mighty of the earth. Be then not anxious about what you should say, Jesus says, for the Spirit will give it to you in that hour (Mark 13:11).[34] The charisms turn everybody into equally competent playmates so that each can come into his or her own right. This is righteousness.

Exploitation of Creation

Moltmann writes that the exploitation of nature is the counterpart of our subjection of the body.[35] We have made our body subservient to the goal of functioning in industrial society where we have to be able to sit day after day behind a desk, or stand for many hours on the factory floor. All this in order that we may silence our restless self by attaining the goals of our consumer ideology, in which the grand vision of human progress is reduced to the aim to possess the latest product advertised. Since we treat our body as a means to a purpose, we cannot help but view nature, of which our body is a part, in the same light. For us, nature is first and foremost a thing to be used: not a marvel to be respected in its own right. There is no difference in principle between smoking a cigarette and poisoning nature with exhaust-fumes. We are strangers to our body and therefore cannot live in friendship with the earth. We spoil the interdependent play of all things, breaking up the 'community of creation' (Moltmann), with grave ecological consequences.

Holistic Spirituality

In the Pentecostal/Charismatic liturgy our mind, emotions and body become an integrated whole which can promote respect for the integrity of creation. Death is the great disintegrator, serving the *diabolos* (literally: 'the one who throws apart'). Releasing us from the fragmentating fear of death, Spirit-baptism liberates us from the necessity to objectivize our body, including nature, in order to manipulate it for our own self-justifying ends. Spirit-baptism therefore makes clear that green is the most important colour of the liturgical year. The world is not designed to be an object to exploit, but to be a place where a young child can peacefully play near the hole of a snake. This integrity of body and nature finds its highest liturgical expression in the Pentecostal/Charismatic dance. According to Huizinga, dance is the purest and most perfect form of play.[36] It teaches us again to live spontaneously, instead of living with ideas about life. Dance is a confirmation of creaturely existence and a celebration of the flesh, expressing the joy of the whole creation about being the dwelling-place of the Spirit. Dance was already central to the liturgy of ancient Israel. Mystics and church fathers properly described redeemed creation as a dance.[37] We thus become entirely caught up in the liturgy in an harmonious interplay with nature in rhythm, space and time.

Closing Remarks: But Will It Play?

I conclude that the Pentecostal/Charismatic renewal can release the liturgy's potential to bring creation to re-creation: as people are equipped to renew the world according to the divine design. That is, as long as they play by the rules. Sound liturgical rules not only prevent disorder, but also preclude an overemphasis on order as they let the Spirit come into his or her own. Yet, the rich experience of Spirit-baptism is already withering away through legalistic misinterpretations; already, many charismatically endowed little people in Latin-America are being overshadowed by big, bossy Pentecostal leaders; already, the prudish and materialistic mentality of western Pentecostals and Charismatics is reducing the body as well as nature to an instrument for ulterior purposes. The raising of a liturgical consciousness therefore seems to be the most important challenge facing both the Pentecostal Movement and the Charismatic Renewal in the years ahead.

Notes

1. See W.J. Hollenweger, *Pentecost Between Black and White* (Belfast: Christian Journals, 1974), 50 ff.
2. Cf. W.J. Hollenweger, "All Creatures Great and Small: Towards a Pneumatology of Life", in D. Martin and Mullen (eds.), *Strange Gifts? A Guide to Charismatic Renewal* (Oxford: Basil Blackwell, 1984), 41-53.
3. J. Moltmann, *God in Creation: An Ecological Doctrine of Creation. The Gifford Lectures 1984-1985* (London: SCM Press, 1985), 5-7, 276-96.
4. Translation G. von Rad, *Wisdom in Israel* (Nashville: Abingdon Press, 1978), 150.
5. This is especially true for the intertestamental literature. See Schoonenberg, "A Sapiential Reading of John's Prologue: Some Reflections on Views of R. Fuller and J. Dunn", *Theology Digest* 33 (1986), 407 ff.
6. Cf. R. Leuenberger, "Wahrheit und Spiel. Zur Frage der Zukunft des evangelischen Gottesdien-

stes", *Zeitschrift für Theologie und Kirche* 67 (1970), 253-55.

7. Cf. F. Buechner, *Telling the Truth: The Gospel as Tragedy, Comedy and Fairy Tale* (New York: Harper & Row, 1977), 49-98; H. Rahner, *Man at Play* (London: Burns & Oates, 1965), 65.
8. J. Huizinga, *Homo Ludens: A Study of the Play-Element in Culture* (London: Routledge & Kegan Paul, 1949).
9. E. Hamilton and H. Cairns (eds.), *'Laws VII', Plato: The Collected Dialogues*, Bollingen Series LXXI (Princeton: Princeton University Press, 1980), 1374 f.
10. Cf. H. Fortmann, *Oosterse renaissance. Kritische reflecties op de cultuur van nu* (Bilthoven: Ambo, 1970), 9-18; J. Thiele (Hrsg.), *Der verliebte Regenschirm: Einladung zu schönen Zeiten* (Stuttgart: Kreuz Verlag, 1990).
11. See e.g. E. Becker, *The Denial of Death* (New York: Free Press, 1973), 201 f.
12. Cf. J. Polkinghorne, *One World: The Interaction of Science and Theology* (London: SPCK, 1986), 51, 54. In this light, Jesus can be seen as the first Spirit-inspired 'mutation' of human life, a protest against the tyrannical necessity of selection and a successful 'adaptation' to the ultimate reality of play. Cf. G. Theissen, *Biblical Faith: An Evolutionary Approach* (Philadelphia: Fortress Press, 1985), 105-28. My concept of 'play' or 'playing order' is close to the 'non-order' of D.W. Hardy and D.F. Ford, *Jubilate: Theology in Praise* (London: Darton, Longman & Todd, 1984), 96-99, 201-201 *passim*. See also *ibid.*, 116-18, for the idea of randomness.
13 Huizinga, *Homo Ludens*, 28.
14. M.A. Vrijlandt, *Liturgiek* (Den Haag: Meinema, 1987), 5.
15. R. Guardini, *Vom Geist der Liturgie* (Freiburg: Herder, 1957), 89-105; English translation: *The Spirit of the Liturgy* (London: Sheed & Ward, 1935).
16. W.J. Hollenweger, "The Producer as Liturgist", *A Monthly Letter about Evangelism* 2/3 (February/March 1967) 1-8.
17. This accords with the ancient idea that rituals guarantee the well-being of the world. See Huizinga, *Homo Ludens*, 5, 14, 16, 54. Cf. W.J. Hollenweger, "Säkulare Liturgien. Versuch einer Interpretation", *Areopag* 6 (1971) 120-140. See further, on a different level, G. Wainwright, *Doxology: The Praise of God in Worship, Doctrine and Life* (New York: Oxford University Press, 1980), 399-434; C. Harissiades, "Le culte chrétien facteur de développement et de civilisation", in A.M. Triacca et A. Pistoia (eds.), *Liturgie, spiritualité, cultures*, Bibliotheca Ephemerides Liturgicae 29 (Roma: Edizioni Liturgiche, 1983), 115-31.
18. See also Huizinga, *Homo Ludens*, 18f., 212. What language does for sound, ritual does for movement. See H. Cox, *The Feast of Fools: A Theological Essay on Festivity and Fantasy* (Cambridge: Harvard University Press, 1969), 74 f.
19. Cf. R.A. Hutch, "The Personal Ritual of Glossolalia", *Journal for the Scientific Study of Religion* 19 (1980), 262-64.
20. Leuenberger, "Wahrheit und Spiel", 254.
21. Cf. Cox, *Feast of Fools*, 78 f., 117-20, 131-38.
22. See e.g. W.J. Hollenweger, "The Social and Ecumenical Significance of Pentecostal Liturgy", *Studia Liturgica* 8 (1971/72), 209-11; K.M. Ranaghan, "Conversion and Baptism: Personal Experience and Ritual Celebration in Pentecostal Churches", *Studia Liturgica* 10 (1974), 68-70.
23. Guardini, *Vom Geist der Liturgie*, 102 f. The disparaging of liturgical rules therefore implies a lack of understanding of the essential play-function of the worship service. In his still widely-used *Spirit-Filled Pastor's Guide* (Springfield: Gospel Publishing House, 1948), 201, 216, Assemblies of God minister R.M. Riggs allows ceremonies chiefly in order not to offend guests from "ritualistic" churches, at the same time counseling the pastor (in connection with children's behaviour) not to "allow his church to be made a place of play at any time"! Yet, a poor liturgy indirectly encourages a fundamentalist attitude, as it fails to develop the 'transitional sphere' (the realm of dreams, rites and symbols in every human being) which enables us to face and integrate painful reality. Cf.

P.W. Pruyser, *Between Belief and Unbelief* (New York: Harper & Row, 1974), 111-14, 198 f., 206 f. *passim.*

24. J.V. Taylor, *The Go-Between God: The Holy Spirit and the Christian Mission* (New York: Oxford University Press, 1979), 198-222.
25. See A. Vergote, "Religieuze moed en deemoed", in J. van der Lans (red.) *Spiritualiteit: Sociaal-wetenschappelijke en theologische beschouwingen*, Voor Willem Berger (Baarn: Ambo, 1984), 93 f.
26. See J.-J. Suurmond, "The Meaning and Purpose of Spirit-Baptism and the Charisms", *Bijdragen, tijdschrift voor filosofie en theologie 51* (1990), 172-94; also published in *EPTA Bulletin* 9/4 (1991), 96-130.
27. As mentioned earlier, a good play (game) needs some necessity (word/rules) in order to contain tension and joy (spirit). As such, it represents authentic life, being a kind of practice session for life-towards-death. Cf. J.D. Crossan, *The Dark Interval: Towards a Theology of Story* (Allen: Argus Communications, 1975), 16-18; J.-J. Suurmond, "The Meaning and Purpose", *passim.*
28. Cf. R.A. Baer, Jr., "Quaker Silence, Catholic Liturgy and Pentecostal Glossolalia - Some Functional Similarities", in R.P. Spittler (ed.), *Perspectives on the New Pentecostalism* (Grand Rapids: Baker Book House, 1976), 158 f.
29. See. B.C. Lane, "Merton as Zen Clown", *Theology Today* 46 (1989), 256-268. Cf. Cox, *Feast of Fools*, 139-157. The Eastern-Orthodox church still knows the ministry of the salos, i.e. the fool in Christ. See K. Ware, *The Orthodox Way* (Crestwood: St. Vladimir's Seminary Press, 1986), 131f.
30. Cf. V. Frankl's paradoxical intention, *Psychotherapy and Existentialism: Selected Papers on Logotherapy* (Harmondsworth: Penguin Books, 1973), 136-54, *passim.*
31. Referred to by Cox, Feast of Fools, 30 f.
32. Cf. Hollenweger, "The Social and Ecumenical Significance", 212-15.
33 J. Comblin, *The Holy Spirit and Liberation*, Liberation and Theology 4 (Maryknoll, New York: Orbis Books, 1989), 26 f. Cf. W.J. Hollenweger, "Liturgiereform als Sozialreform", *Neues Forum* 16 (December 1969), 711-13.
34. K. Stendahl, "The New Testament Evidence", in M.P. Hamilton (ed.), *The Charismatic Movement* (Grand Rapids: Wm.B. Eerdmans, 1975), 55.
35. Moltmann, *God in Creation*, 48 f.
36. Huizinga, *Homo Ludens*, 164.
37. See J.H. Eaton, "Old Testament Worship", in J.G. Davies (ed.), *A New Dictionary of Liturgy and Worship* (London: SCM Press, 1986), 398; Cox, *Feast of Fools*, 49-54.

23

Ecumenical Theology and Pentecostalism

Peter Staples

Comparing Two Styles of 'Doing Theology'

Given the fact that both the Ecumenical Movement and the Pentecostal Movement are two of the most significant and extensive movements in the field of Twentieth Century Church History, the time may well be ripe to ask ourselves whether it is possible to compare their respective 'belief systems' or their respective theologies.[1] Nevertheless, this is by no means a simple operation: especially in a short paper. It is wise to bear in mind that such a comparison may still be too premature for a number of very good reasons.

First: whereas the 'Ecumenicals' have already been elaborating their own systematic ecumenical theology since the 1920s[2], Pentecostals have only recently begun to reflect systematically upon their own theological position. Or, rather, their own theological positions: given the wide diversity of views which are now maintained by Pentecostals and Charismatics on Christology and Trinitarianism. For example: there are the 'Jesus only' groups; so there are now both Unitarians and Trinitarians. Furthermore, both Pentecostals and Neo-charismatics can be found in denominations which run all the way from Independency and Congregationalism, on the one hand, to the hierarchically-organized episcopal Churches, on the other: whilst Christian ministries can now be found along the whole of the gamut which runs from what might be called 'free lance' local ministers (who are 'charismatic' both in the accepted Pentecostal sense and according to the current terminology of the Social Sciences), on the one hand, to those official office-bearers of the mainline Churches who both accept and propagate Charismatic beliefs and practices in their own denominations, on the other.[3] Finally, it cannot even be assumed that all of the Pentecostals share the same views on the so-called 'supernatural' gifts of the Holy Spirit. Glossolalia is a case in point. Whereas the 'initial evidence groups' seem to treat glossolalia as a *sine qua non* of Christian perfection (or part of the so-called Four Square Gospel), others seem to let the Spirit blow 'where it listeth'; and do not insist that every member manifests this particular *charisma*.

In other words: the sheer diversity of Pentecostal views means that it is still difficult, if not actually impossible, to systematize a coherent theological position to which Ecumenical Theologians can eventually respond: or with which the fruits of theological reflection and ecumenical dialogue in the Faith and Order Section of the World Council of Churches could now be directly compared. This does not mean, however, that this cannot and should not be done (see below): but it does mean that such a comparison may well be somewhat premature; for the simple reason that Pentecostal denominations have also had far less time than the ecumenical denominations to elaborate the kind of consensus and convergence texts which would enable them to transcend their own differences and define the limits of acceptable pluriformity.[4] Nor is it evident that every Pentecostal denomination would want to do so: despite the fact that some of them have already accepted full-membership of the World Council of Churches (thousands of smaller denominations have not yet done so); and despite the fact that most of the member churches of the World Council of Churches have been compelled to define their own position towards Pentecostals in their own ranks following the advent of the Charismatic Revival in the 1960s and 1970s. Furthermore: whereas the advent of Charismatic Renewal has generated a certain (not uncritical!) sympathy in most of the main-line ecumenical denominations for typical Pentecostal doctrines and practices (the latter can rightly be called an 'ecumenical' phenomenon nowadays), it is still far from clear how all the Pentecostal denominations which have *neither* established contact with the Ecumenical Movement *nor* engaged in dialogue with the circa 320 ecumenical denominations now propose to respond to these recent developments in the Ecumenical Movement: if they wish to respond to them at all. Until they do so, it would still be too premature to attempt to compare Pentecostalism (in all its diverse forms and with all its many ramifications) with the fruits of Ecumenical Theology.

Secondly: it cannot even be claimed that all of the member-churches of the World Council of Churches have always had a highly-developed theology of the Holy Spirit which can be compared directly with the Pneumatology of the Pentecostals: let alone a fully-fledged understanding of the so-called 'supernatural gifts' such as glossolalia and divine healing. The Church of England is a case in point. When I studied Theology in Oxford in the late 1950s, before the advent of the Charismatic Movement in the 'ecumenical' denominations, I was simply asked to produce one 'tutorial essay' on this particular subject on the basis of H.B. Swete's *The Holy Spirit in the New Testament* (which first appeared in 1909) and *The Holy Spirit in the Ancient Church* (which first appeared in 1912): together with H.W. Robinson's *The Christian Experience of the Holy Spirit* (which first appeared in 1928). This was supplemented for 'finals' by a close-reading of the relevant chapter in Alan Richardson's *The Theology of the New Testament* (which appeared just in time in 1958)! As far as the *filioque* controversy is concerned, this was construed in the late 1950s more as a question of Church Order (i.e. who has the right to make additions to the classical Creeds?) than as a crucial question in Systematic Theology. Meanwhile, times have changed. This was due as much to ecumenical dialogue between the Pentecostal denominations and the Anglican Communion (and to contacts between Anglican Charismatics and non-Charismatics) as it was to subsequent developments in Systematic Theology in England: and to what we have subsequently learned from more recent developments in the field of Ecumenical Theology. Nevertheless, ecumenical theologians should not simply assume that what we have learned from our ecumenical contacts in recent years tells us everything we need to know about Pentecostalism outside the world-wide Ecumenical Movement and the advent of Charismatic beliefs and practices in our own main-line denominations. Obviously, ecumenical 'outsiders' must listen to Pentecostals: whilst Pentecostals must learn to listen to the Ecumenicals.

Thirdly: it is a moot point whether we should simply proceed to compare the fruits of Ecumenical Theology with the first attempts to generate a systematic theology of Pentecostalism: and not simply because the Ecumenicals have had much more time to elaborate their Ecumenical Theology than the Pentecostals have had in which to generate a systematic account of their own theological positions. The main point here is that both the Ecumenicals and the Pentecostals have already generated world-wide Social Movements. Indeed, it can now be stated with little fear of contradiction that the two most important and extensive Social Movements in the whole of Twentieth Century Church History are the Ecumenical Movement and Pentecostal/Charismatic Renewal. It could be argued here, therefore, that it would be much better to compare these two movements as Social Movements; i.e. as socially-organized processes which bear certain formal resemblances to each other: even though their respective 'belief-systems' are by no means directly comparable. In a nutshell: the basic 'ideology' of the Ecumenicals boils down to the belief 'that all should be one' (rather than perpetually divided); whereas the 'ideology' of the Pentecostals seems to require that 'all' should live out their lives 'in the power of the Holy Spirit': in particular by manifesting in themselves both the fruit of the Spirit and the full-range of *charismata* which can be found in such 'foundational texts' as the Acts of the Apostles and the Epistles of St. Paul.[5]

In other words: the 'ideologies' of both of these Social Movements can usefully be compared to the extent that they are both 'theologies'; because all Social Movements do have either an implicit or explicit 'ideology' (or 'codified system of belief').We could also generate descriptions of their respective recruiting practices or patterns of growth and development; but this would simply overlook the important fact that their respective theologies are indeed fundamentally different when we proceed to identify their most essential presuppositions and goals. They also arise in quite different ways. For example: Ecumenical Theology emerges in the context of formal negotiations[6] between divided Churches as they strive to generate a comprehensive theological statement which all Christian denominations could ultimately accept or 'receive' as the 'belief-system' of a United Church which is wide enough and deep enough to include all Christian believers: thus transcending the historical divisions in the Body of Christ. The ecumenically-minded denominations are, in fact, currently negotiating the terms of a New Ecumenical World Order.[7] (Perhaps it will even include the other World Religions?)[8] In order to achieve this, it will obviously be necessary to generate an Ecumenical Theology which is ultimately capable of universal reception: including the Pentecostals.

In the case of Pentecostals, however, the basic goal is rather different from that of the Ecumenical Movement: even if there are some structural resemblances at certain points between their respective theological positions (see below). Furthermore: their processes of theological reflection are also rather different. For example: Pentecostal Theology seems to arise in the form of substantial reflection upon Pentecostal experiences[9] rather than in the context of negotiating the basis of a New Ecumenical World Order: especially at the point at which professional Pentecostal theologians begin to emerge within the ranks of the movement itself in the third or the fourth generation. By comparison, academic theologians have always been in the front ranks of the Ecumenical Movement. This is certainly not the case in Pentecostalism: despite the fact that both movements have explicitly universalistic or global aims; and are indeed directly comparable at this particular point.[10] The point here is that there are some radical differences in the way in which Ecumenicals and Pentecostals 'do' theology. This must surely be kept in mind when comparing their respective theologies or belief-systems.

Identifying the 'Overlaps'

Despite those fundamental differences, however, it is not entirely inappropriate to ask whether there are now any significant overlaps between their respective theological positions; even though neither movement has actually completed its own theological agenda: and such a comparison may well be somewhat premature. Logically, however, there must be some overlaps between them to the extent that both of these Social Movements are indubitably *Christian* movements; which suggests that they must already have at least some theological positions in common: otherwise it would be totally incorrect to locate them both in the same 'universe of discourse'. In the case of the Ecumenical Movement, the ultimate goal of uniting all of the divided or still separated Christian denominations means that, whilst negotiating the 'charter' of the New Ecumenical World Order, the Ecumenicals must also take seriously the theologies of the Pentecostals: for the simple reason that it would be quite impossible for them to achieve their own stated goal *without* the Pentecostal Churches!

Furthermore, it has already been noted that both of these Social Movements do not totally exclude each other; (i) because Charismatics can now be found in all of the Ecumenical denominations; and (ii) because at least some Pentecostal denominations have already joined the World Council of Churches. Moreover, both the World Council of Churches and many of its member-churches (together with the Roman Catholic Church) have already established ecumenical contacts with Pentecostals. But we must still make a firm distinction when comparing the positions of both of these Social Movements between what they have in common (because both are indeed *Christian* Movements rather than Movements of a totally different kind)[11] and those specific doctrines and practices which are now typical of both the classical Pentecostals and Charismatics in the Ecumenical denominations such as glossolalia; which the World Council of Churches - and the majority of its member Churches - has not yet explicitly 'received'. Like many other controversial items on the Ecumenical agenda (such as Papal Primacy, the *filioque*, the episcopate and the Ordination of Women) such matters are still the subject of ongoing ecumenical 'negotiation' and 'reception'.

At this particular juncture, several important points begin to emerge. In order to engage in the processes of ecumenical dialogue, negotiation and reception, Pentecostal theologians will also have to learn to 'do' theology in the ecumenical mode: if they have not done so already. Furthermore, they will also have to consider seriously the divine ecumenical imperative in John 17 (a 'foundational' passage sometimes overlooked by many Protestant Fundamentalists); whilst ecumenical theologians should also learn to 'do' theology in the Pentecostal mode: if they have not already done so. Nevertheless, it is certainly difficult for ecumenical theologians to theologize simultaneously in the Catholic, the Orthodox, the Anglican, the Lutheran, the Reformed, the Methodist and the Pentecostal modes! To say nothing of the styles of the so-called 'Younger Churches'. Finally, given the present global distribution of both the Ecumenical Movement[12] and the Pentecostal Movement[13], it was inevitable that they would meet and intertwine sooner rather than later. So the next question is what happens if and when they do.

Theology in the 'Overlap' between Pentecostal and Ecumenical

Part of the answer can be found in *Presence, Power, Praise*[14]; further details can be found in the documents which deal with ecumenical dialogues between Pentecostal Churches and the Ecumenical Churches; whilst the guidelines for such an ecumenical dialogue have already been set out by Paul van der Laan.[15] Meanwhile, the Faith and Order Section of the World Council of Churches published an important Convergence Text on *Baptism, Eucharist and Ministry* (BEM) in 1982 which has already been submitted to its member-churches for consideration, comment, criticism and 'reception'. It reflects the fruits of more than fifty years of theological reflection in the Ecumenical Movement. The relevant passages on Pneumatology should now be considered carefully by Pentecostal theologians.[16] They require little elucidation because the text is also intended to be understood by church-members as well as by theologians and church-leaders. They read as follows:

> Baptism is a gift of God, and is administered in the name of the Father, the Son and the Holy Spirit. The Holy Spirit is at work in the lives of people before, in and after baptism. It is the same Spirit who revealed Jesus as the Son (Mark 1:10-11) and who empowered and united the disciples at Pentecost (Acts 2). God bestows upon all baptized persons the anointing and the promise of the Holy Spirit, marks them with a seal and implants in their hearts the first instalment of their inheritance as sons and daughters of God. The Holy Spirit nurtures the life of faith when they will enter into its full possession, to the praise of the glory of God (2 Cor. 1:21-22; Eph. 1:13-14). Baptism initiates the reality of the new life given in the midst of the present world. It gives participation in the community of the Holy Spirit. It is a sign of the Kingdom of God and of the life of the world to come. Through the gifts of faith, hope and love, baptism has a dynamic which embraces the whole of life, extends to all nations, and anticipates the day when every tongue will confess that Jesus is Lord to the glory of God the Father.
>
> The eucharist is essentially the sacrament of the gift which God makes to us in Christ through the power of the Holy Spirit. The Spirit makes the crucified and risen Christ really present to us in the eucharistic meal, fulfilling the promise contained in the words of institution. The bond between the eucharistic celebration and the mystery of the triune God reveals the role of the Holy Spirit as that of the one who makes the historical words of Jesus present and alive. Being assured by Jesus' promises... the church prays to the Father for the gift of the Holy Spirit (*epiclesis*)... The Church, as the community of the new covenant, confidently invokes the Spirit, in order that it may be sanctified and renewed, led into all justice, truth and unity [!], and empowered to fulfill its mission in the world. The Holy Spirit unites in a single body [!] those who follow Jesus Christ and sends them as witnesses into the world.[17]
>
> The Church lives through the liberating and renewing power of the Holy Spirit. That the Holy Spirit was upon Jesus is evidenced in his baptism, and after the resurrection that same spirit was given to those who believed in the Risen Lord in order to recreate them as the body of Christ. The Spirit calls people to faith, sanctifies them through many gifts, gives them strength to witness to the Gospel, and empowers them to serve in hope and love. The Spirit keeps the Church in the truth and guides it despite the frailty of its members.
>
> The Holy Spirit bestows on the community diverse and complementary gifts. These are for the common good of the whole people and are manifested in acts of service within the community and in the world. They may be gifts of communicating the Gospel in word and deed, gifts of healing, gifts of praying, gifts of teaching and learning, gifts of guiding and following, gifts of inspiration and vision.

> All members are called to discover, with the help of the community, the gifts they have received and to use them for the building up of the Church and for the service of the world to which the Church is sent.

Although the pneumatological passages in the BEM text require no further elucidation in order to clarify their basic meaning, additional comments are certainly required when the fruits of recent Ecumenical Theology are placed alongside the tenets of Pentecostals and Charismatics. This is necessary in order to establish the extent of the 'overlap' between them.

First, it should be pointed out that the Ecumenical Theology reflected in this particular text is unambiguously Trinitarian; because the Basis of the World Council of Churches was revised during the course of the Third General Assembly in 1961 at the request of the Orthodox Churches. So it now includes an explicit reference to God the Father, God the Son and God the Holy Spirit. This means that it will not commend itself immediately to those Pentecostal denominations which are still Unitarian rather than Trinitarian.[18] Indeed, this was one of the main reasons why it has already been pointed out that it is still quite impossible to think in terms of a systematic Pentecostal Theology. Pentecostal theologians who are now considering the most important fruits of Ecumenical Theology will certainly have to address this basic issue. Furthermore, although there are still a number of basic disagreements in Ecumenical Theology (particularly on questions of Church Order)[19], it should now be realized that this is an Ecumenical issue upon which an ecumenical consensus has already been achieved. It will doubtless be acceptable to many Pentecostals, but this particular doctrine has certainly not yet been received by all of them.

Secondly, it should be noted that the Pneumatological passages in BEM certainly emphasize the 'fruit' of the Holy Spirit: i.e. Faith, Hope and *Agape* (or Love). This means that the overlap between the Ecumenicals and the Pentecostals is already complete when it comes to the 'fruit' of the Holy Spirit. But what about the *charismata*? BEM correctly emphasizes that a 'diversity of gifts' (*charismata*) is bestowed upon the 'community' (i.e. the Church). Several observations are now required. First, those gifts are bestowed upon the Church as the Body of Christ: and not upon individual members of the community. Which means that Ecumenical Theology has understood correctly the ecclesiological context in which St. Paul enunciates the *charismata* in 1 Corinthians 12-14: as well as the subordination of the *charismata* to the 'fruit' of the Spirit (e.g. in 1 Cor. 13:1).

Thirdly, it is already abundantly clear that the *charismata* (when compared with the 'fruit' of the Spirit) are not bestowed upon every member of the community as such because they are 'complementary': as St. Paul himself states quite clearly (though not necessarily in the same words). Their sole purpose is to enhance the 'common good' of all God's people. In other words: their purpose is to 'build up' the Church; and not to 'edify' particular persons! (An observation which, if taken seriously, would go a long way towards the eradication of the so-called 'excesses' of some Pentecostals and Charismatics.)[20] Furthermore, the 'gifts' of the Spirit are specifically enumerated in the BEM text. Expressed in modern language, the ecumenical catalogue includes: the *charismata* of (i) 'communicating the Gospel'; (ii) of 'healing'; (iii) of 'praying'; (iv) of 'teaching and learning': (v) of 'guiding and following'; and (vi) of 'inspiration and vision'. Presumably the explicit use of the plural form (i.e. 'gifts') in every one of those separate categories is to make the simple point that there is no single way of praying, healing and communicating the Gospel. In other words: Ecumenical Theology seems to be emphasizing here that it is 'unity' which is required in the Body of Christ rather than mere 'uniformity'. Indeed, the unity of the Church is, in itself, a work of the Holy Spirit. Which now raises the question of whether the recent retrieval of the Doctrine of the Holy Spirit, both in the Pentecostal Movement and in the Ecumenical Movement, can possibly be regarded as complete whilst the Body of Christ is still divided.[21]

It is clear that this particular statement of Ecumenical Theology is not only based firmly upon the 'foundational' texts of the Christian *oikoumene*, but also reflects the response of Ecumenical Theology to the recent Charismatic Renewal in both classical Pentecostalism and in the member-churches of the World Council of Churches. So the next question is whether the pneumatological passages in the BEM text do or do not constitute a sufficient basis for further dialogue between the Ecumenicals and the Pentecostals: and thus for uniting all the divided Churches. A close-reading of this highly-important Convergence Text seems to suggest that all of the typical beliefs and practices of the Pentecostals have been recognized explicitly by current Ecumenical Theology: with the possible exception of glossolalia. The latter, however, could be implicit in the passage which refers to 'gifts of communicating the Gospel'. This could conceivably be construed as an indirect reference to the phenomenon of *xenolalia* in Acts 2, though this is not explicitly stated. Nevertheless, St. Augustine even suggested that this particular *charisma* is no longer needed once the Church has learned all the languages of the *oikoumene*![22]

Nevertheless, there is no reason why this particular passage could not be made more explicit by ecumenical theologians: provided that glossolalia does not take precedence over the 'fruit' of the Spirit (including *agape* as St. Paul explicitly states in 1 Cor. 13:1); provided that Pentecostals can also appreciate that the special *charismata* cannot properly be required of every member of the Body (as he also states explicitly in the foundational texts which deal with the Gifts of the Spirit); and provided that all of the *charismata* are firmly rooted in the Theology of the Church. In other words: the Body of Christ alone is endowed with all of the *charismata* and not individuals; and, as Augustine suggested, *xenolalia* is no longer strictly necessary once the Body of Christ has become ecumenical in the sense of 'worldwide'. Indeed, the most important procedure for 'testing the spirits' to see whether they are from God is to ask whether they actually 'edify' the Body. But now we seem to touch upon one of the major weaknesses of Pentecostalism. It is rightly *strong* on Pneumatology; but it is still too *inexplicit* on Ecclesiology. Which means that, in the overlap between Pentecostalism and Ecumenical Theology, Pentecostals ought now to respond to the ecumenical retrieval of Pneumatology by stating their own Ecclesiology more explicitly; and also by responding to the claim of the Ecumenicals that the Body of Christ which is still divided is manifesting neither the 'fruit of the Spirit' nor the 'gifts of the Spirit' to the full extent which now seems to be required.

Notes

1. Social Scientists would doubtless prefer the term 'ideologies' in its non-pejorative sense.
2. A process which began at least as early as 1927 at the First World Conference on Faith and Order at Lausanne.
3. This usage goes back to Max Weber. It denotes a type of authority which is based upon the extraordinary gifts of leaders who are capable of attracting a considerable following: or considerable support. Such 'personal *charisma*' can be formally distinguished from another form of *charisma* which is associated with the officially-recognized status of the office-bearer (*Amtscharisma*). These two ideal-types of authority, however, are not necessarily incompatible: and can also be combined in the same person. A good example would be the late Pope John XXIII.
4. The reference here is to the member Churches of the World Council of Churches and the work of the Faith and Order Movement.
5. When reflecting upon the nature and function of Social Movements, I prefer to use the terminology preferred by Social Scientists.
6. Jean-Paul Willaime has recently argued that the Ecumenical Movement has actually ceased to be a Social Movement and has already transformed itself into a species of ecclesiastical diplomacy now dominated by 'experts'. See Jean-Paul Willaime (Ed.), *Vers de nouveaux Oecuménismes: Les Paradoxes contemporaines de l'Oecuménisme: Recherches d'Unité et Quêtes d'identité* (Latour-Maubourg: Les éditions du cerf, 1989), 15 ff. This observation is correct to the extent that it recognises the recent advent of an ecclesiastical-ecumenical elite which is now generating considerable numbers of consensus and convergence texts and also engaging in ecumenical dialogue at the official level. This phenomenon could even be construed as an indication of the 'officialization' of the ecumenical process: especially since the establishment of the World Council of Churches and the advent of official dialogue with the Roman Catholic Church. But this change of emphasis in the ecumenical process does not necessarily imply that it has simply ceased to be a Social Movement as well: especially at the local level. It may well be that the recent tendency in Europe to reduce Ecumenics as a 'science' to Ecumenical Theology, a process which seems to be related to the advent of the new ecclesiastical-ecumenical elite and the obvious need to reflect theologically upon its consensus and convergence texts, has simply transformed the Ecumenical Movement as a Social Movement into an opaque phenomenon which has become temporarily 'invisible'. In which case, the resources of contemporary historiography and especially social science ought to be used in order to establish whether or not the Ecumenical Process has already ceased to be a Social Movement. This is still an open question. Paradoxically: whereas Social Scientists are still re-

searching the Charismatic Movement precisely as a Social Movement, few Ecumenists and Social Scientists are currently doing empirical research into the Ecumenical Process as a Social Movement.

7. This is implicit in the main theme of the Canberra assembly in 1991: Come Holy Spirit - Renew the Whole Creation.
8. Both glossolalia and divine healing can also be found in at least some of the non-christian religions. In this sense, both can properly be construed as 'ecumenical' (or 'global') phenomena. But it still remains to be seen whether Pentecostals (and other Christians) who explicitly reject an ecumenical dialogue with the non-christian religions might still be willing to consider positively their 'pentecostal' practices: and what the significance of that might be.
9. This is explicit in the papers of the Conference on Pentecostal and Charismatic Research in Europe which was held at the State University of Utrecht in 1989. See (Ed.) Jan A.B. Jongeneel, *Experiences of the Spirit* (Frankfurt am Main: Peter Lang, 1991). It has already been pointed out that the only other comparable group in the *oikoumene* which habitually theologizes by specifically reflecting upon Christian experience is that of the Liberals! See Peter Staples in Jongeneel *op. cit.*, 262.
10. Peter L. Berger rightly endorses the view that the third wave of Protestant expansion is indeed a global phenomenon. See his introduction to David Martin, *Tongues of Fire; The Explosion of Protestantism in Latin America*, (Oxford: Blackwell, 1990), vii.
11. Both have the same scriptures as their 'foundational charters' and water baptism at least in the name of Jesus Christ.
12. The Official Ecumenical Constituency now consists of 320 Christian denominations: including the member-churches of the World Council of Churches and the Roman Catholic Church. The latter is not yet a full-member of the Council: but it is a member of the Faith and Order Section; there is regular contact between the WCC headquarters in Geneva and the Pontifical Secretariat for Christian Unity; it is a member of about thirty National Councils of Churches; and it is currently engaged in ecumenical dialogue with all of the main Christian traditions: including the Pentecostals. The Total Ecumenical Constituency (i.e. the members of the officially ecumenical denominations) is now of the order of 1.5 billion. This should be compared with the latest figures on Pentecostals and Charismatics given by David B. Barrett in this *Festschrift*. Such statistics may well suggest at least the possibility of overlapping between Ecumenicals and Pentecostals.
13. See again the contribution of David B. Barrett to this *Festschrift*.
14. Edited by Kilian McDonnell in three volumes (Collegeville, Minesota, 1980).
15. In (Ed.) Jongeneel, *op. cit.*, 196.
16. In the responses already edited and published by Max Thurian, however, I have not been able to find any from explicitly Pentecostal Churches. See (Ed.) Max Thurian, *Churches respond to BEM*, six volumes, (WCC: Geneva, 1986 - 1988; = F. & O. Papers, New Series, Numbers 129; 132; 135; 137; 143; 144).
17. Emphases added in order to indicate the 'foundational character' of the divine ecumenical imperative. Although Baptism in/with the Holy Spirit is generally discussed in connection with Christian initiation, the Eucharistic faith and practice of Pentecostals is still far from clear to ecumenical theologians. Perhaps this should be explained by Pentecostals in more detail to outsiders?
18. It has already been noted that this is still one of the basic theological issues on which Pentecostals are still divided.
19. It has already been observed that Pentecostal beliefs and practices can be found along the whole of the ecclesiological spectrum from Independency to Roman Catholicism. Recently, Ecumenical Theology has also focussed upon 'Fundamental Differences'.
20. The Final Report of the Canberra Assembly of 1991 states in paragraph 69 that if 'filling with the Spirit' as a 'second experience' after Baptism is regarded as 'normative' for all Christians, this may be 'divisive'.

21. It can now be noted that the WCC currently stresses three fundamental points: (i) it is the Holy Spirit which is calling us "to acknowledge the unity that exists among us" and (ii) "to overcome all barriers in order to be able to share our gifts and ministries"; whilst (iii) unity is more explicitly conceived as "*koinonia* in the Holy Spirit". See Report of the Committee on Program Policy (VI.A) and "The Unity of the Church as *Koinonia*: Gift and Calling" (= Statement of the WCC Assembly at Canberra, February 1991). Note especially 1.1 which reads: "The purpose of God according to Holy Scripture is to gather the whole of creation under the Lordship of Jesus Christ in whom, by the power of the Holy Spirit, all are brought into communion with God (Eph. 1)". And also 4.1: "The Holy Spirit as the promoter of *koinonia* (2 Cor. 13:13) gives to those who are still divided the thirst and hunger for full communion. We remain restless until we grow together according to the wish and prayer of Christ that those who believe in him may be one (John 17:21). In the process of praying, working and struggling for unity, the Holy Spirit comforts us in pain, disturbs us when we are satisfied to remain in our division, leads us to repentance and grants us joy when our communion flourishes". Both of these texts can be found in *Mid-Stream* Vol. XXX, No. 3 (July, 1991).
22. J. van Oort has already pointed out that Augustine interpreted *xenolalia* (Acts 2) as a sign that the Church is universal; but such a miracle is no longer needed once the Church, as the Body of Christ, has learned to speak all the languages of the *oikoumene*. See "Augustinus over de kerk" in W. van 't Spijker et al. (Ed.), *De Kerk*, (Kampen: Kok, 1990), 65-94, esp. 86 f. (with references). It is also a fact that missionaries usually learn foreign languages the hard way!

24

Helping the Ecumenical Movement to Move On: Hollenweger and the Rediscovery of the Value of Diversity

Martin Conway

A Friendship in the Context of the Ecumenical Movement

Walter Hollenweger and I first met in the West European working group of the World Council of Churches' study on the Missionary Structure of the Congregation, an inspiring and unforgettable company, whose 'star' was the laconic Hans Hoekendijk, which also included Walter's later friend and colleague Gordon Davies, and of which Walter was soon to take over the secretaryship in succession to Hans Margull. At the time he was still deeply engaged in his encyclopaedic studies of Pentecostalism, but visibly enjoying the new stimulus and challenges of being involved in the World Council of Churches (WCC).

I followed Walter some years later on to the WCC Geneva staff, in time to remember his farewell speech one tea-time in the cafeteria. He began by saying: "On an occasion like this you either crack a few jokes and leave it at that, or else you risk saying the truth for once; I have decided to do the second" - and went on with a fierce critique of the self-satisfaction and in-turned bureaucracy that he had met among his colleagues.

From 1976 onwards we met regularly in Birmingham in the group around Roswith Gerloff, one of his doctoral students, trying to ease into life and strength the project that has become the Centre for Black and White Christian Partnership. This work was greatly encouraged by his awareness of how people of very different cultural and church backgrounds could best enrich and challenge one another. Then in 1986, when I moved to the Selly Oak Colleges, I found myself one of those responsible for Walter's pioneering post and for receiving - all too soon - the request for retirement that has freed him for his contributions to the 1990s.

In these different settings, Walter has continued to point and prod unfailingly into the future of a more widely open church, responding to the ever-unpredictable Spirit that was in Jesus: open to the creative gifts of all who care to join in, open to the experience, insights and emotions of neighbours whose culture may be more oral than written, open to the ever-changing critique of those who do not find good news in Jesus, whether Marxist, Muslim or militant economist. No tame loyalist to the politeness of inter-church talks at any level, Walter is very much a voice of the ecumenical movement, calling in the name and power of Christ for obedience that will break through the barriers of ignorance and scorn. His humour is a notable aid in this.

I particularly treasure his story of the long discussion one Friday evening in the opening session of a parish weekend to which he reported "I have done nothing in preparation for this weekend except to arrange for the regional TV station to broadcast at 10.00 on Sunday morning the service you now have 36 hours to work out together" - and the only person who walked out in protest was the vicar's wife!

More than most, Walter has already contributed very greatly to the still new adventure of the ecumenical movement in this second half of the twentieth century. His 'ferocious curiosity' - the phrase in which he sums up the desirable qualities to bring to the supervision of research students - has made available an astonishing range of opportunities for mission, renewal and unity which the world-wide Church will ignore to our loss. Yet he has - to date - reflected relatively seldom in writing on the nature of the ecumenical movement. This essay, in tribute to his stimulus, tries to do that in the light of some of his characteristic emphases.

What Do We Mean by 'Ecumenical Movement'?

First, a digression into terminology. For since Vatican II, and its catchy but misleading title *De Oecumenismo*, far too much of the thinking and speaking about the ecumenical movement has been caught in the eddies of 'ecumenism': a word which suggests some *corpus* of doctrine or of outlook, some passing understanding of a partial range of phenomena, which will have its day and then fade like so many other once fashionable -isms. No: by the word 'movement' we point to a *pilgrimage* which started in creation, which took a decisive turn in the events leading up to Pentecost, which will come to full fruition in God's promised Kingdom and which meanwhile is always facing us with the challenge of next steps of obedience, whether in terms of friendship, of more sensitive or deeper awareness. And by the word 'ecumenical' we point to the *created world*, to the *whole human family* among whom Christ's people are sent to witness, and to a company of believers who are called both to reflect the full range of cultures and conditions in which our rainbow family pursues its life, and to anticipate the symphony of praise and joy in which we will all celebrate as one in God's final Kingdom.

Thus my definition of the ecumenical movement is "the striving, under the leading of the Holy Spirit, for the proper integrity of Christ's church in her service of the proper integrity of humankind in the purposes of God". That could deserve a long commentary, but in the argument which now follows I will draw out three of its implications.

First, the striving concerned must be pursued at each and every level of church life. It has to do with the way local congregations order their priorities and attitudes: indeed with how any small group or family of Christians will relate to their neighbours along the road or at work. It has to do no less with the responsibilities of synods, church leaders and associations of Christians in a city or region, just as it has many possible consequences for the thinking and action of the leaders and teachers of the churches at national and international levels. Any one new insight or step of obedience (whether to do with e.g. the challenge from the poor to the global economic system or with the proper care of a couple marrying across a sensitive barrier between churches or faiths) involves both the larger horizons of international community as worked on in say the WCC and the local, immediate warmth of neighbourly relationships. "Think globally, act locally" is always an appropriate reminder, either way on.

Second, this striving must always be seen in terms of *movement*, of a next step on from wherever we happen to be, and of further steps leading on ahead, some predictable in advance but many only discernable in detail once we have begun to move on, towards large goals - 'reconciliation', 'peace', 'maturity', 'unity' - that need to be envisaged and thought about, hoped for and celebrated as the horizon for the next steps but that can never be laid down in detail as a blueprint. For these goals are in the gift of the Spirit, not our achievement, even if we have to be prepared to work hard for them to come more nearly into reality. In terms of local inter-church relationships my British Council of Churches (BCC) colleague John Nicholson coined in the 1970s an illuminating mnemonic for the likely stages of ecumenical movement, which Derek Palmer[1] has now publicised as the 'C-Scale'; namely, from a situation of outright *competition* relationships can mellow into a *co-existence* of accepting the others as neighbours, and then warm up into a pattern of *cooperation* in at least certain matters, which can gradually extend until the point is reached for a permanent and overall mutual *commitment* of two or more separate churches, itself pointing towards the eventual establishment of the full-scale *communion* when there need be no more talk or awareness of division between us. Analogous patterns of long-range movement can no doubt be envisaged for other areas of ecumenical striving.

Third, my definition indicates in outline that there are bound to be many different areas of concern in and for the ecumenical movement, which will need their own specific disciplines and decisions yet which need to be taken together in a deliberate inter-twining of commitment. The discipline proper to eucharistic sharing between churches growing together, for instance, needs in many situations to be seen together with the demands of combating racist attitudes and traditions or the challenges of restructuring economic relationships to overcome the inbuilt patterns of exploitation and injustice. Here it has become convenient, though never adequately comprehensive, to refer to three different but necessarily inter-weaving dimensions or strands of ecumenical striving:

- *the 'classical'*: handling the historic theological questions that once divided the churches (Chalcedonian from non-Chalcedonian, Orthodox from Catholic, Catholic from Protestant, Anglican from Methodist, internationally-related from locally-founded, Trinitarian Pentecostal from Oneness Apostolic, and so dismayingly on and on), or which have come to provide theological legitimacy for churches existing in separation; the patient work of dialogue, mutual understanding and sounding the depths of contentious questions, with a view to reaching fuller and more adequate teachings in which the truths which separate churches have stood for can all find their proper place - work illustrated in recent years by the *Baptism, Eucharist and Ministry* texts of the WCC Faith and Order Commission.

- *the 'secular'*: handling the major divisive matters in the human family, both those we inherit, such as all the legacies of imperialism, and those we create anew today, such as the world debt crisis or the dangers of global warming; this calls no less for patient listening and dialogue across the alliances and interest groups, the bringing together of knowledgeable researchers, active enthusiasts and responsible politicians to envisage the necessary commitments and the appropriate next steps in a single world-wide community - all the service of Christians to the large goals of justice and of peace is here.

- *the 'cultural'*: handling all the diversities and relativities of different languages and cultures, of different traditions and different situations which alone make it possible for each human group to think and act in its own way; yet at the same time these diversities must be known in their complex relations alike to the wounding divisions in history, the clashes of truth-claims and peace-expectations, that must be reconciled and overcome, and to the promise in God's good time of depths of mutual acceptance and appreciation that will allow our many diversities to enrich each other for the good of the total human family. Much of the best exploration and study in the field of world mission is today being devoted to this dimension, not least in the patient sifting of disputes and misunderstandings between the great faiths of humankind.

Holding all this together, with the different levels of operation, the many stages in the total movement, the various dimensions of concern and commitment, is inevitably complex. No wonder that the WCC and groups linked with it are often seen to be teetering on the edge of pomposity. The ecumenical movement in any large sense can never be summed up in simple recipes, although many of its roots and fruits are seen in quite ordinary, uncomplicated movements of the human heart, reaching out over some barrier in a friendship and love that is a sign of a new day. The movement is composed as much of a million unsung gestures as of the much-trumpeted 'breakthroughs'; indeed the latter will often never happen without all sorts of ordinary people; beginning to live the new way, just as any breakthrough at some top level encourages and confirms many different people and groups exploring at their own levels the next steps it implies.

The Pendulum Shift in Favour of Diversity

In my not yet forty years of involvement with the ecumenical movement there has been a clear shift of the pendulum from a commitment to unity to an appreciation of diversity. I use this image of the pendulum in the belief that these two are not contradictory but complementary, while recognising that this is far from evident to many people, and that it is a faith-stance which still requires a great deal of working out in practice and eventually in theory.

To stick to my own limited experience, I have seen it happening in several different fields. One has been in the reading of the New Testament. I can remember the stir caused by Ernst Käsemann's address to the Fourth (and so far last) World Conference on Faith and Order in Montreal in 1963, where he appealed to the differences between the various writers and traditions in the New Testament to argue against any biblical justification for a single pattern of church order as a necessary part of the reunion of the churches.[2] By now it is a commonplace of NT scholarship to focus on the different emphases of the different authors, to the point where it is any claimed unity of the NT as a whole that is controversial.

Something similar has been happening on the 'secular' side too. In 1982, for instance, José Miguez Bonino presented to the Faith and Order Commission at its meeting in Lima, Peru, a paper from Latin American experience that raised in very sharp terms the question 'whose *oikoumene*?' What sort of 'one world' is implied in the thinking you are doing about 'one church'? Are you in fact looking to a hegemony of Rome and/or Geneva over the churches in the Third World that will mirror - and perhaps be subservient to - the great economic powers of Europe and North America which have already done so much harm to us? The Faith and Order Commission was, in fact, quite unable to hear, let alone respond to, this challenge (the BEM document mentioned above, though finalised at that meeting, bears hardly a trace of Miguez' concern), but their colleagues in the WCC Programme to Combat Racism or the Commission on the Churches' Participation in Development would have recognized it as central to what they are after. In the 1990s it comes much more easily to think of the world-wide church as comprised of a myriad of local centres of identity and initiative, each quite specific and different, than of any overarching organs of 'truth' or 'right order', let alone of persons authorised to lay down just what these shall be. I suspect that a similar shift has been no less strongly under way in the corridors of the United Nations, and in not a few 'national' parliaments.

Walter Hollenweger has contributed greatly to this shift. By his lively sympathy for an astonishing range of different people, as he frequently illustrates in reference to his own post-graduate students[3], and his 'ferocious curiosity' about their specific questions and discoveries in their own quite specific and non-interchangeable contexts; by his delight in the craft of story-telling which can communicate so much more vividly than abstract generalities, raising questions in the heart and mind of the hearer about one's own life rather than imposing any one else's verities; by his constant questioning of what Europeans, and especially our majority churches, tend to take for granted, and his example of heeding and encouraging those we are tempted to downgrade as 'minorities' - by all of these he has greatly helped along the positive appreciation of our increasingly multi-cultural social context.

Still more, by turning on its head the question of sectarianism so that the essential criterion is not the rightness of the church, over against the sectarian's heresy, but rather the insistence of the latter (whatever he calls himself) on using "his form of worship or his theology to deny that another Christian is a Christian" - and so on "making his own worship or theology the standard of what the church is", thus denying "that the incarnation of God in Jesus Christ is unique"[4]. Hollenweger quite deliberately opens up a very much wider field of truth, and so of catholicity, apostolicity, holiness and indeed unity than the framers of the Nicean Creed could have imagined.

As his very next paragraph admits: "this definition is open to the charge of relativism". It is a charge he answers only by asking a series of questions about the actual function in specific practice of what people regard as central to their faith. These questions remind us that "*the same element of religious practice* [italics in original] can exercise different functions in a different context", and so point to the sweeping conclusion - which concludes nothing! - that "the same pattern of practice and doctrine cannot be of equal value in every society, in every age and for all men."[5] He is well aware how disconcerting this is to many, perhaps most, of his readers. Yet, unless I have missed it, he nowhere seeks to give a general answer; rather he points by the sheer vitality of his curiosity, his sympathies and his spirituality, to the converting value for each new person of setting out on comparable paths of discernment, both of the God who is active through others, and of critique of one's own heritage.

What I miss myself at this point is the drawing - admittedly far from easy - of the crucial distinction between 'diversities' (where people and situations as it were happen to be different because they are created that way), and 'divisions' (where people and groups choose to disagree on some point(s) judged to be crucial to the truth of God).

Hollenweger's argument, summarised above, that the sectarian is the one who deliberately cuts himself off, the orthodox the one who is prepared to continue the conversation, is an important part of this distinction, but not all of it. For there are undoubtedly situations, like that in which the *Barmen Declaration* was written, where the presence of evil and falsity becomes the reason for a division, where some feel compelled, for reasons that cannot be called sectarian, to break fellowship. Sometimes those reasons, as in Hitler's Germany, go on with hindsight appearing justified; sometimes - as with the breach between Rome and Constantinople? - hindsight in later years suggests that they would have been better handled as 'diversities' than as reasons for division. My argument in this article about the value of diversity is not intended to exclude the possibility of a justifiable division where a major evil or untruth is involved.

Another Way in to the Healthy Appreciation of Diversity

Hollenweger learnt the essence of his awareness of diversity in his studies of the Pentecostals, though he has carried it on through all the different ideas and experiences chronicled in his volumes of *Intercultural Theology*. As it happens, the same essential lesson was being learnt in the same years by another group connected with the WCC and coordinated from another office in the same Division of World Mission and Evangelism to which Walter belonged. I am referring to the 'World Studies of Churches in Mission', which from a plan that ripened during the 1950s led to the commissioning of fifteen substantial studies of churches in all the continents, published between 1958 and 1970, and to the convening of a panel to review the total spectrum and draw out whatever 'general principles' could be discerned about the 'vitality of a church'. This was to be "judged by its ability to respond positively to the factors that impinge upon the whole human society in which it is set".[6]

This is not the place to try to go into any detail about the 15 studies. All are published and can be read.[7] I want to focus only on the conclusions to which the review panel came, not least because to my surprise, indeed dismay, the only reference to them in Walter Hollenweger's work I can find is a brief paragraph[8] which ends with the dismissive sentence: "The study concluded with an unsatisfactory reference to 'humble agnosticism' in regard to ecclesiological judgments, which can perhaps be accepted as 'humble' enough but is in no way adequate" (my translation). In turn, and especially in view of the fact that this whole research process has never received the appreciation it deserved, that judgment is seriously inadequate. All the more so when one realises how much the conclusions in question reinforce one of the main lessons of Hollenweger's own writings!

After reading the 15 book-length studies, each a highly specific investigation into the vitality or otherwise of a church in such different settings as Uganda, Japan, Chile, rural Michigan, the Solomon Islands or Birmingham, and each written by a different author from outside the setting in question, inevitably with all sorts of varieties in research approach and in the writing up, the panel members sum up their findings in four deceptively brief theses:[9]

1. This is the Church... in its diversity

Each of the 15 studies, they say, seems to demand the affirmation that 'this is the Church'. Such an affirmation 'arises from intuitive recognition'. To say it about each of these groups of Christians is not just to make a sociological statement that they share a common belief and are organized in a certain way; neither is it to make a deductive assertion that certain biblical definitions apply. It is to make a declaration of faith compelled by an orientation and an inner dynamic which can only be described as 'life in Christ'. At the same time it is of the essence to grasp the astonishing extent of the diversity presented. It is to be accepted as "basic and not superficial. It becomes deeper on closer examination." "Diversity appears as a basic characteristic of churches, as it is of human beings. No universal patterns can therefore be drawn without abstracting from the reality of individual churches."

2. The basic diversity in the Church is a diversity in self-awareness in relation to surrounding culture; and this self-awareness is constantly changing

Each particular 'pattern' of self-awareness the studies describe is comprehensible in its own context, and there are certainly occasional similarities, yet these matter much less than the individuality of each case. 'In our view it is a moot point whether any kind of typology is possible. What is clear is that the relation between Church and culture is basic for the Church's mission. To express it in theological terms: it is within the surrounding culture and in terms of that culture that God challenges the church to obedience."

3. The dynamic of a church's growth and development is an internal dynamic; it is inadequately explained in terms of external agencies, but arises from the interplay of environmental factors and the work of the Spirit

Here the argument is curving back towards the point, crucial also for Hollenweger, of the awareness of the Holy Spirit. The studies show conclusively that it is not whatever role foreign missionaries played, nor anything measurable in the surrounding environment, but something internal to the life of the indigenous community that grows into the local church that makes the decisive difference. "Something more is needed to explain what happened... - and that more is the work of the Spirit.'' ''We cannot deny that conversion is possible, that the Spirit of God is at work gathering his People, working inscrutably in the hearts of men and women and in human societies''. They indicate how at least six of the studies provide ''evidence of an inner dynamic which can impel a community from within, helping it to overcome all kinds of obstacles and to respond in new ways to a changing situation, in a manner reminiscent of the spontaneous expansion of the Church after the first Pentecost.''

4. External criteria derived from Church History are not the most important ones for judging a church's vitality or obedience

Amid the constant change and the constant difficulty of being certain about precisely when it is the Spirit at work and when other spirits, the crucial fact seems to be that all the churches studied had come to ''points of crisis and decision''. Just what these were, how they were discerned, and what sorts of responses were made, all varied with bewildering diversity. Some seem to fail the test of vitality at what looks like a decisive point while others, apparently much less lively, seem to come up with a vital response. Yet as in the letters to the Seven Churches in Revelation 1-3, the ''only criterion of vitality and obedience is the readiness to respond at the point when response is demanded.''

In their final brief chapters the panel emphasise the inescapable finding that any evaluation of 'success' or 'failure' is bound to be made as a function of the theological pre-suppositions of the person making it. There is no 'standard' available, neither from history nor from current experience, which all Christians could use for all our churches with any hope of reaching demonstrably acceptable judgments. ''One cannot take an ideal abstraction of the Church and use it as a plumb-line with which to measure the success or failure of any given congregation... We need to recover our sense of the 'mystery of the seven lamps' - the true being, or presence, of a local church which is a secret known only to God until it is disclosed in his good time.'' ''The churches which are there... have their being in Christ's knowledge of them. The phrase so often repeated in Revelation 2 and 3, 'I know your works', should point us to an unlimited confidence and a very humble agnosticism.''

Here, surely, is the Spirit teaching us through that baffling yet glorious diversity that what matters about our churches, like what matters about ourselves as persons, is that which in them matters to God. Which in turn leaves you and me as some sort of Christians with on the one hand the freedom and responsibility to respond to our own experiences and possibilities in a way as near what we believe to be God's will as we can find (better: as the Spirit can give us), and on the other the joyful faith to believe that God will make out of our responses what he will make, in any case something much more worthwhile than what we can be confident of making! The diversity is baffling or problematic only if we insist on seeing it from a human point of view, very different - though no less calling forth decisive judgments - as we try to approach it from God's, as we have seen that at work in Jesus.

Diversity as a Key to the Way the Ecumenical Movement Moves On

So what does this far-reaching awareness of diversity, Hollenweger's in his stories, the panel's in their more abstract formulations, mean for the nature and process of the ecumenical movement? I hazard an answer in five points:

1. Any particular Christian and church is called and enabled by the Spirit to grow up into the fullness of Christ (Ep. 4:11-16), starting from wherever we are and growing into what we can, by God's good grace, become. In this we need both to be able to know and accept who we happen to be, not resentful of the accidents of history, conditioning and relationships, and yet also to be aware that there are a vast number of other ways of being Christian. We need never feel trapped by being as we are - there is always more to be learnt, to experiment with and to grow by.
2. One prime way of growing into Christ is by the mutual understanding and exchange between significantly different people and groups. All the friendship, the listening, the understanding, the working together, the raising questions about each others' ways and pointing out each other's opportunities, cannot fail to enrich and enhance what we are as Christians. Any particular group of Christians will have its own specific characteristics, and it will be in and through these that the Spirit can enable them to make their unique and creative contribution to God's purposes. Yet they will sabotage that creativity if they cling to their 'own way' as some sort of right or possession, refusing the chances to grow into a still richer creativity that can come from relationships with others. (This is not, of course, an encouragement for any new sorts of imposition by dominant groups of their ways on the others. Although in human relationships one must always be on the watch for unhealthy power structures creeping in, I am speaking here of freely accepted and freely initiated contacts.)
3. This pattern of growing in identity and relationships must not be seen as involving only the church as such, only the 'religious' aspects of life. We are speaking of Christians living among their neighbours, serving and witnessing in and being affected by their surrounding environment throughout their lives. We are speaking of Christians and churches whose basis for being so is that they are sent into the world in mission (John 20:21-22), and of the

ecumenical movement whose ideas and advances have always stemmed from missionary awareness and missionary obedience (a point too often overlooked in formal inter-church talks).

4. Thus at any point in the movement we need a double awareness: on the one hand we need to have a sense of ourselves as part of a much larger whole, and so of the potential that the Holy Spirit is seeking to realise in the whole, and so in turn of what we may be able to contribute towards that potential, in however limited a way; on the other we need a positive enjoyment of all that is wholesome in the many diversities and particularities we are faced with, as part of that potential fullness, so that our vision of the Spirit and of our own part in her work does not become an ideology to be imposed on others, however well-intentioned, but a free offering of love and service that leaves room for the Spirit to enable others to grow in their own ways rather than in mine. "Jesus Christ does not make copies; he makes originals" as the WCC Nairobi Assembly of 1975 put it.[10]
5. Arising from that double awareness - and arising at best in a joyful and free way, not over-earnest let alone guilt-ridden - will be a spirituality that readily pursues a self-examination and self-critique, in the light of what is being learnt about and from others. Not for the sake of navel-gazing but as a central part of what it means to be 'in Christ', the specific identity in which we find ourselves will always be open to new experiment and adaptation, to grow into what can serve God's purposes still more adequately. It is hard to talk about this in the abstract, precisely because it is bound to be very different for different people and churches, yet one soon knows in meeting a new group whether or not they are likely to welcome a new friendship and the self-critique that will be fed by the ideas it will bring.

Here, I hope, is the framework for an understanding of diversity and a practice of relationships that can genuinely hold together a lively appreciation of all the specifics that make human groups and our ever-changing situations unique in our particularities with a commitment to the unity that the one God has since creation intended for us in the full richness of his Kingdom, a unity which it is the business of the world-wide church to be serving and in some - always fragmentary - ways anticipating in the here-and-now.

By Way of Conclusion: The Case of Worship in the World Council of Churches

As an illustration of what can so easily remain impenetrably abstract, and one that I hope is relatively well known among the likely readers of this article, I take the renewal of worship that was such a dominant and joyful feature of the 1983 Assembly of the WCC in Vancouver. For those two-and-a-half weeks, in 30-minute services each morning and six major acts of plenary worship, a gathering of Christians that was outwardly more widely representative than any previous meeting in church history was able to praise and celebrate God in a way that was both admirably fresh and deeply true, *and* - most important - felt to be both, to our great amazement, by almost all the range of churches and cultures that were represented. Here for once Pentecost was happening, with an unforgettable combination of freedom, sharing, joy and God-centeredness, and in a way which at the time, and in the stimulus it has since given to developments in worship around the world, expressed the promise of a reunited church anticipating the peace and fullness in God's final Kingdom.

It is impossible to tell the full story, both because innumerable details contributed to the total impression and because any one person's appreciation of worship is inevitably different from that of the many others - though the published accounts of the Assembly with virtually one voice stress how good it was.[11] But I pick out 6 aspects, each richer than can be put in words, but all of which could - and do - belong to worship in other settings.

First - though this is not intended as an order of value - was the care for participation. The total pattern of worship and many of the details had of course been prepared beforehand, but in a way that positively expected and encouraged the active participation of the many who could worship there. Each service required at least a dozen people to take leading roles, with a deliberate variety of languages, dress styles and denominational backgrounds, each doing something that was 'their own' and yet which contributed to the whole. The music was particularly significant in this: a team of leaders from several different continents, working with a local student choir and players who had brought instruments from many different cultures, led us in a variety of pieces, some ancient and deeply traditional, others from the normal run of church or secular music, some specially written for the occasion, yet all relatively easily sung by a large congregation and all to be actively sung rather than just listened to. At one moment it would be a Russian Orthodox chant, at another an Indian devotional lyric, at another a Zimbabwean Hallelujah or a new hymn from the Caribbean. It did not take long for everyone present to feel that 'our own' cultures and ways of worship were being caught up into the much wider whole.

Second, these acts of worship deliberately involved the participants in many different ways: listening and speaking, singing and praying, looking at vivid colours in decorations and dress, greeting one's neighbours, and frequently in some sort of action that gave a sense of immediacy, even responsibility for something that was going to happen in ways that could not be foreseen. There was the moment when everyone was given a length of fuse wire and invited to shape it into something that spoke of one of the Assembly's emphases, and then to give it to a neighbour. That the shape I received was a thoroughly plain circle (and the one I made a no less ordinary heart) mattered less than the fact that one was actually doing, contributing something as part of the act of worship. Still more effective was the circle of children's paintings, fruits of an invitation to schools around the world, that were waiting for us on the walls as we gathered for the closing service, and the invitation each to take one and to share something of the Assembly with the child whose name and school address was on the back.

Third, this worship was deliberately and joyfully open to the world. Quite literally, in that one long wall of the tent in which it was held was left open the whole time; the worshippers were aware, if they looked, of people coming and going, standing undecided near the edge or getting on with other things in the distance. World-wide horizons were always present in the range of music and languages used, in the topics people brought up in intercessions and in the concerns that featured in the sermons or meditations, no other than those the rest of the Assembly's work was struggling with. Still more, one could not avoid the sense of being there, and of being there precisely in worship, as some sort of representative of one's own culture, one's own sort of people (not only of one's own church), and as one of a body of representatives of as near as might be the whole church of Christ in our day, the total people called by the Spirit to be Christ's visible body and to continue his ministry of caring and of intercession for the entire inhabited earth.

Fourth, the ways in which we worshipped did not involve a choice between the familiar/traditional and the new/experimental so much as an imaginative blending which showed not only that one group's tradition is another's experiment but also that experiment is best set in a context that carries long-range associations, and that tradition is appropriately filled with immediate and contemporary reference. Much in these services, in prayers, in gestures, in the basic shape of the service, came straight from the long-standing traditions of Orthodox and other historic churches; we very seldom had the sense of sharing in a shapeless 'hymn sandwich'. Yet they never failed to direct our hearts to something of what God was wanting for today and tomorrow, for the 'us' who were present and all on whose behalf we were present.

Fifth, this worship, without losing a sense of the serious and sacred, was also friendly and indeed fun to share in. The Assembly as a whole was inescapably seized of the great questions, needs and problems of the world, so we were beyond a superficial mateyness and could meet and greet each other in worship with a ready enjoyment of the other's background and culture. The very variety of people there ensured that as different people gave leadership there would be something interesting and unpredictable, just as the variety of music used ensured that there was something new to learn and enjoy alongside what might be familiar. Pauline Webb, an English Methodist long used to participating in every possible sort of church occasion, nevertheless wrote in the Assembly newspaper: "It is a long time since I have gone with such eager expectation to acts of public worship as I have in these two weeks".

Finally, and in case I am giving the impression of self-indulgent, gimmicky ceremonies, I must stress that this worship was above all remarkable for being centred in a profoundly thoughtful and disciplined way on God and the purposes he has made known in Jesus Christ. The shape of the services was that of the classical liturgies; there could be no mistaking the centrality of the biblical message; the hymns and prayers and actions were all chosen so as to serve the meaning of what was being done in each successive act of worship. The freedom to 'experiment' was most carefully put at the service of the central purpose of classic Christian worship.

It would be misleading to say that these acts of worship derived from the charismatic renewal, although some of the freedom and the sense of participation is widely known there, but I imagine that many 'charismatics' felt very quickly at home in them, as would have done those familiar with Taizé or with the worship of the urban mission teams in Korea or the Philippines... The streams of renewal had been widely drawn on. Here again, the acceptance of diversities in function of the central and overall purpose of God for and with his church showed itself as a thoroughly healthy and forward-looking basis for ecumenical obedience.

That Montreal Conference of Faith and Order had put its finger on the central point: "the truth that the more the Tradition is expressed in the varying terms of particular cultures, the more will its universal character be fully revealed."[12] A generous openness to one another's diversities, alike for the enjoyment of them and the self-critique they enable, in careful awareness of the possibility of the need for judgment and the danger of division when the power of evil creeps in, and above all the expectation that the Spirit will open a way ahead different to that which we could ourselves desire or foresee, these will compose the spirituality, the faith, the prayer in which the ecumenical movement will move on and God be the more richly, the more appropriately glorified.

Notes

1. Derek Palmer, *Strangers No Longer* (London: Hodder and Stoughton, 1990), 81 ff.
2. See P.C. Rodger and L. Vischer (eds.), *The Fourth World Conference on Faith and Order* (London: SCM Press, 1964), 17.
3. For example in *Erfahrungen der Leibhaftigkeit, Interkulturelle Theologie I* (München: Chr. Kaiser Verlag, 1979), 343-45.
4. *The Pentecostals* (London: SCM Press, 1972), 504.
5. *Ibid.*, 507 and 504.
6. The story of this whole study process and of the work of the concluding panel is laid out succinctly

in Steven G. Mackie (ed.), *Can Churches Be Compared?* (Geneva: World Council of Churches, and New York: Friendship Press, 1970), research Pamphlet No. 17 of the Commission on World Mission and Evangelism.

7. The full list is given in *Can Churches Be Compared?* (see note above), 25-26.
8. *Erfahrungen der Leibhaftigkeit* (as in note 3 above), 259-60.
9. I am here following *Can Churches Be Compared?* (see note 6 above), Part Three: "Pointers to a Theological Discussion", 85 ff.
10. In para. 23 of the report of Section I. "Confessing Christ Today", in David Paton, ed., *Breaking Barriers: Nairobi 1975* (London: SPCK and Grand Rapids: William Eerdmans, 1976), 46.
11. See the Editorial in *The Ecumenical Review* (Geneva: WCC), Vol. 36, No. 2 (April 1984), 137, and the following articles by Dieter Trautwein, telling the story of the worship, and Wesley Ariarajah, commenting on the interaction between the worship and the work of the Assembly.
12. From the report cited in note 2 above, 59: from paragraph 69 in the text written by Section II on "Scripture, Tradition and Traditions".

25

The Significance of the Charismatic Renewal for Theology and Church

Jan Veenhof

Introduction

What significance does the Charismatic Renewal (from here on: CR) have for theology and the church? It is my pleasure to consider this question in a *Festschrift* for Walter Hollenweger. For Hollenweger has contributed and still contributes to establishing contacts between the Pentecostal churches and the World Council of Churches. These contacts are an important factor in the effect that the impulses of the Pentecostal churches have on the traditional churches with their fixed confessional structures and rules governing church life. It can be said that the CR can be attributed to the fact that experiences and insights which are alive within the Pentecostal movement, but were long held outside the doors of the official churches, have now been admitted and have led to a renewal of faith and spirituality within those churches. The CR does not strive after a charismatic church of its own, but after a charismatically renewed church. Nor is the CR a strict, uniform organization: it is a movement with various shades, very much because of its affiliation with the characteristic features of the various churches. This variation, at the same time, bears an ecumenical character, because the believers who are touched by the CR recognise and find each other, across the frontiers of church and belief.[1]

Another characteristic of the CR is that from the beginning it wanted to include theology in its endeavours and to make it receptive to the renewal of the life of the church. It is a good cause for various theologians to want to integrate the discoveries and experiences of the CR into their scientific work. With this, they can support the CR and, simultaneously, also give valuable and necessary stimuli to pursuing their profession.[2]

With these introductory remarks I have paved the way for giving an answer to the question concerning the meaning of the CR for theology and the church. In replying to it, I will refer to various data that appear in literature from and about the CR, as well as to views which, inspired by my own participation in the CR, I have gained through my own experiences and investigations. The brief scope of this contribution necessitates short indications and characterizations: even where a wider description would be more desirable.

The Significance for Theology

In order to sketch the significance of the CR for theology, I want to discuss various *loci* (topics), in conformity with the usual order of dogmatic theology, and to indicate what in my conviction are the specific and worthwhile aspects that the CR has to offer with regard to those subjects. The contents of the following sections, therefore, can be seen as a description of what, in my judgment, is worthy of consideration for general theological reflection. In the brief treatment of the various themes I will focus upon creationism and ecclesiology. What can be said about ecclesiology will come up for discussion in the next part of this essay, and creationism in the final part. I shall start with theology as such.

Theology: Method and Contents

History shows that religious renewal movements and academic theology have often been on bad terms with each other or have ignored each other, damaging both. Religious experience which shirks reflection and responsibility often leads to spiritualistic proliferation or fanatic fundamentalism. The theology that does not care about what is active in people's hearts as to religious experience in a concrete-empirical way, often leads to speculative constructions of thought that are interesting only to experts. In order to avoid these derailments, it is necessary to keep experience and reflection together. In this, reflection finds its breeding ground in experience, and must always return to that experience to remain a living and fruitful theology.[3]

When the 'issue' of theology bears an existential character, reflection on it cannot bear the character of purely theoretical analysis. The CR reminds the theologian of the meaning of the Holy Spirit for an adequate theological attitude of thinking. The Cartesian subject-object pattern must be abandoned. In this pattern, man, as the knowing (and, by the power of his *ratio*, ruling) subject, analyses the object (in this case God). We may say that God can become the object of knowing, but we will always have to be conscious of the fact that this object always remains the subject. We know God only because He makes Himself known, which He does through His Spirit, Who brings about the relation with Him.

This pneumatic nature of the knowledge of God is fundamental to theology, concerning both method and content. As far as the method is concerned, we do not need to look for a separate pneumatic method, but should honour this relation in applying certain methods. The more we approach the centre of theology, the more we need to be enlightened by the Spirit.[4] As far as content is concerned: for all doctrinal statements to be in a pneumatological context implies that the investigation into pneumatological components and transverse connections must be of great significance in clarifying and deepening theological definitions of a problem.[5] The following sections may illustrate this.

The Revelation: Word and Spirit

The CR emphasises the close connection between Word and Spirit. They have a 'tandem relationship'[6]. One cannot say a word without breathing and the breath (spirit) goes out with the Word. The Spirit of God is the Spirit of revelation. This is true for the revelation as it has been reflected in the books of the Old Testament. It is also true for the revelation as it has been recorded in the writings of the New Testament. Behind all speaking and writing is God's Spirit. Now, this Spirit did not only speak in the past. He also speaks *now*. John 16:13 says, "Howbeit when He, the Spirit of truth, is come, He will guide you into all truth; for He shall not speak of himself; but whatsoever He shall hear, that shall He speak, and He will show you things to come". What is particularly striking here is the aspect of continuity. The Spirit does not bring revelation that differs in content from the Word that Jesus proclaimed on earth, but He will take care that the word of Christ once spoken remains permanently up-to-date, and will continue to be heard as a relevant and new, surprising word in other and new times.

Often - particularly in orthodox-Protestant circles - the thought is still alive that revelation was restricted to the time in which the Holy Scriptures successively came about. We give thanks to the past for the objective, the Scriptures. For today we rely on the subjective application of those objective Scriptures, and this application is the work of the Spirit, Who enlightens man's heart and mind. The CR recognises - and often more actively than orthodox Protestantism - the necessity of the enlightenment by the Spirit to understand Scripture. It also recognises that this Scripture remains normative in its canonic form. But it does resist one-sided orientation to the past. What has been closed *off* in the past, is not closed *up* in the present. In, with, and in connection with the given Word, the Spirit also speaks today. The Spirit is now not just the Applicator, but also the Revelator.[7] One can rightly speak of a continuing revelation, a *revelatio continua*. Against every biblicistic historicism, as it manifests itself specifically in fundamentalism, the CR pleads for the prerogative and the beneficial significance of prophecy. The *charisma* of prophecy is one of the means by which God, in Christ through the Spirit, wants to speak to people of today.[8]

The Character of God - the Spirit

The CR is deeply affected by the fact that all true renewal is brought about by the Spirit, Who to this end makes use of the *charismata*. 'Charismatic' and 'pneumatic' are coextensive concepts, concerning contents. The emphasis on the *pneuma* is a striking characteristic of the CR. This emphasis does not mean a relegation of Christology, but it does mean that one cannot go along with those who reduce pneumatology to a function of Christology.[9] The CR wants to honour completely the trinitarian confession of God. God is the triune God, which means that God in Himself is relationship, communion, love. Therefore, it squares completely with

His character to move outside Himself, in love, towards man and the world.

The character and the activity of the Spirit is frequently described in the Scriptures. This frequency is reflected in the manifestations of the CR. The CR is particularly fascinated by the fact that the Spirit is the founder of relations. The Spirit is the *pontifex maximus*, the bridge-constructor par excellence. The Spirit joins people with Christ and through Him with the Father, and so He also joins people to each other. The Spirit seizes not only our mind and consciousness, but primarily our heart, the deepest parts of our being, where our feelings and emotions originate. God is very intimately near to us in the Spirit.[10]

In this way the CR distances itself from the view of God which is so wide spread in Christianity; which made this transcendency absolute, and evoked fear of a strict, unapproachable God. Respect and reverence are indeed appropriate in the presence of God, but these may be free of every distrust and fear. God's character is determined in its deepest sense by love, and this love gives security, joy, and freedom.[11]

In the conception of God - as also in other aspects, e.g. the reassessment of the corporeality and the rejection of intellectualism, there exists a line of communication between CR and feminist theology. The CR wants to strip the qualification 'Father' in its application to God of all authoritarian features, and to emphasise specifically the element of intimacy in it. Just like feminist theology (though less frequent and emphatic), representatives of the CR point out that the Spirit includes the feminine and motherly element.[12]

Man and Powers

Man is destined to a relationship in love to God, to his fellow-man, and to himself. However, he no longer lives in paradise, but in a world marked and afflicted by troubles in all those relations. The CR shares this view with all Christian theology. In the CR, a new accent is given to the aspect that in the tragedy of disaster and salvation not only God and man, but also extraterrestrial and superhuman powers, angels and demons, play a role. In this, the CR resists the opinion which is still very influential among the public at large, that only those things that can be observed with our measuring instruments are true and real.[13]

In referring ahead to the section on 'Christus medicus', it seems meaningful to me to say something here about a theme about which there is much to do in connection with the CR, i.e. exorcism. As we already knew, exorcism is controversial, particularly due to derailments that occurred in practice. Fortunately, the CR realises that recognition of the legitimacy of exorcism must go with great care in applying it. Spokesmen of the CR argue that, in cases of illness or problems of a somatic and psychic nature, it is not correct to say that the problems are caused by demons, just as it is neither correct to design some kind of demonological metaphysics in the reflection. It is rather necessary in the contacts with patients to look for 'anthropological components' in the problems and complaints; these components are often blockages in the relations just mentioned, which can only be broken by the power of love.[14]

In this context, it is of great importance that the CR sees man as a unity of body, soul, and spirit, in which 'spirit' - just like the concept of 'heart' - indicates the personal nucleus of man. With this 'holistic' anthropology, intellectualism and rationalism have been cut off at the root. On the other hand, the significance of both the psychic (feelings, emotions) and of corporeality is honored.

The Person of Jesus Christ: Bearer and Sender of the Spirit

The CR receives the doctrinal tradition of the first ecumenical councils and accepts their statements on the person of Jesus Christ. The characteristic feature of the CR is its special attention to the relation of Jesus Christ and the Spirit. In the New Testament, we find two lines with respect to that relation.[15] The first line is the line from the Spirit to Jesus. Jesus is the bearer of the Spirit. Jesus is the Messiah, the Christ, because He has been 'anointed' with the Spirit. Jesus is equipped with the Spirit, and in His entire behaviour, in words and in deeds, He is borne, led and inspired by this Spirit. Apart from this line, there is the line from Jesus to the Spirit. After His exaltation, the Bearer of the Spirit becomes the Sender of the Spirit. This line is constitutive for everything that the CR teaches and practices concerning the gift of the Spirit to and in people.

Yet, on the other hand, the CR is also fascinated by the first line. For a long time this line was underexposed in theological reflection and in spirituality. Now it is gradually being rediscovered. This reassessment is reflected in seeking a pneumatologically oriented Christology. In this respect, I want to mention in particular the ideas of two Dutch theologians, the Protestant H. Berkhof and the Catholic P. Schoonenberg, who (and that is certainly no coincidence) have regularly shown their intense interest in the CR. The further development and specification of such a *pneuma*-Christology is an enticing as well as a large-scale task.[16]

The Work of Jesus Christ: Christus Medicus

When dogmatics deals with the work of Christ, all attention is usually centered on the events of the cross and the resurrection, and their meaning for the establishment of salvation. The CR wholeheartedly endorses their weight, but also pays emphatic and conscious attention to the work of Jesus Christ during His earthly actions in Israel. Jesus made the salvation of the Kingdom of God available in both words and deeds. Alongside preaching, these deeds (for the major part acts of healing) have a meaning of their own, as the visible and concrete shape of salvation. In all this, Jesus showed Himself, as we saw in the previous section to be the Bearer of the Spirit. By the power of the Spirit He casts out the demons and stops illnesses.

The work of Jesus as a healer found its continuation in the young Christian church (compare 1 Cor. 12:9, James 5:14-16). Here too, the CR resists the thought that it should be and may be restricted to that first period. *Christus medicus*, Jesus is healer - also now! Currently, He heals through people in whom that same Spirit works who also carried Him. The thought is incorrect that in the service of the church forgiveness continues, whereas healing is eliminated. That boils down to a 'splitting' in salvation corresponding to a 'splitting' of the one being: dualism of soul and body.

But then again, the CR departs from the idea that the salvation of God in Jesus is now also healing in the overall sense of the word. That healing penetrates the deepest parts of human life and from there that human life is 'sanitised' in its full breadth, in all relations in which it occurs. In this connection, 'sanitise' is a meaningful word. It is no coincidence that the concept *sanus* (healthy) has a direct coherence with the word *sanctus* (holy).[17]

Being Filled with Power unto Service

In orthodox-Protestant spirituality, much emphasis has been put and is still put on the *perfectum* of salvation. Christ *has* accomplished reconciliation. Everything has been fulfilled. But when the implications and consequences of that *perfectum* come up, the tone often becomes hesitant. Again and again we hear that, as far as we are concerned, we do not come beyond falling and picking ourselves up again, and falling once again. The thought that the righteous man remains a sinner sometimes functions even as an alibi for the lack of appearance of real changes. The CR deems this view too minimalistic, as seen from the New Testament. No doubt, the *perfectum* may remain and must remain, according to the CR. But this *perfectum* is of such a nature that it also determines our *praesens*. That *praesens* is not empty; it is rather filled with the power of the Spirit, Who wants to live and work in people and wants really to renew them.

Typical of the CR is that it distinguishes yet a third part in the working of the Spirit, apart from the gifts of faith and renewal (or sanctification), i.e. the filling with the Spirit. This being filled with the Spirit - the CR prefers this concept to the more common 'baptism with the Spirit' in Pentecostal circles - implies that believers who have received and experienced righteousness and sanctification are now also equipped with power to participate in the ongoing work of God in church and world as assistants of the Spirit. The *charismata* are an essential part of the set of instruments with which they can perform this task. What the New Testament lists as fruits of the Spirit (cf. Gal. 5:22-23) corresponds with sanctification and is equally applicable to all Christians. The gifts of the Spirit correspond with being filled, and are individually different. It should be noted, however, that the fullness of those gifts is or should be present in the totality of the church.

Fortunately, the way in which this being filled is realised in the lives of people has not been 'dogmatically' determined in the CR. This can happen by an instantaneous, shocking experience, but also by a gradual process. What matters is that it should happen.

It is the special merit of the CR that it powerfully underlines the value and significance of this third aspect in the working of the Spirit. Also in this connection, it can be sure that it is legitimated by the New Testament, and has a message to theologians and the churches, which all too easily have come to regard a situation of pneumatic minimalism as normal.[18]

The Future and the Present Tension

There is a close-knit connection between the Spirit and the future. This connection has already been expressed in the Pauline letters, in which *pneuma* is typified as first fruits, and as a down-payment, an advance. The duality of the 'already now!' and 'not yet!' of salvation is revealed in the qualification 'first fruits'. In the CR, the emphasis is sometimes on the 'already now!' as a result of the overwhelming experience of the presence of salvation, particularly in praise services. Then again, the other view stands out with power, so that a one-sided *theologia gloriae* is avoided. The experience of salvation in the midst of an immense quantity of disaster raises an enormous tension. It is the tension that rings out in the pregnant language of Romans 8 where, in one breath, there is talk of the Spirit as first fruits and of sighing by Christians (vs 23). Tension forces activity and warfare, against disastrous, deadly iniquity. We can learn from the CR that this service can only be kept up by the continuous assistance of the Spirit, Who makes us pray and hope.[19]

The Significance for the Church

In the above, light has been shed from different angles on the significance the CR can have for the church and indeed has. In this section, therefore, a brief mention of some central data will suffice. It is the merit of the CR that it has rediscovered what, according to the New Testament, the church is and must be: a community, which is borne, kept together, and led by the Spirit. This congregation is originally a charismatic community, not one in which some people order and others follow (or don't!); not one in which some people are stuck with all the tasks and others only take, but one in which all people have the task of complementing and helping each other in order that everyone may be able together to fulfil the common calling: the edification of the body of Christ and its service in and to the world.

The CR sincerely desires to promote the well-being of the church as a whole with its (re)discovery. Its intention is that this church should once again encounter the Biblical model of the early church. Real renewal of the church is possible only through inspiration - in our time! - from the source. In addition to the revealing activity of the Spirit, the CR wants to understand that Biblical church model, including the *charismata*, as a current possibility and mandate, not as a purely historic matter that has been outmoded. The CR's aim is to find a balance between individual and community which can fulfil a sample function for all kinds of forms of congregational edification and congregational renewal. Therefore, the CR is not individualistic. The 'I' of the individual believer cannot be isolated from the 'we' of the community. In that community nobody is just a consumer. Thanks to the *charismata*, everybody has a task of his own and everybody is part of the communal process of giving and receiving. The intention is that the congregation should become a centre of communication, where everybody becomes involved, feels at home, and can express himself.

The communion is experienced in a unique way in the liturgy of praise services. In celebrating our communication with God and with each other, our corporality and emotions can be fully expressed. These are feelings of joy, but also of sorrow. These feelings must be catered for, which happens in pastoral care. One can say that the liturgy in a sense leads to pastoral care. The pastoral care is especially exercised in small teams, and in it the healing in the above sense plays an important role. Both liturgy and pastoral care deserve the serious attention of the entire church, which can profit from them, although it does not need to adopt everything without further consideration. Precisely in our rational and technical culture, people look for transcendence, for somatic and psychic integration, for a sheltering community, for possibilities of expressing their feelings. The official churches, with their often impersonal structures, their verbalism and traditionalism, are insufficiently able to meet this desire. The CR can offer the necessary help here, a help that can also stimulate the churches to self-analysis and self-correction.[20]

Criticism and Appreciation

I have mentioned various positive aspects of the CR above, from which theology and the church, in my conviction, can take advantage. The CR also has its weak points. It is, for instance, remarkable that at least some of the representatives of the CR have difficulty with the theological appreciation of creation. This appears, for instance, from certain dissertations on the *charismata*. Classical Pentecostalism thinks that these gifts are strictly supernatural in origin and nature; they are not related to the properties and qualities that people bring along with them from childhood. Most representatives of the Pentecostal Movement judge more carefully on this issue, but the dualism of supernatural and natural continues to exercise its influence. In my opinion, this dualism is not legitimate. A gift of the Spirit is not less a *charisma*, when it turns out to have a human foundation; as is for instance argued with respect to glossolalia.[21] Of course, this does not mean that every *charisma* should have a human basis. The Spirit is free, but that freedom does not exclude the utilization of what is available and is thus not restricted.

It is the relation of creation and salvation that is at stake here. At times the CR has been accused of paying too little attention to and having too little involvement in the world with its social and political problems. Broadly speaking, this reproach is unfounded.[22] The CR does have need of a fundamental contemplation of the status of creation and nature. More than in the past, the CR should have an awareness of the fact that grace is not hostile towards nature; and that this world, despite everything, is still God's good creation. Creation and salvation can neither be identified nor contrasted. When the CR becomes completely serious about this, various consequences will result.

In the charismatic pastoral care, there will have to be more, and even more conscious awareness of the importance of the opinions and experiences of doctors and psychologists. Furthermore, its relationship to alternative medicine will have to change. The CR often has a certain suspicion of and dislike for this medicine. It is now necessary that a clearer distinction should be made between human information, and the use that is made of it. Only then will a meaningful discussion be possible.[23]

Purely determining the relationship between creation and salvation is also important for a dialogue with other cultures and religions. It is Hollenweger's credit that he desires to approach the questions related to this dialogue from the angle of pneumatology; for it is precisely the Spirit that connects creation with salvation: the spirit of re-creation is none other than that of creation.[24] A further expansion of the concept of a cosmic pneumatology, as developed by Calvin, would be very useful for further reflection on these questions.[25]

Conquering the dualism just mentioned can also contribute to the breaking of another dualism, that of the distance between charismatic Christians and other church members, as it is often visible in local churches. Many have already pointed out the danger of charismatic Christians overwhelming others with their experiences, so that the others resist forms of belief that are new and strange to them.[26] Acknowledging that we as Christians are all people with human feelings and normal, human susceptibility to irritations and frustrations, can help to find the right way for and with each other: the way of patience to explain new things, and of openness to consider new things.

I offer these critical notes because I am convinced of the value of the CR, which lies in what I would call its creed: God can be experienced in Jesus through the Spirit today, by the entire person! Through this creed in all its realizations and applications, the CR confronts us with this question: does the Spirit not have more in store for you than you have assumed so far? In binding this question to our hearts - there lies the significance of the CR for church and theology.

Notes

— The article was translated from the Dutch by drs. A. Pellegrom, Houten, the Netherlands

1. The literature on the CR is immense. I name here the following publications: Edward D. O'Connor, *Spontaner Glaube. Ereignis und Erfahrung der charismatischen Erneuerung* (Freiburg, etc.: Herder, 1974); Michael P. Hamilton (ed.), *The Charismatic Movement* (Grand Rapids: Eerdmans, 1975); Kilian McDonnel O.S.B. (ed.), *The Holy Spirit and Power. The Catholic Charismatic Renewal* (New York: Doubleday, 1975); Siegfried Grossman, *Haushalter der Gnade Gottes. Von der charismatischen Bewegung zur charismatischen Erneuerung der Gemeinde* (Wuppertal: Oncken, 1978); Arnold Bittlinger (ed.), *The Church is Charismatic. The World Council of Churches and the Charismatic Renewal* (Geneva: World Council of Churches, 1981); Hans-Diether Reimer, *Wenn der Geist in der Kirche wirken will. Ein Vierteljahrhundert charismatische Bewegung* (Stuttgart: Quell, 1987); Hans Jörg Kägi, *Der Heilige Geist in charismatischer Erfahrung und theologischer Reflexion* (Zürich: Theologischer Verlag, 1989). A good historical, spiritual, and theological orientation is given in the Dutch article by J.J. Suurmond, "Een introductie tot de charismatische vernieuwing", in *Kerk en Theologie* 40 (1989) 33-50.
Contacts between the Pentecostal and the mainline churches, as they have taken place in the Netherlands, are described in a dissertation written by Paul N. van der Laan under the guidance of Hollenweger, "The Question of Spiritual Unity. The Dutch Pentecostal Movement in Ecumenical Perspective" (Ph.D. Dissertation University of Birmingham, 1988). A Dutch version of this dissertation is forthcoming under the title: *Eén van Geest. De Nederlandse Pinksterbeweging in oecumenisch perspectief* (Kampen: Kok). Dutch speaking theologians have published a great number of books on pneumatology: H. Berkhof, "Die Pneumatologie in der niederländischen Theologie", in Otto A. Dilschneider, *Theologie des Geistes* (Gütersloh: Mohn, 1980), 27-44; and A. Geense, "Pneumatologische Entwürfe in der niederländischen Theologie", in *Theologische Literaturzeitung* 106 (1981), 786-96. Much has also been published in Dutch about the CR and specific aspects of it. Due to restricted space, I do not mention this Dutch literature in the following notes. Instead, I refer to the above mentioned publications and to my article on the Paraclete mentioned in note 7.
2. Actually, I can refer to all authors who are mentioned in the notes to this contribution. I also mention J. Rodman Williams, who produced two interesting writings, i.e. *The Era of the Spirit* (Plainfield NJ: Logos International, 1971), and *The Pentecostal Reality* (Plainfield NJ: Logos International 1972.
3. Compare Kägi, *c.l.*, specifically 265-78.
4. Compare J. Veenhof, "The Holy Spirit and Hermeneutics", in Nigel M. de S. Cameron (ed.), *The Challenge of Evangelical Theology. Essays in Approach and Method* (Edinburgh: Rutherford House, 1987), 105-22.
5. Compare Christian Schütz, *Einführung in die Pneumatologie* (Darmstadt: Wissenschaftliche Buchgesellschaft, 1985), 31 f.
6. See Suurmond, *c.l.*, 34.
7. See J. Veenhof, "Holy Spirit and Holy Scripture. Considerations Concerning the Character and Function of Scripture in the Framework of Salvation History" in: *The Interpretation of Scripture Today, Reformed Ecumenical Synod Theological Conference Chicago 1984* (Grand Rapids: Reformed Ecumenical Synod, 1984), 1-19. Also published in: *The Scottish Bulletin of Evangelical Theology* 4 (1986) no. 2, 69-84. In my contribution "Der Paraklet" in Dilschneider (see note 1), 129-139, I wrote about the theological meaning of John 16:13 and the other Paraclete's words.
8. For prophecy I refer to George Vandervelde, "The Gift of Prophecy and the Prophetic Church", in George Vandervelde, *The Holy Spirit: Renewing and Empowering Presence* (Winfield BC, Ca-

nada: Wood Lake Books), 93-118. Also to Walter J. Hollenweger, *Geist und Materie, Interkulturelle Theologie III* (München: Kaiser, 1988), 316-24. Both refer to David E. Aune's important book, *Prophecy in Early Christianity and The Ancient Mediterranean World* (Grand Rapids: Eerdmans, 1983).

9. Karl Barth has sometimes been accused of such a reduction. This reproach is not totally unfounded. Yet it does not do complete justice to his work as a whole. Compare Schütz's cautious analysis, *c.l.*, 128-131, who also bears in mind P.J. Rosato's monograph, *The Spirit as Lord. The Pneumatology of Karl Barth* (Edinburgh: T.& T. Clark, 1981).
10. Compare my contribution "Der Paraklet", 135-39, with reference to e.g. Dilschneider and Mühlen.
11. These motives are particularly reflected in charismatic songs.
12. In historical argumentation, certain early-Christian traditions - in particular Syrian theology - are referred to as having presented the Spirit as feminine. The Syrian word for 'Spirit' was - at least in that time - feminine. One proponent of this conception of the Spirit is the identification of *pneuma* and *sophia*, found in the *Sapientia Salomonis*; compare Alfred Adam, *Lehrbuch der Dogmengeschichte I* (Gütersloh: Mohn, 1970, 217, and further G. Quispel, "Jewish Gnosis and Mandaean Gnosticism. Some Reflections on the Writing Brontè", in: Jacques-E. Ménard (ed.), *Les textes de Nag Hammadi. Colloque du Centre d'Histoire des Réligions (Strasbourg, 23-25 octobre 1974)* (Leiden: Brill, 1975), 82-122. A turn appeared when, in Syria and other places, Mariology began to develop. That took place in the fourth century, a time of many changes. In that period, Mary took 'on', as it were, all sorts of typically 'paracletic' functions, such as comforting and protection. The Spirit was interpreted more as 'neutrum' or as masculine. It is remarkable how the overshadowing of pneumatology by Mariology, especially in common spirituality, is being corrected in more recent Roman Catholic theology. Such an 'overburdening' of Mary is no longer necessary from the perspective of a renewed confession and experience of the Spirit - such is the tenor of the considerations involved. From here, it is possible, as Catharina J. Halkes, the Roman Catholic pioneer of feminist theology, does, to speak of the Spirit as 'Our Mother'. For the relationship of pneumatology and Mariology see Heribert Mühlen, *Una Mystica Persona. Die Kirche als das Mysterium der heilsgeschichtlichen Identität des Heiligen Geistes in Christus und den Christen: Eine Person in vielen Personen* (München etc.: Ferdinand Schöningh, 1968), 461-78. See also Yves Congar, *Der Heilige Geist* (Freiburg: Herder, 1982) on "Die Mütterlichkeit in Gott und die Weiblichkeit des Heiligen Geistes", 424-32.
13. This popular positivistic view is behind the times, with respect to the developments in the newer natural science; compare Hollenweger, *c.l.*, 271-99.
14. Compare Hollenweger, *c.l.*, 105-20.
15. A clear distinction between these two lines is found in Hendrikus Berkhof, *The Doctrine of the Holy Spirit* (Richmond: John Knox Press, 1964).
16. For a completed conception of Berkhof compare his *Christian Faith* (Grand Rapids: Eerdmans, 1986). Representative of Schoonenberg's view is his article "Spirit Christology and Logos Christology", in *Bijdragen* 38 (1977), 350-75. For the relation of the Spirit and Christ see also James D.G. Dunn, *Jesus and the Spirit. A Study of the Religious and Charismatic Experience of Jesus and the First Christians as Reflected in the New Testament* (London: SCM Press, 1978); and Thomas A. Smail, *Reflected Glory. The Spirit in Christ and Christians* (London etc.: Hodder and Stoughton, 1975).
17. See Part One of Dunn's study which is devoted to a sketch of The Religious Experience of Jesus. In the CR, Jesus' healing activity is the model for the ministry of healing in our days. An influential leader and author in this ministry is Francis MacNutt; compare his *Healing* (Notre Dame Ind.: Ave Maria Press, 1974).
18. On both the baptism in the Spirit and the *charismata* there is a substantial quantity of widely-va-

rying literature. I mention here the following scientific monographs on baptism in the Spirit: James D.G. Dunn, *The Baptism in the Holy Spirit. A Re-examination of the New Testament Teaching on the Gift of the Spirit in Relation to Pentecostalism Today* (Philadelphia: The Westminster Press, 1970); Frederick Dale Bruner, *A Theology of the Holy Spirit. The Pentecostal Experience and the New Testament Witness* (Grand Rapids: Eerdmans, 1970); Harold D. Hunter, *Spirit-Baptism. A Pentecostal Alternative* (Lanham etc.: University Press of America, 1983). In connection with the *charismata* I mention two German writings which are meant for a wider public: Arnold Bittlinger, *Im Kraftfeld des Heiligen Geistes. Gnadengaben und Dienstordnungen im Neuen Testament* (Marburg an der Lahn: Oekumenischer Verlag Dr. R.G. Edel, 1968); and Heribert Mühlen (ed.), *Geistesgaben heute* (Mainz: Matthias-Grünewald-Verlag, 1982). Topos-Taschenbücher Bd. 116. See also the literature mentioned in note 1.

19. Compare Kägi, *c.l.*, 258-65, who points to the coherence between cross and Spirit.
20. Compare, in addition to the literature mentioned in note 1, Heribert Mühlen, *Die Erneuerung des christlichen Glaubens. Charisma-Geist-Befreiung* (München: Don Bosco, 1976).
21. See e.g. W.E. Mills (ed.), *Speaking in Tongues. A Guide to Research on Glossolalia* (Grand Rapids: Eerdmans, 1986). Against dualism, see my contribution: "*Charismata* - Supernatural or Natural?" in Vandervelde, *o.c.*, 73-91.
22. Compare Larry Christenson, *A Charismatic Approach to Social Action* (London: Lakeland, 1974).
23. I am in complete agreement with Hollenweger concerning his open approach to various alternative kinds of medicine, which can be reduced to natural forces created by God, yet which cannot be explained scientifically. See his "Verhängnis und Verheissung charismatischer Heiler", in: Oswald Eggenberger *et al.*, *Heilen, was verwundet ist. Heilkunst zwischen alternativer Medizin und gottlichem Geist* (Freiburg/Zürich: Paulus Verlag/Theologischer Verlag, 1990), 155. Also compare his *Geist und Materie*, 21-59.
24. I think that in this way I can summarize a principal theme in Hollenweger's *Interkulturelle Theologie*.
25. For Calvin see Werner Krusche, *Das Wirken des Heiligen Geistes nach Calvin* (Göttingen: Vandenhoeck und Rupprecht, 1957), 15-32 and 95-125. In connection with Calvin's wide pneumatological devotion, the richly-documented article by I. John Hesselink is interesting: "The Charismatic Movement and the Reformed Tradition", in *Reformed Review* 28 (1975) no. 3, 147-56. Also informative is Garth B. Wilson's contribution, "The Doctrine of the Holy Spirit in the Reformed Tradition: a Critical Overview", in Vandervelde, *o.c.*, 57-72.
26. Compare Reimer, *c.l.*, 101 f.

26

Charismatic Renewal in the Roman Catholic Church: Reception and Challenge

Peter Hocken

This article examines the response of the Roman Catholic Church to the Charismatic Movement, particularly the reaction of Church authority. The points of greatest sensitivity and tension will be identified, together with the nature of the challenges to the Church and to the Charismatic Renewal.

General Catholic Reaction to the Charismatic Movement

Catholic reactions to the spread of the Charismatic Movement within the Roman Catholic Church from 1967[1] must be understood in the context of the recently-concluded Second Vatican Council. Prior to the revolutionary Decree on Ecumenism of November 1964, it would have been unthinkable that a revival-renewal movement originating outside the Roman Catholic Church should be accepted and welcomed by Church authorities. But with the beginnings of Catholic Charismatic Renewal in 1967[2], the context of its appearance and of the Church's response to it was strongly permeated by the atmosphere and programme of renewal inspired by Pope John XXIII and initiated by the Council Fathers. The first thrust of Catholic Pentecostalism developed among young graduates, many of whom had already prayed and worked together for spiritual and liturgical renewal on college campuses: especially at Notre Dame, South Bend, Indiana. This background marked out the first Catholic Charismatics from their Protestant counterparts: for the Catholic pioneers had more cohesion as a group, and as university graduates were more disposed to recognize the role of theology. They immediately interpreted their experience as the realization of the prayers of John XXIII for an outpouring of the Spirit through the Council as at 'a new Pentecost'.[3] Just as the Catholic participants saw this new movement among Catholics as a fruit of the Council, so the Catholic authorities naturally saw this strange phenomenon in this post-Conciliar context.

The responses of the Catholic authorities to Charismatic Renewal never manifested the degree of suspicion nor the specific objections that had characterized the earlier reactions of Protestant Church leaders. Early Protestant reactions often focused on the manifestation of glossolalia, expressing fears about its possible pathological character.[4] There is no focus on glossolalia in any of the statements of Roman Catholic Episcopal Conferences. Whereas Protestant authorities often expressed doubt about the contemporary availability of the New Testament charism, not one of the many Catholic statements questioned the authenticity of glossolalia as a gift of the Spirit.[5]

The Catholic episcopal statements on Charismatic Renewal say very little about prophecy[6], which needs discernment like all other manifestations, but its existence in the contemporary Church does not pose any doctrinal problems such as those raised by the Lutheran Church - Missouri Synod.[7] In general, the Catholic Bishops never questioned the basic orthodoxy and acceptability of Charismatic Renewal. While generally welcoming it, they drew attention to possible imbalances and abuses, and to the necessity of discernment. If anything, the Papal statements were the most positive and encouraging.[8] The over-all result was, perhaps surprisingly to some Protestants, a more positive Roman Catholic response than from the Churches of the Reformation.

Two Tensions

Valid Option or Essential Gift?

An early Catholic tendency was to categorize the Charismatic Movement as a 'spirituality'.[9] In the Catholic context, this meant accepting it as a valid expression of Christian faith, but essentially making it one valid option among many. In the initial stages, this approach helped to gain official Catholic acceptance for the movement, allowing it a right to exist; but, in the long run, it weakened the movement's challenge to the Church. Most Catholic Charismatics have instinctively sensed that 'the Renewal' is for the sake of the whole Church, and that its acceptance as one valid spirituality among many represents a marginalization alien to its inner character. This sense was grasped by those who compared the Charismatic Movement with other Renewal movements (such as the Liturgical Movement), seeing these movements not just as permissible options but as essential works of the Spirit for the renewal of the Church.[10]

This tension has persisted throughout the quarter-century of Charismatic Renewal in the Catholic Church. Some, particularly participants, see the movement as directed towards the whole Church;[11] others, mostly non-participants, see it as one among a number - not now of spiritualities, but of organized movements of renewal. This tension is seen particularly at the institutional level, where Catholic Charismatic Renewal is treated as one of a number of lay movements in the Catholic Church. It easily ignores the fact that both in its origins and in its essential character the Charismatic Movement is different from the organized lay movements that proliferate in the contemporary Catholic Church.[12]

Ecumenism

The other constant point of tension concerns the ecumenical dimension of the Charismatic Movement. There is much evidence to suggest that this element presents the greatest challenge to the Roman Catholic Church; and still remains the most acute point of sensitivity. It was not surprising, given traditional Catholic emphasis on the centrality and uniqueness of the Catholic Church in the Catholic understanding of salvation, that the first U.S. Bishops' statement on Charismatic Renewal says:

> In calling it a Pentecostal movement we must be careful to dissociate it from classic Pentecostalism as it appears in Protestant denominations, such as the Assemblies of God, the United Pentecostal Church, and others. The Pentecostal movement in the Catholic Church is not the acceptance of the ideology or practices of any denomination, but likes to consider itself a renewal in the spirit of the first Pentecost.[13]

In other words, there is an acceptance of Charismatic Renewal, but often in a way that diminishes or ignores the identity of the over-all Movement and the significance of its historical origins. While the essentially ecumenical character of Charismatic Renewal was recognized by some Catholic leaders,[14] this was not seen as central in the Episcopal statements.

Moreover, the years of fastest growth in Charismatic Renewal among Catholics in the USA saw the mushrooming of 'non-denominational' Charismatic churches and ministries. Often Christian unity was presented as a brushing aside of historic differences, rather than a confronting of them in love and penitence. Thus it became a pastoral and theological necessity for Catholics to make clear the distinction between being 'ecumenical' and being 'non-denominational'.[15] Ecumenical renewal would therefore respect Church membership and Church differences, where non-denominational renewal would not.

Institutionalization of Charismatic Renewal

Catholic acceptance of Charismatic Renewal has involved an element of institutionalization. In itself, such a process is both necessary and inevitable. National and international structures were established from the worthy concern to promote Charismatic Renewal so that it would be integrated into the full life of the Church: Catholic Charismatics spoke of the Renewal being placed 'at the heart of the Church'.[16] This process is not primarily a formalization, but the new thrust of the Spirit taking on more embodied forms. The key question is not whether or not institutionalization occurs, but whether it occurs in a way that is faithful to the initial grace of the Holy Spirit.

This process has involved the establishment of National Service Committees for Catholic Charismatic Renewal in almost every country with a Catholic presence and freedom to associate. It includes forms of official relationship with Catholic Episcopal Conferences. There has also been a proliferation of diocesan structures, with Diocesan Liaisons frequently being appointed to connect the Bishop and Charismatic Renewal within his Diocese.

At the international level, the institutionalizing process was reflected in Pope John Paul II's nomination in 1987 of Bishop Paul Cordes, Vice-President of the Council for the Laity, to serve as Episcopal Adviser to the International Catholic Charismatic Renewal Office (ICCRO) in Rome. This appointment was more integrated into Vatican structures than the previous role played by Cardinal L.J. Suenens at the request of Pope Paul VI.

New Charismatic Communities have been drawing up official statutes and seeking canonical recognition: local communities from the local Bishop, international groupings from the Vatican. The Pontifical Council for the Laity has recently issued a Decree officially recognizing the Catholic Fraternity of Charismatic Covenant Communities and Fellowships.[17]

This structuring process has tended to separate Charismatic Renewal among Catholics from the wider Charismatic Movement in, across (and outside) virtually all Church traditions. One reason advanced for this is that the Catholic authorities can only exercise authority over and legislate for Catholic groups. But assuredly more powerful in this process are long-standing Catholic patterns of self-containment and supervision. From this angle ecumenism makes things more complicated and confusing!

A Second Ecumenical Breeze

The second half of the 1980s has, however, seen a resurgence of ecumenical convictions among Charismatic Christians. This has been most evident in the formation of major inter-denominational Charismatic bodies: the North American Renewal Service Committee (NARSC - 1985); the European Charismatic Consultation (ECC - 1988); and the International Charismatic Consultation on World Evangelization (ICCOWE - 1989). While these structures all grew out of pre-existing Charismatic bodies,[18] their formation clearly represented a new commitment to ecumenical cooperation and a stronger institutional embodiment of ecumenical convictions.

This renewed ecumenical thrust manifested an awareness among many leaders that the Charismatic Movement is ecumenical by its nature; and that any loss in ecumenical expression represents a loss in something essential to this work of

God: and a diminution of its distinctive vitality and power. This second wind of ecumenism is both more reflective and more responsible than the first phases of exuberant Charismatic interchange (see for example the NARSC Statement of Policy).[19] Most of the leaders on these new ecumenical committees are now respected figures within and often beyond their own Churches, having regular access to Church leaders. It is noteworthy that many of the Charismatic leaders most committed to the ecumenical character of Renewal are the pioneer figures who remember the excitement of the ecumenical origins of the Renewal.[20]

A Heightening of the Tensions

This new ecumenical upsurge has in many ways heightened the areas of tension already noted in the Catholic response to Charismatic Renewal. It has been a largely unconscious challenge to the prevailing official policy of welcoming Catholic Charismatic Renewal in a way that distanced it from the Renewal among other Christians. From the standpoint of the Catholic authorities, this movement may seem to have been ambiguous and insufficiently Catholic in its origins. The subsequent consolidation of Catholic Charismatic Renewal and a diminution in ecumenical interaction would then be seen as the correction of an original defect. From this perspective, efforts to revive the earlier ecumenical thrust are experienced as undoing this consolidation. Such an interpretation can be found in Bishop Cordes' address to Catholic Charismatic Leaders in Rome in October 1989:

> The Catholicization of the Charismatic Renewal began in the 1960s, and it not only enabled many people to gain a fuller understanding of the Catholic faith, but was also of enormous help in enabling our faith to rediscover the inexhaustible power of the Holy Spirit. It has obviously been a long journey, with some difficult stretches and some very real dangers, and it could not have been concluded without the guidance of the Popes and the orientations of many bishops.[21]

This heightened tension also represents a concern of the Catholic authorities that ecumenical expressions of Charismatic Renewal may be ignoring essential convictions of Catholic faith concerning the nature of the Church. Their concerns focus on the following points:

(i) the fear that recognition of one movement of Charismatic Renewal wider than individual denominations involves or will lead to the positing of a Charismatic Super-Church, consisting of all those who are one in the Spirit, over and against the historic Churches in their divided particularity. Thus John Paul II told Renewal leaders in 1981 that: "Genuine ecumenical effort does not seek to evade the difficult tasks, such as doctrinal convergence, by rushing to create a kind of autonomous 'Church of the Spirit' apart from the visible Church of Christ''.[22]

(ii) the concern that Charismatics are wrongly separating Jesus from the Church; so that ecumenical evangelization proclaims together the same Jesus without reference to Church, and ecumenical community is founded on common faith in Jesus abstracted from the question of Church.[23]

The Challenges

In any sovereign move of the Holy Spirit, there is always a two-way challenge corresponding to a two-fold thrust of the Spirit. One is the Spirit's challenge to the Churches as they are: i.e., corresponding to the Spirit's work of convicting the world of sin, righteousness and judgment (John 16: 8-11). The other is the challenge of the Churches to the new thrust of the Spirit: i.e., corresponding to the Spirit's work of confirming all in the traditions that is the work of the Spirit, which is all that glorifies Jesus Christ (John 16: 12-15).[24]

It is no accident that the challenge is strongest in the area of ecclesiology. The Spirit's presence will sift received ecclesiologies, thus challenging both rigid formulations of the relationship between Jesus and the Church and an individualism that emphasizes a personal relationship to Jesus to the neglect of the Church.

An ecumenical work of the Spirit necessarily challenges all forms of ecclesiastical self-sufficiency and self-containment which, by definition, weaken or deny the Lordship of Christ. In this context, attempts to create a wholly separate Catholic Charismatic Renewal, which is only accidentally related to the same movement among other Christians, will involve changing the Spirit's work into something more familiar or congenial to received Catholic patterns.

An ecumenical reception of Charismatic Renewal by all the Churches is impossible without an openness to a deep process of repentance and purification, and without a deep love for the real work of the Lord in each tradition. The Spirit's challenge will not only expose our areas of weakness and infidelity, but will also require the purification of our apparent areas of strength. The prophetic power of Charismatic Renewal is bound up with its ecumenical character.

The Spirit's challenge from the Catholic Church to the Charismatic Renewal will insist on all that is of God in the Catholic understanding of the relationship between Jesus and the Church. In this respect, the Charismatic Renewal needs the challenge from Catholic authorities: particularly in the light of the individualistic culture in which the Renewal Movement sprung up. It is a mistake to dismiss Vatican concerns as mere remnants of pre-ecumenical conservatism. The ecclesiological questions raised are of importance for all Christians: true ecumenism means real interaction between our inherited ecclesiologies; not their rejection as irrelevant.

The Spirit cuts both ways. It challenges the Churches to open up to a movement of life that transcends historic divisions; and it challenges the Renewal to take seriously the Spirit's witness in the Churches. Let us see how this process applies to the ecumenical character of the Charismatic Movement. As one work of the Spirit across all Church traditions, it does bring a new degree of unity in the Spirit. This creates a new situation for the Churches, deeply challenging their proprietorial attitudes and corresponding modes of operation. Accepting the authenticity of Charismatic Renewal requires the radical questioning of all self-contained 'denominational' separatism.

However, there is also a radical challenge to Charismatics who believe that their Churches stand within the realm of God's saving grace. First of all, it is their responsibility to present to Church leaders for discernment the Charismatic Renewal as the Spirit has given it; this includes its ecumenical character. Secondly, they have to articulate the relationship between the new Charismatic unity in the Spirit and the unity/disunity of the historic Churches. In particular, they have to explain convincingly how a Charismatic unity in the Spirit does not replace confessional and ecclesial unity, but represents a powerful God-given thrust in the midst of historic divisions to realize the organic unity which the Ecumenical Movement is now seeking.

It is not the task of the Vatican and Church leaders to produce the theology to underpin such convictions. It is the responsibility, first, of qualified people within the Charismatic Movement. It is then the task of Church authority to respond and discern. The problems highlighted by official Catholic hesitations over the ecumenical character of Charismatic Renewal are that (i) Catholic Charismatics have often played down the movement's prophetic thrust out of their deep desire to obtain Church approval; and (ii) theological reflection within Renewal circles has not generally grasped the full extent of the Spirit's challenge.[25] This is further exacerbated by the reluctance of contemporary theologians to take this work of the Spirit seriously.[26]

The fact that Catholic hesitations concerning the ecumenical dimension have been expressed in the Vatican does not negate the comments made earlier about the positive welcome of Charismatic Renewal by the Catholic authorities: and especially by the Popes. The statement of John Paul II against an autonomous 'Church of the Spirit' occurs in a discourse that is overwhelmingly positive, and other Papal discourses to Charismatic gatherings have been remarkably commendatory without similar warnings.

Without holding together the ecclesial, the charismatic and the ecumenical, the only possibilities are either (i) wholly denominationalized forms of Renewal no longer forming one movement of the Spirit and increasingly at odds with each other; or (ii) forms of Renewal that may well be one with each other, but which still remain unrelated or marginal to the life of the historic Christian Churches.

Neither of these would gladden the heart of Professor Hollenweger, who has been a consistent defender of the prophetic character of the Spirit's work.[27]

Notes

1. Some Catholics were baptized in the Spirit prior to 1967, in most cases through contact with Pentecostals or Protestant Charismatics, both in the Netherlands and the U.S.A., but there was no corporate expression of Charismatic Renewal among Catholics prior to the Duquesne week-end of February 1967.
2. It was not until 1972-73 that the language of 'Catholic Charismatic Renewal' replaced the earlier terms 'Catholic Pentecostal Movement' or 'Catholic Pentecostalism'.
3. For Pope John's prayer, see Edward O'Connor *The Pentecostal Movement in the Catholic Church* (Notre Dame, Ind.; Ave Maria Press, 1971), 287-88.
4. See for example the documents from Episcopalian, Lutheran and Presbyterian Churches in the U.S.A. on glossolalia issued between 1960 and 1965 in Kilian McDonnell (ed.) *Presence, Power, Praise* (hereafter: *PPP*) Vol. I (Collegeville, Minnesota: Liturgical Press, 1980)
5. The Catholic bishops of Puerto Rico even state that "many of the faithful have been alienated by the gift of tongues because they do not understand it" (*PPP* I, 366-67).
6. The only Catholic statement listed in McDonnell's collection that mentions prophecy specifically is that from the Antilles (*PPP* II, 262).
7. See *PPP* II, 321 (C. 4). Lutherans have often argued against the compatibility of charismatic renewal with Lutheran convictions on the grounds of (i) it being a modern form of the 'enthusiasm' condemned by Luther, i.e. all appeals to subjective experience rather than the objectivity of Word and sacrament, (ii) the acceptance of prophecy inherently subverting the unique authority of the Scriptures as the Word of God. The Rev. C. Donald Photenhauer of Minnesota was suspended from the ministry of the Missouri Synod primarily on the latter grounds (See Conrad J. Christianson, Jr. *Sola Scriptura? Traditions in Conflict, Lutheranism and Pentecostalism*).
8. The Papal addresses are: (i) Paul VI to International Leaders Conference in October 1973 (*PPP* III, 12); (ii) Paul VI to International Conference participants in May 1975 (*PPP* III, 71-76); (iii) John Paul II to International Leaders Conferences in May 1981 (*New Covenant* 11/2 August 1981, 7-9); (iv) in May 1984; (v) in May 1987 (ICCRO *International Newsletter* XIII/3 May-June 1987, 2-4); (vi) John Paul II to Italian Renewal leaders in Nov. 1980 (*Osservatore Romano*, English edition 5 Jan. 1981); (vii) John Paul II to priests' retreat in September 1984 (T. Forrest (ed.) *Be Holy!* 123-27).
9. This argument was most fully developed by Kilian McDonnell in "The Distinguishing Characteristics of the Charismatic-Pentecostal Spirituality" *One in Christ* X/2 (1974), 117-28.
10 This position was adopted by Stephen B. Clark and George Martin in *As the Spirit Leads Us* (ed. Kevin & Dorothy Ranaghan) and by Cardinal Suenens in *A New Pentecost?*, 113. It was endorsed by the bishops of the Antilles in 1976 (*PPP* II, 267).
11. This formulation covers both those who saw the Renewal as directed towards the entire Catholic Church and those who emphasized its ecumenical character and saw it as affecting all Christian Churches and ecclesial communities. The ecumenical character of Charismatic Renewal in fact requires some modification to the comparison made with other renewal movements.
12. Chapter Five of the author's book *One Lord One Spirit One Body* examined the major differences between the Charismatic Movement and the organized movements. It was disappointing but possibly significant that no reviews have commented on this Chapter.
13. *PPP* I, 209.

14. "It is evident that the charismatic renewal is a major ecumenical force and is *de facto* ecumenical in nature" (*Theological and Pastoral Orientations on the Catholic Charismatic Renewal: Malines Document I* VI. D, quoted in *PPP* III, 54).
15. Attempts to explain this distinction were made by Kilian McDonnell *The Charismatic Renewal and Ecumenism*, 102-03 and Cardinal Suenens *Ecumenism and Charismatic Renewal: Theological and Pastoral Orientations*, 81, 84.
16. See ICCRO Themes for the Renewal "At the Heart of the Church", *International Newsletter serving the Charismatic Renewal in the Catholic Church* XV/1 (January-February 1989), 3-4.
17. Decree dated November 30, 1990. This fraternity represents the Catholic membership of the International Brotherhood of Communities (IBOC).
18. NARSC grew out of the fellowship established in the regular meetings of U.S. Renewal Leaders at Glencoe, Missouri (see Vinson Synan "Joint Witness Leads to World Evangelization" *AD 2000* 1/1 February 1987, 1); ECC represented a coming together of the European Charismatic Leaders Conferences (begun in 1972) and the Acts 1986 Committee formed by Michael Harper; ICCOWE grew out of the Singapore Consultations of 1987 and 1988 (see Vinson Synan "Pentecost Vigil", *AD2000* 3/3 July-August 1989, 4-7).
19. Printed in *AD2000* 1/1 (February 1987), 3.
20. Most obviously, this is true of Canon Michael Harper (Anglican); Larry Christenson (Lutheran); Vinson Synan (Pentecostal); Kevin Ranaghan (Catholic); Fr Tom Forrest (Catholic); Fr Laurent Fabre (Catholic); David Berly (Baptist).
21. Mimeographed version of Cordes' address to Catholic Charismatic Leaders, 18. A French translation of this talk was printed under the title "Communion et Oecuménisme" in an insert to *Il est Vivant!* 73 (November-December 1989).
22. *New Covenant* 11/2 (August 1981), 9.
23. Both these concerns were expressed by Bishop Paul Cordes in the address cited in note 21.
24. This two-fold work of the Holy Spirit is examined in Chapters 8 & 9 of the author's book *One Lord One Spirit One Body.*
25. Some French Renewal leaders have done more than others in this regard.
26. Yves Congar is one of the few major Catholic theologians to take the Charismatic Renewal seriously (see *I Believe in the Holy Spirit* Vol. II, 145-212) but he was perhaps past his greatest creativity as a theologian when he took up this question.
27. See Walter J. Hollenweger, "Towards a Charismatic Theology", in Simon Tugwell e.a. *New Heaven? New Earth?* (Springfield, Illinois: Templegate Publishers, 1976), 9-13.

Bibliography of Walter J. Hollenweger

Paul N. van der Laan

The Bibliography includes:
— Books/Monographs
— Books Edited
— Collective Works/Introductions to Books of Other Authors
— Articles

Books/Monographs are numbered arithmetically (1 ff.). Later publications appear under the number of the first publication. Translations are numbered a, b, c, etc. under the number of the original publication.

Books Edited are numbered arithmetically (50 ff.) and follow the same principle as Books/Monographs.

Collective Works/Introductions to Books of Other Authors and Articles are numbered as follows:

The two first numbers indicate the year (e.g. 88), the last two numbers are the arithmetic number in the year.

The entry is filed under the year of its first publication (in any language) following the same principle as Books/Monographs.

The numbers refer to the system developed by Professor Hollenweger. His system made no distinction between Collective Works/Introductions and Articles. It also included manuscripts, lectures, public speeches, sermons and radio features. In this bibliography only the published materials are listed. Since we distinguished between Collective Works/Introducions and Articles and left out the unpublished materials, the numbers might not seem to tally.

Books/Monographs

1. *Der 1. Korintherbrief: Eine Arbeitshilfe zur Bibelwoche 1964/65*. Klingenmünster: Volksmissionarisches Amt der Pfälizischen Landeskirche, 1964.
2. *Geist- und Bibelverständnis bei Spiritualisten der Gegenwart. Eine frömmigkeits- und dogmengeschichtliche Untersuchung unter besonderer Berücksichtigung der Schweizerischen Pfingstmission und ihrer historischen Wurzeln*. Zürich: Akzessarbeit University of Zürich, 1960, Ms.
3. *Handbuch der Pfingstbewegung* 10 vols. - dupl. Geneva. New Haven, Conn.: Available from ATLA, Board of Microtexts, Divinity School, Yale University, 1965/67 (Dr. Theol. Diss. University of Zürich).
4. *Enthusiastisches Christentum: Die Pfingstbewegung in Geschichte und Gegenwart*. Zürich/Wupperthal: Zwingli-Verlag and Theol. Verlag R. Brockhaus, 1969.

4a-1. *The Pentecostals*. English edition. London: SCM, 1972.

4a-2. *The Pentecostals*. Second edition. London: SCM, 1976, paperback.

4b-1. *The Pentecostal and Charismatic Movements*. American edition. Minneapolis, Minn.: Augsburg Publ. House, 1972.

4b-2. *The Pentecostal and Charismatic Movements*. Second edition. Minneapolis, Minn.: Augsburg Publ. House, 1976.

4b-3. *The Pentecostals*. Third edition. Peabody, MA: Hendrickson, 1988.

4c. *El Pentecostalismo: Historia y doctrinas*. Latin American edition. Buenos Aires: La Aurora, 1975.

5. *New Wine in Old Wineskins: Protestant and Catholic Neo-Pentecostals*. Gloucester: Fellowship Press, 1973.

6. *Evangelisation gestern und heute*. Stuttgart: J.F. Steinkopf, 1973.

6a. *Evangelism today. Good News or Bone of Contention?* English edition. Belfast: Christian Journals Ltd, 1976.

7. *Marxist and Kimbanguist Mission: A Comparison*. Birmingham: Birmingham University, 1973. Partly reprinted in "The Amazing Grace of Kimbangu", *The Scotsman* no. 140.600 (14 July 1973), 1.

7a. *Marxistische und kimbanguistische Mission, ein Vergleich*. German edition. *Evangelische Theologie* 34/5 (Sept./Oct. 1974), 434-47.

7b. *La misión kimbanguista: una comparación*. Spanish edition. *Estudios ecuménicos* 25 (1975), 26-41, 8.

8. *Pentecost between Black and White. Five Case Studies on Pentecost and Politics* Belfast: Christian Journals Ltd., 1974.

8a. *De Geest spreekt alle talen: Een analyse van de Pinksterbeweging*. Oekumene VIII/1. Dutch edition, Baarn: Bosch & Keuning, 1976.

8b. *Christen ohne Schriften: Fünf Fallstudien zur Sozialethik mündlicher Religion*. Erlanger Taschenbücher 38. German edition. Erlangen: Verlag der Ev.-Luth. Mission, 1977.

9. *Glaube, Geist und Geister: Professor Unrat zwischen Bangkok und Birmingham*. Frankfurt: Otto Lembeck, 1975.

9a. *Mr. Chips. Fact and Fiction*. English edition, Ms. only.

10. With Theodor Ahrens, *Volkschristentum und Volksreligion im Pazifik: Wiederentdeckung des Mythos für den christlichen Glauben*. Schriftenreihe der Missionsakademie an der Universität Hamburg: Perspektiven der Weltmission, Bd 4. Frankfurt: Otto Lembeck, 1977. Hollenweger's contribution: "Kilibob und der Mythos der Weissen", 81-105, 117-24.

11. *Konflikt in Korinth. Memoiren eines alten Mannes: Zwei narrative Exegesen zu 1. Kor. 12-14 und Ez. 37*. Kaiser Traktate 31. Munich: Kaiser, 1978 and 1987-5.

11a. *Conflit à Corinthe*. French edition. Supplément à la Voix Protestante: Région Est, No. 1, (January 1979).

11b. *Conflict in Corinth. Memoirs of an Old Man*. English edition. New York: Paulist Press, 1982.

11c. *Memoirs of a Babylonian Exile*. Indian edition (part reprint). Madras: The Christian Literature Society, 1985.

11d. *Conflito a Corinto: Esperienze ad Efeso. Saggi di interpretazione narrative della Biblia*. Italian edition (together with no. 13). Serie Biblica, no. 46. Torino: Claudia-

na, 1986.
11e. *Konflik di Korintus & Buku kenangan seorang tua. Dua cerita yang memberi terang tentang cara Kitab Suci ditulis.* Indonesian edition. Yogyakarta: Penerbit Yaasan Kanisius, 1984.
12. *Erfahrungen der Leibhaftigkeit. Interkulturelle Theologie 1.* Munich: Kaiser, 1979.
13. *Erfahrungen in Ephesus. Darstellung eines Davongekommenen: Drei narrative Exegesen zu 1. Mose 8.15-22; Joh. 6.1-15 und Offb. 21.1-6.* Kaiser Traktate 46. Munich: Kaiser, 1979 and 1985-3.
13a. *Experience in Ephesus.* English edition, Ms.
14. *Wie aus Grenzen Brücken werden: Ein theologisches Lesebuch.* Munich: Kaiser, 1980.
15. *Besuch bei Lukas: Vier narrative Exegesen zu 2. Mose 14, Lukas 2.1-14, 2. Kor. 6.4-11 und Lukas 10.1-10.* Kaiser Traktate 64. Munich: Kaiser, 1981 and 1986-2.
15a. *Hard Times.* English edition, Ms.
16. *Umgang mit Mythen. Interkulturelle Theologie 2.* Munich: Kaiser, 1982.
16a. *Myths of Renewal and Renewal of Myths.* English edition, Ms.
17. *Jüngermesse/Gomer: Das Gesicht des Unsichtbaren.* Munich: Kaiser, 1983.
17a. *Hokhma 32.* French edition, 1-11.
18. *Zwingli zwischen Krieg und Frieden, erzählt von seiner Frau.* Kaiser Traktate 76. Munich: Kaiser, 1983 and 1984-2. Reprint: Kindhausen, Switzerland: Metanoia Verlag, 1992.
18a. *Anna Zwingli-Reinhart à sa fille Regula.* Partial French translation in: *Réforme* (1984), 2047-57.
18b. *Zwingli - Prophet or Secularizer.* English edition, Ms.
19. *Das Fest der Verlorenen: Die Bibel erzählt, getanzt und gesungen.* Kaiser Traktate 82. Munich: Kaiser, 1984.
19a. *The Feast of the Lost.* English edition, Ms.
20. *Der Handelsreisende Gottes/Totentanz zum neuen Leben (Passionsliturgie): Im Rössli zu Emmaus (Osterliturgie).* Munich: Kaiser, 1985.
21. With Hans-Jürgen Hufeisen, *Das Wagnis des Glaubens: Ein Spiel über die Mission für Sprecher, Instrumentalisten, Bewegungstheater und Gemeinde.* Munich: Kaiser, 1986. Dramatised version under the same title by Metanoia Verlag, Postfach 15, CH 8963 Kindhausen, Switzerland, 1991.
21a. *The Adventure of Faith.* English edition, Ms.
22. With Hans-Jürgen Hufeisen, *Im Schatten Seines Friedens: Ein Weihnachtsoratorium.* Renningen: Peter Marquardt, 1986, privately published.
23. *Mirjam, Mutter/Michal: Die Frauen meines Mannes: Zwei Monodramen.* Freiburg, Switzerland: Exodus Verlag, 1987.
24. *Ostertanz der Frauen,* 1987, privately published be Peter Marquardt, Silberger Weg 19, D 7253 Renningen, Germany. Enlarged and reprinted version by Metanoia Verlag, Kindhausen, 1991.
25. *Geist und Materie: Interkulturelle Theologie 3.* Munich: Kaiser, 1988.
25a. Abridged French version of nos. 12. 16 and 25 under the title *L'Expérience de l'Esprit. Jalons pour une théologie interculturelle.* Geneva: Labor et Fides, 1991.
26. With Heyno Kattenstedt. *Jörg Ratgeb, Maler und Bauernkanzler erlebt die Passion*

Jesu Christi (oratorio). Kindhausen, Switerzland: Metanoia Verlag, 1992.

27. *Veni Creator Spiritus: Eine Pfingstliturgie.* Kindhausen, Switzerland: Metanoia, 1991.
28. *Hiob oder die Wette Gottes.* Kindhausen, Switzerland: Metanoia, 1991.
30. *Requim für Bonhoeffer. Den Toten aller Völker.* Privately published by Peter Marquardt, Renningen, 1989 (see 24). With Music and Choreography published by Metanoia Verlag, Kindhausen, 1991.
31. *Kommet her zu mir alle, die ihr mühselig und beladen seid. Die zehn Aussätzigen.* Zwei Segnungsgottesdienste. Kindhausen, Switzerland: Metanoia Verlag, 1991.
33. *Fontana. Die Frau am Brunnen und der siebte Mann. Herr, bleibe bei uns, denn es will Abend werden.* Salbungsliturgie zu Luk. 7.36-50. Kindhausen, Switzerland: Metanoia Verlag, 1991.
35. With Peter Bubman. *Der Knabe und die Mondin.* A Ballet Liturgy for Ballet and Orchestra. Munich: Strube Verlag, 1991.

Books Edited

50. *Tracts of the Traktatverlag der Schweiz.* Pfingstmission, ca. 1951-55:
    No. 1: *Der Untergang des Abendlandes.*
    No. 10: *Wo sind unsere Toten?.*
    No. 13: *Ein Mann lebt nach Tod und Begrägnis.*
    No. 14: *Sprung ins neue Jahr*
    No. 17: *Hemmungen.*
    No. 204: *Ich sah 3 Millionen Menschen, die sich vor Gott beugten.*
    No. 206: *Wir können nicht anders.*
    No. 207: *Tatsachen.*
51. *Concept.* Issues in English, French, German, Spanish and Italian. Geneva: WCC, 1965-1971.
52. *Monthly Letter about Evangelism - Monatlicher Informationsbrief über Evangelisation - Lettre meninelle sur l'évangélisation.* Geneva: WCC, 1965-1971 (some issues in Spanish and Portuguese).
53. With Georges Casalis and Paul Keller (eds.). *Vers une église pour les autres: A la recherche de structures pour des communautés missionaires.* Geneva: Labor et Fides, 1966.
54. *The Church for Others and the Church for the World: A Quest for Strutures for Missionary Congregations.* Final Report of the Western European Working Group and North American Working Group of the Department on Studies in Evangelism. Geneva: WCC, 1967.

54a. *Die Kirche für andere und die Kirche für die Welt im Ringen um Strukturen missionarischer Gemeinden.* Schlußberichte der Westeuropäischen und der Nordamerikanischen Arbeitsgruppe des Referats für Fragen der Verkündigung. German edition. Geneva: WCC, 1967.

54b. *La iglesia para otros. Una busqueda de estructuras para congregaciones missioneras.* Spanish edition. La Paz (Bolivia): Instituto Boliviano de Estudio y Accion Social, 1967.

54c. *Uma igreja para o mundo. Estudo das estruturas missionárias da congregaçâo.* Portuguese edition. S. Paulo: Ediçôes Oikoumene, 1969.

55. *Die Pfingstkirchen: Selbstdarstellungen, Dokumente, Kommentare.* Die Kirchen der Welt VII. Stuttgart: Ev. Verlagswerk, 1971.

56. *Studies in the Intercultural History of Christianity.* Frankfurt, Bern, Paris, New York: Lang, 1974 ff. German, French and English.

57. *Pentecostal Research in Europe: Problems, Promises and People. Proceedings from the Pentecostal Research Conference at the University of Birmingham (England) April 26th to 29th, 1984.* Studies in the Intercultural History of Christianity 39. Frankfurt: Lang.

58. *Kirche, Benzin und Bohnensuppe: Auf den Spuren dynamischer Gemeinden.* Zürich: TVZ, 1971.

Collective Works/Introductions to Books of Other Authors

1955

55.09 Dr. A. Guggenbühl (W.J. Hollenweger acting secretary), "Antwort auf die Angriffe gegen William Branham und gegen die Verkündigung biblischer Wahrheit". *Branham-Komitee*, 1955, 1 ff.

1965

65.10 "Christus intra et extra muros ecclesia". In: H.J. Marqull, ed. *Mission als Strukturprinzip*, 1965, 55-57, 145-46.

65.10a "Christus intra et extra muros ecclesia". In: Th. Wieser, ed. *Planning for Mission*, 1966, 56-60.

65.10b "Christus intra et extra muros ecclesia". In: Georges Casalis ed. *Vers une église pour les autres*, 1966, 32-35.

1966

66.04 "Emil Brunner. Eine Geschichte in Porträts". In: H.J. Schulz, ed. *Tendenzen der Theologie im 20. Jahrhundert*, 1966, 360-67.

66.20 Vorwort: "Wert und Problematiek des Sprachenredens". In: Arnold Bittlinger. *Glossolalia: Wert und Problematiek etc.*, 1966, 5 ff.

1967

67.16 "Vollmacht in der Kirche". In: Hanno Heibling, ed. *Kirche im Wandel der Zeit*, 1968, 26-32.

67.18 Vorwort. In: Jack Mendelsohn. *Der Urwalddoktor von Peru. Dr. Theodor Binder und sein 'Amazones-Hospital Albert Schweitzer'*, 1968.

1968

68.04 "Ein wegweisender Versuch, Kommentar". In: *Ev. Presseverband für Baden,*

1968, 14-16.
68.20 "Funktionen der ekstatischen Frömmigkeit der Pfingstbewegung". In: Th. Spoerri, ed. *Beiträge zur Ekstase*, 1968, 57-72.

1969

69.02 "Dialogisch predigen". In: Ernst Lange. *Predigtstudien für das Kirchenjahr*, 1969, 203-10.
69.10 "Der Gottesdienst". In: H.J. Girock, ed. *Notstand in der Kirche?* (16 January 1969), 69-94.
69.21 "Aufbau der Kirche und Anspruch der Welt". *Von Uppsala nach?*, II/1.
69.25 "Interkommunion ist viel zu wenig". In: Arnold Bittlinger. *Das Abendmahl in Neuen Testament und in die frühen Kirche*, 1969, 66-71.
69.26 "Enthusiastisches Christentum in Brasilien". In: Theo Tschuy, ed. *Explosives Lateinamerika. Der Protestantismus inmitten der sozialen Revolution*, 1969, 97-106.
69.28 "Anstelle eines Nachwortes". In: Heinrich Hellstern, *Mississippi*, 1969, 66-68.
69.29 Some chapters for: "Offene Kirche-kritische Kirche". In: W. Simpfendörfer. *Offene Kirche - kritische Kirche*, 1969, 66-68.

1970

70.06 "Adventisten". In: Hans-Dieter Bastian, ed. *Lexicon für junge Erwachsene. Religion, Gesellschaft, Politik*, 1970.
Also the subjects: Altkatholische Kirche, Anglikanische Kirche, Baptisten, Brüdergemeinde, Freikirche, Jehovas Zeugen, Methodisten, Mormonen, Neuapostolische Gemeinde, Quäcker, and Sekten.
70.07 With A.H. van den Heuvel. "Silvester: Psalm 121". *Predigtstudien V/1*, 79-90.
70.11c "Flori i canti. Un contributo messicano all hermeneutica teologica". In: Raniero La Valle, ed. *Le Chiese e la guerra*, 1972, 141-55.
70.23 "Nachwort". In: Liebje Kuylman-Hoekendijk, *Christen nach Mass? Plädoyer für die Vielfalt*, 1970.
70.25 "Protestantisches Missionsverständnis". *Università del sacro cuora, Le missioni e l'unita dei Cristiani* (8 Sept. 1969), 45-58.
70.25a "Il Concetto di Missione nel Protestantesimo". *Università del sacro cuora, Le missioni e l'unita dei Cristiani* (8 Sept. 1969), 171-83.
70.25b "Where no Nightingales are Singing. A Dialogue with Ignazio Silone". *Le missioni e l'unita dei Cristiani*, 1970.

1971

71.20 "Einführung". *Die Pfingstkirchen*, 1971, 15-25.
71.21 "Ein Forschungsbericht". *Die Pfingstkirchen*, 1971, 307-46.
71.29 "Der inhalt des einen Zeugnisses. Die Ausrichtung des einen Zeugnisses, Gottesdienst". In: Ff. Hasselhof and H.Krüger, eds. *Ökumene in Schule und Gemeinde*, 1971, 220-42; 550-54.

1972

72.28 "Einführung". In: Christian D. Schmidt. *Zeit des Gerichts oder Gericht der Zeit?*, 1972, 7-9.

72.31 "Le Pentecôtisme et le Tiers Monde. Problèmes théologiques d'une église prolétarienne". In: K. and D. Ranaghan. *Le Pentecôtisme catholique aux Etats-Unis*, 1972, 226-35. See also 69.15b. The Lutheran World Federation, Geneva, has also a German and an English version of this essay (dupl.).

1973

73.01 "Camp meetings". In: J.G. Davies, ed. *A Dictionary of Christian Liturgy and Worship*, 1973, 110 ff.

73.01a "Experimental Forms of Worship". In: J.G. Davies, ed. *A Dictionary of Christian Liturgy and Worship*, 1973, 178 ff.

73.01b "Liturgies Pentecostal". In: J.G. Davies, ed. *A Dictionary of Christian Liturgy and Worship*, 1973, 241.

73.01c "Open Air Meetings". In: J.G. Davies, ed. *A Dictionary of Christian Liturgy and Worship*, 1973, 285.

73.01d "Pentecostal Ordination". In: J.G. Davies, ed. *A Dictionary of Christian Liturgy and Worship*, 1973, 295 ff.

73.01e "Spirituals". In: J.G. Davies, ed. *A Dictionary of Christian Liturgy and Worship*, 1973, 340 ff.

73.01f "Pentecostal Worship". In: J.G. Davies, ed. *A Dictionary of Christian Liturgy and Worship*, 1973, 311 ff.

73.11 "Ostersonntag: Markus 16.1-8". In: Ernst Lange, ed. *Predigtstudien für das Kirchenjahr 1972/73*, 1973, 16-28.

73.16 "The Gift of the Spirit". *Bible Reading Fellowship Publication*, 1973.

73.22 "Bibelarbeit: Lk 15.20-32". *Wovon leben die Menschen? Bibelarbeiten über Psalm 73, Mk. 8.31-38 und Lk. 15.20-32*, 1973, 138-41. Reprint: Deutscher Evangelischer Kirchentag Düsseldorf, 1973. Dokumente Stuttgart 1973, 143-52.

73.31a "Herr Frei kehrt nach Philadelphia zurück". *Farbe bekennen - Heil für die ganze Welt, Missionsjahrbuch der Schweiz 1973*, 1973, 79-81.

73.31b "Mr. Chips Goes to back to Philadelphia". *Minutes and Reports of the Assembly of the CWME of the WCC 31-12-72 / 12-1-73 Geneva*, 1973, 15-17.

73.32 "Professor Unrat geht nach Bangkok". In: Ph.A. Potter, ed. *Das Heil der Welt heute. Ende oder Beginn der Weltmission*, 1973, 247-57.

73.37 "Contribution to Christianity 2000", (1 July 1973), 13-16.

73.38a "Viele haben vergessen, wie man spielt, Interviews with Sr. Leonore Navarro and Dr. H.R. Weber". *Farbe bekennen. Heil für die ganze Welt?*. Missionsjahrbuch der Schweiz 40 (1973), 33-36.

1974

74.01 "Charismatic and Pentecostal Movements, A Challenge to the churches". In: Dow Kirkpatrick, ed. *The Holy Spirit*, 1974, 209-33.

74.01a "Charismatische und pfingstlerische Bewegungen als Frage an die Kirche Heute". In: Otto Lemebeck und Jos. Knecht. *Wiederentdeckung des Heiligen Geistes*, 1974,

53-75.
74.03 "Professor Unrat auf einer christlichen Party, Erzählung". *Reihe 1000*, 1976, 21-24.
74.03a "Saints in Birmingham". In: A. Bittlinger, ed. *The Church is Charismatic*, 1981, 87-89. Incorporated in no 9a.
74.09 "Schöpferische Freiheit". In: W. Zauner and H. Erharter, eds. *Schöpferische Freiheit - Österreichische Pastoraltagung 27-29 December 1973*, 1974, 33-46.
74.18 Vorwort. In: Morton Kelsey. *Träume-Ihre Bedeutung für den Christen*, 1974, 5.
74.18a Vorwort. In: Morton Kelsey. *Träume-Ihre Bedeutung für den Christen*, 1982, 3.
74.24 With Johanna Wehrli, "1. Kor. 1.4-9, Charmante Christen". *Predigtstudien 11/2*, 1974, 218-25.
74.25 "Evangelism: Bone of Contention or Good News?". In: John E. Francis, ed. *Contemporary Evangelism*, 1974, 61-76. Incorporated in 6a, 76-97.
74.37 "Pentecostal Singing in Tongues". In: Grove, *Grove's Dictionary of Music and Musicians*, 1974.
75.14a "Professor Unrat auf der Suche nach dem vergessenen Glaubensartikel in der pfingstlichen Theologie". In: H.W. Heidland et. al. *Die Charismatische Erneuerung und die Kirchen*, 1977, 43-55.

1975

75.17 "Disputation zwischen zwei Anwälten der Behinderten, Reformpolitiker und Vertreter von Aktionsgruppen". *Deutscher Evangelische Kirchentag, Frankfurt 1975, Dokumente*, 1975, 317-22.
75.18 "Bibelarbeit über Matt. 22.36-46". *Deutscher Evangelische Kirchentag, Frankfurt 1975, Dokumente*, 1975, 108-13.
75.19 "Conversion: L'homme devient homme". In: *Chemins de la Conversion. Rapports échanges, et points de vue de la XLVe semaine de missiologie de Louvain 1975*, 1975, 78-101.

1976

76.01 "Touching and Thinking the Spirit: Some Aspects of European Charismatics". In: Russel Spittler, ed. *Perspectives on the New Pentecostalism*, 1976, 44-56.
76.02 Preface: "Towards a Charismatic Theology". In: Peter Hocken e.a., eds. *New Heaven? New Earth?*, 1976, 9-13.
76.17 "Der Lebendige Geist und die Angst". In: H. Schmidt et. al. *Der Geist und die Geister: Drei Beiträge zu der Vielvalt religiöser Formen in unserer Zeit*, 1976, 39-59.
76.18 "Mr. Chips in Switzerland. International symposium on prospects for worship, religious architecture and socio-religious studies". In: J.G. Davies, ed. *Looking to the Future*, 1976, 13-33.
76.19 With Harold Tonks, "Eine Vision durch das Chaos hindurch, Offenb. 4.1-8". *Predigtstudien IV/2*, 1976, 271-77.
76.20 "Mr. Chips at a Black Church in Birmingham". *Pastoral Studies Spring School*, 1976, 25-27.

1977

77.04 With Harold Tonks, "Das Geschrei der Unmündigen und der Gesang der Christen Matth. 21.14-17". *Predigtstudien V/2*, 1977, 47-51.

77.12 Preface: "Inspiration from Latin America". In: Derek Winter, *Hope in Captivity - The Prophetic Church in Latin America*, 1977, 11-13.

77.13 With H. Tonks, "1 Joahnnes 3.1-6: Schaut her!". *Predigtstudien VI/1*, 1977, 46-51.

77.14 "The Ecumenical Dimension of the Charismatic and Pentecostal Movements and the Charismatic Dimension of the Ecumenical Movement". *Spirituality and Ecumenism*, 1977, 55-60.

77.15 "Schöpferische Liturgie, Dokumentation über den 16. Ev. Kirchbautag, Kassel 1976". In: Rainer Bürgel and Ulr. Conrads, *Umgang mit Raum*, 1977, 89-98, 128.

77.22 "The Role of Theology in a Pluralistic World. Staff Conference at St. Paul's College 22/24-4-1977". *The Future of Religious Studies in the Colleges*, (23 April 1977), 1-15.

1978

78.04 "Erfahrung der Welt - Erfahrung des Glaubens". *Lichte der Reformation*, 1978, 16-20. Incorporated in no. 12, 13-16.

78.06 With H. Tonks, "Ostermontag: Hes. 37.1-14. Was neu ist das Leben?". *Predigtstudien VI/2*, 1978, 17-24.

78.07 With H. Tonks, "Trinitatis: Eph. 1.3-14, Erwählung in die Freiheit". *Predigtstudien VI/2*, 1978, 88-95.

78.08 Preface: "Creative Scholarship". In: Mary Hall, *A Quest for the Liberated Christian, examined on the basis of a mission, a Man and a Movement as Agents of Liberation*. Studies in the Intercultural History of Christianity 19, 1978, 8-10.

78.09 "The Responsibility of a Minority Church", *Regina*, 1978, 16-23.

78.14 "Immanuel, das heißt: Gott mit uns". In: H. Leuendorff, ed. *Daß ich schaue Bethlehem*, 1980, 7-10.

78.19 "Barabara". In: Drutmar Crember, ed. *Sing mir das Lied meiner Erde-Bitten um den Geist*, 1978, 179 ff. Incorporated in no. 12, 198 ff.

78.21 "Heiligenabend Mattäus 1.1-7, 18-21, 22-25, Geboren von der Jungfrau Maria. Ein Briefwechsel zum Geheimnis der Jungfrauengeburt". *Predigtstudien I/1*, 1978, 56-63.

1979

79.06 "Le livre oral. Portées sociale, politique et théologique des religions orales". In: G. Poujol et R. Labourie, eds. *Les Cultures Populaires. Permanence et émergences des cultures minoritaires locales, ethnisques, sociales et religieuses*, 1979, 123-34. German: Incorporated in no. 12, 69-84.

79.11 "Freischwebende Religiosität, Eine Herausforderung an unsere Spiritualität". In: Th. Schober und Hans Thimme, ed. *Gemeinde in diakonischer und missionarischer Verantwortung*, 1979, 227-31.

79.12 Personal contribution. In: Heinz Ed. Tödt et. al., eds. *Wie eine Flaschenpost - Ökumenische Briefe und Beiträge für Eberhard Bethge*, 1979, 194-196.

79.13a "Towards a Church Renewed and United in the Spirit". In: A. Bittlinger, ed. *The Church is Charismatic - The World Council of Churches and the Charismatic Renewal*, 1981, 21-28.

79.14 "Allein auf verlorenem Posten". *Themenstudien 3*, 1979, 96-103.

79.27 Several contributions. In: G. Kugler, ed. *Forum Abendmahl*, 1979, 62-64; 67-71; 165-71.

79.28 "Bekehrung". Article: Praktische Theologie. *Theol. Realenzyklopädie* 5, 1979, 480 ff.

79.30 Nachwort: "Wider das Geschäft mit der Angst". In: Josy Doyon, *Hirten ohne Erbarmen - Zehn Jahre Zeugin Jehovas, der Bericht eines Irrweges*, 1979, 326-30.

79.37 "Der Grund des Glaubens". In: *Deutscher Evangelischer Kirchentag*, Nürnberg, 1979, 98-106.

1980

80.10 "Chancen und Schwierigkeiten interkultureller Theologie". In: J. Brantschen/Selvatico. ed. *Unterwegs zur Einheit - Festschrift für Heinrich Stirnimann*, 1980, 854-74.

80.13 "Roots and Fruits of the Charismatic Renewal in the third world: Implications for Mission". In: D. Martin and P. Mullen, eds. *Strange Gifts. A Guide to Charismatic Renewal*, 1984, 172-91.

80.20 "Vom Umgang mit Mythen". In: Rainer Bürgel, *Bauen mit Geschichte*, 1980, 49-57.

1981

81.11 "Wir sind Gäste am Tisch des Herrn". In: Fritz Baltruweit, ed. *Fürchte nicht. Lieder und Gedichte zum Kirchentag*, 1981, 54-56. Incorporated in no. 17.

81.19 With John Adegoke, Markus 9.17-27 - Heilung, Theorie und Praxis, *Predigtstudien III/2*, 1981, 225-31.

81.20 "Geleitwort eines Betroffenen". In: Werner Keller, *Zur Freiheit berufen - Die Geschichte der presbyterianischen Kirche in Kamerun*, 1981, 20-31.

81.21 "Making the Invisible Unity Visible". In: James Haire. *The Character and Theological struggle of the Church in Halmahera, Indonesia*, 1981, x-xii.

81.22 "Die Kimanbuistenkirche". In: A. Lehmann, ed. *Gottes Volk in vielen Ländern - Ein Lesbuch*, 1981, 193-209. Reprint from no. 8b.

81.23 Introduction. In: A. Bittlinger, ed. *The Church is Charismatic - The World Council of Churches and the Charismatic Renewal*, 1981, 1-4.

81.24 "Szenen aus dem ökumenischen Alltag". In: H.Dauber and W.Simpfendörfer. *Eigener Haushalt und bewohnter Erdkreis. Oekologisches und ökumenisches Lernen in der 'Einen Welt'*, 1981, 12-27.

81.27 Foreword: "Karl Barth as a Narrative Theologian". In: David Ford, *Barth and God's Story*. Studies in the Intercultural History of Christianity 27, 1981, 6-8.

81.34 Preface: "The Challenge of Apostles and Prophets". In: James E. Worsfold. *The Catholic and Apostolic Ministry of the Apostle and Prophet*, 1981, 3-5.

81.35 "Papst und Pfingstler, Ökumene und Charisma". In: R. Flasche and E. Geldbach. *Religionen, Geschichte, Ökumene*, 1981, 171-80.

1982

82.16 "Religiöse Standortbestimmung im Rahmen einer Einführung in eine moderne Mythologie". *EKD Texte 4*, 1982, 2-8.

82.19 "The House Churches-a Challenge for Intercultural Theology". In: Joyce V. Thurman. *New Wineskins-A Study of the House Church Movement.* Studies in the Intercultural History of Christianity 30, 1982, 8-10.

1983

83.07a "Afrikanische unabhängige Kirchen". *Ökumene Lexicon - Kirchen. Religionen. Bewegungen,* 1983, 25-26.

83.07b "Charismatische Bewegung". *Ökumene Lexikon - Kirchen. Religionen. Bewegungen,* 1983, 213-15.

83.07c "Heiligungsbewegung". *Ökumene Lexicon - Kirchen. Religionen. Bewegungen,* 1983, 525-26.

83.07d "Kultureller Kontext". *Ökumene Lexicon - Kirchen. Religionen. Bewegungen,* 1983, 726-32.

83.07e "Pfingstbewegung". *Ökumene Lexikon - Kirchen. Religionen. Bewegungen,* 1983, 951-55.

83.07f "Prophetie". *Ökumene Lexikon - Kirchen. Religionen. Bewegungen,* 1983, 982-984.

83.08 "Charismatische Bewegungen". In: *Taschenlexikon Religion und Theologie I,* 1983, 243-46.

83.13 A contribution. In: Peter Weishaus, *Religion von gestern in der Welt von Heute,* 1983, 76-86.

83.14a "All Creatures Great and Small: Towards a Pneumatology of Life". In: David Martin and Peter Mullen, eds. *Strange Gifts. A Guide to Charismatic Renewal,* 1984, 41-53.

83.21 "Glosolalia". In: *A New Dictionary of Christian Theology* (1983), 225 ff.

83.27 Forword: "Pentecostal Research. Problems and Promises". In: Charles Edwin Jones, *A Guide to the Study of the Pentecostal Movement.* ATLA Bibliography Series 6, 1983, vii-ix.

1984

84.09 "Die Bibel - das Buch der Befreiten". In: H.J. Luhmann and G. Neveling-Wagener. *Deutscher Ev. Kirchentag Hannover 1983. Dokumente,* 1984, 387-89.

1985

85.09 "Was Bonhoeffer von der Negern lernte". In: Madeleine Strub-Jaccoud and Hans Strub, eds. *Wegzeichen gelebten Evangeliums - Festschrift Marga Bührig,* 1985, 78-83.

85.12 "Kultur und Evangelium". *Evangelische Mission - Jahrbuch 17,* 1985, 52-60.

85.17 Preface: "Towards an Indigenous Christianity in India". In: Solomon Raj. *A Christian Folk-Religion in India.* Studies in the Intercultural History of Christianity 40, 1986.

1986

86.06 "Pentecostals and the Charismatic Movement". In: Chesly Jones et. al., eds. *The Study of Spirituality*, 1986, 549-54.

86.13 "La signification oecuménique de la recherche sur le spiritualité pentecôtiste". In: Daniel Brandt-Bessire. *Aux sources de la spiritualité pentecôtiste*, 1986, 13-33.

86.15 Preface: "The Spirit's Call to Repentance". In: Peter Hocken. *Streams of Renewal - The Origins and Early Development of the Charismatic Movement in Great Britain*, 1986, 7 ff.

1987

87.04a "Charismatic Movements". In: Alistair V. Campbell, ed. *A Dictionary of Pastoral Care*, 1987, 32 ff.

87.04b "Intercultural Pastoral Care". In: Alistair V. Campbell, ed. *A Dictionary of Pastoral Care*, 1987, 135 ff.

87.04c "Tongues". In: Alistair V. Campbell, ed. *A Dictionary of Pastoral Care*, 1987, 280.

87.04d "Spirit". In: Alistair V. Campbell, ed. *A Dictionary of Pastoral Care*, 1987, 264 ff.

87.08 "The Pentecostal Churches". In: Peter Bishop and M.Darton, eds. *The Encyclopedia of World Faiths. An Illustrated Survey of the World's Living Religions*, 1987, 133 ff.

87.09 "Wie aus Grenzen Brücken werden. Elemente einer interkulturellen Theologie". *Wissenschaft im Spannungsfeld zwischen den Kulturen*, 1987, 99-114.

87.15 "Prophetie". In: *K.Müller und Th.Sundermeier. Lexikon Missionstheologischer Grundbegriffe*, 1987, 394-99.

1988

88.04 "Was ist das Wort Gottes?". In: *Kreativität im Religionsunterricht*, 1988, 25-36. Dokumentation der Fortbildungstagung für Evangelische Religionslehrer in Mariazell vom 22-27 März 1987. Incorporated in no. 25.

88.05 "Von der monokulturellen Exegese zur interkulturellen Theologie". In: *Kreativität im Religionsunterricht*, 1988, 37-60. See no. 88.04.

88.11 Preface: "African and Western Medicine in Dialogue". In: Abraham âdu Berinyuu. *Pastoral Care to the Sick in Afrika*. Studies in the Intercultural History of Christianity 51, 1988, iii-vi.

88.21 "Junge Kirchen". In: *Theolog. Realenzyklopädie*, Vol. 17, 1988, 454-461.

88.30 Preface: "A Language between Experience and Faith". In: Jean-Daniel Plüss, *Therapeutic and Prophetic Narrratives in Worship*. Studies in the Intercultural History of Christianity 54, 1988.

88.33 Foreword. In: William Robinson, *Let us break bread together: A Guide to the Administration of the Lord's Supper*, 1988, 4 f.

88.38 Foreword: "Pentecostalism, Promises and Problems". In: Iain MacRobert. *The Black Roots and White Racism of Early Pentecostalism in the U.S.A.*, (1988), xi-xv.

1990

90.04 "Black Christian Interpretation". In: *A Dictionary of Biblical Interpretation*, 1990,

90-92.
90.11 Preface: "Can Economists Be Converted?". In: Jane Collier. *The Culture of Economism. An exploration of barriers to faith-as-praxis*. Studies on the Intercultural History of Christianity 65, 1990, ix-x.
90.14 "The theological challenge of indigenous churches". In: F. Turner. A.F. Walls and Wilbert R. Shenk, eds. *Exploring new Religious Movements*, 1990, 163-67.
90.27 "Heilungsbewegungen". In: *Lexikon der Sekten, Sondergruppen und Weltanschauungen*, 1990, 448-55.
90.36 "Elemente einer interkulturellen Theologie". In: Büttner/Winkler, *Musikgeographie, Weltliche und geistliche Bläsermusik in ihren Beziehungen und zu ihrer Umwelt*, 1990, 151-55.

1991

91.06 "Priorities in Pentecostal Research: Historiography, Missiology, Hermeneutics and Pneumatology". In: Jan A.B. Jongeneel, ed. *Experiences of the Spirit - Conference on Pentecostal and Charismatic Research in Europe at Utrecht University 1989*. Studies in the Intercultural History of Christianity 68, 1991, 7-22.
91.33 Foreword: "The Heart and the Head". In: Cornelis van der Laan, *Sectarian Against His Will: Gerrit Roelof Polman and the Birth of Pentecostalism in the Netherlands*. Studies in Evangelicalism 11, 1991, xi-xiii.
91.35 "Fontana, die Frau am Brunnen und der siebte Mann Bible Study". In: Konrad von Bonin, ed. *Deutscher Evangelische Kirchentag Ruhrgebiet 1991*, 1991, 179-90.

Articles

1945

45.01 "Ganz zu Christus hin". *Verheissung des Vaters* 38/07 (1 July 1945), 10 ff.
45.02 "Wir und die Welt". *Verheissung des Vaters* 38/08 (1 August 1945), 11-13.
45.03 "Freiheit, die ich meine". IVerheissung des Vaters 38/09 (1 September 1945), 16.

1946

46.01 "Vom Lernen". *Verheissung des Vaters* 39/01 (1 October 1946), 21-22.
46.02 "Die Reinheit ist mir verloren gegangen!". *Verheissung des Vaters* 39/12 (1 December 1946), 14-16.

1947

47.01 "Preis des Leides". *Verheissung des Vaters* 40/05 (1 May 1947), 15 ff.

1948

48.01 "Zwei Monate I.B.T.I.". *Verheissung des Vaters* 41/12 (1 December 1948), 12 ff.

1949

49.01 "Onesimus". *Verheissung des Vaters* 42/01 (1 January 1949), 4 ff.

1950

50.01 "Der Vogel hat ein Nest gefunden. Saaleinweihung am 13 August in Zürich". *Verheissung des Vaters* 43/09 (1 September 1950), 17-21.

1951

51.01 "Jugendlager Sils". *Verheissung des Vaters* 44/12 (1 December 1951), 14 ff.
51.02 "Ferienlager 'Les Pinsons'". MIVerheissung des Vaters 44/11 (1 November 1951), 16 ff, 24.
51.03 "Durch Busse zur Herrlichkeit". *Verheissung desVaters* 44/10 (1 October 1951), 6-8.
51.04 "Jugendkonferenz Zürich". *Verheissung des Vaters* 44/06 (1 June 1951), 11-13.
51.05 "Welche praktische Massnahmen können wir ergreifen zur Erretung unserer Mitmenschen". *Verheissung des Vaters* 44/02 (1 February 1951), 5-7.
51.06 "Quer durch die Schweiz - ein Tatsachenbericht, Zürich". *Verheissung des Vaters* 44/03 (1 March 1951), 11-13.
51.06 "Quer durch die Schweiz - ein Tatsachenbericht, Bern". MIVerheissung des Vaters 44/10 (1 October 1951), 13-16.

1952

52.01 "Eine Klarstellung loc. cit., Wen soll ich senden? Wer wird uns gehen?". *Verheissung des Vaters* 45/04 (1 April 1952), 16.
52.01 "Wen soll ich senden? Wer wird uns gehen? Jes. 6.8". *Verheissung des Vaters* 45/02 (1 February 1952), 4 ff.
52.02 "Christus unser Beispiel Phil. 2.5-11". *Verheissung des Vaters* 45/07 (1 July 1952), 10-12.

1953

53.01 "Le missionnaire discret". *L'Appel du Maitre* (1 February 1953), 1910-12.
53.02 "Aus meinem Leben". *Jugendbote der Freien Christengemeinde in Österreich*, Heft 3 (1 July 1953), 2-5.

1954

54.01 "Kirche und Sekte". *Verheissung des Vaters* 47/6 (1 June 1954), 5-7.
54.02 "Grosse Evangelisationversammlungen in Freiburg". *Verheissung des Vaters* 47/1 (1 January 1954), 12-14.
54.03 "Über das Studium". MIVerheissung des Vaters 47/1 (1 January 1954), 12-14.

1955

55.01 "Warum ich weiss, dass die Bibel Gottes Wort ist" *Verheissung des Vaters* 48/11 (1 November 1955), 4 ff.
55.02 "Segenstage in Zürich, Evangelist Tommy Hicks predigt zu Tausenden im Züricher Kongresshaus". *Verheissung des Vaters* 48/6 (1 June 1955), 1 ff.

1957

57.01 "Die Grösse Christi Kol. 1.13-28". *Verheissung des Vaters*, 50/8 (1 August 1957), 9 ff.

1961

61.01 "Kirche hinter dem Eisernen Vorhang". *Zwinglibund* 28/9 (1 September 1961), 110-12.

1962

62.01 "Der Mensch im Mittelpunkt" *Der Fürsorger* 30/4-5 (1 October 1962), 99-107.

1963

63.01 "An Approach to Pentecostalism, Religion and Emotion". *Methodist Recorder* III (31 January 1963).

63.02 "Not und Verheissung unserer Bibelarbeit". *Die Pflugschar* 56/4 (1 January 1963), 55-58.

63.03 "Aus dem weltweiten Echo auf Emil Brunners Theologie". *Reformatio* 12/8 (1 August 1963), 441-48.

63.04 "Wurzeln der Theologie Emil Brunners. Aus Brunners Theologischer Entwicklung von ca. 1913 bis 1918". *Reformatio* 12/10 (1 October 1963), 579-87. Incorporated in no. 6 and 6a.

63.05 "Die Reformation". *Die Volkshochschule* 32/10 (1 June 1963), 289-96. Partly incorporated in no. 12, 299-28.

63.05 "Die Reformation". *Evangelisches Schulblatt* 104/1 (1 January 1969), 3-9.

63.06 "Ökumene im Kleinen" *Kirchenbote des Kantons Zürich* (1 June 1963), 11. Partly incorporated in no. 12, 299-328

63.07 "Der Werkmeister in der heutigen Wirtschaftslage". *Werkmeisterzeitung* 70/28 (8 July 1963), 728 ff.

63.08 "Ostpreusen deutsch und frei!". *Evangelische Woche* 44/29 (19 July 1963), 4.

1964

64.01 "Das Prophetische und das Kirchliche in der Reformationszeit: Der Aufbau Schweiz". *Frieden und Freiheit Wochenzeitschrift Recht* 45/38 (10 August 1964), 299-303.

64.02 "Das Prophetische und das Kirchliche in der Reformationszeit,Der Aufbau Schweiz". *Medizin Presse Zürich*, no. 17 (22 June 1964), 1 ff.

64.03 "Geschäftsmann und Christ!". *Evangelische Woche* 18/4 (1 January 1964), 4.

64.04 "Enthusiastisches Christentum in Brasilien". *Reformatio* 13/8 (1 August 1964), 484-88. Enlarged translations of this article are incorporated in no. 4, 99-115. In English: no.4a-1, 4a-2, 4b-1, 4b-2, 4b-3, 75-110. In Spanish: no. 4c, 131-61. In Portuguese: see no. 69.12.

64.05 "Wieder etwas neues?". *Evangelisches Gemeindeblatt für die Diaspora der Zentralschweiz und des Kantons Tessin* 51/6 (1 June 1964), 1 ff.

64.06 "Mensch und Arbeit. Ein kirchlich-theologischer Kurs für Nichttheologen".

Tagesanzeiger (2 October 1964), 21 ff.

64.07 "Toleranz, Liebe, Wahrheit". *Schweizer Monatshefte* 44/2 (1 May 1964), 140-43.

64.08 "In Chile wirken religiöse Socialrevolutionäre". *Tagesanzeiger* (25 April 1964), 1 ff.

64.09 "Oral Roberts: Gott ist ein guter Gott!". *Tagesanzeiger* (14 July 1964), 3.

64.10 "Unternehmertagung auf Boldern". *Neue Zürcher Zeitung Mittagsausgabe*, no. 2719 (22 June 1962).

64.11 "Das Verhältnis zwischen Pfingstbewegung und Oekumene in Afrika, Vervielf". *Seperatum des Ökumenisch-Missionarischen Amtes* (3 April 1964), 1 ff.

64.12 "Ein Gespräch am Runden Tisch: Theologie = Sabotage an der Bibel?, Interview". *Kirchenbote für den Kanton Zürich* 50/5 (1 May 1964), 4 ff.

64.13 "Ökumene im Kleinen". *Kirchenblatt für die reformierte Schweiz* 120/12 (11 June 1964), 187.

64.14 "Die ungemütliche Dynamik". *Die Tat* (26 June 1964).

64.15 "Das Berufsbild des Arztes". *Tagesanzeiger* (26 June 1964).

1965

65.01 "Geschäfstmann und Christ". *Kirchenbote für den Kanton Zürich* 51/3B (16 March 1965), 2.

65.02 "Pfingsten - Stosskraft und Bewegung". *Evangelisches Gemeindeblatt für die Diaspora der Zentralschweiz und des Kantons Tessin* 52/6 (1 June 1965), 7.

65.03 "Der Heilige Geist in der Pfingstbewegung und in der Reformierten Kirche". *Kirchenbote für den Kanton Zürich* 51/6a (1 August 1965), 5-6. To this belongs also "Einspruch", loc. cit. 51/8 (1 August 1965), 8.

65.04 "Ungewohnte Evangelisationsmethoden der Pfingstbewegung in China". *Monatlicher Informationsbrief über Evangelisation* (1 December 1965).

65.05 "Schweizer Kardinäle - eine Rarität". *Tagesanzeiger* (6 February 1965), 27.

65.06 "Im Dienste der Zusammenarbeit: Ein gespräch mit Baron Frary von Blomberg". *Tagesanzeiger* (2 August 1965), 14.

65.07 "Ergriffen im Hallenstadion". *Kirchenbote für den Kanton Zürich* 51/2A (1 February 1965), 2.

65.08 "Wer sind und was glauben die Zeugen Jehovas. Berechnungen des Weltendes mit Pannen". *Tagesanzeiger* (10 July 1965), 4.

65.09 "Die Kirche der Zukunft - eine Realutopie". *Reformatio* 15/2 (1 February 1966), 90-98. See also: "Zum Problem der Kirche". *Reformatio* 15/8 (August 1966), 483-85. Reprinted under the title "Kirche und Charisma". In R.F. Edel, ed. *Kirche und Charisma*, Ökumenische Texten und Studien 35 (Marburg a.d.L.: Edel, 1966), 191-99.

65.09a "Le visage de l'église de demain ou une utopie réalité, Correspondences". *Action protestante du pays de Montbéliard* 33/34 (1 June 1966), 10-16.

65.09b "Le visage de l'église de demain ou une utopie réalité". *La Communaté des Dissémines*, no. 20 (1 December 1965), 5-12. Also in: *Correspondences, Action protestante du pays de Montbéliard* (Centre de Clay, Lyon) 33/34, July 1965, 10-16; and in no. 53, 154-160. Abridged under the title: "Une bombe dans nos paroisses", *La Vie Protestante* 29/6 (11 February 1966), 3.

65.09c "A Vision of the Church of the future". *Laity*, no. 20 (1 November 1965), 5-11.
65.09d "Suggerimenti practica. Diakonia". *Studie e informazioni, Commisione permante per i ministeri* 5/3-4 (1 November 1965), 14-17.

1966

66.01 "The Pentecostal Movement and the World Council of Churches". *Ecumenical Review* 18/3 (1 July 1965), 310-20. Incorporated in no's 4, 496 ff, 4a, 4b, 4c, 438 fff, 4c, 447 ff. Reprinted in: *The World Christian Digest* (Bala, North Wales) 18/21 (December 1966), 26-33.
66.01a "Die Pfingstbewegung und der Ökumenische Rat der Kirchen". *Materialdienst der Ökumenischen Centrale*, no. 2.04 (1 October 1966), 26-33.
66.01b "Pfingstbewegung und Ökumenischer Rat". *Evangelische Woche* 47/33 (19 August 1966), 2 ff.
66.02 "Christentum ohne Scheuklappen". *Kirchenbote für den Kanton Zürich* 52/9B (16 September 1966), 1 ff.
66.03 "Aus der Ökumene". *Kirchenbote für den Kanton Zürich* 52/9B (16 September 1966), 1 ff.
66.05 "Präsenz, Wort und Zeichen als Formen christlichen Zeugnisses in der Welt". *Das missionarische Wort* 19/2 (1 April 1966), 50-63. Incorporated in no. 12, 329-36.
66.06 "Frontdienst in Mississippi: Das Delta Ministry". *Kirchenbote für den Kanton Zürich* 52/7 (1 July 1966), 2.
66.07 "Agenda: The World". *Concept*, no. 11 (1 September 1966), 19 ff.
66.08 "Synode des franzosischen Kirchenbundes". *Kirchenblatt für die reformierte Schweiz* 122/24 (1 December 1966), 376.
66.09 "La conversion et les questions sociales". *La Vie Protestante* 29/42 (18 November 1966), 5.
66.10 "Ein Schweizer Concept". *Schweizer Concept* V (1 September 1966), 3-9.
66.11 "New Literature". *Concept*, no. 13 (1 December 1966), 3-7.
66.12 "The Common Search: Experiment and Tradition". *Pax Romana Journal* 199/4 (1 October 1966), 19-21.
66.12a "La reserche commune: Expérience et tradition". *Pax Romana Journal* 1966/4 (1 October 1966), 19-21.
66.12b "Uma pesquisa comum em faca de experiência e de traduçao". *Carta mensual sobre Evangelizaçao*, no. 1 (1 August 1967).
66.13 "Unter Einsatz des Lebens". *Kirchenbote für den Kanton Zürich* 52/12A (1 December 1966), 1 ff.
66.14 "Der neue Generalsekretär". *Kirchenbote für den Kanton Zürich* 52/3A (1 March 1966), 1 ff.
66.15 "Gerade Du brauchst Jesus". *Kirchenbote für den Kanton Zürich*, 52/1B (16 January 1966), 1.
66.16 "Minutes of the Working Committee of the Department on Studies in Evangelism, Männedorf 22-26 Aug. 1966". *Blue Concept*, no. 12 (1 December 1966), 3-5.
66.17 "Was bedeutet uns der Tod Bernattes?". *Der Blick*, 8/123 (28 May 1966), 2 ff.
66.18 "Die ökumenische Diskussion der Kirchenreform". *Protokoll*, no. 223 (26 June 1966), 16-27.

1967

67.01 "Pfingstbewegung". *Von des Christen Freude und Freiheit, Protestantische Monatshefte* 24/287 (1 September 1967), 26-28.

67.01a "Pfingstbewegung". *Von des Christen Freude und Freiheit, Protestantische Monatshefte* 24/288 (1 October 1967), 25-28.

67.02 "Das Paradox der Kirche Griechenlands". *Kirchenbote für den Kanton Zürich* 53/9B (16 September 1967), 2 ff.

67.03 "Der Regisseur als Liturg". *Deutsches Pfarrerblatt* (1 July 1967), 459-64.

67.03 "Der Regisseur als Liturg". *Monatlicher Informationsbrief über Evangelisation* (1 March 1967), 1 ff.

67.03a1"The Producer as Liturgist". *Ecumenical News, World YWCA* 29/30 (1 February 1971), 1 ff.

67.03a2"The Producer as Liturgist". *Monthly Letter about Evangelism*, (1 March 1967), 1 ff.

67.03b1"Le culte et sa dimension dramatique". *La Vie Protestante*, (2 June 1967), 2 ff.

67.03b2"Le régisseur - un liturge". *Lettre mensuelle sur l'évangélisation* (1 March 1967), 1 ff.

67.03c1"De regisseur als liturg". *De Bazuin* 50/27 (1 April 1967), 6 ff.

67.03c2"De regisseur als liturg". *De Bazuin* 50/28 (15 April 1967), 6 ff.

67.04 "England: Neubesinning der Kirchen". *Kirchenbote für den Kanton Zürich* 53/2A (20 July 1961), 2.

67.04a "England: Neubesinning der Kirchen". *Schweizer Evangelist* (12 March 1967), 187 ff.

67.05 "Frankreich: Gemeine für andere". *Kirchenbote für den Kanton Zürich* 53/5B (16 May 1967), 2.

67.06 "Verlässt die 'Kirche' die Kirche?". *Zürcher Student* 44/8 (1 February 1967), 9. Also in various commentaries

67.07 "Aus der Ökumene". *Kirchenbote für den Kanton Zürich* 53/2B (16 February 1967), 11.

67.08 With M.B. Handspicker. "Pentecostals and the Ecumenical Movement". *The Outlook Journal Presbyterian Church* 74/2 (18 February 1967), 16 f, 21.

67.09 "Ein Gemeinde für andere. Eine Diskussion in romanischen Ländern". *Ökumenische Diskussion* 3/2 (1 June 1967), 97-110.

67.09a "A Church for the others". *Study Encounter* 3/2 (1 June 1967), 84-97.

67.09b "Vers un église pour les autres. Discussion en Europe latine" *Rencontre oecuménique* 3/2 (1 June 1967), 97-110.

67.10 "Zwingli". *Mennonitisches Lexicon* IV (1 June 1967), 648-53.

67.11 "Johann Christian Hoekendijk: Pluriformität der Kirche". *Reformatio* 16/10 (1 October 1967), 663-77. Incorporated in no. 16, 45-46

67.12 "Begegnung mit der Welt". *Botschaft und Dienst, Monatshefte für kirchliche Männerarbeit* 18/8-9 (1 September 1967), 182-186. Incorporated in no. 16, 45-46.

67.13 "New Literature". *Blue Concept*, no. 13 (1 May 1967), 32-35.

67.14 "Il risveglio pentecostale in Italia: religione della fierezza dei poveri". *Concetto Italiano 14*, no. 14 (1 May 1967), 19-32. English in no. 4a, 4b, 251-66. German in no. 4, 284-302. Spanish in no. 4c, 233-52.

67.15 "Kann die Kirche aktuell sein?". *Von des Christen Freude und Freiheit, Protestantische Monatsschrift* 24/281 (1 March 1967), 20-22.

67.15a "Kann die Kirche aktuell sein?". *Von des Christen Freude und Freiheit, Protstantische Monatsschrift* 24/282 (1 April 1967), 24-27.

67.15b "Kann die Kirche aktuell sein?". *Semesterzeitschrift Wintersemester* 167/68 (1 March 1968), 23-25.

67.16 "Vollmacht in der Kirche". *Neue Zürcher Zeitung* 188/314 (23 July 1967), 5.

67.19.1 "Das ist einer von uns. Die Armen Chiles hoffen auf die Pfingstbewegung". *Allgemeines Sonntagsblatt*, (28 May 1967), 12.

67.19.2 "Das ist einer von uns. Die Armen Chiles hoffen auf die Pfingstbewegung". *Kirchenbote für den Kanton Zürich*, 53/12B (16 December 1967), 12.

67.20 "Un arricchimento per tutte le chiese. L'incontro con i Pentecostali italiano". *Nuovi tempi* (18 June 1967).

67.21 "L'evangelizzazione, oggi: che vuol dire?". *La Luce Settimanale delle Chiesa Valdesa* 60/24 (16 June 1967), 2.

67.22 "Schweizer Arbeitsgruppe, Entwurf einer Anleitung zu einer Gemeindeanalyse". *Blue Concept*, Special Issue, no. 15 (1 July 1967), 3-11.

67.23 "The Pentecostal Movement in Europe". *Ecumenical Review*, 29/1 (1 January 1967), 37-47. Also as off-print, Geneva (WCC).

1968

68.01 "Die Arbeit in Uppsala". *Hamburger Sonntagsblatt* (7 July 1968), 16.

68.02 "Uppsala". *Baselbieter Kirchenbote* 60/12 (1 September 1968), 110-12.

68.02 "Uppsala". *Kirchenbote für den Kanton Zürich* 59/9A (1 September 1968), 3 ff. Partly reprinted article.

68.02a "Uppsala". *Schweizer Reformiertes Volksblatt* (13 September 1968).

68.03 "Zum 100: Geburtstag von Leonhard Ragaz". *Volksrecht* 71/174 (27 July 1968), 1 ff.

68.05 "Pfingstbewegung und Ökumene". *Ökumenische Rundschau* 17/1 (1 January 1968), 57-59.

68.06 "Unersetzbarer Verlust für die Menschheit. Martin Luther King". *Neue Presse* 1/82 (6 April 1968), 4.

68.07 "Abendmahl oder Picknick? Der Test der Tradition". *Kontakt* (1 March 1968), 6 ff.

68.08 "Amt und Struktur der Gemeinde. Sechs Fragen". *Ev. Missionsmagazin* 112/1 (1 January 1968), 7-16.

68.09 "Der Pfingstprediger". *Von des Christen Freude und Freiheit* 25/292 (1 February 1968), 26 ff.

68.09a "Der Pfingstprediger". *Von des Christen Freude und Freiheit* 25/293 (1 March 1968), 26 ff.

68.09b "Der Pfingstprediger". *Von des Christen Freude und Freiheit* 25/294 (1 April 1968), 26 ff.

68.10 "Beispiel einer Gemeindeanalyse". *Monatliches Informationsbrief über Evangelisation* (1 May 1968), 1 ff. Fully incorporated in no. 58, 93-99.

68.10a "Hinweise auf eine Gemeindeanalyse". *Neue Zürcher Zeitung* 189/37B (23 June

1968), 21. Abridged reprint.
68.10b "Analysis of a Parish". *Monthly Letter About Evangelism* (1 May 1968), 1 ff.
68.10c "Exemple d'une analyse parroissiale". *Lettre mensuelle sur l'évangélisation* (1 May 1968), 1 ff.
68.11 "The Story of the Study 'The Missionary Structure of the Congregation' told for newcomers to the study group". *Concept*, no. 19 (1 November 1968), 5-12.
68.12 "New Literature". *Concept*, no. 20 (1 December 1968), 33-35.
68.13 "Editorial: On Church Growth". *International Review of Missions* 57/227 (1 July 1968), 271-77.
68.13a "Editorial: On Church Growth". *International Review of Missions* 76/302 (1 April 1984), 207-12. Reprint of article 1968.
68.14 "Evangelism and Brazilian Pentecostals". *Ecumenical Review* 20/2 (1 April 1968), 163-70.
68.15 "Lagebericht aus Südamerika: Die Kirche von Chile an der Wegscheide". *Kirchenbote für den Kanton Zürich* 54/10B (16 October 1968), 2.
68.16 "Gemeinde für andere in Belgien: Kann die Kirche pluralistisch sein?". *Ökumenische Diskussion* 4/3 (1 June 1968), 162-65.
68.16a "The Church for others in Belgium: Can the Church be pluralistic?". *Study Encounter* (1 June 1968), 162-65.
68.17 "Uppsala 1968". *Kirchenbote für den Kanton Zürich* 59/5A (1 May 1968), 6 ff.
68.18 "Gottesdienst in säkularen Zeitalter". *Kirchenbote für den Kanton Zürich* 54/3A (1 March 1968), 11.
68.18 "Gottesdienst in säkularen Zeitalter". *Ökumenische Presse Dienst*, no. 2 (10 January 1968).
68.19 "Dr. Walter Hollenweger: van Pinksterbeweging naar Wereldraad". Interview. *Hervormd Nederland* (6 August 1966), 2.

1969

69.01 "Genf: Die Stadt von morgen?". *Kirchenbote für den kanton Zürich* 55/6B (16 June 1969), 2 ff.
69.02a "Preaching Dialogically". *Concordia Theological Monthly* 42/4 (1 April 1971), 243-48.
69.03 "Exposé und Diskussion über 'Information und Verkündigung' an den Schweizer Massenmedien". *Concept*, no. 23 (1 July 1969), 8-11.
69.04 "Diskussion über 'Information und Verkündigung' an der Schweizer Massenmedien - Teil II". *Concept*, no. 24 (1 November 1969).
69.05 Vorschlag für einen Tatsachenbericht über 'Eine andere Kirche', Zeichen einer 'Kirche für andere' in der Schweiz. *Concept*, no. 23 (1 July 1969), 3-7.
69.06 "Andachten". *Concept*, no. 21 (1 March 1969), 14-17.
69.07 "Bibelarbeit im nachliterarischen Zeitalter". *Glauben und Leben* (6 September 1961), 4-8. Incorporated in no. 50, 135-42.
69.07 "Bibelarbeit im nachliterarischen Zeitalter". *Materialsammlung für die Männerarbeit der EKD-173* 42 (1 June 1969). Incorporated in no. 50, 135-42.
69.07a "Bibelarbeit im nachliterarischen Zeitalter". *Monatl. Informationsbrief über Evangelisation* (1 January 1969), 1. Incorporated in no. 50, 135-142.

69.07b "Bible Study in the post-literary Age". *Monthly Letter about Evangelism* (1 January 1969), 1 ff.

69.07c "Bible Study in the post-literary Age". *United Bible Societies* 79/1969 (1 February 1969), 121-26.

69.07d "L'étude de la Bible à l'epoque post-littéraire". *Lettre Mensuelle sur l'évangelisation* (1 January 1969), 1 ff.

69.07e "Il estudio de la Biblica en una época post-literaria". *Concept*, no. 29 (1 June 1971), 12-14. Reprint

69.08 "El Movimiento Pentecostal y el Movimiento Ecuménico, *Concept*, no. 26 (1 March 1970), 12 ff.

69.08a "El Movimiento Pentecostal y el Movimiento Ecuménico". *Estudios ecumenicos* 1969/2 (1 May 1969), 11-14. Reprint.

69.09 "Liturgieform als Sozialreform". *Neues Forum* 16/192 (1 December 1969), 711--13.

69.11 "Risquer même ce qui est interdit, *Tribune de Geneve*, no. 290 (11 December 1969), I, III.

69.12 "O moviemento Pentecostal no Brasil". *Simposio* 3 (1 June 1969), 5-41.

69.13 "Zwingli writes the Gospel into His World's Agenda". *The Mennonite Quarterly Review* 43/1 (1 January 1969), 70-94. German in no. 12, 299-328.

69.13a "Zuinglio introduce el evangelio en la Agenda de su mundo". *Estudias ecuménicas* 7 (1 May 1970), 18-32.

69.15 "Die Pfingstbewegung und die Dritte Welt". *Kirchenblatt für die reformierte Schweiz* 126/4 (19 February 1970), 53-55. Many more reprints.

69.15a "Die Pfingstbewegung und die Dritte Welt". *Kirchenbote für das ref Volk des Aargaus* (31 July 1969), 6.

69.15b "Die Pfingstbewegung und die Dritte Welt". *Ökumenische Pressedienst* 36/24 (3 July 1969), 11 ff.

69.15c "Die Pfingstbewegung und die Dritte Welt". *Sammlung, Dienst, Sendung*, no. 5 (1 October 1969), 21.

69.15d "Pentecostalism and the Third world". *Ecumenical Press Service* 36/24 (3 July 1969), 13 ff.

69.15e "Pentecostalism and the Third world". *Faith and Unity* 13/5 (1 September 1969), 92 ff.

69.15f "Pentecostalism and the Third World". *Pentecostal Evangel*, no. 2892 (12 October 1969), 34.

69.15g "Le Pentecôtisme et le Tiers-Monde". *Service oecuménique de presse* 36/24 (3 July 1969), 1 ff. Incorporated in no. 72.31

69.15h "Pingstväckelsen och den tredje världen". *Svensk Veckotidning* 29/30 (25 July 1969), 8 ff.

69.15i "Il movimento pentecostale interroga i cristiani classica". *Nuovi Tempi* (1 June 1969).

69.16 "O Herr, wo ist Bethlehem: Der Weihnachtgottesdienst vom 17.12.68 im Ökumenischen Zentrum in Genf". *Lutherische Monatshefte* 8/12 (1 December 1969), 620-23.

69.16a "O Herr, wo ist Bethlehem: Der Weihnachtgottesdienst am 17.12.68 im Ökumenischen Zentrum in Genf''. *Konsequenzen* 3/6 (1 December 1969), 62-64. Many incomplete reprints. Incorporated in no. 16, 102-09.

69.17 "Laienapostolat und Kirchenreform". *Neue Züricher Zeitung* 190/738 (21 December 1969), 52.

69.18 "Traktate oder Traktoren? Die Aufgabe der Mission in unserer Welt". *Evangelischer Pressedienst Kirchliche Presse*, no. 49 (3 December 1969), 1 ff. Many Reprints

69.19 "Christsomol contra Komsomol: Die Lage der Protestanten in Rusland". *Kirchenbote für den Kanton Zürich* 55/10A (1 October 1969), 3 ff. Many reprints.

69.20 "Pentecostalism and the Third World". *Lutheran Standard* 9/19 (16 September 1969), 2-4.

69.22 "The Church for others: Discussion in the DDR". *Study Encounter* 5/1 (1 June 1969), 26-36.

69.23 "Lagebericht aus Brasilien: 'Die Wirklichkeit schreiben ist nicht ratsam". *Gemeindeblatt der Deutschschweizer Gemeinden Genf* 63/6 (1 June 1969), 5.

69.23a "Lagebricht aus Brasilien: Die Wirklichkeit schreiben ist nicht ratsam". *Kirchenbote für den Kanton Zürich*, 55/1B (16 January 1969), 2. Partly reprint.

69.24 "Die ausstehende Reformation,Zur Verbindlichkeit von Zwinglis Gottesdienstmodell". *Neue Zürcher Zeitung* 190/1 (3 January 1969), 15. Partly reprint.

69.27 "Reformpapst oder christlicher Ombudsmann?". *Ecumenical Press Service*, 36/36 (16 October 1969), 14 ff. Many reprints.

69.27a "Reformpapst oder christlicher Ombudsmann?". *Reformierte Kirchenzeitung* 110/22 (15 November 1969).

69.27b "A Reformed Pope or Christian Ombudsman?". *Ecumenical Press Service* 36/36 (16 October 1969), I-II.

69.27c "Un fou de Dieu ou un Pape réforme?". *Service oecuménique de presse* 36/36 (1 January 19696), III-V.

69.27d "En reformerad pave eller en kristen ombudsman?". *Kristet samhällsliv* 50/4 (1 November 1969), 91 ff.

69.30 "O movimento pentecostal e o Conselho Mundial das Igrejas, Speech and Testimony". *First Ecumenical Youth Festival on 1-2 May 1969*, (2 May 1969), 66-68.

1970

70.01 "Billy Grahams Bekehrung". *Kirchenbote für den Kanton Zürich* 56/3B (16 March 1970), 1.

70.01a "Billy Grahams converti une deuxieme fois". *La Vie Protestante* 33/10 (13 March 1970), 1.

70.01b "Billy Graham's second conversion". *The Mennonite* 85/35 (29 September 1970), 694.

70.01c "La conversion de Billy Graham". *Estudios Ecuménicos*, no. 9 (1 December 1970), 64 ff.

70.02 "La parabole des 19 prévenus". *La Vie Protestante* 53/39 (30 October 1970), 3.

70.03 "Le marxiste et les protestants"'. *La Vie Protestant* 33/40 (6 November 1970), 3. Also in German manuscript (70.03a).

70.04 "Question de vérité". *La Vie Protestante* 33/41 (13 November 1970), 3. Also in

German manuscript (70.04a)

70.05 "Un a priori à vérifier". *La Vie Protestante* 33/42 (20 November 1970), 3. Also in German manuscript (70.05a)

70.08 "Charisma und Ökumene: Der Beitrag der Pfingstbewegung zur weltweitem Kirche". *Rondom het Woord* 12/3 (1 July 1970), 300-16.

70.08a "Charisma und Oikoumene". *One in Christ* 7/4 (1 June 1971), 324-43. Abridged reprint of "Charisma and Ökoumene".

70.08b "Spirituality for the World". *Event* 13/10 (1 December 1973), 9-13.

70.09 "Politik der Kirches aus Schweizer Sicht". *Tagesanzeiger* (31 October 1970), 5.

70.10 "Blumen und Lieder in Mexico. Bibelarbeit im nachliterarischen Zeitalter: ein Beispiel". *Monatlicher Informationsbrief über Evangelisation* (1 December 1970), 1.

70.10 "Ein Lagebericht aus Übersee. Bibelauslegung in Mexico". *Kirchenbote für den Kanton Zürich* 56/10A (1 October 1970), 4 ff.

70.10a "Fleurs et chansons au Méxique. L'étude de la Bible à l'époque post-littéraire: un example". *Lettre Mensuelle sur l'évangelisation* (1 December 1970), 1 ff.

70.10b "Les tlamatini". *L'Illustré Protestant* 19/190 (1 November 1970), 13-15.

70.10c "Flowers and Songs in Mexico. Bible Study in the Post-Literary Age: An Example". *Ecumenical Courier* 30/1 (1 March 1971).

70.10d "Flowers and Songs in Mexico. Bible Study in the Post-Literary Age: An Example". *Monthly letter about Evangelism* (1 December 1970), 1. Reprinted exctracts.

70.10e "Flowers and Songs in Mexico. Bible Study in the Post-Literary Age: An Example". *The Mennonite* 86/20 (1 March 1971), 322 ff.

70.11 "Blumen und Lieder: Ein mexikanischer Beitrag zum theologischen Verstehensprozes". *Evangelische Theologie* 31 (1 August 1970), 437-48. Incorporated in no. 8b, 30-48.

70.11a "Flores y Cantos. Una contribucion mejicana al proceso de comprender la teologica". *Concepto latinoamericana* III, Special Issue no. 32 (1 October 1970), 3-16.

70.11b "Flowers and Songs. A Mexican Contribution on Hermeneutics". *International Review of Mission* 60/238 (1 April 1971), 232-44. Abridged reprint.

70.11c "Flowers and Songs. A Mexican Contribution on Hermeneutics". *Movement*, no. 21 (1 July 1975), 19-23. Incorporated in no. 8, 33-54

70.12 "Das Charisma in der Ökumene: Der Beitrag der Pfingstbewegung an die allgemeine Kirche". *Una Sancta* (1 June 1970), 150-59.

70.13 "Heil inmitten der Welt". *IDOC International* (1 October 1970), 47-51.

70.13a "Salvation Today" *IDOC International* (18 July 1970), 61-68.

70.14 "Apostolat in lutherisch. Zwischenbericht von der Fünften Vollversammlung des Luthersischen Weltbundes in Evian 14-24 Juli 1970". *IDOC International* (1 August 1970), 4-7.

70.15 "Spiel als eine Form von Theologie, Zum geplanten Dialog mit der Pfingstbewegung". *Lutherische Monatshefte* 9/10 (1 October 1970), 532-34.

70.16 "A Black Pentecostal Concept: A Forgotten Chapter of Black History: The Black Pentecostal Contribution to the Church Universal". *Concept*, no. 30 (1 June 1970), 1 ff.

70.17 "Seven Words on Salvation Today". *Study Encounter* 6/1 (1 June 1970), 16-25.

70.17a "Sieben Worte zu 'Das Heil der Welt heute'". *Materialdienst der Ökumenischen Centrale*, no. 12 (1 August 1970), 1 ff.

70.17b "Sieben Worte zu 'Das Heil der Welt heute'". *Reformatio* 19/9 (1 September 1970), 594-606.

70.18 "Pentecostalism and the Third World". *Dialog* 9/2 (1 June 1970), 122-29.

70.19 "Redécouvrir le Pentecôtisme". *Communion* 1/1 (1 June 1970), 74-78.

70.20 "Die Pfingstkirchen in der ökumenischen Bewegung, Blick in die Welt". *Monatliche Beilage zu den Nachrichten der Evangelisch Lutherische Kirche in Bayern* (1 April 1970), 2 ff.

70.20 "Die Pfingstkirchen in der ökumenischen Bewegung". *Ökumenischer Presse Dienst Monatsausgabe* (1 February 1970), 5 ff.

70.20a "The Unexpected Dialogue Between Pentecostals and Roman Catholics". *Ecumenical Press Service* (1 February 1970), 4-6.

70.20b "Un dialogue inattendu entre pentecôtistes et catholiques romains". *Service oecuménique de presse Mensuel* (1 February 1970), 5-7.

70.21 "Die Kirche war einst Pionier. Ist sie es heute noch?". *Kirchenbote für die Ev. Ref. Kirchen Basel-Stadt, Glarus, Schaffhausen und der Diaspora der Zentralschweiz und im Kanton Solothurn*, no. 1 (1 January 1970), 3.

70.22 "A Little known chapter in Pentecostal history". *Ecumenical Press Service This Month* (1 April 1970), 8 ff.

70.22a "Les Pentecôtistes noirs: les oubliés de l'histoire". *Service oecuménique de press Mensuel* (1 April 1970), 10-13.

70.22b "Schwarze Pfingstler in den USA, Stiefkinder der Kirchengeschichte". *Ökumenische Presse Dienst Monatsausgabe* (1 April 1970), 12 ff.

70.24 "Was uns verbindet. Was uns trennt". *Leben und Glauben* 45/44 (31 October 1970), 4 ff.

70.26 "Öffentlich machen als Medium der Wahrheitsfindung". *Für eine Offenbahrung* (6 October 1970), 13.

70.27 "Moderner Glaube - rechter Glaube?". *Das Blaue Kreuz* 74/18 (16 September 1970), 2 ff.

70.28 "Die Pfingstbewegung im ökumenischen Gespräch". *Das Wort in der Welt Allgemeine Missionsnachrichten* 1970/5 (1 October 1970), 133-36.

70.29 "Haben die Kirchen in Nigeria versagt?". *Kirchenbote für den Kanton Zürich* 56/4A (1 April 1970), 12.

70.30 "Nicht die Kirchengeschichte ist heilig, sondern was darin geschieht". *Kirchenbote für die Evangelisch-reformierten Kirchen Basel-Land, Basel-Stadt, Glarus, Schaffhausen, der Diaspora der Zentralschweiz und im Kanton Solothurn*, no. 9 (1 September 1970), 5.

1971

71.01 "Blick über die Grenzen". *Leben und Glauben* 46/5 (30 January 1971), 3.

71.02 "Du sollst nicht stehlen". *Leben und Glauben* 46/44 (30 October 1971), 3.

71.03 "Ein X für ein U.". *Leben und Glauben* 46/39 (26 September 1971), 3. Incorporated in no. 14, 63-66.

71.04 "Die Kirchen in der DDR". *Leben und Glauben* 46/48 (27 November 1971), 3.

71.05 "Evangelist in den Slums von Chicago". *Leben und Glauben*, 46/9 (27 February 1971), 3. Incorporated in no. 14, 145-48.

71.06 "Evangelisation in der holländisch-reformierten Kirche Amerikas". *Leben und Glauben* 46/17 (24 April 1971), 3. Incorporated in no. 14, 135-38.

71.07 "Eine Erweckung in Russland". *Leben und Glauben* 46/31 (31 July 1971), 3. Incorporated in no. 14, 45-49.

71.08 "Die Verteidigung der 'freien Welt'". *Leben und Glauben* 46/31 (31 July 1971), 3. Incorporated in no. 14, 138-41.

71.09 "Die, die keine wahlen gewinnen müssen", *Leben und Glauben* 46/26 (26 June 1971), 3. Incorporated in no. 14, 125-28.

71.10 "Das schwarze Dossier der französischen Polizei". *Leben und Glauben* 46/35 (28 August 1971), 3 ff.

71.11 "Was klärt die Frankfurter Erklärung". *Leben und Glauben* 46/13 (27 March 1971), 3.

71.12 "Kriterien für die kirchliche Reformarbeit an Hand der Materialien der sogenannten Action-Research-Groups". *Concilium* 7/6-7 (1 July 1971), 439-43. Incorporated in no. 12, 258-66.

71.12a "Critères pour la réforme de l'Eglise à l'aide des découvertes de ce qu'on appele les action-research-groups, *Concilium* no. 6 (1 June 1971), 115-22.

71.12b "Criteri per un'azione di riforma ecclesiale evoluti sulla scorta del materiale offerto dagli action-research-groups". *Concilium*, no. 6 (1 June 1971), 1196-1206.

71.12c Criteria voor het werk van de kerkhervorming. Aan de hand van het materiaal van de zogenaamde Action-Research-Groups, *Concilium*, no. 6 (1 June 1971), 114-23.

71.12d "Criterios para la reforma de la iglesia. Reflexiones de los 'action-research-groups'". *Concilium*, no. 66 (1 June 1971), 435-41.

71.12e Criteria for Reforming the Church. Based on material presented by the so-called action-researh-groups, *Concilium*, 6/7 (1 June 1971), 116-27.

71.12f "Critérios para o trabalho de reform de igreja". *Concilium* (1 June 1971), 781-89. Also published in Japanese, Korean and Polish.

71.13 "Was tun die Kirchen für den Frieden?". *Kirchenbote für den Kanton Zürich* 57/3A (1 March 1971), 6 ff.

71.14 "Vor 25 Jahren: Friedensarbeit des Ökumenischen Rates". *Die Ostschweiz* 98/42 (20 February 1971).

71.15 "Ich glaube ..". *Zoom Illustrierte Halbmonatsschrift für Film, Radio und Fernsehen* 23/3 (4 February 1971), 16.

71.16 "Die brasilianische Pfingstbewegung: eine proletarische Laienkirche". *Auftrag* 5/3 (1 June 1971), 2-5.

71.17 "Leiblichkeit ist das Ende der Werke Gottes. Zur Arbeit der Abteilung für Weltmission und Evangelisation in Ökumenischen Rat der Kirchen". *Ökumenische Rundschau* 20/1 (1 January 1971), 67-76.

71.18 "Die Gottesdienst für die Welt so nötig wie das tägliche Brot". *Das missionarische Wort* (1 April 1971), 51-61. Incorporated in no. 12, 170-80.

71.22 "Väter und Söhne - in der Bibel und heute". *PRO* 20/15 (15 November 1971), 12-15.

71.23 "Bemerkungen zum Visitationsbericht". *Kirchenbote* (1 October 1971).

71.24 "Ein revolutionärer Minnesänger". *Kirchenblatt für die reformierte Schweiz* 127/19 (30 September 1971), 297 ff.

71.24a "Ein revolutionärer Minnesänger". *Monatlicher Informationsbrief über Evangelisation* (1 October 1971). Abridged reprint of 71.24.

71.24b "A Revolutionary Troubadour". *Monthly Letter on Evangelism* (1 October 1971).

71.24c "Un troubadour révolutionnaire". *Lettre mensuelle sur l'évangélisation* (1 October 1971).

71.25 "The Social and Ecumenical Significance of Pentecostal Liturgy". *Studia Liturgica* 8/4 (1 December 1971), 207-15.

71.26 "Säkulare Liturgien". *Areopag* 6/2 (1 June 1971), 120-43. Incorporated in no. 12, 135-55.

71.27 "Editorial, Issue on Latin America". *International Review of Missions* 60/238 (1 April 1971), 155-59.

71.28 "Polen- Zankapfel oder Brücke zwischen Ost und West". *Leben und Glauben* 46/52 (25 December 1971), 3 ff. Incorporated in no. 14, 63-66.

71.29a "The 'What' and the 'How': Content and Communication of the one Message. A consideration of the Basis of Faith as formulated by the W.C.C.". *Expository Times* 86/11 (1 August 1971), 324-28. Abridged translation of 71.29.

71.29b "The 'What' and the 'How': Content and Communication of the one Message. A consideration of the Basis of Faith, as formulated by the W.C.C.". *Expository Times* 86/12 (1 September 1971), 356-59.

71.30 "Letters and papers from the oikoumene for devotional reading and meditation of the committee of CWME". *Excerpts from forthcoming collection of testimonies* (27 September 1971).

71.31 "Die 'freien Kirchen' von Berkeley". *Kirchenbote für den Kanton Zürich* 57/2A (1 December 1971), 9.

71.36 "In gesprek met Dr. W.J. Hollenweger - Over zending en ontwikkelingshulp". Interview. *Woord en Dienst* 20/11 (29 May 1971), 168-73.

1972

72.01 "Disused churches and other faiths. Letter to the Times". *The Times* (24 October 1972).

72.02 "Pentecostalism - the church's growing point". *Baptist Times* (30 November 1972), 6-10.

72.03 "Weihnachtstext eines französischen Kommunisten". *Leben und Glauben* 47/52-4 (30 December 1972), 3, 23.

72.04 "Harvey Cox - ein amerikanischer Baptist". *Leben und Glauben* 47/48 (25 November 1972), 7. Incorporated in no. 14, 142-45.

72.04a "Harvey Cox - ein amerikanischer Baptist". *Wort und Tat* 27/1 (1 January 1973), 19 ff.

72.05 "Von den Hippies zur Jesusbewegung". *Leben und Glauben* 47/44 (28 October 1972), 24 ff.

72.06 "Afrikanische Katholizität - Geschichte und Theologie der Kimbanguisten". *Evangelische Kommentare* 11/5 (1 November 1972), 675-77.

72.07 "Solschenizyn - ein gefährlicher Schriftsteller". *Leben und Glauben* 47/44 (28 October 1972), 7. Incorporated in no. 14, 49-52.

72.08 "Wie praktisch ist die Praktische Theologie?". *Reformatio* 21/10 (1 October 1972), 542-553. Incorporated in no. 12, 215-25.

72.09 "Die Weisheit der Kinder". *PRO* 21/11 (1 November 1972), 23-26.

72.10 "Pro und contra Ekstase". *Bibel-Report* 1972/1 (1 March 1972), 6 ff.

72.10 "Pro und contra Ekstase". *Die Glocke Ein Zeitschrift junger Menschen* 26/5 (1 May 1972), 12 ff.

72.10a "Pro und contra Ekstase". *Von des Christen Freude und Freiheit* 29/343 (1 May 1972), 11-13.

72.11 "Indianerkirchen in Mexico". *Leben und Glauben* 47/35 (26 August 1972), 7.

72.12 "Philip Potter, der neue Generalsekretär des Ökumenischen Rates". *Leben und Glauben* 47/39, (23 September 1972), 7.

72.13 "Das Suchen nach Solidarität und Authentizität in den sogenannten Solidaritätsgruppen und Subkulturen". *Concilium* (1 July 1972), 349-55. Incorporated in no. 12, 95-105.

72.13a "La recherche de solidarité et authencité dans les groupes souterraines". *Concilium*, no. 75 (1 July 1972), 65-75.

72.13b "The Quest for Authenticity in Solidarity Groups". *Concilium* 5/8 (1 May 1972), 68-79.

72.13c "Het zoeken naar solidariteit en authenciteit in de zogenaamde solidariteitsgroepen en subkulturen". *Concilium* (1 July 1972), 67-78.

72.13d "La busquede d'union y autencidad en los groups y en las subculturas". *Concilium*, no. 74 (1 May 1972), 218-30.

72.13e "Alla ricerca della solidarità e della autencità nei gruppi solidari e nelle sub-culture". *Concilium*, no. 5 (1 May 1972), 92-105.

72.13f "A procura de solidariedade e autencidiade nos grupos solidarios e nas subculturas". *Concilium* (1 July 1972), 619-29.

72.14 "Helder Camara - ein revolutionärer Troubadour". *Leben und Glauben* 47/30 (22 July 1972), 7.

72.15 "Jamaa - eine evangelistische Laienbewegung in Katanga Kongo". *Leben und Glauben* 47/18 (29 April 1972), 7. Incorporated in no. 14, 179-82.

72.16 "Ein Drache fliegt gegen die Wind. Amerikanische Pfingstbewegung und Black Power". *Evangelische Kommentare* 5/5 (1 May 1972), 271-75. Abridged. See also 73.36. Incorporated in no. 8b, 11-29.

72.16a "'Black Power' e Pentecostalismo negli Stati Unite". *Testimonianze* 16/151 (1 February 1973), 28-45.

72.16b "Ein Drache fliegt gegen die Wind. Amerikanische Pfingstbewegung und Black Power". *Evangelische Kommentare* 5/5 (1 May 1972), 271-75. Abridged. See also 73.36. Incorporated in no. 8b, 11-29.

72.16c "Pentecostalism and Black Power". *Theology Today* 30/3 (1 October 1973), 228-38. Abridged. Incorporated in the enlarged form in no. 8, 13-32.

72.16d "Un dragon se alza contra los vientos - El Black Power y el movimento Pentecostal". *El Pentecostalismo*, 1975, 15-49.

72.17 "Au milieu de leur fête". *La Vie Protestante* 35/20 (19 May 1972), 3.

72.18 "Die Invasion Chiles". *Leben und Glauben* 47/22 (27 May 1972), 7.

72.19 "Handwerker Jesus und seine Gesellen". *Allgemeines Deutsches Sontagsblatt* 25/21 (21 May 1972), 10.
72.20 "Kirche, Benzin und Bohnesuppe". *Leben und Glauben* 47/13 (25 March 1972), 3.
72.21 "Frömmigkeit heute!". *Deutsches Pfarrerblatt* 72/11 (1 June 1972), 353-55.
72.22 "Warum hat Jesus nicht gelacht". *Kontakt*, no. 12 (1 March 1972), 16.
72.23 "Die abessinische Kirche". *Leben und Glauben* 47/9 (26 February 1972), 21-25.
72.24 "Pingstvänner, katoliker och politik i Latinamerika". *Svensk Missionstidskrift* 60/2 (1 February 1972), 90-98.
72.24a "Pfingstler, Katholiken und Politik in Lateinamerik". *Reformatio* 22/6 (1 June 1973), 334-41.
72.25 "La culte oecuménique des J.O.". *Horizons protestants Mensuel illustré interregional* 1/7 (1 September 1972), 12-13.
72.26 "Rhodesien: Im Interesse der Rassenreinheit". *Leben und Glauben* 47/4 (22 January 1972), 7.
72.27 "Der rhodesische Kirchenkampf". *Kirchenbote für den Kanton Zürich* 58/2A (1 February 1972), 2.
72.29 "Hermenetical Questions to the Conference, Interview of Hollenweger with L. Navarro and H.R.Weber". *Conference Journal*, no. 1 (31 December 1972), 4.
72.29a "Viele haben vergessen, wie man spielt, in: Farbe bekennen. Heil für die ganze Welt?". *Missionsjahrbuch der Schweiz* 40 (1 July 1973), 33-36.
72.30 "Donald Gee: Portrait of a Pentecostal Gentleman 1891-1966". *Learning for Living* 12/2 (1 November 1972), 9-12.

1973

73.02 "Die Zukunft ist nicht mehr, was sie einmal war". *Leben und Glauben* (27 January 1973), 7.
73.03 "Kirche der Entrechteten". *Blaukreuz Kalender* 78/1973 (1 June 1973), 60-64.
73.04 "Karl Marx 1818-1883 and his Confession of Faith". *Expository Times* 84/5 (1 February 1973), 132-37. Incorporated in German in no. 12, 287-298.
73.05 "Action and Reflection Among Lay Men and Women". *International Review of Mission* 72/245 (1 January 1973), 73-79.
73.06 "Theologiestudium am einer Backstein Universität". *Kirchenbote für den Kanton Zürich* 59/3A (1 March 1973), 2.
73.07 "Missionswissenschaft in Birmingham". *Das Wort in der Welt*, 1973/1 (1 February 1973), 18.
73.08 "Angst vor enthusiastischem Christentum". *Die Mitarbeiterhilfe* 28/2 (1 April 1973), 37 ff.
73.08a "Enthusiasmus in politische Bewegungen". *Die Mitarbeiterhilfe* 28/2 (1 April 1973), 29 ff.
73.09 "Die Rechnung schicken Sie meinem Schwager". *Leben und Glauben* 48/12 (24 March 1973), 7.
73.10 "Ostertext eines tschechischen Marxisten". *Leben und Glauben* 48/16 (21 April 1973), 7.
73.12 "Theologiestudium anders, *Der Überblick* 1973/1 (1 June 1973), 51 ff.
73.13 "Spanningen in missie hier en ginds". *Bijeen - Maandblad over Internationale Sa-*

menwerking 6/1 (1 January 1973), 8 ff.
73.14 "Die Pfingstbewegung in Russland". *Leben und Glauben* 48/21 (25 May 1973), 8 ff.
73.15 "Katholische Pfingstler". *Leben und Glauben* 48/21 (25 May 1973), 7, 34.
73.17 "David Livingstone - der grösste Afrikamissionar?". *Leben und Glauben* 48/25 (23 June 1973), 7. Incorporated in no. 14, 175-78.
73.18 "Schokolade-Boldern in Birmingham". *Kirchenbote für den Kanton Zürich* 59/7 (1 July 1973), 9.
73.19 "Vernunft ist weiblicher Natur". *Schritte ins Offene* 3/4 (1 August 1973), 23-25.
73.20 "Schweiz 2000". *Leben und Glauben* 48/30 (1 August 1973), 7.
73.21 "Ein europäisches Vietnam". *Leben und Glauben* 48/34 (25 August 1973), 7.
73.23 "Wunder". *Leben und Glauben* 48/38 (22 September 1973), 7. Reprint: Deutscher Evangelischer Kirchentag Düsseldorf 1973, Dokumente Stuttgart 1973, 143-52.
73.24 "An introduction to Pentecostalism". *Now* (1 October 1973), 4 ff.
73.25 "Herr MacMillan oder: Der ältere Bruder". *Leben und Glauben* 48/43 (27 October 1973), 8 ff.
73.26 "Evangelisation als Dialog". *Leben und Glauben* 48/47 (24 November 1973), 8 ff.
73.27 "The Christian and the Church of the Future". *Audenshaw Papers*, no. 39 (1 November 1973).
73.28 "Gemeinschaft der Gegensätze". *Der Sämann*, no. 89 (1 November 1973), 2.
73.29 "Wir brauchen die Christen in der Dritten Welt". *Radius* 18/4 (1 June 1973), 42-47.
73.30 "Korntal: Ein Gleichnis aus den Anfängen des Pietismus". *Leben und Glauben* 48/51 (22 December 1973), 8 ff.
73.31 "Mr. Chips Goes to Bangkok". *Salvation Today*, no. 8 (7 January 1973), 1.
73.32 "Professor Unrat geht nach Bangkok". *Evangelische Kommentare* 6/3 (1 March 1973), 146-49.
73.32a "Mr. Chips goes to Bangkok". *Frontier* 16/2 (1 July 1973), 93-100. Incorporated in no. 9a
73.32b "La Salvezza Oggi". *Atti della Conferenza della Commissione Missione e Evangelizzazione Bangkok* (1 June 1974).
73.33 "Der Charme Gottes". *Leben und Glauben* (24 February 1973), 7.
73.34 "Catholic Pentecostalism". *Learning for Living* 13/1 (1 September 1973), 19-22.
73.34a "Catholic Pentecostalism", *Learning for Living* 13/2 (1 November 1973), 64-67.
73.38 "Close Reading". *Salvation Today. Conference Journal of the Bangkok Conference of the CWME*, no. 5 (4 January 1973), 4.
73.38 "Hermeneutical Questions on the Conference. Interviews with Sr. Leonore Navarro and Dr. H.R. Weber". *Salvation Today, Conference Journal*, no. 1 (31 December 1972), 4.

1974

74.01b "Les movements charismatiques et pentecôtistes, Un défi aux Eglises". *Centre d'Etudes oecuméniques* (1 December 1973).
74.02 "Marxist Ethics". *Expository Times* 85/10 (1 July 1974), 292-98.
74.02a "Marxistische Ethik". *Diakonia* 5/6 (1 November 1974), 400-08. Incorporated in

no. 12, 274-86 (enlarged)

74.02b "Marxistische Ethik", *Reformatio* 23/7-8 (1 August 1974), 405-15.

74.03 "Die Heiligen von Birmingham". *Lutherse Monatshefte* 19/9 (1 September 1980), 538-42.

74.03a "Die Heiligen von Birmingham". *Reformatio* 30/11-12 (1 December 1981), 652-62.

74.03b "Professor Unrat bei den Charismatikern". *Reformatio,* 23/11-12 (1 December 1974), 628-35. Incorporated in no. 9, 37-42 and in no. 16, 166-78.

74.03c "Saints in Birmingham". *Research Bulletin ISWRA,* 1981 (1 June 1981), 102-13. Incorporated in no 9a.

74.03d "Saints in Birmingham". *Theological Renewal,* no. 17 (1 February 1981), 27-38.

74.03e "Plaidoyer pour une théologie orale". *Journal des missions évangéliques* 157/1 (1 June 1982), 12-22.

74.04 "Rumpelstilzchen beim Namen nennen". *Evangelische Kommentare* 7/6 (1 June 1974), 366-68. Incorporated (enlarged) in no. 12, 200-14.

74.05 "Ökumene nach 1945. Friedensarbeit des Weltrates der Kirchen". *Berliner Sonntagsblatt* 29/37 (11 August 1974), 5.

74.06 "Fülle des Geistes". *Deutsches Pfarrerblatt* 74/11 (1 June 1974), 361.

74.07 "Herausforderung der Kirche an die Stadt". *Hefte für den Freundenkreis,* Heft 44 (1 December 1974), 22-27. Incorporated in no. 12, 181-87.

74.07a "Kirchen müssen keine Wahlen gewinnen". *Deutsches Allgemeinen Sonntagsblatt* 28/27 (6 July 1975), 10.

74.08 "Leibhaftigkeit des Geistes - Zwei Briefe und Entwürfe einer Antwort". *Deutsches Pfarrerblatt* 74/20 (1 November 1974), 809-12. Incorporated in no. 9, 42-46.

74.10 "Der Evangelist und sein Präsident". *Leben und Glauben* 49/39 (28 September 1974). Incorporated in no. 14, 155-57.

74.11 "Die Anglikanische Kirche und die Kathedrale von Coventry". *Leben und Glauben* 49/47 (23 November 1974), 6 ff. Incorporated in no.14, 78-81.

74.12 "Das schwarze Lächeln Gottes". *Leben und Glauben* 49/41 (12 October 1974), 6 ff. Incorporated in no. 14, 195-98.

74.13 "Die Heilige Geist in der Industrie". *Leben und Glauben,* 49/30 (1 August 1974), 6 ff. Incorporated in no. 14, 88-91.

74.14 "Offizieller Dialog zwischen dem Vatikan und den Pfingstlern". *Leben und Glauben* 49/34 (24 August 1974), 6 ff.

74.15 "Mitbestimmung in der Industrie". *Leben und Glauben* 49/15 (13 April 1974), 8 ff.

74.16 "Quäkerschulen und - schokolade". *Leben und Glauben* 49/26 (29 June 1974), 6 ff.

74.17 "Theologie an einer Backstein-Universität". *Der Sämann* 90/4 (1 April 1974).

74.17a "Theologie an einer Backstein-Universität". *Leben und Glauben* 49/21 (25 May 1974), 6 ff.

74.19 "Bei den Trümmern einsetzen!, Kalenderblatt 31-3-1974". *Zum Heil der Welt* (1 January 1974).

74.20 "Dank an die Arbeiter". *Leben und Glauben* 49/4 (26 January 1974), 8 ff. Incorporated in no. 14, 25-29.

74.21 "Domestizierte Charismatiker? Die katholische Pfingstbewegung in den USA und in England". *Lutherische Monatsheft* 13/2 (1 February 1974), 58-60.

74.22 "Moral". *Leben und Glauben* 49/8 (23 February 1974), 8 ff.

74.23 "Does efficiency imply the destruction of human values? A theological action-research on co-decission in industry". *Research Bulletin of the Institute for the Study of Worship and Religious Architecture* (1 June 1974), 114-18.

74.25a "Ausschau nach dem Gemeinsamen. Zur Kontroverse der Evangelikalen mit den Ökumenikern". *Der Mitarbeiter* 22/4 (1 November 1974), 4-15. Incorporated in no. 9a.

74.25b "Ausschau nach dem Gemeinsamen. Zur Kontroverse der Evangelikalen mit den Ökumenikern". *Lutherische Monatshefte* 13/7 (1 July 1974), 338-42. Incorporated in 12, 121-34.

74.26 "Wenn nichts erfahren wird, gibt es auch nichts zu begreifen". *Kunst und Kirche*, no. 1 (1 April 1974), 33-35.

74.27 "Die Nachkommen Abrahams". *Leben und Glauben* 49/12 (23 March 1974), 8 ff.

74.28 "Mr. Chips Reviews Bangkok". *International Review of Missions*, 63/249 (1 January 1974), 132-36. Incorporated in no. 9a.

74.28a "Professor Unrat denkt weiter". *Ökumenische Rundschau* 23/2 (1 April 1974), 192-204. Incorporated in no. 9, 21-36.

74.29 "Eine Fabrik gehört allen". *Allgemeines Deutsches Sonntagsblatt* 27/2 (2 June 1974).

74.30 "Il movimento pentecostale: verso una spiritualità politica?, conferenza". *La Luce*, no. 48 (6 December 1974), 4.

74.31 "Theologiestudium an einer Backstein Univerität". *Weg und Wahrheit* 28/1 (6 January 1974), 10 ff.

74.32 "Vistar foran en ny ara i det okumeniske arbeid!". Interview with Tor Jorgensen. *Var Kirke* 34/74 (23 August 1974).

74.33 "Unity in the Spirit. Can it subtitute for organic Church union?". *The Church Times*, no. 5799 (18 January 1974), 11, 15.

1975

75.01 "Schokolade-Gwatt in Birmingham". *Der Sämann* 91/3 (1 March 1975), 8.

75.02 "Herzensfriede genügt nicht. Was bleibt von der Jesus-Revolution". *Lutherische Monatshefte* 14/2 (1 February 1975), 67-69.

75.03 "Die Sekten und die Katholizität der Kirche". *Diakonia* 6/3 (1 May 1975), 158-165. Incorporated in no. 12, 229-37.

75.04 "Efficiency and Human Values. A theological Action-Research Report on Co-decission in Industry". *Expository Times* 86/8 (1 May 1975), 228-32.

75.05 "Kimbanguist Church - Historical Background". *Movement The Journal of Radical Christian Ideas and Actions*, no. 21 (1 July 1975), 7 ff.

75.06 "The morning is full of Charismatic Movements today". *Movement. The Journal of Radical Christian Ideas and Actions*, no. 21 (1 July 1975), 3-6.

75.07 "Danced Documentaries: The Theological and Political Significance of Pentecostal Dancing". In: J.G. Davies, ed. *Worship and Dance* (1 June 1975), 76-82. In German: incorporated in no. 12, 85-94 (75.07a).

75.08 "Katholische und quäkerische Tradition". *Kunst und Kirche* 38/1 (1 February 1975), 24 ff.

75.09 "Charismatic Movements Today". *Plumbline A Journal of Ministry in Higher Eduaction* 3/1 (1 April 1975), 4-9.

75.10 "Les mouvements charismatiques aujourd'hui, I - Alléluja". *La Vie protestante* 38/31 (29 August 1975), 1 ff.

75.10 "Les mouvements charismatiques aujourd'hui, II - La théologie orale des pentecôtistes noirs". *La Vie protestante* 38/32 (5 September 1975), 2.

75.10 "Les mouvements charismatiques aujourd'hui, III - Y a-t-il place pour le Saint-Esprit dans la théologie pentecôtiste?". *La Vie protestante* 38/33 (12 September 1975), 2.

75.10 "Les mouvements charismatiques aujourd'hui, IV - Dialogue entre les Pentecôtistes et le Vatican". *La Vie protestante* 38/34 (19 September 1975), 2.

75.11 "China und die Christen". *Leben und Glauben* 50/8 (22 February 1975), 6 ff. Incorporated in no. 14, 18-21.

75.12 "Karl Barth in seinen Briefen". *Leben und Glauben* 50/12 (22 March 1975), 6 ff.

75.13 "Ernst Lange: Wider das Geschäft mit der Angst". *Leben und Glauben* 50/17 (26 April 1975), 6 ff. Incorporated in no. 14, 108-12.

75.14 "Mr. Chips looks for the Holy Spirit in Pentecostal Theology". *Journal of Theology for Southern Africa*, no. 12 (1 September 1975), 39-50.

75.14a "Das vergessene Glaubensartikel". *Das missionarische Wort* 29/4 (1 August 1975), 130-37.

75.15 "Lebende Symbole des Heiligen. Die Religion der Armen ist keine armselige Religion". *Lutherische Monatshefte* 14/8 (1 August 1975), 423-26.

75.15a "The Religion of the Poor is not a Poor Religion". *Expository Times* 87/8 (1 May 1976), 228-32.

75.16 "Die Gaben des Geistes verstehen - Der Vatikan im Dialog mit Pfingstlern". *Evangelische Kommentare* 8/8 (1 August 1975), 494-96.

75.20 "Zur katholischen Pfingstbewegung". *Theologische Literaturzeitung* 100/12 (1 December 1975), 952-60.

75.21 "Erhard Eppler: Wie vernünftig kann ein Politike sein?". *Leben und Glauben* 50/43 (25 October 1975), 6 ff. Incorporated in no. 14, 112-16.

75.22 "Der Turmbau zu Babel". *Leben und Glauben* 50/39 (27 September 1975), 6 ff.

75.23 "Die Evangelisch-Methodistische Kirche". *Leben und Glauben* 50/47 (22 November 1975), 6 ff.

75.24 "Die Selly Oak Colleges in Birmingham". *Leben und Glauben* 50/30 (26 July 1975), 6 ff.

75.25 "Der Geist von Lausanne". *Leben und Glauben* 50/34 (23 August 1975), 6 ff. Incorporated in no. 14, 158-60.

75.26 "Wunden verbinden im Gespräch mit Nichtchristen". *Leben und Glauben* 50/26 (28 June 1975), 6 ff. Incorporated in no. 14, 33-37.

75.27 "Bomben in Birmingham". *Leben und Glauben* 50/1 (4 January 1975), 6 ff. Incorporated in no. 14, 82-85.

75.28 "Glück ist wichtiger für die Engländer als Reichtum". *Leben und Glauben* 50/21 (24 May 1975), 6 ff.

1976

76.03 "Geisteserfahrung und charismatisches Weltverständnis". *Diakonia* 7/6 (1 November 1976), 381-90.

76.03a "Creator Spiritus. The Challenge of Pentecostal Experience to Pentecostal Theology". *Theology* 81/679 (1 January 1978), 32-40.

76.04 "My Fair Lady - ein theologisches Gleichnis". *Kunst und Kirche*, 1976/4 (1 October 1976), 161-164. Incorporated in no. 12, 106-11.

76.05 "Christus in Ost, West, Nord, Süd, Christus im Westen, Das Apostolische Glaubensbekenntnis". *Leben und Glauben* 51/49 (4 December 1976), 18 ff. Incorporated in no. 14, 69-73.

76.05a "Christus in Ost, West, Nord, Süd, Christus im Norden, der heldische Gott". *Leben und Glauben* 51/50 (11 December 1976), 19 ff. Incorporated in no. 14, 131-35

76.05b "Christus in Ost, West, Nord, Süd, Christus im Süden, Christen ohne Schriften". *Leben und Glauben* 51/51 (18 December 1976), 8 ff. Incorporated in no. 14, 171-74.

76.05c "Christus in Ost, West, Nord, Süd, Christus hat viele Farben". *Leben und Glauben* 51/52 (25 December 1976), 10 ff. Incorporated in no. 14, 209-13.

76.05d "Christus in Ost, West, Nord, Süd, Christus im Osten, Das Evangelium vom fremden Gott". *Leben und Glauben* 51/48 (27 November 1976), 14-17. Incorporated in no. 14, 13-17.

76.06 "Woran erkennt man den Heiligen Geist?". *Leben und Glauben* 51/22 (29 May 1976), 6 ff.

76.06a "Woran erkennt man den Heiligen Geist?". *Religion/Lebenskunde - 6. Schuljahr* (1 June 1985), 4-6.

76.06b "Woran erkennt man den Heiligen Geist?, *Zeitschrift für Religionsunterricht und Lebenskunde* (1 February 1979), 1-3.

76.07 "Schwarz und weiss in den USA". *Leben und Glauben* 51/25 (19 June 1976), 10 ff.

76.08 "Nicholas Bhengu". *Leben und Glauben* 51/39 (25 September 1976), 10 ff. Incorporated in no. 14, 184-191.

76.09 "Irland: Was die Zeitungen nicht berichten". *Leben und Glauben* 51/17 (2 April 1976), 6 ff. Incorporated in no. 14, 85-88.

76.10 "Nairobi: Vier afrikanische Kirchen in den Ökumenischen Rat aufgenommen". *Leben und Glauben* 51/13 (27 March 1976), 6 ff. Incorporated in no. 14, 192-95.

76.11 "Zion in Afrika". *Leben und Glauben*, 51/30 (24 July 1976), 10 ff. Incorporated in no. 14, 188-191.

76.12 "Sadhu Sundar Singh, ein christlicher Wandermönch in Indien". *Leben und Glauben* 51/35 (28 August 1976), 10 ff. Incorporated in no. 14, 37-41.

76.13 "Der Libanon". *Leben und Glauben* 51/9 (2 February 1976), 10 ff. Incorporated in no. 14, 29-33.

76.14 "Die Heilsarmee und die Toleranz in der Schweiz". *Leben und Glauben* 51/1 (3 January 1976), 6 ff. Incorporated in no. 14, 102-05.

76.15 "Arm und Reich". *Leben und Glauben* 51/1 (3 January 1976), 5.

76.16 "Glaube, Geist und Geister". *Zur Debatte* 6/4 (1 August 1976), 3 ff.

1977

77.01 "Hans Hoekendijk: ein ökumenischer Souffleur". *Leben und Glauben* 52/15 (9 April 1977), 10 ff.

77.02 "Die Sorgenkinder des Kremlins". *Leben und Glauben* 52/9 (26 February 1977), 10 ff. Incorporated in no. 14, 52-55.

77.03 "Christliche Gurus". *Leben und Glauben* 52/10 (5 March 1977), 10 ff. Incorporated in no. 14, 41-44.

77.05 "Eingeschlafene Utopie". *Kirchenbote für den Kanton Zürich* 63/6B (16 June 1977), 1.

77.06 "Gottvertrauen in Südafrika". *Leben und Glauben* 52/22 (28 May 1977), 10 ff. Incorporated in no. 14, 182-84.

77.07 "Dieter Mendt und Walter Kummer". *Leben und Glauben* 52/26 (25 June 1977), 10 ff. Incorporated in no. 14, 56-59

77.08 "Zur Trennungsinitiative,Gedanken eines Auslandschweizers". *Kirchenbote für den Kanton Zürich* 63/10A (1 October 1977), 7.

77.09 "Gedanken eines Auslandschweizers zum Thema Trennung von Kirche und Staat". *Leben und Glauben* 52/30 (17 July 1977), 10 ff.

77.10 "Die Schweiz aus englischer Sicht". *Leben und Glauben* 52/31 (1 August 1977), 10 ff.

77.11 "Die lästige Dritte Welt". *Leben und Glauben* 52/35 (27 August 1977), 7-9. Incorporated in no. 14, 203-05.

77.16 "Paul Burkhard, ein Troubadour von Gottes Gnaden". *Leben und Glauben* 52/43 (23 October 1977), 8 ff. Incorporated in no. 14, 105-08.

77.20 "Fug und Unfug der Gemeinschaft; oder: Was tun, wenn sich unsere Kinder bekehren". *Schritte ins Offene* 7/6 (1 December 1977), 14-16.

77.20a "Wenn Jugend sich bekehrt". *Lutherische Monatshefte* 17/7 (1 July 1978), 382 ff.

77.20b "When Young People Convert". *International Review of Missions*, 67/268 (1 October 1978), 457-60.

77.21 "The Church for Others - Ten Years After". *Research Bulletin ISWRA* (1 June 1977), 82-96.

77.21a "Dir Kirche für andere-ein Mythos". *Evangelische Theologie* 37/5 (1 October 1977), 425-43. Incorporated in no. 16, 29-45.

77.21b "La iglesia para los demas - un mito". Spanish Summary. *Selecciones de teologia* 18/69 (1 February 1979), 32-37.

77.23 "Konflikt in Korinth. Eine Erzählung aus dem Urchristentum". *Bibelarbeit I 1 Kor. 14.14-20* (1 June 1977), 125-31. Incorporated in no. 11. French (no. 11a), English (no. 11b), Italian (no. 11d), Indonesian (no. 11e), Other editions see no. 11.

77.23 "Konflikt in Korinth. Eine Erzählung aus dem Urchristentum". *Leben und Glauben* 52/49 (3 December 1977), 8 ff.

77.23a "Konflikt in Korinth. Eine Erzählung aus dem Urchristentum". *Leben und Glauben* 52/50 (10 December 1977), 10 ff.

77.23b "Konflikt in Korinth. Eine Erzählung aus dem Urchristentum". *Leben und Glauben* 52/51 (17 December 1977), 8 ff.

77.23c "Konflikt in Korinth. Eine Erzählung aus dem Urchristentum". *Leben und Glauben* 52/52 (24 December 1977), 4 ff.

77.23d "Konflikt in Korinth. Eine Erzählung aus dem Urchristentum". *Leben und Glauben* 52/48 (26 November 1977), 4 ff.
77.23e "Konflikt in Korinth. Eine Erzählung aus dem Urchristentum". *Leben und Glauben* 52/53 (31 December 1977), 4 ff.
77.24 "Die beiden Korintherbriefe verraten uns viel". *Leben und Glauben* 52/48 (26 November 1977), 8 ff.
77.25 "Ave Maria: Mary, the Reformers and the Protestants". *One in Christ* 13/4 (1 October 1977), 285-90. German in no. 12, 112-18.
77.26 "Theology in Relation to Society". In: *Conference on Theological Education - Wadderton 27th - 29th May 1977* (1 June 1977), 5-6.

1978

78.01 "La portée oecuménique et universelle du Renouveau charismatique". *Tychique*, nos. 13-14 (1 January 1978), 53 ff.
78.02 "Die Neuapostolische Gemeinde". *Leben und Glauben* 53/1 (7 January 1978), 10 ff.
78.03 "Ziele der Evangelisation". *Concilium* (1 June 1978), 230-34.
78.03a "Les Fins de l'évangélisation". *Concilium*, no. 134 (1 June 1978), 55-65.
78.03b "Objectivos de la evangeliçazion". *Concilium*, no. 134 (1 June 1978), 52-62.
78.03c "Objetivos de evangeliçazao". *Concilium* (1 June 1978), 445-54.
78.03d "Doelstellingen van de evangelisatie". *Concilium* (1 June 1978), 41-49.
78.03e "Oiettivi dell'evangelizzazione". *Concilium* (1 June 1978), 644-46.
78.05 "Intercultural Theology". *Christian* 6/1 (25 December 1978), 12-25. German: incorporated in no. 12, 33-51.
78.05a "Intercultural Theology". *Research Bulletin ISWRA* (1 October 1978), 9-104.
78.05b "Intercultural Theology". *Theological Renewal*, no. 10 (1 October 1978), 2-14.
78.10 "Papst und Pfingstler". *Leben und Glauben* 53/25 (24 June 1978), 8 ff. Incorporated in no. 14, 217-21.
78.11 "Die Mormonen". *Leben und Glauben* 53/42 (28 October 1978), 8 ff.
78.12 "Madre Maria del Rosario". *Leben und Glauben* 53/47 (25 November 1978), 8 ff. Incorporated in no. 14, 91-95.
78.13 "Eine Lehrerin denkt über ihre Bekehrung nach". *Leben und Glauben* 53/51 (3 December 1978), 8 ff. Incorporated in no. 14, 213-17.
78.14 "Arnoldshainer Akzente, Nachrichten aus der Akademie". *Leben und Glauben* 55/2 (9 January 1980), 8 ff.
78.14 "Immanuel, das heisst: Gott mit uns, Eine narrative Exegese zu Weihnachten". *Evangelischer Pressedienst*, no. 47 (22 November 1978). Incorporated in no. 16, 91-95.
78.14a "Immanuel, das heisst: Gott mit uns". *Gustav Adolf Kalender 1983*, (1 January 1983), 24-27.
78.14b "Immanuel, das heisst: Gott mit uns". *Zeitschrift für Mission*, no. 7 (1 June 1981), 131-34.
78.15 "Narrativité et théologie interculturelle,Un aspect négligée de 1 Cor. 14". *Revue de Théologie et de Philosophie*, no. 110 (1 June 1978), 209-23.
78.15a "Narrative Theologie". *Kirchenblatt für die reformierte Schweiz* 135/4 (15 Fe-

bruary 1979), 50-53.

78.16 "Rom und die Pfingstler". *Lutherische Monatshefte* 17/11 (1 November 1978), 646-48.

78.17 "Weihnachten nur für Christen?". *Evangelisches Frankfurt* 2/6 (1 December 1978), 1. Incorporated in no. 16, 109 ff.

78.18 "Die Dreieinigkeit - ein Stein des Anstosses". *Leben und Glauben* 53/39 (30 September 1978), 10 ff. Incorporated in no. 25.

78.22 "Prophetische Verkündiging". *Das missionarische Wort* 31/2 (1 April 1978), 54-57. Incorporated in no. 12, 337-42.

78.23 "Die Täufer". *Leben und Glauben* 53/29 (22 July 1978), 10 ff. Incorporated in no. 14, 95-98.

78.24 "Samuel Fröhlich und die Neutäufer". *Leben und Glauben* 53/34 (26 August 1978), 8 ff. Incorporated in no. 14, 99-102.

1979

79.01 "Mission in den achtziger Jahren". *Unser Grund zum Handeln* (1 June 1979), 10 ff.

79.02 "Gefährten, Brüder, Zeugen". *Weltmission '79 - Materialen für Gemeinden und Schulen* (1 June 1979), 10-15.

79.03 "Die Blinden der Bibel und die Gestressten von heute". Interview. *Evangelische Pressedienst*, no. 16 (18 April 1979), 4-6.

79.04 "Gottesdienst mit Nichtchristen". *Das Wort in der Welt* 1979/2 (1 April 1979), 13.

79.04a "Gottesdienst mit Nichtchristen". *Gemeindebrief der evangelischen Kirchengemeinde* (1 July 1979), 5.

79.05 "Methodism's Past in Pentecostalism's Present. A Case Study of a Cultural Clash". *Epworth Review* 6/2 (1 May 1979), 35-47.

79.05a "Methodism's Past in Pentecostalism's Present. A Case Study of a Cultural Clash". *Methodist History* 20/4 (1 July 1982), 169-82.

79.05b "Pasado del metodismo en el presente del pentecostalismo. Estudio de un caso de choque cultural en Chile". *Spiritus* 1/1 (1 June 1982), 31-46.

79.07 "Music and Dance in Pentecostal Movements". *WACC Journal* 26/2 (1 February 1979), 23-25.

79.08 "Da muss ein Blättchen ersetzt werden. Die Ökumene und die charismatische Bewegung". *Evangelische Presse Dienst*, no. 23 (6 June 1979), 17-19.

79.09 "Die Pfarrer aber nahmen Reissaus". *Deutsches Allgemeines Sonntagsblatt* 33/24 (17 June 1979), 27. Incorporated in no. 14, 229-31 and in no. 25.

79.09a "Die Pfarrer aber nahmen Reissaus". *Kirchenbote für den Kanton Zürich*, 67/12A (1 December 1980), 3.

79.09b "Die Pfarrer aber nahmen Reissaus". *Leben und Glauben* 53/34 (22 August 1979).

79.09 "Die Pfarrer aber nahmen Reissaus". *Orientierung* 17/44 (15 September 1980), 17-22.

79.10 "Paolo Freire Applied to Theological Education". *Journal of Beliefs and Values* 1/1 (1 March 1979), 6.

79.13 "Towards a Church Renewed and United in the Spirit". *Ecumenical Review* 11/3 (1 July 1979), 305-09.

79.15 "As a minority we can call the bluff of these liturgies called elections". *Reform* (1 February 1979), 3 ff.
79.16 "Ein Deutscher untersucht die ökumenische Sprache". *Leben und Glauben* 54/4 (24 January 1979), 8 ff.
79.17 "Das Wie und Wozu des Festes". *Diakonia* 10/1 (1 January 1979), 16-24. Incorporated in no. 16, 121-29.
79.18 "Pfingsten - Pontifex - Brückenbauer, Der Ökumenische Rat der Kirchen und die charismatische Bewegung". *Evangelische Pressedienst* no. 18 (2 May 1979), 6-8.
79.19 "Interkulturelle Theologie". *Leben und Glauben* 54/30 (25 July 1979), 6 ff.
79.20 "Unheilbar religiös. Über die Mission der Volkskirche". *Evangelische Kommentare* 12/7 (1 July 1979), 400-03.
79.21 "Frau aus Stahl statt 'Maitli us Packpapier'". *Leben und Glauben* 54/26 (27 June 1979), 6 ff.
79.22 "Religiöse Völlerei". *Leben und Glauben* 54/12 (21 March 1979), 8 ff.
79.23 "Charisma - Was die Kirchen schon immer gesagt haben". *Leben und Glauben* 54/22 (30 May 1979), 6 ff.
79.24 "Eine Schwarze Schule in Birmingham". *Leben und Glauben* 54/39 (26 September 1979), 8 ff.
79.25 "Der Ökumenische Rat und die charismatische Bewegung". *Leben und Glauben* 54/16 (18 April 1979), 6 ff. Incorporated in no. 14, 221-25.
79.26 "Das Ende von Jonestown". *Leben und Glauben* 54/8 (21 February 1979), 8 ff. Incorporated in no. 14, 161-64.
79.29 "Erweckung in Schwarz. Eine Schule für schwarze Arbeiterpfarrer in Grossbritannien". *Evangelische Pressedienst* no. 39 (26 September 1979), 8-10.
79.32 "Erfahrungen in Ephesus". *Leben und Glauben* 54/43 (24 October 1979), 8 ff.
79.33 "So könnte ich auch glauben!". *Unsere Kirche* 34/16 (22 April 1979).
79.34 "Charismatiker in der D.D.R.". *Leben und Glauben* 54/47 (21 November 1979), 6 ff. Incorporated in no. 14, 60-62.

1980

80.01 "Vom Mechaniker zum Theologieprofessor". *Leben und Glauben* 55/5 (30 January 1980), 8 ff.
80.02 "Traktate oder Traktoren". *Zeitschrift für Reliogions-Pädagogik ZRP* 2 (1 April 1980), 41-43.
80.03 "Zum Thema: Interreligiöser Dialog". *Theologia Practica*, no. 15 (1 June 1980), 6 ff.
80.04 "Die Schweiz und das Bankgeheminis". *Leben und Glauben* 55/14 (2 April 1980), 6 ff.
80.05 "Hauskirchen in England". *Leben und Glauben* 55/10 (5 March 1980), 8 ff.
80.05a "Zwischen Erweckung und Versektung - Hauskirchen in England". *Die Stimme* 43/1 (1 January 1981), 2 ff.
80.05b "Zwischen Erweckung und Versektung - Hauskirchen in England". *Evangelische Pressedienst*, no. 24 (11 June 1980), 12 ff.
80.06 "The House Church Movement in Great Britain". *Expository Times* 92/2 (1 November 1981), 45-47.

80.07 "W.E. Rose: Frieden auf Erden". *Leben und Glauben* 55/52 (24 December 1980), 6 ff.
80.08 "Michal - eine Frau aus der Bibel auf einer Zürcher Bühne". *Leben und Glauben* 55/47 (19 November 1980), 6 ff. See no. 23.
80.09 "Helmut Gollwitzer, Komplize der Menschen". *Leben und Glauben* 55/26 (25 June 1980), 6 ff.
80.11 "Ein merkwürdiger Protestant". *Leben und Glauben* 55/22 (28 May 1980), 6 ff.
80.12 "Dialog der Erfahrungen in Bossey". *Leben und Glauben.* 55/18 (30 April 1980), 6 ff.
80.13 "Roots and Fruits of the Charismatic Renewal in the Third World: Implications for Mission". *Occasional Bulletin of Missionary Research* 4/2 (1 April 1980), 68-75.
80.13a "Roots and Fruits of the Charismatic Renewal in the Third World: Implications for Mission". *Research Bulletin ISWRA* (1 June 1980), 125-43.
80.13b "Roots and Fruits of the Charismatic Renewal in the Third World: Implications for Mission". *Theological Renewal,* no. 14 (1 February 1980), 11-28.
80.14 "Paolo Freire en Angleterre". *Education des adultes* 30/21 (1 September 1980), 23-28.
80.14a "Paolo Freire in England". *Education des adultes* 30/21 (1 September 1980), 17-22.
80.15 "Zwei merkwürdige Pfarrer". *Leben und Glauben* 55/30 (23 July 1980), 8 ff.
80.16 "Zwingli's Devotion to Mary". *One in Christ* 16/1-2 (1 April 1980), 59-68.
80.17 "Wenn Grenzen Brücken werden". *Leben und Glauben* 55/44 (29 October 1980), 6 ff.
80.18 "Theology Course Unites Black and White". Abridged reprint. *Bulletin University of Birmingham,* no. 385 (3 November 1980), 2.
80.18a "Theology Course Unites Black and White". *University of Birmingham News Release* (18 October 1980).
80.19 "Ein Brücke zwischen schwarz und weiss, Theologische Ausbildung für schwarze Arbeitpfarrer". *Orientierung* 17/44 (15 September 1980), 178-80. See no. 83.35
80.23 "Wenn Soweto vor der Türe steht". *Leben und Glauben* 55/35 (27 August 1980), 8 ff.
80.25 "Professor's two dramas". *Bulletin: University of Birmingham,* no. 386 (10 November 1980).
80.26 "Gomer oder Das Gesicht des Unsichtbaren". *Werkstatt-Predigt Eine homiletische Korrespondenz* 8/37 (1 September 1980), 6-25. Incorporated in no. 17, 29-67.
80.27 "Pluralismus in Kirche und Mission". *Offene Kirche* 1980/1 (1 February 1980), 3-14.
80.28 "Interreligiöser Dialog". *Theologia Practica* 15/1 (1 June 1980), 6 ff.

1981

81.01 "Wenn Pascal heute leben würde". *Leben und Glauben* 56/16 (15 April 1981), 6 ff.
81.02 "A Revival in Black and a New Way of Learning". *Reform* (1 April 1981), 14.
81.03 "Religiöse Aufbrüche können gut oder schlecht sein". Abridged reprint. *Schweiz. Evangelischer Pressedienst* (12 February 1981), 6 ff.

81.03 "Warum freuen sich Theologen nicht über religiöse Aufbrüche". *Leben und Glauben* 52/6 (4 February 1981), 6 ff.
81.04 "The Embrace of Africa with the West". *Reform* (1 March 1981), 7.
81.05 "Ich schäme mich". *Leben und Glauben* 56/11 (11 March 1981), 6 ff. Incorporated in no. 16, 85-90.
81.06 "Hauskirchen in England". *Die Stimme* 43/1 (1 June 1981), 2, 4. see also 80.05.
81.07 "Mr. Rose, now Ph.D., Wrote About Forgiveness". *Reform* (1 February 1981), 3 ff.
81.08 "Bibelübersetzungen". *Leben und Glauben* 52/26 (24 June 1981), 6 ff.
81.09 "Lessons from Indonesia for an Ulster Churchman". *Reform* (1 August 1981), 14.
81.10 "Sister Mary in Search of Liberated Christians". *Reform* (1 June 1981), 4 ff.
81.12 "Die Presbyterinische Kirche in Kamerun". *Leben und Glauben* 56/23 (3 June 1981), 6 ff.
81.13 "W.E. Rose zum Geburtstage". *Der Londoner Bote* 34/309 (1 June 1981), 11-13. See also 80.07.
81.13a "W.E. Rose: Frieden auf Erden". *Leben und Glauben* 55/52 (24 December 1980), 6 ff. See also 80.07.
81.14 "Le double visage de l'église catholique". *La Vie Protestante* 44/21 (22 May 1981), 4.
81.15 "William Paton - Special Kind of Patriot". *Reform* (1 May 1981), 11.
81.16 "William Paton - ein besonderer Patriot". *Leben und Glauben* 56/20 (13 May 1981), 6 ff.
81.18 "Der Ökumensiche Rat und die Charismatische Bewegung". *Orientierung* 45/2 (31 January 1981), 15-18.
81.25 "A l'université de Birmingham avec des pasteurs-ouvriers". *Journal des mission évangéliques*, no. 156 (1 June 1981), 56-63.
81.26 "Pentecost: When the Unthinkable Became Reality". *One World*, no. 67 (1 June 1981), 22.
81.28 "Konflikt der Religionen". *Leben und Glauben* 56/41 (7 October 1981), 6 ff.
81.29 "Karl Barth Tells Such Good Stories". *Reform* (1 October 1981), 9.
81.30 "Bibelarbeiten". *Leben und Glauben* 56/27 (9 September 1981), 6 ff.
81.31 "Was ein Nordirländer von den Indonesiern lernte". *Leben und Glauben* 56/32 (5 August 1981), 6 ff.
81.32 "What Happens When Workers Are Treated Like Children". *Reform* (1 December 1981), 4.
81.33 "Chosen People: The British". *Reform* (1 September 1981), 3.
81.36 "Where the Holy Spirit Brings People who Don't Usually Come to Church". *Reform* (1 November 1981), 5.
81.37 "Karl Barth erzählt biblische Geschichten". *Leben und Glauben* 56/45 (4 November 1981), 6 ff.
81.38 "Evangelische Pfingstchristen in der Sowjetunion - 2.Teil: Zur Geschichte der Pfingstbewgung in Russland". *Glaube in der 2. Welt* 9/10 (1 June 1981), 371-77.
81.39 "Staat und Kirche in England". *Leben und Glauben* 56/51 (16 December 1981), 6 ff.
81.40 "Eine andere Exegese". *Der Graben zwischen Leib, Seele und Geist wurde über-*

brückt. Bericht vom 3. Internationalen Bibelseminar (6 February 1981), 5-10. Incorporated in no. 16, 134-58 (also in English and French).

81.40a "Eine andere Exegese". *Verkündiging und Forschung* 1981/2 (1 February 1981), 5-24.

81.40b "The Other Exegesis, Horizons in Biblical Theology". *An International Dialogue*, no. 3 (1 June 1981), 155-79.

1982

82.01 "Theologie an der Basis, Auf den Menschen hören". *Ev. Monatsblatt Kirche und Mann* 35/1 (1 January 1982), 4.

82.02 "Bei den Kimbanguisten in Afrika: Nachdenken mit den Kimbanguisten". *Leben und Glauben* 57/5 (27 January 1982), 6 ff; and 57/8 (17 February 1982), 6 ff.

82.02a "Op bezoek bij de Kimbaguisten: Gedachten over de Kimbanguisten". *Vandaar* 8/5 (1 May 1982), 6-8; and 8/6 (1 June 1982), 6-8.

82.03 "Der Mythos stirbt nicht. Mythen der Gottesbegegnung". *Werkstatt Predigt-Eine homiletische Korrespondenz* 10/43 (1 March 1982), 29-60. Incorporated in no. 16, 112-21.

82.04 "L'évangélisation aujourd'hui". *Bulletin d'information de l'Eglise d'Augsbourg et de l'Eglise Réformée d'Alsace et de Lorraine* 1982/1 (1 March 1982), 16-18.

82.05 "Der Mythos vom Dritten Weg". *Leben und Glauben* 57/19 (5 May 1982), 5 ff.

82.06 "Die Familie in Geschichte und Gegenwart". *Leben und Glauben* 57/49 (1 December 1982), 6 ff.

82.07 "Erweckung. Praktische Theologie". *Theologische Realenzyklopädie*, Vol. 10 (June 1982), 224, 227.

82.08 "Evangelisation". *Evangelische Erwachsenenbildung* 34/25 (1 May 1982), 15-19. Incorporated in no. 12, 121 ff.

82.09 "Fug und Unfug europäischen Bildungsexportes". *Leben und Glauben* 57/34 (18 August 1982), 6 ff.

82.10 "White Reflections About Black Competence". *Christian Action Journal* (1 October 1982), 16 ff.

82.11 "Brief an W. Simpendörfer". *Der Graben zwischen Leib, Seele und Geist wurde überbrückt. Bericht vom 3. Internationalen Bibelseminar* (6 February 1982), 21-22.

82.12 "Ein neuer Mythos: Der dritte Weg in die Zukunft". *Botschaft und Dienst* 33/4 (1 July 1982), 7-14.

82.12a "Plädoyer für einen dritten Weg". *Reformatio* 31/7-8 (1 July 1982), 402-10.

82.13 "Emil Brunner: Ein Theologe, den alle verstehen können". *Leben und Glauben* 57/27 (30 June 1982), 6 ff.

82.14 "Retrouver l'élan du Moyen Age". *La Vie protestante* 45/23 (11 June 1982), 8 ff.

82.15 "Falkland-Krise. Persönliche Eindrücke eines perplexen Beobachters". *Leben und Glauben* 57/25 (16 June 1982), 6 ff.

82.17 "Die Kolosser sangen ... in der Bibel-Werkstatt". *Werkbrief für Landjugend* 1982/3 (1 June 1982), 30.

82.18 "Die Familie in Geschichte und Gegenwart". *Leben und Glauben* 57/49 (1 December 1982), 6 ff.

82.20 "Die religiöse Schweiz in Zahlen". *Leben und Glauben* 57/46 (10 November

1982), 6 ff.
82.21 "John Taylor gab der ökumenischen Bewegung ein menschliches Gesicht". *Leben und Glauben* 57/45 (3 November 1982), 18 ff.
82.22 "Evangelisation". *Theologische Realenzyklopädie*, Vol. 10 (June 1982), 636-41.
82.24 "Umgang mit Mythen". *Leben und Glauben* 57/12 (17 March 1982), 6 ff.
82.25 "Das Chistentum in der Welt". *Leben und Glauben* 57/38 (15 September 1982), 6 ff.
82.26 "Wie biblisch ist der Sonntag?". *Leben und Glauben* 57/3 (13 January 1982), 6 ff.
82.27 "Einführung in eine moderne Mythology". *Leben und Glauben* 57/15 (7 April 1982), 6 ff.

1983

83.01 "Chinas Christen". *Leben und Glauben* 58/4 (19 January 1983), 6 ff.
83.02 "David war ein Hirtenbub". *Leben und Glauben* 58/25 (15 June 1983), 6 ff.
83.03 "Die Evangelische Gesellschaft im Kanton Bern". *Leben und Glauben* 58/29 (13 July 1983), 6 ff.
83.04 "Elias vor der Bibelkommission Seldwylas". *Leben und Glauben* 58/6 (2 February 1983), 6 ff.
83.05 "Frieden". *Gwatt-Blatt* 49/3 (1 September 1983).
83.06 "Lutherjahr-Zwinglijahr". *Leben und Glauben* 58/45 (4 November 1983), 6 ff.
83.09 "Prospectus for the Study of Theology". *Prospectus* (June 1983).
83.10 "What happens to Scripture in Church and School?". *Journal of Beliefs and Values* 4/2 (1 June 1983), 14-19.
83.11 "Das Erbe Zwinglis". *Tagesanzeiger* (31 December 1983), 45 ff.
83.12 "Glaube - Volk - Kultur, Die evangelische Diaspora". *Jahrbuch des Gustav Adolf Werkes* 53 (1 January 1983), 32-46.
83.14 "Pneumatologie des Lebens". *Evangelische Kommentare* 16/8 (1 August 1983), 446-48.
83.15 "Einheit von Theologie und Praxis". *Kirchenbote für den Kanton Zürich* (3 June 1983), 20.
83.16 "In England ist alles Liturgie, Zur Situation der Kirchen in England". *Kunst und Kirche* 3/1982 (1 June 1983), 118-22.
83.17 "Theologie in der D.D.R.". *Leben und Glauben* 58/12 (16 March 1983), 6 ff.
83.18 "Elija von der interkantonalen Lehrmittelkommision". *Chilebrief 12* (1 June 1984), 2-4.
83.18 "Elija von der interkantonalen Lehrmittelkommission". *Religion/Lebenskunde-Starthilfen zum Lehrplan für die Primar und Sekundarschulen des Kantons Bern*, Propheten I (1 June 1985), 1-4.
83.18a "Elija von der interkantonalen Lehrmittelkommission". *Zeitschrift für Religionsunterricht und Lebenskunde* 12/3 (1 August 1983), 1-4. Propheten I - 5. Schuljahr.
83.19 "Frieden". *Leben und Glauben* 58/34 (17 August 1983), 6 ff.
83.20 "Theologie der Armen - oder: Vormachen wirkt ansteckend". *Missionsjahrbuch der Schweiz 1982/1983* (1 January 1983), 117-20.
83.22 "What is Christianity". *Clarity* 15/4 (1 June 1983), 86-90.
83.23 "Gomer: Das Gesicht des Unsichtbaren". *Leben und Glauben* 58/29 (13 July

1983), 6 ff.

1984

84.01 "The Ecumenical Relevance of Huldreich Zwingli". *One World*, no. 94 (1 April 1984), 21 ff.
84.02 "Weltlich von Gott reden, Liebe für die Unterdrückten". *Evangelisches Monatsblatt Kirche und Man* 37/5 (1 May 1984), 6 ff.
84.03 "Ave Maria, Marialogie bei den Reformatoren". *Diakonia* 15/3 (1 May 1984), 189-93.
84.04 "Tanz in der Kirche". *Leben und Glauben* 59/20 (18 May 1984), 6 ff.
84.05 "Pfingsten - ein Fest der Verlegenheit". *Leben und Glauben* 59/23 (8 June 1984), 6 ff.
84.06 "Für eine reformierte Marienfrömmigkeit". *Leben und Glauben* 59/11 (10 March 1984), 6 ff.
84.07 "Huldreich Zwingli, réformateur de l'église et de la société". *Mensuel*, no. 7 (1 March 1984), 16-18.
84.08 "Herman Kutter in seinen Briefen". *Leben und Glauben* 59/9 (2 March 1984), 6 ff.
84.10 "Huldrych Zwingli: Ein Leben zwischen Krieg und Frieden". *Der Sämann* 100/1 (1 January 1984), 8.
84.10a "Huldrych Zwingli: Ein Leben zwischen Krieg und Frieden". *Kirchenbote für den Kanton Zürich* 70/1A (1 January 1984), 6-8.
84.11 "Die Offenbarung - ein prophetisches Buch". *Leben und Glauben* 59/17 (27 April 1984), 6 ff.
84.12 "Aussenseiter gefragt. Oder: Wozu brauchen wir heute noch Missionare?". *Evangelische Pressedienst*, no. 16a (18 April 1984), 4-6.
84.14 "Can Adventists be Ecumenical?". *Encounter* (1 May 1984), 6 ff.
84.15 "Schwarze Evangelisten in der Schweiz". *Leben und Glauben* 59/22 (10 June 1984), 6 ff.
84.16 "Fritz Berger: Im Dreck die Fahne hochhalten". *Leben und Glauben* 59/31 (3 August 1984), 6 ff.
84.17 "Wenn ich Bunderat wäre". *Leben und Glauben* 59/40 (5 October 1984), 6 ff.
84.18 "Gottesdienst zwischen Lehre und Feier". *Der Sämann* 100/10 (1 October 1984), 2.
84.19 "Monocultural Imperialism versus Intercultural Theology". *International Review of Mission* 73/292 (1 October 1984), 521-26.
84.20 "Was ist von Zwinglis Reformation geblieben?". *Leben und Glauben* 59/44 (2 November 1984), 6 ff.
84.21 "After Twenty Years Research on Pentecostalism". *International Review of Mission* 75/297 (1 January 1986), 3-12.
84.21a "After Twenty Years Research on Pentecostalism". *Theology* 87/720 (1 November 1984), 403-412.
84.21b "La investigacion del pentecostalismo: reinto años despues". *Spiritus* 2/1 (1 March 1986), 5-17.
84.22 "Überzeugt, das er im Himmel auch Heiden antreffen würde: Zwinglis ökumenische Bedeutung". *Entschluss* 39/11 (1 June 1984), 10-13.

84.24 "Dag Hammarskjöld: Reise nach innen". *Leben und Glauben* 59/2 (13 January 1984), 6 ff.
84.25 "The Ecumenical Relevance of Huldreich Zwingli". *One World*, no. 94 (1 April 1984), 21 ff.
84.25a "Huldrych Zwingli, réformateur de l'église et de la société". *Mensuel* no. 7 (1 March 1984), 16-18.

1985

85.01 "Halt dem Verblödungsprozess". *Leben und Glauben* 60/6 (8 February 1985), 6 ff.
85.02 'George Friedrich Händel, ein weltlicher Kirchenmusiker". *Leben und Glauben* 60/8 (22 February 1985), 6 ff.
85.03 "L'expérience de l'Esprit dans l'Eglise et hors de l'Eglise". *Le point théologique*, no. 44 (1 June 1985), 195-209.
85.04 "Leise Sänger, kleine Tänzer". *Deutsches Sonntagsblatt* 38/21 (26 May 1985), 17.
85.05 "Pentecostal Research". *EPTA Bulletin* IV/4 (1 October 1985), 124-53. Incorporated in no. 26.
85.06 "Wenn der Staat seine Bürger betrügt, Zwei mutige Frauen enthüllen die Wahrheit". *Leben und Glauben* 60/15 (12 April 1985), 6 ff.
85.07 "Eine reformierte Gemeindeliturgie für die Kranken". *E.Z.* (24 November 1985).
85.07 "Eine reformierte Gemeindeliturgie für die Kranken". *Kirchenbote für den Kanton Zürich* 71/5B (16 May 1985).
85.07 "Eine reformierte Gemeindeliturgie für die Kranken". *Leben und Glauben* 60/26 (28 June 1985), 6 ff.
85.08 "Vorchristliche und christliche Heilung". *Leben und Glauben* 60/27 (5 July 1985), 6 ff.
85.10 "Dietrich Bonhoeffer and William J. Seymour. A Comparison Between Two Ecumenists". *Norsk Tidsskrift for Misjon* 39/1985 (1 June 1985), 192-201.
85.11 "Jacobs Kampf am Jabok". *Evangelische Kommentare* 18/7 (1 July 1985), 411 ff.
85.13 "Die marktkonforme Religion". *Thelogia Practica*, no. 20 (1 June 1985), 97-103.
85.14 "Eine indische Kirche". *Leben und Glauben* 60/42 (18 October 1985), 8 ff.
85.15 "Rassenkrawalle in England, Hilflose Macht und Ohnmacht". *Leben und Glauben* 60/45 (6 November 1985), 6 ff.
85.16 "Frau Abenteuers Heimkehr und ihre Suche nach einer lebendigen Gemeinde". *Leben und Glauben* 60/21 (24 May 1985), 8 ff.
85.18 "Ihr Treffpunkt ist das Nidelblad, Die Ökumenische Akademie, *Leben und Glauben* 60/46 (15 November 1985), 8 ff.
85.19 "Die Schweiz - klein aber mein". *Kunst und Kirche* 1985/4 (1 October 1985), 228-30.
85.21 "Pingstväckelsen föddes i lidandet". Interview. *Dagen* 41/127 (3 July 1985), 4.
85.22 "Der Handlungsreisende Gottes, Beispiel einer der Bibelarbeiten am 21. Deutschen Ev. Kirchentag". *Leben und Glauben* 60/31 (2 August 1985), 6 ff.
85.23 "Von den Erfahrungen eines Pfarrers auf Haiti, Unchristliches Christentum?". *Leben und Glauben* 60/41 (11 October 1985), 6 ff.
85.24 "Beispiele einer 'züritüütschen' Fassung, So wird das Evangelium verständlich". *Leben und Glauben* 60/32 (9 August 1985), 6 ff.

85.31 "Un défi pour les églises. Réflexions sur les émeutes de Handsworth 9/10-9-1985". *Journal des mission évangeliques* 160/4 (1 December 1985), 171-78.

1986

86.01 "Pfingstlich Zeugnis im wissenschaftlichen Test". *Leben und Glauben* 61/5 (31 January 1986), 6 ff.

86.04 "Nicht nur vom Jenseits träumen, Von der Mitsprache der Kirchen im geteilten 'Vereinigten Königreich'". *Leben und Glauben* 61/2 (10 January 1986), 6 ff.

86.05 'The Chair of Mission at the University of Birmingham". *Selly Oak Journal*, no. 4 (1 January 1986), 12-19.

86.07 "Intercultural Theology". *Theology Today* 43/1 (1 April 1986), 28-35.

86.08 "Das Wagnis des Glaubens". *Leben und Glauben* 61/25 (20 June 1986), 6 ff.

86.09 "Streit gehört zum Wesen der Kirche". *Kirchenbote Basel* (15 April 1986), 1.

86.10 "Wie aus Grenzen Brücken werden". *Zur Debatte* 16/2 (1 April 1986), 6 ff.

86.11 "Die Religion der Verstummten". *Leben und Glauben* 61/39 (28 September 1986), 6 ff.

86.12 "Il fait rire, prier, danser ...". *Le Christianisme au XXe sciècle* 114/82 (22 September 1986), 5.

86.14 "Seelsorge im Westen und in Africa". *Leben und Glauben* 61/42 (17 October 1986), 6 ff.

86.16 "Der Erzbischof von Canterbury". *Leben und Glauben* 61/44 (31 October 1986), 6 ff.

86.17 "Ein Mensch und drei Geischter". *Leben und Glauben* 61/50 (12 December 1986), 24 ff.

86.18 "China-Mission erfüllt?". *Leben und Glauben* 61/28 (11 July 1986), 6 ff.

86.20 "Wenn ich Gorbatschow wäre ...". *Leben und Glauben* 61/15 (11 April 1986), 6 ff.

86.21 "Warum wir eine kritische Presse brauchen". *Leben und Glauben* 61/17 (25 April 1986), 6 ff.

1987

87.01 "Die Schweiz aus erzbischöflicher Sicht. Gespräch nach einem hohen Besuch". *Leben und Glauben* 62/1 (2 January 1987), 24 ff.

87.02 "Das Ende des naturwissenschaftlichen Zeitalters?". *Leben und Glauben* 62/5 (30 January 1987), 24 ff.

87.03 "Der Geist als die schöpferische Kraft". *Diakonia* 18/2 (1 March 1987), 97-103.

87.05 "China Mission erfüllt?". *Leben und Glauben* 61/28 (11 July 1986), 6 ff.

87.06 "Heilet die Kranken!". *Theologia Practica* (1 June 1987), 44-62.

87.07 "Teomilia Maria de Jesus, Priesterin, 12 Brasilianerinnen". *Schritte ins Offene* 17/5 (1 October 1987), 30-32.

87.10 "Interaction Between Black and White in Theological Education". *Theology* 90/737 (1 September 1987), 341-50.

87.11 "Ecce homo, Oratorium zum Kirchentag". *Weg und Wahrheit* 41/23 (7 June 1987), 6 ff.

87.12 "Seelsorge per Computer. Die zweifelhaften Methoden amerikanischer Fernsehprediger". *Leben und Glauben* 62/41 (9 October 1987), 26-28.

87.13 "Kirche und Heimat - Glaube und Patriotismus". *Leben und Glauben* 62/31 (31 July 1987), 24-27.

87.14 "Jona - ein Kind unserer Zeit". *Leben und Glauben* 62/29 (17 July 1987), 26, 29.

87.33 "Das Friedensmahl". *Leben und Glauben* 62/46 (13 November 1987), 12-15.

87.43 "Towards an Intercultural History of Christianity". *International Review of Mission* (1 October 1987), 526-56.

87.44 "Was dem Wohl aller dient, Theologische Argumente und Heilen gehören für die Charismatiker zusammen". *Deutsches Allgemeines Sonntagsblatt* 40/51 (20 December 1987), 19.

1988

88.06 "The Higher Christian Life". *International Review of Mission* 77/306 (1 April 1988), 272-76.

88.07 "Für eine evangelische Marienfrömmigkeit". *Pfarrblatt der Region Basel* 17/22 (29 May 1988), 15.

88.07a "Von der Vielfalt in der Nachfolge: Plädoyer für eine evangelische Marienfrömmigkeit". *Angelus - Röm. Kath. Biel und Umgebung* 79/23 (5 June 1988), 8.

88.07b "Von der Vielfalt in der Nachfolge Plädoyer für eine evangelische Marienfrömmigkeit". *Pfarrblatt* 3/23 (5 June 1988), 4 f.

88.07c "Für eine evangelische Marienfrömmigkeit". *Pfarrblatt* 33/44 (30 October 1988), 13.

88.08 "Der Heilige Geist zum Griefen nahe Verhängnis und Verheissung der charismatischen Bewegung". *Die Zeit*, no. 21 (20 May 1988), 75.

88.09 "Volkstheologie auf koreanisch". *Leben und Glauben* 63/14 (1 April 1988), 37.

88.19 "Grandeur et misère de la théologie". *Les cahiers protestants*, (June 1988), 22-29.

88.20 "Die beste Kritik des Falschen ist die Praxis des Wahren". *Auftrag* 3/88 (1988), 5 f.

88.26 "Neue spirituelle Bewegungen in den Kirchen". *Reformiertes Forum* 37 (15 September 1988), 11-14.

88.37 "Heilt die Kranken! Heilung als Gabe und Aufgabe der Gemeinde". *Studienbriefe*, A 28 (1988),

88.37a "Guérissez les malades! La guérison comme don et mission pour la communauté". *Hokma. Revue de réklexion théologique* 42 (1989), 65-89. Reprint in *Perspectives Missionnaires 20* (1990), 49-61.

1989

89.05 "The Ecumenical Significance of Oral Christianity". *Ecumenical Review* 41/2 (April 1989), 259-65.

89.06 "Healing through Prayer: Superstition or Forgotten Christian Tradition?". *Theology* 92/747 (May 1989), 166-174.

89.06a "Heldbredelse ved bon: Overto aller glemt kristen tradition?". *Praeste Foreningens Blad* 1990/33 (1990), 657-63.

89.07 "Interview". *Heks Nachrichtenblatt des Hilfeswerkes Evanglischer Kirchen der Schweiz*, no. 204 (März/April 1989), 3.

89.12 "Ist der Vater Jesu Christi auch der Gott der Religionen?". *Jahrbuch Mission 1989*

(1989), 39-50.

89.15 "Music in the Service of Reconciliation". *Theology* 92/746 (July 1989), 276-286.

89.15a "Music in the Service of Reconciliation". *The Hymnology*, Annual 1 (1991), 149-60.

89.15b "Music in the Service of Reconciliation". *Themenzentrierte Interaktion* 5/2 (Autumn 1991), 5-15.

89.15c "Musik und Liturgie im Dienste der Versöhnung". *Musik und Gottesdienst* 44/1 (1990), 5-14.

89.16 "The Future of Mission-Mission of the Future, Farewell Lecture Birminghmam". *Occasional Paper no. 2* (Birmingham: Selly Oak Colleges, 1989).

89.16a "Does Mission have a Future". *Movement* (1989), 5-8.

89.18 "Verhängnis und Verheissung charismatischer Heiler, Paulus Akademie". *Heilen, was verwundet ist. Heilkunst zwischen alternativer Medizin und göttlichem Geist* (1990), 133-64.

89.19 "Warum die Bibel?". *Prospectus of Kaiser Verlag and TVZ* (1989), 2.

89.24 "Toleranz im Islam und im Christentum". *Kinder zwischen Kirche und Moschee* 24/90 (28 May 1990), 9-12.

89.25 "Nicht Privatsache, sondern Sache der Liturgie. Heil und Heilung als Gabe und Aufgabe der Gemeinde". *Wege zum Menschen* 41/7 (October 1989), 408-19.

1990

90.05 "Musik und Liturgie im dienste der Versöhnung". *Musik und Gottesdienst* 44/1 (1990), 5-14. See also 89.15a.

90.06 "Kranksein in einer heillosen Welt". *Kirchliche Nachrichten Interlaken* 57/4 (April 1990), 1.

90.09 "Wir alle haben den gleichen Gott". Interview. *Aufbruch*, no. 9 (May 1990), 5.

90.10 "Theologie ist eine Kunst. Circus- und Schaustellerseelsorge der EKD". *Kirche unterwegs in einer säkularen Welt. Zeugnis und Dienst des Laien* (1990). Also in French, Italian and Spanish.

90.29 "Lilje offrierte mir eine dicke Zigarre. Walter Hollenweger: Erinnerungen an Hannover 1967". *Kirchentag aktuell* 18/II (1990), 4.

90.31 "Christsein in einer multikulturellen Gesellschaft". Abendgespräch. *Romero-Haus Protokolle* 24 (1990).

90.32 "Das Problem heute: Verwahrlosung oder schöpferischer Neubeginn". *Helferei*, Heft 1 (1990), 12-15.

90.33 "Vielleicht halt mal eine Woche lang Palaver". *Offene Kirche* 21/3-4 (June 1990), 2-5.

90.34 "Der Heilige Geist in der Theologie Paul Tillichs". *Dialog* 11 (September 1990), 6 f.

90.37 "Das Friedensmahl". *Notabene*, no. 6 (December 1990), 4 f.

90.38 "Die Evangelikalen". *Theologie für Laien: Kurszeitung 32*, no. 2 (December 1990), 27-32.

90.39 "The Koinonia of the Establishment". *Pneuma* 12/2 (Fall 1990), 154-57.

1991

91.01 "The Discipline of Thought and Action in Mission". *International Review of Missions* 80/317 (January 1991), 91-104.

91.02 "Abendmahlsstreit: Wasser in Wein". Interview. *Reformatorische Forum* (1 February 1991), 9-11.

91.05 "Náyons pas peur du Saint-Esprit". *La Vie Protestante*, (22 February 1991), 32.

91.12 "Bilder, die auftauchen". Interview in 'Wirklich traumhaft'". *Kollektenblatt der Evangelischen Gesellschaft des Kanton Bern* 131/2 no. 522 (1991), 15-20.

91.13 "Gottesdienst - nicht nur 'Sache der Theologen'". *Evangelische Kirchenzeitung*, no. 25 (23 June 1991), 11.

91.14 "Biblische Autoren hatten Respekt vor der Volksfrömmigkeit". *Mitteilungen der Evangelischen Landeskirche in Baden* (May/June 1991), 7 f.

91.17 "Das Evangelium sinnlich verkündigen". *Evangelische Information epd Wochenspiegel* 23/30 (25 July 1991), 2.

91.22 "Guérissez les malades". *Approches* 31/141 (September 1991), 5-7.

91.28 "Pentecostalismo: Lenguaje de cuerpos y sentimientos". *Evangelio y Sociedad*, no. 11 (October-December 1991), 7-10.

Missing numbers referring to unpublished manuscripts, lectures, public speeches, sermons and radio features:

29; 32; 34; 55.05; 55.06; 55.07; 66.19; 69.14; 71.19; 71.32-35; 73.35-36; 74.34-36; 77.17-19; 78.20; 79.31; 79.35-36; 80.20-22; 80.24; 81.17; 82.23; 83.24-26; 84.13; 84.23; 85.20; 85.25-30; 86.02-03; 86.19; 87.15-32; 87.34-42; 88.01-03; 88.10; 88.12-18; 88.22-25; 88.27-29; 88.31-32; 88.34-36; 89.01-04; 89.08-11; 89.13-14; 89.17; 89.20-23; 90.01-03; 90.07-08; 90.12-13; 90.15-26; 90.28; 90.30; 90.35; 91.03-04; 91.07-11; 91.15-16; 91.18-21; 91.23-27; 91.29-32.

List of Students of Professor Walter J. Hollenweger

Cornelis van der Laan

I. Ph.D. - Students

1. **John Bayes** — 1989
   Fulfilment on Condition. A Revisionist Appraisal of Christian Fulfilment Theology with Particular Attention to Problems of Verification

2. **Arnold Bittlinger** — 1977
   Papst und Pfingstler. Der römisch katholische/pfingstliche Dialog und seine ökumenische Relevanz *

3. **Brian C. Castle** — 1989
   Hyms: The Making and Shaping of a Theology for the Whole People of God. A Comparison of the Four Last Things in Some English and Zambian Hyms in Intercultural Perspective *

4. **Joseph Colletti** — 1990
   Ethnic Pentecostalism in Chicago: 1890-1950

5. **Jane Collier** — 1989
   The Culture of Economism - An Exploration of Barriers to Faith-as-Praxis *

6. **John R. Davis** — 1990
   Towards a Contextualized Theology for the Church in Thailand

7. **Joseph C. Difato** — 1985
   Pope and Executive. An Examination of Management Science and Catholic Social Teaching in Relation to the Dehumanizing Effect of Business Practice

8. **Roger B. Edrington** — 1985
   Everyday Men: An Analysis of Popular Unbelief and Unbelievers *

9. **D. William Faupel** — 1989
   This Gospel of the Kingdom: The Significance of Eschatology in the Development of Pentecostal Thought

10. Manuel J. Gaxiola-Gaxiola 1990
Mexican Protestantism: The Struggle for Identity and Relevance in a Pluralistic Society

11. Roswith I.H. Gerloff 1991
A Plea for British Black Theologies. The Black Church Movement in Britain in its Transatlantic Cultural and Theological Interaction *

12. Kenneth D. Gill 1990
Towards a Contextualized Theology of the Third World: The Emergence and Development of Jesus' Name Pentecostalism in Mexico

13. Roy E. Graham 1978
Ellen G. White: An Examination of Her Position and Role in the Seventh-Day Adventist Church

14. I. James M. Haire 1981
The Character and Theological Struggle of the Church in Halmahera, Indonesia, 1941-1949 *

15. Mary Hall 1976
A Quest for the Liberated Christian, Examined on the Basis of a Mission, a Man and a Movement as Agents of Liberation *

16. J. Martin Haworth 1982
The Contextuality of Theology: Jan Milic Lochman, Theologian between Czechoslavakia and Switzerland

17. Peter Hocken 1984
Baptised in the Spirit: The Origins and Early Development of the Charismatic Movement in Great Britain

18. George A. Hood 1985
The English Presbyterian Mission in Lingtung, South China - A Study of the Interplay between Mission Methods and their Historical Context

19. Eleanor M. Jackson 1976
Red Tape and the Gospel. The Ecumenical Missionary Struggle of Dr. William Paton 1886-1943

20. Lalomilo Kamu 1989
The Samoan Culture and the Christian Gospel

21. Warren H. Kinne 1989
Ideologies of Communion and Participation in the Mindanao-Sulu Catholic Church from 1971-1983 *

22. Cornelis van der Laan 1987
Gerrit Roelof Polman: Sectarian Against His Will. Birth of Pentecostalism in the Netherlands

23. Paulus N. van der Laan 1988
The Question of Spiritual Unity. The Dutch Pentecostal Movmenent in Ecumenical Perspective

24. Emmanuel Yartekwei Lartey 1984
Pastoral Counselling in Intercultural Perspective: A Study of some African (Ghanaian) and Anglo-American Views on Human Existence and Counselling *

25. Ki-Ban Lee 1989
The Validity of Ricci's Intercultural Mission in China and His Position within the Context of Contemporary Missiological and Theological Proposals

26. Kingsley Lewis 1983
The Moravian Mission in Barbados 1816-1866. A Study of the Historical Context and Theological Significance of a Minority Church among an Oppressed People *

27. Iain MacRobert 1989
Black Pentecostalism: Its Origins, Functions and Theology with Special Reference to a Midland Borough

28. Richard Massey 1988
'A Sound and Scriptural Union'. An Examination of the Origins of the Assemblies of God of Great Britain and Ireland during the years 1920-1925

29. Bongani A. Mazibuko 1983
Education in Mission - Mission in Education: A critical Comparative Study of Selected Approaches *

30. Merrill P. Morse 1989
Kosuke Koyama: A Model for Intercultural Theology *

31. Jörg Müller 1975
Uppsala II: Erneuerung in der Mission. Eine redaktionsgeschichtliche Studie und Dokumentation zu Sektion II der 4. Vollversammlung des Ökumenischen Rates der Kirchen. Uppsala 1968 *

32. George M. Mulrain 1982
Theology of Folk Culture: A Study of the Theological Significance of Haitian Folk Religion *

33. Douglas J. Nelson 1981
For Such a Time as This. The Story of Bishop William J. Seymour and the Azusa Street Revival. A Study of Pentecostal Roots

34. Patrick J. O'Mahony 1987
A Question of Life: Its Beginning and Transmission. A Moral Perspective of the New Genetics in the West, USSR, Poland and East

35. John Mansfor Prior 1987
Church and Marriage in an Indonesian Village. A Study of Customary and Church Marriage among the Ata Lio of Central Flores, Indonesia, as a Paradigm of the Ecclesial Interrelationship between Village and Institutional Catholicism *

37. P. Solomon Raj 1983
A Christian Folk-Religion in India. A Study of the Small Church Movements in Andhra Pradesh, South India, with a Special Reference to the Bible Mission and the Theological Ideas of its Founder, Father Devadas and their Significance to the Mainline Churches in India *

38. Martin Robinson 1987
To the Ends of the Earth - The Pilgrimage of an Ecumencial Pentecostal, David J. du Plessis 1905-1987

39. William Ernest Rose 1979
Sent from Coventry. A Mission of International Reconciliation

40. **John Rutherford** 1983
W.C. Willoughby of Bechuanaland, Missionary Practioner and Scholar

41. **Jose Norberto Saracco** 1990
Argentine Pentecostalism - Its History and Theology

42. **Ioan Sauca** 1987
The Missionary Implications of Eastern Orthodox Ecclesiology

43. **Harold Tonks** 1981
Faith, Hope and Decision Making. A Theological Study in Consistent Relativity, Being an Exposition of the Social Ethical Thought of Professor Arthur Rich of Zürich *

44. **Emil Weber** 1979
Friedrich Dürrenmatt's 'Die Stadt' und die Frage nach Gott

45. **Roger Williamson** 1980
The Reactions of the Churches in the German Federal Republic and the German Democratic Republic to the World Council of Churches' Programme to Combat Racism 1969-1975

46. **Boo-Woong Yoo** 1987
Korean Pentecostalism - Its History and Theology

47. **David Zucker** 1977
The Rabbis: A Jewish Study in Anglo-American Fiction and Sociology (1950-1976)

II. (Mini) M.A., M.Litt., M.Phil. - Students

1. **Pamela M. Binyon** M.A. 1974
The Concepts of 'Spirit' and 'Demon'. A Study in the Use of Different Languages Describing the Same Phenomena *

2. **Ilse Bittlinger-Baumann** M.Phil. 1988
Anders über Godd reden. Kritische Überlegungen zum Gottesbild und neue Wege der Gotteserfahrungen

3. Charles Bradshaw M.A. 1976
A Comparison of the Understanding of Mission in the Work of David Livingstone and Colin Morris

4. Anthony D. Calvert M.A. 1984
The Published Works of William Robinson: An Interpretative and Annotated Bibliography of a Catholic Evangelical

5. I.R. Chelladurai Mini M.A. 1973
Church and Society in Malaysia

6. David H. Dale Mini M.A. 1974
Stanley Kubrick's Film Clockwork Orange. An Exercise in Hermeneutics, a Study in Violence Considered from the Point of View of its Dramatic Interest, Sociological Implications, and Theological Meaning

7. R. Dellagiacoma M.A. 1981
Missionary Society of Verona Fathers in Uganda 1910-1980

8. William G.S. Dixon M.A. 1986
History and Mission of the Anglican Church in Barbedos

9. Eric Forshaw Mini M.A. 1978
The Dialogue between Christians and Socialists in Switzerland between 1900 and 1920 with Special Reference to Ragaz and Kutter

10. Elaine Foster M.Phil. 1990
Black Women: Their contribution to the Growth and Development of Black-led Churches in Great Britain

11. Alison Geary Mini M.A. 1987
Feminist Theology and African Theology: A Liberating Reading of the Bible

12. Jet den Hollander M.Phil. 1990
The Council of World Mission: A Viable Model for Contemporary Mission?

13. Peter Leslie Howard Mini M.A. 1980
The Possibility of a Working Class Church. An Anglican, Evangelical and English Perspective

14. Elanor M. Jackson M.A. 1972
Significant Development in the History of 'Organised Ecumenism' 1910-1968

16. Neil M. McDonald M.A. 1975
The Agressive Freedom: A Comparative Study of Karl Marx and Sren Kierkegaard

15. Iain MacRobert M.A. 1985
The Spirit and the Wall: The Black Roots and White Racism of Early Pentecostalism in the U.S.A.

17. W. David E. Major Mini M.A. 1982
How Indigenous Can an Indigenous Church be? With Special Reference to African Traditional Religion and African Independent Churches

18. Howard Moffat M.Phil. 1991
The Healing Ministry of the Church and Orthodox Medicine

19. Patrick J. O'Mahony M.A. 1984
Swords and Ploughshares. Can Man Live and Progress with a Technology of Death?

20. Eric E. Pemberton M.Phil. 1988
A Study of Caribbean Religions

21. Lynn Price M.Phil. 1989
Interfaith Encounter and Dialogue. A Positive Option or an Irrelevance for Methodist in a Religiously Plural Society? *

22. Ginda Rajagukguk M.Litt 1981
Culture and Gospel. A Theological Investigation Based on a Comparison of the Original Greek of John's Gospel, Chapter 1.1-18, and Three Versions, Namely Javanese, Batak and Indonesian

23. Martin Robinson M.Litt. 1976
Two Anglican Pentecostal Clergymen - A Comparison between the life and work of Alexander A. Boddy and Michael C. Harper

24. Martin H. Simmonds M.Phil. 1988
'A Portrayal of Identity'. A Study of the Life and Worship of the First United

Church of Jesus Christ (Apostolic) U.K.

25. Phillip R. Smith M.Phil. 1987
From a Movement to a Religion: An Examination of the Development of the Baha'i Faith in Britain from 1900-1950

26. Bernard Spencer M.Litt. 1982
American Seventh-Day Adventist Latter Rain

27. Jeffrey F. Spratling M.A. 1980
Conditions for Freedom. A Theological Critique of Marcuse

28. Tomas Stevens Noel M.Litt. 1986
The Church as Signs of the Kingdom: Towards a Latin American Ecclesiology

29. Joyce V. Thurman M.A. 1979
New Wineskins. A Study of the House Church Movement

30. Joyce V. Thurman M.Litt. 1989
How Green is the Spirit *

31. Carol Tomlin M.Phil. 1988
Black Preaching Style

32. John Wilkinson M.Litt. 1991
The Black Christian Tradition in 'Mainstream' Churches: A White Response and Testimony

* Published in the series *Studies in the Intercultural History of Christianity* (edited by Walter J. Hollenweger a.o.).

List of Contributors

Marten Visser

Barrett, David B., Richmond, Virginia, U.S.A. (M.A., B.D. Cambridge, Ph.D.)
— Missionary of the Church Missionary Society, Anglican Research Officer, Research Consultant to the Southern Baptist Foreign Missionary Board, Vatican Consultant on world evangelization.
— *World Christian Encyclopedia: A Comparative Survey of Churches and Religions in the Modern World, AD 1900-2000* (editor), 1982; *Cosmos, Chaos and Gospel: A Chronology from Creation to New Creation*, 1987; *Our Globe and How to Reach It* (co-author), 1990.

Bundy, David, Wilmore, Kentucky, U.S.A. (Th.M. Asbury, Cand. Dr. Louvain)
— Librarian, Associate Professor of Church history at Christian Theological Seminary, Indianapolis.
— *Pietist and Wesleyan Studies* (co-editor); *Middle Eastern Christian Studies* (editor); *Keswick: a Bibliographical Introduction to the Higher Life Movements*, 1975, repr. 1984.

Conway, Martin, Birmingham, U.K. (M.A.)
— Study Secretary of the WSCF, Publications Secretary of the WCC, Assistant General Secretary of the British Council of Churches, President Selly Oak Colleges.
— *The Undivided Vision*, 1966; *Seeing Education Whole*, 1971; *That's When the Body Works - The Canberra Assembly of the WCC as a Foretaste of a Council of the Universal Church*, 1991.

Faupel, D. William, Wilmore, Kentucky, U.S.A. (Ph.D. Birmingham)
— Professor of Bibliography and Research at Asbury Theological Seminary, Associate Rector of St. Johns Episcopal Church, Versailles, Kentucky.
— *The American Pentecostal movement: A Bibliographical Essay*, 1971; *The Higher Christian Life: Sources for the Study of the Holiness Pentecostal and Keswick movements* (advisory editor).

Friedli, Richard, Freiburg, Switzerland (Dr. Theol.)
— University-Chaplain at the National University of Rwanda, Professor of Mission and Director of the Institute for the Study of Religions at the University of Freiburg, co-editor of the series *Studies in the Intercultural History of Christianity*.
— *Fremdheit als Heimat*, 1974; *Le Christ dans les cultures*, 1989.

Gerloff, Roswith I.H., Frankfurt am Main, Germany (Ph.D. Birmingham)
— Founder and Director of the Centre for Black and White Christian Partnership in Birmingham, Minister of Religion, Director of the Ecumenical Centre Christuskirche in Frankfurt, Lecturer in Theology.

A Plea for British Black Theologies, 1992; *Afro-Caribbean Churches in Britain and the Apostolic Succesion*, 1992.

Gill, Kenneth D., Carol Stream, Illinois, U.S.A. (Ph.D. Birmingham)
— Lecturer in Theology, Missions and Research Methods, Library Collection Development and Reference Services at Wheaton College, Publisher for the American Society of Missiology.
— urces for Research (editor), 1982; *Twentieth-century Evangelicalism* (contributor), 1990; *Researching Modern Evangelicalism* (contributor), 1990.

Haire, I. James M., Auchenflower, Queensland, Australia (Ph.D. Birmingham)
— Missionary in Indonesia, Minister, Professor and Principal of Trinity College at Brisbane, Dean of the Brisbane College of Theology.
— *The Character and Theological Struggle of the Church in Halmahera, Indonesia, 1941-1979*, 1981.

Heuberger-Gloor, Marianne, Spiez, Switzerland
— Minister, occasional lecturer (courses, adult education, etc.).
— Gebet für die Kranken. Privatsache oder Sache des Gottesdienstes?, 1991.

Hocken, Peter, Gaithersburg, Maryland, U.S.A. (Ph.D. Birmingham)
— Father, Member of the Mother of God Community in the U.S.A., Coordinator of the theological stream of the International Charismatic Consultation on World Evangelization (ICCOWE).
— *Streams of renewal*, 1986; *One Lord, one Spirit, one Body*, 1987.

Horn, J. Nico, Windhoek, Namibia (Ph.D.)
— Minister, Senior Lecturer at the University of the Western Cape, Researcher at the University of South Africa.
— *Een kudde, een Herder* (co-author), 1987; *From Rags to Riches*, 1990; *Skrifverstaan en Skrifuitleg*, 1990.

Johnson, Todd M., Richmond, Virginia, U.S.A. (B.A., M.A., Ph.D.)
— Missionary, Editor of the *International Journal of Frontier Missions*, Global Plan Coordinator of the AD 2000 Global Evangelization Movement.
— *Countdown to 1900: World Evangelization at the End of the Nineteenth Century*, 1984; *Our Globe and How to Reach It* (co-author), 1990.

Jongeneel, Jan A.B., Bunnik, The Netherlands (Drs. Jur., Dr. Theol. Leiden)
— Missionary in Indonesia, Minister of the Netherlands Reformed Church, Professor of Mission at the University of Utrecht, co-editor of the series *Studies in the Intercultural History of Christianity*.
— *Missiologie I/II*, 1986/1991; *Experiences of the Spirit* (editor), 1991.

Kraft, Charles H., Pasadena, California, U.S.A. (Ph.D.)
— Lecturer at the School of World Mission, Fuller Theological Seminary.

— *Christianity in Culture*, 1979; *Communication Theory for Christian Witness*, 1983.

Laan, Cornelis van der, Houten, The Netherlands (Ph.D. Birmingham)
— General Secretary of the Brotherhood of Pentecostal Assemblies in the Netherlands; editor of *Parakleet.*
— *Pinksteren in Beweging* (co-author), 1982; *De Spade Regen*, 1989; *Sectarian Against His Will: Gerrit Roelof Poelman and the Birth of Pentecostalism in the Netherlands*, 1991.

Laan, Paul N. van der, Lunteren, The Netherlands (Ph.D. Birmingham)
— President Central Pentecostal Bible School.
— *Pinksteren in Beweging* (co-author), 1982; *The Question of Spiritual Unity: The Dutch Pentecostal Movement in Ecumenical Perspective* (Dissertation, Birmingham, 1988).

Lartey, Emmanuel Y., Birmingham, U.K. (Ph.D. Birmingham)
— Lecturer in Pastoral Studies at the University of Birmingham.
— *Pastoral Counselling in Inter-cultural Perspective*, 1987.

MacRobert, Iain, Sandwell, West Midlands, U.K. (Ph.D. Birmingham)
— Principal Lecturer at Sandwell College, President of the Fellowship of Churches of Christ, General Secretary of the Centre for Black and White Christian Partnership.
— *The Black Roots and White Racism of Early Pentecostalism in the USA*, 1988; *Religion, State and Society in Modern Britain* (contributor), 1990.

Mulrain, George M., Birmingham, U.K. (B.A., Ph.D. Birmingham)
— Minister of Religion, Pastor in Haiti, Theological College Yutor and Academic Dean, Mission College Principal.
— *Theology in Folk Culture*, 1984.

Robeck, Jr., Cecil M., Pasadena, California, U.S.A. (Ph.D.)
— Associate Dean for Academic Programs and Associate Professor of Church History, School of Theology, Fuller Theological Seminary.
— *Pneuma: The Journal of the Society for Pentecostal Studies* (editor), 1984-present; *Charismatic Experiences in History* (editor), 1985; *Prophecy at Carthage: Perpetua, Tertullian, and Cyprian*, 1992.

Robinson, Martin, Birmingham, U.K. (Ph.D. Birmingham)
— Pastor, Secretary to the Fellowship of Churches of Christ in Great-Britain and Ireland, Church Growth Consultant to Bible Society.
— *To the Ends of the Earth - The Pilgrimage of an Ecumenical Pentecostal, David J. du Plessis 1905-1987* (Dissertation, Birminghem, 1987).

Staples, Peter, Huis ter Heide, The Netherlands (M.A. Oxford, Ph.D. Nottingham)
— Tutor in New Testament at the University of Nottingham, Priest of the Church of England, Senior Lecturer in 20th Century Church History and Ecumenics at the University of Utrecht.

— *The Church of England 1961-1980*, 1981; *The Liturgical Movement in the Netherlands Reformed Church 1911-1955*, 1983; *Relations between the Netherlands Reformed Church and the Church of England Since 1945*, 1992.

Sundermeier, Theo, Heidelberg, Germany (Dr. Theol.)
— Missionary in Namibia and South Africa, Professor of History of Religions and Missiology at the University of Heidelberg, co-editor of the series *Studies in the Intercultural History of Christianity.*
— *Wir aber suchten Gemeinschaft: Kirchwerdung und Kirchentrennung in Südwestafrika*, 1973; *Das Kreuz als Befreiung: Kreuzesinterpretationen in Asien und Afrika*, 1985; *Nur gemeinsam können wir leben: das Menschenbild schwarzafrikanischer Religionen*, 1988.

Suurmond, Jean-Jacques, Gendt, The Netherlands (M.A., Ph.D. Pasadena)
— Teaching Assistent at Fuller Theological Seminary, Assemblies of God pastor, Director Charismatische Werkgemeenschap Utrecht, Netherlands Reformed Minister.
— *'Och ware het gehele volk profeten!'* (editor), 1992.

Ustorf, Werner, Birmingham, U.K. (Dr. Theol.)
— Professor of Mission at the University of Birmingham.
— *Die Missionsmethode Franz Michael Zahns und der Aufbau kirchlicher Strukturen in Westafrika: eine missionsgeschichtliche Untersuchung*, 1989.

Veenhof, Jan, Thun, Switzerland (Dr. Theol.)
— Professor of Dogmatics and History of Dogma at the Free University of Amsterdam, Minister.
— *Revelatie en Inspiratie*, 1968; *Geist und Liebe*, 1978; *De dubbele Jezus*, 1985.

Yoo, Boo-Woong, Limuru, Kenya (Ph.D. Birmingham)
— Parish Minister, Missionary, Lecturer in Missiology at St. Paul's United Theological College.
— *Biblical Preaching and Its Application to the Korean Church*, 1984; *Korean Pentecostalism: Its History and Theology*, 1988; *Letters from the Equator*, 1989.

Index of Persons

Marten Visser

Indexed are the articles without notes

STUDIEN ZUR INTERKULTURELLEN GESCHICHTE DES CHRISTENTUMS
ETUDES D'HISTOIRE INTERCULTURELLE DU CHRISTIANISME
STUDIES IN THE INTERCULTURAL HISTORY OF CHRISTIANITY

Begründet von/fondé par/founded by
Hans Jochen Margull †, Hamburg

Herausgegeben von/edité par/edited by

Band 1 Wolfram Weiße: Südafrika und das Antirassismusprogramm. Kirchen im Spannungsfeld einer Rassengesellschaft.

Band 2 Ingo Lembke: Christentum unter den Bedingungen Lateinamerikas. Die katholische Kirche vor den Problemen der Abhängigkeit und Unterentwicklung.

Band 3 Gerd Uwe Kliewer: Das neue Volk der Pfingstler. Religion, Unterentwicklung und sozialer Wandel in Lateinamerika.

Band 4 Joachim Wietzke: Theologie im modernen Indien - Paul David Devanandan.

Band 5 Werner Ustorf: Afrikanische Initivative. Das aktive Leiden des Propheten Simon Kimbangu.

Band 6 Erhard Kamphausen: Anfänge der kirchlichen Unabhängigkeitsbewegung in Südafrika. Geschichte und Theologie der äthiopischen Bewegung. 1880-1910.

Band 7 Lothar Engel: Kolonialismus und Nationalismus im deutschen Protestantismus in Namibia 1907-1945. Beiträge zur Geschichte der deutschen evangelischen Mission und Kirche im ehemaligen Kolonial- und Mandatsgebiet Südwestafrika.

Band 8 Pamela M. Binyon: The Concepts of "Spirit" and "Demon". A Study in the use of different languages describing the same phenomena.

Band 9 Neville Richardson: The World Council of Churches and Race Relations. 1960 to 1969.

Band 10 Jörg Müller: Uppsala II. Erneuerung in der Mission. Eine redaktionsgeschichtliche Studie und Dokumentation zu Sektion II der 4. Vollversammlung des Ökumenischen Rates der Kirchen, Uppsala 1968.

Band 11 Hans Schöpfer: Theologie und Gesellschaft. Interdisziplinäre Grundlagenbibliographie zur Einführung in die befreiungs- und polittheologische Problematik: 1960-1975.

Band 12 Werner Hoerschelmann: Christliche Gurus. Darstellung von Selbstverständnis und Funktion indigenen Christseins durch unabhängige charismatisch geführte Gruppen in Südindien.

Band 13 Claude Schaller: L'Eglise en quête de dialogue. Vergriffen.

Band 14 Theo Tschuy: Hundert Jahre kubanischer Protestantismus (1868-1961). Versuch einer kirchengeschichtlichen Darstellung.

Band 15 Werner Korte: Wir sind die Kirchen der unteren Klassen. Entstehung, Organisation und gesellschaftliche Funktionen unabhängiger Kirchen in Afrika.

Band 16 Arnold Bittlinger: Papst und Pfingstler. Der römisch katholisch-pfingstliche Dialog und seine ökumenische Relevanz.

Band 17 Ingemar Lindén: The Last Trump. An historico-genetical study of some important chapters in the making and development of the Seventh-day Adventist Church.

Band 18 Zwinglio Dias: Krisen und Aufgaben im brasilianischen Protestantismus. Eine Studie zu den sozialgeschichtlichen Bedingungen und volkspädagogischen Möglichkeiten der Evangelisation.

Band 19 Mary Hall: A quest for the liberated Christian, Examined on the basis of a mission, a man and a movement as agents of liberation.

Band 20 Arturo Blatezky: Sprache des Glaubens in Lateinamerika. Eine Studie zu Selbstverständnis und Methode der "Theologie der Befreiung".

Band 21 Anthony Mookenthottam: Indian Theological Tendencies. Approaches and problems for further research as seen in the works of some leading Indian theologicans.

Band 22 George Thomas: Christian Indians and Indian Nationalism 1885-1950. An Interpretation in Historical and Theological Perspectives.

Band 23 Essiben Madiba: Evangélisation et Colonisation en Afrique: L'Héritage scolaire du Cameroun (1885-1965).

Band 24 Katsumi Takizawa: Reflexionen über die universale Grundlage von Buddhismus und Christentum.

Band 25 S.W. Sykes (editor): England and Germany. Studies in theological diplomacy.

Band 26 James Haire: The Character and Theological Struggle of the Church in Halmahera, Indonesia, 1941-1979.

Band 27 David Ford: Barth and God's Story. Biblical Narrative and the Theological Method of Karl Barth in the Church Dogmatics.

Band 28 Kortright Davis: Mission for Carribean Change. Carribean Development As Theological Enterprice.

Band 29 Origen V. Jathanna: The Decisiveness of the Christ-Event and the Universality of Christianity in a world of Religious Plurality. With Special Reference to Hendrik Kraemer and Alfred George Hogg as well as to William Ernest Hocking and Pandipeddi Chenchiah.

Band 30 Joyce V. Thurman: New Wineskins. A Study of the House Church Movement.

Band 31 John May: Meaning, Consensus and Dialogue in Buddhist-Christian-Communication. A study in the Construction of Meaning.

Band 32 Friedhelm Voges: Das Denken von Thomas Chalmers im kirchen- und sozialgeschichtlichen Kontext.

Band 33 George MacDonald Mulrain: Theology in Folk Culture. The Theological Significance of Haitian Folk Religion.

Band 34 Alan Ford: The Protestant Reformation in Ireland, 1590-1641. 2. unveränderte Auflage.

Band 35 Harold Tonks: Faith, Hope and Decision-Making. The Kingdom of God and Social Policy-Making. The Work of Arthur Rich of Zürich.

Band 36 Bingham Tembe: Integrationismus und Afrikanismus. Zur Rolle der kirchlichen Unabhängigkeitsbewegung in der Auseinandersetzung um die Landfrage und die Bildung der Afrikaner in Südafrika, 1880-1960.

Band 37 Kingsley Lewis: The Moravian Mission in Barbados 1816-1886. A Study of the Historical Context and Theological Signifcance of a Minority Church Among an Oppressed People.

Band 38 Ulrich M. Dehn: Indische Christen in der gesellschaftlichen Verantwortung. Eine theologische und religionssoziologische Untersuchung politischer Theologie im gegenwärtigen Indien.

Band 39 Walter J. Hollenweger (Ed.): Pentecostal Research in Europe: Problems, Promises and People. Proceedings from the Pentecostal Research Conference at the University of Birmingham (England) April 26th to 29th 1984.

Band 40 P. Solomon Raj: A Christian Folk-Religion in India. A Study of the Small Church Movement in Andhra Pradesh, with a Special Reference to the Bible Mission of Devadas.

Band 41 Karl-Wilhelm Westmeier: Reconciling Heaven and earth: The Transcendental Enthusiasm and Growth of an Urban Protestant Community, Bogota, Colombia.

Band 42 George A. Hood: Mission Accomplished? The English Presbyterian Mission in Lingtung, South China. A Study of the Interplay between Mission Methods and their Historical Context.

Band 43 Emmanuel Yartekwei Lartey: Pastoral Counselling in Inter-Cultural Perspective: A Study of some African (Ghanaian) and Anglo-American viewes on human existence and councelling.

Band 44 Jerry L. Sandidge: Roman Catholic/Pentecostal Dialogue (1977-1982): A Study in Developing Ecumenism.

Band 45 Friedeborg L. Müller: The History of German Lutheran Congregations in England, 1900-1950.

Band 46 Roger B. Edrington: Everyday Men: Living in a Climate of Unbelief.

Band 47 Bongani Mazibuko: Education in Mission/Mission in Education. A Critical Comparative Study of Selected Approaches.

Band 48 Jochanan Hesse (Ed.): Mitten im Tod - vom Leben umfangen. Gedenkschrift für Werner Kohler.

Band 49 Elisabeth A. Kasper: Afrobrasilianische Religion. Der Mensch in der Beziehung zu Natur, Kosmos und Gemeinschaft im Candomblé - eine tiefenpsychologische Studie.

Band 50 Charles Chikezie Agu: Secularization in Igboland. Socio-religious Change and its Challenges to the Church Among the Igbo.

Band 51 Abraham Adu Berinyuu: Pastoral Care to the Sick in Africa. An Approach to Transcultural Pastoral Theology.

Band 52 Boo-Woong Yoo: Korean Pentecostalism. Its History and Theology.

Band 53 Roger H. Hooker: Themes in Hinduism and Christianity. A Comparative Study.

Band 54 Jean-Daniel Plüss: Therapeutic and Prophetic Narratives in Worship. A Hermeneutic Study of Testimonies and Visions. Their Potential Significance for Christian Worship and Secular Society.

Band 55 John Mansford Prior: Church and Marriage in an Indonesian Village. A Study of Customary and Church Marriage among the Ata Lio of Central Flores, Indonesia, as a Paradigm of the Ecclesial Interrelationship between village and Institutional Catholicism.

Band 56 Werner Kohler: Umkehr und Umdenken. Grundzüge einer Theologie der Mission (herausgegeben von Jörg Salaquarda).

Band 57 Martin Maw: Visions of India. Fulfilment Theology, the Aryan Race Theory, & the Work of British Protestant Missionaries in Victorian India.

Band 58 Aasulv Lande: Meiji Protestantism in History and Historiography. A Comparative Study of Japanese and Western Interpretation of Early Protestantism in Japan.

Band 59 Enyi Ben Udoh: Guest Christology. An interpretative view of the christological problem in Africa.

Band 60 Peter Schüttke-Scherle: From Contextual to Ecumenical Theology? A Dialogue between Minjung Theology and 'Theology after Auschwitz'.

Band 61 Michael S. Northcott: The Church and Secularisation. Urban Industrial Mission in North East England.

Band 62 Daniel O'Connor: Gospel, Raj and Swaraj. The Missionary Years of C. F. Andrews 1904-14.

Band 63 Paul D. Matheny: Dogmatics and Ethics. The Theological Realism and Ethics of Karl Barth's Church Dogmatics.

Band 64 Warren Kinne: A People's Church? The Mindanao-Sulu Church Debacle.

Band 65 Jane Collier: The culture of economism. An exploration of barriers to faith-as-praxis.

Band 66 Michael Biehl: Der Fall Sadhu Sundar Singh. Theologie zwischen den Kulturen.

Band 67 Brian C. Castle: Hymns: The Making and Shaping of a Theology for the Whole People of God. A Comparison of the Four Last Things in Some English and Zambian Hymns in Intercultural Perspective.

Band 68 Jan A. B. Jongeneel (Ed.): Experiences of the Spirit. Conference on Pentecostal and Charismatic Research in Europe at Utrecht University 1989 .

Band 69 William S. Campbell: Paul's Gospel in an Intercultural Context. Jew and Gentile in the Letter to the Romans. 1992.

Band 70 Lynne Price: Interfaith Encounter and Dialogue. A Methodist Pilgrimage.

Band 71 Merrill Morse: Kosuke Koyama. A model for intercultural theology .

Band 75 Jan A. B. Jongeneel a.o. (Eds.): Pentecost, Mission and Ecumenism's. Essays on Intercultural Theology. Festschrift in Honour of Professor Walter J. Hollenweger.

Band 76 Siga Arles: Theological Education for the Mission of the Church in India: 1947-1987. Theological Education in relation to the identification of the Task of Mission and the Development of Ministries in India: 1947-1987; with special reference to the Church of South India.

Band 77 Roswith I.H. Gerloff: A Plea for British Black Theologies. The Black Church Movement in Britain in its transatlanctic cultural and theological interaction with special reference to the Pentecostal Oneness (Apostolic) and Sabbatarian movements. 2 parts.

Band 78 Friday M. Mbon: Brotherhood of the Cross and Star. A New Religious Movement in Nigeria.

Band 79 John Samuel Pobee (ed.): Exploring Afro-christology.

Band 80 Frieder Ludwig: Kirche im kolonialen Kontext. Anglikanische Missionare und afrikanische Propheten im südöstlichen Nigeria.

Festschrift Prof. Dr. Walter J. Hollenweger

Tabula gratulatoria

I

Amato Angelo, Pontificia Universita, Rome, Italy
Dr. David B. Barrett, Richmond, Virginia, U.S.A.
Ulrike Birkner-Kettenacker, Oxford, England
Dr. Arnold Bittlinger, Oberhallau, Switzerland
David Bundy, Th.M., Wilmore, Kentucky, U.S.A.
Dr. Jan van Butselaar, Netherlands Missionary Council, Amsterdam, The Netherlands
Prof. Dr. Arnulf Camps, Wijchen, The Netherlands
Dr. Brian Castle, Somerset, England
Dr. Martin Conway, M.A., Birmingham, England
Prof. Rudolf Dellsperger, Ev.-theol. Fakultät, Bern, Switzerland
Prof. Dr. Murray W. Dempster, Costa Mesa, California, U.S.A.
Prof. Dr. Günter Ebbrecht, Evangelische Akademie Iserlohn, Germany
Prof. Dr. D. William Faupel, Wilmore, Kentucky, U.S.A.
Elaine Foster, M.Phil., Birmingham, England
Prof. Dr. Richard Friedli, Freiburg, Switzerland
Niklaus Gäumann, Eichberg, Switzerland
Dr. Roswith I.H. Gerloff, Frankfurt am Main, Germany
Dr. Kenneth D. Gill, Coraol Stream, Illinois, U.S.A.
Rev. Annemarie Graf, Winterthur, Switzerland
Prof. Dr. I. James M. Haire, Queensland, Australia
Rev. Ruedi Heinzer, Krattigen, Switzerland
Rev. Marianne Heuberger-Gloor, Spiez, Switzerland
Dr. Peter Hocken, Gaitherburg, Maryland, U.S.A.
Rev. H. Hoffmann, London, England
Jet den Hollander, M.Phil., Kingston, Jamaica
Dr. J. Nico Horn, Windhoek, Namibia
Dr. Todd M. Johnson, Richmond, Virginia, U.S.A.
Prof. Dr. Jan A.B. Jongeneel, Bunnik, The Netherlands
Rev. Michel Kocher, St. Saphorin s/Morges, Switzerland
Gerhard Koslowsky, Ratingen, Germany
Dr. Charles H. Kraft, Pasadena, California, U.S.A.
Dr. Cornelis van der Laan, Houten, The Netherlands
Dr. Paul N. van der Laan, Lunteren, The Netherlands
Dr. Emmanuel Y. Lartey, Birmingham, England
Hildegard and Dieter Lenz, Bremen, Germany
Dr. Kingsley Lewis, St. John's, Antigua
Dr. Iain MacRobert, Sandwell, England

W. David E. Major, Chester, England
Friedeborg L. Müller, M.Phil. and Dr. Jörg H. Müller, Bochum, Germany
Prof. Dr. Karl Müller, St. Augustin, Germany
Dr. George M. Mulrain, Birmingham, England
Prof. Dr. Olav G. Myklebust, Oslo, Norway
E. and F. Noetzli, Hirzel, Switzerland
Joan Pearce, Birmingham, England
Prof. John S. Pobee, World Council of Churches, Geneva, Switzerland
L. Price, M.Phil., Birmingham, England
Father John M. Prior, Maumere, Indonesia
Prof. Dr. Jannes Reiling, Bilthoven, The Netherlands
Dr. Cecil M. Robeck, Pasadena, California, U.S.A.
Dr. Martin Robinson, Birmingham, England
Prof. Dr. Horace O. Russell, Philadelphia, Pensylvania, U.S.A.
Dr. John Rutherford, Cumbria, England
Dr. J. Norberto Saracco, Civdad Evita, Argentine
Dr. Siegfried S. Schatzmann, Elim Bible College, Nantwich, England
Prof. Dr. Hans Heinrich Schmid, Schwerzenbach, Switzerland
Prof. Marc Spindler, The Hague, The Netherlands
Dr. Peter Staples, Huis ter Heide, The Netherlands
Prof. Dr. Theo Sundermeier, Heidelberg, Germany
Dr. Jean-Jacques Suurmond, Gendt, The Netherlands
Prof. Dr. Werner Ustorf, Birmingham, England
Prof. Dr. Jan Veenhof, Thun, Switzerland
Marten Visser, Utrecht, The Netherlands
Prof. Andrew Walls, Edinburgh, Scotland
Dr. Boo-Wong Yoo, Limuru, Kenya

II

Centrale Pinkster Bijbelschool, Lunteren, The Netherlands
Centre for Black & White Christian Partnership, Birmingham, England
Duke University Library, Perkins Library, Durmham, North Carolina, U.S.A.
Erzbischöfliche Akademische Bibliothek, Paderborn, Germany
Facoltà Valdese di Teologia, Rome, Italy
Interuniversity Institute for Missiological and Ecumencial Research, Leiden, The Netherlands
Rijksuniversiteit, Bibliotheek Faculteit der Godgeleerdheid, Groningen, The Netherlands
Selly Oak Colleges, Central Library, Birmingham, England
Theologische Faculteit, Bibliotheek, Tilburg, The Netherlands
Universitätsbibliothek, Mainz, Germany
Wiss.-Theol. Seminar d.Universität Heidelberg, Heidelberg, Germany
Peter Lang Verlag, Frankfurt am Main, Germany